Wealthy Corinth

WEALTHY CORINTH

A HISTORY OF THE CITY TO 338 BC

J. B. SALMON

CLARENDON PRESS · OXFORD

Oxford University Press, Great Clarendon Street, Oxford OX2 6DP
Oxford New York
Athens Auckland Bangkok Bogota Bombay
Buenos Aires Calcutta Cape Town Dar es Salaam
Delhi Florence Hong Kong Istanbul Karachi
Kuala Lumpur Madras Madrid Melbourne
Mexico City Nairobi Paris Singapore
Taipei Tokyo Toronto Warsaw
and associated companies in
Berlin Ibadan

Oxford is a trade mark of Oxford University Press

Published in the United States by
Oxford University Press Inc., New York

© J. B. Salmon 1984

First published by Oxford University Press 1984
Reprinted 1986
Special edition for Sandpiper Books Ltd., 1997

British Library Cataloguing in Publication Data
Data available

ISBN 0-19-814833-X

3 5 7 9 10 8 6 4

Printed in Great Britain by
Bookcraft Ltd
Midsomer Norton, Somerset

For
VERONICA

Preface

An account of the history of Greek Corinth needs no defence. My choice of the occupation of Acrocorinth by a Macedonian garrison as a terminus is more questionable; but I have written a history of an independent city, and although Corinthians no doubt continued to take a distinct view of their interests after 338, the nature of our evidence does not allow it to be traced. I have tried to make my book accessible not only to specialists: every Greek text quoted has been translated. It may be more difficult for those without experience in handling archaeological evidence to feel at home in some parts of the book, for all too frequently a line still divides archaeological from historical study. I shall be satisfied if I have been able to contribute something to erasing it, and to moderating the equally disturbing tendency to teach Greek history at all levels through Spartan, Athenian, or occasionally Boeotian eyes.

I am grateful for many grants which have enabled me to travel in Italy and Greece, especially in the Corinthia itself: from the Department of Education and Science, the Research Fund of the Queen's University of Belfast, the Wolfson Foundation (which also generously made a grant to defray the costs of typing), the Department of Classics and Archaeology and the Research Grant Fund of the University of Lancaster, and the British Academy.

I thank H. Catling and the authorities of the British School of Archaeology at Athens for invaluable assistance during my visits to Greece; and the Greek Archaeological Service for allowing me access to material in museums under its care.

Corinth was famed in antiquity for its pleasures; they remain attractive, even if their nature has changed. Not the least of them is the hospitality of the American School in Corinth; I hope that I have been able to make some small return to N. Bookidis and C. K. Williams II for their very generous entertainment of myself and my family by treating their city as it deserves.

I am pleased to record my warmest thanks to numerous friends and colleagues for the help they have generously given: J. Boardman, P. Cartledge, G. L. Cawkwell, J. L. Creed, R. M. Errington, W. G. Forrest, C. M. Kraay, M. Popham, R. J. A. Talbert, and C. K. Williams II have all read and criticized parts of earlier drafts. I owe the elimination of many mistakes to them; those which remain are not the result of their advice but of my own determination. I should also like to acknowledge the skills of Pat Kitchen, whose careful preparation of the final typescript greatly lightened the burden of the editorial staff of the Oxford University Press.

More general influences are not so easy to define; but I am sure that I learned more, both as an undergraduate and later, from W. G. Forrest than I am able to recognize. I am greatly indebted to him for suggesting to me the subject which I have found so rewarding, and I hope he will forgive me if I have unwittingly failed to acknowledge his ideas. To Sir Maurice Bowra's infectious delight in all things Greek (and more) my obligation is greater than I know; but I am well aware of the responsibility of A. E. Astin and G. L. Huxley for making the Queen's University of Belfast a most stimulating and enjoyable place in which to begin an academic career. I am grateful to that institution for granting me sabbatical leave in 1976/7, during which much of the book was written. Without the patience, understanding, and support of my parents, my wife, and my children I could not have started, much less completed my work, or enjoyed it as much as I have. I am delighted to have been able to take them all to Greece to share in some of the greatest pleasures I have derived from what they have helped to make.

Lancaster   J.B.S.
September 1982

Acknowledgements

I am grateful to the following institutions and individuals for providing, and/or permitting me to reproduce, plans, photographs, and drawings: the American School of Classical Studies at Athens (Figs. 6-10, 16; Pls. 36-38); l'École Francaise d'Athènes (Fig. 11); the Manchester Museum (Fig. 13; Pls. 39-41); the National Archaeological Museum, Athens (Pl. 42); N. Bookidis, I. Ioannidou and L. Barziotou, and C. K. Williams II (Figs. 6-7, 9, 16; Pls. 36-38); C. and P. Howard (Figs. 8, 9, 11, 13, 15); and A. J. N. W. Prag (Fig. 13; Pls. 39-41).

Contents

List of Plates

(at end)

List of Figures

Abbreviations

All works cited by author's name appear in the bibliography, where the abbreviations used are given; other abbreviations are as follows:

AAA	*Athens Annals of Archaeology.*
AC	*L'Antiquité Classique.*
AD	Ἀρχαιολογικὸν Δελτίον.
Admiralty Handbook	Admiralty. Naval Intelligence Division. Geographical Section. *Greece*, 3 vols. (Geographical Handbook Series, B. R. 516), London, 1944-5.
AE	Ἀρχαιολογικὴ Ἐφημερίς.
AJA	*American Journal of Archaeology.*
AJP	*American Journal of Philology.*
AK	*Antike Kunst.*
AM	*Mitteilungen des deutschen archäologischen Instituts, athenische Abteilung.*
Annuario	*Annuario della Scuola Archeologica di Atene e delle Missioni Italiane in Oriente.*
Ant. Denk.	*Antike Denkmäler*, herausgegeben vom (kaiserlich) deutschen archaeologischen Institut, 3 vols., Berlin, 1891-1926.
AR	*Archaeological Reports*: Supplement to *JHS*.
Arch. Zeit.	*Archäologische Zeitung.*
ATL iii	Merritt, B.D., Wade-Gery, H.T. and McGregor, M.F., *The Athenian Tribute Lists* iii, Princeton, 1950.
BA	*Bollettino d'Arte del Ministero della Pubblica Istruzione.*
BASOR	*Bulletin of the American Schools of Oriental Research in Jerusalem and Baghdad.*
BCH	*Bulletin de Correspondance Hellénique.*
BSA	*Annual of the British School of Archaeology at Athens.*
BIAB	*Bulletin de l'Institut Archéologique Bulgare.*
CAH	*Cambridge Ancient History.*
Céramiques de la Grèce de l'est	*Céramiques de la Grèce de l'est et leur diffusion en occident* (Colloque, Centre Jean Bérard, Naples, 1976), Paris and Naples, 1978.
CHJ	*Cambridge Historical Journal.*
Clara Rhodos	*Clara Rhodos: Studi e materiali pubblicati a cura dell'Istituto storico archeologico di Rodi.*
C. Ord. Ptol.	*Corpus des ordonnances des Ptolémées*: see Index of Sources.
CP	*Classical Philology.*
CQ	*Classical Quarterly.*
CR	*Classical Review.*

Abbreviations

CSCA	*California Studies in Classical Antiquity.*
DdA	*Dialoghi di Archeologia.*
DHA	*Dialogues d'Histoire Ancienne.*
Ét. arch. i	*Études archéologiques: recueil de travaux*, publiée sous la direction de Courbin, P., Paris, 1963.
FHG	*Fragmenta Historicorum Graecorum*, ed. Müller, C. and T., Paris, 1841–85.
FGH	*Die Fragmente der griechischen Historiker*, ed. Jacoby, F., Leiden, 1923–58.
GRBS	*Greek, Roman and Byzantine Studies.*
Hell. Oxy.	*Hellenica Oxyrhynchia*: see Index of Sources.
HSCP	*Harvard Studies in Classical Philology.*
IG	*Inscriptiones Graecae*: see Index of Sources.
IM	*Mitteilungen des deutschen archäologischen Instituts, Abteilung Istanbul.*
JAS	*Journal of Archaeological Science.*
JdaI	*Jahrbuch des deutschen archäologischen Instituts.*
JEA	*Journal of Egyptian Archaeology.*
JHS	*Journal of Hellenic Studies.*
JRS	*Journal of Roman Studies.*
LCM	*Liverpool Classical Monthly.*
LS	Liddell, H.G. and Scott, R., *A Greek-English Lexicon*, 9th edn., Revised by Jones, H.S., Oxford, 1940.
MEFR	*Mélanges d'Archéologie et d'Histoire de l'École Française de Rome.*
MMS	*Metropolitan Museum Studies.*
MN	*American Numismatic Society Museum Notes.*
NC	*Numismatic Chronicle.*
NS	*Notizie degli Scavi di Antichità.*
PCPhS	*Proceedings of the Cambridge Philological Society.*
Phil. Woch.	*Philologische Wochenschrift.*
PP	*La Parola del Passato.*
PPS	*Proceedings of the Prehistoric Society.*
Praktika	Πρακτικὰ τῆς Ἀρχαιολογικῆς Ἑταιρείας.
RA	*Revue Archéologique.*
RE	*Paulys Realencyclopädie der classischen Altertumswissenschaft.*
Rev. Hist.	*Revue Historique.*
REG	*Revue des Études Grecques.*
Rh. Mus.	*Rheinisches Museum.*
RHR	*Revue de l'Histoire des Religions.*
SIG[3]	Dittenberger, W. (ed.), *Sylloge Inscriptionum Graecarum*, 4 vols., 3rd edn., Leipzig, 1915–24.
Staatsverträge ii	Bengston, H. (ed.), *Die Staatsverträge des Altertums* ii: *Die Verträge der griechisch-römischen Welt von 700 bis 338 v. Chr.*, Munich and Berlin, 1962.

ΣΤΗΛΗ   Τόμος εἰς μνήμην Νικολάου Κοντολέοντος, Athens, 1980.
St. Etr.   *Studi Etruschi.*
TAPA   *Transactions of the American Philological Association.*
YCS   *Yale Classical Studies.*
ZGEB   *Zeitschrift der Gesellschaft für Erdkunde zu Berlin.*
ZPE   *Zeitschrift für Papyrologie und Epigraphik.*

Pottery Publications

Vases from the following publications are cited in abbreviated form:

Aetos B   Benton, *BSA* xlviii (1953), 255-361.
Aetos R   Robertson, *BSA* xliii (1948), 1-124.
W   Weinberg, *Corinth* vii.1.

Pottery Style Periods

Abbreviations for the conventional style periods of Corinthian pottery, which
provide the basis for Corinthian archaeological chronology, are given below. For
the dates, see briefly Salmon, *JHS* xcvii (1977), 86 (with references); the margin
for error is c.25 years. I add a simplified version of the chronological chart in
Hope-Simpson and Dickinson, Gazetteer (at end; cf. 23-6) for the Bronze Age.

EH I-II   Early Helladic I-II (*c.*3000-2200)
EH III   Early Helladic III (*c.*2200-2000)
MH   Middle Helladic (*c.*2000-1550)
LH I-III A   Late Helladic I-III A (*c.*1550-1300)
LH III B   Late Helladic III B (*c.*1300-1200)
LH III C   Late Helladic III C (*c.*1200-?)
SM   Submycenaean (?)
LPG   Late Protogeometric (?-875)
EG   Early Geometric (875-825)
MG I   Middle Geometric I (825-800)
MG II   Middle Geometric II (800-750)
LG   Late Geometric (750-720)
EPC   Early Protocorinthian (720-690)
MPC I   Middle Protocorinthian I (690-670)
MPC II   Middle Protocorinthian II (670-650)
LPC   Late Protocorinthian (650-640)
TR   Transitional (640-625)
EC   Early Corinthian (625-600)
MC   Middle Corinthian (600-575)
LC   Late Corinthian (575 and later)

I. The Land and Prehistory

a. Boundaries and Climate

History is nowhere closer to the land than in Greece: to stand on Acrocorinth and to turn from the coastal plain, the Corinthian Gulf, and the mountains of the Perachora Peninsula towards the Isthmus, Oneion, and the passes to the Argolid is to appreciate many of the vital factors affecting Corinthian history (Pls. 1–5). Thucydides drew attention to the commercial benefits Corinth enjoyed by virtue of her position, and archaeological evidence can now demonstrate that the inhabitants of the Isthmus region reaped the fruits of their geographical situation from the Neolithic period; but that they reaped more literal fruits has often been overlooked in favour of the more obvious advantages of location. A map will make the exceptional position of Corinth clear (Fig. 1); but the fertility of the central region of the Corinthia can only be appreciated after closer acquaintance. The rich land between Corinth and Sicyon became proverbial;[1] and Corinth was 'wealthy' to the epic poets before her wealth could have depended to a significant degree upon commerce. Without the resources of her land, Corinth would only have acted as a parasite upon the traffic which passed over her Isthmus; it is therefore no mere convention to root Corinthian history in the Corinthian soil.

There is rarely direct evidence from antiquity for the boundaries of the Corinthia, and what there is often refers to Roman Corinth; but the approximate lines are clear enough (see Fig. 5). In the north-east,[2] the peaks of the Geraneia range form a well-defined border with the Megarid, and an important road between the Peloponnese and Central Greece wound between them;[3] both to the north and to the south the line is less clearly defined by nature, but Wiseman has argued that in the north it reached the shore of the Corinthian Gulf between Megarian Pagae and Corinthian Oenoe

---

[1] References in Parke and Wormell, *Delphic Oracle*, ii. 21, no. 46. Modern works referred to in footnotes have full bibliographical references in the List of Abbreviations and the Bibliography.

[2] For border disputes in this quarter, see below, 71.

[3] Wiseman, 20–2 with fig. 9. Ancient fortifications are preserved in the pass, but it is not clear whether they were constructed by Megara or by Corinth.

Fig. 1   Greece and the Aegean

just east of Mavro Limni, which he demonstrates was Lake Gorgopis, also called Eschatiotis—the last feature in Corinthian territory.[4] In the south, Pausanias places the boundary to the west of the Scironian Rocks, which were in Megarian territory; it is likely that the border between Greek Corinth and Megara was here too.[5]

In the west, the border with Sicyon ran through the fertile coastal plain. Livy (xxxiii.15.1) places the boundary at the River Nemea in 197, and the same torrent-bed, now known as the Koutsomadi or the Zapantis, formed the boundary between Roman Corinth and Sicyon in the time of Strabo (382). A few kilometres to the east is a second torrent-bed, that of the Longopotamos, which would act as an equally well-defined boundary; but careful analysis of the events which preceded the battle in this region in 394 demonstrates that the frontier at that time also was on the Nemea.[6] That it followed the western of the two possible routes through the plain is significant: the Corinthians were able to defend their possession of this rich land against the less numerous Sicyonians. South of the coastal plain, the boundary cannot be traced with any accuracy. The upper Longopotamos valley belonged to Cleonae. Where the boundary stood is unclear, but the closer to the coastal plain it was, the easier it is to understand how Cleonae was able to maintain her independence of Corinth even though she enjoyed Argive support (below, 259–60). The wide plain south of Spathovouni (Pl. 6) must have belonged to Cleonae, for there is no other significant arable land in her territory. The reason for the separation of Corinth and Cleonae may well have been the difficulty of communication between Corinth and the upper Longopotamos. West of Penteskouphi village the land is scored by steep-sided ravines, and even travel on foot is hazardous (Pl. 7). Such features are extremely unstable, and the configuration of this area was no doubt different in antiquity; but that its general character was similar is demonstrated by a bridge, probably fourth century or Hellenistic, which crosses one of the

[4] Wiseman, 22–7; for Eschatiotis, 40 n. 76.
[5] Paus. i. 44. 6–10. Strabo 392 (cf. 171) and Plut. *Thes.* 25.4 refer to a stele placed on the boundary between the Peloponnese and 'Ionia', including the Megarid in the latter. The stele was presumably on the Corinthian/Megarian border, and although references to it cannot be traced earlier than the foundation of Roman Corinth, it was probably first erected before 146. Cf. Wiseman, 17.
[6] Below, 351. The Spartan army invaded Corinthian territory and ravaged it, but was forced towards the sea by missiles thrown from the hills above the plain by light-armed troops. The Corinthians and their allies then camped on the right bank of a torrent-bed which can only have been that of the Longopotamos, for there is no other between this and Corinth. The border must then have been west of the Longopotamos, or the Spartans would have been devastating the territory of their Sicyonian allies.

Fig. 2   The Corinthia: Physical

ravines.[7] The bridge shows the difficulty of communications here, and in the archaic period, when political affiliations originated, there was presumably no bridge to facilitate travel. It is remarkable how rarely Acrocorinth is visible from the Longopotamos valley, although Penteskouphi can be seen more frequently; if the men who farmed the valley, which is narrow but fertile, were not able to look towards Corinth's bastion they may have looked for political allegiance to the south. The south-western boundary of the Corinthia may therefore have left the Nemea river not far south of the coastal plain and followed the northern slopes of Mt. Phoukas instead of ascending to its summit; that would accord with the view of the ancients that Apesas (Phoukas) was in Nemean territory.[8] The border with Cleonae

[7] Wiseman, 82–4. The ground in the region has undergone such alteration that the course of the road carried by the bridge can no longer be determined; it has been covered by much subsequent accumulation. See in general Philippson, *Landschaften*, iii.91.

[8] References in Wiseman, 106 with n. 36.

will then have crossed the Longopotamos valley perhaps to the summit of Skiona and then turned south towards the passes to the Argolid.[9] The exact line of the frontier with Argos is equally uncertain. In the archaic period, and perhaps for a little longer, Argos herself may not always have been able to control territory so far north, for Mycenae maintained her independence until the mid-fifth century. The Spathovouni plain belonged to Cleonae, and Tenea was Corinthian. A frontier which crossed from the peak of Skiona almost due south to that above Klenies would fit these requirements, although in the absence of a natural boundary-line there will probably have been small-scale disputes here for much of the time. Thus only one of the four possible routes into the Argolid passed directly from Corinthian into Argive (or Mycenaean) territory: that of Agion Orion. Three others, the Tretus, taken by the modern road and railway, Agios Sostis, in which Kolokotronis inflicted heavy casualties on the Turks in a notable action during the Greek War of Independence, and the Contoporeia, passed through Cleonaean territory.[10] It is therefore appropriate that none of the military structures which have been identified in these passes can be shown to have been manned by troops defending them against invasion from the south, and that the fort in the pass of Agios Sostis was suitable only for use by Argives against attackers from the north;[11] Corinthians did not have access through Cleonaean territory to the three western passes, and it was hardly worth defending Agion Orion when there were so many alternative routes.[12]

The boundary with Epidaurus in the south-east ran through rugged country (Pls. 8, 31); but it is known to have been disputed in the third century, when Megarian arbitrators decided in favour of Epidaurus, although it is no longer possible to trace the border which they fixed.[13] The point at which the boundary reached the Saronic Gulf has been the subject of much discussion; three authors give relevant information, but it cannot easily be interpreted. Thucydides, in discussing an action on and off this coast in 412, refers to a

[9] For this section of the Corinthian boundary, see Sakellariou and Faraklas, 47.

[10] For all these passes, the ancient references, and a graphic description of the action of Kolokotronis, see Wiseman, 113-26.

[11] Agios Sostis: Wiseman, 116. In the Contoporeia, however, the fort might have been used for defence in either direction.

[12] Wiseman (92, 121) suggests that Agesilaus invaded the Corinthia in 391 through Agion Orion; but the mention of his presence at Tenea (Xen. *Hell.* iv.4.19) does not guarantee that the στενά (narrows) through which he passed (Xen. *Ages.* ii.17) were those of Agion Orion above Tenea: the roads from the other passes will have passed through this place, the most populous in the southern Corinthia.

[13] *IG* iv.1². 71; see Wiseman, 136-8 with references.

deserted harbour in the Corinthia called Speiraeum;[14] it was 'the last before the boundary with Epidaurus'. Pliny (*NH* iv.18) and Ptolemy (iii.16.12-13) both give landmarks along this coast. Each first mentions a promontory, Spiraeum, north of Epidaurus, and then two harbours before Cenchreae; the northern harbour has the name Bucephalus in each author, but Pliny's southern harbour was Anthedus and that of Ptolemy 'the harbour of the Athenians'. Thucydides' deserted harbour called Speiraeum is probably the same as the Spiraeum mentioned in the arbitration inscription: what sort of natural feature this Spiraeum was is not stated, but a road went *down* to it (καταγούσας), so it will not have been the promontory of Pliny and Ptolemy. Unfortunately this information is insufficient to enable the frontier to be identified with certainty. Pliny refers elsewhere (*NH* iv.57) to islands lying off Cape Spiraeum, and this should probably mean that the cape is to be identified with that now known as Spiri; islands cluster off that cape strikingly, but not off Cape Trachyli further south. The two, or perhaps three, harbours mentioned by the geographers should therefore be sought north of Spiri, and suitable harbours are available.[15] It is by no means clear, however, that any of the three bays is to be identified with the Speiraeum of Thucydides, despite the coincidence of the name preserved by Ptolemy, 'the harbour of the Athenians'.[16] Of all the harbours along this coast, the description ἐρῆμος (deserted, isolated) suits Korphos best (Pl. 9). The possible candidates north of Spiri may all have been deserted in 412 in the sense that little or no human activity was normally to be observed there; but Korphos is ἐρῆμος in a fuller sense, for it faces well away from the heavily populated region of the Isthmus, which is easily visible from the slopes above Sideronas and Lychnari, while even Frangolimani and Amoni face more naturally to the north than Korphos. On this ground, the action of 412 is best situated in the Bay of Korphos; in addition, the large bay of Korphos suits the events better than any of the other candidates, which are considerably smaller (below, 337). It will follow that the boundary at that time was further to the south; but exactly where it lay, and how it ran from the mountains above

---

[14] viii.10.3. MSS Πειραιὼν; the correct reading Σπείραιον probably stood in *P. Oxy.* 1247 (Grenfell and Hunt, *The Oxyrhynchus Papyri*, x. 129), and is supported by the toponym Σπίραιον in *IG* iv.1². 71, 18 and by the name Spiraeum given to the promontory in the vicinity by Pliny and Ptolemy (below).

[15] Wiseman, 132-4; Sideronas, Lychnari, Frangolimani, and Amoni, none of them showing much (but Sideronas a little) surface evidence of the classical period.

[16] This may have been a merely literary equation, made in ignorance of the ground by a reader of Thucydides who figured among Ptolemy's sources.

Tenea, cannot now be determined.[17] The land in the region of modern Sophiko, and the approaches to the harbour of Korphos, will have been Corinthian; the status of the upland plain of Angelo-kastro is quite unknown.[18]

Full records of the climate of the Corinthia are not available: the Corinth weather-station recorded only rainfall when the figures for the whole of Greece were published.[19] The rainfall figures, however, are of vital significance. Corinth is among the driest places in Greece: the average annual rainfall is 404.7 mm.,[20] which is wetter (among stations on the mainland) only than Athens.[21] In one year, little more than a quarter of the average was recorded.[22] These bare statistics, however, obscure an even more significant fact: that most of Corinth's rain falls in the form of heavy showers.[23] On average, there are only 40.2 days each year on which at least 1 mm. falls (rain days); at the slightly drier Athens there are twice as many,[24] and nowhere in Greece does so little rain fall in such short periods as at Corinth. Figures for the monthly distribution of rainfall give a similar impression. Only from June to August do less than 20 mm. fall in the month; but only in November and December are there more than five rain days.[25] Throughout the year, then, when rain falls it does so in showers of some violence; and although Philippson asserts that no heavy showers fall in the summer months I have been caught by one in August, and the collective experience I have tapped in the American School at Corinth indicates that they are not in-frequent even in summer.

[17] It has often been argued that Korphos must have been mentioned by Pliny and Ptolemy, on the ground that it is the best harbour between Epidaurus and Cenchreae (Fowler, *Corinth*, i.22; cf. Wiseman, 140); but this is beside the point. Good harbours are not necessarily used—especially if they are in rough country, as here—and mention by the geographers will have depended not on potential, but on actual use.

[18] Wiseman, 140, seems to show a preference for supposing it to be Corinthian (but contrast 130); but since we cannot tell whether the border reached the sea at Cape Trachyli or in the Bay of Sophiko at some point south of Korphos, not even a guess can be made. The figure of 300 stades given by Ps.-Scyl. 55 for the Saronic coast of Corinth can hardly be used to shed light on this question; there are too many variables.

[19] Most conveniently in *Admiralty Handbook*, i.479–90; Philippson, *Klima*; I quote the latter, since it is more easily available. Temperature and humidity figures are given by Sakellariou and Faraklas, 12-13. Suggestions that significant changes in the climate have taken place (esp. Carpenter, *Discontinuity in Greek Civilisation*) are not supported by what evidence we have from pollen analysis, which indicates that there has been no major alteration (Greig and Turner, *JAS* i (1974), 193).

[20] Philippson, *Klima*, 185; cf. 83.

[21] 383.9 mm.: Philippson, *Klima*, 185.

[22] 105.3 mm.: Philippson, *Klima*, 113.

[23] For the general principle, see Philippson, *ZGEB* xxv (1890), 64.

[24] Philippson, *Klima*, 185; cf. 105.

[25] Ibid. 91, 106, 185.

The effect of this character of rainfall is clear enough. Not only is Corinth almost the driest place in Greece: even the rain which falls does so in showers of such force that it rarely permeates beneath the surface of the soil. The water collects so rapidly that it forms innumerable small streams, following the natural slope of the land or roads, and rushes away, carrying much of the soil with it; in much of the Corinthia the rainfall is at least as destructive as it is beneficial. What harms other parts of the Corinthia, however, brings added advantages to the region of Corinth itself. The coastal plain has been built up to a significant degree by the alluvium washed down by these heavy showers. The rain which falls on the mountains to the south of the plain rushes towards the sea, carrying alluvium with it; but neither water nor sediment reaches it directly, but is trapped on the plain and is thus available for agriculture. Channels now cross the plain in profusion, and there is clear archaeological evidence for similar activity in the region of Corinth from the fifth century at the latest.[26] Not only is the plain flat, so that it is able, with relatively simple banking operations, to retain the rain which falls upon it directly; it can also benefit from the water and detritus from the mountains to the south. The geological structure of the immediate vicinity of Corinth improves conditions in a further related way. Numerous levels of clay are found beneath those of poros and poros conglomerate which form the stepped plateaux above the plain; they trap the water with such efficiency that there are no less than sixteen springs within a radius of less than 1 km. from Peirene, the most famous of them all. Thus Corinth was described by Simonides as 'well-watered' (below, 255). These natural springs added to the possibilities for irrigation in the part of the coastal plain near to Corinth, where indeed some of the ancient evidence for installations of this kind has been uncovered; it is even possible that similar operations were undertaken to improve conditions for agriculture on some of the land above the plain, for springs are found at all levels between the foot of Acrocorinth and the plain itself.[27]

b. Prehistory

Its water-supply makes Corinth the most attractive site in the Isthmus region. A survey of population patterns in the Corinthia from the earliest times reveals that its advantages were recognized early, but

[26] Below, 126.
[27] The springs: map prepared by W. B. Dinsmoor, Jr., in Hill, *Corinth*, i.6, pl. 18.

that these benefits were long outweighed by one serious drawback. This is not the place for detailed consideration of the prehistory of the area; but the general prehistoric distribution of population in the Corinthia, and the connections enjoyed by that population, reflect significant facts about the potential of the region which are timeless in character, and can throw important light on Dorian Corinth. I therefore survey the prehistory of the Isthmus region before giving an account of the territory itself. The evidence is generally favourable to Corinth, for few other sites have been extensively excavated; but surface finds enable some conclusions to be drawn, and part of the significance of the period is the small amount of evidence reported from Corinth for much of the Bronze Age.

Despite the imbalance in favour of Corinth, there is little doubt that this was the main site in the region from the earliest times when man rooted himself in permanent settlements (see Fig. 3); and the fact is significant. The 'Neolithic Revolution'—not the least of man's advances—when hunters and gatherers first stopped a nomadic existence and settled to sow and reap the fruits of the same fields, year in, year out, reached Corinth early.[28] Earlier finds, although there is a continuous sequence from the Palaeolithic in the Franchthi cave, are not known in the Corinthia;[29] but the region has not been investigated from this point of view, as have others in Greece, and the character of the evidence from Corinth, where Neolithic material is often disturbed fill, would make it more than ordinarily difficult to recognize phases of occupation earlier than the first use of pottery in Early Neolithic.[30] The earliest Neolithic, however, is especially well represented at Corinth, where the settlement seems to have centred on Temple Hill;[31] evidence has also been found in isolated pockets up to 100 m. away in the east and south.[32] These finds are close enough together to have belonged to a single settlement, probably concentrated on Temple Hill;[33] and all periods of Neolithic,

[28] For a general survey of Neolithic Greece, see Theocharis (ed.), *Neolithic Greece*.

[29] See, however, Weinberg, *CAH* i.1.564-5: caves with possible evidence from these periods just north and just south of the Corinthia.

[30] For elsewhere, see, e.g., Bintliff, *Natural Environment and Human Settlement in Prehistoric Greece*, 236-40 (southern Argolid), 116-17 (general, with references). In the Corinthia, the cave above Klenies might repay full investigation, although only Neolithic has been identified there so far (below).

[31] Kosmopoulos, *The Prehistoric Inhabitation of Corinth*, 40-7; Weinberg, *Hesperia*, vi (1937), 488; Scranton, *Corinth*, i.3.156; Weinberg, *Hesperia*, xxix (1960), 246; Weinberg, *Hesperia*, xliii (1974), 522-7.

[32] South Basilica: Weinberg, *Corinth*, i.5.59. East of Lechaeum Road: Hill, *AJA* xxxi (1927), 72-3; Weinberg, *Hesperia*, xxix (1960), 242-5. South of Temple Hill: Lavezzi, *Hesperia*, xlvii (1978), 402-51.

[33] Cf. Lavezzi, *Hesperia*, xlvii (1978), 432.

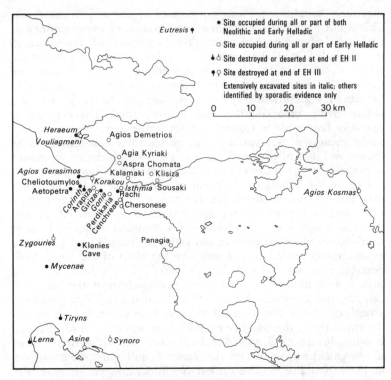

Fig. 3   Prehistory I: Neolithic and Early Helladic

roughly from the sixth millennium to the fourth, are well represented. There is not yet enough information to establish the relative import- ance in the settlement's economy of hunting, herding, fishing, and agriculture, especially as much of the evidence is in the form of disturbed fill, and of what we have only the pottery has been sub- jected to full analysis; but a useful reminder of the character of the 'Neolithic Revolution' is a concave blade of chert—a locally occurring substitute for obsidian—on which remain clear traces of its use as a sickle. The object belongs to a context transitional between Early and Late Neolithic.[34]

Other sites in the Corinthia have produced Neolithic evidence, but none of it has been properly studied. The sites are concentrated where we should expect them, in the vicinity of the coastal plain.

[34] Ibid. 406; 433, no. 3 with pl. 104.

Finds are reported from Cheliotoumylos north-west of Corinth, from Aetopetra, a hill which dominates the plain where the Longopotamos valley reaches it, from Agios Gerasimos, a hill on the coast north of Aetopetra, and from Gonia, east of Corinth; only on the latter site has there been excavation, and all Neolithic phases are represented.[35] A few Neolithic scraps have turned up on the well-excavated sites at the Perachora Heraeum and the Rachi, the ridge above the sanctuary of Poseidon at Isthmia; but it is not clear whether they demonstrate significant or permanent occupation.[36] The finds at the cave above Klenies, however, may well do so; presumably some of the Neolithic inhabitants of the Corinthia took advantage of this natural shelter instead of constructing their own near the coastal plain. If so, they will probably have been herders, for there is little good land in the immediate vicinity; the cave is not far above a natural route for transhumance between the Isthmus region and upland grazing in the mountains between the Corinthia and the Argolid.[37]

Many of the important factors in the economy of the Corinthia throughout its history are already apparent in the Neolithic. However cultural phenomena were transmitted, whether by diffusion or by the movement of peoples, the central geographical position of the Isthmus region ensured that new possibilities became known here early. The ceramic techniques which define the phases of Neolithic were all quickly adopted, and sometimes perhaps first used, here.[38] There are clear connections in the pottery, especially in the Late Neolithic phase, with Orchomenus and Thessaly to the north, with which links may have been maintained by land over the Isthmus;[39] Adriatic contacts, on the other hand, were probably made by sea.[40] The presence of significant quantities of Melian obsidian, along with local red chert, in Late Neolithic contexts at Corinth demonstrates maritime relations to the east; even earlier phases present similar evidence in smaller quantities.[41] Far more significant, however, if perhaps less immediately obvious, is the fact that Corinth supported a Neolithic population which flourished sufficiently to take advantage of its geographical position. In the

[35] Blegen, *MMS* iii.1 (1930), 55-71. Surface evidence of the prehistoric period is best traced in Hope-Simpson and Dickinson, *Gazetteer*, 61-6, nos. A 50-66; 68, no. A 74; 70-3, nos. A 82-92.
[36] Payne, *Perachora*, i.20; Smith, *Hesperia*, xxiv (1955), 142.
[37] References in Sakellariou and Faraklas, Appendix ii, 60 n. 84.
[38] See in general Weinberg, *CAH* i.1.572-608.
[39] Kosmopoulos, *The Prehistoric Inhabitation of Corinth*, 40; Weinberg, *Hesperia*, vi (1937), 492-515. The scraps from the Rachi (above) may have been connected with this traffic.
[40] Lavezzi, *Hesperia*, xlvii (1978), 428-33.
[41] Ibid., 407, 424-5, 432.

day-to-day economy of the settlement, such widespread contacts
were of minimal importance; the basis of Corinth's evident prosperity
lay in the natural resources of her territory, no doubt especially in
the plenteous water-supply and in the agricultural potential of the
coastal plain where the settlements were concentrated.
Small finds at Corinth suggest that metalworking was already
known at Corinth before the end of the Neolithic.[42] In the immediately succeeding phase, however, EH I, despite its conventional
identification as the first phase of the Early Bronze Age, there is no
direct evidence for the use of metal; the situation is similar on the
rest of the Greek mainland, although this does not mean that the
knowledge died out.[43] Even in EH II, when metal finds in the mainland are slightly more widespread, there are none from Corinth
itself and only two small items from the rest of the territory;[44]
but this is probably not significant, since there are few undisturbed
contexts at Corinth. At Zygouries, which was not in the historical
Corinthia, metal finds of this period show links with Crete;[45] they
may have been made through the Corinthia rather than the Argolid.
For much of the Early Bronze Age, the communities of the
Corinthia progressed gradually, building on the achievements of the
Neolithic. The floral and faunal finds, if they have been preserved,
have not been subjected to analysis, and the lack of pure EH strata
makes it impossible to say whether the community now developed
anything approaching the social hierarchy to which the palace at
Lerna bears witness; but the distribution of sites remains concentrated near the fertile coastal plain. At Corinth there are signs that
the area of settlement may have increased to the north.[46] A deep,
skilfully cut well is evidence of a highly developed community life,
for on a site where springs are so easily available a well must have
been dug for convenience, not necessity.[47] The settlement at
Cheliotoumylos, where a similar well was dug, was probably distinct.[48] All the known Neolithic sites continued in occupation,[49]
and new ones were added. Korakou, on the coast just east of

[42] Kosmopoulos, *The Prehistoric Inhabitation of Corinth*, 46, 65: the working seems
to have been done locally, even though there are no known sources of ore in the Corinthia.
Cf. Branigan, *Aegean Metalwork of the Early and Middle Bronze Age*, 62.
[43] Branigan, *Aegean Metalwork of the Early and Middle Bronze Age*, 100, 102.
[44] Cheliotoumylos: Shear, *AJA* xxiv (1930), 405 (needle). Korakou: Blegen, *Korakou*,
104 (pin).
[45] Branigan, *Aegean Metalwork of the Early and Middle Bronze Age*, 110, 113.
[46] For a summary, see Wiseman, *Archaeology* xxii (1969), 217: see also Wiseman,
Hesperia, xxxvi (1967), 23–7; 410.
[47] Weinberg, *Hesperia*, xvii (1948), 200–3: depth 9.60 m.
[48] Shear, *AJA* xxxiv (1930), 404–6; Waage, *Hesperia Suppl.* viii (1949), 415–22.
[49] For excavation at Agios Gerasimos (EH II–III), see *AD* xxvi. B (1971), 68–71.

Lechaeum, began occupation in this period;[50] it is unclear whether its economy depended to a significant degree on fishing in the Corinthian Gulf which it overlooked. The region south of the Isthmus was able to support settlement not only at Gonia but also on the nearby hill at Giriza;[51] surface evidence has indicated yet another settlement not far away at Arapiza, but its extent is not clear.[52] Surface evidence or odd scraps have turned up in other parts of the Corinthia, but the only excavated site is near the tip of the Perachora peninsula at Vouliagmeni.[53] There is no good land in the vicinity, and the probability is strong that the economy of this settlement differed considerably from that of the central part of the Corinthia: fish was presumably a major part of the diet, although there is no confirmation from the finds. It is interesting that obsidian was worked here; but it is not known whether it came from Melos or from Lipari.[54]

The concentration of sites near the coastal plain confirms the natural assumption that the inhabitants of the Corinthia remained dependent on its rich soil for their support. There is no direct evidence, but it was presumably in this period that the Corinthia, like other places in Greece, first made full use of both the vine and the olive.[55] Finds from the Corinthia are virtually indistinguishable from those of the Argolid to the south; continued contact both with the north and by sea with the Cyclades is clear, and links with Crete are apparent for the first time.[56] Many aspects of the culture of Leucas at this period show close connections with the north-east Peloponnese.[57] The links were probably maintained through the Corinthia and along the Corinthian Gulf,[58] but as far as can be told at present it was Leucas which derived the greater benefit from the association, even if the obsidian from Vouliagmeni did make its way across the Adriatic.

The most interesting phenomenon of the Early Bronze Age, however, is the radical change in the settlement pattern of the Corinthia which took place towards the end of it. Nothing after EH II has been

[50] Blegen, *Korakou*.
[51] Blegen, *AJA* xxiv (1920), 6; *AJA* xxvii (1923), 160; *MMS* iii.1 (1930), 71-5.
[52] Blegen, *AJA* xxiv (1920), 5-6; *AJA* xxvii (1923), 159.
[53] Fossey, *BSA* lxiv (1969), 53-69; *AD* xxvii.B (1973), 149-51.
[54] Fossey, *BSA* lxiv (1969), 64.
[55] Renfrew, *The Emergence of Civilisation*, 281-7.
[56] Blegen, *Korakou*, 110-13; above, 12 (metal finds at Zygouries). See in general Caskey, *CAH* i.2.787.
[57] See in general Caskey, *CAH*, i.2.792-3.
[58] The metal industry of Leucas, however, is more problematic; Branigan, *Aegean Metalwork of the Early and Middle Bronze Age*, 114.

identified at Corinth itself,[59] and the site appears to have lacked a major community from now until after the end of the Mycenaean Age. This desertion of what had probably been the largest settlement of the region is to be associated with numerous destructions on other excavated sites in the Isthmus area, both in the Corinthia and further afield. At Zygouries, Agios Kosmas, Tiryns, Asine, Lerna, Synoro, and Vouliagmeni, destruction levels occur at the end of EH II,[60] while at Korakou and Eutresis there are similar levels at the end of EH III.[61] The relationship between these two horizons of destruction separated by perhaps as much as two centuries is not yet clear, and the extent to which the destructions were the work of invaders remains controversial;[62] but one significant conclusion for the Corinthia is safe enough. At the end of EH II, when many settlements both north and south of the Isthmus suffered violent destruction, the site at Temple Hill was abandoned, and did not support a major community for a millennium or more. It is impossible to be sure that the destructions on other sites were not the result of an earthquake; but a more probable explanation is that the disasters were the deliberate work of invaders, whether they came from far or near. Since EH deposits at Corinth cannot be fully investigated, it is not known if the settlement on Temple Hill was also destroyed; but whether it was or not, the widespread attacks on other settlements will have given its inhabitants serious cause for concern. Throughout the millennia of the Neolithic and Early Bronze Ages, there are no signs of serious attacks on settlements anywhere in the region, and experience did not teach the population of Corinth that self-defence was necessary; but the woefully inadequate natural defences of their well-watered site on the low mound at Temple Hill must have been all too apparent to them after the devastation of so many nearby communities even if they had not suffered themselves. They may have been able to save their lives, and even for a short while their livestock, in the event of attack by withdrawing to the heights of Acrocorinth; but their settlement itself was disastrously exposed. Nor could it be given satisfactory artificial defences, for unless Acrocorinth were included within the system—a

[59] Weinberg, *Hesperia*, xxix (1960), 244-5.

[60] References and argument in Caskey, *Hesperia*, xxix (1960), 300-1. Synoro: Döhl, *Tiryns*, vi. 214. Vouliagmeni: *AD* xxviii.B (1973), 150.

[61] Caskey, *Hesperia*, xxix (1960), 302.

[62] For the Isthmus region, see especially ibid., 285-303. The account of Hooker, *Mycenaean Greece*, 11-33 (with references), is perhaps too sceptical of the possibility of invasion. For the recent bibliography, see Schachermeyr, *Die ägäische Frühzeit*, 193-4, 241-2 (cf. 188-92). For a cautionary article on the question of 'The Coming of the Greeks', see McNeal, *Antiquity*, xlvi (1972), 19-28.

fortification no doubt beyond their capacity to man, if not to build—
an enemy would always have the advantage of approach from above.

The fate of the inhabitants of Corinth at the end of EH II remains unclear. It might be guessed that the population of the Corinthia
decreased now that what had probably been its most populous site
was almost deserted; but this is uncertain, since our evidence comes
mainly from surface exploration, which can be notoriously misleading. Korakou appears to have suffered no major dislocation at
this stage, although at Zygouries the EH III settlement which
followed the destruction was diminished in size. The destruction of
Korakou at the end of EH III was not an isolated phenomenon, for
there is a similar level at Eutresis in Boeotia; but no reconstruction
of what happened in the Corinthia between the end of EH II and the
beginning of what is conventionally known as the Middle Bronze Age
can command confidence when so few sites have been excavated and
the general pattern remains controversial. A small trench on the hill
at Giriza suggested that the site may, like Corinth, have been deserted
towards the end of EH, but at what stage remains unclear.[63] At
Gonia, the transition to the Middle Bronze Age seems to have been
peaceful; and even at Korakou, the destruction of the EH III settlement did not prevent subsequent occupation on a similar scale.[64]
The richest finds of the Middle Bronze Age (see Fig. 4) are the
dozen or so graves from the North Cemetery: they yielded part of
a finely decorated gold diadem, and are among the wealthiest of the
period on the mainland.[65] Scraps of gold were found in a grave of
the period at Crommyon.[66] The North Cemetery served the needs
of the settlement at Temple Hill in later periods; but it is close to
the hill at Cheliotoumylos, on which surface evidence of MH occupation has been observed. No other site in the immediate vicinity
has been identified, and it is possible that the hill was now preferred
to the less defensible site at Corinth. Surface exploration indicates
that with the exception of Corinth and Giriza all the EH sites in the
region of the plain continued in occupation in the Middle Bronze
Age; our evidence is consistent with the view that the plain supported
as flourishing, and perhaps as large, a population now as before even
though Corinth itself was largely abandoned. Certainly the area was
no less open to external contacts; in particular, as the Middle Bronze
Age grew older, so Minoan influence became more marked.[67]

[63] Blegen, *AJA* xxvii (1923), 160.

[64] Korakou: Blegen, *Korakou*. Gonia: Blegen, *MMS* iii.1 (1930), 75–80.

[65] Blegen, *Corinth*, xiii.3; cf. Caskey, *CAH* ii.1.124.

[66] *AD* xxiv.B (1969), 103.

[67] Metalwork: Branigan, *Aegean Metalwork of the Early and Middle Bronze Age*, 117,
123; contrast Blegen, *Corinth*, xiii.6. Blegen, *Korakou*, 115. See in general Caskey, *CAH*
ii.1.124; Dickinson, *Origins of Mycenaean Civilisation*, 17–38.

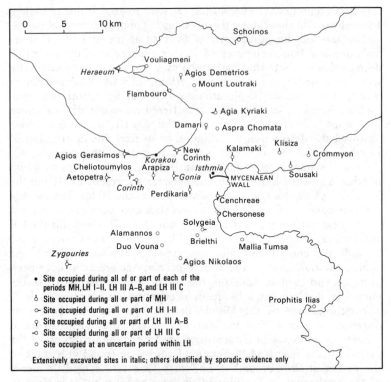

Fig. 4   Prehistory II: Middle and Late Helladic

Towards the end of the Middle Bronze Age there began, a short distance to the south of the Corinthia, a remarkable process which culminated in the Mycenaean civilization of the latter part of the Late Bronze Age. Its impact on the Corinthia cannot yet be determined because we have almost no material from controlled excavations; but certain broad generalizations are possible, even though they are more than usually open to revision in the light of new evidence. There is little doubt that the population reached its highest prehistoric point towards the end of the Late Bronze Age in LH III B. There are no sites of earlier periods in the vicinity of the plain, apart from Giriza, which fail to reveal evidence of this time, and it is well represented on the excavated sites at Korakou and Gonia.[68] Even at Corinth there is evidence of occupation in

[68] See now in detail Rutter, *Korakou and Gonia.*

LH III B, for the first time since EH II, in a deposit which includes a fine pictorial amphoroid krater from just east of Peirene.[69] It is probably significant that evidence now appears for the first time of occupation on numerous sites well away from the coastal plain. Near Galataki a few chamber tombs have been excavated, and there was presumably a settlement close by, perhaps at Brielthi.[70] There are some half a dozen sites in the southern Corinthia where surface exploration has revealed LH sherds and nothing earlier, and to the north of the Isthmus the situation is similar. Such evidence might be misleading; but it is likely enough that the population of the region increased to a level which the plain alone was unable to support, and that the less attractive territory to both south and north was brought under cultivation, especially for vines and olives.

If the Corinthia was now more densely populated than ever before, however, there is little doubt that many of the benefits derived from the fruits of the Corinthian soil were enjoyed elsewhere. Even the surface evidence makes it plain that the rich potential of the region was heavily exploited; but none of the excavated sites can have been the centre of the type of sophisticated palace economy known in the Argolid and Messenia, and it is most improbable that such a site remains to be discovered. Korakou was probably provided with a fortification wall in this period,[71] but no signs of a palace were discovered there or at Gonia; Perdikaria may have boasted a fortification wall, but even this is doubtful.[72] No tholos tombs have been found. If there was no palace site in the region, it might be conjectured that the Corinthia, although it clearly shared the material culture of the late Mycenaean world, was not brought within the system of any of the palace economies. Many regions of the mainland were no doubt in such a position; but even without appealing to the evidence of the Homeric Catalogue of Ships, such a conclusion is extremely improbable for the Corinthia. The rich coastal plain was an obvious target for the rulers of Mycenae for its own sake; when the vital geographical position of the Isthmus is added to the equation, it is impossible to believe that the inhabitants of the Corinthia, settled as they were in numerous small and mostly defenceless communities, were able to retain their political independence. That does not of itself imply that they were

---

[69] Weinberg, *Hesperia*, xviii (1949), 156–7. Scraps found earlier: Broneer, *AJA* xl (1936), 207.

[70] Hope-Simpson, *Gazetteer*, 29.

[71] Blegen, *Korakou*, 98.

[72] Wiseman, 66; Hope-Simpson and Dickinson, *Gazetteer*, 64, no. A 59 with references; Sakellariou and Faraklas, Appendix ii.17.

drawn fully into the economic system of the Mycenaean palace; but
if they were not, contemporary pressures would probably have
created in the Isthmus region a dependent prince similar to those of
Tiryns. The absence of a suitable centre for even such a ruler makes
it probable that the Corinthia was directly exploited from Mycenae.
The evidence of comparative wealth at Corinth and at Korakou
probably marks the dwellings of subordinate officials of the Mycenaean kings.[73] The passage relating to the Corinthia in the Catalogue
of Ships thus reflects what is in any case probable on archaeological
grounds:

> But those who possessed Mycenae, the well-built citadel,
> Corinth the wealthy, . . . [and other places]
> Of their hundred ships the mighty Agamemnon was the leader.
>   (*Il.* ii.569-70, 576.)

But it is impossible to use this evidence as direct confirmation of
the political, much less the economic, status of the Corinthia in the
Late Mycenaean Age; it remains unclear whether the description of
Corinth goes back to Mycenaean times or has a later origin.[74]
    The date of the establishment of Mycenaean control over the
Corinthia cannot be determined. It need not have been much, if at
all, before LH III B; but on the other hand the political control, if
not the tight organization of the economy, may already have been
established to some degree towards the end of the Middle Bronze
Age. Indeed, it has recently been argued that control of communications through the Corinthia to the Corinthian Gulf and the west
was of major importance in the rise of the Mycenaean rulers buried
in the Shaft Graves.[75] Nor can the character of the relationship be
determined; but the archaeological record does allow the recovery
of one of the most significant activities of the kings of Mycenae
in the Corinthia: the Isthmus fortification wall. It can be traced
for something approaching 2 km. from the eastern side of the
Isthmus, and is sometimes as much as 4 m. thick at the base; it was
provided with towers facing to the north. Despite suggestions that

---

[73] For discussion of this question from the Mycenaean point of view, see Bintliff, *Natural
Environment and Human Settlement in Prehistoric Greece*, 299-305, 345-6; Dickinson
(below, n. 75).
[74] Contrast, e.g., Dunbabin, *JHS* lxviii (1948), 60 with Page, *History and the Homeric
Iliad*, 164 n. 34. Either view is plausible; neither is demonstrable. That the Catalogue, at
least in part, reflects Mycenaean conditions is certain (see, e.g., Hope-Simpson and Lazenby,
The Catalogue of Ships in Homer's Iliad); but that does not guarantee the Mycenaean origin
of all its parts. The Bacchiad epic poet Eumelus claimed for Corinth the Homeric references
to Ephyre because there was little on Corinth itself (Huxley, *Greek Epic Poetry*, 61), but
that tells us nothing of the origin of what we have.
[75] Dickinson, *Origins of Mycenaean Civilisation*, 54-6; cf. 87-9.

the wall may have served to retain a road, there is now no doubt that its purpose was defensive, and it must have been intended to prevent incursions into the Peloponnese from the north.[76] The wall is dated to about the time of transition from LH III B to C, and although it is impossible to be sure of its precise chronological relationship to the widespread destructions in the Mycenaean world at about this time, it is clear evidence that the powers of the Peloponnese feared an invasion from the north. Since there was no Mycenaean centre in the Corinthia capable of organizing the manpower needed for the construction of the wall, the plans, the supplies, and the building will have been administered ultimately from elsewhere, presumably from Mycenae itself. This cannot be taken to confirm that the Corinthia was ordinarily subject to Mycenaean control, for the exceptional danger that was thought to demand the devotion of massive resources to the creation of the wall may have called for exceptional arrangements to meet it. None the less, commands from Mycenae were probably no novelty in the Corinthia; only the scale and nature of the project were new. The character of the crisis for which the wall is an important item of evidence remains disputed (below, 50-54); but the Corinthia was no better able to survive the crisis than her Mycenaean rulers, for LH III C evidence has turned up on very few sites in the region, and then only in tiny quantities (below, 39, 47-8).

c. The Land

The potential of the Corinthia was recognized early: its prehistoric inhabitants did not have to read geographical or geological treatises to know that the springs of Corinth and the rich land of the coastal plain provided a site without a rival so long as there was no external threat. The land controlled by Corinth in the historical period comprised an area of some 900 km.[2] I do not have the skills, nor have I had the time to conduct the systematic survey of the region that is still urgently required, both of the character of the soils and of the surface evidence for ancient occupation.[77] What follows is therefore necessarily a preliminary account, based on published work of an equally unsystematic kind but, for the character of the land itself, more especially on numerous walks in the Corinthia. I make no pretence at scientific analysis, nor have I been able, with all too few exceptions, to exploit the inherited experience of those whose

[76] Wiseman, 59-60 (with references).
[77] Cf. Wiseman, 143.

ancestors have earned a living from the soil of the Corinthia for generations; but while modern statistics and impressionistic observation of modern conditions may mislead, even the chance collection of surface evidence can exercise a valuable control. The broad conclusions about the exploitation of the land in antiquity—which is all that a more systematic analysis could hope to provide in the absence of detailed ancient evidence—are not likely to be seriously wrong.[78]

The land ranges in character from the coastal plain to the rough mountains of Geraneia and the south. It is better considered in blocks which share common features than in geographical order, although the blocks are, broadly speaking, disposed in concentric fashion about Corinth itself: the well-watered coastal plain proper; relatively flat areas in the region of the Isthmus, where there is much arable but water-supply is more difficult; gently sloping hills which, often with terracing, will support some cereals, but more frequently olives or vines; and the mountains to the north and south. Both the drawing of boundaries between land of these different types and the placing of some tracts in a given type on the sketch map (Fig. 5) are inevitably somewhat arbitrary in places, and in all regions but the coastal plain there are small areas which do not conform to the character of the block as a whole; but these inaccuracies can be compensated for to some degree by study of the accompanying photographs.

The basic geological structure of the Corinthia is relatively simple. The central area, between Geraneia in the north and Acrocorinth and Oneion in the south, is made up of sedimentary rocks lying close to the horizontal, and laid down in the Late Tertiary or Quaternary Periods. Similar layers are found on the coast of the Saronic Gulf south of Geraneia and south of Oneion. The mountains are almost exclusively limestone. Thus the rocks of the whole region are permeable: the only layers which catch water are those of clay beneath the sedimentary rocks which form bluffs rising above the coastal plain in the region of the ancient city. The distinctive Corinthian clay was not only used to make Corinthian pots; it created springs which provided water to drink from them.[79]

The Corinthian portion of the coastal plain[80] has an area of rather over 30 km.^{2}; it thus comprises about one-twenty-fifth of

[78] For all that follows, see Philippson, *Landschaften*, i.948-64; iii.71-92, 96-102, 160-1.

[79] For the geology of the Corinthia, see in general Philippson, locc. citt.; cf. also Philippson, *ZGEB* xxv (1890), 1-98. A detailed recent treatment: van Freyberg, *Die Geologie des Isthmus von Korinth*.

[80] For the boundary with Sicyon, see above, 3.

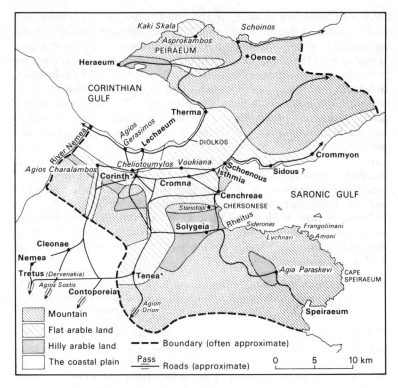

Fig. 5   The Corinthia: Land, Settlements, Roads, and Harbours

the total territory. South of the plain, the land rises in a series of
bluffs (Pls. 10–11, 35); the plain is the lowest of the plateaux which
rise like steps between them, but it has been considerably built up
by alluvium washed down from the south.[81] This has always been
the most heavily populated region of the Corinthia. For much of
the prehistoric period many of those who cultivated the plain lived
at Corinth, and this pattern was resumed early in the first millennium
BC and not disrupted significantly until the earthquake of 1858,
when a new city was built on the coast to the north-east. The great
majority of the earliest settlement sites in the Corinthia have similar
access to the plain. In the historical period there is surface evidence,
beginning in the sixth century, of a settlement of considerable
extent to the western end of the Corinthian section of the plain

[81] Above, 8; cf. Philippson, *Landschaften*, iii.161.

at Agios Charalambos. Here, as at Corinth itself, the settlement was built just above the plain and thus did not encroach upon the prime agricultural land;[82] the hill of Agios Gerasimos, which rises above the plain near the coast, seems to have been used for a similar purpose from the seventh century.[83] The North Cemetery, on the other hand, in which generations of those who had supported themselves from the plain were buried, was in the plain itself.[84] There is scattered surface evidence, which shows a consistent increase from Neolithic to Late Mycenaean, for settlement on a smaller scale just above the plain (above, 10-17). There are a few items from Geometric (below, 156); but by the archaic and classical periods the evidence is, relatively speaking, abundant again.[85] In the modern period, population was denser here in the first part of this century than near the Isthmus despite the distorting effect of the town of Corinth.[86]

We have direct evidence of the excellence of this land in antiquity. Diodorus records that the Partheniae of Sparta, before founding Tarentum, went to Delphi to ask if they might settle here; the Pythia replied,

> 'Good is the land between Corinth and Sicyon,
> But you will not live there, not even if you are all made of bronze.'
> (Diod. viii.21.3.)

The first line of this oracle is given, in distorted form, by many authors as a stock answer to the hopeful request for advice as to how to become rich: 'Get possession of the land between Corinth and Sicyon.'[87] In modern times it is widely used for vines: 'currant' derives from the name of Corinth, but more recently citrus groves have become numerous; cereals are hardly to be found there (Pl. 1). The situation was presumably different in antiquity; but Xenophon's description of the part of the plain on which the battle of the Nemea was fought in 394—λάσιον—literally 'shaggy', 'woolly', so that the Spartans could not see that the enemy were advancing—shows that more substantial plants were grown in parts of it.[88] A similar use is implied by Agesilaus' destruction of trees here a few years later (Xen. *Hell.* iv.5.10); orchards or olive groves might well have shared this rich land with cereals grown among the trees.

---

[82] Wiseman, 100-2.
[83] Wiseman, 99.
[84] For the North Cemetery, see Blegen, Palmer and Young, *Corinth*, xiii.
[85] Wiseman, 102-4.
[86] *Admiralty Handbook*, iii.162: 417 per square mile in the plain, 267 in the Isthmus.
[87] References in Parke and Wormell, *Delphic Oracle*, ii.21, no. 46.
[88] Xen. *Hell.* iv.2.19; see below, 352.

There is nothing in the rest of the Corinthia to match the wealth
of the coastal plain; but a good proportion of it is reasonably productive. Land of this character is much greater in extent than the
coastal plain: the total is nearly 200 km.^{2}, almost a quarter of the
Corinthia, and most of it is in a single block of territory through
which the main communications of the Corinthia run. It begins
at the foot of Geraneia and covers the whole Isthmus region to
Acrocorinth and Oneion in the south. This land is only rarely as
flat as the coastal plain, and it has a great deal less water; in modern
times its productive capacity is increased by artificial irrigation,
and under the emperor Hadrian water was carried to Corinth from
Lake Stymphalus in Arcadia.[89] Here and there the slopes are so
steep that even terracing cannot provide land that is sufficiently
flat for agriculture; but the view from Acrocorinth to the east and
north-east (Pls. 3, 4) shows that the great majority of the region is
cultivated. The Isthmus is divided from the coastal plain by a series
of bluffs of poros and poros conglomerate, between which the land
is relatively flat. New Corinth is built between the lowest of these
bluffs and the sea, on the small delta of the Leukon. West of New
Corinth the lowest bluff almost reaches the coast. From here the
cliff runs south-west and then west towards Corinth and beyond;
above it rise two more before the level of the city is reached. From
Temple Hill the bluffs can be traced eastwards (Pls. 10, 35); the
north city-wall was built on one just above the coastal plain (Pl. 11),
and they continue past the valley cut by the Leukon (Pl. 12) to
Examilia and on towards Isthmia; ancient quarries can be observed
all along their course.[90]

The land of this central region varies considerably in quality. In
modern times, some of it is almost as productive as the coastal plain,
and along the bottom of the valley of the Leukon there is little but
citrus groves; but they are mainly supported by artificial irrigation—
one sprinkler to each tree—and in antiquity these methods were not
available. Much of the land in the immediate vicinity of Corinth,
above the coastal plain to the east, is similarly used now (Pls. 2, 13).
This land will have been a good deal drier in ancient times, but
cereals will grow here, and above the bluffs that rise over the Leukon
valley and throughout much of the region barley is still grown. The
Admiralty Chart of 1890 remarks on the growth of cereals at the
Isthmus itself. There are now extensive vineyards at Examilia, where
there are signs of ancient (but mainly Roman period) occupation.[91]

[89] Paus. ii.3.5.
[90] For these bluffs, see Philippson, *Landschaften*, iii.80–2.
[91] Wiseman, 68–9.

The soil cover in many parts of the Isthmus region is thin, and it is
not long ago that it was covered in pine forest; the coastal region
between Isthmia and Cenchreae, where the rocks are almost without
soil, can support nothing else, although fire has very recently destroyed many of the trees (Pl. 30). But the land has now been
almost entirely cleared elsewhere, and although it cannot support
such a density of population as the coastal plain, almost everywhere
it can produce something.

That this region was exploited early is demonstrated by the
Neolithic evidence from Gonia, just east of the Leukon; other
prehistoric sites are known here, on ridges which form parts of
the bluffs which run west to east from the region of Corinth. That
cultivation was extensive here in the classical period is shown by
the wide sherd-scatter at ancient Cromna;[92] the material dates from
at least the seventh century. There was a smaller settlement to the
north-west at Voukiana from perhaps the fifth;[93] a few graves of
the sixth and fifth centuries have been excavated further to the
north at New Corinth.[94] The best land in this whole area is the
narrow strip along the valley of the Leukon, where the alluvium
(much of it perhaps relatively recent) is often some metres deep;
but Plate 14, if the telegraph-poles can be removed by the imagination, may give an accurate impression of the broad character of
the region as a whole in antiquity: a field of barley with olives
behind.

The most extensive block of land in this category is the Isthmus
region itself; but other smaller areas possess a similar character. The
Leukon valley remains fertile nearly as far as Chiliomodion in the
south. On either side of its narrow strip of artificially irrigated citrus
groves cereals and olives are grown, and the extensive remains at
Tenea, just south of Chiliomodion, which begin with a grave in MG I
(below, 156), demonstrate a considerable population in this region
and further west towards Cleonae and the passes to the Argolid.
Tenea was, to judge from the scatter of surface sherds, the largest
settlement in the Corinthia outside Corinth.[95] The presence of men
from Tenea among the colonists at Syracuse indicates that this
region was already so heavily exploited for agriculture by the mid-
eighth century that its population was growing too great for its
resources (below, 63). Further to the west, even vines can grow
beneath the slopes of the mountains without artificial irrigation,

[92] Wiseman, *Hesperia*, xxxii (1963), 271–3; Wiseman, 66–8.
[93] Wiseman, *Hesperia*, xxxii (1963), 273–5; Wiseman, 70.
[94] Wiseman, 70–2.
[95] Wiseman, 92–3.

and olive groves are numerous (Pl. 15); some cereals are found. The Longopotamos valley, the northern part of which belonged to Corinth, also supports vines, along with olives and a few citrus groves; but the valley is narrow, except where it approaches the coastal plain, and its sides are heavily eroded (Pl. 16). Communications between here and Penteskouphi village are made difficult by steep-sided and unstable ravines (above, 3–4); but near the village, on the lower slopes of the peak of that name, there are vineyards (pl. 17), and from here eastwards, from the foot of the north face of Acrocorinth down the steps of the bluffs towards the coastal plain, there are olive groves and some cereals. The character of the land here is well shown in Plate 1, where the National Road in the centre marks the approximate southern boundary of the coastal plain. Plate 18 shows a typical example, the Potters' Quarter plateau; the first evidence of habitation here belongs to the early eighth century, and it is likely that at that date it was the definite, if restricted, agricultural potential of the area which attracted settlers (below, 83). Together with the land to the east of Corinth (Pls. 13, 27), these plateaux between the coastal plain and Acrocorinth provided the city with an unusually extensive area of cultivable land within the walls: $c.3$ km.^{2}, allowing $c.1$ km.^{2} for the settlement itself. There may have been further land available between the Long Walls to Lechaeum; but during the Corinthian War, when the city was under the greatest military pressure, this land was not under its control, for the Spartans were in possession of Lechaeum (below, 362-3).

There is a finger of similar territory pointing eastwards beneath Geraneia along the north coast of the Saronic Gulf from the Isthmus. At its widest point was the settlement of Crommyon, near the modern Agioi Theodoroi; habitation is attested here from the early eighth century—the date of a dozen or more graves (below, 48)—and there is extensive evidence for later occupation.[96] Both here and at Sidous further west there were fortifications by $c.400$, for they were captured in 392 by the Spartan Praxitas (below, 363); but it is not quite clear from the text of Xenophon whether the reference in either case is to a wall round the settlement or to a smaller fortified position to which the inhabitants of this border region could flee in case of attack.[97] At other points along this coast the barren foothills of Geraneia reach close to the sea, especially at the western end near the Isthmus; much of this land is now occupied by petrochemical

[96] Wiseman, 18-19.
[97] Xen. *Hell.* iv.4.13: 'He attacked and took first Sidous and then Crommyon, and after placing garrisons in these fortifications (τείχεσι) . . .'.

and other industrial installations. Sidous cannot be precisely located but should be in the wider part of the flat coastal area half-way between Crommyon and the Isthmus.[98] It was famous in antiquity for its apples (below, 126). Nothing similar is grown here now, but there are orchards south of the canal, although they are mainly almonds.

The Perachora peninsula was known in antiquity as the Peiraeum, the 'land opposite'—a meaning exactly the same as that of the name of the main modern settlement at Perachora;[99] that the name is admirably appropriate is shown even more by the view from Acrocorinth (Pl. 2) than by the map. The peninsula is largely mountainous; but two plains are reasonably productive. That of Perachora village stretches to Bissia in the centre of the peninsula; the land is mainly used for barley and olives, but there is little sign on the surface of extensive ancient settlement here.[100] The coastal valley of Asprokambos, on the other hand, has a good deal of evidence, including graves and probably a sixth-century temple, from the archaic period on.[101] Xenophon, in his brief description of the campaign of Agesilaus in the Peiraeum in 390,[102] remarks that in that year 'the Corinthians were keeping all their animals safe in the Peiraeum, and were sowing and reaping crops over the whole Peiraeum.' The latter item is no doubt exaggerated, for much of the peninsula cannot support crops; but although the especially intensive cultivation of the region was exceptional, as a war emergency measure, the passage is a useful indication that this area may have been more heavily exploited in antiquity than it is now. Even in the early years of this century the official statistics record a much greater use of the land than more recently.[103]

Most of the productive land in the Corinthia is in the plain or the flat land near the Isthmus; but there are smaller, less flat tracts of land elsewhere which, while they certainly present greater difficulties, are not without value, and considerably increase the population the territory is able to support. The most extensive block of land of this character is between Oneion and the mountains of the southern and

[98] Wiseman, 19-20.

[99] Τὸ Πείραιον refers rather to the peninsula as a whole, from Oenoe in the north and the region of Loutraki westwards, than to any particular settlement within it: Wiseman, 32-3.

[100] Wiseman, 32; for a summary, with references, of the scattered evidence in the region, Wiseman, 36-7.

[101] Wiseman, 34-6, with references.

[102] *Ages.* ii.18; see below, 364-6.

[103] Most conveniently in Sakellariou and Faraklas, Appendix i.4. The figures are clearly incomplete, but the drop between 1911 and 1961 is none the less striking. In 1911, 3.85 km.² are recorded as having grown annual crops and 3.13 km.² as fallow; fifty years later the figures were 0.89 and 0.86 km.² respectively.

south-eastern Corinthia, and is bounded on the west by the better land east of the Leukon valley (Pl. 19), where there was a classical site on the western of the two hills known as Duo Vouna.[104] Much of this region, especially towards Athikia in the south, has bare limestone hills where there is too little soil for cultivation (Pl. 20); but although further to the north the soil is always stony, it supports numerous olive groves, particularly towards the coast (Pls. 21-2). There is similar land between Athikia and Chiliomodion. From Galataki almost to the top of the long ridge of Oneion, which slopes much less steeply to the south than to the north, there are olive groves, where the trees are planted further apart than on the coast, mixed with pine forests on the slopes which are too steep to retain soil. The land here is often forbidding, and communications are not easy; but it is rarely useless, and there is sufficient evidence on the surface here to show that it was probably exploited in antiquity for purposes similar to those for which it is used now. Mycenaean habitation is known on a number of sites in the region (above, 17). There is evidence from Athikia already in MG I (below, 156), and the famous kouros known as the Apollo of Tenea was found close by.[105] The temple at the Solygeian Ridge above Galataki was presumably not built in a totally deserted region by Corinthians who believed what Eumelus told them of their origins (below, 49-50), and there is surface evidence from the classical period on a number of sites close to the shore.[106] The settlement at Solygeia, near Galataki, seems to have been the most important in this region. There are extensive surface remains, including a cemetery and well-cut water-storage tunnels; and the need to defend the village was a consideration in the minds of the Corinthian commanders when Nicias invaded in 425.[107] But cereals would not do well here, except perhaps to some degree near the coast. Very few are grown now.

The hilly land which stretches up from the Leukon valley between Acrocorinth and Skiona to the south is remarkably intensively exploited for olives and cereals in modern times (Pl. 23); but there is little evidence of occupation here in antiquity. Further to the west, the land is broken up by the ravines between Penteskouphi village and the valley of the Longopotamos (Pl. 7); but on the west of that valley, on the northern slopes of Mt. Apesas (Phoukas), there are olives and vines where the land has not been eroded and the

---

[104] Wiseman, 90.

[105] Milchhöfer, *Arch. Zeit.* xxxix (1881), 54-6. For chance finds of slightly later pottery, Wiseman, 90.

[106] Wiseman, 53, 58.

[107] Thuc. iv.43.1-44.2.

slope is not too steep. The general descent from south to north is gentle, but there are many ravines here which make cultivation impossible. Elsewhere in the Corinthia there are almost always relatively narrow strips of land of this character where, as here, the flatter land slopes up towards the mountains. Olive groves especially, but also sometimes vineyards, are often found here, as beneath the northern face of Acrocorinth (Pl. 24). Tracts of territory of this kind are found in otherwise mountainous regions in the southern Corinthia and the Peiraeum. Near the village of Sophiko a good deal of barley is grown on the flatter land, and the road from the village to Korphos now passes through olive groves for some way (Pl. 25). The only known classical site in this region is on the hill of Agia Paraskevi, some 2 km. ENE of Sophiko. The earliest surface evidence here belongs to the fourth, perhaps the fifth, century, and the hill is crowned by a relatively large fortification, c.120 × 90 m., which boasts seven towers. Obsidian blades, not necessarily prehistoric in date, found here demonstrate that cereals were grown in the region in antiquity: many of them show the distinctive sickle sheen acquired during use in harvesting.[108]

In the Peiraeum, the small coastal valley of Schoinos is used for similar purposes today, and there is some evidence of occupation there from the sixth century; but the bay, with the fort of Oenoe behind, was of some military significance, and these scraps may not indicate exploitation for more peaceful purposes.[109] The land to the south side of the peninsula between Perachora village and the Heraeum is more varied: vines are found here along with olives, but in parts the rock is too close to the surface to support anything but pines. It is by no means certain that there was a permanent settlement of any size at or near the Heraeum; the remains here may rather represent structures for temporary use by worshippers at the sanctuary.[110] There is evidence of occupation in the seventh century at the EH site by Lake Vouliagmeni; and sherds of a similar and later date have been found by the east shore of the Lake, in an area that is now especially well cultivated.[111]

Between three-fifths and two-thirds of the Corinthia is now almost without productive capacity. The great proportion of this land is limestone mountain. The main blocks are Geraneia, including the Peiraeum, in the north, and those which separate the Corinthia from Epidaurus and the Argolid in the south; but there are other

[108] Wiseman, 127-8.

[109] For the remains—more extensive in the later Roman period—see Wiseman, 30.

[110] Tomlinson, *BSA* lxiv (1969), 233-40.

[111] Fossey, *BSA* lxiv (1969), 55; *AD* xxvii.B (1973), 150; Payne, *Perachora*, i.9.

heights south of the Isthmus which contribute to the character of the Corinthia and determine its communications. The most obvious, because of its mainly isolated position, is Acrocorinth—despite its relatively low height (575 m.). Its striking shape, especially from the north and east to the traveller approaching the Isthmus from Central Greece, intensifies this effect even from a distance against the backdrop of the higher mountains beyond (Pl. 26). From close by, the gently rising slopes beneath the crags above detract a little from its grandeur (Pl. 27); but from a distance its cliffs arrest the eye, and it appears to dominate the surrounding area like a giant pillbox. The verse quoted by Strabo (382), 'Corinth's brow frowns and is hollowed out', probably refers to the aspect of Acrocorinth— often called simply 'Corinth'—from the city, for from here the towering cliffs and the gully on the northern face (Pl. 28) fit the description perfectly.[112] The almost sheer faces of the citadel, not quite unscalable but offering easy access only to the west, provide an admirable place of refuge; but they are too high for a regular acropolis which could serve as the defensible nucleus of a settlement. The ridge which gives the easiest access to the west is joined (Pl. 29) to the contrasting pinnacle of Penteskouphi (473 m.). To the south-east of Acrocorinth the long limestone ridge of Oneion stretches between the Leukon valley and the coast, its north face almost sheer in parts (Pl. 4); despite its very slightly greater height (584 m.), its shape and position make it less eminent than Acrocorinth, but it provides a more effective barrier which Epaminondas took care to secure before his third invasion of the Peloponnese after earlier suffering difficulties here (below, 376). A fort at the eastern end, above the narrow pass between mountain and coast, affords a splendid view of the Isthmus and movements in the Saronic Gulf (Pl. 30).[113] South of Acrocorinth, Skiona has a more gentle slope but rises to a considerably greater height (701 m.) before falling away equally gradually towards the valley of Tenea (Pl. 23).

Much of the mountainous territory in the far north and south of the Corinthia is now covered with forests of Aleppo Pine, *Pinus halepensis* (Pl. 31), which provide sustenance for the larvae of

---

[112] Strabo (followed by many modern authors; e.g. Wiseman, 9) referred it rather to the fact that some of the Corinthian territory is rough and full of gullies. This is possible, and even the city of Corinth might be said to 'frown', from above the bluffs on which it was built, at a traveller approaching from the plain (see Pl. 11); but the city is not in any obvious sense 'hollowed out', and the description is more striking and effective if it refers rather to the citadel.

[113] Stroud, *Hesperia*, xl (1971), 127-43.

processionary moths which feed in colonies in innumerable webs; but in modern times the tree is useful to man mainly for its resin, which is collected particularly intensively on the heavily wooded slopes of the mountains of the south-eastern Corinthia near Sophiko. The Peiraeum, the ravines west of Penteskouphi, the upper parts of Oneion, and the mountains towards the coast in the south-east are densely covered; but Acrocorinth, Skiona, and the more rounded slopes through which the passes to the Argolid run are now bare. Such forests were extensive even in the Isthmus region quite recently (above, 24). Without detailed investigation it is impossible to say how great the tree cover in antiquity was; but it is likely that the deforestation of Greece in the classical period, for which there is considerable evidence of a general kind, was a relative matter. Much, perhaps all, of the timber used for the construction of Corinthian ships, and the wood for building which was extensively exported from the Corinthia in the classical period may have grown in the ancient predecessors of these forests. Where soil cover is thin, the Aleppo Pine often grows in twisted shapes; but that would not preclude its use for fuel. It would not be surprising if much of the now heavily cultivated land south of Acrocorinth and Penteskouphi was wooded in the archaic period. The general slope of the land here is gentle enough to prevent the disastrous effects of erosion which are visible on the white marls further to the west (Pl. 32), and in a more limited area on the eastern slopes of Acrocorinth. Forests close to the city will have been the first to be exploited, and these parts may have been cleared early. Once trees had gone from the steeper slopes beneath the sheer face of Acrocorinth and from Skiona, they would not grow again; but the more undulating land between retained its soil and could be cultivated. It is perhaps significant that it is the remotest areas of the Corinthia from the ancient city, the south-east (Pl. 33) and the Peiraeum with Geraneia, which now show the most extensive forest cover; if these parts had been heavily exploited in antiquity, the slopes are so steep that regeneration might not have occurred. An incidental remark of Xenophon's (*Hell.* iv.5.4) proves that wood for fuel was freely available in the early fourth century on the heights of Mt. Loutraki.

Only a tiny proportion of the Corinthia is more than 10 km. from the sea, and the central region of the territory, perhaps a quarter of the whole, is within a similar distance from both the Saronic and the Corinthian Gulf; but there are few natural harbours within easy reach of the best sites for settlement. The prevailing winds blow from the north-west in summer and the north and east in winter; thus the Corinthian Gulf is more frequently rough than the

Saronic,[114] but it has no harbours in the Corinthia except in the Peiraeum: at the Heraeum and along the north coast. The harbour at Kaki Skala will have served the not inconsiderable settlement at Asprokambos;[115] but it is far away from the heavily populated regions. The shore of the coastal plain provides admirable beaching for warships; but it has no shelter, and for this reason an artificial harbour was excavated as early as c.600 at Lechaeum (below, 133-4). Since the character of the shore is similar all along this coast, Lechaeum was placed solely because this was the closest point to Corinth. The Saronic Gulf near Corinth is usually calmer than the Corinthian, but has more bays in which to shelter from what waves there are. Both Isthmia and Cenchreae provide some natural protection, which at Cenchreae—since it is both more sheltered and marginally closer to Corinth—was extended in antiquity at an unknown date by the construction of moles on each side of the harbour (Pl. 30).[116] Cenchreae was fortified by the mid-fourth century, for it is described by Pseudo-Scylax (54) as a τεῖχος; but the walls were probably built much earlier, for it would have been reckless to expose the port to the threat of Athenian raids during the Peloponnesian War.[117] Corinth thus had easier access to the Corinthian Gulf, once the harbour at Lechaeum was constructed, than to the Saronic; the journey to Cenchreae was three times as great as that to Lechaeum. It might be argued that this greater convenience of western than of eastern communications by sea from the city was partially responsible for the concentration of Corinthian commercial interests in the west, but geographical considerations at a wider range were probably more significant in this respect: no Greek city had a more favourable approach to the west, and Corinthians would have looked in this direction even if their immediate access to the Corinthian Gulf had been a great deal more difficult.

There are other natural harbours, most of them small, on the more sheltered Saronic coast of the Corinthia; but they were little used precisely because they were too far away from the well-populated parts of the territory. The north part of this coast, apart from Cenchreae and Isthmia, provides only open beaching: this is to be found both in the region of Crommyon and south of Oneion, and

[114] Philippson, *ZGEB* xxv (1890), 64-5.
[115] Wiseman, 36.
[116] It is possible that the harbour once provided more natural protection than it does now: Scranton, Shaw, and Ibrahim, *Kenchreai*, i.4, 6-14.
[117] Wiseman, 75 n. 42, argues that if the course of the wall built in 480 was the same as that of the Hellenistic fortification, that would demonstrate that Cenchreae was already fortified in 480; but a wall which used the Agios Demetrios Ridge (see Wiseman, 60) might end just north of Cenchreae, whether the port was itself fortified or not.

Nicias took advantage of both stretches in his attack on the Corinthia in 425 (below, 319–20). Further to the south, there are many small, sheltered inlets which may have been used in antiquity; but the hinterland is so rough here (Pl. 34) that they cannot have been much more significant than they are now (above, 6 with n. 15). The bay of Korphos was the scene of military action towards the end of the Peloponnesian War; but the place saw little if any normal use, for Thucydides describes it as ἐρῆμος, 'deserted', 'isolated' (above, 5–6). It is now used only by fishing vessels and pleasure craft, and the pine-clad mountains above it rise so close to the sea that there is room only for a few olives along the coast. It will have been more convenient for the inhabitants of the region of Sophiko to conduct such business as they had to undertake by sea northwards, from the coast near Solygeia, than to the east at Korphos. The two approaches were approximately equidistant; but from Korphos they had to make their way round Cape Spiri before making contact with any other part of the Corinthia—although there would be little competition for the fish in these waters.

Corinth is not a natural centre for communications in the Corinthia. For the long-distance traveller by land, the Isthmus imposes obvious constraints. It can be approached from the north by three different routes, but thereafter the choice is simple: to follow either the east/west corridor provided by the coastal plain, or the equally clear route up the valley of the Leukon (Pl. 5) to Chiliomodion (Tenea) and the passes to the Argolid. The Longopotamos valley, though narrower, is a possible route; but for those going south it would be natural to turn in that direction at the Isthmus itself instead of first travelling west along the eastern part of the coastal plain. Corinth does not lie exactly on either of these main routes, and the approach to the city from them, especially from the plain, involves no easy climb. For much of the prehistoric period, therefore, after Corinth was almost abandoned at the end of EH II, the site was probably ignored by the main roads in the territory; even when Corinth was a flourishing city, traffic passing through the Corinthia would not need to make the detour to the city itself.

Communications at a shorter range, within the Corinthia, were determined by the character of the land and the location of settlements: they will have differed as particular sites were occupied or abandoned. The direct evidence for roads is meagre. Some have been found in excavation, but the best evidence we have for the general pattern is in the gates which pierced the circuit of the city-walls; some are named in our literary sources, and some have been excavated (see Fig. 6). The Teneatic Gate has not been identified on

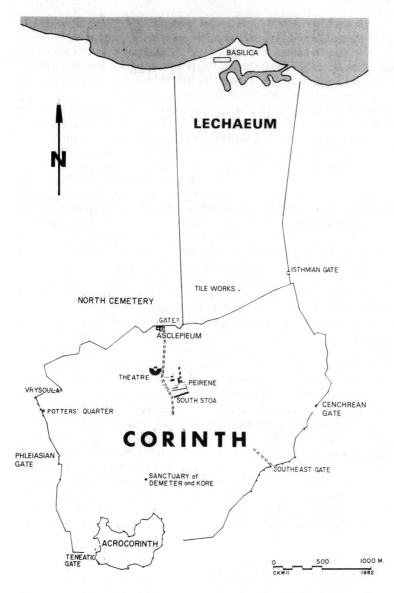

Fig. 6   Corinth: Fortifications

the ground; but Pausanias (ii.5.4) mentions it along with a 'mountain road' from Acrocorinth, and it must have been close to Acrocorinth on the ridge between the citadel and Penteskouphi. It was necessary to allow access through the wall here to the south, but this will not have been the main route from Corinth to Tenea: it is hardly shorter than the road along the Leukon valley, and involves an unnecessary steep climb from the city up to the Gate.[118] The second gate in the western part of the circuit, the Phleiasian, provided access from Corinth to the natural route south along the valley of the Longopotamos;[119] but this route was probably not heavily used (above), and to reach the valley from the gate it was necessary to pass through difficult country (above, 3-4). Cleonae and Nemea, along with Phleious and Arcadia beyond, were best approached from Corinth itself by this road; but longer-distance traffic for these destinations would most conveniently pass not through Corinth but down the Leukon valley, or (less probably) along the coastal plain and then south at the Longopotamos, the Nemea, or even beyond. The corn bought by Phleious from Corinth during the 360s, the transport of which so impressed Xenophon (*Hell.* vii.2.17-23), seems to have passed along the Nemea (Aeschin. ii.168). It was probably imported corn which had been purchased at Lechaeum.

The northern part of the city's circuit was cut by a number of gates giving access to the roads which traversed the plain, where the natural routes lay. This portion of the wall is very badly preserved; but there is other evidence which enables the approximate course of roads here to be traced from an early date. Pausanias mentions a road to Sicyon (ii.5.5), distinct from that which led to Lechaeum (ii.3.2). Sicyon might be reached from Corinth by first taking the road north to the plain and then turning west; but it is likely that from the earliest times a road ran west from the region of Temple Hill and descended into the plain near the hill of Cheliotoumylos. The North Cemetery, first used in the early eighth century, was probably placed beside this road where it reached and traversed the plain; and there are other burials, some even earlier, west of the Lechaeum Road Valley which were probably dug beside the same road as it left the early settlement.[120] Traces of the road have been

---

[118] See Wiseman, 81, with references; and esp. 93 n. 3, on Stroud's observation of traces of the hill road to Tenea south of the Teneatic Gate.

[119] For excavations here, see Carpenter, *Corinth*, iii.2.74-6. The gate was the scene of an action during Epaminondas' second invasion of the Peloponnese (below, 377). On the Phleiasian Gate and its use by Aratus in 243 during his successful attack on Acrocorinth, see further Wiseman, 81.

[120] Fig. 7: Graves 1, 4, 14?, 31-6, 38-9. See also below, 76.

discovered at various points along its course.[121] Similar evidence indicates a road striking immediately north along the Lechaeum Road Valley from the settlement well before the Long Walls were built to enable the Corinthians to defend their access to the sea at Lechaeum. The road naturally followed the course of the stream fed by Peirene, and graves of the ninth and eighth centuries have been found over some distance along this line.[122] Other roads may have descended into the plain from the region of the city—especially in the early period, when there was no city-wall; but they cannot be traced. Since Corinth was the main site in this region, the most important east/west road in the plain no doubt ran as close as possible to the city, just beneath the lowest bluff. A gate, known now but not necessarily in antiquity as the Isthmian Gate (Pl. 35), allowed this road to pass through the East Long Wall;[123] a similar gate will have pierced the West Long Wall. The western continuation of this road could have served the large settlement at Agios Charalambos if it ran close beneath the bluffs for its whole course. No doubt the plain was crossed by numerous minor tracks and paths, but it is impossible to tell whether there were any of major significance. Even a road along the coast west from Lechaeum might not have seen very heavy traffic; but there must have been a gate in each Long Wall near the coast to give access from either direction to Lechaeum.

A road passing through the 'Isthmian Gate' might provide the shortest route from Corinth to the western side of the Isthmus; but for the Isthmian sanctuary itself there was an alternative approach, through the Cenchrean Gate in the east city-wall, almost due east of Corinth. Diogenes Laertius describes this gate as 'leading to the Isthmus',[124] and it was by this way that Pausanias, coming from Cenchreae, reached the city (ii.2.4). After passing through the Cenchrean Gate,[125] the road will have descended to the main route south from the Isthmus along the valley of the Leukon. From here, it will have run beneath the bluffs to Isthmia, passing through or near the large settlement at Cromna on its way; the innumerable tons of poros quarried here in antiquity (above, 23) must have been transported along this road. A road to Cenchreae will have diverged from it in the region of Cromna, and probably carried the stone which was exported from the Corinthia in the fourth century to be used under the direction of the temple commissioners

[121] For references, see Wiseman, 84-5; add Broneer, *Corinth*, x.5-6, 142.
[122] Fig. 7: Graves 2, 5-7, 11, 15?, 37. See also below, 76.
[123] Parsons, *Corinth*, iii.2.94-113; see also Wiseman, 84-5, 86.
[124] vi.78; cf. Wiseman, 86.
[125] For excavations here, Carpenter, *Corinth*, iii.2.55-7.

at Epidaurus.[126] It is probable that the road from Isthmia to the Leukon Valley carried most of the traffic passing south from the Isthmus. Two of the routes from central Greece, that along the Saronic coast through Crommyon and Sidous, and the (probably more frequented) road through Geraneia (above, 1), reached the eastern side of the Isthmus. The third route ran from Boeotia along the Halcyonic coast and through the plain of Perachora village— from where the Heraeum at the tip of the Peiraeum could be reached; even though this road from the north approached the Isthmus on the Corinthian Gulf coast, it had easy access to Isthmia. There are no known major centres of habitation in the region of New Corinth which would require a heavily travelled road along the Leukon Valley from the coast to the vicinity of the Cenchrean Gate; but a coast road will have run from the springs at Loutraki (Therma) to Lechaeum.

The main access from Corinth for the traveller to the south along the road which followed the Leukon Valley was through what has been called in modern times the South-East Gate, the last in the city circuit, just beneath the lower slopes on the north-east side of Acrocorinth (Pl. 13).[127] To the south, the main road must have followed much the same path to Tenea as the modern route takes to Chiliomodion; there were then four possible passes to the Argolid, three of which ran through Cleonaean territory on the way. Two of these, from Cleonae itself, are described by Pausanias (ii.15.2): 'one is for fit men: it is short. The other is in the pass called Tretus; while it is narrow and has mountains on all sides it is more suitable for wheeled traffic.' These passes are easily identifiable as those of Agios Sostis and the Dervenakia (which carries the modern road) respectively;[128] a fit man travelling to either pass from Corinth might take the more direct route through the Phleiasian Gate and along the upper valley of the Longopotamos, for although this would involve a rougher journey it avoids a considerable detour towards Tenea. The Contoporeia, further to the east but still passing through Cleonaean territory (above, 5), might reasonably be approached from Corinth either along the valley of the Leukon or that of the Longopotamos; but the traveller intending to use the pass of Agion Orion, a good deal further east, would be most unlikely to reach it by any other route than the main road along the Leukon.

There will have been other less frequented roads which reached

---

[126] Below, 122. For roads in this region, cf. Wiseman, 64. Some of those he conjectures may have seen little use in the classical period, for the land near Examilia and Xylokeriza shows more significant surface evidence in later times.

[127] Carpenter, *Corinth*, iii.2.44 n. 2, 48-55.

[128] Wiseman, 113-16; above, 5.

this main route to the south at various points along the upper valley of the Leukon. A track may have left Cenchreae and run below the north face of Oneion; it probably reached the Leukon Valley road as far south as the foothills of Oneion allowed, for its main function will have been to link Cenchreae with Tenea and the south-western Corinthia. The land south of Oneion has no easy routes from east to west; but there was probably at least one road from Solygeia to the west—to the western of the Duo Vouna, where there are signs of a small settlement of the classical period, towards Athikia further south, or both. A coastal road will have run from Isthmia to Cenchreae (cf. Paus. ii.2.3), and then passed through the narrow gap between Oneion and the sea to the region of Solygeia. Further south there can have been little traffic along the coast; this road will have climbed the pass now taken by the modern road to Sophiko and the land cultivated by the inhabitants of the classical site at Agia Paraskevi. No doubt a track or path provided access from here to the isolated habour at Korphos; but it was probably rarely used. High passes to the territory of Epidaurus lay further south.

Corinth derived immense benefit from her position near the Isthmus, washed both by the Corinthian and by the Saronic Gulf; but for communications within the territory this position brought disadvantages not shared by island cities or those situated on peninsulas such as Attica. Transport by land was prohibitively expensive in antiquity. A long journey with cargo by sea round the coast of a peninsula or an island might be preferable to the use of one or more carts over a much shorter distance; but the two seas obliged the great proportion of traffic within the Corinthia to travel by land. Journeys from Corinth to the Heraeum or the north side of the Peiraeum might well be made by sea, and the Saronic Gulf will have seen similar traffic; but other communications within the Corinthia, including all those between the major centres of population, had to be carried out in whole or in large part by land. Even the traffic which left Corinth destined for shipment on the eastern sea had to make a considerable journey to reach Cenchreae. These drawbacks were no doubt more than compensated for by long-range traffic over the Isthmus both by land and by sea. Even though the main land routes passed either side of Corinth, it would be a single-minded traveller who would not divert his path to the city and himself with its delights; the sanctuary of Poseidon at Isthmia must also have exerted a powerful attraction. Already c.600 Periander built the diolkos to exploit the traffic which could pass from one gulf to the other and avoid the perils of Cape Malea. If fortune did not smile constantly upon Corinth when determining her position, she looked only momentarily aside.

II. The Origins of the City

The literary evidence for the origins of Dorian Corinth is of little value; I shall therefore not follow Will in detailed discussion of the tradition.[1] The Greeks believed that the two greatest Dorian cities, Argos and Sparta, were founded by the Heracleidae, descendants of Heracles who returned to claim their inheritance. The foundation of Dorian Corinth was also attributed to the Heracleidae; but the Corinthian story was fitted into the account only with difficulty and at a late date. The alleged founder was Aletes, who in some sources was in the fifth generation after Heracles;[2] but one author explicitly placed him a generation later (Vell. Pat. i.3.3), and there are òther signs that for some he belonged to the generation after the Return.[3] In some versions, indeed, Aletes' foundation of Corinth apparently had nothing to do with the Return: he is said to have consulted the oracle at Dodona and taken Corinth with Zeus' blessing.[4] There is no trace of Heracleidae here. Associated with this story is the proverb δέχεται καὶ βῶλον Ἀλήτης, 'Aletes accepts even a clod', which scans as the last part of hexameter;[5] it is probable that these words are to be recognized as a fragment of Eumelus, and that in his version the Heracleidae played no part.[6] Aletes in Eumelus' account probably founded Corinth independently; but later a

---

[1] *Korinthiaka*, 258–95.

[2] Paus. ii.4.3; Schol. Pind. *Ol.* xiii.17 c. Satyrus (*P. Oxy.* 2465, fr. 3.ii.12–20; cf. Hammond in Hammond and Griffith, *History of Macedonia*, ii.17) explicitly associates Aletes' capture of Corinth with the Heracleidae.

[3] Cf. Didymus ap. Schol. Pind. *Ol.* xiii.17 c Drachmann. Didymus denied that Aletes was the founder of Corinth but claimed that he ruled thirty years after the arrival of the Dorians; this is perhaps the result of a conflation of one system, in which Corinth was founded at the time of the Return, and another, in which Aletes belonged to the following generation (see further Huxley, *Philologus*, cxix (1975), 142 n. 11). Diodorus' reigns of Corinthian kings etc. (vii.9) add up to thirty years fewer than are needed to take us back from Cypselus' revolution in 657 to 1104, the Apollodoran date for the Return: perhaps another indication that Corinth could be dated in the subsequent generation, but this is not what Diod. vii.9.2 implies, and cf. Forrest, *CQ* xix (1969), 106–10.

[4] In most detail in Schol. Pind. *Nem.* vii.155 a; see Parke, *The Oracles of Zeus*, 129–31.

[5] Diogenian. iv.27; Zenob. iii.22; Duris *FGH* 76 F 84 (where, perhaps by contamination from the myth of the Return, it is a question of Aletes returning to Corinth after exile).

[6] This story does not exclude them; but the fact that the oracle concerned is Dodona, and not Delphi, makes it probable that in this version they were not present (cf. Parke, *The Oracles of Zeus*, 130–1). It is possible, however, that Dodona was involved later in order to explain the phrase Διὸς Κόρινθος: cf. Schol. Pind. *Nem.* vii.155 a.

connection with the Heracleidae was worked up. The tenuous and artificial nature of the link is also shown by the fact that the Temenids in Argos and the Agiads and Eurypontids in Sparta all traced their descent back to Heracles through Aristomachus;[7] the Corinthian list reached back to Heracles quite differently.[8]

The legend of the Return was no doubt intended to explain the fact that certain Peloponnesian cities spoke the Doric dialect and shared certain cult practices and institutions. Corinth's legend was different from all others in that it made her foundation neither an integral part of the Return nor part of the secondary Argive expansion like the foundation of Megara and Sicyon.[9] It might be concluded that Corinth's origins were known to have been independent of Argos;[10] but to base such a conclusion on the literary evidence alone would be hazardous. That Corinth was an Argive foundation has indeed been argued by Dunbabin. His case was based heavily on the archaeological evidence from the Heraeum at Perachora, and I have argued elsewhere that it gives no support to his view.[11] But that does not demonstrate that Corinth was not founded from Argos, for Eumelus may have claimed a false independence for his city;[12] in view of the untrustworthy nature of the tradition, the origins of Dorian Corinth are best studied through the material remains.

In the prehistoric period, while the well-watered site of Corinth was probably never completely deserted, it had not been settled in strength since before the end of the Early Bronze Age. Extensive subsequent occupation can first be traced in the LPG period, *c*.925–875, when a long series of graves begins the continuous development of the archaeology of Dorian Corinth (below, 75–6; see Fig. 7). Between LH III C and LPG there is evidence of brief, small-scale occupation late in LH III C, along with a contemporary child-grave in a cist, in the later sanctuary of Demeter on the slope of Acrocorinth.[13] Two Submycenaean graves have been excavated in the central area.[14] The only other remains which have a context are a few vases found on a burnt hearth to the west of the Museum (the

---

[7] e.g. Paus. ii.18.7; for the generations back to Heracles, Hdt. vi.52.1; vii.204; viii.131.2.

[8] Paus. ii.4.3; Apollod. ii.174; Schol. Pind. *Ol.* xiii.17. b–c. *P. Oxy.* 2465, fr. 3, ii.17–20 (Satyrus).

[9] Salmon, *BSA* lxvii (1972), 193.

[10] Cf. Huxley, *Philologus*, cxix (1975), 141.

[11] *BSA* lxvii (1972), 179–92. Dunbabin (*JHS* lxviii (1948), 63–5) used other arguments, but none of them any more persuasive. For the epithet Acraea for Hera, cf. Salmon, *BSA* lxvii (1972), 194–5, 202–4; 179 n. 99 for Dunbabin's geographical argument.

[12] Dunbabin, *JHS* lxviii (1948), 66–8.

[13] Rutter, *Hesperia*, xlviii (1979), 348–91.

[14] Williams, *Hesperia*, xxxix (1970), 14–15.

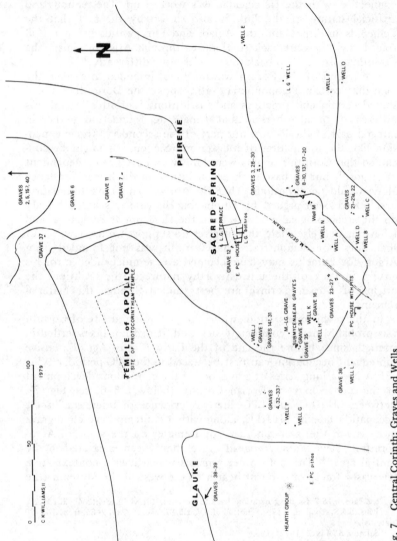

Fig. 7 Central Corinth: Graves and Wells

Figure 7: Key
Geometric Graves and Wells marked without numbers or letters remain unpublished; I am much indebted to C. K. Williams II for the plan on which this figure is based. All graves and wells are given an approximate location as follows:

N   from Sacred Spring area northwards

SE   south of Sacred Spring and east of Middle Geometric Drain

SW   south of Sacred Spring and west of Middle Geometric Drain

Graves

1 (SW). LPG. Williams, *Hesperia* xxxix (1970), 16-20.
2 (N). LPG. Weinberg, 9 (W 20-1).
3 (SE). LPG. Williams, *Hesperia* xlii (1973), 4-6.
4 (SW). LPG/EG. Weinberg, *Hesperia* xvii (1948), 204-6.
5 (N). LPG/EG. Weinberg, 10-15 (W 22-53); Wiseman, 95 n.43.
6 (N). EG. Williams, *Hesperia* xliii (1974), 24 n.21.
7 (N). EG/MG I. Nichols, *AJA* ix (1905), 411-21; Weinberg, 16-18 (W 54-66).
8 (SE). MG II. Morgan, *AJA* xli (1937), 543, pl.13.2, grave D; Weinberg, 25-7 (W 73-7); G. D. Weinberg, *Corinth* xiii, 68, no.516.
9-10 (SE). MG II. Morgan, *AJA* xli (1937), 544-5, pl.13.2, graves F-G; Weinberg, 28 (W 80); G. D. Weinberg, *Corinth* xiii, 199, no.1511.
11 (N). MG II? Hill, *AJA* xxxi (1927), 73. The closest vase known to me is Young, *Corinth* xiii, 24-5 (17-1: MG II).
12 (N). MG. Williams, *Hesperia* xlii (1973), 3 fig.1.
13? (SE). MG II. W 78; perhaps from a grave (Weinberg, 28).
14? (SW). MG II. W 83-5; perhaps from Grave 31, or from one or more other burial(s). Cf. Weinberg, 29.
15? (N). MG II. W 68; perhaps from a grave (Weinberg, 19).
16 (SW). Early EPC. Broneer, *AJA* xxxvii (1933), 567; Weinberg, 34 (W 102).
17 (SE). EC. Morgan, *AJA* xli (1937), 543 n.1 (W 197-8); cf. Weinberg, 55.
18-19 (SE). Morgan, *AJA* xli (1937), 544-5, pl.13.2, graves A-B; Weinberg, 28 (W 81); G. D. Weinberg, *Corinth* xii, 68-70, no.517.
20 (SE). Morgan, *AJA* xli (1937), 543-4, pl.13.2, grave C; G. D. Weinberg, *Corinth* xiii, 276-7, fig.64; 233, nos.1808; 250, no.2000; 281, nos.2264-5.
21-21a (SE). Weinberg, 30 (W 87-8, 89-97).
22 (SE). Morgan, *Hesperia* xxii (1953), 134 with 132 fig.1 top left (south of gr.1). Perhaps early; for the type, cf. Grave 1.
23-27 (SW). Williams, *Hesperia* xli (1972), 145.
28 (SW). Williams, *Hesperia* xliii (1973), 4.
29-30 (SE). Williams, *Hesperia* xliii (1974), 1.
31 (SW). Stillwell, *AJA* xl (1936), 43; Weinberg, 29 (W 86); Scranton, *Corinth* i.3, 5.
32 (SW). Weinberg, *Hesperia* xvii (1948), 206-7.
33? (SW). Weinberg, *Hesperia* xvii (1948), 207.
34 (N). Williams, *Hesperia* xxxix (1970), 16.
35 (SW). Williams, *Hesperia* xxxix (1970), 20.
36 (SW). Williams, *Hesperia* xlv (1976), 100.
37 (N). Williams, *Hesperia* xliii (1974), 24.
38-39 (SW). Broneer, *Corinth* x, 10.
40 (N). Wiseman, 95 n.43.

Wells

A (SE). PG. Williams, *Hesperia* xlii (1973), 3 fig.1, 4 (Well 72-7).
B (SE). MG/LG. Williams, *Hesperia* xlii (1973), 3 fig.1, 4 (dug in 1953).
C (SE). MG II? Broneer, *Hesperia* xx (1951), 293-4. Four MG II skyphoi were found in the well; but they may have come from disturbed graves in the vicinity. The fragmentary material, which is much later, perhaps gives the date at which the well was dug.
D (SE). LG. Williams, *Hesperia* xlii (1973), 3 fig.1, 4 (Well 72-3).
E (SE). LG. Weinberg, *Hesperia* xviii (1949), 153-4.
F (SE). LG. Williams, *Hesperia* xlii (1973), 3 fig.1 bottom right.
G (SW). LG. Weinberg, *Hesperia* xvii (1948), 208-14.
H, J, K (SW). LG. Williams, *Hesperia* xxxix (1970), 13 fig.4 (dated by Williams, *Hesperia* xl (1971), 23).
L (SW). MG II/LG. Williams, *Hesperia* xlv (1976), 100 (Well 75-3).
M (SE). EPC. Williams, *Hesperia* xli; (1972), Weinberg, 37 (W 116-34).
N (SE). EPC Williams, *Hesperia* xli (1972), 147 (Well 71-5).
O (SE). LG/EPC. Williams, *Hesperia* xlii (1973), 3 fig.1 bottom right.
P (SW). EPC. Williams, *Hesperia* xlii (1973), 3 fig.1 bottom left.

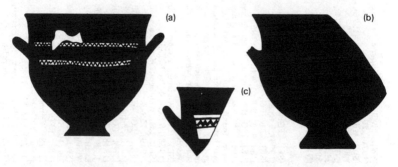

Fig. 8   From The Hearth Group: (a) W 1; (b) W 3; (c) W 4

Hearth Group: Fig. 8).[15] A few other scattered scraps have turned up;[16] and two whole or nearly whole vases have been recovered from disturbed contexts.[17] The LPG period probably witnessed an increase in the population of the site. There are five graves of this short period, and subsequently the numbers rise further; and while it is hazardous to draw conclusions from the relative wealth of graves, one of the earliest is richer than anything known at Corinth for centuries (Fig. 7, Grave 1). If this evidence is representative, it implies an increase in population; but the record is far from full. If the population grew, that could be explained either by natural increase or by the arrival of newcomers; the latter conclusion would be encouraged if it were possible to prove discontinuity in the material record. The pottery provides, at first sight, some evidence for an opposite conclusion. A not infrequent type of Corinthian LPG skyphos has a deep shape with a low foot, and three or five reserved lines in the handle zone; the central line is covered with a diluted scribble (Fig. 9).[18] There are no contemporary parallels known to me outside the Cyclades;[19] these skyphoi may therefore be the successors of the untidy deep specimens with tall flaring feet and wavy lines in the handle zone from the Hearth Group and

[15] Weinberg, *AJA* xliii (1939), 596–9; cf. Weinberg, 3. The pots, W 1–5; their chronology, Weinberg, 5; Desborough, *PGP* 203–4; *Last Mycenaeans*, 85.
[16] Broneer, *Hesperia*, xx (1951), 293, pl. 89 b (cf. Desborough, *Last Mycenaeans*, 85); SM to early PG, South Stoa area. Williams, *Hesperia*, xl (1971), 3; early to late PG, Sacred Spring area. Weinberg, *Corinth*, i.5.4; PG, not illustrated or more closely dated.
[17] Shear, *AJA* xxxv (1931), 426; LPG lekythos from a Roman grave in the North Cemetery. W 6 (Weinberg, 5–6; Desborough, *PGP* 67–8, 203); LPG jug from disturbed fill in the Museum area.
[18] W 38; Williams, *Hesperia*, xxxix (1970), 19, no. 26.
[19] Coldstream, *GGP* 165 n. 2, pl. 34 a; cf., however, Kraiker, *Kerameikos*, i.126–7, pl. 38 bottom left.

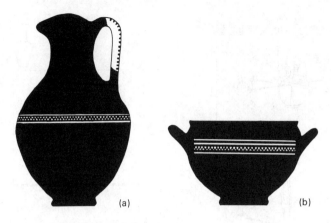

(a)   (b)

Fig. 9   Oinochoe and Skyphos from Grave 1

the South Stoa at Corinth.[20] But a more probable explanation is that the shape of the scribble skyphoi was adapted from the high-footed vases of Attica,[21] while the decoration was matched to that of the common scribble oinochoai of LPG to make what Miss Benton has called dinner-sets (Fig. 9).[22]

Pottery styles thus provide no argument against discontinuity of settlement; other aspects of the material record offer some evidence in favour of it. Grave types in the long Corinthian series from LPG onwards are remarkably consistent. Out of about ninety graves to the end of Geometric, some seventy are of a type not often found elsewhere: a rectangular pit, often very carefully cut, covered by a single well-finished rectangular slab (Pl. 36).[23] There is sometimes a separate cache at the head of the grave, covered by a separate slab,

[20] Hearth Group: W 1, 4; South Stoa: Broneer, *Hesperia*, xx (1951), 293, pl. 89 b.

[21] Cf. Desborough, *PGP* 77–92 (examples with a decoration like that of the Corinthian skyphoi with low feet; *PGP* 86–7). Low-footed examples are known, but they are not common (e.g. Smithson, *Hesperia*, xxx (1961), 166, no. 45), and it is easier to believe that Corinthian potters, who in LPG never gave their vases high feet, put a low foot on the common Attic shape.

[22] *BSA* xlviii (1953), 260 (MG II). Corinthian scribble oenochoai: W 20, 23; Williams, *Hesperia*, xxxix (1970), 18, no. 20. Attic examples are common: Desborough, *PGP* 51–2. Corinthian potters appear to have also transferred the scribble decoration to the pyxis, on which it is unusual elsewhere: Coldstream, *GGP* 197 with n. 3.

[23] This is best seen in the North Cemetery, where more than three-quarters of the Geometric burials were of this type: cf. Young, *Corinth*, xiii.18 (a typical example, pl. 102, grave 16). There are some fine examples from the Agora south-central area: Morgan, *AJA* xli (1937), 543–5, pl. 14.1. Four of the six Potters' Quarter graves are of the same type: Stillwell, *Corinth*, xv.1.7–11.

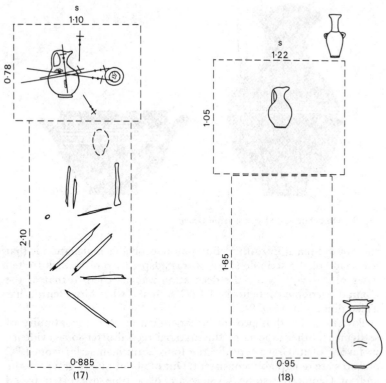

Fig. 10   North Cemetery Graves 17 and 18. From Blegen, Palmer and Young, *Corinth*, xiii, pl.102.

for some or all of the grave goods (Fig. 10).[24] Other types occur in sufficient numbers to be significant: the monolith sarcophagus is almost universal from the late eighth to the fifth centuries,[25] but is known already in LPG (as we might expect) for child burials;[26] and a type best known as the slab sarcophagus, made out of six stone slabs neatly fitted together, appears at least as early as MG II and has a primitive predecessor as far back as LPG (Pl. 37).[27] A few

[24] North Cemetery: Young, *Corinth*, xiii.24; perhaps already foreshadowed in LPG: Grave 1 (for numbered graves in the following notes, see Fig. 7).

[25] Young, *Corinth*, xiii.50.

[26] Grave 2; cf. Lawrence, *Hesperia*, xxxiii (1964), 89–91; Grave 7 (sarcophagus of adult size found near a large deposit of EG/MG I vases; but cf. Young, *Corinth*, xiii.20 n. 13). One mud sarcophagus: Grave 35.

[27] North Cemetery: Young, *Corinth*, xiii.18–19; cf. also Grave 11. The rich LPG Grave 1 is perhaps best interpreted as a primitive example of this type.

burials were made in vases,[28] but other types are so unusual that they must be taken as abnormal. The two SM graves are like none of these later types (Pl. 38). Each had a layer of stones round the lip of the grave, and a floor of pebbles; neither feature is recorded subsequently, and the mud-brick cover found in each SM burial is later replaced by a single poros slab. Perhaps a more significant difference is that one of the SM graves contained two corpses: for the second a new pebble floor was laid above the first;[29] there is no other Corinthian double burial. The differences between the SM and the later graves should not be exaggerated; all are inhumations. But the differences remain and may well be significant;[30] a further argument of a quite different kind points in the same direction.

The Hearth Group proves settlement in SM/early PG; but it is isolated as habitation evidence in its area (see Fig. 7). Not only is the next evidence for occupation here more than three centuries later;[31] in addition the closest area that was demonstrably occupied before the LG period, when the settlement area expanded considerably, is some 100 m. away.[32] I argue below (75-7) that from LPG onwards settlement was concentrated in the upper end of the Lechaeum Road Valley; the distance between this area and the Hearth Group, and the absence of subsequent occupation near the latter, suggest that it may not have belonged to the Dorian settlement. A further sign is that the region between the Hearth Group and the upper Lechaeum Road Valley was used for burial intermittently after LPG:[33] we should not expect habitation areas over such a relatively short distance to be separated by a cemetery.[34] A similar argument may perhaps be applied to the few scraps of

[28] North Cemetery: Young, *Corinth*, xiii.20.

[29] The graves described: Williams, *Hesperia*, xxxix (1970), 14-15. For pebble floors in the Argolid, see Hägg, *Die Gräber der Argolis*, 126-7, 153.

[30] Williams notes (*Hesperia*, xxxix (1970), 20) that the orientation of the SM graves is different from that of later graves in the same region; that may be significant, but orientation seems to have been variable from MG II onwards in the North Cemetery (Young, *Corinth*, xiii.16).

[31] Two wells of the seventh century (Weinberg, 42, 49).

[32] Well G (Fig. 7), and a pithos which may have been used during LG as a water-butt (Weinberg, 35: identified as a grave by Coldstream, *GGP* 98, but claimed by Weinberg as evidence of habitation).

[33] LPG: Grave 1. LPG/EG: Grave 4. Other graves in this area are of uncertain date within the Geometric period, for their contents (if any) were merely handmade vases which cannot be accurately placed; Graves 14?, 31-2, 33?, 34-6.

[34] This argument would lose its force if the excavator's most recently expressed opinion concerning the burial practices of Geometric Corinth were correct, that graves were placed in the settlement area itself. But the argument for discontinuity based on the distance between the Hearth Group and other early habitation evidence would remain. For discussion, below, 75-7.

LH III C to early PG date found in the South Stoa area (above, 42 n. 16). They are probably habitation debris; like the Hearth Group, they were separated from the settlement of the upper Lechaeum Road Valley by a cemetery.[35]

If the Hearth Group area was abandoned and not settled again for at least two centuries, it is probable not only that the LPG settlement in the upper Lechaeum Road Valley was in some sense a new foundation, but also that those who founded it did so at the expense of the small community to which the Hearth Group belonged. There is literary evidence that the Dorians defeated and drove out the earlier inhabitants of Corinth. Thucydides refers to Dorians attacking the Aeolian inhabitants of Corinth from a base on the Solygeian Ridge (below, 49), while in the Aletes legend he gained access to a hostile Corinth with the help of a daughter of Creon, who opened the gates(!) for him (Schol. Pind. *Nem.* vii.155 a), or by agreement with the kings after driving out the other inhabitants (Paus. ii.4.3). But it was inevitable that hostility should be part of the legend; this evidence can give no support to the conclusions which may be drawn from the archaeological evidence.

That Dorian Corinth was founded at about the beginning of the Geometric period was concluded by Dunbabin.[36] The record can now be traced back into LPG, and the positive evidence for discontinuity is a stronger ground than the mere absence of earlier finds that Dunbabin was able to offer. Dunbabin also used literary evidence to support his conclusion. A Corinthian king-list is preserved by Diodorus (vii fr.9); Dunbabin argued that it 'has a second beginning with Bacchis, eponym of the Bacchiads', and that Bacchis should be considered both as a historical figure and as contemporary with the foundation of Dorian Corinth. Computing the generations back from Diodorus' date for the end of the kingship in 747, Dunbabin suggested *c*.900 for Bacchis—which agrees remarkably with the archaeological evidence. But the list arouses too many suspicions to enable it to pretend to corroborate the date suggested by the material record. Bacchis' predecessors cause disquiet.[37] I do not doubt that

[35] Below, 75–7. The other deposit of EPG/LPG sherds from central Corinth (Williams, *Hesperia*, xl (1971), 3) shows nothing: it comes from the settlement area of LPG and later.

[36] *JHS* lxviii (1948), 62–3.

[37] Diodorus vii.9.2–4 gives the succession Aletes, Ixion, Agelas, Prymnis, Bacchis. Ixion's name did not inspire Dunbabin's confidence, but a new fragment of Satyrus (*P. Oxy.* 2465, fr. 3.ii.14–15) gives instead the less disturbing Anaxion. Agelas, however, is also the name of Bacchis' successor (Diod. loc. cit.); cf. Dunbabin, *JHS* lxviii (1948), 62. Dunbabin did not note that in Aristotle's *Constitution of the Corinthians* Bacchis was the third king of Corinth (fr. 611.19 Rose). His source was probably Eumelus; in his account Aletes will have founded the city and Bacchis will have been his grandson. Later versions will have added kings in an attempt to provide Corinth with a pedigree comparable to those of the royal houses of Argos and Sparta.

Bacchis was historical;[38] but even a certainly historical Bacchis could not guarantee the value of the list of his successors. Scepticism about at least the last of them, Telestes, is imposed by his name: it is too much to believe that the last of the kings had a name related to τέλος, 'end'.[39] It is possible that much of the rest of the list is genuine; but unless Eumelus mentioned Bacchis' successors it is not likely that information was provided in the tradition: the Bacchiads left Corinth in the mid-seventh century, and they probably never returned (below, 195).

Literary sources can, however, in one respect give important general confirmation of the chronology suggested by the archaeological evidence. The grave difficulties which were faced by later chronographers in their attempts at fitting the Corinthian tradition to the received picture of the Return of the Heracleidae—which caused the invention of kings, the forcing of Aletes into a legend to which he did not belong, not to mention the rejection of the version of Eumelus—are eloquent evidence that in Eumelus there were too few kings. Now Eumelus no doubt falsified; but if he did so in this respect, it will have been in order to give Corinth *more* kings than he knew of. Since in his version the Corinthian lists were significantly shorter than either the Argive or the Spartan, the reality which lies behind the lists is that Dorian Corinth was younger than either Sparta or Argos.[40]

It would be of interest to determine whether other areas of the Corinthia show a similar pattern to Corinth; but discussion is difficult when there has been so little excavation. Gonia and Zygouries have nothing after LH III B; there is a destruction level on the latter site at the end of the phase.[41] LH III C is well represented at Korakou, but the site then seems to have been deserted.[42] A few scraps of

[38] Many (e.g. Oost, *CP* lxvii (1972), 23) have supposed that he was invented to explain the name of the Bacchiads; but they derived their name from somewhere, and a historical eponym (if not a historical eponymous ancestor) is as likely an explanation as any.

[39] Diod. vii.9.5-6; Paus. ii.4.4.

[40] At least in Argos, both genealogies and archaeology support this relative chronology. On the archaeology, which indicates newcomers *c.*1100 or after, see below, 52. Genealogies fit: Temenus, the eponym of the Temenids, was himself in the generation of the Return. Sparta is more difficult, for the archaeology is hazy. Little has been found which must be before *c.*900; but an argument *ex absentia* in a place where the evidence is exclusively from sanctuaries hardly shows that there were no Dorians in Sparta before that date. The eponyms of the royal houses were one generation further removed from Heracles than Temenus. That may mean that Dorians reached Sparta later than Argos; but the king-lists are very difficult to use—especially when rivalry between the two Spartan royal houses was added to all the usual reasons for falsifying genealogies (see briefly Cartledge, *Sparta and Lakonia*, 341-6).

[41] Desborough, *Last Mycenaeans*, 84. For Gonia, see now Rutter, *Korakou and Gonia*, 529-35.

[42] Desborough, *Last Mycenaeans*, 85-6; in more detail now Rutter, *Korakou and Gonia*. A grave(?) at New Corinth is published briefly by Wiseman, 72.

LH III B and C have turned up at Perachora and probably at Isthmia, while on the latter site there are sherds related to the Hearth Group at Corinth.[43] There seems to have been progressive depopulation in the Corinthia from the end of LH III B. The earliest subsequent evidence in the Corinthia is later than at Corinth and consists of graves—at Athikia, Tenea, Zygouries, and Crommyon; but it is significant that they always take the Corinthian forms.[44] The natural conclusion is that these areas were settled in the same way as Corinth itself; and this is especially interesting at two of the sites. Zygouries was, in classical times, not in the Corinthia: it was part of the territory of Cleonae; but the origins of its inhabitants may have been the same as those of the Corinthians if the Zygouries evidence is representative. More important is the case of Crommyon. The graves here, of MG II date where they contained gifts, are mainly of the usual Corinthian type, with a single slab cover; and some of them exhibit the Corinthian pecularity of the cache for grave goods.[45] Hammond has argued that Crommyon was absorbed by Corinth only in the late eighth century;[46] but funeral practice favours a close Corinthian connection a good deal earlier. I have argued elsewhere on other grounds that the Corinthia north of the Isthmus, including Crommyon, was settled at the same time as the parts which lay within the Peloponnese; the movement involved the displacement of the Megarian Heraeis and Piraeis (Plut. *Mor.* 295 B) from the land they had occupied in the historical Corinthia, respectively the Perachora peninsula and the region immediately south of the Isthmus, since the earlier foundation of Megara from Argos.[47]

The question of the origin of those who settled Dorian Corinth towards the end of the Protogeometric period remains. There is nothing in the archaeological record which might be pressed into

[43] Desborough, *Last Mycenaeans*, 86, 85.

[44] Below. For Geometric graves from the Corinthia, below, 156. Three graves of a similar type to that at Zygouries were found on the same site without grave goods (Blegen, *Zygouries*, 66–7, graves ix–x, xv); they are more likely to be Geometric than MH in date (MH: Blegen, *Zygouries*, 67). A further grave without offerings was intermediate in type between Corinthian and Argive (Blegen, *Zygouries*, 43–5; grave vii in its second use).

[45] Of 15 graves, 8–9 had single slab covers; 4 had two slabs (no doubt because large ones were not easy to come by), and there were 5 caches separated from their graves by upright slabs (*AD* xvii.B (1961/2), 52–3). The slabs were rougher than at Corinth; Crommyon presumably lacked skilled cutters.

[46] *BSA* xlix (1954), 93–102.

[47] *BSA* lxvii (1972), 192–6, 202–4. The problem with this reconstruction, as Professor Andrewes points out to me, is that it imples local rather than tribal organization in the Megarid at a remarkably early date. The nature of the organization remains, however, unclear; it is easier to accept this difficulty than to find an alternative explanation for the Heraeis (though the Piraeis could be explained away: ibid., 195 n. 221; cf. Wiseman, 41–2, n. 109). Megarian burial practices at this time are unknown.

providing an answer. The Corinthian style of LPG is so close to Attic that no features which might have been derived from the place of origin of the Corinthians can be identified;[48] other artefacts are found so rarely that they are no more helpful. The burial practices do at least offer evidence for a negative conclusion. They show a remarkably consistent pattern (above, 43-5), which is sufficiently distinct from the practice of the Argolid to make Dunbabin's view that Corinth was founded from Argos (above, 39) most improbable.[49] But positive conclusions cannot be drawn, for there are no precise parallels for the Corinthian custom;[50] the speciality of the separate cache for grave goods is unique.

A version of the tradition concerning the origins of Dorian Corinth has been reconstructed by Huxley.[51] A fragment of Aristotle (fr. 554 Rose) refers to Hippotes the father of Aletes as laying a curse on the Malians, to the effect that their ships would always leak, because they refused to join him when he sailed on a colonizing expedition. The destination of Hippotes is not given in the fragment, but Corinth is an inevitable answer; that Corinth was, in one tradition, founded by sea is supported by Thucydides' account of the Dorians attacking Aeolian Corinth from the Solygeian Ridge, close to the coast in the south-east Corinthia.[52] The credit of this story is perhaps improved by the fact that it may be independent of the legend of the Return of the Heracleidae;[53] but it is impossible to rely on such an uncorroborated element in the tradition, and it is safest to ignore it. The arrival of the Dorians by sea and their establishment for a brief period at the Solygeian Ridge may well have been found in Eumelus.[54] It is remarkable that a sanctuary

[48] Handmade wares may have reached Corinth (like the Argolid and Laconia) with the settlers (below, 50); but they point to no one place of origin, though similar wares are widespread in northern Greece. There can be no connection between these wares and the handmade pieces of quite different character found especially at Korakou and taken by Rutter as showing intrusions from Romania or Bulgaria: *AJA* lxxix (1975), 17-32 (but cf. Walberg v. Rutter, *AJA* lxxx (1976), 186-8).

[49] The commonest grave type in the Argolid is the stone cist (Hägg, *Gräber der Argolis*, 100-61, with tables 23-4, 39-40; Courbin, *Tombes géométriques d'Argos*, i. 107-14). In addition, graves in the Argolid are not infrequently reused, although such cases are usually Geometric (for Corinth, above, 45): Hägg, *Gräber der Argolis*, 157-9.

[50] Elis, PG: Desborough, *Dark Ages*, 74; some graves, however, contain more than one corpse. LH III C graves of similar type have been found at Perati, but the excavator showed that they depended on the special circumstances of the site (briefly ibid., 107). The LH III C examples from Medeon in Phocis have multiple cover slabs (Vatin, *Médéon de Phocide*, 45).

[51] *Philologus*, cxix (1975), 140-2.

[52] Thuc. iv.42.2; above, 27.

[53] Hippotes was brought into the legend of the Return (refs. in Huxley, *Philologus*, cxix (1975), 140 n. 1); but his departure from Malis and the arrival of his son (?) in the Corinthia belong to a different stage in the story.

[54] Dunbabin, *JHS* lxviii (1948), 67.

on the ridge received its first votives in the seventh century, when Eumelus' verse no doubt began to take hold on Corinthian imaginations.[55] There was an apsidal temple on the site which may have been built by those who believed what Eumelus told them of their early history.[56]

Since there are no reliable indications specific to Corinth, the evidence (such as it is) for the origins of the other major Dorian cities of the Peloponnese must be considered. This has been the subject of dispute for many years, and cannot be fully treated here; but the general case may clarify that of Corinth, and vice versa.

At first sight our evidence discourages any attempt to treat the foundations of Argos, Sparta, and Corinth as related to each other. The ancients could not assimilate Corinth satisfactorily to the Return of the Heracleidae; it would be dangerous for modern scholarship to try to fill the gaps in ancient inventions. The tradition that the Dorians arrived at Argos and Sparta in a single movement has serious doubt cast upon it by the archaeological record (above, 47 n. 40); and the material remains at Corinth confirm that the settlement of Corinth was not directly connected with that of Argos. Each site must be treated separately. It even remains a matter of dispute whether it is right to speak of a Dorian invasion at all. Snodgrass has stressed that no intrusive elements can be traced which demonstrate the arrival of outsiders in Greece.[57] Desborough has taken the appearance of cist tombs as a sign of invasion from the north-west Greek mainland; but there are many in Athens, which tradition held was not reached by invaders, and they have also been explained as a revival of a Middle Helladic practice which never quite died out in Mycenaean times.[58] The fine handmade pottery found from LPG onwards in the Argolid, the Corinthia, and (in less distinguished form) Laconia has been explained as a revival of 'a native art using indigenous materials';[59] but it is as likely that this ware represents an intrusive element. The distribution of the Doric dialect was once confidently thought to indicate the arrival in the Argolid, the Corinthia, and Laconia of Dorian newcomers; but it has been suggested more

---

[55] Verdelis, *Praktika*, 1958, pl. 111; *Archaeology*, xv (1962), 188, fig. at bottom. For Eumelus' date in the second half of the eighth century, see Huxley, *Greek Epic Poetry*, 62.

[56] The temple had two phases, the second belonging to the sixth century (Verdelis, *Praktika*, 1958, 140): the first cannot be dated except by reference to the votives.

[57] *Dark Age*, 313-24.

[58] Desborough, *Last Mycenaeans*, 37-40; *PPS* xxv (1965) 221-3; criticized by Snodgrass, *Dark Age*, 177-84, 314-15. Desborough is more cautious in *Dark Ages*, 106-11.

[59] Snodgrass, *Dark Age*, 97; the class: 94-7, 329. Contrast, however, Desborough, *Last Mycenaeans*, 83 (but cf. *Dark Ages*, 168-9).

recently that Doric speech might already have been spoken in the Peloponnese in Myceanaean times.[60]

It is difficult to know where to turn in the face of all these uncertainties. Neither archaeological nor dialect evidence can establish intrusions in the Dorian parts of the Peloponnese. This allows the conclusion that Argos, Sparta, and Corinth were inhabited by the survivors of the decline of Mycenaean civilization in these regions; but it does not demonstrate it, and there are important counterarguments. The dialect evidence is ambiguous. Both main groups, East and West Greek, were in close contact at some stage. The evidence of the Linear B tablets is compatible with the supposition that Doric was already spoken in Mycenaean times by a majority of the inhabitants of those parts of the Peloponnese which later spoke Doric; but an equally plausible hypothesis is that Doric was introduced by intruders from an area outside the peninsula but yet close enough to the Mycenaean world (perhaps even within it) to account for the linguistic features which East and West Greek share.[61] Other evidence supports the arrival of new peoples.

The three Dorian tribes (Hylleis, Pamphyloi, and Dymanes) are attested directly at both Sparta and Argos and indirectly at Corinth;[62] this demands the hypothesis of a common origin for the Dorians in these areas. They were probably also intrusive. In both Corinth and Argos there were non-Dorian inhabitants,[63] while at Sparta the helots were non-Dorians subjected at an early date.[64] The existence of two population groups, both Dorian and non-Dorian, argues strongly for disparate origins for the peoples of each area; it will hardly be doubted that the Dorians were in each case the last to arrive.[65]

---

[60] Hooker, *Mycenaean Greece*, 170–2 with references, esp. Chadwick, *PP* xxxi (1976), 103–17.

[61] Hooker, *Mycenaean Greece*, 171–2, 179–80 (following Chadwick, art. cit.), suggests that Doric was spoken by the subjects of the Mycenaean bureaucracies: an administration recorded not only in a palace script but also in a palace dialect in the tablets. But this leaves the close relationship between the Mycenaean administrative language and the vernacular of classical Arcadia difficult to explain: the simplest view is to take Doric as intrusive and Linear B (leading to Arcadian) as the Mycenaean vernacular. See further on this hypothesis Cartledge, *Sparta and Lakonia*, 77–9 with 100–1.

[62] Sparta: Tyrt. fr. 19.8 West. Argos: Wörrle, *Untersuchungen*, 11 with n. 1; Kritsas, ΣΤΗΛΗ, 498, l. 6.

[63] Corinth: below, 413–6. Argos: Wörrle, *Untersuchungen*, 11–13 (Hyrnathioi); Kritsas, ΣΤΗΛΗ, 498, l. 6.

[64] Cartledge, *Sparta and Lakonia*, 75–101, esp. 92–100.

[65] Roussel (*Tribu et cité*, 221–56) argues that the tribal structure of the major Dorian states in the Peloponnese originated more recently than the arrival of settlers after the collapse of the Mycenaean world. His reconstruction cannot be fully discussed here; but it is easier to explain the three Dorian tribes as an inheritance from the Dorian past than to suppose that they developed at Argos and spread under Argive influence to Sparta, Corinth,

The archaeological record shows no certainly intrusive artefacts or practices; but two of the relevant sites show changes which are best explained by the hypothesis of intrusive population. There are no such signs from Sparta, where the finds are from sanctuaries,[66] but at Argos both the area of settlement and the location of cemeteries changed at some time after about 1100;[67] indeed, at nearby Mycenae and Tiryns graves were dug in areas previously occupied by settlement.[68] Such significant changes provide strong evidence for serious disruption and probably for new elements in the population.[69] If the evidence from Corinth is representative, there was a similar situation on that site (above, 39–46).

Finally, the nature of the tradition should not be wholly ignored. Much was invented in order to achieve a simple pattern of a single invasion, the Return of the Heracleidae; it would be too optimistic to hope that the tradition could answer questions of detail. But it remains true, and significant, that the origins of the Dorian cities of the Peloponnese were explained in terms of new settlers. The cases of Argos and Sparta should perhaps be seen as essentially one tradition, for our story of Temenus, Cresphontes, and the sons of Aristodemus probably originated in the seventh or sixth century, when Argos and Sparta fought a mythological as well as a more real dispute over the hegemony of the Peloponnese; the story of one party will have been grafted on to an already existing legend of the other. The Corinthian version, however, was originally independent; it included the same element of invasion, and it has a special value. The basic form of the Corinthian story was to be found in Eumelus, and that it attributed the foundation of Corinth to invaders is guaranteed by the name of Aletes, 'the wanderer'. Eumelus composed his 'Corinthiaca' in the second half of the eighth century; that places the tradition far earlier than is usually possible, and indeed not many generations after the events themselves.

Sicyon, and Megara. Roussel adopted his view in part precisely because the tribes are attested only in *poleis*, and should therefore be intimately associated with the idea of the *polis*; but it is most improbable that an Argive practice was adopted in the very moment, *ex hypothesi*, of the construction of the independent identity of each of the other four cities. The three in which tribes other than the Hylleis, Pamphyloi, and Dymanes are attested cannot be accommodated to Roussel's pattern: that the other tribes were subsequently added to allow the entry into the *polis* of remoter districts fits the Argive case adequately (ibid., 247–9), but will not do for Sicyon (despite 250–2) or for Corinth.

[66] See, however, for a more doubtful argument based on pottery styles, Cartledge, *Sparta and Lakonia*, 81–90; cf. 93 on the choice of the site at Sparta.

[67] Desborough, *Last Mycenaeans*, 80–2, 251; *Dark Ages*, 72–3; Snodgrass, *Dark Age*, 363; for full evidence and discussion, see Hägg, *Gräber der Argolis*, 20–7, 42–4.

[68] Desborough, *Dark Ages*, 69–72; cf. Snodgrass, *Dark Age*, 316; Hägg, *Gräber der Argolis*, 97, with the evidence in detail, 64–71, 75–87.

[69] Cf. Snodgrass, *Dark Age*, 315–16.

To judge from what happened at Argos and Corinth, where the establishment of new inhabitants was separated by more than a century, it is inaccurate to speak of a single Dorian invasion: we have to envisage, rather, the settlement of different sites by peoples with a common origin at widely differing dates. It is significant that Argos and Corinth share an unusual feature among Greek city sites. Neither has a normal acropolis: both Larisa and Acrocorinth are far higher than is usual. The new inhabitants of Corinth thus altered the settlement pattern of the region by occupying the well-watered site which had not held a major community since EH II, when experience taught that it was perilously difficult to defend (above, 13-15). The Dorians had apparently not yet learned to concentrate their settlements about a hill of regular acropolis type, for they chose to live beneath a much higher mountain to which they could retire in time of danger; the case of the Spartans, who could flee to Taygetus, is similar. These peoples probably came from outside the Peloponnese. The acropolis idea was now firmly rooted in the peninsula, and the archaeological record hardly allows room for them here immediately before the Mycenaean time of troubles *c*.1200; in addition both the tribal and the dialect evidence would be difficult to explain if they were descendants of Mycenaean Peloponnesians who left their original homes then or later.

For the rest, only conjecture is possible. The different groups who settled in Argos, Sparta, and Corinth may have reached the Peloponnese at different times and/or by different routes; they may rather all have been members of a single group of nomadic people who reached the peninsula at the latest *c*.1100, and the foundations of the cities may represent the decisions of separate sections of the group to settle in turn in different places. It is even possible that the great destructions in the Mycenaean world *c*.1200 are to be attributed to such a group. Nomads are notoriously difficult to trace archaeologically; they might well have wandered about the Peloponnese for more than a century without leaving evidence even of their burials. Such a hypothesis has the advantage of economy. It allows the obvious conclusion to be drawn from the combined evidence of the Mycenaean fortification wall at the Isthmus (above, 18-19) and the approximately contemporary destructions in the Mycenaean world *c*.1200; and it will explain not only the destructions but also the gap between them and the earliest evidence of subsequent settlement by intruders in some of the affected areas. But it has the disadvantage that it is at present, and perhaps in principle, impossible to test.[70] The invaders may even have reached the Peloponnese from

[70] On all this, see ibid., 385-6; on 'transhumance pastoralists' at Sparta, Cartledge, *Sparta and Lakonia*, 94-6.

Doris, as Herodotus (viii.31, cf. i.56.3), and perhaps more importantly Tyrtaeus (fr.2.12-5 West), claimed—or, indeed, in the case of Corinth, from Malis by sea.

III. The Bacchiads

During the century before the Bacchiad aristocracy was overthrown
c.650 many of the economic features which made Corinth unusual
among Greek cities had already begun to develop (below, esp. 95–100).
It is unfortunate that our evidence allows very little to be concluded
about the character of political life during these vital years. The
earliest period is even more obscure. Corinth, like all Greek 'cities'
(the term is anachronistic) of the period, was ruled by hereditary
monarchs;[1] no doubt they were descended from the chief who led
the Dorians into the Corinthia—perhaps Bacchis himself, in view of
the name of the Bacchiads. But the accounts which have been
preserved[2] are unreliable even for the names of the kings (above,
46–7); otherwise they contain little but lengths of reigns calculated
to accord with chronographical preconceptions. Aristotle tells us
that Bacchis was lame, but that this did not prevent him from
fathering many children (fr. 611.19 Rose). Diodorus preserves a
record of usurpation towards the end of the line, and such events
are only to be expected in a hereditary monarchy; but that hardly
increases the credit of the details Diodorus gives, especially as one
of the kings involved—the last of the line—has a name which is
related to τέλος, 'end'.

Our sources on the overthrow of the monarchy are no more
reliable. Diodorus records that Telestes was killed[3] by his relatives,
and Pausanias that 'Arieus and Perantas killed Telestes out of hatred'
(ii.4.4); at the least we may take it that the last king did not relinquish
his authority without a struggle. Diodorus continues, 'The Bacchiads,
descendants of Heracles, were more than 200 in number and held

---

[1] Diod. vii.9.3, if literally interpreted, gives an unusual form of hereditary succession in
which the royal power, on the death of each king, passed to the oldest living descendant of
Aletes. This is made the basis of an elaborate discussion by Broadbent, *Studies in Greek
Genealogy*, 39–59 (followed by Oost, *CP* lxvii (1972), 12); but it is probably careless writing
by Diodorus. Kings chosen in this way will have been remarkably old when they died even
if their reigns were only half as long as Diodorus states.

[2] Diod. vii.9; partially, Paus. ii.4.4.

[3] vii.9.6, ἀναιρέθεντος: just possibly, 'removed'. Telestes is reported by Diodorus to have
been deprived of this throne in his youth by an uncle; but this circumstantial detail cannot
be taken as a sign that the story is genuine against the strong suspicions aroused by the
construction of Telestes' name.

authority; all of them ruled the city in common, and for ninety years
until the tyranny of Cypselus, who overthrew them, they chose each
year one of their number to be *prytanis* and exercise the functions of
the king' (vii.9.6). This gives the mid-eighth century (747) for the fall
of the hereditary monarchy. That would accord with the date of
similar developments elsewhere; but it seems more likely that the
ninety years[4] is the product of later chronographers' compilations
than that it rested upon a genuine list of Bacchiad *prytaneis*. The
latter will hardly have been preserved in and after the tyranny when
the Bacchiads were in exile (below, 195).

Herodotus described the Bacchiads as follows: 'It was an oligarchy
called the Bacchiads. They ran the city, and married only among
themselves' (v.92 β 1). The general description could have been given
of any of the aristocracies of archaic Greece; and the specific information that the Bacchiads married only among themselves cannot be
given great weight. The story of Cypselus, born to a Bacchiad mother
and a non-Bacchiad father to become the destroyer of the Bacchiad
regime (below, 186), might easily have attracted a false statement
that the Bacchiads as a rule only married each other.[5] If they did,
however, they were probably more exclusive than other aristocracies,
and it may be significant that they bore a name which asserted a
claim to a common ancestry. Many aristocracies did not emphasize
such a connection; the Bacchiads (and perhaps the Penthilidae of
Lesbos) may have been more restrictive than others. In Attica and
Chalcis it may have been doubtful whether a man belonged to a
'good family' (Eupatridae) or was able to 'feed a horse' (Hippobotae):
but in Corinth Bacchiad identity would be clear—though if Cypselus'
case is anything to go by it could be conferred by a Bacchiad mother.
No man could achieve Bacchiad status by his own efforts; only by
his father's.

Bacchiad institutions are difficult to reconstruct, but they will
have been simple: they were born to rule, and not to rules.[6] No
council is recorded, but it must have existed. Diodorus gives the
number of Bacchiads as over 200; it may have contained about that
number. It is difficult to see why such a figure should have been
invented—but equally difficult to imagine how it might have been
preserved. Two magistracies seem reasonably secure. Both Diodorus

---

[4] Strabo's figure of 200 years (378) may be corrupt; but it could be a rounded-off total
of the reigns from Bacchis onwards and the years of the aristocracy before Cypselus in
some unknown chronographic scheme—although this would be quite different from the
figures in Diod. vii.9.2-4.

[5] An insignificant exception (if it is true) is recorded by Zenobius v. 8 (below, 70).

[6] See most recently Oost, *CP* lxvii (1972), 10-16.

(vii.9.6) and Pausanias (ii.4.4) mention an annual *prytanis*;[7] presumably he was the eponymous magistrate, but his functions are irrecoverable. For the *polemarch* some information is preserved in Nicolaus' account of the rise of Cypselus: one of his functions was to exact fines imposed by other magistrates (below, 188, 189-90), and the title proves that another was to lead in war. No other titles are known,[8] but Nicolaus' version of Cypselus' polemarchate indicates that there were, as we might have guessed, other magistrates with judicial functions. The implication of Cypselus' tenure of the polemarchate at an age which enabled him to enjoy a long tyranny subsequently is that, if he was typical, magistracies were held at a relatively early age; presumably the practice was for Bacchiads to undertake office[9] and then sit in the council for life. Nicolaus implies that the demos exercised some constitutional functions, and Will has concluded that certain formal rights were theoretically enjoyed by the demos but had been abrogated by the Bacchiads;[10] but this is to place too much reliance on a passage full of anachronisms (below, 188-9). No doubt members of the demos enjoyed property-rights in practice—and perhaps in proper constitutional form after the legislation of Pheidon (below, 63-5). They may have been consulted in an embryonic assembly irregularly, or even once a year for elections; but this will have been an informal practice, as was usual in an aristocratic state, not a defined constitutional right. There is no direct evidence for the three Dorian tribes at Corinth, though there are indirect signs that they existed.[11] The name of one non-Dorian tribe, the Aoreis, is now given by a decree from Delos recently identified as Corinthian (below, 413-6); it need not have been the only such tribe.

By Cypselus' time the Corinthia was a unified state, with its political centre at Corinth; but how this was achieved under the Bacchiads is unclear. Different Greek states accomplished such a synoecism at different periods. There are signs of local particularism

[7] Perhaps confirmed by the presence of a *prytanis* at Corcyra (Gschnitzer, *RE* Suppl. xiii (1973), 737); but see below, 205 n. 79. Nic. Dam. *FGH* 90 F 57.6 has Cypselus killing 'Patrocleides, who was king' (βασιλεύοντα); this no doubt refers, inaccurately, to the *prytanis*.

[8] Will, *Korinthiaka*, 299-300, argues for a *basileus*, on inadequate grounds.

[9] By what method of appointment is unclear. If Diodorus' method of choosing kings at vii.9.3 is applied to the prytaneis it becomes more credible (above, 55 n. 1).

[10] *Korinthiaka*, 303-6.

[11] Dunbabin, *Western Greeks*, 55; Roebuck, *Hesperia*, xli (1972), 114. The argument is tenuous: the connection is made through Corcyra Nigra (where the three Dorian tribes are attested), itself not even founded directly by Syracuse. But the conclusion would be next to certain even without evidence. The Hylleis, at least, are attested at Corcyra (Calligas, *BSA* lxvi (1971), 87).

in Attica until the reforms of Cleisthenes; while in Arcadia Mantinea
only achieved synoecism in the fifth century. Our literary evidence
preserves no such evidence for the Corinthia; but at least physically
Corinth in the earliest years was but one of many separate villages
scattered about the Corinthia: the settlement near Temple Hill was
very small (below, 75-7). But the archaeological evidence does not
allow any conclusions about political structure in this very early
period; and the signs are that the Corinthia enjoyed some form
of unity.[12]

It would be dangerous to rely on the absence of preserved traditions
concerning the synoecism of Dorian Corinth to prove that the
Corinthia had always been unified; but the notice of the *Suda* s.v.
πάντα ὀκτώ gives positive ground for believing that the tradition knew
nothing of such a synoecism. The passage runs, 'When Aletes
synoecized Corinth in obedience to an oracle he divided the citizens
into eight tribes and the city into eight parts' (below, 413). The
synoecism could not have been ascribed to Aletes, the mythical
founder of Corinth, except in defiance of any tradition that may
have referred to a synoecism in a later period. It seems not only
that no report of a later unification has been preserved, but that none
existed. This does not prove that no synoecism took place; but two
arguments can be urged in favour of such a conclusion. Archaeological
evidence from tomb types tends to show that those who settled at
Temple Hill and others who reached as far away as Crommyon
north of the Isthmus and Zygouries in the territory of Cleonae—not
to mention those who lived at Tenea and Athikia—were all part of
the same group of invaders (above, 48). Since they arrived in a
single movement and communications between them were easy
(above, 32-7), they may well have preserved the early links they
enjoyed with each other, although Cleonae—with which communications were more difficult (above, 3-4)—became in the end a
separate state and may have diverged early. The name of the Bacchiads
provides a further clue. The claim to a common descent implies that
when the name was first used the Bacchiads, with estates no doubt
scattered in various parts of Corinthia, had enjoyed unity for
generations. They must have used their name from the mid-eighth
century at least; that leaves little room for a time when the Dorian
Corinthia was not unified.

Politically speaking, the Corinthia will have been synoecized from
the very beginning; and it would be unreasonable to deny that
Corinth was the centre. But in the early years, it was merely a small

---

[12] Cf. Roebuck, *Hesperia*, xli (1972) 105-6.

village. At least one other close but separate settlement can perhaps
be traced at Anaploga in the ninth century;[13] the EG grave at Mavrospelaies near the North Cemetery (below, 156) may indicate that
there was another settlement close by. Occupation in other parts
of the Corinthia can be traced in graves of the ninth century. In
the following hundred years the population of Corinth increased,
perhaps dramatically. It is unclear whether this growth was reflected
in the rest of the Corinthia, although there was relative over-
population at Tenea by the mid-eighth century (below, 63); but the
settlement about Temple Hill had increased greatly by the middle of
the seventh century. Already in respect of population Corinth could
be called a true city (below, 75-80).

The population growth can hardly be attributed directly to the
Bacchiad government; but there remains a difficult question as to
whether the Bacchiads began the construction of large-scale public
monuments in their growing urban centre. The earliest public structures of the Bacchiad period which have been identified are at
Perachora. Hera Acraea was given a primitive apsidal temple c.800.
It was replaced, probably because it collapsed, c.735;[14] at the same
time or later a dining-room was added to the goddess's complement.[15]
In the city, the earliest phase of the Sacred Spring is to be dated
before the tyranny, along perhaps with the Cyclopean Spring (below,
78); but they are minor structures—though not insignificant, for
they must have been designed for public use. Whether they, and the
Perachora temples, were provided by the Bacchiad government as a
public service must remain doubtful; they may have been erected at
private (though no doubt Bacchiad) expense. But the scale of the
predecessor of the present temple of Apollo shows that it can only
have been a public undertaking. Evidence has recently been published
which seems to date its construction unequivocally in the Bacchiad
period; but there remain reasons for doubt.

Excavation has revealed a stratum on Temple Hill which contained
many working chips of limestone of the same type as was used for
the blocks of the early temple. Within this stratum were found

[13] An unsuccessful attempt was made to dig a well there (*AD* xix.B (1964), 101). It
remains uncertain whether this was a habitation area in MG I, when the well was filled (I
am indebted to Keith de Vries for information about the chronology); a potters' establishment can be traced here later (below, 103 n. 12), and there may have been similar
activity in the ninth century.
[14] Salmon, *BSA* lxvii (1972), 161-5, 175-8.
[15] Ibid., 174-5; now convincingly identified as a dining-room by Tomlinson, *BSA* lxxii
(1977), 197-202, esp. 197-200. Tomlinson gives reason to doubt the obvious interpretation of the evidence, that the building was constructed c.735 (*BSA* lxvii (1972), 174):
BSA lxxii (1977), 199-200, 202; but the date remains unclear.

fragments of an almost complete LG/EPC oenochoe, along with fragments of EPC ware.[16] Robinson concluded that the building was under construction c.700;[17] But there are difficulties with such a chronology. The limestone-chip stratum includes material which looks later than EPC.[18] The roof of the temple consisted of clay tiles which are almost exactly the same as those of the early temple of Poseidon at Isthmia. The two buildings were probably therefore roughly contemporary;[19] and although Broneer[20] has suggested an early seventh-century date for his building there is no published evidence to support such a conclusion and some against it. The perirrhanterion which stood at the entrance has a stylistic date in the mid-seventh century.[21] This allows some latitude; but the fragments of wall-paintings recovered from the temple are in a style which owes nothing to Geometric and should belong c.650:[22] the closest parallels are on the Chigi Vase, later than 650.[23] A date for both the temples c.650 is further suggested by the small finds. Each temple was destroyed by fire; in the fills of discarded debris the earliest concentration belongs to the third quarter of the seventh century in each case.[24]

The temple of Poseidon has been convincingly restored by Broneer with a wooden peristyle.[25] Robinson suggests that the building at

[16] Robinson, *Hesperia*, xlv (1976), 211–12.

[17] Ibid., 234–5.

[18] I am much indebted to Professor Robinson for allowing me to study this material. Much of it is eighth century, but much is too fragmentary for close dating; there are many bases of ray-based kotylai which should belong well into the seventh century.

[19] Cf. Broneer, *Isthmia*, i. 50; the span of 25–50 years suggested by Robinson, *Hesperia*, xlv (1976), 234, seems too long.

[20] *Isthmia*, i. 55; cf. 1.

[21] Broneer, *Isthmia*, i. 3 with refs., 11–12; Dörig, *AM* lxxvi (1961), 74. Dated to the reign of Cypselus by Clement and Thorne, *Hesperia*, xliii (1974), 401.

[22] See in particular the horse(?) mane, Broneer, *Isthmia*, i, pl. A 1 (IA 474). Contrast the Geometric painting on the Corinthian (Salmon, *BSA* lxvii (1972), 185–6) model of the late eighth century from Ithaca: Robertson, *BSA* xliii (1948), 101–2, pl. 45.

[23] Broneer, *Isthmia*, i. 33–4.

[24] At Corinth there were few votives, but they date no earlier than LPC (Roebuck, *Hesperia*, xxiv (1955), 150–3). Broneer rightly points out (*Isthmia*, i. 50 n. 42) that the pottery found at Corinth with the tile debris does not necessarily give the date of the roof; but many of the finds are too early to belong with the destruction, and they are best taken as discarded votives. At Isthmia the votives were more numerous; they go back in quantity only to LPC (Broneer, *Hesperia*, xxvii (1958), 27–8; xxviii (1959), 301. For the Circular Pit, see now Broneer, *Isthmia*, ii. 135–6).

[25] *Isthmia*, i. 3–56. He suggests that since the cella was a hecatompedon it may originally have had no peristyle (*Isthmia*, i. 12; cf. 35, on the possibility that the walls of the cella may at first have been unpainted); but the suggestion is made only to be rightly rejected. Even if it is correct, the wall-paintings and the perirrhanterion (both of c.650) will belong to the second stage; so will the roof tiles, for the addition of a peristyle will have demanded a new roof. It is the Isthmian roof that was contemporary with that at Corinth; even the improbable first stage at Isthmia would not support a date of c.700 for the Corinthian structure.

Corinth may only have been a cella on the ground that nothing from a stylobate could be recognized among the numerous limestone fragments.[26] This is an uncertain argument where the material is so fragmentary and the foundations cannot be excavated; it is better to leave the question open. Whether the Corinth temple had a peristyle or no, the rhythm of the development of architectural skills at Corinth is far easier to understand the closer to the middle of the seventh century we place the buildings at Isthmia and Corinth. The advances they represent on earlier buildings are immense. Blocks measuring at least 0.78 × 0.65 × 0.24 m. could now be squared, lifted, and built right up to the eaves.[27] Clay tiles were employed for a roof, hipped at each end, which weighed at least sixteen tons[28] —not to mention the skills of overall design. We have no earlier buildings for comparison; but the earlier the temples of Apollo and Poseidon are placed in the seventh century, the less probable the tempo of subsequent development becomes. The plan of Temple C at Thermon, designed no doubt by Corinthian architects, differs little from that at Isthmia,[29] but architecture then progressed rapidly. The Thermon building is dated by its clay metopes to the second half of the century (below, 121); if the temple at Isthmia was erected at least half a century earlier the enormous strides in temple design in the late eighth century and the second half of the seventh and later will have been improbably separated by fifty years or more of virtual stagnation.

There is considerable evidence that from the second half of the seventh century Greek temple architecture owed a great deal to Egypt; but it is not likely that contact with the Nile was sufficient before c.660 to allow the Corinthian buildings to have been similarly inspired. An independent evolution at Corinth of ashlar masonry soon after 700 is not impossible; but if archaeological evidence will allow a date of c.650 for both temples, the probability that the Greek debt to Egypt, which can be traced rather later, began in the mid-century will provide a further argument for the conclusion that these important new developments were made under the aegis of Cypselus.[30] There is no trace of his building programmes in the

---

[26] *Hesperia*, xlv (1976), 228 n. 82.

[27] Ibid., 225-8.

[28] Ibid., 231-4.

[29] Terracotta had, however, been developed for the purposes of decoration by the time of the Thermon temple, which boasted terracotta metopes and decorated eaves tiles; they were not used at Isthmia (Broneer, *Isthmia*, i. 50).

[30] On the debt to Egypt, see esp. Coulton, *Greek Architects at Work*, 32-50; for the importance of the chronology of the temples at Corinth and Isthmia in the history of early Greek temple design and its relation to Egyptian models, esp. 49-50.

literary tradition; but archaeology shows that he provided Corinth
with an elaborate system of fortifications (below, 220-1), and a
tyranny is far better suited to ambitious building schemes than an
aristocracy. The new temples were ostentatious, as if a comparison
with what had gone before was deliberately invited. Cypselus, like
many other tyrants, will have created magnificent buildings to call
attention to his own standing as well as to that of the gods for whose
worship they were intended. If the temple at Corinth lacked a
peristyle, it is possible that it was provided by the Bacchiads in their
last years and that Cypselus demonstrated his superiority by giving
Poseidon not only a peristyle but also more elaborate wall-paintings.[31]
Such a comparison would have been telling enough, but Cypselus
probably provided for the construction of both.

Other aspects of Bacchiad activity which can be traced concern
regions outside the Corinthia: the most important is the colonizing
movement of the late eighth century.[32] Corinthians were commercially active in the west for half a century or more before the
foundation of Syracuse in the mid-730s and that of Corcyra perhaps
rather later.[33] It was once believed that the colonies were designed
in part for a commercial purpose; but the connection between the
foundations and the trading voyages which preceded them was
probably indirect. Pithecusae, the earliest Greek settlement in the
west, may have been a commercial foundation; but even this may
reasonably be doubted,[34] and the absence of significant Greek

---

[31] The few fragments that remain are more impressive at Isthmia (Broneer, *Isthmia*,
i. 33-4) than at Corinth (Robinson, *Hesperia*, xlv (1976), 228-30). Robinson suggests that
Apollo's paintings were on the interior walls (*Hesperia*, xlv (1976), 228); but the grounds
are not strong, and paintings inside such a building can only have been very dimly seen. It
is perhaps better to restore the Corinthian temple with wall-paintings outside, as at Isthmia,
even though that may imply a peristyle too.

[32] Drews has recently suggested that Corinthians settled at Sinope *c*.750 (*JHS* xcvi
(1976), 22-6), on the ground that in Eumelus the eponym of Sinope was a daughter of
Asopus, the eponym of the river between Corinth and Sicyon (fr. 8 Kinkel). Eumelus' few
fragments have preserved another Pontic name (Borysthenis: fr. 17 Kinkel), and his interest
in the region cannot be denied; but it is rather to be explained by the myth of Medea and
Colchis (Huxley, *Greek Epic Poetry*, 63-8) than by Corinthian voyages and a settlement
for which there is not the slightest archaeological evidence.

[33] Below, 83-94. Syracuse: Coldstream, *GGP* 322-7 with refs. The substantial agreement
between Thucydides' colonial dates (vi.3-5), the finds in the colonies, and the absolute
archaeological chronology which can now be established from essentially non-Greek evidence
should still the doubts which have rightly been cast, on purely literary grounds, on
Thucydides' accuracy. Corcyra has been less extensively excavated, and is not fixed by any
obviously reliable literary source. Strabo (269) made it contemporary with Syracuse, but
Eusebius gives a date of a generation later. For the moment, the question remains open.

[34] For the commercial view, see most recently Coldstream, *GG* 221, 225-33; but the
cautionary arguments of Graham (*JHS* xci (1971), 42-5) remain unanswered, and cf. Cook,
Historia, xi (1962), 113-14.

(much less Corinthian) finds in Sicily before the foundation of the colonies makes such a motive for the Sicilian foundations most improbable.[35] If such considerations were not relevant in the further west it is superfluous to introduce them at Corcyra.

The western colonizing movement was in general designed to relieve over-population in the mainland;[36] there is a good deal of specific evidence for Corinth, relating especially to Syracuse. The mere fact that sufficient colonists could be provided—perhaps at one time, perhaps on separate occasions a generation apart—for what quickly became flourishing cities proves that there were ample Corinthians to spare; it is but a short step from here to conclude that the Corinthia was suffering from over-population. There is evidence that Corinth grew in population from *c*.800, and the same can perhaps be observed in other parts of the territory (below, 156). Strabo (380) records that Tenea, in the southern Corinthia, sent 'most of the colonists who sailed with Archias, who founded the colony at Syracuse'; it may be questioned whether a majority of the settlers came from Tenea, but there are no grounds for doubting the essence of the report. Each colonist expected a plot of land in the new foundations: the light-headed Aethiops bartered his for a honey cake on the way to Syracuse (Archilochus fr. 293 West), and enabled us to confirm the natural assumption—already strengthened by the participation of settlers from inland Tenea, who can only have been farmers—that the colonists left the Corinthia in order to secure for themselves more substantial plots than they farmed near the Isthmus.

An extremely suggestive passage in Aristotle concerns land tenure at Corinth, and may have been connected with the foundation of the colonies. Neither date nor context is given, but Aristotle records that the legislator, Pheidon, was one of the earliest lawgivers: he will certainly have preceded the tyranny of Cypselus. His concern was to ensure that the number of plots was equal to the number of citizens even though plots were unequal in size (*Pol.* 1265 b 12-16). The passage has usually been interpreted to mean that the number of plots and citizens was to remain constant after being fixed by Pheidon;[37] but ἴσος should mean equal rather than constant, especially where each term of the equation (τοὺς οἴκους . . . καὶ τὸ πλῆθος τῶν πολιτῶν; the properties . . . and the number of citizens)

---

[35] Coldstream, *GG* 233.
[36] Ibid., 221-2, 233-42.
[37] e.g. Will, *Korinthiaka*, 318-19; Zörner, 116; Roebuck, *Hesperia*, xli (1972), 115-16 n. 68; Oost, *CP* lxvii (1972), 13.

is given.[38] Aristotle may have understood the legislation to mean not only that plots and citizens were to be equal in number for the moment, but also that they were to remain constant in the future; but this is uncertain.[39] Even if he did he was not necessarily right: Pheidon may not have concerned himself with future development.

The possible practical effects are numerous, but at this early period there will hardly have been men who owned land in the Corinthia who were not citizens: Pheidon did not increase the number of citizens to balance the number of plots. Rather, some landless men may have been deprived of citizenship or excluded from the rights of citizenship which were now defined for the first time; and/or some citizens with little or no land will have been given plots. The foundation of the colonies is an admirable context for both. The reduction in the number of citizens was effected automatically; while the distribution of plots was facilitated by the departure of the colonists, many of whom will have left plots behind them. Most such plots were no doubt small, and many will have remained in the hands of relatives of their departed owners; but any vacant holdings may have been distributed to Corinthians who were unwilling to leave.

Other interpretations of the legislation are possible. Pheidon may, for example, have been attempting to define citizenship, and he may have excluded the landless but free inhabitants of the territory from the rights he defined. But this is not how Aristotle reports the laws, and such a definition is more likely to derive from a particular practical difficulty than from a desire to solve a theoretical problem; the foundation of the colonies provides exactly the practical issue that is required. Pheidon may have legislated before the colonies were founded in the hope of alleviating the problems of land hunger

[38] With his translation Will, followed by Zörner (locc. citt.), compares the legislation of the Bacchiad Philolaus for Thebes 'concerning the birth of children, which they call the laws of adoption ... which were intended to maintain the number of plots' (Ar. *Pol.* 1274 b 3-5). He suggests that the purpose of both Pheidon and Philolaus was to prevent subdivision of plots, the former by making it illegal for a plot to be divided and the latter by discouraging the rearing of children. But Aristotle's words imply the opposite conclusion for Philolaus, that his purpose was rather to keep *up* (σῴζηται) the number of plots. It is significant that the laws were called adoptive. Adoption is designed to keep within the family a plot which it is in danger of losing; the intention was therefore not to prevent subdivision, but rather to retain within an artificially extended family a plot which would otherwise have passed to another. But there is in any case no reason to believe that Pheidon at Corinth and Philolaus at Thebes hoped to achieve the same purpose.

[39] The conclusion has been encouraged by Aristotle's remarks on the control of the birth rate before he adduces the example of Pheidon (1265 b 6-12); but his specific argument against Plato based on the Corinthian law relates rather to the fact that Pheidon's plots were of unequal size (as Plato's were not), and that point is made *after* the details of the legislation are given (1265 b 15-16). Aristotle may of course have had both points in mind.

which the colonies later solved more successfully; but if so, it is
difficult to see how he obtained land to distribute to those citizens
who had little or none: hardly from Bacchiads, or even from other
wealthy Corinthians. The most plausible context for the legislation
is thus the time after the foundation of the colonies; it was designed
merely to regulate land tenure in the Corinthia in the new conditions, and was not an answer to any pressing problem except in
so far as it may have increased the holdings of some Corinthians
who remained at home.

Land hunger provides an entirely sufficient explanation for the
colonies. A Bacchiad founder for each is recorded: Archias for
Syracuse and Chersicrates for Corcyra.[40] It is a reasonable inference
that the Bacchiads determined to relieve the pressure on resources—
and no doubt increasing discontent—by settling excess population
elsewhere. A sufficient explanation, however, is not necessarily a
complete one; and some late sources introduce matters of high
politics. The story of Chersicrates is merely that he was 'deprived
of his rights' (ἀποστερούμενος τῶν τιμῶν) by the Corinthians;[41] but
for Archias there is more detail. An Argive, by name Habron, revealed a plot of Pheidon of Argos against Corinth and fled there.
His grandson Actaeon was murdered by Archias, and the wrath of
the gods was turned against the city. Delphi advised that Actaeon's
death be avenged; Archias, who had been on the embassy to Apollo,
sailed to Syracuse (where he was murdered in turn) instead of
returning to Corinth.[42] Chersicrates and Archias could hardly have
procured settlers for their colonies if they had acted independently,
as our sources suggest; but the stories might reflect the choice by
the Bacchiads of two of their number who were under clouds to lead
the colonies. Such a decision is in principle entirely credible; but
these versions are patently romantic inventions. What is reported of
Chersicrates was probably suggested by the analogy of Archias; and
there is enough that is suspect about his tale to cause its rejection
three times over. It is a distortion of the myth of the Boeotian
Actaeon; but there are two further reasons for disbelief. A similar
story occurs as an explanation of the expulsion of the Bacchiads;
and although this is no better history it does fit a real context
(below, 71-2). Finally, Archias was not the only Corinthian to perform

[40] Strictly, Archias is not specified as Bacchiad, but as Heracleid (Thuc. vi.3.2); but the
story of Actaeon (for what it is worth: see below) implies that he was Bacchiad (Plut. *Mor.*
772 C-773 B, esp. 772 E). Chersicrates: Ap. Rhod. iv.1212 with Schol. Ap. Rhod. iv.1212,
1216; Timaeus *FGH* 566 F 80.
[41] Schol. Ap. Rhod. iv.1216; perhaps not from Timaeus (as Jacoby, *FGH* 566 F 80); cf.
Andrewes, *CQ* xliii (1949), 70-1 n. 5.
[42] Plut. *Mor.* 772 C-773 B; cf. Diod. viii.10.

great deeds at Syracuse while under taint of murder: Timoleon was his model (below, 390).

The two colonies will have been made up largely of settlers from the Corinthia. For Syracuse, the evidence of burial types confirms this natural assumption; but it also indicates that there may have been some colonists of a different origin: cremation occurs at Syracuse but never at Corinth. It has been suggested that this is a sign of Chalcidian settlers (and see below, 66–7). Argives are indicated both by burial practice and by the more general archaeological record: a group of kraters made locally c.700 has strong affinities with contemporary Argive ware and is perhaps to be attributed to an immigrant Argive potter, while the burial of two youths in a pithos is closer to Argive than to Corinthian custom.[43] That the colony was essentially Corinthian would not exclude volunteers from elsewhere, and it was normal in later times for such ventures to be widely advertised; the practice was probably already to be found in the eighth century. There are no similar traces at Corcyra, but that colony has been less well explored.

Once the decision to found a colony (or two) had been taken, there remained the question of location. It is natural to suppose that the Bacchiads relied upon information brought from the west by Corinthians who had undertaken commercial voyages; but more may have been involved. It was hardly coincidence that the earliest Sicilian colonies were concentrated in such a short space of time. The Bacchiads may merely have followed the Chalcidian example at Naxos; but there are suggestive links between Corinth, Chalcis, Syracuse, and Delphi. Part of a Delphic foundation oracle for Syracuse is preserved by Pausanias: 'Ortygia lies in the misty sea of Thrinacria (Sicily), where the mouth of the Alpheius bubbles and mixes its waters with the spring of broad flowing Arethusa'.[44] This is probably genuine;[45] and it has often been suggested that the Syracusan spring Arethusa was named after that in Chalcis. It seems that Chalcidians had visited Syracuse before the colony was founded. The Chalcidian colony at Naxos was established with the blessing of Delphi, for the city had an altar of Apollo Archegetes, and there are possibly genuine foundation oracles for other Chalcidian colonies.[46] The probability is strong that Chalcis and Corinth determined together to carve up the central east coast of Sicily; greater Chalcidian

[43] See Coldstream, *GG* 234. The Argive 'king of Syracuse', Pollis, is probably a fiction of confused literary imaginations; see esp. Dunbabin, *Western Greeks*, 93–4.

[44] Parke and Wormell, *Delphic Oracle*, ii.2, no. 2.

[45] Ibid., i.67–8.

[46] Forrest, *Historia*, vi (1957), 165.

knowledge of the island may have joined with Corinth's growing influence at Delphi to make a powerful combination. A less accurate Corinthian knowledge of Sicilian conditions may be reflected in the sites of Naxos and Syracuse. Archias had to expel Sicel inhabitants from Syracuse, as is revealed by archaeological evidence;[47] Ephorus claimed that Theocles, the oecist of Naxos, chose that site in part because of the weakness of its previous inhabitants (*FGH* 70 F 137a), and although this hardly inspires confidence it is not incompatible with what material evidence there is.[48]

Plutarch (*Mor.* 293 A-B) preserves a story that the Corinthian colonists at Corcyra expelled Eretrians from the island; this raises the difficult question of the Lelantine War. Thucydides, after stating that in the past, land wars between Greek states had been a matter of mere border quarrels, writes, 'neighbours fought against each other. It was for the war which took place once a long time ago between Chalcis and Eretria that other Greeks most ranged themselves on one side or the other' (i.15.2-3). The proportion of the Greek world which participated should not be exaggerated, for Thucydides offers this case as a contrast to the normal rule that wars in early Greece were *only* border quarrels;[49] but it must have been to some degree exceptional to attract Thucydides' attention. He gives his war neither name nor date; the latter has sustained lively controversy. I follow Forrest and others in placing it in the late eighth century;[50] the best evidence is that Hesiod won the prize at the funeral games of Amphidamas of Chalcis, who died in the war.[51]

There is no direct evidence that Corinth took part; but the indirect signs are strong. The main aspect of the conflict must have been the dispute between Chalcis and Eretria over control of the Lelantine Plain. This is indicated by a strict interpretation of Thucydides' words; he does not claim the war as an exception to his general rule that wars in the past had been border disputes, but rather to the rule that only neighbours had fought each other. Our war was a border conflict in which allies not directly involved helped either party. Plutarch confirms this by referring to the struggle as fought 'over the Lelantine Plain' (*Mor.* 153 F). It is difficult to say

[47] Coldstream, *GG* 234.
[48] Ibid., 233-4.
[49] De Ste Croix, 219 n. 21.
[50] *Historia*, vi (1957), 161-4; but Ameinocles' date in Thucydides can no longer be used in support (Forrest, *CQ* xix (1969), 106 n. 4; cf. below, 222-3) For archaeological arguments which confirm this date, though they cannot on their own establish it, see Coldstream, *GGP* 368-9.
[51] Hes. *Erg.* 654-7; Plut. *Mor.* 153 E-F.

how far we should search for other participants; but it is safest to
include only those states which can be connected with one of the
Euboean cities. Plutarch makes the adherence of Pharsalus to Chalcis
certain: Cleomachus of Pharsalus died while taking part in a successful cavalry action on Chalcis' behalf during the war (*Mor.* 760 E–761
B). Herodotus makes Samos a probable ally for Chalcis and Miletus
for the Eretrians.[52] It is not strictly necessary to look further for an
explanation of Thucydides' description; but the addition of Corinth
to the Chalcidian alliance is imposed by the evidence which ranges
her both with Chalcis in Sicily (above, 66–7) and against Eretria at
Corcyra. Megara is perhaps to be included in the Eretrian alliance,
but this is more doubtful. There is no reason to associate any border
dispute that may have taken place in this period between Megara
and Corinth (below, 71) with the Lelantine War; but the Megarians
were expelled from Leontini by its Chalcidian settlers and forced to
found a colony of their own at Megara Hyblaea. It is true that they
were originally accepted at Leontini on amicable terms; but this may
have been before the outbreak of the war—or before Megara had
committed herself (in eastern waters?) to Eretria. To bring the first
Messenian War into the reckoning is too cavalier. Corinth is attested
as a Spartan ally by Pausanias,[53] but this must be rejected along with
the rest of Pausanias' romance; nothing associates either Sparta or
Messenia with the main combatants.[54]

A Chalcidian alliance of Pharsalus, Samos, and Corinth opposed to
Eretria, Miletus, and perhaps Megara is quite sufficient to explain
Thucydides' description. The nature of the war can only be the
subject of conjecture. Our evidence would be satisfied if it began
as a dispute over the Lelantine Plain but for various reasons the
Euboean cities could call on the help of allies—not necessarily
in the original area of conflict. Corinth's closest recorded action
in Chalcis' favour was undertaken at Corcyra; but the dedication
of spoils at Delphi commemorated by Eumelus (fr. 11 Kinkel) may

[52] v.99.1. Erythrae may perhaps be added to Samos, and Chios to Miletus, on the basis
of i.18.3; but there is no word here of Chalcis and Eretria.
    [53] iv.11.1,8. Eumelus fr. 13 Kinkel, written for a Messenian choir at Delos, implies if any-
thing that Corinth favoured Messenia, at least at the beginning of the war (esp. Bowra, *CQ*
xiii (1963), 151–3); but it is doubtful whether so small a fragment can yield such precise
conclusions, and I prefer to date the lines before the outbreak of the war (see Huxley,
Greek Epic Poetry, 62). No political point should be read into the words 'the Muse . . . who
wears free (unrestrained) dancing sandals'.
    [54] That Sparta (and Messenian traitors) used the oracle at Delphi is not sufficient evidence
(contrast Forrest, *Historia*, vi (1957), 167–8): the Pythia will not have excluded neutral
states. Samian help for Sparta (Hdt. iii.47.1) could be dated well after the late eighth
century.

have been a thank-offering for an action nearer home—if the battle was part of the Lelantine War at all.[55] It is difficult to see how the conflicts in the west could have given Chalcis any direct help in the Lelantine Plain (the return of the Eretrians from Corcyra might even have hindered, had they not been denied readmission); but the enmity caused by the central dispute will have had its effect else-where, and the Corinthian role may have been restricted to the aid afforded to the Chalcidians in the west. Samos and Miletus perhaps undertook similar action in the east, but we have no details.

Whether there was any positive purpose behind the extension of the conflict beyond Euboea is doubtful. Strictly, Thucydides implies that the war was a mere border dispute. It suits his argument to belittle the importance of the war, for the passage is intended to show how much greater Thucydides' own subject was than all previous conflicts; but nothing more is necessary. What was unusual about the dispute over the Lelantine Plain was that the combatants had extraordinarily widespread connections; the ripples generated in Euboea therefore reached the corners of the then Greek world. Where Chalcidians came into contact with Eretrians outside Euboea the enmity of the Lelantine dispute caused friction: hence the undated conflict at Pithecusae (Strabo 247), and the various actions of allies of the main disputants elsewhere. The conflict was fought on such a wide geographical scale merely because Chalcidians punched Eretrian noses wherever they could find them—and were helped by their allies.

If this is so, it will be misleading to speak of the Chalcidian alliance winning in the west and the Eretrian in the east: there were no prizes to be won outside Euboea. These hostilities were essentially a matter of revenge—although the Bacchiads will have had their own motives for choosing the propitious site of Corcyra. The essence of the dispute was the struggle for the Lelantine Plain; Chalcis was probably the victor here.[56] Elsewhere the results of the quarrel were various; but it is wrong to argue that since the Eretrians were in the main excluded from western colonization, the war was fought partly in order to exclude them. The exclusion was a consequence, not a purpose, of a conflict which originated in Euboea and was resolved—perhaps earlier than the associated disputes elsewhere—when Chalcis made good her claim to the Lelantine Plain.

[55] And if, indeed, it was a Corinthian action; other possibilities cannot be excluded.

[56] On geographical grounds Chalcis had the stronger claim; loss of the plain would almost imply Chalcis' destruction. But, if anything, archaeology suggests that Chalcis suffered more than Eretria, perhaps more from exhaustion than from defeat. See esp. Boardman, *BSA* lii (1957), 27-8; Coldstream, *GG* 200-1 (on Lefkandi).

Coldstream suggests that the war drained the energies of both Euboean cities, and that they thus 'lost the commercial initiative' to Corinth.[57] It is undeniable that after *c*.700 Euboean pottery gives way to Corinthian on western sites; but Corinth's geographical advantages are as probable an explanation as Euboean exhaustion. Euboean wares are found in significant quantity in the west until just before the end of the eighth century because Euboeans, having discovered the western routes (below, 92-3), remained commercially active here for some time afterwards. But the Isthmus and Cape Malea were powerful barriers; once Corinthians began to exploit their advantages the Euboeans, whether debilitated by the Lelantine War or no, will have found competition difficult.

If this treatment of the war is on the right lines, it will not have been a major episode in Corinthian history. Corinthians aided Chalcis by ejecting Eretrians from Corcyra; but they brought more benefit to themselves by choosing Corcyra than to the Chalcidians by first driving out the Eretrians. The victory recorded in Eumelus need not have been either of great importance or part of the war at all.[58] Unless the Corinthians were so committed to Chalcis that they sent help to Euboea itself—of which there is no sign—the war will have absorbed little Corinthian energy. This interpretation makes the war as unimportant in international affairs as is consistent with our evidence, and far greater claims have been made for it;[59] but to take it as a commercial conflict would be to make it almost unique in Greek history.[60] It is better to restrict conjecture to what is necessary to explain our evidence.

We have some traces of Corinthian relations with states closer to home.[61] Border disputes which Thucydides so disparaged no doubt took place; but evidence is preserved only for the border with the Megarid. Zenobius (v. 8) records a possibly genuine tradition that the daughter of a Megarian king Clytius married one Bacchius (presumably a Bacchiad), and that Megarians were forced to go to Corinth to mourn when she died; but this tells us nothing of normal relations.[62]

[57] *GGP* 369-70, cf. 376.

[58] Above, 68-9 with n. 55. That we know of no other suitable context is not an argument for associating this battle with the Lelantine War.

[59] Esp. Burn, *JHS* xlix (1929), 31-4; more cautiously Forrest, *Historia*, vi (1957), 160-4 esp. 164; d'Agostino, *DdA* i (1967), 20-37.

[60] De Ste Croix, 218-20.

[61] Corinth is recorded by Pausanias (iv.15.8; 19.1,3) as a Spartan ally in the Second Messenian War, perhaps fought in the Bacchiads' last years; but this is no more credible than his report of similar aid in the eighth century (above, 68). Pausanias' lists of allies reflect conditions of the fifth and fourth centuries rather than those of the eighth and seventh. See Cartledge, *Sparta and Lakonia*, 139.

[62] See, on this and its distortions, Salmon, *BSA* lxvii (1972), 198.

Plutarch—perhaps influenced by the better-known history of the fifth century—states that Corinthians were always plotting to subject Megara to their rule (*Mor.* 295 B). Other sources purport to preserve more detail. The proverb Διὸς Κόρινθος was sometimes (see also above, 38 n. 6) explained by a story that Corinthian ambassadors who went to Megara to assert the claims of 'Zeus' Corinthus' (the eponym of the city) were themselves stoned in place of Corinthus. This is hardly reliable; even if it reflects the truth it cannot be dated, and will have been no more than an episode in the border disputes which might have been assumed without evidence.[63] In an epitaph—no doubt composed long after the event—the Megarian Olympic victor Orsippus, who won the foot-race in 720 and was distinguished as the first Greek to run naked, was praised because 'He pushed the borders of his country to their greatest extent, when enemies tried to lop off much territory' (*IG* vii.52). The enemies are not identified; but the Corinthians are perhaps the most likely—though not the only possible —candidates. The scale of the conflict is unknown, but if it was from Corinth that Orsippus took land his success was presumably no more permanent than any other in a lasting dispute: rival claims in this region helped to bring about the First Peloponnesian War.[64]

The greatest threat against Bacchiad Corinth may have been Argive. Nothing is known of the relations between Corinth and Argos before the seventh century. The two territories were separated at this date by those of Cleonae and (probably) Mycenae (above, 3-5). The material record demonstrates that there was some contact; but it was not intense and (as far as pottery goes) there was little actual exchange. In the second quarter of the seventh century Pheidon was, in Ephorus' imaginative words, 'restoring the lot of Temenus';[65] his attention was, our sources allege, turned to Corinth on two apparently separate occasions. The two versions of the first story have widely differing chronological implications. Pheidon plotted against Corinth but his plans were revealed by an Argive (either Habron or Melissus) who fled to Corinth, where he was given thanks and protection. But gratitude did not persuade the Corinthians to give satisfaction when Actaeon (either the grandson or the son of the Argive traitor) was murdered; and the story ends either with the departure of Archias for Syracuse or with the expulsion of

---

[63] Ibid., 197-8.

[64] Below, 262. On Orsippus, ibid., 198-9. For a different reconstruction of relations between Megara and Corinth in the late eighth century see Hammond, *BSA* xlix (1954), 93-102.

[65] For the date, which remains controversial, see Salmon, *JHS* xcvii (1977), 92-3 with refs. On the 'lot', see Kelly, *A History of Argos*, 41-6.

the Bacchiads from Corinth. One version of the story thus places Pheidon's plot before the foundation of Syracuse, and the other nearly a century later. Andrewes has shown that the second is both the more satisfactory and the earlier-attested version; after discarding the romance of Actaeon as a version of the Boeotian myth, we are left with an unsuccessful attempt by Pheidon to gain control of Corinth some time before the coup of Cypselus.[66] The second story, recorded by Nicolaus of Damascus, is that 'Pheidon, out of friendship, gave help during a dispute at Corinth, but he died when an attack was mounted' (*FGH* 90 F 35); this Pheidon has usually, and correctly, been identified as the Argive tyrant rather than the Corinthian lawgiver.[67]

The two stories have often been taken as showing two separate attempts by Pheidon to secure control of Corinth;[68] but this is to give too much credit to unreliable sources. If there is any truth to be gained from the Actaeon stories, it is merely that Pheidon had designs on Corinth; the details—that Corinth was the first object of his attentions, or that he asked for troops from Corinth with the intention of doing away with them (both in Plutarch)—must be discarded. These stories have some value in confirming that Pheidon's ambitions were directed towards the Isthmus; but for the rest they are worthless. Nicolaus' notice remains; but it is too brief to be of much assistance. Pheidon's death must be placed after his intervention at Olympia in 668, and this makes it probable that his action in Corinth was connected with the struggles which issued in Cypselus' tyranny; but Nicolaus' account of Cypselus' rise itself contains no mention of Pheidon (*FGH* 90 F 57; below, 188). Argive intervention may only have been indirectly related to Cypselus' coup; but we must allow for the possibility of excerptor's omissions, not to mention Nicolaus' own. The identity of the faction through which Pheidon hoped to gain control cannot be recovered, although Forrest makes an attractive case for Cypselus himself.[69]

The only alliance which can be reconstructed for Bacchiad Corinth is that with Chalcis; but Corinth's most fruitful relationship may have been with Apollo. Delphi played a part in Corinth's colonization,

[66] *CQ* xliii (1949), 70-1. The Archias version: above, 65-6. The other: Schol. Ap. Rhod. iv.1212; Alex. Aet. fr. 3, 7-10 (Powell, *Collectanea Alexandrina*, 122)

[67] Esp. Andrewes, *CQ* xliii (1949), 77-8 n. 9; cf. Zörner, 71 n. 2. Contra, Jacoby ad loc.

[68] Will, *Korinthiaka*, 352-3; Zörner, 68-71.

[69] *Emergence*, 116-19. Sadly, the strongest arguments can both be easily answered. If any Bacchiads really fled to Pheidon's enemy Sparta, they may have done so only after they had been in Corcyra for some time (below, 195 with n. 29, 218). Delphic approval of Pheidon is clear from the last lines of the oracle preserved in the Palatine Anthology (xiv.73; cf. Salmon, *JHS* xcvii (1977), 93); Delphi also approved of Cypselus, but the reference to Argos may have been made before the Bacchiads lost Apollo's favour.

and Corinthian influence with the Pythia must have been strong. The shrine of Apollo enjoyed recognition from other than local visitors only from about the middle of the eighth century, to judge from the material remains (below, 86-8). A significant proportion of the votives of Corinthian manufacture, which far outweigh all others from the very beginning, will have been dedicated by Corinthians, even though Corinthian pottery was already popular elsewhere. The only formal evidence of Corinthian interest in Delphi is the foundation oracle for Syracuse and the dedication of spoils that is recorded by Eumelus; but Forrest has shown that Delphi was closely associated with the allies of Chalcis in the Lelantine War, and both geography and archaeology suggest that the most important influence was Corinthian, though Thessaly may have played some part.[70] It is curious that Corinth does not figure in the Delphic list of excellences compiled *c*.700 (Anth. Pal. xiv.73); but the Pythia may not have thought pottery worth a mention. It was presumably Bacchiads who represented Corinth in the consultations of political importance in this period; but they lost the confidence of Apollo, for he supported Cypselus in his attempt on the tyranny (below, 186-7, 219-20). What caused him to change his mind we cannot say; perhaps he really saw which way the future lay.

Many of the foundations for the subsequent development of Corinth were laid during the period of Bacchiad rule. Politically, the most momentous was the decision, surely taken by the Bacchiad government as such, to adopt the hoplite method of fighting. The date of the decision, I have argued elsewhere, will have been before the coup of Cypselus, and the new technique is probably already implied by the flautist—whose music kept the phalanx in step—on a Protocorinthian battle scene *c*.675.[71] The precise context of the change cannot be recovered; it might have been a matter of self-defence against Pheidon's linen-corseleted phalanx—or Pheidon might have pressed it on his Bacchiad allies to bring cohesion to his total forces. When vase-paintings begin to give evidence for the Corinthian phalanx, they indicate that the normal weapon was the spear, and not the sword which is attested at an early stage of phalanx warfare elsewhere; but the Chigi Vase—if it represents Corinthian practice—shows that hoplites at Corinth used throwing as well as thrusting spears: a technique not found in the phalanx of the classical

---

[70] *Historia*, vi (1957), 165-7. Note also 172: Apollo refused to sanction a settlement of Partheniae from Sparta on a site between Corinth and Sicyon, but sent them off to Tarentum instead.

[71] Salmon, *JHS* xcvii (1977), 85-93. The flautist, 89-90.

period.[72] Whatever the nature of the weapons of the phalanx in the Bacchiad period, they were soon turned, under Cypselus' leadership, against the Bacchiads themselves.

For other social and economic developments the extent of Bacchiad responsibility remains unclear. The single most important factor was the foundation of the colonies, which relieved pressure on resources at home. There were other consequences. The produce thus released could be used to exchange against the work of skilled Corinthian hands, and both Corinthian and other colonies provided a market for pots and perhaps other commodities too (below, 95–100); but the Bacchiads will hardly have foreseen these results, much less founded the colonies partly in order to achieve them. Strabo informs us that they 'reaped the fruits of the market without fear' (378). Much ink has been spilt in an attempt at determining whether the claim is that they took part in commerce themselves or merely grew fat on harbour-dues; but the passage is hardly worth the effort: it is probably a construction of Strabo or his source, based on the evident riches of the Bacchiads and Corinth's later commercial importance. Land must have been the basis of their wealth: it was established before there was any other possibility. The more quick-witted of them will have taken advantage of the increasing opportunities from the mid-eighth century, and some truth probably lay behind the subsequently embroidered tale of Demaratus, the Bacchiad who made his fortune by trade with Etruria, took craftsmen there with him when the Bacchiads were expelled, and eventually fathered a king of Rome.[73] Eumelus learned skills which will have been beneath many an aristocrat—indeed, his Bacchiad birth has been unnecessarily denied on such a ground. These may have been exceptions, but some of the surplus produce of the land of nameless members of the family will have provided items for export; many of the skills learned in the Corinthia will have been paid for by similar Bacchiad surpluses to achieve Bacchiad ostentation. All of this, however, was a matter of private initiative; of action by the government as such there is no sign. Many of the foundations of Corinth's future were laid during the Bacchiad period; but they were laid by the ambition, the greed, and the skills of individuals.

[72] Ibid., 90–2.
[73] The most detailed version; Dion. Hal. *Rom. Ant.* iii.46.

IV. Corinth: The Settlement

For the whole of the Geometric period, our evidence for occupation in the region of Temple Hill is indirect. The earliest dwelling is a house near the Sacred Spring, built in the first half of the seventh century.[1] A house of a similar date has been uncovered in the south of the Roman Agora.[2] A few terrace walls of Geometric date have been identified, and some of them may have been built to secure level ground for houses; but the buildings themselves have not been discovered.[3] The settlement area of Geometric Corinth must therefore be determined from indirect evidence: wells and graves.

Especially at Corinth, where Peirene gave a never-failing water-supply, wells are clear evidence of occupation in the immediate vicinity; but to draw conclusions for occupation from graves is more difficult. Their distribution shows a clear pattern. Burials were not normally made in central Corinth after MG II.[4] The largest group comes from the area of the Roman Bema. There was at that time a slope here on the south-east side of the Upper Lechaeum Road Valley; the earliest burial here is LPG.[5] There is no other accurately datable grave before MG II (Graves 8–10, 13?); but many must be Geometric, and some were probably dug in the ninth century.[6] These graves are so concentrated that they cannot have been scattered among dwellings: this must be a designated cemetery area.[7] Graves were also dug west of the Babbius Monument and further to the south: the western side of the Valley. Again, the earliest burial is LPG; another is to be dated soon afterwards (Graves 1, 4). No others can

---

[1] Williams, *Hesperia*, xl (1971), 5–10.

[2] Williams, *Hesperia*, xli (1972), 145–9.

[3] Weinberg, *Hesperia*, xxix (1960), 252; cf. Williams, *Hesperia*, xl (1971), 3, 23 n. 20; xli (1972), 144.

[4] In view of the absence of datable graves in LG, Grave 16 (Fig. 7) is to be taken as an exception. The EC Grave 17 is similarly exceptional, and is to be explained by the discovery of the Geometric graves in the vicinity. Two other sarcophagi without gifts may have been used at the same time, and the region was subsequently devoted to a hero cult; cf. Morgan, *AJA* xli (1937), 545–6; Broneer, *Hesperia*, xi (1942), 143–5.

[5] Grave 3. For a map of the graves mentioned here, and references to publications, see Fig. 7.

[6] Graves 18–30. Some contained Geometric handmade pottery or bronze pins etc.; but none can be accurately dated.

[7] Cf. Williams, *Hesperia*, xlii (1973), 2 with plan, 3, fig. 1; xliii (1974), 5.

be dated, but they may cover the period between EG and MG II (Graves 14?, 31-2, 33?, 34-6). Graves here are less concentrated than those of the south-east cemetery. Other Geometric graves are more scattered. There is a line running north from Peirene: this covers most of the Geometric period,[8] and the graves must have been dug beside the road which led along the Lechaeum Road Valley.[9] Two empty graves of the usual Geometric type with a single cover slab (above, 43) were found in the Odeum (Graves 38-9).

The graves in the northern area were dug beside a road leading out of the settlement; the same happened in the west.[10] The road in the area of the largest Geometric cemetery, to the south-east, will have led to Acrocorinth, Anaploga, or both.[11] The natural conclusion from this distribution of graves is that the settlement was to be found in the small, but not impossibly limited, area in the Upper Lechaeum Road Valley between these cemeteries; but this has recently been doubted by the excavator of many of the graves. He suggests that 'the Early Iron Age custom in Corinth was to bury the dead close to their own houses, rather than in common grave fields isolated from the area of habitation'.[12] If this is right, it would be impossible to use graves to determine the limits of settlement. It is with great reluctance that I venture to question the excavator's opinion; but the evidence seems to me to point in a different direction.

In the north, graves certainly lined a road that led out of the settlement: they follow the path of the Lechaeum Road over a considerable distance. Elsewhere there is no published evidence which disturbs a similar conclusion, and some which encourages it. In both the west and the south-east the earliest burial is nearest to the presumed area of habitation; this would be natural if graves were dug in the closest available places beyond the settlement, but in the north the chronological pattern is different. The strongest evidence is to be found in the distribution of wells in central Corinth. It is remarkable that in the LG period, immediately after the latest regular burials in the central area, wells were dug either in or beyond earlier cemeteries. Wells were not sunk in the north: Peirene and its stream made them superfluous. But in the west they were placed

[8] From south to north: Graves 7, 11, 6, 37, 15?, 5, 2, 40.
[9] Cf. Weinberg, *Hesperia*, xxix (1960), 252.
[10] See the plan in Williams, *Hesperia*, xlii (1973), 3, fig. 1; this road presumably led eventually to Sicyon.
[11] Williams, *Hesperia*, xliii (1974), 3, 5.
[12] Williams, *Hesperia*, xlii (1973), 4.

very close to earlier graves,[13] while in the south-east they were first dug beyond the cemetery (Wells B, D, perhaps C). The south-eastern burials, since they were more numerous, may have been respected for longer than the western, but wells were none the less sunk here soon afterwards (Wells M, N). It seems that in the LG period the original settlement area became inadequate, and houses were therefore built above or beyond earlier cemeteries. Since Peirene was so close wells were not needed in the north; but it has been suggested that terrace walls show that an area north of Peirene which had been used for burials in the ninth century was converted for dwellings in the second half of the eighth.[14] The evidence for settlement in or beyond the areas once used for graves is to be dated after the last known burials;[15] a chronological distinction should therefore be drawn between graves and habitation in these areas, and the natural assumption that separate places were designated for the dead and the living is confirmed. Other published evidence for Geometric habitation, terrace walls and sporadic sherds, comes from regions which are enclosed by the known cemeteries.[16]

From the mid-eighth century the evidence provided by wells for the expansion of the settlement area increases. LG wells were not only dug in or beyond the cemeteries but also further to the east (Wells E, F) and the west (Well G). EPC wells have been found in much the same areas (Wells M, N, O, P), and it is unnecessary to trace such activity any further: even in LG habitation had almost reached the limits of the region which has been extensively excavated, and wells were commonly sunk in all these places subsequently. The rapid expansion of the settlement area is probably partially explained by increasing population; but another factor will have been that the average dwelling-place now occupied a greater area than before. Ninth-century houses will hardly have been as large as those of the early seventh recently excavated (above, 75). The extent of

[13] Wells H, J, K, L (cf. Williams, *Hesperia*, xl (1971), 23-4); for a map of these wells, and references to publications, see Fig. 7.

[14] Weinberg, *Hesperia*, xxix (1960), 252.

[15] Cf. Coldstream, *GG* 174. There is one certain, one probable, and one possible exception. Grave 16 is a clear case. Grave 12 might be taken as the most southerly in the north/south series; but this would restrict the settlement area improbably, and this burial is best taken with Grave 16 as an exceptional case of interment among houses. The PG Well A will be earlier than most of the graves in the south-east cemetery; but its position will allow it to be within the habitation area as defined by the graves. Its contents have not been published; it is therefore unclear whether it belongs with Dorian Corinth or with the earlier settlement, other remains of which have turned up in this area (above, 42 n. 16).

[16] Terrace walls: Williams, locc. citt. above, 75 n. 3. For the north, see above. MG II sherds have turned up in small numbers in the western cemetery area (Williams, *Hesperia*, xliv (1975), 7). This area was certainly occupied in LG (above, 76-7 with n. 13); the settlement may have encroached here in the earlier phase.

population growth cannot therefore be accurately measured by
the extent of increase in the settlement area. The growth which
did take place is probably mainly to be explained by an increase
in the number of skilled craftsmen who found that their work
could best be sold at Corinth. Such a trend can be directly traced
in the region of the Sacred Spring, where a metal workshop was
established in the first half of the seventh century. Pottery workshops have not been found at Corinth itself, but other skills developed
rapidly around 700 (below, 95-100); they will have been best exercised at Corinth unless the raw materials were available more easily
elsewhere.

It is difficult to trace development beyond the end of the eighth
century; excavation has rarely been undertaken outside the Roman
Agora. One case shows how limited our knowledge is: a kilometre
north of the Roman Agora, fifth- and fourth-century settlement
has been revealed.[17] From the seventh century public buildings of
various kinds can be traced. The earliest major project was the
seventh-century temple of Apollo on Temple Hill (above, 59–62),
replaced in the middle of the sixth (below, 180); there are numerous
small cult-places in the central area,[18] but the only other large
known temple is that of Olympian Zeus probably built by Periander
in the region of the Gymnasium (below, 228). Springs were constructed rather earlier: the Sacred Spring had a supply chamber with
a stone floor sealed with bronze joints perhaps already in the eighth
century.[19] The Cyclopean Spring may be of a similar period,[20]
although its primitive appearance is no guarantee of an early date.
The publication of other springs in the city gives little attention
to chronology;[21] but embellishments at Peirene probably reach
back into the seventh century and Glauke was probably not much
later. The development of the Sacred Spring is now much better
known after recent excavations.[22] Secular buildings other than
springs cannot be traced earlier than the fifth century. This is the
probable date of the race-track which ran past the Sacred Spring,[23]
and there are structures in the region of the South Stoa which

[17] Robinson, *Hesperia*, xxxi (1962), 124.
[18] Williams, *Hesperia*, xli (1972), 149-51 with refs.; xlii (1973), 6-12; xliii (1974), 1-6;
xlvii (1978), 5-12. See also in general Williams, 'Pre-Roman Cults'. I am extremely grateful
to the author for allowing me to read a copy.
[19] Williams, *Hesperia*, xl (1971), 3-5.
[20] Hill, *Corinth*, i.6.46-80.
[21] Hill, *Corinth*, i.6.
[22] Williams, *Hesperia*, xxxviii (1969), 38-62; xxxix (1970), 21-31; xl (1971), 10-22;
xlii (1973), 27-32.
[23] Williams, *Hesperia*, xxxix (1970), 1; 1 (1981), 2-21.

probably served some public purpose.[24] More imposing buildings were erected to the north and east of Temple Hill (below, 180-1). This scattered evidence, however, gives little idea of the appearance of the city, and it even remains uncertain where the agora was to be found.[25] This can hardly be taken to show that the city had no agora; but it demonstrates how restricted our evidence is.

Roebuck, in a valuable study of the early development of Corinth, has suggested that 'the urban monumentalization of the heart of the growing "city" was long delayed'; and that 'Corinth was still (sc. in the sixth century) a group of scattered villages, essentially rural in character'.[26] There is no positive evidence for a sprawling urban centre; but the fact that the agora cannot yet be traced even in the fourth century should prevent the drawing of premature conclusions. Roebuck points out that many industrial establishments were some distance from Temple Hill;[27] but these places where clay was worked may have been chosen because of the availability of the necessary materials, and the implications for the development of Corinth itself are uncertain. It should not be argued that the large scale of sales of pottery in the Potters' Quarter shows that the development of an agora at Corinth for marketing purposes was slow.[28] Corinthian potters did not have to search for a market before the second quarter of the sixth century: their customers came to them—and probably continued to do so even when the export market declined. It is significant that both metalworking and dyeing can be traced in the central area, beginning in the seventh and sixth centuries respectively (below, 99, 119). Metal and dye-workers, who were not constrained by local origins of their raw materials, deliberately chose a central position.

Roebuck seems to imply not only that there were many separate villages close to Corinth (which is no doubt accurate), but also that the settlement at Corinth itself remained physically little more than a village. Such a conclusion is improbable. It is not easy to draw a line between village and city; but already by the mid-seventh century Corinth could boast one of the most imposing temples of its day, and in the early sixth Periander built a large temple dedicated to Olympian Zeus. The springs of Glauke and Peirene provided large quantities of

---

[24] Williams, *Hesperia*, xli (1972), 151-74. Possibly also the 'Tavern of Aphrodite' (Morgan, *Hesperia*, xxii (1953), 134-40; more recently Williams, *Hesperia*, xlii (1973), 19-23); the purpose of the structure remains unclear.

[25] Williams, *Hesperia*, xxxix (1970), 33-5 with refs., 35 n. 47.

[26] *Hesperia*, xli (1972), 122.

[27] Ibid.; see below, 96-7, 122.

[28] Cf. Roebuck, ibid., 121-2.

water by the mid-sixth century. Each was a monumental structure; in addition, Glauke was fed from some distance away, which implies that the population in the central area was increasing so much that Peirene would not suffice. The defensive wall built by Cypselus shows that already the urban centre of Corinth was worth defending (below, 220-1). Further factors, apart from monumental public buildings, which may be taken as defining characteristics of a city, are large urban population and economic specialization: both can be traced at Corinth well before the end of the seventh century, and Periander's decision to build an artificial harbour at Lechaeum, the closest point on the coast to Corinth, demonstrates the scale of trade to and from the settlement (below, 133-4). Our limited evidence strongly favours the conclusion that Corinth was already, in respect of amenities, population, and economic activity, a true city by the time of the tyrants.

V. Exploration

It is no more possible to write a satisfactory social and economic history of Corinth than of any other Greek state. We have almost none of the statistics necessary for serious study of any economy and (perhaps more significantly) our literary sources take little interest in such factors; where they do they are either very general (e.g. Thuc. i.13: below, 133) or frustratingly isolated (e.g. Hdt. ii.167: below, 163). But an attempt must be made. The result will inevitably be speculative in part; but all speculation must start from the evidence and must attempt to explain it. Many of our sources are archaeological; they therefore have the advantage that they cannot lie, if only they are properly interpreted and evaluated.[1] My aim is to trace developments from the foundation of the city to the fourth century; but a strictly chronological treatment is impossible, and I shall in general distinguish only three stages: the first down to the foundation of Syracuse, the second the subsequent century or rather less, and the final from c.650 onwards. The length of this last stage will seem excessive; but no satisfactory division within this long period can be made. We know far more about the political history of Corinth in the fifth and fourth centuries than in the seventh; but in some respects the reverse is true of economic history, for the archaeology of the archaic period is often better known than that of the classical. More importantly, no major change in the nature of the economy can be traced within the whole of this period. What made Corinth exceptional among Greek cities—the abnormally high proportion of her inhabitants who supported themselves other than by agriculture—was already true of the seventh century.

In the earliest years the economy must have been almost exclusively based on the land. The material remains allow us to identify one exception in potters—although this specialist skill need not have occupied all their time, and they may have worked plots as well as wheels. Work in metal may have been a similar specialization; but

---

[1] Cf., however, Grierson, *Trans. Royal Hist. Soc.*[5] ix (1959), 129: 'It has been said that the spade cannot lie, but it owes this merit in part to the fact that it cannot speak.' I owe this reference to Mr G. E. M. de Ste Croix.

most other skills (carpentry, building, weaving, etc.) were so rudimentary that they could be learned as they were needed. The nature of the economy cannot be recovered. Early Corinthians may have been rather meat- than cereal-eaters, for the arable farming on which Hesiod concentrates in the *Works and Days* may have been of relatively recent origin in Greece when he composed his work *c.*700; but there is no evidence from the Corinthia itself.[2] If this is true, we have no means of telling whether the stock belonging to any one man or family will have fed on land that was in some sense his own or on common land. If the latter, difficult problems of landownership may have accompanied the switch from pasture to arable; we cannot know how they were solved.

There is more direct evidence for Corinthian contact with the outside world about 900 than for a century afterwards. Corinthian vases of LPG date or retaining PG features have turned up at Medeon in Phocis,[3] in the Argolid,[4] and in Boeotia.[5] In view of the absence of Corinthian EG and the almost total absence of MG I outside its place of origin,[6] these finds are probably significant; but what they signify is unclear. They are hardly evidence of extensive trade; they may indicate nothing more than that the early Corinthians travelled in nearby regions merely to see where they were, left guest-friend gifts, and then settled down to a more circumscribed local life. Corinth was not entirely turned in on itself; its potters followed, in a sober way, the development of Attic throughout the ninth

[2] See in general Snodgrass, *Dark Age*, 378–80; *Archaic Greece*, 35–7; Murray, *Early Greece*, 46–7; above, 53. If Corinth was founded by nomads, they may have remained pastoral after settling down. Hes. fr. 204, 46–51 West (cattle and sheep in, among other places, Corinth) can hardly be taken as serious evidence.
[3] Pyxis: Coldstream, *GGP* 197 with n. 3 (cf. *Praktika*, 1907, 111). A number of Corinthian LPG or slightly later oinochoai, along with handmade aryballoi, were uncovered in a later excavation of the same cemetery (cf. Vatin, *Médéon de Phocide*; Coldstream, *GG* 40); they remain unpublished, and I am grateful to Miss Nicopoulou for her generous permission to look briefly at them. Coldstream (*GG*, 40, 50) suggests that these vases, along with the contemporary adoption of the cist as a form of burial, may indicate that settlers from Corinth reached Medeon; but the built cist is not common at Corinth, though it does occur at the relevant period (above, 44), and Corinthian influence need not indicate Corinthian settlers.
[4] Mycenae: Desborough, *BSA* 1 (1955), 241, no. 2 (Coldstream, *GGP* 113 n. 6). Argos: Argos C 2414 (unpublished: I am indebted to Mrs Protonotariou-Deilaki for permission to study the vase). Both are similar to the oinochoe, Fig. 9. Weinberg, 8, suggests that some LPG vases from Asine are Corinthian; but those which have been illustrated (Frödin and Persson, *Asine*, 429, fig. 227) are decorated in a manner unknown at Corinth.
[5] Thebes: Desborough, *PGP* 198 (cf. 195), pl. 29 c.
[6] For a few MG I vases from the Aegean, below, 93 n. 57. Vases of a similar date have turned up in the Megarid (Weinberg, 24 with pl. 11 top left; found (circumstances not recorded) at Megara with Nat. Mus. 13678, a Corinthian MG I amphora); the Megarid probably produced little pottery of its own and used either Corinthian or Attic.

century.[7] No doubt there were similar interchanges in other fields which cannot now be traced; but their scale must have been small.

For the whole of the ninth century there is little to report. The settlement at the head of the Lechaeum Road Valley probably grew no larger: even in the early eighth century graves were dug in the same places as those of the late tenth and the ninth; it is not until even later that evidence begins to accumulate for an increased size of the settlement (above, 75–8). There are a few scattered graves from the rest of the Corinthia; but the evidence is too thin to allow conclusions (below, 156).

Until *c.*800 the majority of the inhabitants of Corinth were probably buried in graves close to the settlement in which they had lived; but from the beginning of MG II many graves were dug in the North Cemetery, some 1.5 km. north-west of the city. Those who were buried there had probably lived at Corinth itself; the establishment of a new cemetery implies that the population was increasing.[8] The small MG II cemetery near the Potters' Quarter[9] probably demonstrates that the plateau was occupied soon after 800, probably for the first time; there is no sign that pots were made here so early, and the inhabitants may have come from Corinth because there was no longer room for them there. Some confirmation may be found in the number of MG II graves from central Corinth; it is probably greater than that for all earlier periods combined (Fig. 7). Certainly after 750 the settlement at Corinth grew: the ground which had held cemeteries in earlier times was occupied in LG by houses (above, 77). Excess population in the Corinthia is indicated by the foundation of two colonies soon after the middle of the century (see above, 63); the establishment of the North Cemetery and the occupation of the Potters' Quarter plateau suggest that the trend was already established by *c.*800. There is no evidence to show why the increase took place; but the phenomenon was common in Greece at this time.[10]

There was probably some connection between this trend and the other major development of the early eighth century: the Corinthian westward expansion. A few scraps of MG I have been found outside the Corinthia (above, 82 n. 6); but after *c.*800 Corinthian vases

[7] Coldstream, *GGP* 92–5.

[8] The cemetery may have served a separate settlement in its earliest years (Coldstream, *GG* 174), even though it was later used for Corinth itself; but it remains evidence for population increase in this general area.

[9] Stillwell, *Corinth*, xv. 1.6–11.

[10] Snodgrass, *Archaic Greece*, 19–25; there are not sufficient graves to make similar calculations for the Corinthia.

travelled abroad in increasingly large numbers. Some went eastwards; but most were carried along the Corinthian Gulf or beyond. The foundation of the colonies added a new element to the traffic between Corinth and the west; but all the evidence from before that time may be considered together.

Corinthian vases reached Medeon in some quantity in LPG (above, 82 n. 3); the traffic was resumed in MG II.[11] Perhaps the earliest vase found on these sites comes from Delphi: a magnificent stemmed krater (Fig. 11); it exhibits both accuracy and restraint, the best features of this phase, and should be dated soon after 800.[12] Other vases reached the site before the end of the phase.[13] Their presence is noteworthy of itself; their interest is increased by the fact that those for which a context is recorded had no connection with the cult of Apollo.[14] The stemmed krater, along with other pieces, came from a house deposit beneath the ramp of the fourth-century temple,[15] while others were found in a complex of eighth-century houses.[16] It is also significant that two Corinthian MG II pots from Delphi were mended in antiquity; no doubt they were prized household possessions.[17] Similar Delphic contexts produced even more Corinthian LG; the house deposit beneath the ramp and the complex of houses mentioned above continued into this period,[18] and other domestic deposits produced Corinthian LG.[19] But Corinthian of this date is also found in a quite different context, connected with the cult. Corinthian vases appear in quantity from *c*.750 in a deep, extensive layer which reaches to the mid-sixth century; it is what remains of the votive deposit of Apollo, thrown out as a result of the destruction by fire of his temple in 548.[20] Some few bronzes from this layer

---

[11] Preliminary reports on the later graves, *AD* xix.B (1964), 224; esp. Vatin, *Médéon de Phocide*, 7–35. Corinthian LG: Vatin, ibid., figs. 71, 75, 77–8, perhaps 76. The MG II finds remain unpublished.

[12] *BCH* lxxiv (1950), pl. 39.1 bottom left; probably the earliest of its type; more elaborate and later examples are Young, *Corinth*, xiii. 25, 17–3 and W 73.

[13] Some examples: *BCH* lxxiv (1950), pl. 39.1 bottom right, top centre left; Lerat, *RA*[6] xii. 2 (1938), 211, pl. 3 top; Weinberg, *AJA* xlv (1941), 33, figs. 3–4. There are more unpublished than published pieces.

[14] Rolley, *Fouilles de Delphes*, v.2.103.

[15] *BCH* lxxiv (1950), 322.

[16] Ibid., 328.

[17] Both kraters/kantharoi: *BCH* lxxiv (1950), pl. 39.1 bottom right; Lerat, *RA*[6] xii. 2 (1938), 211, pl. 3 top.

[18] *BCH* lxxiv (1950), 322, pl. 39.1 top centre, 328, 329, figs. 40–2, pl. 39.2–5; not all Corinthian LG is published.

[19] Lerat, *BCH* lxxxv (1961), 338–52 (cf. Coldstream, *GGP* 98); *RA*[6] xii. 2 (1938), 207–14 with 211, pl. 3 bottom; 216, fig. 13 top left, top right, bottom left.

[20] Lerat, *BCH* lxxxv (1961), 328. Parts of this level are referred to in numerous publications: Perdrizet, *Fouilles de Delphes*, v.133–52; Amandry, *BCH* lxii (1938), 305–31;

(a)   (b)

Fig. 11   Corinthian MG II at Delphi: (a) Stemmed Krater; (b) Krater/Kantharos.
From *BCH* lxxiv (1950), pl.39.1.

perhaps belong in the first half of the eighth century, or even at the
end of the ninth.[21] The origin of these items cannot be determined,
but after 750 Corinthian bronzes are probably almost as great a
proportion of the total as Corinthian pottery.[22]

The closest significant site to Delphi is Ithaca; here, in unexpected
contrast to Delphi, all the material is from sanctuaries. Corinthian
MG II turns up in the Aetos sanctuary at about the same time as
at Delphi. Among the earliest vases are many drinking-vessels, some
of which reach back to the beginning of the eighth century.[23] Other
shapes occur in smaller numbers and begin almost as early.[24] LG
vases are far more numerous.[25] A poorer sanctuary at Polis received

lxviii/lxix (1944/5), 36-51; Lerat, *BCH* lxxxv (1961), 323-9. Only a few scraps of pottery
from this layer have been published. The earliest is Perdrizet, *Fouilles de Delphes*, v.138,
fig. 548: late in MG II (cf. Young, *Corinth*, xiii. 26-7 (18-1)). Already LG, and not early, is
Amandry, *BCH* lxviii/lxix (1944/5), 37, fig. 1 centre towards bottom: a nick-in-rim skyphos
with five lines beneath the chevrons (cf. Salmon, *BSA* lxvii (1972), 168-9).

[21] Cf. for the figurines Rolley, *Fouilles de Delphes*, v.2.23 (no. 1); 47-9 (no. 32); ibid.,
v.3.11 (no. 254). Tripods and modifications to the chronology: ibid., v.3, esp. 135 with
n. 5.

[22] Herrmann, *JdaI* lxxix (1964), 17-71, confidently attributed most of the Geometric
bronzes from Delphi to Corinth. Rolley in *Fouilles de Delphes*, v.2 is more cautious; but
at least the hammered horses (ibid., 73-6) and the hammered birds (ibid., 90) are surely
Corinthian, and despite Rolley's doubts it is unreasonable to deny a Corinthian origin to
his group 1-4 (cf. ibid., 26). Rolley states that nothing like these last was found on Ithaca;
but see below, 86 n. 26. The presence of this object at Ithaca deprives Rolley of an argument against a Corinthian origin which is in any case of doubtful force.

[23] The earliest is probably Aetos B 619; its shallow shape is similar to that of Payne,
Perachora, i.12.1 (for which see Salmon, *BSA* lxvii (1972), 161). Aetos B 622-3 (more than
two examples) will be little later. Glazed protokotylai (Aetos R 289, B 615, R 16, B 621,
B 616-18) begin early in MG II (cf. Salmon, *BSA* lxvii (1972), 162). Decorated protokotylai
probably cover much the same period (Aetos B 620, 624, 626-7).

[24] e.g. kraters: Aetos R 55, B 787, 790, 793; cup: Aetos R 46; giant oinochoai: Aetos
B 881-2, 885-6 (dated by Coldstream *GGP* 353 n. 8).

[25] Ibid., 353, n. 11.

a few Corinthian offerings from c.750.[26] At Ambracia, Corinthian Geometric fragments have been found beneath the later colony; while at Vitsa Zagoriou in the mountains of Epirus much Corinthian Geometric has been uncovered recently in a large cemetery. The earliest pieces from both sites have been dated by the excavator in the early eighth century; but the finds have not yet been fully published.[27]

Across the Adriatic (Fig. 12) there are a few pieces which date from just before or about the same time as the foundation of Syracuse, scattered on sites from near Taras to Etruria;[28] but the only site on which Corinthian appears in significant quantities is Pithecusae. The earliest sign of Corinthian influence, a decade or so before the end of MG II, is a local copy of a Corinthian type;[29] but there are some original Corinthian pieces which may have been made at about the same time.[30] From the earliest years Corinthian predominates among the imported wares at Pithecusae, and the number of finds is large; but there was a great deal of local and Euboean material too.[31] Corinthian may have played a similar role at the slightly later Euboean foundation at Cumae, but there is no evidence from the earliest years at this site.[32]

It would be natural to guess that the Corinthian vases which reached Delphi soon after 800 were connected with the sanctuary of Apollo; but there are serious reasons for doubting such a conclusion. In the first place, the sanctuary was probably too insignificant at this date to attract Corinthians in any numbers. There are no pottery votives which belong much before c.750. Some bronze

[26] The earliest published vase is mid-LG: Benton, *BSA* xxxix (1938/9), 21, no. 11, pl. 11 e; a few unpublished kotylai and protokotylai might be earlier. A bronze female statuette (Benton, *BSA* xxxv (1934/5), pl. 16) is earlier; cf. Coldstream, *GG* 176.

[27] Ambracia: Vocotopoulou, *AAA* iv (1971), 335; *AD* xxvi.B (1971), 331. Vitsa: *AD* xxii.B (1967), 348; xxiv.B (1969), 250; cf. xxiii.B (1968), 288; Vocotopoulou, *AAA* vi (1973), 215. The Geometric bronze horse from the settlement at Vitsa, *AD* xxiii.B (1968), 289 with pl. 233 δ, is also perhaps Corinthian. Isolated finds further afield: Coldstream, *GG* 186.

[28] Satyrion: Lo Porto, *BA* xlix (1964), 76, 77, fig. 23 = *NS* 1964, 224, 223, fig. 44.2 (probably not much after 735: cf. Payne, *Perachora*, i. 12.4, and see Salmon, *BSA* lxvii (1972), 172-4). L'Incoronata: Orlandini, *Acme* xxix (1976), 36. Sicily: below, 92 n. 53. Capua: Johannowsky, *DdA* i (1967), fig. 16 (perhaps local copies). S. Marzano: d'Agostino, *MEFR* lxxxii (1970), 604. Etruria, probably local copies: Blakeway, *BSA* xxxiii (1932/3), 196 with pl. 31 no. 73; *JRS* xxv (1935), 133 with pl. 21, B 3 (Falerii); Brown, *Etruscan Lion*, 13 with pl. 6 a (Veii).

[29] A chevron protokotyle like Aetos B 624: Coldstream, *GGP* 354-5.

[30] Buchner, *Expedition*, viii.4 (1966), 11, nos. 1, 3; cf. Coldstream *GGP* 355 n. 3.

[31] For the local, see esp. Buchner, *AR* 1970/1, 66-7; in addition to this independent style, there were many local copies of Corinthian types (e.g. Buchner, *DdA* iii (1969), 87-9, figs. 21-2; 90, figs. 22-3 (grave 233-1).

[32] Coldstream, *GGP* 355-6.

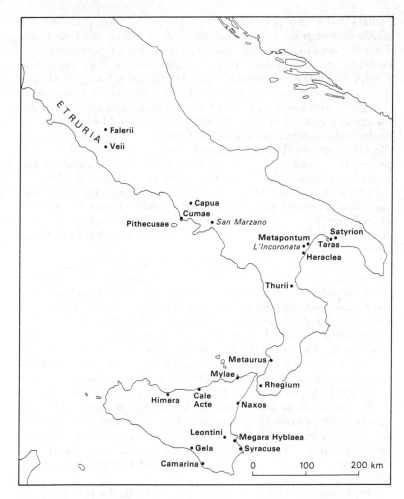

Fig. 12   South Italy and Sicily

tripods have been claimed to reach back to *c*.800; but the chronology
of these objects is insecure, and Rolley—despite his date in the first
half of the eighth century for some of them—places the Panhellenic
reputation of Apollo and his oracle no earlier than *c*.750.[33]   It is

---

[33] *Fouilles de Delphes*, v.3.143. On the chronology of tripods in general, see Rolley,
ibid., 105-45: they can never be dated by their contexts, and there are precious few other

perhaps more important that every Corinthian vase from the site which dates significantly before the end of MG II was found in a domestic deposit, and that the great majority of pots from such contexts are Corinthian. This, of itself, proves that Corinthian pottery had some commercial value for the inhabitants of Delphi; the conclusion is strengthened by the fact that two of them were thought worth mending. It is curious, if Corinthians went to Delphi for reasons connected with the cult, that they sold (or gave) vases to the Delphians but did not offer them to the god whom they had come to worship. The large quantity of pottery votives after c.750 proves that vases were not then thought to be unsuitable; and Corinthians dedicated significant numbers of vases to Hera at Perachora throughout MG II. The positive evidence that Corinthian vases had an exchange value at Delphi combines with the absence of evidence for Corinthian dedications to Apollo before the mid-century to indicate that it was for secular reasons that Corinthians made the journey.

If it was the prospect of profitable commercial exchanges which brought Corinthians to Delphi in the first half of the eighth century, the commodities involved remain problematic. The pots clearly held some value; but they are so few that if they were the main item the exchanges were of minimal significance. They were probably an unimportant sideline; but we can only guess at the identity of the other items. The restricted number of vases shows in any case that the traffic was not heavy. There was little enough for Corinthians to seek at Delphi; Delphians might covet what Corinthians had to offer, but they probably had little to give in exchange save a higher price than could be had in the Corinthia. Rough handmade MG II and LG hydriai made their way from Corinth to Delphi[34] and were no doubt taken for the sake of their contents; they probably show that Corinthians offered wine or oil as well as pots, but some of them could have been the empty wine-carriers of Corinthians who had made thirsty journeys.

Delphi was therefore no special case in MG II; the evidence from Medeon makes it probable that it is only because other sites have been less well explored that no comparable material has turned up

points of reference (112-13; note esp. 113 n.1). The absence of votive vases before c.750 might (despite Rolley, ibid., 135) be taken to indicate that the date of the earliest bronzes should be somewhat reduced (see below). The supposed derivation of the mid-eighth-century temple of Apollo Daphnephoros at Eretria from the earliest temple at Delphi, which literary sources claim as made of bay-wood (Bérard, *AK* xiv (1971), 59-73; Cold-stream, *GG* 88), is too fanciful to support conclusions for the chronology of Delphi (cf. Rolley, *Fouilles de Delphes*, v.3.143).

[34] Lerat, *BCH* lxxxv (1961), 342-3, mentioning other unpublished examples.

elsewhere. Many sites on the Gulf will have been visited as often as Delphi. There are sporadic finds from sites close to Delphi which probably illustrate such exchanges in the LG period.[35] No Corinthian Geometric has yet turned up in Achaea;[36] but the local style shows influence from Corinth in LG which was almost certainly exerted in some cases by Corinthian imports.[37] Even at Delphi, however, the amount of evidence suggests that the contacts were neither frequent nor important. Soon before 750, Corinthians began to visit Delphi in large numbers to worship Apollo and to offer him votives; but their gifts have little importance for economic history.

The traffic which brought Corinthian vases to Delphi and perhaps other sites on the Gulf from 800 was of minor significance; it is different with the finds from Ithaca. The shrines in which the vases were dedicated were too unimportant to attract worshippers from so far away. That at Aetos later declined: we do not even know the name of the deity to whom it was sacred;[38] and the Polis sanctuary, despite its fine bronze tripods,[39] was never of very great importance. There is nothing else which can have persuaded Corinthians to make journeys to this barren, if delightful island; we must conclude that Ithaca was merely an intermediate point on the voyages which the pots attest: no doubt some (perhaps not many) of the Corinthians who were passing thought it prudent to gain the goodwill of the deity of Aetos before proceeding. The sanctuary had received votives for some time before the arrival of the first Corinthian dedications;[40] it would have been natural for visitors who stopped at the island to dedicate to the local deity. The votives have usually been thought to demonstrate that Corinthians settled on the island,[41] but this is neither necessary nor likely; it is difficult to see what point there could have been to such a settlement.

[35] Amphissa: *BCH* lxxxix (1965), 778, 779, fig. 1 centre and left; *AD* xviii.B (1963), 130, pl. 166 *a* left, 167 *a*. Elatea (bronze horse): Herrmann, *JdaI* lxxix (1964), 29 n. 49.

[36] There are three vases (two conical oinochoai, one aryballos) in the Sicyon Museum which are exactly like Corinthian MG II; they were found at Moulki, in the Sicyonian part of the coastal plain (Dunbabin, *JHS* lxviii (1948), 60 with n. 22). A Corinthian origin is uncertain; if there were Sicyonian potters they will presumably have made vases very close to Corinthian, and the fabric might not be distinguishable.

[37] Two skyphoi from Aegium are close to Thapsos Class pieces: Patras Mus. Inv. BE 365-6; I am much indebted to Mr Mastrokostas for his generous permission to study them. These vases are unusual for Achaean LG, and although the more orthodox local LG I style shows debts to Corinth (Zapheiropoulos, *Praktika*, 1952, 406-12; Coldstream, *GGP* 227), the same traits are apparent on Ithaca, which may have provided the inspiration for Achaean.

[38] Robertson, *BSA* xliii (1948), 122.

[39] Benton, *BSA* xxxv (1934/5), 56-68.

[40] Robertson, *BSA* xliii (1948), 121; Coldstream, *GGP* 353.

[41] Robertson, *BSA* xliii (1948), 122-3; Coldstream, *GGP* 353; cf. *GG* 187. Snodgrass, *Dark Age*, 339, is more cautious.

The only evidence for the destination of the first Corinthians to dedicate on Ithaca is the material from Ambracia and Vitsa. We must conclude that there were some exchanges between Vitsa and Corinth in the early eighth century. The finds from Ambracia make it likely that contact was made either exclusively or in part along the route to inland Epirus which begins there. It would be rash to assume that this was the only, or even the most important, destination of those Corinthians who dedicated at Aetos. There must have been some profit at Vitsa, whose inhabitants valued Corinthian vases as much as the Delphians; but it is unlikely that pots were the main items offered, and the identity both of the others and of what the Epirots provided in exchange remains obscure. Corinthians may have come here for Epirot slaves. The iris may have grown in profusion here for collection as the raw material for the perfumes and scented oil which were widely disseminated from Corinth in the late eighth century and after.[42] Corinth was the destination of some Epirot corn in the late fourth century (below, 129). A similar trade 400 years earlier cannot be ruled out entirely; but the production of a significant surplus was then probably beyond the abilities of the Epirots, and the immediate vicinity of Vitsa is ill suited to cereal crops. The inhabitants of Vitsa had access to considerable quantities of iron,[43] and may have been able to offer some to the Corinthians. Tin and amber might have reached Greece down the Adriatic in the eighth century; but Vitsa is too far inland to be connected with such traffic, and it remains doubtful whether it existed at all.[44] Dodona is as unlikely to have attracted pilgrims from Corinth in the early eighth century as Ithaca; the earliest Corinthian find is LG.[45]

It is probably mere accident that only three Greek sites outside the Gulf have revealed Corinthian in significant quantities. If it was not the Aetos sanctuary which attracted Corinthians to Ithaca they may have gone as frequently to different islands in the vicinity, and

---

[42] Below, 117-18. The number of Corinthian Geometric aryballoi is not large enough to indicate widespread use of their perfumed contents until EPC. Conical oinochoai may have been used for a similar purpose, and they are very numerous in MG II; but they did not travel far from the Corinthia.

[43] Iron weapons and other objects were buried in some of the graves along with Corinthian vases: see refs. above, 86 n. 27.

[44] Tin: Coldstream, *GGP* 353 (cf. Will, *Korinthiaka*, 39); but it is unlikely that the Adriatic tin trade was ever of great importance (Villard, *La Céramique grecque de Marseille*, 157 n. 5). Amber: Dunbabin, *Perachora*, ii.520-3, modified in respect of Dunbabin's criterion of colour by Strong, *Catalogue of the Carved Amber*, 14. Most amber which reached Greece in the eighth and seventh centuries probably came from Etruria; there is no evidence that the upper Adriatic was opened to the Greeks before the sixth.

[45] The rim of a Thapsos Class krater, *BCH* lxxxix (1965), 777-8, fig. 2 = *AD* xviii. B (1963), 149-50, pl. 187 β; not necessarily before Syracuse. Metal finds are no earlier: cf. refs. in Parke, *Oracles of Zeus*, 274-5. See in general Coldstream, *GG* 185-6.

isolated finds from Leucas and Cephallenia may reflect precisely that.[46] Ambracia may have been special in that it was a point of departure for inland Epirus; but Vitsa will hardly have been alone among inland sites in receiving Corinthian ware. It cannot be excluded that some of the journeys for which Ithaca was an intermediate point were made to the south. There is one Messenian group of Corinthian LG vases; of itself this shows only that one Corinthian vessel had passed that way, but there may have been others.[47]

The Corinthians who dedicated at Aetos from soon after 800 may have passed beyond the Adriatic to Etruria. The earliest Corinthian ware found in the west is at Pithecusae, and is at least twenty-five years after the earliest from Ithaca; but this gap is not necessarily significant, for we can only be sure of tracing Corinthians —even assuming extensive excavation—where they lived or dedicated to the gods. Euboeans reached Etruria soon after 800, and left behind them chevron skyphoi in Etruria and Campania.[48] That does not prove that Corinthians reached so far so early, even if we know that they pressed on beyond Ithaca; but the Corinthian finds at Pithecusae prove that Corinthians arrived there by *c*.760.[49] and they may have made similar journeys some years earlier. If so, the main items of exchange are as uncertain here as elsewhere. Dunbabin suggested before the excavation of Pithecusae that the Greeks acquired metals—especially iron—in Etruria,[50] and confirmation has recently been sought in the discovery that iron, probably mined on Elba, was worked at Pithecusae in the eighth century;[51] but Graham has rightly doubted the cogency of the argument. It was not necessary for the Euboeans, at least, to go as far as Elba to secure

[46] Leucas: Herrmann, *JdaI* lxxix (1964), 29 n. 47 (bronze horse). Cephallenia: Marinatos, *AE* 1964, 23, pl. 3.3 left (LG kotyle sherd). There is no evidence that Corinthians put in on the Acarnanian coast; the Corinthian ceramic influence that is found there (*AD* xvii.B (1961/2), 184, pl. 212 *a* no. 9; cf. Coldstream, *GGP* 225 with n. 4) may have been exercised through Ithaca and not from Corinth direct.

[47] Coldstream, *GGP* 218; for the dig, Marinatos, *Praktika*, 1953, 243. The kotyle was copied in Messenia at about this time: Coldstream, *GG* 162 (Nichoria).

[48] Esp. Ridgway, *St. Etr.* xxxv (1967), 311–21; Johannowsky, *DdA* i (1967), fig. 8 b; d'Agostino, *DdA* iii (1969), fig. 14. Preceded (?) by a few pendent semicircle skyphoi: Ridgway and Dickinson, *BSA* lxviii (1973), 191–2; *NS* 1972, 256. *DdA* viii (1974–5), 97, fig. D.

[49] The Corinthian at Pithecusae might have been taken by Euboeans; but the ware does not seem to have reached Euboea itself in any quantity (below, 107; cf., however, Ghali-Kahil, *AD* xx.B (1965), 285).

[50] *Western Greeks*, 3, 7–8.

[51] Esp. Klein, *Expedition*, xiv.2 (1971/2), 34–9; Buchner, *Expedition*, viii.4 (1966), 12; refs. in Ridgway, *St. Etr.* xxxv (1967), 318, n. 49. Cf. however, Bakhuizen, *Chalcis-in-Euboea*, 66–7 n. 83.

iron-ore: the ironworking at Pithecusae may have been for local use only.[52] Iron may have been a major factor; but it is safest to leave the question open. Corinthian voyages to the far side of Italy—if they took place at this date—probably had, like those to Delphi and western Greece, a commercial purpose; but the exact nature of the exchanges must remain obscure. In Sicily, there is little evidence of Corinthians before Syracuse was founded; a few earlier Corinthian vases reached the island,[53] but they might have been taken by Euboeans, for their traces are both clearer and earlier.[54] But the choice of the site of Syracuse demonstrates that Corinthian eyes had seen the place before it was selected. Those who knew the site presumably went there in search of profit; they did not necessarily find it.

The manner in which the western routes were opened to Corinthian travellers must remain a matter for conjecture; but probably not all the exploration was carried out by Corinthians. Euboeans reached Etruria at about the time of the earliest Corinthian dedications at Aetos, and this is probably not coincidence: one group will have followed the lead of the other. Euboeans almost certainly led. They travelled to the Levant before the end of the ninth century and to Etruria in the early eighth.[55] They will not have reached the west down the Corinthian Gulf; to cross the Isthmus was difficult (below, 137-8), there is no sign of their presence in the Gulf, and Euboean contact with Ithaca is both tenuous and later than Corinthian.[56] The Corinthians therefore explored their Gulf and its approaches in the early eighth century; but they probably did so precisely because they already knew, from Euboeans, of the opportunities of the far west. Paradoxically, they may have gained the information on eastern journeys. One or two late ninth-century

---

[52] *JHS* xci (1971), 44. Snodgrass, *Dark Age*, 335-6, argues that the chevron skyphoi from Etruria and Cumae, which date before the earliest evidence from Pithecusae, 'should tip the scales against [the] explanation (that the Pithekoussai finds speak only for the situation of [the] colonists in their new home)'; but the Euboeans who left chevron skyphoi in Etruria and who may then have settled at Pithecusae will have needed iron in their new homes whether they had gone to Etruria for iron or for something else. The hypothesis of Bakhuizen, *Chalcis-in-Euboea*, esp. 65-9, that Chalcidians first reached the west in search of a market in which to sell their iron technology and/or its products, is highly improbable.
[53] Frederiksen, *AR* 1976/7, 67; Villard and Vallet, *MEFR* lxviii (1956), 12, pl. 1.1.
[54] See Frederiksen, *AR* 1976/7, 66-7 with refs.
[55] Coldstream, *GGP* 345-6, 354-5; *GG* 223-4.
[56] See Coldstream, *GGP* 366-7 for the evidence, such as it is. Aetolian Chalcis has often been claimed as a foundation of the Euboean city of the same name, but this is mere conjecture; the absence of Euboean finds in this area does not encourage its adoption (cf. Bakhuizen, *Chalcis-in-Euboea*, 63 n. 69). On Euboeans at Corcyra before the Corinthian colony, see above, 67.

Corinthian vases have turned up on Aegean islands;[57] and if Corinthians had looked beyond their borders shortly before 800 it is to the east that they would have turned their attention. Corinthian increases in both quantity and range in the Aegean subsequently (below, 107-8); but the amounts compare very unfavourably with those of the western finds. The Corinthians were not pioneers except in Epirus; but they took rapid advantage of their ideal geographical position once the way had been pointed out by Euboeans.

The importance of Corinthian commercial activity in this period should not be exaggerated. Even in early LG the finds are not abundant, and those of MG II are still fewer. None the less the contacts, once established, gradually intensified; and since pottery was probably not the main item of exchange the importance of the traffic cannot be calculated on the basis of the surviving evidence. The novelty of the appearance of Corinthians in these parts is itself significant. Their adventures were no doubt extremely limited in the context of the whole Corinthian economy; but they were responsible, at least indirectly, for the effective solution to the problem of over-population. Corinthians brought back with them from the west knowledge of suitable colony sites—and perhaps the very idea of colonization, first adopted by the Euboeans at Pithecusae, Cumae, and Naxos in Sicily. Once the Bacchiad government was convinced that it was necessary to transplant Corinthians, they found no difficulty in placing the colonies; the sites were already well known.

The direct effect of the western traffic is difficult to assess in the absence of evidence for the commodities exchanged and the economic status of those involved. The popularity of Corinthian vases gave rise to a modest expansion of pottery production, but this can only have increased the prosperity of the few existing potters: not a broadly significant trend. Other items will have been more important; and although we have no evidence for what the Corinthians offered it can hardly have been anything but primary produce. The extent to which the exchanges brought direct benefits to those who suffered from the growing population pressure is difficult to determine. Even a man whose plot was unable to support himself and his family for a full year might, if he had access to a seaworthy boat, make sufficient profit on short voyages along the Corinthian Gulf soon after his harvest to make all the difference between starvation and survival; if he was more adventurous he might make greater profits

[57] MG I amphora, Rheneia: Coldstream, *GGP* 94 (cf. *GG* 90). MG I skyphos, perhaps two, Thera: Pfühl, *AM* xxviii (1903), 195 (K 29-30; cf. W 59-60).

further afield. For Hesiod, to take to the sea seemed a last resort
(esp. *Erg.* 618-94; cf. also 236-7); but, even in Boeotia, he allowed
that men might be driven to trade by 'debt and hunger' (*Erg.* 646-7).
But a far greater proportion of the traffic probably depended on the
produce of wealthier men. Hesiod's advice was to commit only a
small part of a substance to the sea (*Erg.* 689-94); those who could
afford to take it were hardly among the least well off in the Corinthia.
Such men would probably not themselves have undertaken the risk
and effort of the journey; that may have created opportunities for
others who could not provide the cargoes themselves but were
prepared to undergo the dangers in return for a (no doubt small)
share of the profit (see further below, 149-52).

The dedications made in the Geometric temple of Hera Acraea at
Perachora show an increase in quantity and quality in the years
before 735;[58] this may reflect improved circumstances for these
Corinthians who had participated in the western traffic. But profitable exchanges in the west cannot have benefited more than a small
proportion of the population; that the problems remained acute is
demonstrated by the foundation of the colonies. The overall effect
of the western traffic may have been to increase hardship in the
Corinthia. Surplus production of some estates may have fed poor
Corinthians before 800 for want of any other means of disposal;
but it could now be exported: in many cases, a handsome profit will
have been preferred to a healthy neighbour.

[58] For the pottery, compare Salmon, *BSA* lxvii (1972), 161-2 with 168-72. The bronzes
from the deposit are impossible to date, but there is nothing which must be early (Payne,
Perachora, i.69-75).

VI. Expansion

The proportion of Corinthians who left for the new colonies is unknown; but the primary purpose of the foundations was to relieve population pressure, and the number of those who remained will have been broadly determined by what was seen as the optimum number of inhabitants for the territory. In view of the still overwhelmingly agricultural nature of the Corinthian economy, the main effect of the foundations will have been to restore the balance between resources and population. At first the colonies no doubt had to import some primary products, presumably from mainland Greece: vines and olives take some years to establish. This trade may have been of some importance for Corinth for a decade or so; it may have continued even though little would grow in the Corinthia which was ill suited to the colonies (below, 135-6). It has often been suggested that the mainland supplied 'luxury goods'; but what they were is unclear. Pottery perhaps qualifies, and after the foundation of the colonies Corinthian exports to the west increased enormously (below, 105-6). But even this expansion in pottery production was of very limited importance (below, 101), and other commodities which demanded skills that the early colonists may have lacked—artwork in general, metalwork, and perhaps some few others—will have been of even smaller significance: the colonies presumably developed such skills for themselves before long.

The foundation of the colonies was rapidly followed by a great increase in general prosperity. The increased quantity and quality of offerings made to Hera Acraea at Perachora during the last years of the Geometric temple was nothing to the improvement of the late eighth and the early seventh centuries.[1] Nothing can demonstrate that the prosperity reflected by these offerings was enjoyed by a majority of Corinthians; but it is most improbable that they were made by only a small proportion while the rest suffered in grinding poverty. Much of the improvement was related, either directly or indirectly, to the decrease in population.

An immediate effect will have been that many individual plots were now more capable of providing for those who farmed them;

[1] See Payne, *Perachora*, i for the metal objects, and Dunbabin, *Perachora*, ii for the rest.

every Corinthian colonist had previously been an extra mouth for a Corinthian plot to feed. Other holdings may have been increased in size. The legislation of Pheidon the Bacchiad was probably designed precisely to deal with the land in the Corinthia which had been left vacant on the departure for the west of its previous occupants (above, 63-5). Even those who did not sail to the west benefited indirectly from the colonies, for the archaeological record shows that there was an increased market in the Corinthia for skills that could be sold in return for food.

The most obvious case of such a skill is that of vase-making; we have evidence not only from widespread finds of the vases themselves but also from one of the centres of production: the Potters' Quarter. It was situated at the north-west corner of the plateau that runs between two ravines which descend from the western end of Acrocorinth, some 2 km. from the centre of the city. It is well provided with clay and water, two of the vital raw materials;[2] the third, timber for firing, was probably to be found on the slopes of the plateau and elsewhere in the vicinity (above, 30). Already in 700 pottery production here had passed beyond the stage of a cottage industry. From the earliest use of the Quarter for making pots there were installations designed to facilitate the operation. Numerous water-channels were found crossing and recrossing each other in apparent irregularity; but they all lead to a single depression which often holds standing water. The associated sherds date from c.750-c.650.[3] There is nothing to associate the channels specifically with the production of pottery; but there can be little doubt that they were connected with it. They testify to extensive activity. One channel has built sides and a date a little before 700;[4] it provides confirmation that the channels in general were at least that early. These installations were improved c.650 when a crushed stone pavement was laid above them, and they were replaced by a single built channel.[5] This and its predecessors are too large in scale to have been built to serve a single establishment. The numerous early channels were perhaps the result of competitive enterprise by individual workshops; but by the mid-seventh century they combined to provide themselves with a common, superior service. It is significant even that more than a single family of potters worked on

[2] Stillwell, *Corinth*, xv.1.3.
[3] Ibid., 11: that publication uses the term Geometric Protocorinthian to cover the whole period from LG to MPC.
[4] Ibid., 12; Coldstream, *GGP* 104: the Channel Deposit. Representative sherds published by Stillwell, *AJA* xxxviii (1933) 605-10; see further below, 146 n. 41.
[5] Stillwell, *Corinth*, xv.1.11.

the same site by 700; that by c.650 the various establishments co-operated to provide amenities for the benefit of all is a yet greater advance.

The Potters' Quarter may have been founded as a direct result of the rapidly increasing popularity of Corinthian ware. Chronology suggests such a conjecture: the date of the first manufacture on the site is much the same as that of the steep rise in the graph of Corinthian production as a whole. The character of the finds from the Quarter gives some support. Most exports bore simple, geometric decoration, and this has been well called a mass-produced ware: the techniques of potter and painter were extraordinarily fine, but the vases could be made at speed (Fig. 13). Throughout this period Corinthian painters were perfecting figured drawing in the consistent development which reached its peak with the Macmillan Painter c.650; but very few figured fragments of this period turned up in the Quarter.[6] No doubt other examples will come to light when the pottery is fully published; but it is tempting to suppose that the majority of figured work was done elsewhere. Perhaps it is not too fanciful to suggest that the development of the Quarter was a conscious attempt by an enterprising potter—either accompanied or soon followed by others—to exploit an expanding market by producing large quantities of fine vases with simple geometric decoration.

There is little evidence of such a direct nature for skills other than those of the potter, and the expansion of vase production cannot have given opportunities to very large numbers (below, 101); but there is a great deal of evidence that other crafts were increasingly practised. Building skills c.800 must have been rudimentary, to judge from the temple at Perachora; it was built of mud-brick on a foundation of small undressed stones and had a thatched roof.[7] Building skills had improved by c.735 if the dining-room at the same site was erected at that time, for it had dressed—if not very well-fitted—stones of larger size for its foundation.[8] The building techniques of the eighth century, and progress towards its end, are probably fairly reflected in the models of Corinthian origin dedicated at the Perachora Heraeum and at Aetos on Ithaca: at Perachora there is a progression from steeply pitched and curved roofs of thatch to straighter, less sloping

[6] See, however, Dunbabin and Robertson, *BSA* xlviii (1953), 179: Sacrifice Painter, no. 6; ibid., 177: Aegina Bellerophon Painter, plaque; 178: Head in Air Painter, no. 19: Benson, *AJA* lx (1956), 220: Painter of the Hopping Birds.

[7] Payne, *Perachora*, i. 28-9.

[8] Above, 59 with n. 15; Payne, *Perachora*, i.111. See in general Drerup, *Griechische Baukunst*, 106-7.

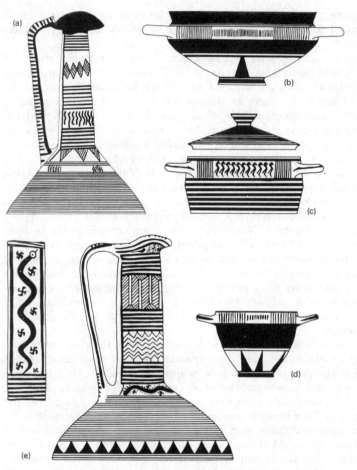

Fig. 13   Protocorinthian Linear Ware: (a) Conical Oinochoe, Manchester III C 2;
(b) Skyphos, Manchester 1971.8; (c) Pyxis, Manchester III C 1;
(d) Kotyle, Manchester II D 23; (e) Conical Oinochoe, Manchester III C 3.
Cf. T. B. L. Webster, 'Greek Vases in the Manchester Museum', *Memoirs
of the Manchester Literary and Philosophical Society* lxxvii (1933), 1-7.

examples, while at Ithaca the chequers probably indicate tiles, and
the walls are painted with Geometric figures. The Ithaca example
represents the last stage of ambitious Corinthian building before a
rapid development.[9] The chronology of the temples of Apollo at

[9] Cf. Salmon, *BSA* lxvii (1972), 185-7 (n. 151 for the tiles; cf. Drerup, *Griechische
Baukunst*, 119-20).

Corinth and Poseidon at Isthmia remains disputed; but certainly by c.650 Corinthians were able to build walls of fully squared stone up to the eaves and hipped roofs made of large tiles.[10] Both buildings at Perachora might have been constructed by men who had learned their skills casually in the construction of their own houses; but the later temples show skills of quite a different order, developed specifically for monumental architecture. Boat-building may by now have been specialized—though perhaps carried out by the individuals who made the woodwork for temple roofs. Corinthians had perhaps always been able to make fishing-boats, and some of the early western journeys may have been made in such precarious vessels; but considerable advances in naval architecture must have been made before the first trireme was built perhaps in the late seventh century (below, 222-3). The introduction of new items of armour c.700 must have given wider opportunities to those skilled in bronze-work. The Corinthian helmet, already present soon after 700, demanded a high degree of skill.[11] The development of the hoplite phalanx c.675 will have increased the demand for bronze armour and iron weapons even further;[12] the number of heavily armed combatants immediately increased. Recent excavations have provided fascinating documentation. Near the Sacred Spring a house was found which in its second phase—ending with the destruction of the house c.640—was used for ironworking; a furnace and much iron slag was discovered. In the earlier phase of the building there was no sign of such activity;[13] thus at some time in the first half of the seventh century a metalworkshop was established in a house previously occupied by a family with no such interest. The development may have been very closely connected with the hoplite reform; among the finds was a mould for the production of spearheads.[14]

The foundation of the colonies increased the disposable surplus of many Corinthian plots: it was disposed of, in part, precisely in payment for the skills which developed at exactly this time. Another specialist skill, to judge from the outstanding success of Corinthian vases in the west, was trade (below, 147-54). All such skills increased the opportunities available for work off the land, and all the work at least of production will have been undertaken in independent workshops. Even in Hesiod's Boeotia such a pattern is evident, and no household was large enough to employ such craftsmen for its own

[10] Above, 59-62; cf. Snodgrass, Archaic Greece, 60-1.
[11] Snodgrass, Early Greek Armour, 20-8, esp. 27-8.
[12] Salmon, JHS xcvii (1977), 85-93.
[13] Williams, Hesperia, xl (1971), 5-10.
[14] Ibid., 30-1, no. 31.

use alone.[15] Whether those who learned the new skills devoted their
whole effort to them is more doubtful; many, perhaps most, may
have continued to work their own plots. Even those who acquired no
skills were more able, now that the population had been significantly
reduced, to gain seasonal work on the larger estates, unskilled labour
provided by greater building and other activity, or casual work
loading or manning vessels for the export trade.

Thus the colonies helped in numerous ways to improve conditions
for ordinary Corinthians, and the increase in prosperity which is
proved by the archaeological record will have been enjoyed by a
wide spectrum of those who remained behind. The only evidence
which might be taken to indicate widespread poverty is in the
North Cemetery, where the graves of the Protocorinthian period
(*c*.720–*c*.640) contained very few offerings; but this impression
is belied by the fact that almost every burial was made in a well-
cut poros sarcophagus.[16] Those who conducted the burials could
provide a by no means cheap receptacle for the corpse; they probably offered few gifts not because they could not afford them but
for some reason connected with burial fashion.[17]

[15] Cf. Starr, *Economic and Social Growth*, 80–1.
[16] Young, *Corinth*, xiii. 51.
[17] The Lechaeum Cemetery (C. W. J. and M. Eliot, *Hesperia*, xxxvii (1968), 345–67) may
support this conclusion. The first dated burial was early seventh century (ibid., 347–50:
grave B 20), but the next is more than a century later (351: grave C 15). The excavators
suggested that some of the many empty sarcophagi from the Cemetery belong to the inter-
vening period (346 n. 7).

VII. Pottery

a. Production

There is some literary evidence for the importance of Corinthian pottery. The references are mainly to periods after the archaic, when Corinthian production was a fraction of what it had been;[1] but in one version the invention of the potter's wheel is ascribed to Corinth (Plin. *NH* vii.198). Our sources are, however, overwhelmingly archaeological. Thanks to the American excavations of the Potters' Quarter we have direct evidence for one of the centres of production.

Since there is far more evidence for pottery than for any other manufactured item, there is a constant danger of exaggerating its importance. Cook has shown that at any one time in fifth-century Athens 500 men or so at most can have been involved in the whole process, including unskilled labour. At Corinth, he suggests, the maximum number may have been half that: Corinthian vases were, on the average, both smaller and simpler than classical Attic.[2] The conclusion is inevitable that pottery production was an almost insignificant sector of the Corinthian economy even though many Greeks used the ware. A second danger, however—also commented on by Cook—is more difficult to guard against. Corinthian pottery was widely exported and is easily identified; but Corinthian vases abroad are not evidence for Corinthian trade except in the very general sense of trade in items produced at Corinth. Corinthian vases need not have been exported by Corinthian traders or in Corinthian ships. Most important of all is the final difficulty: to what extent is it possible to draw conclusions for the nature of trade in Corinthian products in general from that in Corinthian pots?

The finds from the Potters' Quarter reflect the enormous expansion of the export market in the seventh century. There is little evidence for early buildings; but the last quarter of the seventh century saw the erection of the South Long Building. Its walls were made of mere rubble and the roof probably of thatch; but it was at

---

[1] Athen. 236B, 488D. For Thericles the Corinthian, a late fifth- or early fourth-century potter, see Nachod, *RE* s.v. for refs.; there is nothing to demonstrate that Thericles worked at Corinth.

[2] *JdaI* lxxiv (1959), 118-21; for reactions, cf. Johnston, *Trade Marks on Greek Vases*, 50-1 with 65 n. 19; add Snodgrass, *Archaic Greece*, 126-34.

least 65 m. long and perhaps more, and was planned as a single unit.
It faced a road on the other side of which stood Cypselus' fortification wall (below, 220-1); behind the building were yards with a
profusion of small shelters, pits for storing or working clay, and
water-channels.[3] The extent of organization required for such a
structure is clear; but the size of the project raises more questions
than it solves. Nothing can tell us whether it was a single establishment, whether it was the result of co-operation between a large
number of independent potters or small workshops, or whether
those who worked in it were free or slave. The figured vases found
in the Quarter prove that the painters influenced their fellows over
matters of detail only rarely.[4] This might favour the hypothesis of
separate workshops within a single building; but since we should
have expected influences to operate within such a small area even
if the work was done in different buildings, the argument has little
force. It is hardly likely that Periander or any other Corinthian
provided the South Long Building for rent.

The export market for Corinthian was to collapse not long after
600; before it did so, Corinthian potters were confident enough to
erect the North Long Building. It was on the same large scale as the
South Long Building, and its purpose—to judge from the extraordinary amount of pottery found smashed on the road outside it—
was similar; its date seems to have been about 600, although it
continued in use and underwent alterations into the fifth century.[5]
The South Long Building probably saw its greatest use in the early
sixth century, for the majority of sherds from the road outside it
were MC; but it remained in use after the construction of its counterpart to the north, for late sixth- and fifth-century activity is attested.[6]
It may have been used for both production and sale until the latter
was concentrated mainly in the northern structure. The road in front
of the North Long Building was covered to a great depth with
smashed vases; they may have been casualties from the displays of
wares for sale. It is perhaps too fanciful to take them as unsaleable
pots, thrown out during the period when Corinthian was losing
its first place to Attic.

The export market for Corinthian pottery diminished rapidly
after c.575; but activity in the Potters' Quarter does not seem to
have fallen off in proportion. There remained a large home market

---

[3] Stillwell, *Corinth*, xv.1.15-17.
[4] Amyx and Lawrence, *Corinth*, vii.2.83.
[5] Stillwell, *Corinth*, xv.1.20-1.
[6] Ibid., 16.

for Corinthian ware;[7] and the vases shattered outside the North Long Building include a good deal of late sixth- and fifth-century material.[8] New installations, especially cisterns, were constructed during the latter part of the sixth century;[9] small shrines, perhaps built before 500, continued in use well into the fifth.[10] In the fourth century, at least one new centre in the Quarter took up production: the Terracotta Factory. The first phase of that building belongs to the fifth century; but at that time it may have been a private house.[11] The Potters' Quarter seems not to have suffered from the general decline of Corinthian to the same degree as other centres; a reason can be tentatively put forward which fits well with the character of manufacture in the Quarter in its early years. I suggest above (97) that the Quarter concentrated upon production in quantity; this probably explains the large size of the buildings on the site. In the later sixth century, when Corinthian vases were no more sophisticated than the subgeometric ware of the seventh, the size of the installations may have given the potters of the Quarter an advantage over the small workshops which had taken a greater pride in their figured work. Since production was now mainly for the home market, we might have expected workshops closer to Corinth to survive while far-flung establishments like the Potters' Quarter withered; but the advantages of size seem to have out-weighed the disadvantages of distance.

Only a proportion of Corinthian vases were produced in the Potters' Quarter; two other centres have been approximately but not precisely located.[12] There will have been many others, but we are unable to compare them with the Potters' Quarter.

b. Export

The vases themselves provide our only evidence for the nature of

[7] Cf. (e.g.) the Corinthian vases of the period published by Palmer in *Corinth*, xiii; and the Vrysoula Deposit (Pemberton, *Hesperia*, xxxix (1970), 265–307).

[8] Stillwell, *Corinth*, xv.1.21. In the absence of a full publication the period of greatest vase-breaking (if not directly vase-making) activity cannot yet be determined.

[9] Ibid., 26–7.

[10] Ibid., 22–6.

[11] For structures in the Quarter after the sixth century, see ibid., 29–53. There were several minor installations—shrines, walls, graves, and pits—as well. The Factory: ibid., 34–49.

[12] Amyx and Lawrence, *Corinth*, vii.2.69–70: the Anaploga Well contained numerous mis-fired pots, wasters, etc. from a potters' establishment not yet identified. The Vrysoula Deposit was found not far from the Potters' Quarter, and was made up in part of discards from a potter's workshop; but probably not one in the Quarter itself (Pemberton, *Hesperia*, xxxix (1970), esp. 269).

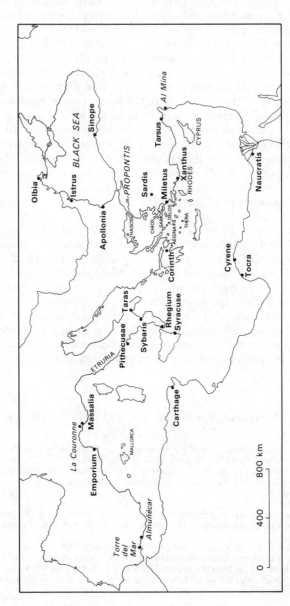

Fig. 14 The Mediterranean

the export market.[13] By far the greatest amount of Corinthian pottery was exported to the west (see Figs. 12, 14). Even before the foundation of any Corinthian colonies there was a significant, if small, export market in the Corinthian Gulf and the western Greek mainland, and the colonists at Pithecusae used a great deal of Corinthian ware; when the colonizing movement gathered momentum Corinthian found an enthusiastic market not only in Corinthian but also in other colonies. The most impressive statistics are those of Megara Hyblaea, where the finds up to 1961 have been fully published: well over half the total finds from the foundation of the colony to *c*.575 are Corinthian. There were rather under 15,000 catalogued Corinthian pieces, but that is a conservative estimate of the total number of vases they represent; 30-40,000 is perhaps more accurate, but that will naturally be only a small proportion of the total number actually imported.[14] In the absence of equally full statistical publications of other sites we do not know to what extent Megara Hyblaea was typical: but for all sites in Italy up to the Straits of Messina and for the whole of Sicily, until about the middle of the sixth century, Corinthian dominated the import market. There was sometimes competition from locally produced wares; but Corinthian was always a significant, and sometimes an overwhelming, proportion of the fine pottery in use.[15] Corinthian faced competition from Euboean in the late eighth century,[16] and throughout the seventh small amounts of East Greek ware reached Sicilian sites in particular;[17] in the first half of the sixth century Attic is found here in increasing quantities. Corinthian was equally dominant in the colonies of North Africa; but the Greeks reached these coasts rather later.[18] At Carthage there are local copies of

[13] I have not attempted to make the complete collection of material suggested by Will, *Ét. arch.* i (1963), 163: that is a job for a historian of the Corinthian pottery industry, not for a historian of Corinth.

[14] Vallet and Villard, *Mégara Hyblaea*, ii; for the principles on which the statistics are based, see pp. 9-10.

[15] References must be selective to remain manageable. Dunbabin, *Western Greeks*, 224-58, summarizes the evidence up to 1948; cf. Vallet, *Rhégion et Zancle*, 161-3. Little has changed since then except that significant local styles have been identified; cf. esp. Vallet and Villard, *Mégara Hyblaea*, ii.139-99. As more work is done on these styles, more will no doubt be isolated; it appears, for example, that a greater part of the market at Sybaris was taken by local wares than at Megara Hyblaea, and that imported Corinthian was correspondingly reduced: cf. esp. *NS* 1972 Suppl., 148, 437-8; *NS* 1970 Suppl. iii.232. To attempt to give references to all material since 1948 would be excessive; see, e.g., Bernabò-Brea and Cavalier, *Mylai*, 105-6; Lo Porto, *Annuario*, xxxvii/xxxviii (1959/60), 7-230 (Taras); and reports in *NS*, indices s.v. ceramica, etc.

[16] Coldstream, *GGP* 374-5; see further above, 70.

[17] See esp. Dunbabin, *Western Greeks*, 472-8; Vallet and Villard, *Mégara Hyblaea* ii.77-91. See now *Céramiques de la Grèce de l'est*.

[18] Cf. esp. Boardman and Hayes, *Tocra*, i-ii; Stucchi, *Cirene 1957-66*, 150-1; *L'Agora di Cirene*, i.37-44; Boardman, *BSA* lxi (1966), 149-56.

Corinthian *c*.730 (below, 140-1); true Corinthian is found shortly afterwards and until the early sixth century, but never in large quantities.[19]

In other parts of the western Mediterranean either the amount or the character of Corinthian differs. On the Italian coast between Rhegium and Etruria few Greek colonies which were inhabited early enough for Corinthian to be expected there have been well explored; but they show less Corinthian than sites on the Greek side of the Straits of Messina.[20] The character of the Corinthian found here is much the same as that from Sicily, South Italy, and North Africa: it was used as ordinary tableware. In Etruria, however, the character of the finds is markedly different. From the mid-eighth to the mid-seventh century some Corinthian reached Etruria, though not in very large quantities; but from *c*.650 there arrived significant numbers of quite exceptional vases. Outstanding among them is the Chigi Olpe of *c*.650, which has a good claim to be the finest known product of any Corinthian workshop; but many superb pieces made similar journeys. The total number of Corinthian vases from Etruria is not large; but their quality probably gave them a very high exchange value. These vases are found in Etruscan tombs; luxury goods bought for their artistic quality and with a view to being buried with the Etruscan dead.

The amounts of Corinthian found in southern France and in Spain are more restricted. A little Protocorinthian reached Spain in the first half of the seventh century; but it is always found in Punic contexts.[21] Corinthian first reached this far western end of the Mediterranean in any quantity not long before 600; the majority comes from Massalia and her colony at Emporium,[22] but it is also known elsewhere.[23] Villard has suggested that the high quality of the pieces from Massalia means that the market here was of similar character to that in Etruria;[24] but the finds from other sites in this region are more ordinary.

In other parts of the Greek world Corinthian commanded a far smaller part of the market than in its area of western domination. It is often the major imported ware; but it is only on sites where there was no local production that it approaches the percentages regularly found in the west. On some Boeotian sites where only sanctuaries or tombs have been excavated, Corinthian often forms

[19] Cf. esp. Boucher, *Cahiers de Byrsa*, iii (1953), 11-29.

[20] Vallet, *Rhégion et Zancle*, 153-6.

[21] Trias de Arribas, *Ceramicas griegas*, 452, 491 (Almuñécar, Torre del Mar).

[22] Villard, *La Céramique grecque de Marseilles*, 13-15; Trias de Arribas, *Ceramicas griegas*, 31-6.

[23] Lagrand, *Gallia*, xvii (1959), 185-7 (La Couronne).

[24] *La Céramique grecque de Marseilles*, 15, 35.

a very high proportion of the finds: it is usually small vases—kotylai, aryballoi, and alabastra;[25] the position may have been similar at Medeon in Phocis, but the site has not been fully published.[26] In Athens, about 10 per cent of the total finds of fine pottery from the Agora are Corinthian from *c*.750 to *c*.600;[27] Attic cemeteries of the same period contain a good deal of Corinthian.[28] Much the same proportions of Corinthian were found in the sanctuary of Artemis Orthia at Sparta.[29] In the Argolid, presumably both on geographical grounds and because archaic Argive ware was not a major fabric, the proportion of Corinthian vases is greater. The majority of pieces dedicated in the Argive Heraeum were Corinthian from the late eighth century to the early sixth,[30] and Corinthian bulks large in the dedications at the shrine of Agamemnon at Mycenae.[31] In the rest of the Peloponnese far less Corinthian has turned up. A recent publication of pottery from Olympia has almost none;[32] Messenia and Arcadia are not well known in this period, but they have little Corinthian material. By contrast, Aegina used little but Corinthian from the late eighth to the late seventh century.[33] In Euboea, although Protocorinthian was often copied there, not much has yet been found; Corinthian fares little better.[34]

In the islands of the Aegean and on the western coast of Asia Minor, Corinthian is almost always present; but it is only in special circumstances that it makes up anything like a majority of the finds. At Delos, both in graves and in the sanctuary of Hera, most finds were Corinthian;[35] but that is because there was no local ware and because Corinthian aryballoi and alabastra were thought to be the most suitable vases for dedication both to Hera and with the dead.[36]

[25] Orchomenus: de Ridder, *BCH* xix (1895), 182-202; Rhitsona: Ure, *Aryballoi and Figurines.*

[26] Cf. Vatin, *Médéon de Phocide*, 74-7; *AD* xix.B (1964), 224.

[27] Brann, *Agora*, viii.27-8.

[28] e.g. Phalerum: Pelekidis, *AD* ii (1916), 25-40. Kübler, *Kerameikos*, vi.1.124-46.

[29] Droop in Dawkins, *Artemis Orthia*, 113-15; cf. 52. See Catling, *AR* 1976/7, 41 for the Menelaion.

[30] Waldstein, *Argive Heraeum*, ii.124-73; cf. also Blegen, *AJA* xliii (1939), 423-7. Caskey and Amandry, *Hesperia*, xxi (1952), 187-93, publish more finds from the Heraeum, of which Corinthian makes up only 5 per cent of the total. It seems that for some (unknown) reason the cult to which this deposit related required the dedication of vases not normally made at Corinth but produced locally; this makes it clear how much fashion could dictate the proportion of Corinthian on any given site. See in general Kelly, *History of Argos*, 79, 83.

[31] Cook, *BSA* xlviii (1953), 50-7.

[32] Gauer, *Olympische Forschungen*, viii.

[33] Kraiker, *Aigina*, 35-84; Furtwängler, *Aegina*, 448-55.

[34] Boardman, *BSA* xlvii (1952), 12; lii (1957), 3.

[35] Dugas, *Délos*, x.61-152; *Délos*, xvii.79-112.

[36] Dugas, *Délos* x.3.

On other Cycladic islands local workshops were in evidence; but there is a scattering of Corinthian on almost every excavated site.[37] Much the same is true of sites in the eastern Aegean. Roebuck, writing in 1959, suggested that gaps he observed at Miletus and Chios were significant, and reflected political hostility between Corinth and these two states;[38] but such an explanation was always improbable, and the gaps have subsequently been filled.[39] Rhodes and Samos have produced the finest pieces, and the majority of vases belong between *c*.700 and *c*.575.[40] There is little information from the North Aegean except from Thasos;[41] the history of the finds there issues an instructive warning. The Corinthian material excavated up to 1957 was exceptionally meagre,[42] but almost immediately afterwards Corinthian turned up in far greater quantities; its rarity among the earlier finds was purely accidental.[43]

A certain amount of Corinthian reached inland sites in Asia Minor—perhaps especially Sardis, although the relatively large number of finds there may reflect rather the extent of excavation than that of imports.[44] On the non-Greek sites on the southern coast of Asia Minor and in the Levant, Corinthian is present but not common; East Greek fabrics greatly outnumber it.[45] Corinthian is almost absent from Cyprus.[46] A good deal, however, reached Naucratis

[37] e.g. Siphnos: Brock and Young, *BSA* xliv (1949), 51-2; Thera: Dragendorff, *Thera*, ii. 190-3, 221; Pfühl, *AM* xxviii (1903), 193-206, 284; Paros: Rubensohn, *Das Delion von Paros*, 117-20, 125; *AD* xviii. B (1963), 274.

[38] *Ionian Trade and Colonization*, 77-9.

[39] Chios: Boardman, *Emborio*, 153-4. The amount is small (but no smaller than on many other sites); but it compares with that of sixth- to fourth-century Attic. For Miletus a full publication of the archaic pottery is still eagerly awaited; but preliminary reports show that Corinthian was as common at Miletus itself and at Didyma as at Emborio: esp. Naumann and Tuchelt, *IM* xiii/xiv (1963/4), 44-5; von Graeve, *IM* xxiii/xxiv (1973/4), 110-12. References to Corinthian from elsewhere published before 1959 are collected by Roebuck, *Ionian Trade and Colonization*, 77-9. The British material from Old Smyrna is now in Anderson, *BSA* liii/liv (1958/9), 138-51; on Troy, see now Blegen and others, *Troy*, iv.257.

[40] Samos: esp. Walter, *AM* lxxiv (1959), 57-68. Rhodes: *Clara Rhodos* iii, iv, and viii; Kinch, *Vroulia*; Johansen, *Acta Archaeologica*, xxviii (1957), 1-192; Blinkenberg, *Lindos*, i. 311-28.

[41] Cf., however, *AD* xvi. B (1960), 219-20; xx. B (1965), 447-51.

[42] Ghali-Kahil, *Études thasiennes*, vii.

[43] Ibid., 49-50; cf. e.g., *AD* xviii. B (1963), 258.

[44] Refs. up to 1959 in Roebuck, *Ionian Trade and Colonization*, 78 n. 27; on Sardis, see now preliminary reports in *BASOR* clxii (1961) onwards.

[45] Hanfmann in Goldman, *Tarsus*, iii.128-9, 138-40, 153; references to Corinthian on other sites, 153 n. 194. Xanthus: Metzger, *Xanthos*, iv.58, 190.

[46] Gjerstad, *Swedish Cyprus Expedition*, iv.2.275; *Greek Geometric and Archaic Pottery found in Cyprus*, 11-12, 38-42, 81. There are only two or three pieces of PC and C in Karageorghis, *Salamis*, iii-v, vii. It is not that Greek pottery in general is rare in Cyprus; for East Greek wares and Attic, see (e.g.) Gjerstad, *Swedish Cyprus Expedition*, iv.2.276-81, and see in general 317.

from the beginning.[47] In the Greek colonies on the Black Sea Corinthian is known; but amounts are again small, and almost insignificant in comparison with Chiot and other East Greek wares. On the north coast, little material reaches back much before 600, and there thus remains only a short part of the period in which we might have expected Corinthian; the southern, Turkish coast is archaeologically almost an unknown quantity.[48]

In the years after c.600 Corinthian lost its place as the major exported fabric of the Greek world to Attic; but the process was not the same in all areas. In Attica, Corinthian falls off rapidly after c.600.[49] The fabric is not entirely absent in the early years of the sixth century,[50] and a few pieces continued to arrive much later.[51] Even in the fifth and fourth centuries Corinthian was the commonest among the tiny proportion of imports. Curiously, Corinthian remained dominant in one restricted section of the market even in the fourth century. Certain types of rough domestic ware—especially louteria and mortars—of Corinthian origin have turned up in large numbers. Clearly Athenians preferred Corinthian products to Attic in these shapes; but we can hardly suggest why.[52] At Corinth the pattern is strikingly different. A small amount of Attic is found in the late seventh century;[53] but from not long after the beginning of the sixth Attic is surprisingly common.[54] The flow was maintained throughout the fifth century, with an interruption during the Peloponnesian War;[55] but a majority of finds in household use was always Corinthian.

In the main western markets of South Italy, Sicily, and North Africa, Attic begins to appear in significant quantities c.575;[56] but

---

[47] Austin, *Greece and Egypt*, 23 with n. 8 (p. 60), with refs.

[48] See most conveniently Boardman, *Greeks Overseas*, 238-66, with refs., 281-2. See also Venedikov, *Apolonija*, 75 (Apollonia); Dimitriu and Cosa, *Dacia*, ii (1958), 82 (Olbia); Alexandrescu, *Histria*, iv.64-6. In general on the north coast, Gajducevic, *Bosporanische Reich*, 46. The south coast and the Propontis are so ill explored or, if explored, ill published that nothing can be made of the few pieces of Corinthian that are known.

[49] Brann, *Agora*, viii. 28.

[50] e.g. Kübler, *Kerameikos*, vi.1.146-50.

[51] Cf., e.g., Knigge, *Kerameikos*, ix, pl. 80, index s.v. Korinthische Gefässe.

[52] Sparkes and Talcott, *Agora*, xii.218-23, cf. 36-7, 42; for the catalogue, 367-71 (ranging in date from the late sixth to the fourth century). Other Corinthian domestic wares have been found in the Agora, but in far smaller amounts: ibid., 190 with n. 8.

[53] e.g. Weinberg, *Hesperia*, xvii (1948), 225: D 58-9.

[54] References in Roebuck, *Hesperia*, xli (1972), 125.

[55] See in general esp. Dunbabin, *Perachora*, ii.334-49; Corbett in Dunbabin, *Perachora*, ii.350-8; Palmer, *Corinth*, xiii.152-66; McPhee, *Hesperia*, xlv (1976), 380-96. On the Peloponnesian War, below, 176.

[56] Cf. esp. Dunbabin, *Western Greeks*, 242-5; Vallet, *Rhégion et Zancle*, 163. For Attic at Megara Hyblaea, Vallet and Villard, *Mégara Hyblaea*, ii.95-125; for Taras, Lo Porto, *Annuario*, xxxvii/xxxviii (1959/60), 180-230 (high-quality vases found in graves, like the earlier Corinthian from the same cemetery); for Tocra, Boardman and Hayes, *Tocra*, ii.4-5.

Corinthian is found until about the middle of the century. Even later, large numbers of specialized Corinthian shapes occur—round aryballoi and miniature kotylai in particular, intended for dedication either in graves or in sanctuaries.[57] Attic began to invade the fine-art market in Etruria soon after 600;[58] but Corinthian continued to enjoy great success here until the end of the figured style c.550.[59] Corinthian is not found in Massalia or in Spain, even in small quantities, much after the early sixth century.

On the Greek mainland, Corinthian is less frequent after 575, with the exception of specialized shapes. Round aryballoi and miniature kotylai (especially the latter) reach Boeotia, Phocis, and the Argolid well after 550 in some numbers.[60] The export of Corinthian vases other than these specialized shapes never quite ceased altogether. Even Athens received some in the fifth century, and major mainland markets of the seventh never entirely stopped buying Corinthian.[61] Since finds from this period are usually less fully published than those of earlier times, and since Corinthian from c.550 is rarely striking, many pieces probably remain unreported; but after c.575 exports must have been a tiny fraction of what they had been. The position is similar in the Aegean: a rapid decline after c.575, with a few specialized shapes able to maintain themselves rather longer.[62]

The enormous volume of exports increased the amount of work available in pottery production at Corinth; but it is doubtful whether the large export market had many other significant effects. Roebuck has argued that certain groups (beginning with the Thapsos Class in LG) and shapes (especially aryballoi and, later, alabastra) were produced specifically for the export market, for they are not often found in the Corinthia;[63] but all of them are well represented at Perachora, and although they do not appear in the North Cemetery

[57] Dunbabin, *Western Greeks*, 243-4. Miniature kotylai especially are found in large numbers well after 550: Boardman and Hayes, *Tocra*, i.40 (hundreds); *Tocra*, ii.9, 14. On the dating, Boardman and Hayes, *Tocra*, ii.9. On the pottery trade to Tocra in general, Boardman in Gadallah (ed.), *Libya in History*, 89-91.

[58] Vallet, *Rhégion et Zancle*, 158-9.

[59] See the catalogue in Payne, *Necrocorinthia*.

[60] Vatin, *Médéon de Phocide*, 76; *AD* xix.B (1964), 224; Cook, *BSA* xlviii (1953), 53-5 (Agamemnoneion); Frickenhaus, *Tiryns*, i.103-4; Ure, *Aryballoi and Figurines* (cf. Payne, *Necrocorinthia*, 331, under no. 1486); other refs. (not only on the mainland) in Dunbabin, *Perachora*, ii.290.

[61] Cf., e.g., *AD* xxi.B (1966), 102; xix.B (1964), 77-9; xx.B (1965), 124 (Aegina); Cook, *BSA* xlviii (1953), 58 (Agamemnoneion); *AD* xviii.B (1963), 62-3 (Argos); xix.B (1964), 225 (Medeon).

[62] For a summary, Roebuck, *Ionian Trade and Colonization*, 79-82; Attic at Smyrna: Boardman, *BSA* liii/liv (1958/9), 152-70. For aryballoi and miniature kotylai of late date, Dugas, *Délos*, xvii.88; Dragendorff, *Thera*, ii.192; Payne, *Necrocorinthia*, 335.

[63] *Hesperia*, xli (1972), 117-21.

that is probably for reasons of burial fashion.[64] A high proportion of very fine vases was exported, especially to Etruria between *c*.650 and *c*.550. In this sector, Corinthian painters were relatively more dependent on exports than in any other; but such production accounted for only a tiny percentage of the whole. In broad terms, the main influence of the export market was to increase the scale of Corinthian production; but that scale itself encouraged significant change. The shapes are simple and quickly made, and the decoration of most vases suits rapid production in quantity. Until about the mid-seventh century most Corinthian vases have a fine but unpretentious subgeometric decoration: the effect is disciplined and delicate, and high-quality vases could be produced at speed (Fig. 13). But in the second half of the century more vases carried figured decoration (Pl. 39). Whether that was the result of changed taste in the export or the home market it is impossible to say; and it may have been a matter of more ambitious painters rather than of changing taste among customers. The increased output of figured ware implies more painters; figured vases cannot have been painted as quickly as linear.[65] But the ever-increasing demand brought added pressures; and much of the history of the Corinthian style is that of ever-greater speed of production and consequent deterioration. Animals were elongated to enable the field to be covered with fewer beasts, and the average Corinthian painter became more cursory and careless (Pl. 40). The victory of Attic in all export markets has often been attributed to precisely this fall in standards; however that may be, the demand for production at speed was a major cause of the decline.

The vases themselves are consistent with the view that Corinthian workshops remained the small establishments that must have been the rule in earlier times; but the evidence from the Potters' Quarter demonstrates that at least this centre was organized in such a way as to derive significant advantage from the size of the market. I have suggested that the very establishment of the Quarter was a deliberate

[64] The distribution of types probably depends on the nature of the sites that have been excavated in the west and in the Corinthia. The shapes which Roebuck claims were made for export were especially suitable for dedication, whether in sanctuaries or in graves: that will explain why they are found only rarely at home, where the only significant votive deposit is at Perachora (a site which Roebuck almost ignores) and where burial custom was different (above, 100). The Thapsos Class workshop may have concentrated on export even though there is some from Perachora and now even a little from Corinth itself; but many Thapsos Class pieces from Delphi and Aetos were presumably dedicated by Corinthians: they were not taken abroad as part of the export trade.

[65] The number of identifiable painters is far greater in Corinthian than Protocorinthian: cf. the lists in Benson, *Geschichte der korinthischen Vasen*. Much will no doubt be added by Benson in his publication of the pottery from the Potters' Quarter. It must be remembered, however, that the painters of linear ware can hardly be identified or counted.

attempt to exploit the expanding market; by *c*.650 many workshops already co-operated to provide common installations, and the scale of the co-operation was even greater in later years (above, 96-7, 101-2). It is probably no accident that the South Long Building dates to the late seventh century, when the vases themselves suggest that the manpower of pottery production increased as the proportion of figured work rose; the construction of the North Long Building not long afterwards and on a similar scale proves that such large establishments were reckoned a success. But their advantages cannot have been comparable to those achieved by scale in a modern, industrial economy. The production process itself did not alter: each man remained alone with his clay, his wheel, and his paint. The main achievement will have been to avoid unnecessary duplication. Strictly, the evidence shows only that in the mid-seventh century there was a common water-supply, and rather later common buildings; but kilns and unskilled labour were probably shared too.[66]

Organization in the export business is harder to trace. The export market must have originally developed purely by chance: Corinthians who visited Delphi and elsewhere for other purposes found that vases they had brought for their own use would fetch a good price. The point at which vases were taken deliberately for sale need not have been long after these unpremeditated exchanges. Corinthian vases at Pithecusae, and perhaps even at Delphi and Vitsa, are numerous enough well before the foundation of Syracuse to have been taken as commercial items. The business expanded rapidly. In every colony in the area of Corinthian domination, there is so much Corinthian from the beginning that we must posit traders who specialized—not necessarily exclusively—in pots. The colonists did not bring their taste for Corinthian with them from the mainland, where it was far less popular. The merchants must therefore have taken a deliberate decision to exploit the new market; they were greeted with the success their enterprise deserved, and established a pattern for their successors to exploit over little less than two centuries. Similar enterprise among the potters is probably to be inferred from the evidence of the Potters' Quarter; their heads were not so firmly stuck in the clay that they were unaware that their increased sales depended on exports. There is eloquent evidence that at least one

[66] Kilns have not been found: no doubt they were temporary structures (Stillwell, *Corinth*, xv.1.17). Some of the Penteskouphi plaques depict the firing process—probably exclusively for pots, despite the attempt of Orlandos, *Matériaux de construction*, i.99, to identify one of the kilns depicted as a furnace used in the production of metal (cf. ibid., 69-70). Note the batch of vases dumped after firing, Stillwell, *Corinth*, xv.1.16.

Fig. 15   Penteskouphi Plaque Showing a Vessel Carrying Vases. (From *Ant. Denk.*i, pl.8, 38).

painter knew the facts: one of the Penteskouphi plaques shows vases being loaded on to a vessel (Fig. 15).

If merchants could establish a market in the west, they might try to break into that which already existed in other parts of the Greek world: the extensive finds of Corinthian demonstrate that they both tried and succeeded. The reasons for their success are more complicated here, for there were usually substantial local schools; but three main factors can be isolated. It does not seem that there was a fine-art market here in the same sense as there was in Etruria; but much of the Corinthian on mainland and Aegean sites is of higher than usual quality. It will have been used for the same purposes as lesser ware; but it would serve as 'best plate'—and could presumably fetch a higher price. More ordinary Corinthian ware often sold in competition with local products of hardly lesser quality. In such circumstances we might have expected Corinthian, with its added transport costs and with profits expected by the merchants, to price itself out of the market; but this factor may have been cancelled out either by the reduced costs of production on a large scale or—an unquantifiable factor—by the fact that Corinthian rated as the Wedgwood of the seventh century: a merchant who could advertise his vases as Corinthian may have been selling status as well as pots. Probably most important, however, was the market in specialized vases for dedication. On almost every site the greatest concentration of Corinthian is in graves and sanctuaries, and the commonest shapes are particularly suitable for dedication (Pl. 41): aryballoi, alabastra, and kotylai (the latter often miniature, especially in the sixth century). This distribution is no doubt partly to be explained by the fact that sanctuaries and cemeteries are both better explored and better published than settlements; but it remains clear that dealers in Corinthian vases made a special effort to exploit the demand for votives or grave goods. Almost everywhere it was this market which lasted the longest. Attic had no similar products, and did not develop them; the organization of this aspect of the Corinthian export market was strong enough to endure well after the general sale for Corinthian had diminished. A further factor may have been that taste in these religious spheres was more conservative than in others.

When Corinthian exports declined, they gave way everywhere to Attic; probably not for internal reasons, but because they were suppressed. The most difficult sector of the market to explain on such grounds is the fine-art market in Etruria. Attic pieces began to reach Etruscan sites in some quantity soon after 600, but for nearly half a century the products of Corinth were able to compete very effectively. It has sometimes been suggested that towards the end of the MC period Corinthian painters began to recognize the serious nature of Attic competition and conceded the inferiority of their own products by covering the main decorated zone in a red slip and giving the vase a superficially Attic appearance.[67] But there can be no question of Corinthian artists striving in general to create an Attic effect; the slip was probably added to provide a background of better contrast than the almost pure white of Corinthian clay when white paint was used as a colour for flesh in figures both male and female.[68] This merely increases the difficulty of explaining the sudden and almost total collapse of Corinthian in Etruria c.550; the reason may have been rather that Corinthian was not taken than that Etruscans would not buy it. Perhaps the great contraction in the production of more ordinary pots at Corinth created a momentum which dragged down even the finest painters whose vases might have remained competitive on their own merits; perhaps the sentiment of the market in more ordinary vases affected the merchants who had in the past carried the best Corinthian to Etruria, so that they declined to carry more.

The failure of Corinthian in the market for ordinary use is, to a modern eye, easier to understand. It may have been merely a matter of appearance: Corinthian ware becomes flabby in the first half of the sixth century (Pl. 40); the painters were perhaps more self-satisfied than their predecessors in the long Protocorinthian and Corinthian tradition, and their Attic competitors produced far tauter and more vigorous work. Technical matters may also have been relevant. Corinthian clay is not as hard as Attic, and the glaze often peels off the surface. It is uncertain whether the latter would have been apparent in use in antiquity; but Attic may have retained

[67] Robertson, *History of Greek Art*, 123; Cook, *Greek Painted Pottery*, 60.
[68] See on these vases Payne, *Necrocorinthia*, 104–11. I am much indebted to Prof. J. Boardman for his assistance with this question.

its quality longer than Corinthian, and some knocks which would smash or chip a Corinthian vase might have left an Attic product unharmed. Such a technical criterion may have affected all markets but that in specialized shapes for dedication—which remained buoyant for longer. The question of appearance will have been more important in the market for 'best plate'; but although there is little to choose between the worst Attic and Corinthian, sixth-rate Corinthian may have suffered from the growing reputation of first-rate Attic. If one reason for the success of very ordinary Corinthian had been the reputation of the best Corinthian products, once the latter lost their status the former will have followed suit.

It is thus possible at least to guess why Attic seemed preferable to customers; but what they were offered may have been equally important. Corinthian remains significant in the west for a generation longer than elsewhere. Western taste may have lagged behind that of the rest of the Greek world; but it is more likely that the reason is to be sought in the momentum of the mechanisms of distribution, which had always been on a larger scale in the west. It can perhaps be further concluded that the men who were involved in the western trade were not significantly concerned with the Aegean. It is in any case likely that individual merchants would concentrate their business in relatively restricted areas; local contacts would be of immense help, and the Isthmus will have been a natural boundary to a man's interests. A more specific argument can be offered. If merchants were involved in the pottery trade both in the Aegean and in the west, they would have observed that Attic sold far better than Corinthian in the Aegean after 575, and they would have changed their western cargoes accordingly; even if they were Corinthians they will have felt a greater concern for their own business than for the welfare of Corinthian potters. But most western carriers seem not to have taken Attic until some time later; had they done so it would have been as popular in the west as elsewhere. We should conclude that most of the men who carried vases to the west had not observed conditions in the Aegean.[69]

Exactly what caused merchants to carry Attic rather than Corinthian to the markets of the Aegean is a matter for speculation; but it is significant that Corinthian declines perceptibly earlier in Athens than elsewhere. After 600 the merchants who brought Corinthian to Attica may have reasoned that since Corinthian could no longer compete successfully in Athens, Attic might also command a greater sale elsewhere. Aeginetans may have played a significant part in this

[69] There is, however, at least one counter-example: Johnston, *BSA* lxx (1975), 148-9.

process. Although Corinthian reached Aegina well into the sixth century, it suffered from Attic competition hardly later here than in Attica itself.[70] Aeginetans are known to our literary sources as traders, and on geographical grounds they are highly plausible candidates as carriers of both Corinthian and Attic. They may have been responsible for carrying Attic to Corinth itself. If Attic could deny Corinthian a market in Athens and reduce its hold on Aegina, it was worth trying to break into the market at Corinth too; but no sentiment will have prevented Corinthian carriers from making a similar attempt. All this is speculation, more or less rash; but the important point remains that merchants must have played a major part in the victory of Attic. The primary responsibility lay with the taste of consumers; but taste was allowed to have its effect in the Aegean because of the acute observation and commercial enterprise of traders—and its effect in the west was delayed by the momentum of the processes of distribution. The speed with which the change in the Aegean was accomplished is eloquent testimony to commercial flexibility and initiative: when consumer tastes changed, merchants were quick to respond.

[70] Sixth-century Attic from Aegina has not been fully published, but even Protoattic was imported, and MC imports are far fewer than Corinthian of earlier times: Kraiker, *Aigina*, 20, 83-4.

VIII. Production and Export

Common sense demands that pottery played only a small role in the total productive and export capacity of the Corinthia; but other items are far more difficult to trace. The evidence of pottery helps us to identify a further Corinthian export. Most vases were carried for their own sakes; but from the late eighth century to the mid-sixth a high proportion of finds consists of small closed vases such as aryballoi and alabastra, designed to contain perfume or perfumed oil. It was recorded at the time of discovery of one EC aryballos that it smelt strongly of scent.[1] The origin of their contents is uncertain. The original impulse was no doubt eastern; but the perfume carried in Corinthian vases was probably not itself of eastern origin even in the earliest period. Pliny (*NH* xiii.5) notes that Corinthian iris perfume was long popular; the period to which this tradition referred presumably included that of the Corinthian containers suitable for the perfume. Some of the plants from which Corinthian perfume was derived may well have grown in the Corinthia; others may have come from further afield. Illyrian iris was famous.[2] Pliny (*NH* xxi.40) names as the origin of the best specimens places far to the north of Vitsa Zagoriou, where Corinthians were active in the eighth century (above, 86, 90); but his discussion will reflect Roman conditions.

The wide distribution and large number of the containers might be taken to indicate a very extensive export; but not every export of this kind of vase will indicate one of perfume. Some of them, especially in the late eighth and early seventh centuries, are exceedingly delicate; but similar vases were also used as oil flasks,[3] and they may well have been exported empty. Corinthian aryballoi and alabastra were especially suitable as votives at certain sanctuaries if they were filled with perfume;[4] an empty vase would have created an appearance more generous than the reality. The contents of some

---

[1] Payne, *Necrocorinthia*, Catalogue no. 486, from Acrae in Sicily.
[2] Refs. in Beaumont, *JHS* lvi (1936), 184 n. 174; cf. also Hesych. s.v. ἀμβροσίη; Athen. 681 B.
[3] I do not share Payne's view (*Necrocorinthia*, 5-6 n. 3) that early aryballoi are too delicate to have contained oil.
[4] Cf. Dugas, *Délos*, x.5.

vases of this kind found in tomb groups will have been used during the rite;[5] but oil was as suitable for burial use as perfume. Tombs often contain far more vases than can conceivably have been necessary for the rite; many of the surplus may have been dedicated empty. It is thus impossible even to guess at the scale of Corinthian perfume exports and/or production. It is unlikely that the market in Corinthian perfumes collapsed at much the same time as that in their containers; what vessels were used subsequently is not known, but Dionysius II, the exiled tyrant of Syracuse, is reported by Plutarch (*Timol.* 14.3) to have spent time in Corinthian *parfumeries*.

When there is no means of using vases as evidence for Corinthian exports, problems begin to multiply. In time much progress may be made in the identification of products of Corinthian bronze and other workshops; but at present little is certain, and even less is of much significance. A Corinthian school of late geometric bronze-making has been convincingly identified, and specimens have been found in most parts of the Greek mainland, even as far away as Macedonia; but the number of finds is small.[6] In subsequent periods far less confidence can be placed in attributions to particular schools. There is much literary evidence for the quality of Corinthian bronze-work of all kinds over a long period,[7] and there are scattered signs of bronze-working at Corinth in the archaeological record.[8] The Corinthian helmet was known at Corinth soon after 700, and its name presumably indicates that it was invented at Corinth;[9] but Corinth cannot have enjoyed a monopoly in the manufacture of such a vital piece of military equipment. Bronze vases and statuettes were no doubt made in some numbers,[10] and the same may have been true of tripods and cauldrons.[11] But the scale of the export of such objects must have been very limited. Strictly from the point of

[5] Kurtz and Boardman, *Greek Burial Customs*, 209.

[6] See esp. Herrmann, *JdaI* lxxix (1964), 17–71. At least in respect of the horses, Corinthian seems the best established of Herrmann's schools, despite the doubts of Rolley (above, 85 n. 22). Macedonia: Benton, *JHS* lxxii (1952), 119; central Greece: *AD* xxvii (1972), 330–1 with Pl. 280 *a*. For other examples, above 86 n. 27 (Vitsa), 89 n. 35 (Elatea), 91 n. 46 (Leucas); Herrmann, art. cit., 28 n. 46 (Tegea). See now Coldstream, *GG* 174–7.

[7] Refs. in Payne, *Necrocorinthia*, 349–50.

[8] Orlandos, *Matériaux de construction*, i.100; Williams, *Hesperia*, xlii (1973), 15–17; Mattusch, *Hesperia*, xlvi (1977), 380–9.

[9] Snodgrass, *Early Greek Armour*, 27–8.

[10] See esp. Payne, *Necrocorinthia*, 210–31; Perachora, i.123–67; Vocotopoulou, *BCH* xcix (1975), 729–88, esp. 784. The bronze vases found at Trebenischte were originally attributed to Corinth; but opinion has recently moved in other directions (Wallenstein, *Korinthische Plastik*, 83–5 with refs.); the famous Vix krater has also been identified as Corinthian, but falsely so (ibid., 85 with refs.).

[11] Willemsen, *Olympische Forschungen*, iii, esp. 175–80; Herrmann, ibid., vi, esp. 107–112; Payne, *Perachora*, i.126–30.

view of trade, most Corinthian bronzes which found their way abroad probably did so by means of casual exchange; but those which reached the great sanctuaries of Olympia, Delphi, and Dodona may represent an exception.

Such items made up only a tiny proportion of the products of metalworkshops in general. It will hardly ever be possible to identify the place of origin of the few knives, tools, and other objects of general use which have been preserved; but neither Corinth nor anywhere else will have enjoyed a major export trade in them. Most states could probably support their own workshops for the production of such everyday items. Specific confirmation of this general argument is to be found in the accounts of the fourth-century building commissioners at Epidaurus. Almost every kind of skilled craftsman employed in the scheme came from elsewhere; but local metalworkers were available.[12]

The case may have been different with Corinthian fabrics (see Pl. 42). Athenaeus preserves references to garments, apparently rich ones, of Corinthian manufacture;[13] a similar concern is reflected in the reference in Antiphanes to Corinthian στρώματα (rugs or blankets).[14] By themselves these items would prove little; but recent excavations have uncovered evidence for the production of fabrics at Corinth, and the scale was considerable. Just north of Peirene there was a large dyeing installation: it originated well before the mid-sixth century and continued work, with alterations and extensions, into the fourth.[15] The installations are large, and the production process must have been highly organized for manufacture in quantity; the same benefits of scale may have been achieved here as in the Potters Quarter. It is a reasonable conjecture, in view of the literary references, that much of the production was exported; the importance of textile exports in the early Greek world has been properly emphasized.[16] There is evidence for similar work in the fourth century at Anaploga, although no indication of the scale was found;[17] later there was a third-century dye-works on the Rachi at Isthmia, and perhaps another of similar date at Tenea.[18] Presumably the raw material—apart from dyes etc.—was wool; the mountains

---

[12] Burford, *Temple Builders*, esp. 233.
[13] 525 D = Democritus of Ephesus *FGH* 267 F 1; 582 D, from Machon: see Gow, *Machon*, 129.
[14] Athen. 27 D = Antiphanes fr. 236 Edmonds.
[15] Esp. Williams, *AD* xxiii.B (1968), 134.
[16] Starr, *Economic and Social Growth*, 65–6.
[17] *BCH* lxxxvii (1963), 726; *AD* xviii.B (1963), 79.
[18] Kardara, *AJA* lxv (1961), 261–6. Tenea: *AD* xxv.B (1970), 159: the date of the installation is not clear, but the vats are similar to those on the Rachi (Wiseman, 93).

of the Corinthia, including those above Tenea, could have supported many sheep.[19]

The most impressive evidence for Corinthian exports besides pottery relates to building materials. This is not the place for discussion of Corinth's contribution to the development of the Doric order, although it was certainly significant and perhaps decisive: the early temples at Isthmia and Corinth, that of Olympian Zeus, and the present temple of Apollo—not to mention the heavy Corinthian involvement at Corcyra, Thermon, and Calydon—all show that Corinth's part in the process was of major importance.[20] More important in the present context is the evidence for Corinthian work on the public buildings of other states. This is not merely a matter of the use by other states of Corinthian skills in design; this was common from the seventh to the fourth century, but its strictly economic importance was small. Far more significant was the use of Corinthian building materials: that could provide substantial employment.

Corinthian materials can be traced most clearly in roof-tiles and architectural terracottas. From the time of the early temple of Apollo at Corinth temples were given roofs of large terracotta tiles, and from shortly afterwards the eaves were decorated with members in the same material (above, 60-1). At least in the artistic sense, Corinthian influence in the Isthmus region, the Corinthian Gulf, and the north-west mainland was overwhelming: almost every known specimen bears a close resemblance to Corinthian types.[21] What is less clear is the extent to which these objects were made in Corinth and exported, made on the spot by Corinthians, or made locally by local craftsmen; but that export from Corinth was significant from the earliest times is demonstrated by the finds from Delphi. From the earliest examples *c*.650 to the end of the fourth century over 70 per cent of the finds have been identified, on grounds of fabric, as Corinthian. Another 10 per cent were probably made by Corinthian craftsmen at Delphi; the remaining 20 per cent or less came mainly from treasuries and other buildings dedicated by areas with their own flourishing terracotta industries, such as Corcyra and Sicily.[22] Almost every building at Delphi, if it had clay and not marble tiles, was roofed by Corinthians.[23]

---

[19] Cf. Xen. *Hell.* iv.5.1: not all these sheep, however, will have been pastured normally in the Peiraeum: some will have been evacuated there as a war emergency measure.

[20] Cook, *BSA* lxv (1970), 17-19.

[21] Payne, *Necrocorinthia*, 252-62; see now for the early material Williams, ΣΤΗΛΗ, 345-50.

[22] Le Roy, *Fouilles de Delphes*, ii, *Terres cuites*, 220 with n. 1.

[23] For some exceptions, see Le Roy, *Fouilles de Delphes*, ii, *Terres cuites*, 63-91, 139-40.

Finds from other sites have not been so fully studied; and the question is complicated by evidence that craftsmen who learned their skills in Corinth might make architectural terracottas elsewhere. The fabric of the late seventh-century metopes at Thermon is mainly local, although fine clay for the surface was imported from Corinth;[24] the style is Corinthian, but the inscriptions sometimes include non-Corinthian features. Most of the architectural terracottas from Calydon were made in local clay, and a mis-fired piece proves that manufacture was done on the spot; the lettering is mainly, but not perhaps exclusively, Corinthian. Probably much of this work was done locally by craftsmen who had brought their paint and their tools—especially moulds—with them from Corinth.[25] The export of the finished product, as to Delphi, might provide a good deal of unskilled work in Corinth both in manufacture and in transport; but such work was lost to the Corinthia if production was undertaken on the site where the building was to stand. Some areas even in the specially Corinthian ambit were able at least from the sixth century to provide their own craftsmen: Corcyraeans roofed the temple of Artemis, and Corcyraean terracottas were exported to Delphi in the second half of the century for the Corcyraean treasury.[26]

In the fifth century the majority of tiles in the region of the workshop of Pheidias at Olympia are Corinthian; but it is not clear whether they were imported or made on the spot by Corinthians who had brought with them not only their paints and their tools but also their clay.[27] In the following century tiles made in Corinth might be specified even for public buildings in Eleusis.[28] If Corinthian could secure a market in Attica it is even more likely that it would be exported to sites where there was no local production. The place of manufacture of the tiles used in the temple of Asclepius at Epidaurus is never given in the building accounts, and the origins of the men who contracted for their supply are unknown; but the conjecture that the tiles were Corinthian is attractive.[29] In the absence of careful study of the fabric of finds from Epidaurus and elsewhere,

[24] Payne, *Necrocorinthia*, 254 with n. 2.
[25] Dyggve and Poulsen, *Das Laphrion*, 201-2. For lettering at Thermon and Calydon, see Jeffery, *Local Scripts*, 225-6.
[26] Le Roy, *Fouilles de Delphes*, ii, *Terres cuites*, 65-70.
[27] Mallwitz and Schiering, *Olympische Forschungen*, v.132-4. For fifth-century tiles of Corinthian manufacture in Boeotia, Tomlinson and Fossey, *BSA* lxv (1970), 246.
[28] *IG* ii.2². 1672, 72-3. In this case the tiles are 'from Corinth'. The mention of 'Corinthian' tiles, which is more frequent in Attic documents, does not necessarily demonstrate Corinthian manufacture, for a certain type of tile was known as Corinthian—in contrast to Laconian—to identify its shape. The case is probably similar with the Corinthian *geison* at *IG* ii.1².463, 71-2.
[29] Burford, *Temple Builders*, 182.

precision is impossible; but Corinth exported a great many tiles and roof decorations for large public buildings, especially temples, from the mid-seventh to the fourth century. Curiously enough, just as with fabrics, the archaeological record provides confirmation; a large complex known as the Tile Factory has been excavated not far from the centre of Corinth: it is known to have been in operation from at least the second half of the sixth century well into the fourth.[30]

Terracotta sculpture has been found in some quantity at Corinth,[31] and was exported to other sites. Well over fifty pieces have been catalogued in the recent publication of the material from Delphi; they are almost if not quite exclusively of Corinthian origin.[32] Athens had a significant school of terracotta sculpture, but she still imported more Corinthian work than she used local;[33] other sites will presumably have imported an even greater proportion of Corinthian.[34] Work of this kind can have employed only a few men; but these finds may have wider implications. The sculpture was often in the form of acroteria; their export from Corinth may have some bearing on the origin of the roof itself, and that will be of greater general economic significance.

In the fourth century Corinth was heavily involved in other aspects of the building schemes of other states. The most impressive evidence, because it is the most nearly complete, concerns the temple of Asclepius at Epidaurus, built in the second quarter of the fourth century. Lycius contracted to quarry and deliver all the stone for the colonnade, to supply the greater part of the timber for the roof, and to transport the stone for half the cella; the latter was quarried by Archicles, while the remaining half was quarried and delivered by Euterpidas. All these men are, unusually, specified in the accounts as Corinthians.[35] It is not stated that these materials were to be brought from the Corinthia; but at least the stone probably was. Its appearance encourages that view; the conclusion is made next to certain by the specification of Corinthian stone both for the Tholos at Epidaurus and for the fourth-century temple of Apollo at Delphi.[36] The case of timber is more problematic. Some was taken from Corinth to Epidaurus for another project rather

---

[30] A kiln which was associated with the factory is illustrated by Orlandos, *Matériaux de construction*, i.71-4 (late fifth century); for a preliminary report, see *AA* 1942, 143-4.

[31] Weinberg, *Hesperia*, xxvi (1957), 289-319.

[32] Ducat, *Fouilles de Delphes*, ii, *Terres cuites*, 231-69.

[33] Nicholls, *Hesperia*, xxxix (1970), 115-38; the Corinthian ranges from the mid-sixth to the late fifth century.

[34] Some examples are noted by Payne, *Necrocorinthia*, 261-2.

[35] *IG* iv.1². 102, 5-6, 14-19, 24-5.

[36] Burford, *Temple Builders*, 169; below.

later,[37] and Lycius must have been only one of a number of large-scale timber-merchants in the Corinthia;[38] one Athenian document appears to mention a Corinthian in the timber business.[39] It is uncertain whether these merchants dealt in wood cut in the Corinthia. There was originally much forest. It will have been heavily exploited by the fourth century, but there is no reason to believe that the supply was now exhausted. At Delphi in the fourth century, a good deal of timber was imported from Sicyon—and carried by a Corinthian;[40] but that does not necessarily mean that the Corinthia could no longer provide it.[41]

All this evidence, along with that which relates to roof-tiles, concerns materials exported from Corinth to Epidaurus; another major export was the skills of Corinthian craftsmen. Some of those who worked on the temple are identified as Corinthians in the accounts.[42] Burford identifies many others on the ground that they worked Corinthian materials, but this is a doubtful principle: even if it is in general valid it can only establish that the men concerned usually worked in Corinth; they might have been either metics or Corinthian citizens (a distinction to which we shall return).[43] But it remains probable on general grounds that many craftsmen were hired at Corinth for work at Epidaurus. That city had too few skilled men herself; and Corinth was a major source of supply.

The accounts for the building of the fourth-century temple at Delphi are less complete, and they take a different form; but heavy Corinthian involvement in both men and materials remains clear. Pausanias informs us that the architect of the temple, one Spintharus, was Corinthian (x.5.13). The stone for stylobate, columns, and entablature has been identified as Corinthian; there is reference in the documents to 'the works in Corinth', which must be quarrying, and Corinthians are mentioned as having transported the stone.[44]

[37] *IG* iv.1². 110, B 3-11.
[38] Burford, *Temple Builders*, 200.
[39] *IG* ii.2². 1672, 157, 170.
[40] Bourguet, *Fouilles de Delphes*, iii.5, no. 36.
[41] Cf. Burford, *Temple Builders*, 176 n. 2; above, 30. The plaque Payne, *Necrocorinthia*, 117, Fig. 41 probably represents tree-felling (ibid., 116 n. 12).
[42] *IG* iv.1². 102, 29-31: Cleandridas and Dorcon, who both dressed stone.
[43] Burford, *Temple Builders*, 237-45 with refs. One probably significant counter-example is found: an Argive who contracted to erect the colonnade of Corinthian stone (*IG* iv.1². 102, 13-14).
[44] See the refs. collected by Orlandos, *Matériaux de construction*, ii.4 with n. 5. 'The works in Corinth': Bourguet, *Fouilles de Delphes*, iii.5, no. 19, 20, 87-8. 'Poros from Corinth': ibid., no. 25 II A, 1-2. Transport: no. 19, 98-9; no. 23 II, 66-8.

There is no sign that timber was imported from the Corinthia, although Sicyon supplied a good deal (above). The roof-tiles, to judge from the absence of finds, were not of tèrracotta; but a Cnidian contracted to provide what was probably a temporary roof of tiles of the Corinthian type, and they were probably made in Corinth.[45] The Delphic accounts more frequently give the origins of those who worked on the project than the Epidaurian; Corinthians appear frequently.[46]

Our specific, documentary evidence relates mainly to the involvement of Corinthian men and materials at Epidaurus and Delphi; but we may assume that many other large public-building schemes of the fourth century relied heavily on Corinth where there was no need for transport of materials over long distances by land. There is no evidence from an earlier period which compares to the fourth-century building accounts from Delphi and Epidaurus; but a good deal of stone used at Delphi has been identified as Corinthian,[47] and it was possible to transport Corinthian stone across the Gulf already in the seventh century, for it was used in the Treasury of Cypselus.[48]

Since transport did not pose insuperable problems for the seventh century, building schemes at Delphi especially, but also other places, were probably supplied not only with architectural terracottas but also with wood and stone from the Corinthia.[49] Even in the fourth century the expertise necessary for the construction of large buildings was available only in Corinth and Athens and, to a lesser extent, Argos (below); Corinth will have been an even more natural centre in the seventh and sixth centuries, given her important role in the development of the Doric order.

From the earliest period of monumental building, Corinthian skills and Corinthian materials were always of the first importance.[50] Burford has argued that of the mainland Greek states only Athens and Corinth, and to a lesser degree Argos, could provide from among their own inhabitants the craftsmen needed for the construction of

[45] Bourguet, *Fouilles de Delphes*, iii.5, no. 26 I A, 33–44; cf. Le Roy, *Fouilles de Delphes*, ii, *Terres cuites*, 214–15.

[46] Best found in *SIG*[3] i, pp. 386–8.

[47] Pomtow, *Philologus*, lxvi (1907), 268–9, 273–86. It would, however, be difficult to distinguish Corinthian from (for example) Sicyonian stone without proper technical analysis.

[48] The appearance of the few remains makes this conjecture almost certain. Both the building and its blocks were small, and the relative ease of transport may have established a trend, which explains the remarkably high proportion of stone imported to Delphi for later buildings.

[49] Early quarrying near Corinth: Robinson, *Hesperia*, xlv (1976), 209–10.

[50] Hermione, for example, paid expenses for a journey to Corinth (*IG* iv. 742, 12–13); probably the matter was connected with a public-building scheme, like the many similar payments recorded in the Epidaurian accounts *IG* iv.1[2]. 102.

large temples: when other states undertook buildings of this kind, they had to call upon men who had learned their skills, and often practised them, in these cities.[51] But whether such undertakings were as important for the Corinthian economy as Corinthian participation was for other states is very doubtful. Temple-building cannot have been a continuous occupation even for those skilled men who went from place to place as contracts were available. For those who learned their crafts in Corinth the schemes were no doubt a welcome source of employment; but while they were important for individuals, those who took advantage of them were at least temporarily lost to the Corinthian economy. Far more important than exports of skilled labour were exports of materials; they could provide work in the Corinthia itself. A contract for Corinthian stone would provide substantial work both in quarrying and in transport; an order for Corinthian tiles will have had a similar effect on a smaller scale. As for timber, even if it was not felled in the Corinthia the work available in Corinthian timber-yards may not have been negligible.[52] But the demand for labour which depended on public building schemes must have fluctuated wildly.

Behind the Corinthian involvement in public undertakings may lie a ruder but more important concern in everyday construction work. Stone for house-building will presumably have been local; but tiles and timber may have been supplied to many other places from Corinth. A contract for house-building under the Epidaurian commissioners specifies Corinthian tiles. They were not necessarily imported from the Corinthia, but it has reasonably been conjectured that they were.[53] If Epidaurians found it more convenient or less expensive to import Corinthian tiles for houses, many others may have been in the same position. More reliable indications of the importance of Corinthian exports of tiles can be expected only from study of the finds themselves; but the humble domestic roof-tile has received scant attention in archaeological publications. There is certain evidence for the import of Corinthian timber at Epidaurus for house-building under the commissioners in the late fourth century.[54] That a Corinthian supplier could compete successfully

[51] *Temple Builders*, 199-201.
[52] It is impossible to determine under what terms the quarries and (if they existed) the forests of the Corinthia were exploited. Burford suggests that they may have been owned by the state (ibid., 174, 177-9); there is no evidence.
[53] *IG* iv.1². 109 II, 97, 148, 151; Burford, *Temple Builders*, 182. The adjective 'Corinthian' is perhaps more likely in this domestic context to signify place of manufacture than in the cases noted above, 119 n. 28.
[54] *IG* iv.1². 110 B, 3-11. The fact that the purchase was made 'according to the agreement (ἐξαίρεσις) of the cities' should not be used to argue that timber export from Corinth

may imply that there were none in Epidaurus to speak of: Corinthian tiles may often have been supported by timber supplied from Corinthian yards, and the employment thus provided will have been both more stable and more extensive than what was generated by public-building schemes.

A constant effort has to be made, in respect of all items of production and export so far discussed, not to exaggerate their importance for the total Corinthian economy merely because evidence for them has survived. The case is quite opposite in respect of Corinthian agriculture: the paucity of evidence should not lead us to underestimate its importance. Paradoxically, we have more general evidence for the eighth century than for any later period: the legislation of Pheidon provided for every Corinthian to own his own plot (above, 63-5). Evidence for subsequent centuries is meagre indeed. A Corinthian farmer is reported to have deserted his plot and his vines for philosophy (Ar. fr. 64 Rose). Agricultural activity is rarely represented in Corinthian painting; but what we have may perhaps be significant, for scenes which show everyday life, apart from those of aristocratic interest, have almost nothing but items of interest to potters or painters.[55] The fruit-tree on a Protocorinthian vase of *c*.650 from Megara Hyblaea is so unusual in the vase-painting tradition that it must have been drawn from life.[56] There is some evidence for artificial irrigation systems: water collected above the clay-bearing strata in the bluffs above the coastal plain could in two places be delivered under controlled conditions to the plain or to a small valley just above it.[57] A few agricultural products are mentioned in the literary sources. Sidous in particular produced good apples, and the same may have been true of the Corinthia as a whole (Athen. 82 A-C); the naming of a variety of radish as Corinthian may reflect extensive production as well as the supposed origin.[58] Corinthian wine is mentioned rather for its bad than its good quality. Alexis described it as torture to drink; but we do not know the context,

to Epidaurus was so common that it was made the subject of a special agreement. The agreement was probably made for the purposes of the building scheme as a whole; it may have consisted (for example) of the waiving by Corinth of export dues on material destined for use under the commissioners, and it was probably not restricted to timber. Cf. Burford, *Temple Builders*, 37.

[55] See Payne, *Necrocorinthia*, 116 with n. 12. The Penteskouphi plaque (*Ant. Denk.* ii, pl. 40, 9) appears to represent ploughing, and ibid., pl. 23 15 b may show some agricultural implement.

[56] Vallet and Villard, *Mégara Hyblaea*, ii.40 with 39, Fig. 14.

[57] Robinson, *Hesperia*, xxxi (1962), 127-9 (fourth century or earlier); xxxviii (1969), 1 (fourth century; cf. 5).

[58] Athen. 56 F; cf. Plin. *NH* xix.75-6. For medicinal uses of Corinthian plants, *NH* xxiv. 69, 157.

and wine may have stood metaphorically for a quite different Corinthian horror (Athen. 30 F = Alexis fr. 290 Edmonds). The sheep which produced the wool used in the manufacture of Corinthian fabrics were presumably reared mainly in the Corinthia (above, 119-20).

Until recently the evidence for agricultural exports was even less impressive; but attention is now being given to Corinthian transport amphorai with important results. Such rough vessels can only have been exported for the sake of their contents; and they travelled from the Corinthia from the time of the earliest exchanges with Delphi in the first half of the eighth century (above, 88). Study of these unexciting finds is only just beginning; but it is already clear that substantial numbers reached the west from the eighth century onwards. In the second half of the fourth century a cargo went down as far west as Mallorca, and although finds from the eighth to the fourth century (and later) are concentrated in the west, they are known from the Black Sea, especially Olbia, throughout the classical period, and from North Africa. Two types have been identified, and there is reason to believe that one was intended for oil and the second for wine; the former is found from the earliest years, though for some reason it seems not to have been exported in the fourth century, while the latter occurs only from the late sixth century.[59] It is not yet possible to draw quantitative conclusions from these Corinthian transport vessels, either at Corinth or elsewhere: until recently they will have been thrown away, or at least unrecorded, in most excavations. The only other evidence for Corinthian agriculture is in the nature of the land itself (see further below, 154-8).

[59] See for all this Koehler, *Proc. 9th Conf. Underwater Archaeology* (1978), 231-9 with refs. More than twenty archaic examples were identified at Megara Hyblaea: Vallet and Villard, *Mégara Hyblaea*, ii.50-1. Numerous examples have turned up recently at Metapontum, and see Frederikson, *AR* 1976/7, 57, 61 (Heraclea, Metaurus); Orlandini, *Acme*, xxix (1976), 32 (L'Incoronata).

IX. Imports

Our evidence for Corinthian imports can be briefly recorded. The most recent evidence is also the most impressive. Excavation has revealed a building with two phases, known as the Punic Amphora Building, near the west end of the South Stoa. Activity in it covered perhaps half a century, and ceased towards the end of the third quarter of the fifth century, almost certainly as a direct result of the Peloponnesian War. Enormous quantities of Corinthian and imported transport amphorai were recovered; the commonest imported items were Chiot and Punic amphorai, and some of them—perhaps not all—had been used to contain dried or salted fish.[1] Such an unexpected find is instructive: further excavation will no doubt alter the pattern as significantly.

Other evidence is negligible by comparison. From at least the eighth century a few vases reached Corinth which were made elsewhere, and there are other occasional non-Corinthian finds; but little signifies more than casual exchange. Some objects might have been acquired by Corinthians on their travels and brought back, for example to dedicate at Perachora; others may have been brought by non-Corinthian visitors (below, 145-7). From soon after 600 the import of Attic pots reached a significant level. When marble was employed in Corinthian buildings or sculpture it was imported, for the Corinthia had none; but in the main, local stone was used.[2] Such imports were of minimal importance; more significantly, all metals must have been imported. There were no mines of any kind in the Corinthia;[3] and gold, silver, bronze, and iron, along with ivory, are already known in Corinthian graves of the late tenth and early ninth centuries.[4] Imported ivory was the raw material for the

---

[1] Williams, *Hesperia*, xlvii (1978), 15-20; xlviii (1979), 107-24; xlix (1980), 108-11. For the connection with the war, see esp. xlviii (1979), 118.

[2] Some marble is known; e.g. the roof of the fifth-century temple of Poseidon at Isthmia (Broneer, *Isthmia*, i.90-3); sphinx (Protonotariou-Deilaki, *AAA* vi (1973), 181-8); Apollo of Tenea (above, 26).

[3] It is, however, just possible that the Bay of Sideronas in the south-east Corinthia (above, 6) had something to do with iron, σίδηρος, at some stage: iron slag has been found on the island in the bay, along with traces of fourth- and fifth-century occupation (Wiseman, 132 with n. 24).

[4] Snodgrass, *Dark Age*, 264-5 with n. 48.

impressive Corinthian school of ivory-work, especially seals, which is best represented at Perachora.[5] The first Corinthians who reached Etruria and/or Epirus in the early eighth century may have been searching for iron; but the case remains unproved (above, 91–2). It is impossible even to guess at the sources of the metals used in the Corinthia.[6] The almost total absence of Corinthian vases from Cyprus in the seventh and early sixth centuries (above, 108) perhaps indicates that copper was not carried from the Copper Island in Corinthian vessels; but this is an uncertain argument.[7] Some timber may have been imported, partly for re-export, in the later period; but this question too must remain open (above, 123).

There is a little more evidence for corn imports. In the crisis of the 320s, when there was a general lack of corn, Cyrene sent enormous quantities to almost all parts of Greece. Corinth received 50,000 measures; only Athens took more (100,000), and only Argos and Larisa as much.[8] Lycurgus asserts that when Leocrates was living at Megara in the 330s he acquired corn from Cleopatra of Epirus and took it to Corinth via Leucas rather than (as the Athenian law demanded) to Athens.[9] This concerns only one shipment; but it does show that Corinth might compete with Athens as a destination for corn. A story told of Hieron I of Syracuse has him making a gift of (among other things) a shipload of corn to one Architeles of Corinth, who had not only sold Hieron all the gold he wanted but made him a present of more.[10] Even if the story is invented (which is likely enough) it may indicate that corn would have been welcome at Corinth; but an inventor may have concerned himself rather with whether corn was a suitable gift for Hieron to give than for a Corinthian to receive.

This is the only specific evidence I know of; but a passage in Thucydides is almost certainly relevant. He informs us that one reason which persuaded the Athenians to dispatch twenty vessels to Sicily in 427 was that they 'wished to prevent the import of corn from there to the Peloponnese' (iii.86.4). Of all the Peloponnesian states Corinth is the most likely to have been affected. The expedition may have been the second stage of a plan to deny imports,

[5] Stubbings in Dunbabin, *Perachora*, ii.403–51.
[6] For the silver used in Corinthian coins, see below, 172–3.
[7] See further below, 143–4. Copper might have reached Corinth from Cyprus in non-Corinthian vessels, but this seems unlikely, at least in the early period.
[8] Tod, ii, no. 196.
[9] *In Leocr.* 26. It may also be relevant that an Apollonia sent barley to Delphi in the fourth century (Bourguet, *Fouilles de Delphes*, iii.5, no. 3 II 1–22); but the identity of the place is unclear, although Corinth's Adriatic colony is the most likely candidate.
[10] Athen. 231 E–232 B = Theopompus *FGH* 115 F 193.

especially of corn, to Corinth which began with the blockade instituted by Phormio two years earlier. Polyaenus may record a successful evasion of precisely that blockade by a Corinthian convoy of corn
ships.[11] The Athenians may have exaggerated the importance of corn
imports for Corinth by comparison with their own case; but they
are unlikely to have invented a Corinthian dependence on imports.

The extent of that dependence is difficult to determine; but at
least some corn was probably imported from an early period. It is
impossible to calculate with any accuracy what the Corinthia could
produce in antiquity; but it is most improbable that enough cereals
were grown to support the whole population. The most suitable
land in the Corinthia, the coastal plain and the flat regions near the
Isthmus, along with a few small tracts elsewhere, comprises rather
over 20,000 hectares (above, 19-26). Barley was the most commonly
grown cereal, and most land under ancient conditions will have
yielded no more than sixteen hectolitres per hectare.[12] The rich
coastal plain may have given a slighter better yield, but if half the
land was left fallow each year production in these parts of the
Corinthia could hardly have exceeded 200,000 hectolitres, and
was presumably a great deal less. Some land may have been fertilized
with manure and sown each year, and barley will also have grown
in other parts of the territory; but these factors cannot have cancelled
out the amount that had to be retained from each crop for next
year's seed.

When it can first be traced in the early fifth century, the total
population of the Corinthia is unlikely to have exceeded 70,000 and
may have been a good deal smaller (below, 165-9). Since the annual
requirement for an adult was *c*.3 hectolitres, it is theoretically
possible, on the most optimistic calculation, that the Corinthia was
nearly, if not quite, self-sufficient in cereals if we allow a lower
consumption for children; but such a reconstruction is extremely
improbable. A yield of 200,000 hectolitres is a maximum that was
almost certainly not reached in practice. Even so, it allows too little
for seed and wastage, and the calculation assumes that all the best
land grew cereals. Olives were probably grown among the barley
as well as on the rougher marginal land which could not support

[11] *Strat.* v.13.1: Ariston defends the convoy against an unidentified enemy. He is not
stated in this passage to be Corinthian, but v.13.2 refers to the Corinthian of that name
who played a prominent part in the defence of Syracuse (below, 334-5). The two passages
were no doubt at least intended by Polyaenus to refer to the same individual, and v.13.1
may thus refer to Phormio's blockade (below, 308); but the events could equally well
have taken place in Sicily.
[12] All calculations of yield and consumption in this section are based on Starr, *Economic
and Social Growth*, 152-4.

cereals, and fruit-trees—perhaps especially apples—may also have stood with barley on the better land; but much of the central Corinthia probably grew vines—not to mention vegetables—and these could not share the land with barley. If a more plausible estimate of *c*.100,000 hectolitres total cereal production is taken, approximately half of the total consumed in the Corinthia had to be imported.[13]

Besides importing corn for local consumption, Corinth may also have acted as a centre for the distribution of corn imported by other states. During the 360s the efforts of the Corinthians to supply the beleaguered city of Phleious impressed Xenophon, who probably observed them himself.[14] That was an exception, necessitated by war; but if any inland Peloponnesian states had to import corn—a need which probably only arose in years of harvest failure—it would have been natural to make use of the mechanisms which already existed at Corinth. A passage in Thucydides indicates that Corinth performed a similar function in respect of other items. He makes the Corinthians who speak in favour of war at the Congress of the Peloponnesian League in 432 argue that inland states should not ignore the Athenian threat to maritime cities, or their own 'exports of agricultural produce, and their imports in return of what the land gains from the sea' would suffer.[15] The scale of these exchanges should not be exaggerated, especially as the whole Corinthian speech is remarkable for its lack of realism (below, 306-7); but there was probably some truth behind the argument, which presumably referred to Corinth herself. Certainly the Corinthia, which imported a good deal for local consumption, was a convenient point of entry for essential imports, perhaps especially metal, to inland states such as those of Arcadia; they could hardly exchange anything against them but agricultural produce.

[13] The shipment from Cyrene reflects an abnormal situation, and should not be used as a basis for calculation. Corinth, with about half the Athenian population, received half the amount sent to Athens; but this means little, for Argos and Larisa—which took the same as Corinth—can hardly have been as dependent on imported corn in normal years. Since we do not know the extent to which the Cyrenaean corn could remedy the total deficiency, the time taken to consume it, or the proportion of it which replaced corn normally grown in the Corinthia, calculations are without point.

[14] *Hell.* vii.2.17-23; Aeschin. ii.168. See further above, 34.

[15] i.120.2. I am much indebted to Steve Hodkinson for discussing this passage with me.

X. The Corinthian Economy

a. Trade: Extent

From the early eighth century, trade provided opportunities both
for traders themselves and for others at sea and on shore. The extent
of these opportunities cannot be determined solely by the evidence
for specific exports and imports; it is too patchy. There are few
commodities for which a quantitative approach can be attempted;
one of them is pottery. At Megara Hyblaea the commonest Corinthian shape was the kotyle; fragments of at least some 6,000 were
found up to 1961 which dated to between c.710 and c.625, and they
may represent something of the order of 15,000 vases.[1] If we allow
for examples not yet found, the annual rate of arrival cannot have
been more than 2,000 and was presumably a great deal less. That
is perhaps an impressive figure for a single shape at a single site, but
it becomes less so when the mechanics of transport are considered.
Kotylai are easily stacked; allowing for packing in straw or some
similar material, 2,000 could be loaded into panniers which could
easily be carried by two donkeys to Lechaeum, and they would take
up little space on a vessel. Some other shapes were more difficult
to pack, but the number of vessel journeys required for the transport
of all fine Corinthian vases ever taken to the west will be small:
probably 100 per annum would be a considerable overestimate. No
doubt vases were usually taken only as a part of the load of any
one vessel (below, 135); but the export of pottery alone can have
accounted for only a small number of vessel movements. Other
directly traceable exports will have accounted for even fewer; but
textiles, which are bulky, may have been more significant, while the
transport amphorai which already left Corinth in some numbers
by c.700 were not easy to stack. As for imports, 3,000 *medimni*
seems to have been the capacity of a grain-ship of average size from
the fourth century. Less than 100 movements of such vessels per
annum would account for enough to feed half the population of
Corinth for a year;[2] earlier vessels, however, will have been smaller.
Other imports, such as metal, cannot be quantified.

[1] Vallet and Villard, *Mégara Hyblaea*, ii. 39; cf. 9–10.
[2] For the figures, see above, 130–1. The average capacity of vessels: Casson, *Ships and
Seamanship*, 183–4.

Such movements of specific items are put into perspective by direct evidence for the scale of Corinthian trade. 'Because the Corinthians had their city on the Isthmus they have always had a market. In ancient times the Greeks travelled through the Corinthia to make contact with each other rather by land in and out of the Peloponnese than by sea, and the Corinthians were powerful through their riches, as is shown by the ancient poets; for they called the place wealthy. When the Greeks took more to the sea, the Corinthians acquired a fleet and put down piracy; they provided a market for traffic of both kinds and made their city powerful by the revenues they gained' (Thuc. i.13.5). This passage is not entirely trustworthy. The land route across the Isthmus was probably not commercially important before the development of maritime traffic: transport by land was notoriously difficult. This statement, like much of i.1-17, is probably little more than intelligent reconstruction. Observing for himself Corinth's contemporary importance for maritime trade, Thucydides probably guessed that since this trade was (as he thought he knew) a comparatively recent development and yet even the ancient poets called Corinth wealthy, the trade which explained her riches must in the earliest times have been conducted by land. The passage remains, however, eloquent evidence for Corinthian maritime trade in his own day—and for some time past. His insistence on the importance of Corinth's position perhaps strictly implies that he refers to the transit trade, not to that in goods produced or consumed in the Corinthia; and much of Corinth's public wealth derived from levying dues on traffic which passed through her territory, especially on the diolkos; but the word ἐμπόριον (market) shows that he had more than the transit trade in mind. Since his purpose is to explain Corinth's early lead in naval affairs, Thucydides uses the past tense; but his description must have applied to the Corinth he saw. We cannot tell how far back from his own time his evidence is to be taken as valid;[3] fortunately, the evidence of the spade brings some precision.

By nature, the shore at Lechaeum was similar to that all along this coast. That the harbour here was artificial is indicated by its description by a geographer of the Roman period as λιμὴν χωστός, 'excavated

---

[3] He evidently believed that it applied at least by the late eighth century: the logic of the passage is that Ameinocles built his triremes, 300 years before 'the end of this war' (i.13.3), after the development of maritime trade. But the date for Ameinocles is too early. A more realistic one, in the late seventh century (below, 223), will take maritime commerce back to c.650 if Thucydides had evidence for the connection between it and the first triremes; but the connection was probably dependent rather on Thucydides' powers of reconstruction than on specific evidence.

harbour' (Dion. Calliph. 108-9); the material dug out for the purpose
was heaped into mounds which can still be seen, and they consist—as
far as can be discovered without excavation—entirely of pebbles such
as occur all along this shore (Pl. 43). The harbour itself has not been
archaeologically investigated, but it is hardly likely that the port was
still a mere open shore in the classical period; important evidence for
the date of the harbour was discovered during excavations of the
exceptionally large basilica between the basin and the shore. Immediately south of the coast there was originally a marsh, and the
spit between marsh and shore was later artificially strengthened with
accumulations of large stones. This must have been done when the
marsh was dug out to make the harbour; between the stones sherds
were found which date the strengthening of the spit to the reign of
Periander.[4] Since the evidence for chronology was found near the
western limit of the later basins, at the far end from the entrance,
the harbour built by the tyrant appears to have been no smaller
than that of later times. There is no reason to doubt that his engineers
were capable of the project: he at least contemplated driving a canal
through the Isthmus, and his father dug one at Leucas (below,
202, 210-1).

There can be little doubt that the harbour at Lechaeum was
primarily, perhaps exclusively, intended for vessels carrying cargoes.
For warships the main need was for runways or a beach for launch-
ing: at Lechaeum the shore already provided admirable facilities.
It would have been no easier to defend war vessels drawn up by
Periander's harbour than those beached on the shore itself. The
new basins, indeed, had a positive disadvantage for war vessels: the
entrance was so narrow that a fleet could only put to sea one or
two at a time. On the other hand, the irregular perimeter of the
harbour was particularly suitable for vessels which were to be
loaded:[5] it provided a great length of quay in a small area. It was
far more convenient to use the calm water in the harbour than to
load vessels on or close to the shore and then push them out into
a possibly rough sea. After the harbour was built, warships may
have used part of its perimeter; but there was still room for them
to be launched directly into the sea from between harbour and
shore, and this practice may well have continued. Some of the
craft which used the harbour were probably fishing vessels; but
the majority will have carried cargoes.

[4] Pallas, *AD* xvii.B (1961), 75. For discussion of Lechaeum and its installations, see
Wiseman, 87-8, with refs.
[5] Cargo vessels and warships probably already differed in this period (below, 152-3); but
what is crucial for the present issue is whether they were to be loaded, not their construction.

Periander will hardly have devoted as many resources as the harbour required to assisting the small number of movements which can, to a degree, be quantified. Since the port was presumably built in order to service—and, no doubt, levy dues upon—an already existing pattern of trade, the scale of trade which passed through Lechaeum was already, by the second half of the seventh century, considerably greater than our evidence for specific items indicates. This conclusion is strongly supported by the fact that vases can have made up only a small proportion of the cargo of any single vessel. If it were loaded with pots alone, a ship could carry so many that they would be impossible to sell. Merchants' marks indicate a similar conclusion. They are rarely repeated; where they seem to give the number of vases in a batch—or at least the number of a particular shape in a batch—the total is always small. Johnston concludes that 'the vases were marketed casually by a large number of traders'.[6] No counter-evidence is provided by the fact that vases are the only visible cargo on the Penteskouphi plaque fragment which represents vase exports (Fig. 15). The vessels which carried vases from Lechaeum therefore carried other items too—which continued to be carried when Corinthian vases could no longer find a market.

This disparity between the general evidence for the scale of Corinthian trade and specific exports and imports which can be established or inferred leaves an unquantifiable, but large, gap which can only be filled by conjecture.[7] Some of the movements from Lechaeum may have been internal to the Corinthia; but exchanges with the Perachora peninsula cannot have been extensive. At a wider range, some imports, especially corn and metals, can be identified with confidence, for they were necessities which the Corinthia could not produce itself; but the substantial imports of preserved fish in the fifth century demonstrate that imports were not restricted to necessities. To identify exports is more difficult. What the Corinthia could export depended not only on local conditions, which can to some extent be determined, but on what could find a market elsewhere. The identifiable exports can have made up only a small proportion of the total even during the best period of Corinthian pottery. Other manufactured goods, perhaps especially textiles, probably made up some of the shortfall. One raw material on which these exports depended was the wool of

[6] *Trade Marks on Greek Vases*, 36–8; cf. *Greece and Rome* xxi (1974), 140–1 (quotation from p. 141); *BSA* lxviii (1973), 187. For a similar situation with regard to Attic at a later period, cf. *Greece and Rome*, xxi (1974), 144; *Trade Marks on Greek Vases*, 51.
[7] For all the details, see above, 103–31.

Corinthian sheep, and probably the most significant export item also grew in the Corinthia: surplus agricultural produce. There is little doubt, even though precise calculations are impossible, that the territory could produce both olive oil and wine in greater quantities than were needed for local consumption. There is at least some evidence in the Corinthian transport amphorai exported for the sake of the oil or wine they contained; and under ancient conditions no alternative is possible.

The difficulty of identifying exports should not lead us to under-estimate the scale of Corinthian trade. The export of oil or wine to places which were in principle capable of self-sufficiency in these items is not precluded. The vital issue was whether Corinthian produce could be sold elsewhere at a price which enabled it to compete with local. Price variations in the ancient world cannot be traced except—sometimes—in the special circumstances of the corn market; but various factors may have worked in favour of Corinthian wine or oil. The success of Corinthian vases in the west proves that commercial skills were already well developed by the late eighth century; they could be exercised on other items too. If wine and oil were produced in greater quantity than could be con-sumed in the Corinthia, that might reduce their price sufficiently to enable them to compete elsewhere. Most of the good land in the Corinthia, especially the coastal plain, was very close to Lechaeum; that would eliminate the heavy costs of land transport, and might make Corinthian produce saleable in places where local oil or wine had to come some distance by land. In the cases of both these items, the harvest had to be processed before consumption; Corinthians may have been able to speed up the process after observing the advantages that large-scale operations could bring in pottery and other workshops. Quality might suffer, but the speed could produce opportunities for sale. Corinthian produce may in general have sold rather for its price than its quality: Alexis' description of Corinthian wine as torture to drink may, if it was intended literally (above, 126-7), indicate that it was sold to those who could get no other. Indifferent quality does not exclude sales if the price is right.

b.   The Isthmus Carrying Trade

The trade so far discussed consisted of movements to and from the Corinthia; but trade of another kind certainly provided some employment. The decisive evidence is that in the early sixth century Periander constructed the diolkos to assist—and no doubt more importantly to derive income from—the carrying trade across the

Isthmus.[8] It enabled vessels to be carried from one side of the
Isthmus to the other, and our only evidence for its use concerns
military vessels.[9] It has been concluded that it was used only for
military purposes;[10] but that is a rash argument from silence. Our
sources tell us so little of trading practices and routes that their
failure to mention such traffic over the Isthmus means nothing.
The physical remains give no clue as to whether the primary use
was military or commercial. Thucydides shows that triremes could
be transported;[11] a small merchant vessel, even fully loaded, could
certainly have been carried, but the upper weight-limit can hardly
be determined.[12] Aristophanes implies such frequent traffic on the
diolkos that only commercial movements can have been intended:
'What's this Isthmus business? You're shoving your prick up and
down even more than the Corinthians shove ships across their
diolkos' (*Thesm.* 647-8).

If the diolkos was used primarily for merchant vessels, that does
not prove that Periander intended it to be so used; but the tyrant
is not likely to have been concerned with his war fleets alone. All
the known instances of the transport of war fleets involve non-
Corinthian, or at least partly non-Corinthian, ships. The diolkos was
of far greater use to the vessels of other cities than to those of
Corinth. She had ports on either side of the Isthmus and had no
need of the diolkos—though it might prove useful for her allies
(below, 227); and in an emergency it would enable her to reinforce
her fleet on one Gulf by transporting that on the other. If military
considerations alone had been involved, it would probably have been
simpler and cheaper to build more vessels; but military arguments
may have strengthened what was already a powerful commercial case.

It remains uncertain whether there was a significant carrying trade
over the Isthmus before the construction of the diolkos; Periander

[8] For excavations, see the references in Wiseman, 74 n. 7. For the date, esp. Verdelis, *AM* lxxi (1956), 57-9; the best evidence are the sherds found beneath the blocks of the diolkos, for the letters and other masons' marks carved in them could belong much later (Jeffery, *Local Scripts*, 375). For all that follows, see Cook, *JHS* xcix (1979), 152-3; Snodgrass, *Archaic Greece*, 147; (briefly) Salmon, in Coldstream and Colledge (eds.), *Greece and Italy in the Classical World*, 197. I am indebted to Professor Cook for allowing me to see a copy of his note in advance of publication and for subsequent discussion.

[9] Refs. in Cook, *JHS* xcix (1979), 152, n. 7.

[10] Lehmann-Hartleben, *Hafenanlagen*, 47.

[11] iii.15.1 (a plan not put into effect); viii.8.4. Special preparations may, however, have been needed for triremes: Cook, *JHS* xcix (1979), 152 with n. 11.

[12] Cook (ibid., 153 with n. 16) shows that it was weight rather than size that was critical. The strain on hulls could have been countered to some degree by ropes secured round them (ὑποζώματα: cf. Casson, *Ships and Seamanship*, 91); cradles and padding would merely have increased the strain on the axles. Cook's view that it 'would have been a very small ship that was not too heavy when fully laden' may therefore be too pessimistic.

may have hoped to create rather than to satisfy a demand. Vessels will probably not have been loaded on carts and carried across by road; if vessels themselves were not carried, the mechanisms of the carrying trade, if it existed at all, will have been very different from those permitted by the diolkos. From the early eighth century a good deal of traffic passed from the Aegean to the west. Euboeans reached Etruria soon after 800, substantial amounts of Euboean pottery are found in the west to the end of the eighth century, and during the seventh there was a steady, if small, stream of East Greek imports into Sicily. If these movements crossed the Isthmus, they will presumably have taken the shortest route. It is perhaps significant that the earliest signs of settlement at its western end appear in the late eighth century:[13] a small settlement may have grown up as the carrying trade developed. There were, however, grave difficulties in the way of trade across the Isthmus. If vessels themselves could not be carried, not only would cargoes have to be broken for carriage over the Isthmus, but a different boat would have to be hired on the other side. A journey to Sicily from Euboea and back would have involved so many changes of vessel and so much loading and un-loading that it may have seemed preferable to brave the dangers of Cape Malea. There are almost no signs of Euboeans in the Corinthian Gulf.[14] The practical effects of the carrying trade might have been achieved in a different way before the diolkos. Cargoes might have been taken from west or east to Corinth, sold there, and shipped independently beyond the Isthmus; but what evidence we have is against this. If Euboean and East Greek vases could be sold at Corinth for shipment to the west in the late eighth and seventh centuries respectively, they could presumably have been sold at Corinth for use there; but no certain example of Euboean from the Corinthia is known to me, and there are only a few pieces of East Greek which date before the diolkos.[15] No doubt the trade between areas east and west of the Isthmus involved far more items than the pottery which is our only direct evidence; but vase finds discourage the view that such trade was conducted over the Isthmus.

The extent of employment provided in the Corinthia by the carrying trade and the diolkos which served it—the transport of vessels and the services which might be performed for passing

[13] Verdelis, *AM* lxxi (1956), 57 (cf. Coldstream, *GGP* 405). The eastern end of the diolkos at Schoenous (Strabo 380) has not been located, and there is little evidence in this region on the surface (Wiseman, 46).

[14] Above, 92; for a different view, see Murray, *Early Greece*, 74, 140.

[15] Shefton in Dunbabin, *Perachora*, ii.368, 373-4; Weinberg, *Hesperia*, xvii (1948), 216 (D 5), 223-4 (D 53-4); Williams, *Hesperia*, xlviii (1979), 14-24.

crews—depended on the number of vessels carried; but in all periods this is difficult to quantify. Some items which passed from east to west of the Isthmus or vice versa can be identified; but only if (for example) a wreck carrying Chiot wine-jars were to turn up in the Corinthian Gulf could we be reasonably sure that it had been carried towards its destruction on the diolkos. Aristophanes indicates that traffic was not infrequent; but it is likely that the diolkos became progressively less suitable for use as the size of the average merchant vessel increased. Probably the craft of Periander's day could be carried fully laden; but in later periods it may have been necessary for most vessels to unload cargo. Such a complicated process was sometimes preferred to the dangers of Cape Malea; but very heavy traffic would have led to intolerable congestion, especially at either end, on a single track which could carry vessels in only one direction at a time.[16]

c. Trade: Range and Direction

The scale of Corinthian trade to the west is demonstrated by that of Periander's installations at Lechaeum; for its range and direction we have almost no evidence save the imports and exports which can be identified: above all, the pottery of the eighth to the sixth centuries. Since pottery was concerned in only a small proportion of the movements from Lechaeum even in the best period of Corinthian ware, the unrepresentative character of this evidence will be obvious, and Cook has drawn attention to the dangers of using pottery as an index of trade in general;[17] but it can yield some conclusions if it is warily interpreted.[18] The direction of Corinthian trade may clearly have shifted significantly after we lose the evidence of pottery; but we have no means of tracing any developments that may have taken place. We cannot hope to achieve anything approaching a full picture; but evidence should not be ignored merely because it is incomplete.

At the simplest level, the distribution of Corinthian vases demonstrates that the range of Corinthian trade covered, directly or indirectly, the whole Greek world and beyond from the eighth to at least the early sixth century. Such a conclusion is obvious, but not illuminating; more valuable is the study of patterns of distribution.[19] Corinthian vases were carried almost exclusively by sea; they are

[16] See further Cook, *JHS* xcix (1979), 153.
[17] *JdaI* lxxiv (1959), 115.
[18] Corinthian exports of materials for public-building schemes can tell us nothing of the normal patterns of trade: below, 147.
[19] For the details, above, 103-16.

rarely found far inland. The exports to Sparta probably travelled further by land than most. Even at Olympia there is not much Corinthian; and the general paucity of fine pottery dedications at the site probably reflects the lack of local potters and the difficulty of supplying the deficiency by imports which had to come by land. Arcadia is not very well known archaeologically in the period of Corinthian predominance; little Corinthian has been found among the material that is known.

The overwhelming preponderance of Corinthian vases in North Africa, Sicily, and Italy up to the Straits of Messina demonstrates that a conscious effort was made to establish and maintain a market for Corinthian vases in these areas; but in other parts of the western Mediterranean there was probably no such effort, for Corinthian occurs in far smaller quantities or (in Etruria) different quality.[20] The traders who worked between Corinth and the main area of Corinthian domination probably did not often progress beyond the Straits of Messina; this would fit well with the literary evidence which indicates a primacy for Phocaeans in these waters (Hdt. i.163). Phocaeans, however, did not reach here much, if at all, before the end of the seventh century.[21] There must have been some earlier movements from Lechaeum to Etruria, to account for the fine-art vases which travelled;[22] but the finds are too few to establish heavy traffic. Some of the Corinthian vases which reached the far west after *c*.600 may have done so in the hands of Phocaeans. They probably reached Spain not by the southern route, along the north coast of Africa, but rather through Italian waters.[23] Corinthian vases appear in the far west in small but perhaps significant quantities just at the time of the construction of the diolkos; the Phocaeans may then have used it and picked up some vases before heading on down the Corinthian Gulf. If they took this route the reference in Herodotus to their presence in the Adriatic might receive a partial explanation.[24] Similarly, knowledge of Corinthian vases, if not the vases themselves, reached Carthage already in the late eighth century, and Punic contexts in Spain have yielded Protocorinthian of the mid-seventh; but the numbers are too restricted to demonstrate significant traffic here from Corinth. The vases might have been picked up by Carthaginians or Levantine Phoenicians in Sicily; and the fact that Corinthian is

[20] Etruscan bucchero is known at Corinth (MacIntosh, *Hesperia*, xliii (1974), 34–45); but hardly in sufficient quantity to disturb the conclusion.
[21] Vallet and Villard, *PP* xxi (1966), 166–90; Morel, *PP* xxi (1966), 378–420; *BCH* xcix (1975), 853–96.
[22] See also above, n. 20.
[23] Boardman, *Greeks Overseas*, 214.
[24] Ibid., 228.

the commonest Greek pottery in Punic contexts is probably a reflection rather of the popularity of Corinthian in Sicily than of frequent calls by Corinthian vessels at Carthage or by Carthaginian at Corinth.[25]

The vessels which carried pottery from Lechaeum to where it was sold also carried other goods (above, 135). Since there are few alternative candidates in these parts for a major role in western trade, most vessels which carried pots probably had their cargoes made up almost completely at Lechaeum. In Herodotus' story of Arion, the singer insisted on being taken from Taras to the mainland in a Corinthian vessel.[26] If the story at least reflects the realities of *c*.600, Corinthian craft were well known and well (if undeservedly) trusted in the west at that time; but it may rather reflect the realities of Herodotus' day and indicate that they were in a similar position in the fifth century. To show that traffic between Corinth and the west was heavy is not to prove that Corinth dominated the western trade, and East Greek vessels were certainly to be found in Sicilian waters; but Corinth enjoyed great advantages from her position and Corinthian vessels were probably commoner in the west than any others.

It is hardly mere coincidence that the area in which Corinthian vessels were most frequently found in the west was precisely that of corn exports in the classical period. Herodotus (vii.158.4) shows that Sicily was believed to have a surplus of corn; a purpose of the Athenian expedition to Sicily in 427 was to try to prevent Sicilian corn from reaching the Peloponnese, and in the second half of the fourth century the arrival of shipments from Sicily could alter the price of corn at Athens.[27] Much North-African corn was sent to Greece in the crisis of the 320s (above, 129). In the archaic period production may not have been as great as it was to become; but the goods brought from Corinth had to be exchanged for something, and corn is by far the most likely conjecture. Pots were hardly the only items offered in exchange for corn.[28] To suppose that they were would lead to a serious underestimate of the total amount of corn carried; more importantly, it would imply that Corinth suffered serious difficulties of corn supply after the demise of her pottery. But vases accounted for only a small proportion of movements

[25] For LG, see Coldstream, *GGP* 386-7.
[26] i.23-4. The discussion of the legend by Schamp, *AC* xlv (1976), 95-120, is excessively speculative and historically inaccurate.
[27] De Ste Croix, 217-18; Talbert, *Timoleon*, 165-6. For Corinth, see above, 129-31.
[28] As in the too schematic reconstruction of Vallet, *Rhégion et Zancle*, 207 (followed by Mossé, *Tyrannie*, 27); cf. Vallet and Villard, *Rev. Hist.* ccxxv (1961), 314-16.

between Corinth and the west; the commodities carried along with them in the early period—mainly agricultural produce—continued to be taken later. Corinth's requirements for imported corn were probably always brought mainly from Sicily and North Africa; but Epirus was involved in the later fourth century and may have been earlier.

It is difficult to determine what proportion of the traffic which left Lechaeum was bound across the Adriatic, what never reached the Italian coast, and what stayed within the Corinthian Gulf. Finds of Corinthian pottery are far more restricted in the Ionian Sea, the eastern Adriatic, and even the Gulf itself than in the further west, but to conclude that most vessels which left Lechaeum travelled long distances would be rash. Archaeological exploration on the Greek side of the Adriatic has been less thorough and less well published than on the Italian. Even if we could be sure that Corinthian pottery was less used on the closer sites, the reason may have been related rather to local taste and production than to the general pattern of Corinthian trade. Short-range traffic from Lechaeum was probably at least as heavy as long-range; but the evidence is inconclusive.[29]

It is geographical arguments which help to show that a majority of cargoes bound for the west which included Corinthian pottery were made up at Corinth. The construction of the diolkos altered the facts of geography. The proportion of movements down the Corinthian Gulf which started from Lechaeum must have been reduced when Periander's project came into use; but it is unlikely that this had any serious effects on the volume of trade originating at Lechaeum. The diolkos opened the west to competitors from east of the Isthmus; but vessels travelling from Lechaeum will still have enjoyed the advantages of not having to pay dues and transport costs at the diolkos, and the men who worked them had well-established contacts in the west to exploit. There may, however, have been some connection between the construction of the diolkos and the demise of Corinthian vases in the west which followed soon afterwards. The primary reason was one of taste; but the

[29] Perhaps the most significant item is that in the late fourth century Corinth imported Epirot corn; but whether she did so much earlier is unclear. This may have been the basis of the friendly attitude of Epirots towards Corinthians in the fifth century (Thuc. i.47.3); but the relationship may rather have been political, connected with Corinth's conflict with Corcyra (below, 276). At least the effect of the friendship was political (Thuc. loc. cit.). The knowledge of Corinthian skills evident in buildings at Thermon and Calydon need not have reached these parts through Corinthian traders (but see below, 150). That the sites of the colonies of the tyrants were sufficiently known to enable cities to be founded here does not show that previous trade had been extensive (above, 92).

dangers of Cape Malea might have dissuaded traders from giving Sicilians an opportunity to buy Attic if the Isthmus had not been easy to cross. Dunbabin suggested that the victory of Attic pottery had very little effect on western trade from Corinth on the ground that the newly fashionable vases were carried in Corinthian vessels;[30] but this is unlikely. There is no reason to exclude Athenian carriers, and once Attic domination was established vessels bound for the west might have come from almost any part of the Aegean to fill a spare corner with Attic vases. Since vessels operating from Lechaeum would otherwise not have used the diolkos, they are less likely candidates than those based east of the Isthmus; the latter would in any case either have to use the diolkos or to round Cape Malea. Mercantile marks on Attic pottery are not known in Corinthian script; but there are signs of heavy Ionian involvement.[31] Johnston has demonstrated that one Sostratus of Aegina dealt extensively in Attic vases in the west;[32] he may have carried them by way of the diolkos.[33] Some Attic may have been taken to the west in Corinthian vessels, but the issue is in any case of very minor significance; trade in pottery had always made up so small a proportion of the total traffic that its elimination affected few but potters.

Our evidence for trade from Cenchreae is far less satisfactory; we have no sign of the extent of operations as we do at Lechaeum. The distribution of Corinthian vases demonstrates that Cenchreae saw some movements; but the volume of trade in pottery was far smaller in the east, and here there is not the same probability that loads which included Corinthian vases also contained other goods produced in the Corinthia; there was sufficient demand for Corinthian almost everywhere in the Aegean to make it worth while to divert to Cenchreae for a batch of vases. It remains probable that a good deal besides vases was carried, for if there was a market for Corinthian goods in the west it was probably no different in the east; but we have no quantitative evidence. Even the study of pottery shows that Corinthian products might turn up in unexpected places, for Athenians preferred rough domestic vessels of some shapes to come from Corinth; such inexplicable preferences may have involved other items too.

For the range of movements from Cenchreae, pottery can yield positive conclusions only for the vases themselves; and even here

---

[30] *Western Greeks*, 242-3. Followed by Finley, *History of Sicily*, 34; Holladay, *Greece and Rome*, xxiv (1977), 48.
[31] Johnston, *Greece and Rome*, xxi (1974), 141, 143; *Trade Marks on Greek Vases*, 2, 52.
[32] *PP* xxvii (1972), 416-23.
[33] See, however, Johnston, *Trade Marks on Greek Vases*, 51.

there are signs that a significant group of finds reached their ultimate destinations from Cenchreae indirectly. On sites in southern Asia Minor and the Levant, together with Cyprus, Corinthian is less common than East Greek wares; the position is much the same in the Black Sea, and the proportion of Corinthian to East Greek in these areas beyond the Aegean is much the same as that of Corinthian to local on most Aegean sites. East Greek vessels were well known in these waters; since Corinthian was in regular use on East Greek sites, it may have been carried to the further east and the Black Sea by East Greek traders, perhaps not directly from Cenchreae but indirectly from their home ports. The proportion of Corinthian to East Greek on these sites leaves little room for vessels which would normally carry a high proportion of Corinthian among their vases; Corinthian craft were not often to be seen outside the Aegean. There is a good deal of Corinthian from Naucratis; but the prime responsibility here may have been Aeginetan rather than Corinthian.[34] Whether Corinthian vessels began to sail out of the Aegean after the early sixth century it is impossible to say in the absence of evidence from Corinthian vases. There may have been some traffic in corn from the Black Sea and/or Egypt to Corinth, and the corn-ships which Xerxes allowed to pass through the Hellespont were bound for Aegina and the Peloponnese (Hdt. vii.147.2–3); but Corinth's corn probably came overwhelmingly from the west.

Evidence for the relative importance of traffic to east and west is difficult to find. Certainly Corinthian vases sold better in the west than elsewhere; but in the Aegean there was competition from local schools, and the known distribution of Corinthian would hardly call for comment if we knew that traffic was heavier from Cenchreae than from Lechaeum. Corinthian trade was probably more heavily concentrated in the west than in the east; but that is rather suggested by common sense than proved by the evidence of pottery.[35] Corinth was better placed than any major maritime city to exploit the western routes, and this remained true even after the construction of the diolkos. Her traders will naturally have concentrated their energies in the west: they will probably have done so far longer than we have the evidence of pottery for. Even this factor, however, might be cancelled out if what Corinth had for sale found a more ready market in the east or (perhaps more important) if the east could better provide what was needed at Corinth; but we can make

---

[34] Boardman, *Greeks Overseas*, 125.

[35] The amphorai from the Punic Amphora House at Corinth come in approximately equal amounts from east and west (Williams, *Hesperia*, xlviii (1979), 118); but it would be hazardous to take this as representative.

no allowance for such factors. At least there was far less loading space at Cenchreae than at Lechaeum.

Other evidence sometimes demonstrates exchanges of one kind or another with various parts of the Mediterranean world. Some momentous developments resulted: in the history of Greek art many of the earliest and most fruitful innovations stemmed from acquaintance with the products of the Near East; and, perhaps most important of all, the origins of the Greek alphabet are to be sought in the same area. None the less, such interchanges cannot be used as evidence for the geographical concentration of Corinthian trade. Only persistent traffic has any importance in this respect; yet while artistic influence may be exerted by imports which have some economic significance in themselves, this is almost always excluded at Corinth by the absence of evidence for imports in any quantity. The establishment of workshops for foreign craftsmen in Corinth would be of some interest; but no such case can be traced.[36]

The case of the alphabet is similar. Greeks first learned to adapt the North-Semitic alphabet for their own use at some place where they shared a settlement with Semites, possibly at Al Mina.[37] The precise manner of its transmission to Corinth remains uncertain, although in view of the confusion of Semitic sibilants shared by all Greek scripts it probably came through a Greek intermediary.[38] The close relationship between the Corinthian and the Cretan, Theran, and Melian scripts makes it probable that one of these islands was the immediate source; but the letters ϕ, χ and ψ (which are not known in these islands) presumably came from elsewhere.[39] A single individual may have been responsible for bringing the alphabet to Corinth; but his journey need not have conformed to the normal patterns of movement to and from Corinth at the time. The date of the arrival remains unclear. Writing may not have been widespread at the time of the foundation of Syracuse, which did not use a Corinthian script;[40] it was probably therefore illiterate in its

---

[36] Dunbabin suggested that a mould of *c*.650, in North Syrian style but Corinthian clay, found in the Potters' Quarter, was made by an eastern visitor; but the presence of a Syrian import at Corinth shows that the mould might have been made from an imported positive (*Greeks and their Eastern Neighbours*, 37).

[37] Jeffery, Local Scripts, 5-12; *Archaic Greece*, 25-6; cf. also Coldstream, *GG* 295-302; Johnston, *BSA* lxx (1975), 167; Snodgrass, *Archaic Greece*, 78-84.

[38] Jeffery, *Local Scripts*, 25-8.

[39] Jeffery, ibid., 119, inclines to the view that Crete was the source, on the ground that Protocorinthian pottery shows affinities with Cretan. The argument is weak; a similar (but equally weak) argument in favour of Thera could be advanced on the grounds that actual Corinthian imports of the relevant period are more frequent there.

[40] The fact that Corcyra did proves nothing either for the date of literacy at Corinth or for that of the foundation of Corcyra (above, 62); see ibid., 18-19.

earliest years. Writing had reached Corinth by *c.*700; that is the date
of the earliest known inscription.[41]

Objects found in Corinth but made elsewhere show the wide range
of contacts Corinth enjoyed; but they are no more significant of
general trends. An Egyptian mirror or a Rhodian vase found in the
Corinthia demonstrates contact of some kind: but nothing is found
in such quantity that we must posit more than casual exchange.[42]
Egyptianizing scarabs appear in their hundreds at Perachora from
perhaps the late eighth to the end of the seventh century, along
with a few other objects of similar composition and Egyptian
appearance. They were not made in Egypt; but their place of origin
remains unclear.[43] The Corinthian finds might have been made at
Corinth; even if they were not, they may have been brought as part
of a very few cargoes.[44]

Much of this evidence points to the Levant; it might be argued
that while no single item may be pressed, the cumulative evidence
has some effect. In particular the alphabet, much of the eastern
influence on Corinthian art, and the Egyptianizing objects found in
large numbers at Perachora might (but must not necessarily) be
referred to Phoenicia; and the presence at Corinth of various proper
names with the root Phoinik-[45] has been taken to imply a Phoenician
influence at Corinth. The argument is strengthened by the concentration of much of the evidence in the late eighth century.[46] The
Phoinik- names cannot be placed chronologically; but influence in
the opposite direction is shown by the Corinthianizing LG pottery
found in the lowest stratum of the Tanith sanctuary at Carthage.

It may prove that this concentration is significant; but present
evidence is against it. The Phoinik- names probably have nothing to
do with Phoenicians, and intensive movements of Phoenicians to
Corinth are almost ruled out by the absence of significant quantities
of finds of Phoenician type; the Corinthian models for the pottery
from Carthage were probably seen in Sicily.[47] Corinthian journeys
to Phoenicia were probably no more frequent. Corinthian is not

[41] The Channel Deposit (above, 96 with n. 4); unless the inscription can be shown to
be incompatible with this date (see ibid., 120-1), it must be dated by its context.
[42] The most fruitful site is Perachora: Payne, *Perachora*, i (metal, terracotta figurines;
but probably many of the latter published as Argive are Corinthian); Dunbabin, *Perachora*, ii.
[43] James in Dunbabin, *Perachora*, ii.461-516.
[44] Cf. Buchner and Boardman, *JdaI* lxxxi (1966), 1-62 (Lyre Player Seals at Pithecusae);
Shefton in Dunbabin, *Perachora*, ii.369 n. 3 (Laconian at Kavalla).
[45] Dow, *AJA* xlvi (1942), 69-72; Wiseman, 10.
[46] Earlier confidence in the importance of Phoenicians before this date was misplaced:
Snodgrass, *Dark Age*, 352; Boardman, *Greeks Overseas*, 37-8. On the possible eastern
connections of sacred prostitution at Corinth, see below, 398-9.
[47] Coldstream, *GGP* 386-7.

known in the Levant before the last years of the eighth century, and
even then the quantity is small. Lack of excavation in eighth-century
levels in Phoenicia hampers enquiry,[48] and positive conclusions are
discouraged by the possibility that there may have been an as yet
undiscovered Corinthian counterpart to Al Mina; but there is no
evidence at present for heavy Corinthian involvement in eastern
traffic at such a range. The concentration of evidence is significant
in showing that eastern influences were stronger than any others
at Corinth; but it remains uncertain whether the Phoenicians were
responsible in every case.[49] Even if they were, that merely indicates
that they had a good deal to offer; not that the routes along which
the influences were transmitted were frequently used.

d. Trade: Mechanisms

There are at least some signs of the range and scale of Corinthian
trade; direct evidence for its mechanisms is almost absent. We know
something of these matters in fourth-century Athens, thanks to
forensic speeches; but our only evidence for Corinth is the brief
passage of Lycurgus which records the shipment of Epirot corn by
Leocrates, and a shipowner mentioned in a fourth-century inscription
from Troezen.[50] The movements revealed by the building accounts
of Epidaurus and Delphi were, if the Athenian pattern is anything
to go by, abnormal; in these cases orders were placed by the consumer, but usually the trader purchased a cargo and went to seek a
market. Before the fifth century, we do not even have comparative
evidence from Athens. Whatever the mechanisms of trade, there were
some constant factors: loading and unloading, transport to harbours,
and perhaps the crewing of vessels will have provided some employment. The greatest difficulties concern the status of the traders
themselves, and especially the means by which they acquired the
goods they carried.

In the earliest period some trade will have been conducted by
producers. In Boeotia *c.*700 Hesiod saw it as possible, if undesirable,
for a farmer to put some of his produce on board his own ship and
risk it at sea for profit (*Erg.* 618–94). Some of the earliest exchanges
for which we have evidence may have been conducted in a similar
fashion; but probably already in Hesiod's time few cargoes made up
in the Corinthia were carried by those who had produced them
(above, 93–4). The most significant evidence from this early period is

[48] Ibid., 388.
[49] Snodgrass, *Dark Age*, 352.
[50] *IG* iv.823, 27.

the rapid success of Corinthian vases in the west in the late eighth century. It is fashionable to draw attention to the difficulty of distinguishing, especially in the early period, between trade and piracy; but while theft can generate imports it can hardly explain exports. The widespread use of Corinthian in the west demonstrates sophisticated two-way traffic, which in turn proves the development of commercial skills. By the late seventh century these skills had extended the scale of Corinthian trade sufficiently to persuade Periander to build the Lechaeum harbour; in the early sixth the strength of these patterns of distribution was enough to delay the victory of Attic over Corinthian in western markets. The speeches made before Athenian courts show that in the fourth century normal practice was for producers to sell to specialist traders;[51] at least there is little doubt of the existence of specialist traders working between Corinth and the west from the late eighth century. Their status remains problematic. The crucial issue is the extent to which a trader was dependent on third parties for his activity. A man who could provide, from his own resources, both a vessel and goods for trade was a man of considerable substance; but if the use of one or both could be acquired indirectly, that would open up opportunities to a far wider range of men.

Even for fourth-century Athens, the evidence from the orators for the relationship between traders and the vessels which carried their goods is not full enough to establish a pattern. Some owned their own vessels, while others hired them and sometimes secured the services of the owner or a third party as ship's captain; but it is impossible to determine which was the commonest practice. In any case, the Corinthian norm may have differed from the Athenian. At an earlier period, there is no direct evidence; but the vocabulary of maritime commerce, which has been subjected to detailed examination by Bravo, indicates that vessels were often owned by persons who did not travel with them.[52] But we have no direct evidence of the Corinthian vocabulary; the practice may have been different there. The central issue, however, is the question of how a trader acquired his cargo. If mechanisms existed at Corinth for the acquisition of goods by men who could not provide them from their own resources, the vessel will hardly have presented a problem.

In fifth- and fourth-century Athens, a good proportion of cargoes were bought on credit. The bottomry loan, made on terms which waived even repayment of capital in case of total loss, was in

[51] Finkelstein, *CP* xxx (1935), 336.
[52] *DHA* iii (1977), 1–59, modifying his earlier discussion in *DHA* i (1974), 111–87.

widespread use; its advantages were great for both parties to the transaction. For the creditor, it provided a source of profit: since the effect of the loan on these terms was to require the creditor to share the risk, rates of interest were relatively high. By the same token, even a trader who could afford to finance himself would have been well advised to prefer credit. In the event of total loss, he would suffer little damage if he could save himself: the bottomry loan was perhaps the nearest the ancient world came to the concept of insurance.[53] We have no evidence for Corinth; even bankers, the pivot of the system in Athens, are not reliably recorded there before the third century.[54] But it would be extremely surprising if traffic at Lechaeum and Cenchreae was not financed in the late fifth and fourth centuries in much the same way as at the contemporary Peiraeus; even if Corinth had to learn from Athens, the advantages for all parties were so great that the lesson cannot have been ignored.

The bottomry loan cannot be traced, even in Athens, much earlier than the last quarter of the fifth century; it is first mentioned, apparently as normal practice, in 421.[55] De Ste Croix has suggested that it may have been evolved to finance the heavy shipments of corn to fifth-century Athens;[56] the guess is plausible, but it is (as he admits) no more than a guess, and the bottomry loan may have had a longer history. Calligas has identified as bottomry loans those which are recorded on a series of lead plaques from Corcyra inscribed *c*.500. Credit was certainly given at Corcyra on a large scale: no preserved total is less than 100 dr., and the largest is 660 dr. There can be no proof that these loans were made in order to finance maritime trade—much less that they took the form of bottomry loans; but at least their find spot—in a temple near the harbour at Corcyra—encourages the conjecture.[57] If it is right, the Corinthian connections of Corcyra are significant: there is no more likely centre in the archaic world for the development. But since there is no specific evidence, the question of the means by which cargoes were acquired in archaic Corinthian trade must be approached in other ways.

There has recently been a strong tendency to emphasize the close dependence of archaic trade upon the landowning aristocracy.[58] But a careful distinction must be made between professional trade

[53] See esp. de Ste Croix, 'Ancient Greek and Roman Maritime Loans'.
[54] *SIG*³ 1075. For some false trails, see Bogaert, *Banques et banquiers*, 94-6.
[55] Harvey, *ZPE* xxiii (1976), 231-3.
[56] 'Ancient Greek and Roman Maritime Loans', 44.
[57] *BSA* lxvi (1971), 79-94.
[58] Cf. Bravo (above, 149 n. 52); Mele, *Prexis ed emporie*, is a good deal more extreme.

and the activities of aristocrats who voyaged abroad for different but sometimes related purposes.[59] We hear of a number of such individuals in the archaic period: Solon sailed with his own produce to finance a journey of enquiry, θεωρία, while Sappho's brother Charaxus disposed of his (presumably) wine in Egypt and became infatuated there.[60] We even have a Corinthian example in Demaratus the Bacchiad (above, 74). A pattern of mingling piracy with peaceful exchange, raids with the giving and receiving of gifts, is apparent in the epic, and could no doubt be found at Corinth as elsewhere.[61] The earliest exchanges for which we have evidence, from Delphi through Ithaca to Vitsa Zagoriou and Etruria, may well have been made in this way. No doubt Demaratus had his successors in the later seventh and sixth centuries. We do not hear of them; but contacts at this level of society provide the most likely explanation of the spread of knowledge of Corinthian architecture in north-west Greece in the later seventh century.

The scale and character of Corinthian trade from the late eighth century shows that not all exchanges were made by these means. No aristocrat would stow vases for commercial exchange even in a spare corner in his vessel; and the development of commercial expertise and the considerable scale of Corinthian trade speak strongly in favour of more sophisticated mechanisms. There remains, however, a powerful argument in favour of the dependence of even the more professional type of commerce upon the landowning aristocracy: only they could provide the capital required. Once coinage came to be used for the purpose of providing credit for maritime commerce, liquid capital could be invested. But at an early period, when land was the basis of wealth and its produce the main item of export, only substantial landowners could possess the necessary capital. Small-scale ventures might be undertaken in their own vessels by producers who sought to dispose of an insubstantial surplus, as Hesiod attests; but for trade on a greater scale the resources possessed by wealthy landowners were required. They would not normally travel in person; the contempt for this kind of trading activity which screams from the pages of fifth- and fourth-century literature is already apparent in the epic (*Od.* viii.158–64). But they might dispose of their own surplus by entrusting it, along with a vessel in which to carry it, to dependants.[62]

---

[59] Compare the distinction made by Murray, *Early Greece*, 69–70, between long- and short-haul trading; but the difference is not so simple, since professional trade took pottery to the west (below).

[60] Ar. *Ath. Pol.* 11.1; Strabo 808 (cf. Hdt. ii.135).

[61] Bravo, *DHA* iii (1977), 24; Humphreys, *Anthropology and the Greeks*, 165, 167.

Some such pattern may well have been behind the first organized commercial voyages from Corinth; but the stage of direct dependence on the landed aristocracy was probably soon passed. It is not likely that those men concerned themselves with anything but the disposal of their own agricultural surplus and the acquisition in exchange of items to support their ostentation at home; and the success of Corinthian vases in the west suggests that other factors were involved from an early date. Those who traded the vases may have travelled as dependants of wealthier men; but they could exchange vases on their own account. That, and similar exchanges of other items, may have been the origin of operations that were independent of the wealthy;[63] the scale and, by before the end of the seventh century at the latest, the stability of the patterns of Corinthian trade were a strong encouragement to both parties to develop mechanisms which would increase that independence. For the trader, that would improve his chances of success; but there were equal advantages for the wealthy. To engage in trade through dependants might maximize the return; but it would also increase the risk, both of loss and of taint by association.

It is impossible to prove that the direct dependence of Corinthian trade on the wealthy was broken relatively early; but the link can only have been severed by means of some form of credit which fixed the rate of return to the creditor before the voyage was undertaken. That would give the trader sufficient independence to allow him to benefit from initiative. We have no evidence; but mechanisms are not difficult to imagine.[64] Even though coins were not introduced for this reason (below, 170-2), they could have been so used from an early date, as they were later. Even before the first coins, credit for maritime commerce may well have been available. The introduction of coinage implies that silver bullion had a generally accepted exchange value; bullion could have performed the same function as coins did later. There is a persistent tradition that iron spits were employed as currency before coins; it is not clear whether such a use was known at Corinth, but some other item may have performed a similar role. Even credit in the commodity to be traded is possible. What was crucial for the independence of the trader was that the loan was made on fixed terms which gave him the opportunity for enterprise. If his intention was to carry wine to Sicily, to take a loan

[62] Bravo (above, 149 n. 52); Humphreys, *Anthropology and the Greeks*, 166-7; Snodgrass, *Archaic Greece*, 137.

[63] Contrast Bravo, *DHA* iii (1977), 25; that aristocrats exported vases—or any other such item—seems to me highly improbable.

[64] Cf. ibid., 3.

of fifty jars of wine would offer exactly that flexibility if he undertook to repay a stipulated amount of some other commodity, whether specified by himself or by the creditor. Such a transaction would involve no greater risk for either debtor or creditor than a loan made in coin at a later period; indeed, for the creditor it might involve less. There was no opportunity for fraud between the handing-over of the loan and the making-up of the cargo;[65] more importantly, the loan might be secured on landed property.[66] Greed might have provided a large part of the motivation of creditors in such transactions. The fact that traders were citizens (below, 159–63), who would not fail to return to Corinth, would increase the confidence of creditors.

Since the very existence of maritime credit cannot be demonstrated for the archaic period, its character can hardly be accurately defined. Such loans will usually, I take it, have been secured in some way, perhaps by the land, the produce, or even the person of the trader: he would not necessarily have lived by trade alone. What the creditor would take as security will have determined how wide a range of persons could undertake trading voyages. In fourth-century Athens, loans were often secured on the return cargo. That was perhaps partly because traders were usually metics or foreigners who could offer no landed security—at least in Attica. Traders from Corinth were more often citizens and might be able to offer more attractive security; but that does not exclude the possibility that some loans were secured on the return cargo once Corinthian trade had developed some stability. The essential principle of the bottomry loan—the waiving of repayment in the event of loss at sea—may already have been known to the seventh century: we hear of it only at a time when credit was given in the form of coin, but it is not incompatible with an earlier age, at least when the patterns of trade were sufficiently established to give confidence.

The character of vessels used for trade before the mid-sixth century is difficult to determine. Vessels which appear on eighth-century vases were driven mainly by oars. The first clear signs of purpose-built merchant ships are not before the late sixth century,[67] but they had probably then existed for a good deal longer. The vessel shown in Figure 15, probably of the late seventh century, appears to have proportions very like those of the rounded merchantman, and its sail is prominent; no oar-ports are shown. Corinth, with her skilled carpenters and her considerable trade, is as likely a place

---

[65] Contrast the allegations in Ps.-Dem. xxxv. 19–21.

[66] Bravo attempts unconvincingly to trace such a loan in Theog. 1197–1202.

[67] Humphreys, *Anthropology and the Greeks*, 168–9.

as any for the development of sail-driven merchant craft; in the seventh century, they were not necessarily large. The first design may have been for a successful independent trader: at least such a man was more likely than any other to seek the advantages of greater carrying capacity and smaller crew. A man of landed wealth might be more capable of providing the necessary capital; but he would also be less likely to feel the need. No doubt some trade continued to be conducted in oared vessels, which would need a larger crew; but they did possess sails, and not all oars would have to be manned on a trading voyage. There is good evidence that more than one trader might use the same vessel (whether purpose-built or not). The word ἔμπορος, which came to mean 'trader', did so after passing through a stage at which it signified a man who travelled on a ship but did not belong to its complement;[68] the history of the word implies traders who hired space on the vessels of others. There were probably some traders working from Corinth who owned their own specialized vessels by the late seventh century; those who did not will have found little difficulty in hiring a whole vessel or space on one if they were able to acquire a cargo to carry.

Any account of the mechanisms of trade in the archaic period must inevitably be conjectural;[69] but there are powerful arguments for placing the development of an independent status for traders, at least at Corinth, relatively early.[70] The skills which were responsible for the establishment and maintenance of a market for Corinthian vases for a century and a half, and for the expansion of trade from Lechaeum to such an extent that Periander built his harbour there, are more likely to have been developed by independent men than by those who depended on the wealthy. Exports of pottery, perfume, and textiles were of little or no interest to the wealthy; and perhaps above all, the close association of the wealthy with trade on such a scale as the hypothesis of dependence demands is at variance with all we know of that class.[71] If Corinthian aristocrats were directly responsible for Corinthian trade—even though they did not travel in person—either they were far more flexible than their successors in the classical period or their successors were an exception among their contemporaries. Those who traded from Corinth may

[68] Bravo, *DHA* iii (1977), 30.
[69] Humphreys, *Anthropology and the Greeks*, 169.
[70] Similar arguments might, however, be applied to Aegina and parts of the eastern Aegean.
[71] This would not of course preclude association in individual cases. Even at Athens, some such transaction is probably implied by Lys. xxxii.24–5 (late fifth century: Bravo, *DHA* iii (1977), 3–4), even though the evidence of Isoc. vii.31–2 adduced by Bravo (ibid., 4–5) is less persuasive.

have been of greater substance than the metics who can be traced at Athens in the fourth century, if creditors insisted on land or its produce as security; this archaic pattern probably continued later and encouraged a greater citizen involvement in Corinthian than in Athenian trade (below, 159-63). But it is most unlikely that trade soiled more than a few men of any pretensions.

e.   Agriculture and the Economy

The range of opportunities offered at Corinth was greater, for a longer period, than anywhere else in the Greek world. With respect to the diversification of her economy, Corinth was in the first rank from at least the late eighth century to the end of the fourth and beyond. No doubt Corinth was overhauled by Athens during the fifth century; but by then the pattern of the Corinthian economy had been established for nearly two centuries. But none of this should lead us to underestimate the importance of the role of agriculture. Even in fourth-century Athens, it played a far more significant part than any other single activity, and probably accounted for a greater proportion of the economy than all others put to-gether.[72] The comparison with Athens alone creates a strong case for a similar conclusion for Corinth; more detailed arguments point in the same direction.

Many other economic activities at Corinth relied on the produce of the land. Probably the most significant export was agricultural surplus: certainly it was this which fuelled a substantial proportion of Corinthian trade from the earliest times, and even the export of textiles depended on the wool of Corinthian sheep. In the fifth and fourth centuries, hardly less than half of the population consumed corn produced within the territory. If we add other produce, used both for internal consumption and for export, perhaps three-quarters of the total economy will have depended, directly or indirectly, upon the fruits of the Corinthian soil, and the proportion may well have been even higher.

The proportion of Corinthians who supported themselves to some extent from the produce of their own plots was probably equally high. In the eighth century, the legislation of Pheidon the Bacchiad provided that each Corinthian citizen should have his own plot (above, 63-5). It is not clear whether the intention was also for the number of citizens and plots to remain constant in the future; even if it was, there was presumably an increase subsequently. The

[72] Cf. Jones, *Athenian Democracy*, 90-1, summarizing his previous discussion.

requirement that all citizens should own land was probably not maintained until the end of the fourth century; but it is unlikely that more than a very small proportion was entirely without land. Many of the non-agricultural activities which can be traced were best undertaken casually, by those who normally worked their own plots, at times when there was little to do on the land: quarrying, transport by land, loading and unloading vessels at Lechaeum or Cenchreae, manning the diolkos, and perhaps much of the skilled work in building would not provide sufficient reliable employment for individuals who had no other means of support. Other skills—perhaps especially pottery and metalwork—could be depended upon more permanently; but the proportion of the population dependent on them was always small. Even trade, which necessitated absence from the Corinthia for long periods, did not inevitably exclude its practitioners from relying in part on their own plots. Voyages undertaken when work in the fields was slack would allow ample room for enterprise. A trader who could afford a slave or who had an adult son might use the whole of the sailing season without leaving his plot to suffer; conversely, the son might travel before coming into his inheritance.[73] Such activities in fifth- and fourth-century Athens were as a rule not undertaken by citizens, but there was greater citizen involvement at Corinth (below, 159–63). No citizen would be without land if he could retain it; the different opportunities available at Corinth enabled citizens to continue to support themselves on plots which elsewhere might have proved insufficient.

Corinthian agriculture was probably directly affected by the diversification of other aspects of the economy. No doubt in early times each family hoped to be self-sufficient on its plot. We have no evidence for the subsequent development of specialization in agriculture, and the ideal of self-sufficiency, although it is mainly expressed in literature which reflects the views of the higher ranks of society, may have acted as a powerful brake; but it is difficult to imagine that concentration on crops which were particularly suited to the character of an individual plot or to the general nature of the Corinthian economy was resolutely resisted. The regularity of corn imports might encourage the planting of (for example) corn-land with vines to produce wine for exchange against imported corn. Such changes were presumably first made on the larger estates, with their greater reserves of capital and labour and their wider margin of safety; but they were not precluded on smaller plots.

[73] Cf. Humphreys, *Anthropology and the Greeks*, 168; there was probably, however, more regularity in the Corinthian pattern.

A trader who had seen the realities of the market at first hand might be among the first to recognize the potential of his plot: his enterprise might give him both the capital and the labour required for the change if he could purchase a slave to tend his vines. A good harvest, a single successful trading venture, or even a few weeks of short rations might provide a more ordinary farmer with sufficient capital to invest in fruit- or olive-trees to plant in next year's fallow; the returns would not be immediate, but they would eventually be tangible.

Population patterns in the Corinthia offer further support for the vitality of Corinthian agriculture. The only sites which have been seriously investigated are Corinth itself and some of the sanctuaries elsewhere; but chance finds and surface evidence indicate that the population was widely distributed over the Corinthia. Corinth was the political centre; but there were large settlements elsewhere, populated by those who cultivated the surrounding territory. Chance finds of Geometric graves are perhaps not representative; none the less, they have been made in precisely those parts of the Corinthia in which distinct settlements could be expected. It is difficult to be sure whether the EG grave at Mavrospelaies near the North Cemetery is to be connected with the settlement at Corinth itself or with some other, perhaps at Cheliotoumylos;[74] if the latter, the place was so close to Corinth that it was not heavily occupied later. But other Geometric finds, at Crommyon and Tenea, are from sites which held a substantial population later, while the graves from Athikia are followed by settlement into the classical period.[75]

Only extent of sherd-scatter can indicate the relative importance of settlements in the Corinthia; but it provides instructive evidence. Each of the substantial sites, judged by this criterion, is to be found in an easily defined block of territory.[76] Crommyon on the Saronic Gulf coast beyond the Isthmus, Cromna between Oneion and the Isthmus, Corinth itself above the eastern and Agios Charalambos the western part of the coastal plain, Tenea in the upper Leukon Valley, and Solygeia between Oneion and the mountains of the south-east Corinthia all show evidence of habitation over a wide area. There are few parts of the Corinthia with any agricultural potential which are not within a radius of well under 5 km. from one of these centres, although one or two such sites perhaps remain to be discovered

[74] Lawrence, *Hesperia*, xxxiii (1964), 89–91; cf. Coldstream, *GGP* 92.
[75] Crommyon: above, 48. Tenea: Charitonides, *AJA* lix (1955), 125–8. Athikia: Lawrence, *Hesperia*, xxxiii (1964), 91–3; Weinberg, 19; Charitonides, *AJA* lxi (1957), 169–71. For chronology, see Coldstream, *GGP* 94.
[76] For all the details, see above, 19–28.

immediately beyond the Isthmus: Sidous is placed in this region by our literary sources but has not yet been identified, and there may have been a similar settlement at or near Loutraki (Therma). There were smaller villages in the less attractive regions of the south-east Corinthia and the Peiraeum.

This evidence is inadequate to provide a satisfactory basis for discussion of the economic relationship between Corinth and its territory; it does not allow even an estimate of the proportion of the population which lived at Corinth. Most skilled manufacturing work was presumably undertaken in Corinth unless constraints were imposed, as on the potters who worked in the Potters' Quarter, by the availability of raw materials (above, 79); but that would not exclude small workshops in the larger villages which served local needs. There is even some positive evidence for dyeing establishments outside Corinth, although in each case the date is probably after the fourth century: that at Tenea was in what appears to have been the largest centre of population outside Corinth and also close to the mountain pastures of the south-east Corinthia, while that on the Rachi may have been related in some way to the sanctuary at Isthmia (above, 119–20). Metalwork, on the other hand, was perhaps undertaken exclusively at Corinth, where it can be traced in the archaeological record from the seventh century; once mechanisms for the delivery of the heavy raw material to Corinth had been devised, it was easier for consumers to transport their own purchases from the workshop.[77] Many of the opportunities for casual employment were available not at Corinth but in the quarries or at Lechaeum, Cenchreae, or the diolkos; but all these were within easy reach of the city itself. Corinth, along with Lechaeum and to a lesser extent Cenchreae, presumably acted as a centre for the distribution of imported goods; but bulk purchases of goods for export might be made direct from producers—and if in the early period trade was financed by credit in kind the central market might play no part at all, at least in exports. Traders would work from Corinth or at any rate from her ports; but if they also owned plots from which they derived part of their support they would presumably live near to them.

The role of the city in the economy of the Corinthia is irrecoverable; but at least one conclusion is certain. A substantial proportion of the inhabitants of the Corinthia lived outside Corinth, and they did so because that gave them more convenient access to the fields from which they derived at least part of their livelihood. The

[77] Cf. Snodgrass, *Archaic Greece*, 139–40.

overwhelming importance of agriculture in the Corinthian economy
has often gone unrecognized because of the paucity of direct evidence
for it and the much greater extent of evidence for other activity,
both in the total evidence for the Corinthia and in relation to the
evidence for similar activity elsewhere in Greece. Corinth is often
designated as a 'trading' or an 'industrial' city;[78] most extreme is
the statement of Kagan, that 'by the sixth century Corinth had
become predominantly a commercial state.'[79] The truth is different.
The Corinthian economy was more highly diversified for a longer
period than any other in the Greek world; even so, it still followed
the universal rule of the ancient world that agriculture was dominant.

[78] e.g. Busolt, *Griechische Geschichte*, i.631; *Staatskunde*, i.182; cf. Bengston, 225.
[79] *Politics and Policy*, 20; cf. also *AJP* lxxxi (1960), 294.

XI.   Citizens, Metics, Foreigners, and Slaves

I have attempted to trace something of the economy of the Corinthia; but it is a quite different task to trace the work that was undertaken by Corinthian citizens. The question of slave involvement can—regrettably—be rapidly dismissed; not because it is of small importance, but because we have not a scrap of evidence: there is no hope of reaching even an approximate answer. From a relatively early period some production—of pots and perhaps other items—may have been undertaken by slaves. The nature of production in specialist establishments was well suited to them, for they could be employed permanently; whether they were actually employed is not known. Slaves are less likely to have been kept solely for agricultural work, which was more seasonal; but many household slaves will no doubt have helped in the fields when there was much work to be done, and some larger estates may have been able to find enough work to make the keeping of slaves worth while. The total slave population of the Corinthia is unknown (below, 165, 168).

It is hardly to be doubted that the sector of the Corinthian economy in which metics and foreigners were most heavily involved was trade. I have written above of Corinthian trade in its broadest sense, of trade conducted to and from the Corinthia; but whether it was conducted by Corinthians is a quite different matter. In fourth-century Athens, not only was much trade in the hands of metics, but much was in those of foreigners whose normal residence (in so far as they had one, being engaged in a wandering profession) was elsewhere. The bankers and shipowners and captains were as variable. We have almost no evidence for Corinth; it is probably mere coincidence that the only specific evidence known to me of normal trading activity at Corinth relates to Leocrates, the Athenian who was alleged to have traded corn from Epirus to Corinth while registered as a metic at Megara (above, 129).

In archaic times our only direct evidence is from the pottery trade. The establishment of markets for Corinthian must be attributed to Corinthian potters and merchants. It is hardly likely that foreigners came to Corinth in the eighth century to secure vases for export after scanning Greece and concluding that Corinth was the most suitable site for such an enterprise. The initial impetus must have been almost exclusively Corinthian; but once the markets had been established, non-Corinthians may have followed. None the less, a high proportion of merchants' marks found on Corinthian vases exhibits specifically Corinthian script, and hardly any are positively not Corinthian. The sample of marks is small, and it cannot demonstrate firm conclusions; but if it shows anything, it is that it was probably Corinthians who carried most vases.[1] If so, the same will have been true of other items carried from Lechaeum.

The men who conducted the eastern trade will have been far more variable. Traders from many states in the Aegean, from Rhodes to Aegina, may often have called at Cenchreae to pick up vases and probably other items too. Aeginetans may have been especially important. They had a reputation as traders; since they used Corinthian almost exclusively at home in the seventh century, they may have been responsible for carrying almost every Corinthian vase which reached sites on the Saronic Gulf and beyond, and many other Corinthian products besides.[2] I do not mean to assert positively that Aeginetans were so heavily involved; merely to show that there is no hope of identifying the hands in which eastern movements from Cenchreae were concentrated. Brann has suggested that Corinthian vessels were responsible for carrying the great majority of ceramic imports—not only Corinthian—which reached Athens from *c*.725, and even that they carried olive oil away from Attica;[3] but this picture of the domination of Athenian and even general Aegean trade by Corinthians goes far beyond both evidence and probability. Aeginetan vessels are just as likely as Corinthian, and indeed imports were probably not brought by vessels from any one centre in particular. Corinthian imports to Athens—or to any other site east of the Isthmus—can only suggest that the vessel which brought them had called at Cenchreae: there is no means of identifying the origin of the vessel. There are even indications that some of the vases may have reached their destinations indirectly (above, 143-4).

It would be excessive to deny, merely on the ground that the origins of traders cannot be proved, that Corinthian citizens were extensively involved in Corinthian trade. The balance may perhaps be redressed by consideration of the case of the diolkos. Movements

---

[1] Johnston, *Greece and Rome*, xxi (1974), 141; cf., however, *BSA* lxviii (1973), 185-8. See now further Johnston, *Trade Marks on Greek Vases*, 234-5.

[2] For foreign, perhaps especially Aeginetan, involvement in trade in Attic vases, see above, 143.

[3] *Agora*, viii. 27-8.

which used Periander's installation must almost all have begun outside the Corinthia; but just as it is dangerous to suppose that all movements from Cenchreae were in Corinthian hands, so we may not assume that all traffic which used the diolkos was the responsibility of non-Corinthians.[4] It would not accord with normal Greek practice if Corinthians were given preferential treatment in the matter of dues payable at the Isthmus; but some of the Corinthians engaged in western trade might have made up part of their cargoes bound for the west in the Aegean and crossed the Isthmus at the diolkos.

In general, the proportion of Corinthians involved in Corinthian trade was probably higher, even in the fourth century, than in the Athenian case. Since Corinthian trade was among the earliest to develop, Corinthians were almost exclusively responsible for it in the eighth century. At least well into the sixth the number of foreigners who engaged in trade to and from Corinth probably remained small—not so much because Corinth did not provide attractive opportunities as because social mobility was not yet sufficiently developed in other parts of the Greek world to enable many foreigners to come to Corinth. No doubt the proportion of foreigners and metics increased with time, but it probably never reached the same level as in Athens. One reason for the heavy involvement of foreigners in classical Athenian trade was that Athens offered business, and in this respect Corinth was similar from at least the seventh century; but another factor in Athens was that the political structure of the Athenian Empire encouraged the whole Aegean to look to Athens, and nothing similar operated at Corinth. A further factor may have been the very speed of the growth in Athenian trade in this broad sense, which depended on the rapid increase in Athenian population, itself related to political developments in the Aegean. Athenian trade grew so quickly that it could perhaps not be supported by Athenians alone;[5] Corinthian development was more gradual. For these reasons, foreign participation in Corinthian trade, at least in the archaic period, must have been much less extensive than in classical Athens. That, of itself, will have created a momentum which may have had an effect into the fourth century; and in addition, Athens exerted a greater attraction than Corinth after the mid-fifth century at the latest. That was no doubt fortunate for those Corinthians who supported themselves partly by trade; they had lived with plots

---

[4] Contrast Cook, *JHS* xcix (1979), 152-3.

[5] Davies, *Democracy and Classical Greece*, 99-11; Jones, *Athenian Democracy*, 8-9, 161-80; Meiggs, *Athenian Empire*, 262-5.

too small to support them in the archaic period, and effective foreign competition would have left them with no means of survival.

A similar conclusion is probable for other sectors of the Corinthian economy. Unless Corinth was quite exceptional, the ownership of the means of production was heavily concentrated in Corinthian hands: the right to own land and property was reserved for citizens. Athens was presumably exceptional in granting it to—very few— privileged foreigners; Corinth may not have done so at all. Thus all the agricultural produce of the Corinthia was probably grown on land owned by citizens; and before the introduction of coinage, all credit in the form of agricultural produce—which formed the basis of a significant proportion of Corinthian trade—could only have been given by Corinthians. Bullion or—later—coins might have been lent by others to finance trade; we have no means of telling to what extent this was done, but at least by the fifth century Corinth may have been as attractive a city for foreigners to make this form of investment in as Athens, where this vital role was played more by foreigners and metics than by citizens.[6]

The land and buildings on and in which all other forms of production were carried on will have been owned by Corinthians. The fourth-century Athenian evidence demonstrates that the legal restriction on ownership of property did not prevent metics from owning large businesses in non-agricultural production; but, if our evidence is at all representative, it shows that citizens were extensively involved too.[7] At a lower level, however, there were no legal restrictions on metics and foreigners: they were as free to sell their skills and their labour or to lend money as any Athenian citizen; but we have no evidence for Corinth. It is not even formally certain that Corinth registered metics and specified rights and duties for them; but that is probable on general grounds.[8] It is unlikely that citizen involvement was any less extensive at Corinth than at Athens: the legal restrictions on metics and foreigners will hardly have been fewer in Corinth, and they may have been more numerous. The Athenian pattern provides a maximum for the participation of non-citizens which was probably not reached at Corinth. Most developments from the eighth to the sixth century were, I take it, initiated by citizens, for Corinth was in most fields ahead of or at least contemporary with her neighbours: most advances were stimulated

[6] Jones, *Athenian Democracy*, 91 with 152 n. 77.
[7] Ibid., 91, 152-3 n. 78.
[8] At Xen. *Hell.* iv.4.6, pro-Spartan Corinthians complain that under the 'union' of 392 they have no more rights in their own city than mere metics (below, 357). This cannot prove formal registration.

internally. How quickly foreigners came to Corinth to practise the same skills we cannot say; in Athens the names of those active in making and painting vases indicate heavy foreign, and even slave, involvement, but we know all too few names of Corinthian potters. It is safe to guess that foreign participation in crafts at Corinth increased with time; but although we have no direct evidence, citizens were probably always more significantly involved than at Athens.

One factor determining the proportion of citizen participation was the extent to which others came to Corinth to seek employment or profit; this cannot be quantified. But another factor was the attitudes to such activity among Corinthians; here a fascinating aside of Herodotus offers considerable assistance. He remarks (ii.167.2) that of all Greeks the Corinthians despised craftsmen (χειροτέχναι) the least. It is difficult to determine the nature of his evidence. It may have been a matter of law: that craftsmen at Corinth were free from some formal restriction which encumbered those of other states. But such a formal disability is likely to have been the exception rather than the rule, and it is not easy to see why Herodotus remarked on the case of Corinth when it can hardly have been unique. It would fit better with Herodotus' non-legal interests if his view resulted from a real and striking difference in social attitudes; this would be exactly the kind of observation he—in contrast to the narrower Thucydides—might make. We should conclude, in particular, that even the highest reaches of Corinthian society were markedly less hostile towards craftsmen than their counterparts in other cities; for in view both of Herodotus' own class and of his attitude towards the Corinthian tyranny he must have gained his Corinthian information from men of the highest standing. It must be emphasized that his expression is negative in form: craftsmen were held in less dishonour at Corinth than elsewhere. The implication is that dishonour still attached, at least in the best circles, to those who practised a craft; it was only that Corinthians felt less strongly about it than others.

Whatever the reasons for this exceptionally liberal attitude, there can be little doubt that its existence encouraged a greater citizen participation in crafts than elsewhere. Indeed, the attitude may well have been determined by the fact that more Corinthian citizens were craftsmen than was normal; and this would fit extremely well with the most probable (if wholly speculative) account of the development of crafts in the Corinthia. Corinth was among the earliest states in which sophisticated skills were practised on a large scale. Since most of the men who introduced them were Corinthians, that will have set a pattern for the future both in attitudes and in participation. Corinthian craftsmen would not only teach their skills to slaves but also to their sons. Corinth was probably therefore exceptional not only in the amount of non-agricultural employment which she could provide, but also in the high degree of citizen involvement in such activity. Other states, where the development of skills was both slower and later, had more room for foreign and slave participation; and this was both a cause and an effect of their more hostile attitude to craftsmen in general. Herodotus made his observation in the second half of the fifth century, and it is not clear whether the Corinthian attitude was maintained in the fourth; that century produced no Herodotus.

XII. Population

Only very broad estimates of the population of the Corinthia can be made. It is at least clear that the population was too great for resources before the foundation of Corcyra and Syracuse. There are no further indications of population trends; but we do have evidence which covers much of the fifth and fourth centuries.[1] The only source which explicitly claims to give a number for any population group in the Corinthia must be rejected: Athenaeus quotes Timaeus for a total of 460,000 slaves, but the figure is impossibly high and cannot be satisfactorily replaced.[2] Our fullest information concerns Corinthian hoplite contingents from the Persian Wars to the expedition of Timoleon to Sicily: a period of nearly a century and a half. There is no good reason to doubt Herodotus (ix.28.3) when he gives a total of 5,000 Corinthian hoplites at Plataea. All figures for subsequent campaigns are smaller. This has been taken to demonstrate that the total number of Corinthians possessing the hoplite census fell significantly after 479;[3] but such a conclusion is too simple. The figures for occasions when anything approaching a full levy is possible[4] are as follows: 3,000 hoplites—along with thirty ships—prepared for the Leucimme campaign, although only 2,000 seem actually to have been sent;[5] 2,700 to serve under Brasidas at Megara in 424; 2,000 in Boeotia after Delium and for the Spartan invasion of the Argolid in 418; 3,000 at the Nemea in 394; and 2,000 hoplites,

[1] For earlier estimates, see Beloch, *Bevölkerung*, 119-21 (cf. *Griechische Geschichte*, iii.1.275-6); Sakellariou and Faraklas, 83-7. Cf. also Wiseman, 10-12 (considerably over-estimated).
[2] *FGH* 566 F 5. Simple emendation in the text of Athenaeus is impossible: Gomme, *JHS* lxvi (1946), 128; esp. Westermann, *HSCP* Suppl. i (1941), 451-70 = Finley (ed.), *Slavery in Classical Antiquity*, 73-92. Athenaeus (272 B) quotes a Delphic oracle which described the Corinthians as χοινικομέτραι (corn-measurers), and explains it by the large number of slaves at Corinth for whom corn had to be measured out. The true meaning might be interesting for a number of Corinthian issues, but cannot be recovered.
[3] Cf. esp. Griffith, *Historia*, i (1950), 240-1; Kagan, *PP* xvi (1961), 335-7; de Ste Croix, 334-5. Beloch, on the other hand, typically preferred to doubt Herodotus' accuracy: *Bevölkerung*, 119.
[4] Thus I exclude (e.g.) the force sent to Potidaea in 432.
[5] There is a discrepancy between Thuc. i.27.2 and 29.1. Gomme (*HCT* i.163-4) argues that one of the figures must be corrupt; this is unnecessary, though possible. In view of the figures for occasions soon after Leucimme, only 3,000 can have been anything like a full levy.

200 cavalry, and ten ships for the reinforcements sent to Timoleon in Sicily.[6] When the circumstances of the campaigns are taken into account, these figures imply a remarkably uniform total for the whole period.

At the time of Plataea, presumably the whole hoplite force, including those younger and older than the normal serving ages, was called out. On all subsequent occasions, however, it would have been unexpected for the Corinthians to commit every available man whatever his age. The only possibly significant comparison is between the 5,000 at Plataea and the 3,000 on the Leucimme campaign. Old men and boys will account for some of the difference, and some of the colonists sent to Epidamnus (Thuc. i.26.1, 27.1) may have been Corinthians; but a disparity perhaps remains. It may not be significant, for we might have expected a stronger commitment at Plataea than for Leucimme, and fewer triremes may have been manned for Mycale at the same time as Plataea than for Leucimme; the vital requirement in 479 was for the defeat of Mardonius. But it is possible that the Leucimme figures reflect casualties suffered during the First Peloponnesian War.[7] If so, the deficiency had been all but made up within a decade, for in 424 the full levy cannot have fallen far short of 5,000. The 2,700 troops sent to help Brasidas were not the only hoplites in service: there were presumably still 500 on garrison duty in the north-west as there had been in 425 (Thuc. iv.42.3); over 200 Corinthians had been killed during Nicias' invasion (Thuc. iv.44.6), and the old men and boys will account for the rest. The force of 2,000, presumably a two-thirds levy, which arrived in Boeotia after Delium will have been affected by the same considerations, while those who invaded the Argolid in 418 may have been fewer than a full two-thirds call-out for political reasons (below, 330).

A force of 3,000 Corinthians at the Nemea has been thought to be small for a battle fought in Corinthian territory; but it is precisely for such a battle that we should have expected the old men and boys, and perhaps others too, to be left behind to defend the city in case of defeat. Both when Myronides defended the Megarid against Corinthian attack in the First Peloponnesian War and when Nicias invaded the Corinthia in 425, at least the old men remained at Corinth;[8] the threat to the city was far greater in 394. This factor alone might explain why only 3,000 of a total hoplite force of 5,000 engaged at the Nemea; but political considerations probably

[6] Thuc. iv.70.1, 100.1; v.57.2; Xen. *Hell.* iv.2.17; Plut. *Timol.* 16.3 with Diod. xvi.69.4.
[7] Cf. de Ste Croix, 344.
[8] Thuc. i.105.3–106.2; iv.44.4.

also played a part. There was a strong pro-Spartan faction at the time, and the fact that the Corinthians in the city at first refused to admit the defeated army demonstrates that sympathy for Sparta was strong among those who had remained behind;[9] some Corinthians who were called up for the Nemea may have declined to turn out. The figures for the reinforcements sent to Timoleon are remarkably high: 2,000 hoplites, 200 cavalry, and ten ships is an enormous force for a campaign of unknown length so far from home. A state which could send so great a force might well be expected to have had a full hoplite levy, including all age-groups, of well over 5,000. Such an argument is necessarily imprecise, and some (or indeed all) of the force may have been mercenaries; but the figures we have afford no evidence that Corinth's hoplite strength diminished seriously between Plataea and the 340s. The most plausible interpretation of them suggests that it remained much the same throughout the period, though the First Peloponnesian War may have caused a temporary decline.

The only evidence for other sections of the Corinthian population is the figures preserved for Corinthian fleets; but we have them only for the fifth century. Corinth provided forty vessels for both Artemisium and Salamis (below, 254); the figures for the Corcyra affair and the Archidamian War are more variable, but it is unlikely that Corinth was able to put to sea many more than forty triremes from her own resources alone.[10] More than thirty-five were at sea at one time during the Sicilian Expedition;[11] during the Ionian War it was probably rare for Corinth to have anything like as many as forty triremes in service, but this reflects rather the fact that fleets were now at sea for long periods than a reduction in capacity. It seems that for the whole of the fifth century Corinth could man forty triremes; but more than that could only be manned with difficulty.[12] Two hundred rowers per vessel gives a total of 8,000; some, but presumably not many, may not have come from Corinth. There is no means of telling what proportion of the 8,000 were citizens, what metics, and what slaves. The use of slave rowers in contemporary fleets is known at Corcyra, and metics served at Athens; 8,000 will therefore be a maximum for Corinthian

---

[9] The old men, who will have been detailed *en bloc* to defend the city, may have been more favourable to the Spartans, with whom they had fought the long Peloponnesian War.

[10] Below, 430. Ninety were manned for Sybota, but certainly not with Corinthians alone.

[11] Ten in Sicily under Gylippus and over twenty-five in the Gulf under Polyanthes: below, 332-3.

[12] The limit of forty might have been imposed by the availability either of men or vessels; but Corinth was not short of the latter.

rowers.[13] If the same age-limits were applied to service in the fleet as to hoplite service (and they may well not have been) the maximum for Corinthians below the hoplite census will be raised to perhaps 10,000. These figures may be a great deal higher than the actual citizen population; but we may conclude that the proportion of hoplites to others in the citizen body in the fifth century was no smaller than 1:2, and that it may have been as great as 1:1. The proportion at Athens in the same period was (very broadly) similar.[14]

We thus reach a maximum of *c*.15,000 adult male citizens in the fifth century. Since we possess no later figures for fleets, it is possible that the total of citizens below the hoplite class altered significantly in the fourth century; but there is no reason to suppose that it did so. Fifteen thousand adult male citizens will give a maximum total citizen population, including children, of approximately 50,000. If metics at Corinth were liable to service neither as hoplites nor in the fleet, they will have to be added to reach the total free population. There may not have been many (above, 161-3); but if there were, they were probably required to serve in the Corinthian forces. Fifty thousand will therefore be not only a maximum for the total citizen population, but also the probable actual total for the free population. For slaves, we have no evidence besides the obviously inaccurate figure recorded by Athenaeus. Since there was nothing in the Corinthia like the silver-mines of Attica to swell the slave population, the total is not likely to have exceeded 20,000—an average of more than one for each citizen family; the actual figure may have been a good deal smaller.[15] The maximum total of 70,000 is determined by figures for citizen population which cover most of the fifth century. No serious shift in the nature of the Corinthian economy can be detected for some time before our earliest figures at the time of Plataea; the total was probably therefore similar for some time before 480. But the

[13] Thuc. ii.103.1 implies that the Athenians under Phormio took slaves captive during the actions in the Corinthian Gulf in 429. Welwei, *Unfreien im antiken Kriegsdienst*, ii. 122-3, argues that this indicates a Corinthian use of slaves in her fleet, at least in the difficult first years of the Archidamian War; but the conclusion is most uncertain. We do not know how many slaves were captured; even if there were many, none of them need have been Corinthian. The remarkable consistency of the size of Corinthian fleets from Artemisium to the expedition to restore Euarchus—with the exception of Sybota—argues for a consistent policy of manning for the whole of this period; but whether that policy was to allow (or require) significant numbers of slaves or metics to serve, we cannot say.

[14] Jones, *Athenian Democracy*, 8-10.

[15] To quote figures from Athens for comparison would be misleading, since the two states can be shown to have differed on the matter of using slaves for mining, and probably did so in other respects too.

further we depart from the reasonably secure figures for citizens in the fifth century—both chronologically and by building on them as a basis for calculating other groups—the more hazardous the estimates become.

XIII. Coinage

It might be supposed that the study of Corinthian coinage can provide considerable help for the economic historian;[1] in fact, it gives remarkably little. The history of the mint can be traced in the coins; but the influences which shaped that history are almost always a matter for conjecture alone, and we know too little of the reasons which might lead, in the Greek world in general, to increased or decreased output to place any confidence in such a record as an index either of political or of economic history.[2]

The earliest coinage on mainland Greece was issued by Aegina; her first coins are to be placed perhaps in the second quarter of the sixth century. Corinth seems to have followed soon afterwards, perhaps within the same twenty-five years.[3] It is impossible to discuss the purpose of these first coins specifically with reference to Corinth; but Kraay's persuasive account of the motives which lay behind the introduction of coinage in Greece is particularly appropriate to the Corinthian case. He has shown that coinage cannot have been intended to facilitate trade, either at a local level or on a wider scale. He suggests that coins were first issued in order to serve the purposes of the minting authorities. Cities would find it convenient if payments made to them—taxes, fines, etc.—were in the form of coins whose purity and weight were fixed; while payments made by the state from time to time for building schemes, mercenaries, and other purposes could be much simplified if trustworthy coins were available.[4]

---

[1] In all that follows my debt to the published work of Dr C. M. Kraay will be obvious. My obligation to him for his generous help is even greater; I am extremely grateful for the time he devoted to informing my numismatic ignorance; and I remain responsible for my own errors.

[2] See in general esp. Kraay, *Archaic and Classical Greek Coins*, 326-7.

[3] Ibid., 41-3, 79-80. Price and Waggoner, *The Asyut Hoard*, esp. 122-4, have suggested that Kraay's dates are to be revised downwards slightly. I am unable to judge the issues (for a brief comment, see Kraay, *NC* cxxxvii (1977), 197-8); but this change of date makes little serious difference for Corinthian history. More important is the implication of Price and Waggoner (123-4), for which they offer no argument, that Corinth was the first mainland Greek state to strike coins; but since the earliest coins of Aegina, Corinth, and other early mints do not themselves show evidence of an order, there is no ground for rejecting the ancient tradition which gave Aegina priority.

[4] Kraay, *Archaic and Classical Greek Coins*, 317-22; esp. *JHS* lxxxiv (1964), 76-91.

Corinth in particular would have derived substantial benefit from the introduction of her own coinage, especially because the dues which she levied in the second quarter of the sixth century were probably more varied than in any other city; at any rate, she had quite exceptional opportunities. Maritime cities usually had only one major port at which harbour-dues could be levied; but Corinth could derive income from two, and could in addition make charges for the use of the diolkos. Strabo may affirm that the Bacchiads already charged harbour-dues; the fact need not be doubted even if the value of the evidence is uncertain (above, 74), and Periander will certainly have charged for the facilities he provided at Lechaeum and for the diolkos. The amount of traffic on which such payments were levied had probably become so great by *c*.575 that the Corinthian government greeted the idea of coinage with relief; the business of collecting dues in kind (and, perhaps, of subsequently disposing of them) or even in bullion will have been more than complicated. It may also be no accident that the introduction of coinage at Corinth coincides in point of time with a building scheme for which many payments were necessary: the present temple of Apollo (below, 180). This point can hardly be pressed; but there would have been many attractions for Corinth in adopting the new Aeginetan practice. We are unable to guess why the Aeginetan standard was not adopted at the same time; perhaps it was a matter of local pride, but more probably Corinthian coins were issued in accordance with an already existing weight-standard which happened to differ from the weights used for Aeginetan coins. Before the first Corinthian coins, silver bullion will have been weighed in terms of whatever weight-standard was in use at Corinth; the adoption of a different standard merely on the ground that Aeginetan coins were first in the field would have caused great confusion.[5]

Coinage was not introduced specifically in order to serve the needs of trade; but it may well have been used for that purpose soon after the first coins. Bullion may have been used in credit transactions for maritime trade some time before the introduction of coinage; if so, the convenience of using coins instead will rapidly have become apparent, but the mechanisms of trade will not have been altered significantly. If bullion had not been in frequent use for such a purpose, it might have taken longer to recognize that credit could be more conveniently given in coin than in kind. From the earliest issues to the second half of the fourth century, at least in Corinth, the association between coins and trade was mainly that they

[5] See below, Endnote A.

offered a means of providing credit. If they had acted as an item of
trade themselves we should have expected them to travel much
further, and in far greater quantities, from Corinth than they in
fact did.[6] Their main function was to be lent at Corinth for purchase
of items to be traded.

The first Corinthian coins bore on the obverse the type which
remains standard for staters throughout the history of the mint:
Pegasus, with koppa, the initial of the issuing state.[7] The reverse
dies at first have no true type, but towards the end of the sixth
century the equally unchanging reverse type of (for staters) the
helmeted head of Athena was introduced.[8] During the fifth century, Corinthian issues are heavily concentrated in the first half.
Some 80 obverse dies are known before *c*.450, but Kraay has shown
that only 17 belong to the subsequent half-century, and that of
these, 11 were minted in a short period before 430 during which
a number of changes of detail were introduced in the Athena
head types.

This leaves very few issues for the period of the Peloponnesian
War. Part of this gap is perhaps to be filled by moving up some of
the issues which have been thought to belong to the fourth century;
but there was a period in the late fifth century when Corinth was not
minting while Leucas was: a series of pegasi from Leucas is not
represented at Corinth.[9] Activity in the Corinthian mint may have
been resumed some time before the end of the fifth century; but not
a great deal before, since the Ionian Shore hoard, dated to 375/370
by the reasonably sure chronology of its Taras issues, contains only
the earliest issues of the next Corinthian sequence, many of them in
good condition.[10] Corinthian minting was clearly under severe
pressure during the Peloponnesian War; Kraay has made the plausible
conjecture that the war made it difficult, if not impossible, to
obtain supplies of silver. Corinth did not, as far as is known, have
access to her own supplies; and technical analysis of Corinthian
coins before the end of the fifth century shows that silver of two
distinct compositions was minted: one closely related to Athenian,
the other to Aeginetan. Presumably each issue at Corinth used
silver from one source, either Attic or Aeginetan; but it is impossible
to say whether the supply came in the form of bullion or of

[6] Kraay, *Archaic and Classical Greek Coins*, 317–22; esp. *JHS* lxxxiv (1964), 76–91, esp.
79–80. See further Murray, *Early Greece*, 225.
[7] For all that follows, see Kraay, *Archaic and Classical Greek Coins*, 80–5.
[8] The exact date of this change remains a matter of dispute; cf. Price and Waggoner,
The Asyut Hoard, 78; Kraay, *NC* cxxxvii (1977), 195–6.
[9] Kraay, *Archaic and Classical Greek Coins*, 84, 124.
[10] Kraay, *MN* xvi (1970), 23–30.

Athenian and Aeginetan coins for melting down and reminting.[11] During the years of the war Attic silver will have been much harder to acquire; Aeginetan may have been no easier even though the (unknown) source which supplied Aegina at an earlier date no longer did so after the expulsion of the Aeginetans at the beginning of the war.[12] Lack of silver will have caused the state serious embarrassment, for the war demanded considerable expenditure on the payment of crews (though payment during the Ionian War was made by the Persians), and for the construction of vessels; we have no means of telling how these problems were solved.

In the late fifth or early fourth century the Corinthian mint resumed its activity; but it was on a significantly greater scale than at any earlier time. From now on, some 227 obverse dies were used before *c*.340; that is well over twice the number found in comparable earlier periods. The reason for this greater activity cannot be determined.[13] No doubt it reflects in part the increased availability of silver after the Peloponnesian War, although the series may well have begun in the last years of the war, perhaps with the reminting of coins from other mints paid to Corinthian rowers in the Peloponnesian fleets. The source of silver employed is unknown: coins of this phase have not been subjected to the same analysis of composition as those of the earlier period. A small gold issue in the early fourth century was probably the result of Persian subsidies given at Corinth to the allies at the beginning of the Corinthian War; it may have been used to finance the Corinthian fleet which operated in the Gulf in the early years of the war (below, 353-4). Bronze coins were probably first issued at about the same time to facilitate small-scale transactions.[14]

Even the increased output of issues in the first half of the fourth century was greatly surpassed subsequently. This phase of Corinthian

---

[11] Kraay, *Composition*, 16-20, 33-4. This analysis finally puts out of court the possibility, long canvassed, that Corinth derived her silver supplies from the mines of inland Epirus which later supplied the metal for the coinage of Damastium.

[12] Thuc. ii.27.1. On Aeginetan coins from the mid-fifth century to 431, see Kraay, *Archaic and Classical Greek Coins*, 47.

[13] On all this, see ibid. 85-6. Kraay guesses that the increased number of coins may have been used for the hire of mercenaries, and certainly in the years after the Peace of Antalcidas Spartan allies were allowed to contribute cash for campaigns instead of serving in person; but the few signs we have indicate that Corinth generally did not take advantage of the new arrangements (below, 372-4). After 365, when there were some twenty-five years of this phase of the coinage still to run, Corinth engaged in little military activity until Timoleon went to Sicily (below, 379-83).

[14] Pegasus and Trident bronzes were found in Phase 3 of the Sacred Spring, which belongs in the early fourth century (Williams and Fisher, *Hesperia*, xl (1971), 20-1, 37, 40 (nos. 11-12, 14-17). I am much indebted to Dr Williams for drawing my attention to this evidence.

coinage comes only partly within the scope of this book; but the expedition of Timoleon to Sicily led to an extraordinary flowering of activity in the Corinthian mint. Before Timoleon reached Sicily Corinthian coins are found there only rarely; but every Sicilian hoard buried between the mid-century and *c*.290 contains pegasi in very large numbers: they never make up less than 70 per cent of the contents, and although some of them were minted elsewhere the vast majority were issued at Corinth. This greatly increased output is reflected in various technical innovations designed to cope with the new demand.[15] Most of the coins issued at this time seem to have reached Sicily, and the new development must have been connected with Timoleon's expedition; but only conjecture can suggest the nature of the connection.

Kraay has shown that conditions in Sicily, where in the mid-fourth century there was very little coinage in circulation, were partly responsible; and that the first Corinthian coins which entered this 'coinage vacuum' arrived very soon after Timoleon himself. He suggests that the first Corinthian coins reached Sicily as payment for his troops; and that the numerous issues of pegasi from other mints in north-west Greece—including, besides Leucas and Ambracia (which had both issued coins of Corinthian type for more than a century), many states which now made such issues for the first time—were the result of a Corinthian effort to raise money in this area in support of Timoleon.[16] On historical grounds, these coins probably arrived not with Timoleon's original force (which received but bare support from Corinth), but with the reinforcements dispatched a few years later (below, 390-1). The coins used for the payment of troops may have been supplemented by others brought by the settlers who went to Sicily at Timoleon's invitation. They gathered at Corinth from various places in Greece before their departure,[17] and they may have been required to take Corinthian coins rather than those of their home cities. This might provide a partial explanation of how Corinth acquired the silver for the massive minting of this period; but it remains difficult to see why pegasi continued to pour into Sicily until the early third century.[18]

[15] Kraay, *Archaic and Classical Greek Coins*, 86-7.
[16] Esp. *Actes du 8éme Cong. Int. Num. 1973* (1976), 99-104; cf. also *Greek Coins and History*, 53-62; *Archaic and Classical Greek Coins*, 86-8, 126-8; Talbert, *Timoleon*, 161-78.
[17] Plut. *Timol.* 22.4-23.6; Diod. xvi.82.3.
[18] That they did so implies a considerable change in the character of trade between Corinth and the west, for it had been conducted before without significant movements of coin; but the nature of the change is irrecoverable (see refs. above, n. 16).

XIV.   Indices of Prosperity

To determine with precision the relative prosperity of Corinth from time to time is an impossible task. The only factor which can be identified and, to a degree, assessed in the state of our evidence is war; but there are also some direct indices. That which has been most frequently used in the past is the supposed decline in the number of Corinthian hoplites between Plataea and the Nemea; but I have argued that the decline is a mirage (above, 165–7). If this is a reliable index, the Peloponnesian War did not have the serious effect that has been imagined; consideration of the probable effects of the war bears out the conclusion.

It should not be too readily assumed that the economic consequences of the war were serious. Agricultural production will have been affected only marginally. Two-thirds of the hoplite levy were, in the first years of the war, absent in Attica for some weeks. There were similar calls on the rowers before the capture of the greater part of the Corinthian fleet at Pylos, and from 425 there were 500 troops on permanent garrison duty in the north-west; but none of this is likely to have caused serious disruption to harvests.[1] Even the invasion of the Corinthia in 425 appears to have done only a small amount of damage in the fields, although 212 Corinthians lost their lives. Thucydides mentions only that Nicias laid waste to land in the region of Crommyon (iv.45.1). He does not seem to have been able to ravage systematically near Solygeia, even if the battle itself will have caused some damage (iv.42–4). The eastern Corinthia may have been subjected to a few minor raids which Thucydides did not think worth a mention; but they can hardly have been significant. Other forms of production, since they were not seasonal, may have been more seriously affected by the absence of men on military service; but it is difficult to believe that such a factor made a great difference. In general, the main effects of the war on the productive capacity of the Corinthia were two, neither of them very

[1] Westlake, *Essays*, 94, 107, supposes the invasions of Attica to have been a serious factor; but there was little to be done on the land when the crops were ripening, and it was at precisely this stage—and for precisely this reason—that the invasions were mounted. It was only when a second invasion was proposed in 428, to help the Mytilenaean revolt, that the allies complained: Thuc. iii.15.2.

serious: the loss of manpower through war casualties, and the devotion
by individual Corinthians of time and effort to the war which might
otherwise have been employed in productive purposes.

Corinthian trade will certainly have suffered more extensively;
but the contraction is difficult to quantify. The most dramatic
evidence is the apparent collapse of the extensive business conducted
in the Punic Amphora Building (above, 128); but the archaeological
record also allows us to trace the effects on Corinthian imports of
Attic pottery. The best evidence is to be found in the North Cemetery, for the patchy publication of fifth-century vases from elsewhere precludes proper analysis; the finds from the Cemetery show
a marked decline in Attic imports during the last third of the century.
One shape is instructive. Attic lekythoi were imported in large
numbers for funerary use throughout the fifth century until they
cease abruptly at about the time of the outbreak of the war;
Corinthian potters then began to turn out an exceptionally high
number of copies of Attic vases, but as the Archidamian War continued they developed the shape independently of Attic until contact was established again during the Peace of Nicias.[2] This provides
striking illustration of the fact that mere political hostility would
not disrupt trading contacts; during the Peace of Nicias—even though
there was no formal state of peace between Athens and Corinth
(below, 331)—relations were resumed after disruption during the
war itself. Even then, Attic imports did not entirely cease, although
they may have reached Corinth indirectly; it is significant that
Corinthian vase-painters appear to have started during the war to
execute commissions for specific occasions because orders could
no longer be placed at Athens.[3]

Trade between Corinth and Athens probably almost ceased
during the years of actual war; but the effect of that cessation will
depend on the proportion of Corinthian trade which was conducted
with Athens during peacetime, and that cannot be guessed at. For
trade with other centres we have no evidence from pottery; there
can be no doubt that the Athenians attempted to disrupt Corinthian

[2] Cf. in general Palmer, *Corinth*, xiii.121-2, with discussion of lekythoi (see also Kurtz,
Athenian White Lekythoi, 138-9); C. W. J. and M. Eliot, *Hesperia*, xxxvii (1968), 347,
364-5. For Attic imports from the sixth to the fourth century, Palmer, *Corinth*, xiii.152-66.

[3] Hence the development of Corinthian Red-Figure; cf. Herbert, *Corinth*, vii.4.3-4. For
Attic imports, cf. Pease, *Hesperia*, vi (1937), 258. A list of eleven Attic vases of this period
from the North Cemetery: Palmer, *Corinth*, xiii.121 n. 105; cf. Kurtz, *Athenian White
Lekythoi*, 139. Attic Red-Figure published by McPhee, *Hesperia*, xlv (1976), 380-96,
almost certainly includes pieces made (if not imported) during the war; and cf. Herbert,
Corinth, vii.4.3. The rough domestic vessels made in Corinth which found a market in
Athens (above, 109) cannot be dated precisely enough to test traffic in the reverse direction.

trade, perhaps especially imports of corn, but how successful the attempts were is uncertain. The blockade of Naupactus started in the winter of 430/29 will have had some effect; but it is easy to exaggerate its consequences. According to Thucydides, the Athenians sent the expedition to Sicily in 427 partly in order to prevent Sicilian corn from reaching the Peloponnese; this proves that the blockade was by no means fully effective,[4] and there were formidable difficulties in the way of success. In the early years of the war the Athenians attempted to blockade Megara by stationing three triremes at Budorum (ii.93.4); but they enjoyed only partial success, for Nicias later captured Minoa partly in order to improve the chances of intercepting ships bound for Megara.[5] This demonstrates that the Athenians attached some importance to interference with the shipping of their enemies; but it illustrates even more clearly how the dice were heavily loaded against the blockading force unless it possessed a base almost at the very mouth of the harbour concerned. Lechaeum and Cenchreae were both free of pressure at such a close range. The straits at the entrance to the Corinthian Gulf were more suitable for blockading vessels; but that still left the Gulf itself open. Very many vessels must have been able to evade the Athenians successfully.[6]

It does not admit of doubt that both the carrying trade over the Isthmus and the Corinthian import/export trade were disrupted by the war; but the effect may have been greater on the financial resources of the state as a whole than on those of individual citizens. A reduction in the number of movements will automatically have reduced the income from dues unless rates were raised; and the history of the Corinthian mint proves that silver was difficult to acquire during the war years (above, 172–3). Employment in trade and related activities will have been similarly reduced; but the opportunities which the war itself provided may have been a sufficient compensation. We have no direct evidence, but it is hardly to be doubted that payment was made for service in the fleet; for individuals such payment—while it will certainly have strained the resources of the state—will have compensated for the curtailment of employment opportunities brought about by the war. During the major part of the Ionian War, many Corinthians may have been almost permanently employed in the fleet; and by this time payments were made by Persia.

---

[4] Corinth is not mentioned as a destination for the corn, but was almost certainly the main target: above, 129–30.

[5] Thuc. iii.51, esp. 2. For the topography, Gomme, *HCT* ii.334–6.

[6] Westlake, *Essays*, 88.

The First Peloponnesian War may have had a greater impact;[7] but it is certain that the wars of the first third of the fourth century caused very extensive dislocation. During the Corinthian War the fighting was centred on the Corinthia itself for nearly a decade; for almost the whole war Corinthian exiles and Spartans conducted raids in the Corinthia from Sicyon or Lechaeum. Agriculture must have suffered severely, especially in the most productive land in the territory, the coastal plain. The Perachora peninsula was attacked, according to one of Xenophon's accounts (*Hell.* iv.5.1), precisely because of its economic value as pasture and as the origin of the supplies of those in the city. The strategic reason adduced by Xenophon in his other account (*Ages.* ii.18) was perhaps more important; but Agesilaus inflicted serious damage. The region lost a high proportion of its inhabitants when he received their surrender: he either sold them into slavery or (in the case of the politically active) delivered them into the hands of their enemies. Only those inhabitants of the peninsula who were away from home at the time (who may have been many, given the military situation) will have escaped. Non-agricultural production was probably mainly concentrated within the protection of the city-walls; but some raw materials may have been difficult to acquire. Trade at Lechaeum, at least, will have ceased entirely for that major part of the war when it was held by the Spartans, and there was not the same opportunity for service with the fleet that had been available during the Peloponnesian War. The fifteen years which followed the Peace of Antalcidas no doubt allowed considerable recovery. Agricultural production, except of olives and their oil, will have been quick to respond, and some spare—though not very good—land may have been made available in the Peiraeum to diminish any pressure of population that may have existed in other parts of the Corinthia. In 371 warfare returned; but it was not so intensive as in the Corinthian War: Epaminondas ravaged the Corinthia at least once, but his main attention was directed elsewhere. In 365 the Corinthians negotiated neutrality for themselves, and seem to have remained immune from attack until the morrow of Chaeronea. It is unfortunate that we possess no figures for Corinthian hoplite contingents during these years: the war can have had no serious effect by the time of the Nemea in 394, but recovery will have been complete when reinforcements were sent to Timoleon in the late 340s.

---

[7] We have too few details of the war to enable us to make an assessment of its probable economic consequences. We do not know, for example, whether the Athenians made a sustained effort to interfere with Corinthian shipping. It is possible that the number of

Such indices as we have of the general prosperity of the Corinthia never contradict, and sometimes support, conclusions based on the probable consequences of wars. The burials in the North Cemetery have sometimes been used to draw conclusions for general prosperity or otherwise; but they do not provide reliable evidence. The wealth of burials may vary at least as much with burial fashion as with the general standard of living; and it is unclear to what extent the practice of the North Cemetery is to be taken as typical for the Corinthia as a whole. In the seventh century, for example, tombs are notably lacking in fine burial gifts; but this is a period when other evidence, if it indicates anything, is in favour of a great improvement in general conditions (above, 100). The late fifth-century evidence allows, and perhaps encourages, the conclusion that the war had but a small effect. Burials from the Protocorinthian period to c.450 are almost exclusively made in monolithic sarcophagi, but from the mid-fifth century tile graves become increasingly common until they predominate from c.425; in the fourth century sarcophagi are almost unknown. Tile graves were presumably less expensive than sarcophagi, and Palmer has suggested that the change is to be partly attributed to the generally diminished wealth of Corinthians during the war;[8] but this explanation is improbable. It is possible to detect a pattern in the burials of the period, for tile graves usually contained fewer offerings than contemporary sarcophagi; but this merely reflects the obvious fact that some graves were richer than others; the wealthy could afford both sarcophagi and gifts, while the less fortunate had to use tiles and could offer fewer vases. Since there is no general decline in the number of offerings made in the late fifth-century graves, the adoption of tiles for burial is probably more a matter of fashion than a sign of general impoverishment. It is to be noted that the early fourth-century graves show no sign of the decline which must have taken place during the Corinthian War;[9] the safest conclusion is that the North Cemetery cannot be used as evidence for the general level of prosperity.

The history of the Corinthian mint is equally without significance in this respect. The lack of issues in the Peloponnesian War certainly reflects difficulties suffered by the state; but it cannot be taken to

Corinthians of hoplite census was smaller at the time of Leucimme than at that of Plataea (above, 166).

[8] *Corinth*, xiii. 74.

[9] Fourth-century slab-covered graves tended to contain more offerings than their tile contemporaries (Palmer, ibid., 75), and slabs were no doubt more expensive than tiles; the distinction is probably similar to that of the fifth century between sarcophagi and tiles.

demonstrate a more general decline. If any general trend can be traced, it is that the early fourth century was a time of intense difficulty; yet the mint in these years was more active than ever before. There can be no correlation between the history of the mint and general economic conditions (above, 173).

Public building programmes are more instructive, even though they can only be used with caution. The main requirement for the erection of public buildings is sufficient resources for the city itself; and they are not necessarily absent when the majority of citizens are poor. More importantly, the absence of large building schemes at any particular time cannot be taken to prove that the general level of prosperity was then low: political considerations played a large part in decisions to build. It is no accident that the greatest period of activity at Corinth was that of the tyranny: Cypselus and Periander wished to emphasize their own magnificence and that of the city they ruled, but the succeeding oligarchs felt no such pressure; and in a stable oligarchic state it was less important for the wealthy to demonstrate their generosity than in democratic Athens. Equally, the extent of public building was determined not only by resources but by requirements.[10] None the less, there is some correlation between periods during which on other grounds we should expect Corinth to have suffered economic hardship and periods when public building programmes were under pressure.

The tyranny saw the greatest concentration (see Fig. 16). Cypselus fortified the city and probably dedicated temples, magnificent for their time, to Apollo at Corinth and to Poseidon at Isthmia; these schemes were of a quite different order to the projects of the Bacchiads at Perachora and the Cyclopean Spring at Corinth. Periander provided the Lechaeum harbour, the diolkos, and a massive temple to Olympian Zeus. The subsequent century, however, saw only the temple and altar of Hera Acraea at Perachora and the present temple of Apollo at Corinth: even the latter was necessitated by the destruction of Cypselus' building by fire.[11] A similar conflagration at Isthmia led to a new temple for Poseidon not long after the invasion of Xerxes.[12] The Long Walls from Corinth to Lechaeum date from c.450.[13] At Corinth the third quarter of the fifth century witnessed the construction of the second phase of the North Stoa; the first must belong some time earlier. The Painted Building close by has also been dated to the third quarter of the

[10] Burford, *Temple Builders*, 203.
[11] For the date, see now Robinson, *Hesperia*, xlv (1976), 217-18.
[12] Broneer, *Isthmia*, i.57-173, esp. 101.
[13] Parsons, *Corinth*, iii.2.84-125, esp. 121.

fifth century.[14] In the last quarter of the fifth century the Centaur
Bath, with an impressive mosaic in its main room, was built;[15] but
whether the project was public or private is uncertain. The history
of the North Building is unclear. It was first suggested that a monumental colonnade was added in the late fifth or early fourth century
to an already existing stoa with shops and a smaller colonnade to the
front;[16] but the shops may in fact have been later than the colonnade.[17] There are difficulties with each reconstruction of the area;
what is clear, however, is that a large and impressive, if very badly
preserved, stylobate with columns was built here in the late fifth
or early fourth century. Presumably it belonged to a stoa which
faced on to the Lechaeum Road. Earlier suggestions that a further
stoa may have been built in the fifth or fourth century beneath the
Roman Central Shops, just north of the South Stoa, must now be
discounted;[18] the South Stoa itself was not erected until the late
fourth century.[19] Large new temples are not known after that built
for Poseidon at Isthmia just before the mid-fifth century; but that
building was damaged by fire in 390 (Xen. *Hell.* iv.5.4) and subsequently repaired.[20] The roof had to be entirely replaced, and although
marble tiles had been used in the fifth century those of the fourth
were of terracotta;[21] some of the fifth-century stone blocks were
recut for the repairs, but others had to be replaced. A small temple
was made from reused blocks opposite the North Building probably
in the third quarter of the fourth century.[22] The theatre at Corinth
was dated in the original publication to the late fifth century;[23] but
this is too early, and the exact time of the construction remains
uncertain.[24] A theatre was in use at Isthmia in the mid-fourth
century, and it may have been built *c*.400.[25] The early fortification
wall built by Cypselus was probably replaced, at least in the Potters'

[14] Scranton, *Corinth*, i.3.157-79; cf. Coulton, *Stoa*, 46, 228.
[15] Williams, *Hesperia*, xlv (1976), 109-15; xlvi (1977), 45-53.
[16] Stillwell, *Corinth*, i.1.212-28.
[17] Coulton, *Stoa*, 52-3.
[18] Williams, *Hesperia*, 1 (1981), 28-9, n. 42.
[19] The publication: Broneer, *Corinth*, i.4; for the date, cf. Williams, *Hesperia*, xlix (1980),
121.
[20] Broneer, *Isthmia*, i.1, 101-2.
[21] Ibid., 90-6.
[22] Askew, *Corinth*, i.2.8-9; for the date, Williams, *Hesperia*, xlv (1976), 116.
[23] Stillwell, *Corinth*, ii, esp. 131.
[24] See most recently Gebhard, *The Theater at Isthmia*, 16-17, who perhaps implies
(but does not state) that the earliest stone construction at Corinth is late fourth century.
There is, however, some evidence for an earlier wooden, and perhaps trapezoidal, form;
Xen. *Hell.* iv.4.3 implies that Corinth had a theatre in 392.
[25] Gebhard, *The Theater at Isthmia*, 9-26, esp. 24-6.

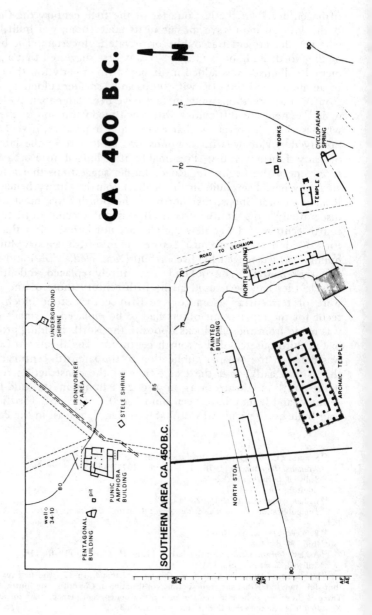

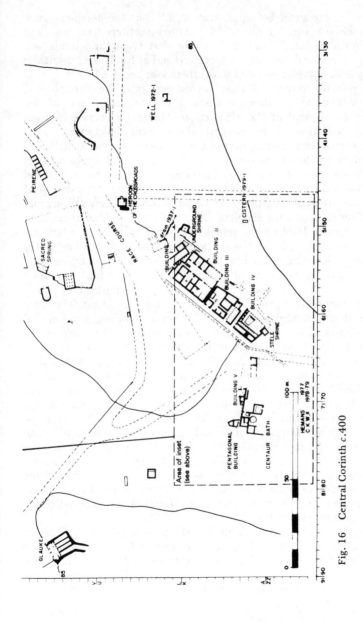

Fig. 16   Central Corinth *c.*400

Quarter, in the years before or after 400;[26] but the north-east part of the circuit was rebuilt *c*.300.[27] Other sections have no clear archaeological date,[28] but it is likely that Cypselus' circuit was replaced piecemeal, as seemed necessary and as funds were available; the city-wall provides no clues to prosperity or decline.

It is possible to detect at least a broad pattern in the chronological concentration of building schemes. From the beginning of the tyranny to the end of the fifth century, there may have been considerable variation in the amount of resources devoted to public building from time to time; but there seems to have been no difficulty in raising the materials for whatever the government chose to provide. The tyrants were far more lavish than their successors; but the period after about the middle of the fifth century saw the construction of a number of public buildings in Corinth and the Long Walls, and when fires damaged the temples of Apollo and Poseidon there were no shortages to hold up the rebuilding. The new temple at Isthmia, at least, could be provided with expensive marble tiles when a clay roof might have sufficed. For the North Building the architectural evidence gives a date only of about 400; but a date during or soon after the Corinthian War is historically almost impossible, and it may be confidently placed before 395 at the very latest. The same is true of the theatre at Isthmia. The North Building, and some of the buildings of the third quarter of the century which may belong after 431, give some support to the view that the economic consequences of the Peloponnesian War have been exaggerated. Public buildings are most instructive in helping to confirm poverty in the early fourth century. Nothing can be assigned definitely to this period, but better (because positive) evidence is that cheap terracotta tiles were employed to replace the marble roof on the temple at Isthmia; this reconstruction is securely dated after the disruption and devastation of the Corinthian War, although how soon repairs were carried out after the fire of 390 is not known. A possibly similar indication of diminished public wealth is the construction from reused blocks of a small temple opposite the North Building; but this probably belongs some time after the end of the intense fighting of the early fourth century.

A final index which has been thought to indicate public financial difficulty in the late fifth century is the building history of the Corinthian fleet; but this is no more persuasive. In 433 Corinth put

---

[26] Before: Stillwell, *Corinth*, xv.1.53–62; after: Carpenter, *Corinth*, iii.2.76–8, 82. The evidence is insufficient to allow a decision.

[27] Parsons, *Corinth*, iii.2.121–3, 294–6.

[28] Carpenter, ibid., 44–83, 126–7.

ninety vessels to sea for the Battle of Sybota; some were destroyed during the engagement. In the Archidamian War and afterwards Corinth hardly ever manned more than half that number; but that is to be explained rather by the difficulty of providing crews than by a reduced total of triremes in service. Something like forty Corinthian vessels were captured at Pylos in 425; but more than thirty-five were none the less at sea at a single time in 413 (above, 167). These latter were probably newly built; they had certainly been considerably modified, for their bows were especially strengthened.[29] If Corinth built the fifteen triremes assessed on her by the Spartans in winter 413/12 (below, 338), she will have had fifty vessels or more. These figures do not allow us to conclude that Corinthian resources had suffered severely from the war, for they show that Corinth was always able to provide at least as many vessels as she could man; but it is dangerous to use them as a positive argument that the war had little effect, for the provision of these vessels might have been at a cost far greater than we can know.

The only serious change in the general level of prosperity which can be traced is the decline of the early fourth century caused by the Corinthian War. It is hard to believe that there were not other fluctuations over the long period from the seventh to the fourth century, even if we have no evidence which enables us to trace them. But there is no sign that the general prosperity of the seventh century, and especially its second half, was seriously affected at any time before the early fourth. Even the disruption of the Corinthian War and the 360s may have been rapidly repaired—though there is hardly any confirmation to be found in the fact that admirers of Neaera were well able to pay the exorbitant prices her madam charged (Ps.-Dem. lix.26-32).

[29] For the fleet under Polyanthes in the Gulf, Thuc. vii.34.5; the ten sent to Sicily were probably similar (below, 345).

XV.   The Tyranny

a.   The Revolution

We have very little trustworthy information on the events of the revolution which brought Cypselus to power c.655.[1] Herodotus devotes the bulk of his account to the escape of the infant Cypselus from the Bacchiads after oracles had predicted his tyranny (v.92 β–ε 1). This folk-story is given in a context of hostility to the tyranny, for Socles is arguing against the reimposition of Hippias as a tyrant on Athens; but all the same, Cypselus is the hero. Since the favourable motif cannot have been attached to the tyrant after the fall of his house, Herodotus gives us a version of what was said in the seventh century. Even more valuably, two of the three oracles he records must go back to the same time, for they are as favourable to the tyrant as the story in which they are embedded:[2] the fact that they are in verse guarantees their status as verbatim seventh-century sources.

Cypselus, according to Herodotus, was the son of a Bacchiad mother and a non-Bacchiad—indeed non-Dorian—father. His mother Labda was lame, could find no Bacchiad husband, and married 'Aetion, son of Echecrates, from the deme Petra; by descent he was a Lapith of the family of Caeneus' (v.92 β 1). Aetion consulted Apollo at Delphi about his childlessness, and received the following reply:

> Aetion, no one gives you honour, though you richly deserve it.
> Labda is pregnant, and will bear a boulder which will come crashing
> Down on the exclusive rulers, and will set Corinth to rights.
>
> (v.92 β 2.)

This will hardly have been given to Aetion; but the tone, favourable to Cypselus, places it before the fall of the dynasty. Further precision

---

[1] It is fortunately no longer necessary to add to the extensive bibliography on the date: the earlier chronology is generally accepted (cf. Oost, CP lxvii (1972), 16 n. 26), so long as the date of 657/6 for Cypselus' accession is not pressed as exact (for sources, see Servais, AC xxxviii (1969), 30–2). 584/3 for the fall of the tyranny may be precise, if the chronographers took their information from a list of eponymous magistrates or from some other possibly reliable source; but since we cannot know what evidence was used we cannot test its validity. See in general Servais, ibid., 28–81.

[2] This has long been recognized: Oost, CP lxvii (1972), 18 with refs.

is possible. Forrest has argued that it would have been tactless to attack the Bacchiads for being exclusive if Cypselus had himself been an exclusive ruler for long;[3] a date for the oracle not long, if at all, after the revolution is also indicated by δικαιώσει, 'set to rights'. An alternative meaning—but one not intended to be understood because of the general tone of the lines—is 'punish': a clear instance of Delphic concern to be right whatever happened.[4] The oracle will have originated at a time when it was uncertain whether Corinth would be punished or set to rights by Cypselus. Apollo was willing to attack the Bacchiads unambiguously; but he did not care to commit himself so soon to the view that the tyrant's rule would turn out well.

The Bacchiads, continues Herodotus, heard of the oracle, and it enabled them to interpret another, given to them before; but it is hostile to Cypselus, and the date of its origin cannot be fixed:

> An eagle is pregnant among the rocks and will give birth to a lion,
> Strong and a devourer of flesh; it will loose the knees of many.
> So take this to heart, Corinthians, you who live about the beautiful
> Peirene and frowning Acrocorinth.

> (v.92 β 3.)

The Bacchiads determined to kill the child, but Herodotus in his most delightful manner tells how he smiled at those entrusted with his murder, who at first shrank from their task; when they hardened themselves and returned, Labda had hidden him in a κυψέλη, a beehive.[5] They failed to find him and he was named Κυψέλος. Fullgrown, he 'consulted the oracle at Delphi and received a double-edged response; he put his trust in it, made an attempt on Corinth, and gained power there. This was the oracle:

> Happy is the man who enters my house,
> Cypselus son of Aetion, king (*basileus*) of famous Corinth,
> Himself and his sons, but his sons' sons no longer.

> (v.92 ε 1-2)

Again, the tone proves an early origin for the first two lines; the last was no doubt added when the tyranny finally fell. When he gained power, Cypselus 'drove out many, deprived many of their possessions, and even more of their lives' (v.92 ε 2). He ruled for thirty years, died in his bed,[6] and handed power to his son Periander.

---

[3] *Emergence*, 111.
[4] Cf. den Boer, *Mnemosyne*[4], x (1957), 339.
[5] Roux, *REA* lxv (1963), 279-89.
[6] On the translation of διαπλέξαντος τὸν βίον εὖ, cf. Zörner, 28.

More details are given by Nicolaus of Damascus (probably following Ephorus). His account (*FGH* 90 F 57) begins with a rationalized
version of Herodotus' fairy-story: the men sent to kill the infant
decided not to do so—they were touched by his smile—and instead
warned Aetion, who fled with his son to Olympia and then to
Cleonae. When Cypselus reached manhood he returned to Corinth
after consulting Apollo at Delphi and soon made himself popular
'because he was brave and moderate and seemed to favour the
demos more than the other Bacchiads, who were insolent and
violent' (*FGH* 90 F 57.4). He became polemarch and achieved even
greater popularity in that office. Persons who were fined by a court
of law were required to appear before the polemarch and be imprisoned until the fine—part of which went to the polemarch himself
—was paid. Cypselus, however, imprisoned no man but accepted
security for some and himself gave it for others; he waived his
portion of the fines entirely. He saw that the Corinthians were
hostile to the Bacchiads but had no leader; so he offered himself
to them and turned the demagogue. He told how an oracle had
predicted that he would overthrow the Bacchiads, so that they had
tried to kill him before and were still plotting against him. In the
end, he gathered a party about himself and killed Patrocleides (or
Hippocleides: *FGH* 90 F 57.1), 'a lawless and hateful man' who
held the office of *basileus*; the demos quickly appointed Cypselus
basileus (cf. *FGH* 90 F 57.1) in Patrocleides' place. Once in power,
Cypselus recalled those who had been exiled by the Bacchiads,
restored rights to those who had been deprived of them, drove the
Bacchiads into exile, and confiscated (ἐδήμευσε, 'made public') their
property. His rule was mild and he had no bodyguard; he died after
being in power for thirty years.

One fact stands out from both accounts: the tradition was remarkably favourable to Cypselus and hostile to the Bacchiads. Nicolaus'
version has this tone consistently; and although Herodotus uses his
story as an argument against tyranny the signs are unmistakable that
it originally stood in a version of which Cypselus was hero. That the
favourable view was able to survive in an age that was hostile to
tyrannies proves that it reflects the truth: Cypselus was remembered
with sympathy because that was how his contemporaries saw him.[7]

To derive more detail from our evidence is hazardous. Some have
placed a good deal of confidence in Nicolaus;[8] but his account of

[7] Esp. Andrewes, *Tyrants*, 45–9.
[8] Recently Oost, *CP* lxvii (1972), 10–20, see esp. 16 n. 27 (quoted with approval by
Lloyd, *JHS* xcv (1975), 53 n. 58); Zörner, esp. 49–61. See rather Murray, *Early Greece*,
142.

Cypselus' rise to power is deeply suspect. It reeks of two fourth-century tendencies: rationalization and assimilation to contemporary practice. Many of the details belong to the textbook tyrant of fourth-century theorists—especially demagoguery and accusations of plots by the tyrant's enemies. There was probably valid information to be found in the fifth and fourth centuries by those who would look; but Nicolaus' general tone is such that even those details which seem plausible for the seventh century have doubt cast upon them by their context. It is safer to reject every detail of Cypselus' early career and his revolution that Nicolaus gives unless there is some special reason to accept it.

Firm application of such a principle leaves us with very little. Herodotus' evidence for the tyrant's parentage may be accepted: it is not strictly part of the legend and there was no reason to invent it.[9] That Cypselus spent his youth in exile is difficult to credit. For a fourth-century writer it was necessary to explain how the infant Cypselus survived the hostility of the Bacchiads to attack them in his turn: he thus had to be taken beyond the reach of his enemies. Olympia—to which Periander, at least, was conspicuously generous (below, 227-8)—and Cleonae were suitable guesses; but the exile solves a problem which does not exist, for Bacchiad hostility to Cypselus must be rejected along with the fairy-story. A fourth-century exile might return, survive oligarchic attacks, and even gain office if he had the powerful protection of the demos; that it happened in Bacchiad Corinth is impossible.[10] Cypselus no doubt spent his early years in Corinth; and he spent them in the favour of the Bacchiads, for there is reason to accept not only that he was polemarch but also some details of his tenure of the office. An imaginative writer will hardly have invented a military title and yet given Cypselus civil functions to perform:[11] either the title, or the function, or both will have been preserved in the tradition. It is hard to believe that in the fourth century a proportion of fines

[9] It is over-sceptical to doubt that Labda was Bacchiad (Berve, *Tyrannis*, 16). Pausanias' account of Cypselus' ancestry (ii.4.4; v.18.7-8) differs from that of Herodotus: he was descended from Melas, son of Antasus, who came from 'Gonoussa above Sicyon' and was admitted to Dorian Corinth by an unwilling Aletes. This is not incompatible with Herodotus, and both versions make Cypselus' non-Dorian but well-born descent clear (cf. the Arcadian king Cypselus: Paus. iv.3.6; viii.5.6, 29.5). Pausanias' story was no doubt embellished to attribute prescience of the tyranny to Aletes; but that of Herodotus remained uncontaminated. The name Cypselus seems to appear in a Linear B tablet: Chadwick, Killen, and Olivier, *The Knossos Tablets*, 264 Og (2) (4467); but since it was found at Cnossus it is less likely to be relevant than Berve, who attributed it to Pylos, supposed (*Tyrannis*, 522).

[10] Exile in Olympia cannot be supported by the story that Cypselus vowed to give all the goods of the Corinthians to Zeus if he were to gain the tyranny; it is false (below, 196).

[11] Cf. Salmon, *JHS* xcvii (1977), 97 n. 51.

was reserved for a magistrate;[12] we should conclude (with surprise) that the outlines of this part of Nicolaus' account rest on genuine tradition, even if Cypselus' extreme generosity remains doubtful.[13]

For the events of the coup we have only Nicolaus.[14] Herodotus' brief version probably already implies that violence was used;[15] the same might have been guessed without evidence. It is likely enough that the last Bacchiad eponymous magistrate was murdered, and he may well have been called Patrocleides (or Hippocleides). He was probably 'lawless and hateful' in the opinion of Cypselus' supporters, and the revolution may have been effected with the help of a 'party' (ἑταιρικόν); but we cannot rely on these details merely because Nicolaus gives them. It remains doubtful whether the demos appointed Cypselus as king (*basileus*), though they were probably willing—like Apollo in the third of Herodotus' oracles—to address him as such. A formal appointment might have been made, but no reliance can be placed upon it.[16]

Our sources do not try to clarify the factors which worked in Cypselus' favour. Nicolaus lays emphasis on the demos;[17] but this evidence has the strength of sand. Nicolaus uses the word demos in the sense of the democratic party opposed to the oligarchic Bacchiads; this is anachronistic, and demonstrates only that the account was based on a tradition which held Cypselus to have been a generally popular ruler.[18] The same tradition was doubtless responsible for Aristotle's view that Cypselus was among the many early tyrants who came to power 'through demagoguery' (*Pol.* 1310 b 29–31). Our sources make no other statement about the nature of Cypselus' support; but indirect inference is possible.

That the revolution was at least as much a matter of hostility to the Bacchiads as of adherence to Cypselus is certain. Even Herodotus does not emphasize the wickedness of the tyranny by contrast with

[12] It is this fact which makes reconstruction by analogy from (for example) the Athenian polemarchs improbable. I owe this observation to Professor Forrest.

[13] Cf. Schaefer, *RE* Suppl. viii (1956), 1121-2.

[14] I take it that Polyaen. *Strat.* v.31 is worthless; Berve, *Tyrannis*, 523.

[15] v.92 ε 1: ἐπεχείρησε and ἔσχε (in this sense) are both normally used in military contexts in Herodotus. To conclude that strictly military action was involved (as, apparently, Zörner, 47) is to go too far.

[16] Modern scholars have tended to accept this statement of Nicolaus: e.g. Oost, *CP* lxvii (1972), 19; (at length) Zörner, 153-60. Contrast Berve, *Tyrannis*, 161-7, 523. No fourth-century tyrant, of course, was appointed king; but if Nicolaus' source thought he knew (from the oracle, for example) that Cypselus' title was king, he would have assumed that the appointment was made by the demos.

[17] Followed by Zörner, *passim*, esp. 58-61.

[18] That the favourable view rests ultimately on opinion contemporary with the tyrants does not increase the credit of Nicolaus' details (contrast Oost, *CP* lxvii (1972), 18-19): the existence of a favourable view would justify such inventions as Nicolaus gives.

the regime it supplanted—an obvious technique if the tradition had allowed sympathy for the Bacchiads. Nicolaus, for whom the Bacchiads in general were 'insolent and violent' and Patrocleides in particular 'lawless and hateful', is more explicit; Strabo (378: also no doubt following Ephorus) describes them as tyrants themselves. The tradition was hostile to the Bacchiads; but it is doubtful whether these sources can demonstrate that it was their violence and hatefulness, lawlessness and insolence which earned them the enmity of their contemporaries. These are general words of disapproval, to justify the hostile tradition. More specific accusations are made in the first oracle: the Bacchiads were 'exclusive rulers', and Cypselus would crash down on them like a boulder and 'set Corinth to rights'. The exact sense of the second item is difficult to get. It may carry the restricted meaning, normal in the fifth century and after, that the Bacchiads did not act with justice, in the strictly legal sphere. It is more likely that the earlier, wider meaning is intended, and that they acted in general without rules: that their government— not only their administration of justice—was arbitrary.[19] The oracle is *ex parte*; but it is contemporary evidence for what Cypselus claimed—indeed, it *is* what Cypselus claimed. Since he succeeded, it also shows what significant public opinion of the time wanted.

There is no direct evidence for the groups which made up that significant public opinion. I have argued elsewhere that the strength behind the political upheavals in the mid-seventh century was provided by hoplites: Cypselus was successful because he enjoyed their support. As polemarch, even though he is given only civil duties by Nicolaus, he must have had a military function, and could exploit the strength of the new phalanx. Cypselus could not have defeated the Bacchiads in the face of hoplite opposition; the hoplites must therefore have been at least neutral, and they probably gave him willing help. But that merely explains how Cypselus was strong enough to succeed; the hoplite reform will get us no further, for although a majority of hoplites supported Cypselus we do not know why they did so. Hoplites will have supported Cypselus for a variety of reasons; but none of them depended on the fact that they were hoplites.[20]

The nature of the support Cypselus enjoyed is clarified by the complaints made against the Bacchiads. The first item in the oracle, the exclusive character of Bacchiad rule, was potentially almost a universal grievance: 'it was an oligarchy called the Bacchiads. They

[19] See on all this especially Forrest, *Emergence*, 111-12.
[20] *JHS* xcvii (1977), 97-101.

ran the city, and married only among themselves' (Hdt. v.92 β 1).
Thus the great majority of Corinthians played no part; but discontent on this score can only have been felt by a tiny proportion
of those excluded: where there is a closed ruling class it is among
those closest to admittance that exclusion is most deeply resented.
In this case there is some evidence. When the tyranny fell, Corinthians were content with a constitution under which the central organ
of government was a council of eighty men (below, 231, 234): if
numerous voices had been raised *c*.655 for a part in government, so
small a council would not have satisfied the demands for active
participation which the tyranny could not have eradicated. The
oracle proves that such demands were made; but they were not
widespread. They can hardly even have been made by more than
a minority of hoplites, for the later constitution was too narrow
to satisfy a body of politically active citizens as large as the
phalanx.[21]

The identity of those who felt excluded, and their reasons for
feeling so, can only be the subject of conjecture. It has often been
suggested that Cypselus was a representative of one particular such
group: the non-Bacchiad aristocracy. They certainly existed:
Cypselus' father Aetion boasted a proud ancestry that was not
Bacchiad, indeed not Dorian; but Cypselus himself was more
fortunate. He rose to the polemarchate before his coup, and must
have been treated by the Bacchiads as one of themselves.[22] No
doubt non-Bacchiads with long family trees were prepared to support
Cypselus in order to gain admittance; but Cypselus himself cannot
stand as evidence that his revolution had such an aspect. More
importantly, his non-Dorian descent cannot show that he led a
suppressed non-Dorian population to political recognition equal to
that of the Dorians. This racial factor was of some importance at
Sicyon, at least in the time of Cleisthenes; but there is no similar
evidence for Corinth, and what we have points in a different direction. The fact that the non-Dorian Aetion could marry even a lame
Bacchiad girl and have a son who was treated as a Bacchiad suggests
that at least in the higher reaches of Corinthian society racial
distinctions were of small significance; and Aetion and his like
cannot have supported the pretensions which his lineage proclaims
without dependants—presumably of similarly non-Dorian descent—
whose standing was not very different from that of the dependants

---

[21] Salmon, ibid., 99.
[22] For possible explanations of Cypselus' position, cf., e.g., Oost, *CP* lxvii (1972), 12–13;
Jeffery, *Archaic Greece*, 147.

of his Dorian rivals. To explain Cypselus' revolution in racial terms remains pure conjecture.[23]

We can at least be sure that both non-Bacchiad aristocrats and non-Dorians (both aristocrats and others) existed; but for every other group which conjecture suggests may have demanded political power we cannot even show that—much less that it played a part in the coup. Trade, and the other skills which developed after the foundation of the colonies, all presented opportunities for enrichment (above, 95-100); but it is difficult to assess the effect of this on political development. It can be excluded that the merchants, potters, smiths, and others who took direct advantage of the opportunities improved their circumstances and changed their attitudes to such an extent that they sought political influence. Such demands will have been restricted to those who held some pretensions already; but the ambitions of outstanding non-Bacchiads who had participated indirectly in the recent expansion, especially by devoting their agricultural surpluses to overseas trade, may have been sharpened by their increased wealth. The new developments are more likely to have provided further stimulation for those who were already dissatisfied with their exclusion than to have stimulated new complainants.

Since only quite exceptional Corinthians followed Cypselus in resentment at their exclusion from political power, many of his adherents will, have been concerned with quite different issues. It is probably at this level that the rapid developments after *c*.730 were most significant: as ordinary Corinthians had in some numbers successfully negotiated a major shift away from their traditional patterns of life, so it will have been easier for them to conceive of dissatisfaction with Bacchiad leadership, and offer their support to Cypselus. The second major ground of complaint indicated by the oracle, that Corinth needed to be 'set to rights', might have been shared by every Corinthian who was not a Bacchiad—and some, indeed, who were. Such a view will have been based on specific grievances about what Bacchiads had or had not done; and it has often been suggested that Cypselus was able to succeed partly because of the errors of Bacchiad foreign policy in the last half century of their rule. Andrewes cites the failure to maintain control over Corcyra, defeats at the hands of Megara, and pressure from

---

[23] Contrast Jones, *TAPA* cx (1980), 189; he ignores the evidence of Nic. Dam. in asserting that 'Cypselus remained an outsider'. The hypothesis of Roussel (not applied explicitly to Corinth in this respect; but cf. *Tribu et cité*, 248) would allow Aetion to have belonged to a 'Dorian' tribe; see briefly above, 51-2 n. 65.

Pheidon of Argos;[24] but none of these is a clear instance of Bacchiad failure.[25] Land tenure was the subject of the legislation of Pheidon of Corinth, at some time before the tyranny; but the best explanation of his activity makes it improbable that it gave rise to discontent which Cypselus might have exploited (above, 63-5).

Another possible approach is through the actions of Cypselus when he gained power: some of his measures were probably designed to meet discontent which had been a factor in the fall of the Bacchiads. His colonizing programme demonstrates that Corinth had no lack of bodies to send to new sites. The Corinthia may have been suffering from population pressure once more; if the Bacchiads were unwilling to found further colonies that may have been a serious complaint. It is perhaps more likely that the problem of population was not acute, but that many Corinthians saw the success of Syracuse and Corcyra and wished for similar opportunities (below, 215); that would explain why the Bacchiads would not accede to the requests. Nicolaus' report that Cypselus as polemarch had been conspicuously generous to those from whom his function was to collect fines might indicate a number of failings among Bacchiads. Other polemarchs might have acted with excessive rigour. Perhaps more probably, Bacchiad polemarchs, since they were responsible for the collection of fines, may have become the target for general complaints about Bacchiad justice. But Nicolaus' account may have arisen from only a few cases, and cannot therefore establish that such a factor played a major role.

It is disappointing that we have so little evidence for specific grounds of complaint against Bacchiads; but if we had more, it would probably be misleading. In the oracle, the grievance is general: that Corinth needed to be 'set to rights'; but the individuals who supported Cypselus probably did so because they were concerned by particular issues. Each man who followed Cypselus did so for his own reasons. Most of these will have involved what was seen as a wrong, a foolish, or an unjust Bacchiad decision;[26] but to attempt a more exact definition would be to assume a uniformity where none existed. In a broad sense the Bacchiads fell because they were exclusive and arbitrary; but that was a focus of discontent because of numerous disagreements between Bacchiads and others over particular issues, and their disagreements were prior. Specific evidence for one would give it greater importance than the many

[24] *Tyrants*, 44-5; cf. Will, *Korinthiaka*, 362; Berve, *Tyrannis*, 15.
[25] Forrest, *Emergence*, 109; see below, 218 (Corcyra); above, 71-2.
[26] Cf. Forrest, *Emergence*, 119-22.

others which must have existed: in some respects, it is better to remain in the dark than to have only partial light.

b. Cypselus in Power

For Cypselus' policies after his revolution[27] we have some information in Herodotus, though it is contaminated by its hostile context; for the rest, we have little more than Nicolaus. Herodotus has it that many Corinthians were exiled, many had their possessions removed, and even more were killed (v.92 ε 2): this must refer to Bacchiads in particular, and even so it is doubtful whether death was suffered by more than a few. Nicolaus speaks rather of exiles, and is perhaps more accurate.[28] They fled, in his account, to Corcyra; Plutarch refers to Bacchiads at Sparta (*Lys.* 1.2), and there are possible traces of them as far away as Macedonia, Caunus, and Etruria.[29] Corinthian tradition remained hostile to Bacchiads, and they probably never returned even when the tyranny fell. Nicolaus' assertion that their property was 'made public' may be nothing more than a restatement in fourth-century terms of Herodotus' accusation that Cypselus stole the possessions of many. The tyrant presumably appropriated what the fleeing Bacchiads were forced to leave behind —especially their land; but what he did with it in detail we cannot say.[30] He may have discontinued a major Bacchiad festival, the Isthmian Games.[31] That he restored those sent into exile or deprived of citizen-rights by the Bacchiads (as is stated by Nicolaus) is possible; but since this was an expected feature of fourth-century revolutions we can place little reliance on it. On the other hand, fourth-century tyrants rarely dispensed with bodyguards; we, like Aristotle (*Pol.* 1315 b 27-8), may believe that Cypselus did.

Some information is to be found in our sources about Cypselus' taxation. Periander is said to have contented himself with taxing the harbours and the agora (below, 199); that may imply not only a contrast with what was expected of a typical tyrant, but also with

---

[27] See also below, 205-9 (institutions); 209-17 (colonies).

[28] Nicolaus' account of Cypselus in power is far less suspicious than what he says of the way in which it was gained: it bears few of the marks of fourth-century invention which abound in the latter; and see below, 197 n. 39.

[29] Sources and references in Berve, *Tyrannis*, 523; none of the traces outside Corcyra is obviously worthy of credit.

[30] Will, *Korinthiaka*, 477-81 (cf. Snodgrass, *Archaic Greece*, 96), argues at great length that the land was distributed to the landless supporters of Cypselus; that may be true, but there is no evidence.

[31] Solinus vii.14; it is best to admit (with Berve, *Tyrannis*, 19) that the motive is irrecoverable—if the account is to be accepted at all.

Cypselus: Periander may have abolished some of the taxes his father levied. That remains uncertain; and the only details we have of Cypselus' taxation are suspect. The earliest evidence is provided by the Pseudo-Aristotelian *Oeconomica* (1346 a 31–b 6): 'Cypselus the Corinthian vowed to Zeus that if he gained control of the city he would dedicate all the possessions of the Corinthians; so he ordered them to be registered. When that had been done, he took a tenth of what each man had, and told him to work with what remained. The next year he did the same thing, so that in ten years Cypselus had all that he had dedicated, and the Corinthians had earned more for themselves.' Agaclytus (*FGH* 411 F 1) added that the dedication to Zeus took the form of the famous colossus of gold that was to be seen at Olympia. The addition deserves little credit. That the colossus existed and was dedicated by Cypselus or a member of his family we cannot doubt;[32] but the purpose, and even the identity, of the dedicator are so confused in our sources that there can be no question of a genuine tradition, and the statue can give no support to what Pseudo-Aristotle says of Cypselus' method of raising revenue to dedicate to Zeus.[33] That account itself gives strong grounds for doubt; van Groningen has shown that Corinth could not have survived more than a year or two of such levies.[34] It is possible that what is in question is a tax on revenue rather than capital;[35] but after such reinterpretation the passage can command little credit. It gains none from the argument that Cypselus might well have tried to silence opposition to his taxes by claiming a religious purpose:[36] the vow to Zeus was merely one of the many guesses made to explain the dedication of the colossus.[37]

---

[32] The earliest source is Plat. *Phaedr.* 236 B; for subsequent accounts, cf. Servais, *AC* xxxiv (1965), 146–7.

[33] On the whole question of the colossus, see Servais, ibid., 144–74. For the motive for the dedication and the contradictory sources, ibid., 152 with n. 31.

[34] *Aristote: le second livre de l'Économique*, 51; cf. Will, *Korinthiaka*, 482–5. The difficulty is not reduced by Ar. *Pol.* 1313 b 26–8; a 20 per cent levy, bringing Dionysius of Syracuse the whole property of his subjects within five years, would have been even more ruinous.

[35] Will, *Korinthiaka*, 484–5, comparing a similar tax imposed by Peisistratus.

[36] Zörner, 167–9.

[37] It has often been suggested that the taxation and the colossus were connected early, in order to support the argument of the Corinthians that they should be allowed to substitute the name of the city for that of the tyrant as the dedicator of the colossus (below, 227–8); Schachermeyr, *RE* xix (1937), 708–9; Will, *Korinthiaka*, 466–8. If so, the taxation would gain in credit; but it is unlikely that a story worked up so early would have impressed itself so feebly on the tradition that later writers felt as free to invent in connection with the colossus as they did.

c. Periander in Power

The tradition was generally favourable to Cypselus; it was different for his son. According to Herodotus Periander began his rule more mildly than his father but became far bloodier[38] after receiving advice from Thrasybulus of Miletus to get rid of all outstanding Corinthians (v.92 ζ-η 1); 'Periander did away with those whom Cypselus had omitted to put to death or send into exile' (v.92 η 1). Unlike his father he felt it necessary to maintain a bodyguard.[39] His cruelty and perverted habits are often illustrated. He killed his wife Melissa,[40] made love to her corpse,[41] and stripped all the Corinthian women of their finery to burn it for her spirit.[42] He sent 300 Corcyraean boys for castration in Lydia when his son was killed in Corcyra;[43] and he killed both Rhadine, who was intended for his bride, and her cousin who loved her.[44] Aristotle tells us that he was generally thought to be the originator of many measures that were typical of the repressive tyrant (*Pol.* 1313 a 35-7).

There remain, however, signs of a different attitude. Already in Herodotus Periander began his rule more mildly than his father; and in the story of Arion (i.23-4) Periander helps the hero.[45] Aristotle was more explicit. In a valuable fragment of his *Constitution of the Corinthians*,[46] while the tyrant's bodyguard and some repressive measures are recorded, we also read: 'In other respects he was moderate: he raised no other taxes but was satisfied with those on the market and the harbours; and he was neither unjust nor insolent, but hated wickedness.' Periander was numbered by some among the Seven Sages;[47] the tradition cannot have been

[38] Cf. Parthen. *Amat.* 17.1; Schol. Plat. *Hipp. Mai.* 304 E.

[39] Hdt. v.92 η 3. Cf. Heracl. Lemb. 20 = Ar. fr. 611.20 Rose; Diog. Laert. i.98. There were 300 bodyguards according to Nic. Dam. *FGH* 90 F 58.1: perhaps genuine (unless the number is textually corrupt); there will have been little point to inventing such a figure. Nicolaus' treatment of Periander (like his account of Cypselus in power) carries more conviction than his version of Cypselus' early career; cf. esp. Schachermeyr, *RE* xix (1937), 711. At least the seventh and sixth centuries are not reconstructed in the image of the fourth; the main difficulty is the attribution to Periander of the typical measures of a tyrant.

[40] Hdt. iii.50.1; Diog. Laert. i.94.

[41] Hdt. v.92 η 2-3; Nic. Dam. *FGH* 90 F 58.2.

[42] Hdt. v.92 η 1-4; Plut. *Mor.* 1104 D; cf. Diog. Laert. i.96 = Ephorus *FGH* 70 F 178.

[43] Hdt. iii.48.2-53; Nic. Dam. *FGH* 90 F 59.2-4; Diog. Laert. i.94-5.

[44] Strabo 347; cf. Rose, *CQ* xxvi (1932), 88-92. The tyrant is not named in the story, but is, no doubt, Periander rather than Cypselus; but note Rose, ibid., 90.

[45] Zörner, 26-30 (following Will, *Korinthiaka*, 451-2), exaggerates the extent to which Herodotus includes material which lies ill with his generally hostile conception: that Periander (for example) regretted the way in which he had treated Lycophron is hardly a sign of grace.

[46] Heracl. Lemb. 20 = Ar. fr. 611.20 Rose.

[47] References and sources in Berve, *Tyrannis*, 529-30.

wholly hostile. Some of the sayings of Periander are significant even though they were probably falsely attributed; he was said to have remarked that the safety of a tyrant was better guarded by the goodwill of the citizens than by the spears of a bodyguard.[48]

The favourable elements of the tradition cannot demonstrate that everything unfavourable is later accretion. Some of the stories of Periander's cruelty can be explained away, others must be rejected, and many of them relate merely to the private history of his family. But the bodyguard by itself demonstrates a change in the character of the tyranny, and it is doubtful whether all the stories are to be rejected: that of the youths of Corcyra is likely enough, though it may not be typical, for Periander had the death of his son to avenge. The ambiguous tradition will mean that conflicting views were held of him during his lifetime. The broad character of the group responsible for the hostile judgement is clear enough. Soon after Periander died, the tyranny itself fell. The forces which destroyed it must have existed well before Periander's death, and they were certainly exerted by those men who profited from the fall of the tyranny: those who ran oligarchic Corinth. The identity of those from whom the favourable tradition derived is more hazy. It is better to leave their definition negative in form: they were not represented in the central organs of Corinthian government after *c*.585.

Even without taking into account Periander's strong, if not brutal, character, the development of opposition is only to be expected. By careful management and skilful following of public opinion Cypselus was able to avoid appearing as arbitrary as the Bacchiads; but those ill-defined Corinthians who helped to drive out the Bacchiads because they were exclusive will have resented the claims made by his son.[49] Even if they did not, the very energy of the second tyrant made it easier for disagreements to arise. Forrest has drawn attention to the instructive parallels between Augustus and Cypselus, Tiberius and Periander:[50] second-generation tyrants face increased problems, as Aristotle at least half recognized (*Pol.* 1315 b 11-39). Natural unwillingness to accept Periander's supremacy may have been accentuated by his own character. It is likely enough, at the least, that he had a bad temper, and perhaps that he was 'something of a brute';[51] the tension that already existed on political grounds between the tyrant and the great men of Corinth may have been increased by his personal defects (compare, again, Tiberius).

---

[48] *Gnom. Vat.* 451. Cf. ibid., 450; Diels-Krantz, *Vorsokratiker*, 10.3 ʒ; Diog. Laert. i.97.
[49] See esp. Ar. *Pol.* 1313 b 30-2: tyrants are especially mistrustful of their friends.
[50] *Emergence*, 115-16.
[51] Andrewes, *Tyrants*, 52.

For Herodotus, Periander had to be taught the techniques of tyranny by Thrasybulus of Miletus, though he learned the lesson well; Aristotle reversed the roles, no doubt because it seemed unthinkable that Periander had anything to learn about repression.[52] It is likely enough that Periander protected himself by suppressing his rivals, though how many he removed is unclear; but other measures reported of him present far greater problems. Aristotle gives a list (*Pol.* 1313 a 36–b 32) of the typical measures of a tyrant, many of which were said to have been introduced by Periander; but he ascribes only one explicitly to Corinth: the numerous dedications of the Cypselids were one example of the policy of impoverishing citizens so that they could not maintain their own military force and were so hard at work that they could not plot.[53] Other accounts are more specific. 'Periander . . . did not allow people to live in the city, and he completely forbade luxury and the acquisition[54] of slaves. In other respects he was moderate: he raised no other taxes but was satisfied with those on the market and the harbours; and he was neither unjust nor insolent, but hated wickedness. He threw all the madams into the sea (cf. Hermippus *FHG* iii.40, fr. 16); and he set up a council ἐπ᾽ ἐσχάτων,[55] and they did not allow expenditure to exceed income' (Heracl. Lemb. 20 = Ar. fr. 611.20 Rose). The prohibition of the acquisition of slaves appears also in Nicolaus, while that of living in the city figures in a less paradoxical form in Diogenes Laertius, following both Ephorus and Aristotle: 'he did not allow people to live in the city at will' (i.98). Nicolaus adds other items: 'He prevented the citizens from remaining idle, and was always finding some work for them to do; and if any person was

<hr/>

[52] Hdt. v.92 ʓ 2–η 1; Ar. *Pol.* 1284 a 26–33; 1311 a 20–2. Burn, *Lyric Age*, 192; Berve, *Tyrannis*, 528.

[53] 1313 b 18–22, retaining the MSS reading μήτε at line 19. Cf. Theophrastus ap. Phot. s.v. Κυψελιδῶν ἀνάθημα. Numerous other measures appear in Aristotle's list; but no particular one can be safely attributed to Periander, even though it may have been the general opinion that he instituted many of them. He may have used some, but we cannot say which; even Aristotle seems to have had his doubts: cf. φασι (they say). Aristotle's treatment in the *Cor. Pol.* seems to have been relatively sympathetic, to judge from Heracl. Lemb. 20 = Ar. fr. 611.20 Rose. Oost, *CP* lxvii (1972) 26 n. 66, puts more weight on this passage of Aristotle's *Politics* than it will bear.

[54] κτῆσις: which might strictly mean either acquisition or possession (LS s.v.); but the latter is hardly right here.

[55] The words have been variously, but not yet convincingly, interpreted. Dilts (Heracl. Lemb. 20) translates 'at the last'; Burn (*Lyric Age*, 192) perhaps makes a translation 'concerning funerals' the basis of his view that Periander tried, like Solon (Ruschenbusch, ΣΟΛΩΝΟΣ ΝΟΜΟΙ, fr. 72 a–c), to curb expenditure on rites for the dead. One might also try a council 'for the poor' (LS s.v., I.3); or even perhaps 'to crown it all'. None of these is exactly like any use of ἔσχατος known to me; Heracleides probably failed to understand Aristotle's original.

sitting in the agora, Periander punished him in fear that he might be plotting something against him' (*FGH* 90 F 58.1).

That Periander attacked luxury is almost certain. Already Herodotus told how he stripped all the Corinthian women of their finery. The story is that he burned all the best garments to keep the chill from his dead wife's spirit; but it is difficult to resist the conclusion that this is a telling perversion of the tyrant's attempts to prevent rich Corinthian women from wearing what he thought showy.[56] Why the acquisition of slaves was prohibited is disputed; but the aim was probably sumptuary, and it is in this context that Heracleides (though not Nicolaus: below, 201) puts the measure. What appears in our sources as a general prohibition may have been more specific: the tyrant may (for example) have limited the number of slaves in any one household, for it is not likely that Periander wished to prevent the ordinary Corinthian from buying a household slave.[57] One function of the council ἐπ᾽ἐσχάτων, if Heracleides is correct, was presumably to restrict private individuals. A fragment of the fourth-century comic poet Diphilus (F 32 Edmonds) shows that a law which had this effect existed in fourth-century Corinth, and it may have originated with Periander; it fits well with his other work, and was not a measure commonly attributed to tyrants. Attacks on luxury were well known in archaic Greece, and were not only (indeed, not usually) made by tyrants;[58] whether in Periander's case the motive was the same as for Solon, the lawgivers Zaleucus and Charondas, and perhaps Pittacus, or whether his aim was to prevent ostentation by potential rivals, remains unclear.[59]

The measures against idleness ascribed to Periander are equally comparable with other activity in the archaic period. Many tyrants are credited like him with giving their subjects work, or even financial or other help, in order to prevent them from having the leisure to conspire; but these are almost certainly misinterpretations of measures taken for quite different reasons.[60] In Athens the law

---

[56] Schachermeyr, *RE* xix (1937), 707.

[57] Another possibility is that Periander outlawed debt slavery, like Solon in Athens. That is not what our sources say; but they may represent distortions of just such a measure. μὴ δούλους κτᾶσθαι Κορινθίους (that (one) should not buy Corinthians as slaves) might easily have been misunderstood as μὴ δούλους κτᾶσθαι τοὺς Κορινθίους (that the Corinthians should not buy slaves); but we cannot make history out of such conjectures.

[58] Cf. Zörner, 201-3.

[59] Cf. also Didymus ap. Phot. s.v. Κυψελιδῶν ἀνάθημα; but this conjecture has no value as evidence: above, 196 with n. 33.

[60] e.g. Ar. *Pol.* 1313 b 18-22 (see above, 199); Ael. *Var. Hist.* ix.25; Peisistratus equipped men idling in the agora with ploughing-teams and seed corn 'in fear that their leisure would breed conspiracy' (cf. Ar. *Ath. Pol.* 16.3).

against idleness was probably not made by a tyrant;[61] such legislation could spring at least as much from the spirit of the age as
from a tyrant's fear for his safety. But it is doubtful whether
Periander tried to stamp out idleness as such;[62] he may merely
have provided Corinthians with work in his extensive building
programme (below, 201-2), which is a quite different thing. Nicolaus,
who is our only source for this aspect of Periander's work, says that
he was 'always finding some work' for his subjects to do; the motive
of attacking idleness may have been supplied by later theorists. The
detail that Periander punished those found sitting idle in the agora
would imply disapproval of laziness; but it may have been invented
as a pointed contrast to the practice of Peisistratus, who, if he
found anyone in a similar state, offered him the means of livelihood
(above, n. 60), or it may be a distortion of a restriction placed by
Periander on certain individuals (below, 205). Periander's prohibition
of the acquisition of slaves is associated in Nicolaus with the attack
on idleness; the logic of the connection is obvious, but the slave
regulation could be explained in many other ways.

No details of Periander's public works have been preserved in our
literary sources; but archaeology provides a great deal of evidence.
It is likely that he took part in (and perhaps began) the long development of Peirene, and he may have built Glauke; but the date of
construction at most of Corinth's springs is unclear. A number of
small sanctuaries in the city are to be attributed to his time; but
many of them are so small that they may have been private (above,
78). The sanctuary of Demeter and Kore on Acrocorinth was either
founded under Periander or enjoyed increased attention under him.
The remains do not include impressive buildings;[63] but they may
have been politically significant. In Athens Peisistratus encouraged
the growth of popular cults like that of Demeter at Eleusis and
Dionysus in Athens;[64] it may be no accident that Periander's reign
in Corinth saw both the beginning or the increased popularity of
the cult of Demeter and Kore on Acrocorinth and Arion's progress

[61] The responsibility probably lay either with Dracon (Stroud, *Drakon's Law on Homicide*,
79-80, with full discussion and refs.) or with Solon. Theophrastus attributed the law to
Peisistratus and thought that he passed it in order to render the country better worked and
the city more tranquil (Plut. *Sol.* 31.5); that is better evidence for fourth-century theory
than for the origin of the law (cf. Stroud, ibid., 80).
[62] Comparison has been made (e.g. Will, *Korinthiaka*, 509-10) with the order of Cypselus
that the Corinthians should work with what remained to them after they had paid him the
taxes he demanded; but the connection is forced and the evidence for Cypselus' taxation
invented (above, 196).
[63] Refs. to preliminary reports in Wiseman, in Temporini (ed.), *Aufstieg und Niedergang*, .
ii.7.1, 448 n. 31.
[64] Andrewes, *Tyrants*, 113-14; cf. Ar. *Pol.* 1319 b 24-5.

in the development of the dithyramb in honour of Dionysus.[65] Peisistratus' purpose was to give impetus to cults which were independent of the old priestly families.[66] Periander's intention will not have been exactly the same, for his main aristocratic enemies, the Bacchiads, were in exile, as those of Peisistratus were not; the exact significance of the development remains obscure. A large temple, of which only a few scraps found near the Gymnasium remain, belongs to the first half of the sixth century.[67] This impressive building is more likely to have been erected by a tyrant than under the subsequent oligarchy; but the hypothesis cannot yet be archaeologically confirmed. The location of the temple and the identity of the god to whom it was dedicated are unclear; but a good case can be made for identifying it as a temple of Olympian Zeus, and this would help to confirm Periander's responsibility for it (below, 228).

Obscurity remains the fate of Periander's religious projects; but his other public works yield more interesting information. His most impressive construction was an artificial harbour at Lechaeum (above, 133–4). He is said to have intended to dig a canal through the Isthmus (Diog. Laert. i.99); but he had to content himself in the end with the diolkos, a paved way over which ships could be carried from one side of the Isthmus to the other. In providing these facilities Periander seems to have been primarily concerned to benefit merchant shipping rather than his own war fleet (above, 134, 137). No doubt he constructed them partly in order to levy dues on them: Heracleides records that he only imposed taxes on the market and the harbours (which will presumably include charges for the diolkos). None the less, a similar income could have been raised by other means without such outlays of effort and capital, and Periander's choice of projects must have been determined in part by a calculation that they would serve a useful purpose. It is most improbable that the schemes were intended, even in part, to relieve unemployment in the Corinthia; after the extensive colonizing activity of both tyrants there can have been few Corinthians unable to support themselves left at home.

If Periander did not necessarily view idleness as a moral issue he may well have disapproved heartily enough of whoring to take action against it. He may not literally have had all madams thrown into the sea as Heracleides reports; but presumably he did try to suppress their activity. He may merely have been concerned that

[65] Hdt. i.23; cf. Pind. *Ol.* xiii.18–19.
[66] Andrewes, *Tyrants*, 113.
[67] Wiseman, 84, with references (nn. 26–7).

Aphrodite's (and, indirectly, presumably his own) business should not suffer from competition;[68] but it is just as likely that he tried to remove what he took to be a blot on the moral landscape without thought for the goddess.

It is particularly difficult to interpret Periander's regulations concerning access to the city. That nobody was allowed to live in the city is impossible; if the measure was a matter of regulating where Corinthians were to live, he will at the most have prevented further settlement in the city, and perhaps then required some dispersal from it.[69] But the tyrant may rather have concerned himself with access to Corinth for those who lived elsewhere in the Corinthia. This is not strictly what the evidence says; but such a restriction might well have been reported as our sources have it. The prohibition, whatever its nature, affected all Corinthians according to Heracleides and Nicolaus; but they may be wrong. The unfavourable view of Periander originated with a small group which ran Corinth after the tyranny; a restriction placed on precisely that group might well have been falsely reported as universal.

At first sight, a general restriction on access to the city, or even on living there, is given plausibility by archaic parallels reported from elsewhere. It was a commonplace that tyrants tried to keep their subjects out of the city in order to reduce the possibility of riots. Such an explanation is never made explicit for Periander; but it would have appealed to many in antiquity, including Aristotle (*Ath. Pol.* 16.2-3, 5). It will not bear examination. Both the Peisistratids and the Orthagorids are said to have required the rural population to wear κατωνάκαι (garments appropriate for peasants) to shame them into staying away from the city;[70] but such a regulation was neither enforceable nor effective. Tradition probably preserved information about a measure which could not be understood; it was therefore distorted and explained by the commonplace that a tyrant will keep his subjects out of the city if he can.[71] The commonplace

---

[68] Compare, in Ptolemaic Egypt, the complaint that private brothels were being run to the detriment of the 'houses of Aphrodite': *C. Ord. Ptol.* 47, 25-7, cf. 18. See, on the sacred prostitutes of Aphrodite, below, 398-9.

[69] It is possible that our sources on this question derive from a misunderstanding of information about the Corinthian local tribes: the Corinthia was divided into three (or more) parts for this purpose, and one of them was the city (ἄστυ); see below, 413-9. If the city divisions of the tribes were in some way privileged, it might have been necessary to deny registration in them to some who might have claimed to be qualified; but our sources cannot safely be interpreted in such a cavalier fashion.

[70] Pollux vii.68; *Suda* and Hesych. s.v. κατωνάκη.

[71] Theopompus (*FGH* 115 F 311) is less general than the sources quoted in n. 70. His story is hardly more plausible; but it indicates that the later sources distort an earlier (cf. Ar. *Lys.* 1155-6) and more specific version.

itself is suspect. It is sometimes adduced to explain facts better understood otherwise;[72] and the one clearly attested case of a tyrant regulating access to his city, that of the son of Promnesus who allowed ten days' stay in the city of Cephallenia each month (Heracl. Lemb. 64 = Ar. fr. 611.64 Rose), is neither a major restriction nor a sign of serious concern. The only other case known to me is that of the three tyrants/oligarchs of Erythrae who 'allowed none of the people within the walls, but made their judgements in a court which they had prepared outside, in front of the gates' (Hippias of Erythrae *FGH* 421 F 1). We know too little to judge these cases fairly; but they do not make a general restriction more credible for Periander by establishing a trend that tyrants commonly restricted access to their cities to reduce the risk of disorder.

Modern commentators have offered an economic interpretation which is also claimed as an explanation of the slave regulation and the supposed attack on idleness. The tyrant is said to have wished the slave population of the Corinthia to remain static in order to prevent further slave competition pressing upon either the rural or the urban free labourer; while at the same time, living in the city and idleness were outlawed in order to halt a drift of the hard-pressed rural population into an overcrowded city unable to provide work for all its inhabitants.[73] None of these suggestions can be disproved; but they have a strong flavour of modern theoretical economics, and probability speaks strongly against them. If such problems had existed early in Cypselus' day, they hardly remained after the extensive programme of colonization which continued under both Cypselus and his son Periander. He would, I take it, have preferred to found more colonies if they had been necessary rather than to hope that the difficulties would evaporate if he legislated against their effects.

Access to the city will not have been limited because that was part of the technique of tyranny: Periander had not read his Aristotle. A restriction on Corinthians in general will have been motivated by fear that Corinthians in general would participate in riots; but there is neither evidence nor probability that they were inclined to disorder. If they were, it is difficult to see how the favourable view of Periander survived (and, perhaps, how he survived); it certainly did not do so among the great men of Corinth. The scope of the restriction was probably more limited.[74] To forbid

---

[72] Esp. Ar. *Pol.* 16. 2-3, 5 (loans to small farmers and the δικασταὶ κατὰ δήμους under Peisistratus).

[73] Pleket, *Talanta*, i (1969), 47-9; cf. Will, *Korinthiaka*, 510-12.

[74] Cf. Burn, *Lyric Age*, 191.

the city to named individuals or specific groups[75] would make excellent sense for a second-generation tyrant under pressure from ambitious or jealous enemies. The attack on luxury is perhaps to be interpreted partly in the same sense; and Nicolaus' story that Periander punished those who were idle in the agora in the fear that they were plotting against him might well have originated in punishments of those who defied a ban of this kind. Periander was perhaps civilized enough to restrict those whom he did not trust instead of doing away with them altogether: he did not lop off the heads of corn he merely suspected of being higher than the rest.[76]

d. The Tyrants and the State

We have no explicit evidence of how, if at all, the Corinthian state was organized under the tyrants; but a good case can be made for attributing many of the Corinthian institutions of the classical period to Cypselus. Nicolaus says that on the fall of the tyranny 'the demos established (the text is corrupt, but the sense is clear) the following constitution: it set up a group of eight *probouloi*, and from the rest chose a council of nine men ⟨from each tribe⟩' (*FGH* 90 F 60.2: below, 231). Nicolaus thus attributes the council and *probouloi*, and perhaps the tribal arrangements on which they were based, to the period immediately after the tyranny;[77] but this probably rests on the invalid assumption that since the constitution was used in post-Cypselid Corinth it was designed to serve a city without a tyrant.[78]

The structure of government was shattered by Cypselus' revolution; a main point of the coup was to remove from power those who had held a monopoly of it. The practices of Bacchiad Corinth are only imperfectly known; but they are very different from those of the post-Cypselid period.[79] The tyrants are more likely to have been

[75] Compare, on a larger scale, the Roman practice of banning the Latins from Rome at the time of politically sensitive meetings of the *comitia tributa*.

[76] The story of Thrasybulus and the ears of corn might derive from a tradition that Periander 'cut the great men down to size': part of the favourable view of him which originated with ordinary Corinthians. Κολούω sometimes carries a less drastic meaning than in Herodotus (Powell, *Lexicon*, s.v.); cf. Plat. *Legg.* 731 A, *Apol.* 39 D.

[77] Accepted by Busolt, *Staatskunde*, i.363 with n. 4; apparently, Jeffery, *Archaic Greece*, 153.

[78] Cf. (attributing the *probouloi* to the Bacchiads) Schaefer, *RE* xxiii (1957), 1221; Roebuck, *Hesperia*, xli (1972), 114.

[79] See above, 56–7. Schaefer (*RE* xxiii (1957), 1222) argues that the *probouloi* were a Bacchiad institution, since the office is found in Corcyra (*IG* ix.1.682). That may be a coincidence; if it is not, control of the colony by a Corinthian tyrant provides as plausible a context for the introduction of *probouloi* at Corcyra as the time of its foundation. *Probouloi* are not easily compatible with the aristocratic Bacchiad state: they belong to a more complicated age.

responsible for the changes than the oligarchs who followed them. Cypselus will not have swept away Bacchiad arrangements and put nothing in their place: he made an explicit claim to have saved Corinth from the arbitrary rule of a clique, and to rule without formal arrangements would have been no better. Periander is stated to have been an *aesymnetes* by two sources, neither of them trustworthy;[80] the position of the tyrants may have been made formal in this way, but the evidence cannot establish the conclusion. Nicolaus reports that Cypselus was made *basileus*; but this evidence is also of doubtful value (above, 190).

The most important aspect of any new arrangements would have been the formation of a council; and we have (scarcely reliable) evidence for the existence of one under Periander, who is credited by Heracleides, following Aristotle, with a council ἐπ' ἐσχάτων. Its function was supposedly to prevent expenditure from exceeding income; no doubt it undertook other tasks too. Peisistratus and his sons could live with the Solonian constitution in Athens; arrangements devised by the Cypselids to suit themselves and the ambitions of their powerful supporters might well have lasted. It has often been conjectured that the eight local tribes originated with the tyrants;[81] certainly they are presupposed by the classical constitution, which was so extensively based on the eight tribes that a catchword 'eight of everything' (πάντα ὀκτώ : *Suda* s.v.) developed.[82] The notice of the *Suda*, which attributes the tribes to Aletes, is perhaps to be explained by reluctance after the fall of the tyrants to admit that they were responsible. If it was they who gave Corinth her constitution and tribal structure,[83] only general arguments can be invoked to determine whether the work was done by Cypselus or his son (or by both); but probability is strongly in favour of

---

[80] Diog. Laert. i.100; Theodorus Metochites p. 668 Müller. Periander is identified as *prytanis* in the poem quoted by Diog. Laert. i.97; but this is hardly reliable evidence.

[81] Dunbabin, *Western Greeks*, 55; Will, *Korinthiaka*, 612 n. 2 (with caution); Berve, *Tyrannis*, 18. See now Jones, *TAPA* cx (1980), 187.

[82] Roebuck (*Hesperia*, xli (1972), 115-16) attributes the tribal reorganization to the Bacchiads, on the ground that it fits well with a time at which the Corinthia absorbed part of the Megarid (but see above, 45); he suggests that the introduction of the tribes marks, in effect, the synoecism of Corinth. It seems to me extremely improbable that the Bacchiads would have altered the tribal system through which they had established their domination (cf. Jones, *TAPA* cx (1980), 188); Attica, at least, was synoecized well over a century before Cleisthenes' locally based tribal division.

[83] To what extent tyrants in other cities made similar changes it is impossible to say: Solon might have been a tyrant, but chose to legislate instead. In so far as tyranny was mainly a reaction against the aristocratic past, it is likely that the Cypselids were not alone. Peisistratus provides no counter-example, in view of Solon's work; indeed, if we knew enough of other cities Peisistratus' exception might well have proved the rule.

Cypselus.[84] It was in his time that the need for new arrangements was greatest.[85]

If the constitution was mainly the work of Cypselus little can be said of his motives except that something was needed to replace Bacchiad institutions. The council of eighty is of some interest; it was smaller than the Bacchiad council, if the latter numbered 200 (above, 56). If eighty places satisfied the ambitions of Cypselus' supporters, that gives striking emphasis to the restricted nature of the group which demanded political power in Corinth: it was smaller than the Bacchiads themselves. The oligarchy which followed the tyrants was distinguished by its ability to ensure that its decisions accorded with the wishes of the population at large; the Corinthian governing class probably began to learn its complementary skills of moulding and following popular opinion under the leadership of the tyrants. It is possible that the *probouloi* were introduced by the tyrants at least in part for precisely this purpose (below, 238-9); but the part the tyrants played, by introducing them, in the development of *probouleusis* as a technique of government cannot have been central: they were anticipated at Sparta.[86]

The details of the tribal structure remain controversial (below, 413-9); but it is clear that membership of the tribes was initially determined by residence, and this alone makes it possible to clarify Cypselus' purpose in introducing them. The kinship tribes of Bacchiad Corinth will have been disrupted by the expulsion of the Bacchiads; most positions of tribal supremacy were now vacated, at least in the Dorian tribes—unless Bacchiads belonged to only one of them, which is improbable. Non-Bacchiads could perhaps have stepped into the gaps; but this would probably have represented such a change in the traditional structure that it seemed better to establish new tribes to form the basis for the organization of the state· than to risk criticism for excessive tampering with hoary

[84] Heracl. Lemb. 20 says that Periander set up the council ἐπ' ἐσχάτων and that it regulated expenditure. What appeared in Aristotle's *Cor. Pol.* may have been that Periander gave an already existing council this function. Cypselus would hardly have gone without—of all things—a council.

[85] Cf. (briefly) Berve, *Tyrannis*, 26. Oost argues (*CP* lxvii (1972), 21-8) that Cypselus claimed to restore the traditional Bacchiad kingship in his own person; if so, the changes will have been made by Periander, but Oost's case is exceedingly weak. The murder of Patrocleides/Hippocleides, which Oost claims as symbolic (ibid., 22), hardly needs explanation in a revolution; and that Cypselus was sometimes called *basileus* (cf. ibid., 23) is no indication of his formal position. Oost's remaining arguments (ibid., 24-8) are no more persuasive, and a claim to be returning to a hereditary monarchy does not fit the political realities of the seventh century.

[86] See esp. Andrewes, *Probouleusis*; the date, Salmon, *JHS* xcvii (1977), 93, 99 with refs., esp. Forrest, *Phoenix*, xvii (1963), 157-79.

institutions. Almost certainly the old tribes were not abolished any more than Cleisthenes destroyed the four Ionian tribes of Attica, although our evidence refers only to the non-Dorian Aoreis and one of its ph(r)atries, the Omacchiadae (below, 414); but the Oligaethidae, mentioned by Pindar and defined as a ph(r)atry by the Scholiast, may have belonged to one of the Dorian tribes.[87]

It is therefore possible to explain the new local tribes without supposing that they were intended to achieve a positive purpose; a new arrangement may have seemed necessary after the disruption to the old that Cypselus' revolution brought with it. Positive purposes might be suggested but seem to me improbable. It has often been supposed that the change was intended to facilitate the admission of non-Dorians to the citizen body; but our evidence indicates rather that at Corinth the distinction between Dorians and others was insignificant (above, 192–3). In any case, the establishment of a local tribal structure was not necessary to achieve such a purpose if (as this hypothesis demands) those in power were sympathetic to non-Dorians. It is significant that at Sicyon, where the tribal factor had an important effect, the old tribes were retained but their political positions reversed. It is possible that the kinship tribes were replaced for political purposes because the hereditary principle, on which they were based, was under attack; but the seventh century is very early for such a development, which only reached Athens with the reforms of Cleisthenes. Nor is it likely that Cypselus attacked a principle which was the basis of his most significant supporters' claims to political power.

The new tribes were probably not only local in character but made up a similar way to the Cleisthenic tribes of Athens: the Corinthia was divided into three (or perhaps more) regions, and each tribe consisted of part of each region (below, 413–9). Such a complicated arrangement must have been designed for a purpose; but only conjecture can suggest an answer. Cleisthenes' purpose in introducing his ten tribes seems to have been twofold: to discourage disputes between differing regions of Attica by giving people from different regions a common interest in one tribe; and to ensure that only a small part of an aristocrat's traditional following would be in the same tribe as the aristocrat himself.[88] That Cypselus had a purpose of the latter kind is improbable: after the revolution, the only possible targets were those aristocrats who

[87] Pind. *Ol.* xiii.97 with Schol. ad loc. In Attica, phratries had more life than the tribes: cf. Lewis, *Historia*, xii (1963), 38 with n. 144.
[88] Cf. esp. Lewis, ibid., 22–40, esp. 36–40.

remained and no doubt supported him. Of disputes between differing regions of the Corinthia there is no sign; but they may well have taken place. In Attica the tyranny of Peisistratus was preceded by a period in which local factions threatened the unity of the state. The situation in pre-Cypselid Corinth was different in important respects; but there must have been struggles between the Bacchiads and their aristocratic rivals. There was one disturbing difference between these disputes and those of a century later in Attica. None of the Attic factions had secure control of Athens; but the Bacchiads were masters of Corinth, and the attempts to dislodge them may well have been a serious threat to the fabric of the state. In Attica the tribes were introduced when the factions of the 570s re-emerged after the tyranny; Cypselus' similar reforms may have had a similar purpose when the unity imposed by the Bacchiads seemed to be in danger. Even if we knew that there had never been disputes between local factions in the past, Cypselus may have believed that to establish locally based tribes would be to risk a threat of disintegration if he did not attempt to impose some artificial unity. The Corinthians may have been the first to rest their tribal structure on purely local factors;[89] if they were, the consequences will have been unknown and the possibilities may have been alarming. The Corinthian phalanx had no doubt fought in the past in tribal contingents,[90] in each of which were to be found men from all over the Corinthia; Cypselus may have decided upon the complicated tribal pattern in order to ensure that his new tribal contingents came from as wide an area. The arrangements may therefore reflect difficulties not observed in the past but anticipated for the future.

e. **Colonies**

Our sources serve us better for Cypselus' colonies than for any other aspect of his work as tyrant. The main connected accounts are in Nicolaus and Strabo. 'He led out those who were not friendly to him to a colony so that he could rule those who were left behind more easily; he sent them to Leucas and Anactorium, and appointed his bastard sons Pylades and Echiades as their oecists' (Nic. Dam. *FGH* 90 F 57.7). 'And the Corinthians, sent by Cypselus and Gorgus, took that shore (sc. Leucas) and went on to the Ambracian Gulf. Ambracia and Anactorium were founded, and they cut through the

---

[89] Sparta had probably preceded Corinth in tribal reform; but in Sparta the old tribes may have been an integral part of the new scheme (Forrest, *Sparta*, 43–5).
[90] Compare Sparta: Tyrt. fr. 19, 8 West.

isthmus of the peninsula and made Leucas into an island.[91] Strabo implies that the three colonies he mentions were conceived as a single enterprise: that Ambracia was the main foundation, and that Leucas and Anactorium were established at the same time as part of the same scheme. Gorgus, the leader of the whole scheme, was the oecist of Ambracia;[92] and the greater size of Ambracia in the classical period[93] probably reflects the intentions of those who planned the whole enterprise. Certainly the site of Ambracia is the most favourable of the three, for it possessed a great deal more good agricultural land.

The Corinthian origin of both Leucas and Ambracia is supported by other texts, though they refer neither to Cypselus nor to his sons.[94] There is no reason to doubt that the tyrant was responsible for the foundations even though the sites have not been sufficiently tested to provide archaeological confirmation: the colonies will have remembered the names of their founders. Gorgus is credited by Strabo (452; cf. 59) with a canal through the spit which joined Leucas to Acarnania.[95] There are no geological reasons to doubt the account,[96] and it should probably be accepted. The city of Leucas was situated to the south of the spit: if the latter was impassable, that would have meant either a long detour to the south of the island or embarkation some way to the north of the city for a journey to the north or into the Ambracian Gulf. In the fifth century Leucas could bear that difficulty, for Thucydides twice refers to Peloponnesian fleets being dragged over the isthmus, which I take it implies that the passage could not be navigated (iii.81.1; iv.8.2); but the inconvenience was real, and if a canal was attributed to Cypselus and Gorgus it is likely that the spit was known once to have been passable. The canal probably tended to become silted up, so that periodic dredging was necessary to keep the passage clear.

---

[91] Strabo 452. Plut. *Mor.* 552 E makes Periander the founder of Leucas and Anactorium (and Apollonia: below, 211); but the context of the information detracts from its credit, and it cannot stand against the evidence of Nic. Dam. and Strabo.

[92] Strabo 325; Ps.-Scymn. 453–5; cf. Anton. Lib. 4.4.

[93] Calculated on the basis of military strength: for Leucimme, Ambracia and Leucas provided much the same number of vessels (Thuc. i.27.2), but at Sybota there were twenty-seven Ambraciot and ten Leucadian (Thuc. i.46.1). It is highly unlikely that Leucas could match the number of hoplites raised by Ambracia in 425: an army of 3,000 (Thuc. iii.105.1) still left many to spare (Thuc. iii.110.1; 112–13).

[94] Leucas: Hdt. viii.45; Thuc. i.30.2; Ps.-Scyl. 34; Ps.-Scymn. 465; Plut. *Timol.* 15.1; Ambracia: Thuc. ii.80.3; Harpocr., *Suda* s.v.

[95] Other authors refer to the fact that the canal was dug, but do not attribute responsibility: refs. in Oberhummer, 8 n. 2.

[96] Despite numerous statements to the contrary; see Philippson, *Landschaften*, ii. 474–9, esp. 477–8.

Pseudo-Scylax, in the second half of the fourth century, describes Leucas as an island (34), and says that it was separated by a channel from Acarnania; either the channel was clear in his day or his source knew of an earlier time when it was.[97]

These three foundations were fully Corinthian in the sense that they were led by Corinthians; but Thucydides describes Anactorium in 433 as 'common to Corcyra and (Corinth)' (i.55.1), while Themistocles arbitrated between Corinth and Corcyra concerning Leucas and judged that Corinth should be fined and that the two claimants should share rights as metropolis (below, 272-3). Other cities in these western waters were sometimes said to have been Corinthian foundations, sometimes Corcyraean, and sometimes both. Apollonia according to Thucydides was Corinthian,[98] and Stephanus of Byzantium gives more details (s.vv. Ἀπολλώνια, Γυλάκεια): there were 200 Corinthian colonists under a Corinthian founder Gylax, after whom the city was first named Gylaceia. Strabo (316) and Pseudo-Scymnus (439-40), however, made the place a joint foundation of Corinth and Corcyra; Pausanias (v.22.4) claimed Corcyraean involvement, but corruption of his text makes it unclear whether he allowed any part to Corinth. Plutarch (*Mor.* 552 E) dates Apollonia to the reign of Periander, but this information is rendered untrustworthy by the attribution of both Leucas and Anactorium to the same tyrant (above, 210 n. 91). Plutarch's notice at least makes it likely that Apollonia was founded during the tyranny; that accords with other traces which place it in the late seventh or early sixth century.[99] Epidamnus was agreed to be a Corcyraean foundation; but Thucydides states that the oecist was Phalius son of Eratocleides, a Corinthian descended from Heracles, that he was sent for by Corcyra from her mother city according to the ancient custom, and that Corinthian colonists went with him.[100] Epidamnus' foundation date is given as 627 in Eusebius; if that is approximately correct—and such archaeological information as is available at least does not contradict it—it is uncertain whether the responsibility was that of an ageing Cypselus or a youthful Periander.[101] Potidaea, in the north-east, stood alone among Corinthian colonies; it is credited by Nicolaus to Periander, whose son Euagoras

[97] Oberhummer, 10-11.

[98] i.26.2; cf. Plin. *NH* iii.145; Dio xli.45.1.

[99] Van Compernolle, *AC* xxii (1953), 60-4. Archaeological evidence is compatible with, but cannot prove the truth of, such a date (Hammond, *Epirus*, 426).

[100] Thuc. i.24.1-2; cf. Strabo 316; Ps.-Scymn. 435-6.

[101] Eusebius (ed. Schoene ii. 88-9) placed the foundation after the accession of Periander; but that is hardly reliable evidence. For the archaeology, cf. Hammond, *Epirus*, 426 with refs.

is said to have died while founding the place (*FGH* 90 F 59.1); no source associates any city but Corinth with the foundation.

Potidaea was probably settled by Corinthians. alone, but our information about the Adriatic cities may have been distorted by the fifth-century disputes between Corinth and Corcyra in this region (below, 272-80). For Ambracia there is no evidence of anything other than a Corinthian origin; but that proves no more than that the Corcyraeans were unable to make any impression there in the fifth century. Thucydides' description of Anactorium and the disagreements of our sources over Apollonia might reflect either shared foundations in the seventh century or disputed control in the fifth.[102] At Leucas, Themistocles' decision hardly proves that Corcyra really had a part in the foundation: only that in the circumstances of the fifth century it was politic (or in Athens' or Themistocles' interest) to pretend that she had. In the 430s, however, Corcyra made notoriously little effort to support Epidamnus until Corinth became involved; the mainly Corcyraean origin reported by our sources for that city therefore probably reflects the truth.

Our evidence for the origins of the colonists is untrustworthy; fortunately there is no doubt about the status of the three southern cities themselves. The oecists of Ambracia, Leucas, and Anactorium were sons of Cypselus. There is strictly no evidence that they were also tyrants; but there can be little doubt that they were.[103] Thus these cities were purely Corinthian at least in the sense that they were ruled by the sons of the Corinthian tyrant. Apollonia and Epidamnus were not—as far as we know—founded by relatives of the tyrant; but in other respects they were probably similar to the colonies of the Ambracian Gulf. Gylax was a Corinthian, though he is not attested as a Cypselid; the fact that he (unusually) gave his name to the colony indicates that he was more than a mere oecist, and that he ruled his city much as the sons of Cypselus ruled theirs. Phalius at Epidamnus is also not recorded as a member of

---

[102] We cannot rely on the authority of Thucydides to determine the truth in either case. Aristotle's statement (*Pol.* 1290 b 8-14) that the descendants of the original colonists at Apollonia were few and ruled the other inhabitants cannot be taken to support Stephanus' information that the colony was founded by 200 Corinthian settlers (as it seems to be by van Compernolle, *AC* xxii (1953), 54): Aristotle's account could be true if there were well over 200 original settlers.

[103] For the two Cypselids attested as tyrants in Ambracia, see below, 277-8 with n. 2. Corcyra was ruled under Periander by a relative of the Corinthian tyrant (Hdt. iii.52.6-53), and this is likely to reflect the method of government adopted for other cities in the region; cf. Lloyd, *JHS* xcv (1975), 56 with n. 90.

Cypselus' family;[104] but he may have been a tyrant whatever the origin of his colonists, for Corcyra was under Corinthian control when Epidamnus was founded (below, 218-9). Euagoras the oecist was no doubt intended to act as tyrant under Periander at Potidaea, but he died before the colony had been long established; there is no information about what arrangements were made subsequently.

Molycreium, a small city just west of Naupactus, is described by Thucydides (iii.102.2) as a Corinthian colony. It has usually been attributed to the tyrants, along with the Corinthian possessions of Sollium, in Acarnania probably opposite Leucas, and Chalcis, a little west of Molycreium. The tyrants may have been responsible for Corinthian activity in these places; but a more plausible context can be found in the fifth century (below, 227-8). Doubt of a different kind attaches to a fourth city: Heracleia. A famous golden phiale probably found at Olympia bears the inscription, in Corinthian letters, 'The Cypselids dedicated this from Heracleia.'[105] Serious consideration cannot be given to any Heracleia but that on the Ambracian Gulf;[106] but the precise circumstances cannot be recovered. 'Cypselids' may mean the sons of Cypselus who founded cities on the shores of the Ambracian Gulf; but the dedication was probably made some time later, by Cypselids who survived here well after the fall of the dynasty in Corinth.[107]

The state of the Adriatic coast before the foundation of the colonies is obscure. Corinthian contacts are attested in the mid-eighth century not only with Ambracia and Leucas but also with Vitsa Zagoriou in inland Epirus (above, 86, 90-1); Thucydides remarks (i.47.3) that in the fifth century Corinth had long enjoyed good relations with the inhabitants of the area, and Periander consulted the oracle of the dead at Ephyra in Thesprotia.[108] But none of this shows that the colonists were welcomed, though they seem quickly to have reached an accommodation with the Epirots. In the fifth century the Illyrians pressed hard on Epidamnus (Thuc. i.24). Appian reports (*BC* ii.39) that the city was founded by Corcyraeans

[104] That he is called a descendant of Heracles (Thuc. i.24.2) does not exclude a relationship with the tyrant, who might have called himself Heracleid through his mother if·he had thought it to his advantage to make the claim.

[105] Casson, *AJA* xxxix (1935), 513-14; for the find-spot, Servais, *AC* xxxiv (1965), 149 n. 24.

[106] Steph. Byz. s.v., no. 21; Plin. *NH* iv.5.

[107] Below, 228 with n. 165. Hammond (*Epirus*, 426 with n. 5) seems to claim Heracleia for a Corinthian colony; but the word order of the inscription indicates the translation 'The Cypselids dedicated this (from the spoils taken) from Heracleia.' rather than 'The Cypselids from Heracleia dedicated this.'

[108] Hdt. v.92 η 2; for references to excavations and discussions, Dakaris, in Stillwell, MacDonald, and McAllister, *Princeton Encyclopaedia*, 310-11.

in association with Taulantians, who had previously been expelled from the site by Liburnians. The context of the account inspires little confidence; for Apollonia we do not even have evidence to doubt.

There is some information about Acarnanian relations with the first colonists on and near the Gulf of Ambracia; much of it is suspect. Pseudo-Scymnus (459–61) reports that Anactorium was founded by Corinthians and Acarnanians; but that story probably has its origin in the fact that the place was appropriated by Acarnania (with Athenian help) during the Archidamian War.[109] Pseudo-Scylax (34) states that the Acarnanian inhabitants of Leucas, suffering from internal strife, accepted 1,000 Corinthian colonists, who then killed the Acarnanians and took the place for themselves. The number of Corinthians is reasonable; but if it is based on genuine tradition that does not guarantee the truth of the rest of the account. The walls of Leucas, if they were built when the colony was founded, might indicate that the colony needed to defend itself; their appearance does not discourage the conjecture, but recent evidence seems rather to demonstrate a date in the mid-fourth century or later.[110] Acarnania was bitterly hostile to Corinth at the time of the Archidamian War; but that may have been the result of the fifth-century conditions. Two early inscriptions may reflect fighting between colonists and natives in the region of the Ambracian Gulf.[111] A Corcyraean named Arniadas was buried in Corcyra with an epitaph, dated between 650 and 550 by letter-forms, which recorded that he died 'fighting by the ships on the flowing Araththus'. Arniadas might have been one of a Corcyraean force which helped Ambracia in its early years against the Epirots; but he might equally have died fighting against the Corinthian colonists.[112] The Cypselid dedication from Heracleia (above, 213) probably testifies to fighting between the colonists and the natives; but date and circumstances are obscure.[113] We know nothing of relations between Potidaea and the

[109] Below, 318, cf. Oberhummer, 76.

[110] For this information I am indebted to Tom Gallant.

[111] Anton. Lib. 4.4 refers to a war between the colonists and the Epirots; but this is unreliable evidence (below, 220 n. 133).

[112] Jeffery, *Local Scripts*, 234, no. 11. Contrast Oberhummer, 75–6 with Will, *Korinthiaka*, 529 n. 3. For relations between Corinth and Corcyra in this period, below, 218–9, 222, 276.

[113] Hammond (*Epirus*, 427) argues that the Eleans were the first to colonize on the Ambracian Gulf: that Rogous, which he identifies as the obscure Elean colony Buchetium, is a more attractive site than Ambracia and must have been settled first. Quite apart from the fact that Hammond's location of Buchetium at Rogous is a mere guess (though a plausible one, accepted by Dakaris, *Cassopaia and the Elean Colonies*, 135), the chronology of the whole of Greek colonization could be rewritten on the basis of such arguments. Dakaris

previous inhabitants. Euagoras the oecist died at or soon after the time of the foundation;[114] he may have been killed in conflict with the natives or with Greeks from the older Euboean foundations in the region, but many other fates are possible.

The purpose of the colonies can only be determined by inference. They—in contrast to Corcyra and Syracuse—will have been expected to remain under Corinthian control through their tyrant/oecists; but this does not necessarily show that they were founded for some purpose which demanded continued control. It would be natural for a tyrant to establish tyrants in his colonies whether the latter had a continuing function to perform or no. In the cases of his sons Cypselus had an obvious personal motive in addition; there was a less obvious, but hardly less powerful, motive at Apollonia and Epidamnus: close political allies were as worthy of reward as sons.

It is certain, however, that the purpose of almost all the colonists was to secure opportunities which they lacked at home. It is true that Nicolaus treats the colonies as a means of removing Cypselus' enemies from Corinth (*FGH* 90 F 57.7); but such men must have been insignificant. The tyrant had few enemies; and he would hardly have handicapped his sons by giving them malcontents for citizens.[115] Most colonists no doubt volunteered in the hope of improving themselves; but that is not necessarily to say that the colonies were designed to relieve conditions that were becoming dangerous in Corinth.[116] The success of Syracuse and Corcyra will have made similar foundations attractive to men who had a sufficient but small livelihood in the Corinthia. Perhaps some thousands of families were settled;[117] but that hardly proves earlier over-population in the Corinthia. Corcyra provided most of the colonists at Epidamnus and perhaps some elsewhere; even when Syracuse and Corcyra were founded Corinth did not provide all the colonists (above, 66).

For the colonists themselves the desire to improve themselves with plots in the new foundations is an entirely sufficient explanation; but for the tyrants different motives are possible. No doubt

(ibid., 134) argues that 'it is not feasible that the Eleans could have founded colonies along the Ambracian Gulf when the Corinthians were in control'; but the Eleans will not necessarily have been unwelcome to the Ambraciots. Franke (*Die Münzen von Epirus*, 52) puts the Elean colonies in the fifth century; nothing can show that he is wrong.

[114] Nic. Dam. *FGH* 90 F 59.1.
[115] Cf. Will, *Korinthiaka*, 528.
[116] As argued by (e.g.) Oost, *CP* lxvii (1972), 27.
[117] 1,000 colonists are reported at Leucas (Ps.-Scyl. 34); the figure cannot be checked, but is reasonable enough.

they acted in part to satisfy the prospective colonists; but they might have taken the opportunity to pursue other objectives. This question can only be approached through the sites chosen for the colonies: various possibilities have been offered. 'Imperialism', without further definition, is suggested by Graham; but the only colonies which clearly had such a purpose were founded far later by Athens and Sparta in order to secure or extend already existing empires.[118] To describe the colonies as imperial means little more than that the tyrants expected to retain control over them—though the success of Cypselus may have persuaded Periander to extend the principle (below, 224). Cypselus may have hoped to neutralize a Corcyra which was still friendly to the Bacchiads (below, 218-9).

The sites of some colonies have encouraged the belief that commercial considerations were involved. Ambracia stands near the end of the most important land route northwards to Epirus,[119] and Leucas was in a useful position for Adriatic voyages; Potidaea was well situated to exploit trade with Macedonia. Anactorium, on this view, will have been intended to secure for Ambracia the entry to her Gulf; while Epidamnus and Apollonia each stood at the western end of a not unimportant route inland. A more specific suggestion has been that the colonies were intended to secure Corinth's supplies of silver from the mines of inland Epirus;[120] but there are too many colonies to be explained on these grounds, and the downward revision of the date of the first Corinthian coins casts doubt on the whole argument (above, 170). The colonies may have served as bases for actions against pirates. Thucydides says that Corinth 'destroyed piracy', and the reference is to the period of the tyranny (below, 223).

These factors may have been taken into account; but they are unlikely to have been of major importance. Cypselus did not need to found three colonies in the region of the Ambracian Gulf to suppress piracy. One would have sufficed, and Ambracia, at least, is not particularly suitable for the purpose. Greater difficulties attach to the question of directly commercial motives. Some of the colonies could serve the convenience of those who carried on the trade from Corinth along these routes, which had been opened more than a century before; but it is doubtful whether they will

[118] *Colony and Mother City*, 30-4. Athens: Brea and Amphipolis, perhaps Thurii; Sparta: Heraclea in Trachis (ibid., 34-9). Also perhaps the colonies of Dionysius I of Syracuse: cf. ibid., 208-9.

[119] Philippson, *Landschaften*, ii.118-21; Hammond, *Epirus*, 33-7, 148-9.

[120] Beaumont, *JHS* lvi (1936), 181-4; followed (with doubts) by Will, *Korinthiaka*, 535-8.

have made a serious material difference. It is even more doubtful whether Cypselus will have chosen the sites of his colonies in order to increase the comfort of such merchants (see further below, 405-6).

Either necessity or ambition made new colonies attractive to numerous Corinthians; if the colonies were founded on these grounds alone their locations are easy to explain. All the sites near the Ambracian Gulf were well known at Corinth before, and Ambracia in particular was attractive; it would be surprising if Cypselus had not chosen the Ambracian Gulf for settlement. Leucas was only less attractive because its fertile land was not so extensive; in other respects it was an ideal site, so long as the canal was planned from the beginning. Anactorium was different; it was designed to secure the entrance to the Ambracian Gulf, probably because Cypselus feared a threat from Bacchiad Corcyra (see below, 218-9). There is no direct evidence for Corinthian contacts with the Adriatic north of Corcyra before Apollonia and Epidamnus were founded; but they are the best sites along this coast. Apollonia may have been settled mainly by Corinthians; but Epidamnus was not, and Corcyraeans may have been heavily involved also at Apollonia. Why Corinthian tyrants should have provided colonies for Corcyraeans is unclear; but these cities, along with Potidaea, were founded significantly later than those on the Ambracian Gulf. The latter may have opened the eyes of the tyrants to the possibilities of naval domination further afield (below, 224).

f. Foreign Policy

We know little of Cypselus' relations with other cities; this is perhaps no accident, for the fourth century saw Periander as exceptionally warlike, and Aristotle may imply a contrast between Cypselus and Periander in this respect.[121] There was no doubt some special motive in the marriage of a daughter of Cypselus to an Athenian Philaid which issued in an Athenian Cypselus, eponymous archon in 597/6;[122] but it cannot be recovered. Periander himself married Melissa, also called Lyside, the daughter of Procles tyrant of Epidaurus, probably while Cypselus was still alive. The pretty story of how Periander fell in love with her while she was pouring wine wearing simple clothes hardly shows that the marriage was not a matter of policy.[123] Cypselus' interest in Epidaurus apparently initiated a special

[121] *Pol.* 1315 b 27-9; cf. Nic. Dam. *FGH* 90 F 58.3.

[122] Davies, *Athenian Propertied Families*, 295.

[123] Pythaenetus of Aegina, *FGH* 299 F 3. For the marriage, see also Hdt. iii.50.1; v.92 η 1-4; Diog. Laert. i.94.

relationship which lasted until the end of the fifth century (below, 329-30). Its basis was perhaps a shared fear of Argos; but it may be significant that Periander's marriage was recorded by Pythaenetus in his History of Aegina. Probably at some time in the early seventh century that island broke free of its early dependence on Epidaurus.[124] Relations were no doubt strained in consequence, and Corinth and Epidaurus may have been brought together by their shared enmity for Aegina.[125] Athens was similarly hostile.

Cypselus' relations with Corcyra have usually been approached mainly through Thucydides' statement that 'the earliest sea battle of which we have knowledge' was fought between Corinth and Corcyra 260 years 'before the end of this war', that is *c*.664 or *c*.681 (i.13.4); but uncertain chronology makes this report difficult to use. Even if the date is approximately correct it is unclear whether the battle took place before or after Cypselus' revolution; and there are strong arguments for revising the date drastically on the ground that it is based on an excessive forty-year generation count.[126] The result of the battle is equally uncertain. Thucydides reports it in a context of Corinthian primacy in naval affairs, and it may have been a Corinthian success;[127] but the argument is of doubtful force.

A better starting-point is Nicolaus' statement that when the Bacchiads were driven out of Corinth they went to Corcyra (*FGH* 90 F 57.7). This implies that Corcyra was then friendly to Bacchiads, and therefore hostile to Cypselus. This helps with the date of the battle. If it was fought under Bacchiads, whatever its result they are unlikely to have been welcomed at Corcyra; they cannot have been strong enough to force an entry, and we should conclude that the battle had not yet been fought. Herodotus, it is true, asserts that Corinth and Corcyra were hostile from the very foundation of the colony (iii.49.1); but this is probably an anachronism, and the origin of the hatred will have been precisely the arrival of the Bacchiads in flight from Cypselus.[128] Corcyra, founded but two or three generations ago with a Bacchiad oecist and probably other Bacchiads as leading colonists, was an obvious place of refuge.

Whether Cypselus thought it necessary to subdue Corcyra remains unclear; but Periander certainly controlled the island towards the end of his life. Corinthian control had been established by the time of the foundation of Epidamnus, which saw close co-operation

[124] Hdt. v.82-8. Cf. Dunbabin, *BSA* xxxvii (1936/7), 90-1; Jeffery, *Archaic Greece*, 150.
[125] Wormell, *Hermathena*, lxvi (1945), 13.
[126] Forrest, *CQ* xix (1969), 99-100; Lloyd, *JEA* lviii (1972), 277-9.
[127] Zörner, 63.
[128] Cf. Jacoby ad *FGH* 90 F 57.7; Forrest, *CQ* xix (1969), 106 n. 3.

between Corinth and Corcyra;[129] but it is unclear which tyrant was responsible for the foundation. Thucydides says that in 435 Anactorium was common to Corinth and Corcyra (i.55.1). If this is taken to prove a joint participation in its foundation, then it was Cypselus who first established control over Corcyra, for Anactorium was his work; but Thucydides' remark need not prove anything about the origins of the city (above, 212). The fate of the Bacchiads when Corcyra was reduced is unknown: it was probably now, if ever, that they went to Sparta and perhaps elsewhere.

Cypselus enjoyed the favour of Apollo; that god supported the tyrant, at least after he had established himself, and may have played a significant role even before the coup (above, 186-7). He was rewarded with impressive offerings: a bronze palm-tree with frogs and snakes beneath, and a treasury to hold it and no doubt other offerings;[130] it was the earliest treasury known to have been constructed at Delphi, and the dedications will have done Cypselus as much good as Apollo. The same will have been true of the magnificent temple which Cypselus probably built for Apollo at Corinth early in his reign.[131] The tyrant called one of his sons Pylades (Nic. Dam. *FGH* 90 F 57.7): that was the name of a hero of Cirrha, the city which controlled Delphi and with which Cypselus must have been on excellent terms.[132] Cypselus probably sought, and if he did he certainly received, Delphic approval for

---

[129] Cf. Forrest, ibid.; contrast Graham, *Colony and Mother City*, 31. The co-operation at the time of the foundation of Epidamnus is of course compatible with the Corcyraean independence which Graham suggests; but in view of the earlier enmity, an independent Corcyra will probably have founded a colony without reference to Corinth, whatever the normal procedure for the foundation of second-generation colonies.

[130] The palm: Plut. *Mor.* 164 A, 399 E-F, 724 B; see esp. Deonna, *RHR* cxxxix (1951), 162-207; cxl (1951), 5-58 (but see Will, *Korinthiaka*, 487-8 n. 2). The treasury: Hdt. i.14.2; Plut. *Mor.* 164 A, 400 D-E. For references to French work on the treasury itself, Will, ibid., 542 n. 2; cf. Jeffery, *Local Scripts*, 104, no. 21.

[131] Above, 59-62. Earlier doubts that the temple was dedicated to Apollo have been unnecessarily revived by Wiseman, in Temporini (ed.), *Aufstieg und Niedergang*, ii.7.1, 475, 530. Pausanias refers to a temple of Apollo on the right of the road leading from the forum to Sicyon, and this fits the building on Temple Hill exactly (ii.3.6); this perfectly clear statement is not affected by uncertainty about other parts of Pausanias' route. If we reject this natural identification, then Pausanias did not mention the temple which dominated the forum from Temple Hill at all. Wiseman's tentative suggestion that the archaic temple was dedicated to Athena receives no support from the fragment of an inscription of c.575-550 which reads φοινι[κ . . .] (Jeffery, *Local Scripts*, 131, no. 18); the word could equally well represent the independently attested Corinthian month as the epithet of Athena (above, 146 n. 45).

[132] Schol. Eur. *Or.* 33; Forrest, *Historia*, vi (1957), 172; (in general) *BCH* lxxx (1956), 47. Cragaleus, the eponym of the Cragalidae of Cirrha (Aeschin. iii.107-8), had some connection with Ambracia (Anton. Lib. 4); but the exact significance remains obscure.

his colonies.[133] Whether he also cultivated the favour of Zeus at
Olympia is less clear; the family had close connections with Olympia,
but the responsibility was probably Periander's.(below, 228).

Cypselus may have devoted more effort to defence than to
aggression; a wall in the Potters' Quarter which has a clear date in
the third quarter of the seventh century[134] can only have been
defensive. Its faces were of stone, and the interior filled with rubble;
the average width was 2.40 m., and cross-walls at intervals of c.5 m.
gave added strength.[135] A wall on such a scale must have been a
fortification; and its discovery in the Potters' Quarter has a special
importance. The defensive problems of Corinth were exceptional.
Acrocorinth was a natural fortress; but artifical defences of the
lower city which did not include the citadel would allow an enemy
the advantage of approach from above.[136] Both the citadel and
the lower city therefore had to be included in the fortifications;
thus a very long circuit was required. The shortest such system
might not have included the Potters' Quarter, for the eastern edge
of the ravine to the east of the plateau on which the Quarter was
built provided a suitable course; but a wall built here would have
left the easiest approach to Acrocorinth, from the west, dangerously
exposed. Only by following the western edge of the Potters' Quarter
plateau (Pl. 44) could the most vulnerable approach to the citadel
be adequately defended. This course was followed by the later
circuit (Fig. 6); the discovery of Cypselus' wall at exactly this crucial
point demonstrates that the early system was based on the same
plan.[137] It is not clear whether Cypselus felt it necessary to fortify
the citadel once he had brought its western approach within the
system; and the line of his wall from the east cliffs of Acrocorinth
may not have followed the same course above the valley of the
Leukon as the later city-wall. But the broad pattern of Corinth's

[133] An oracle of Delphic (cf. Cragaleus, above, n. 132) Apollo for Ambracia is recorded
by a late source (Anton. Lib. 4.4; Parke and Wormell, *Delphic Oracle*, ii. no. 394). But its
context—a dispute between Apollo, Artemis, and Heracles over priority in the city—does
not inspire confidence in the historical details (despite Berve, *Tyrannis*, 19, 524); none is
given by the fact that Gorgus is said to have been Cypselus' brother.

[134] Stillwell, *Corinth*, xv.1.14; the South Long Building, erected in the last quarter of
the century (above, 101–2), took account of the existence of the wall (ibid., 15).

[135] Ibid., 14.

[136] A late Roman wall was built at Corinth which did not include the citadel; but such a
system was greatly inferior. See Gregory, *Hesperia*, xlviii (1979), 264–80, esp. 278–9.

[137] Stillwell, *Corinth*, xv.1.62, suggests that the Potters' Quarter wall was part of a
separate system for the Quarter alone; that the tyrant, or even the potters themselves,
devoted such resources to the defence of just the Quarter is incredible. If the wall was built to
defend the approach to Acrocorinth (Winter, *Greek Fortifications*, 64), it is placed remarkably far away from the citadel; a much less costly (and more easily manned) defence
for the approach alone could have been devised.

defences for the rest of her history was established as early as the seventh century: to the north of the city they followed the line of one of the bluffs above the plain, and from either end of this northern course the wall ran south, using what slopes were offered by the terrain, to reach the cliffs of Acrocorinth.

Cypselus' purpose in building these massive defences is unclear. The scheme is hardly to be explained by the supposed desire of tyrants to keep their subjects at work, and Cypselus will not have built the wall to keep the Bacchiads at arm's length; no other particular enemy is recorded and no guess imposes itself. General considerations may have been more important than the fear of particular enemies. Corinth's defensive problems were exceptional on purely topographical grounds. The primitive Dorian founders of Corinth may have been prepared for the destruction of their homes so long as they could flee to Acrocorinth and save themselves; but in Cypselus' time Corinth was worth defending, with its increasingly impressive public, and presumably increasingly wealthy private, buildings. But it was in a hopelessly exposed position; and the intervention of Pheidon of Argos may have indicated how vulnerable the city was even though he lost his life (above, 71-2). Any wall that was to serve a useful purpose had to follow much the same line as Cypselus chose; the length of the circuit is imposed by the topography. Cypselus may have felt it necessary to provide the city with walls because at the Isthmus it was open to attack from almost every direction. The recent development of the phalanx may have provided a further general motive; but we cannot know anything of the capabilities of the early phalanx in respect of storming cities without the slightest natural defence. Paradoxically, the early date of the fortifications makes it easier in one sense to understand their scale: there were few if any precedents to limit Cypselus' imagination once he had decided that a system was necessary.[138]

The signs are that Cypselus was not aggressive; by contrast, his son was characterized by Aristotle as warlike: πολεμικός (*Pol.* 1315 b 27-9). Nicolaus is more specific: 'he was for ever making expeditions and was warlike: he built triremes and used both seas' (*FGH* 90 F 58.3). Our sources give few details of this constant activity. Herodotus gives a personal motive for an expedition against Procles of Epidaurus, Periander's father-in-law (iii.50-2): Epidaurus was taken and Procles captured because he had caused Periander's son Lycophron to believe that his father had been responsible for his mother's death.

[138] There has been some reluctance to accept so large a circuit so early: Winter, ibid.; Lawrence, *Greek Aims in Fortification*, 215-16.

The true reason cannot be discovered, though it was probably related to that for which Cypselus made the original alliance with Epidaurus. If Cypselus did not establish control over Corcyra, Periander certainly did so. Towards the end of his rule he entrusted the island to Psammetichus his nephew (Nic. Dam. *FGH* 90 F 59.4); Lycophron had probably ruled there before that.[139] The implication of Nicolaus' account of Psammetichus' journey from Corcyra to take up the tyranny in Corinth is that Periander retained control of the island at least until shortly before his death. We have one other scrap in the lines of the Theognidean corpus (891-4) which curse the Cypselids after describing the destruction of Cerinthus in Euboea, the ravaging of the Lelantine plain, and civil strife in an unidentified, probably Euboean city. The reference must be to an otherwise unknown undertaking of Periander[140] in Euboea, perhaps connected with the foundation of Potidaea; its scale and purpose remain obscure.[141]

This is very little detail to support the reputation of Periander. His active interests were no doubt more widespread than those of his father, whose recorded activity was restricted to the west. The description of Periander as warlike may rely more on what was believed of the typical tyrant than on what was known about Periander; but his energy is supported by an attractive conjecture of Forrest. The tenth entry in the thalassocracy list of Eusebius, dated 730-669, is given as the Carians, but this is impossible; the solution is to emend, and Forrest has argued persuasively that the Corinthians are the best candidates. He has also shown that what lies behind the list is a fifth-century account from which Thucydides took his details of Corinthian naval affairs: 'The Corinthians are said to have been the first to engage in naval activity in a manner very close to that of the present, and triremes are said to have been built first in Greece at Corinth. Ameinocles the Corinthian appears to have made four vessels for the Samians too; and Ameinocles went to Samos about 300 years before the end of this war. The earliest sea battle of which we have knowledge was fought by the Corinthians against the

---

[139] Lycophron: Hdt. iii.52.6-53; Diog. Laert. i.94-5. A similar story is told of a son named Nicolaus by Nic. Dam. *FGH* 90 F 59.1-2. He adds that Lycophron, another son of Periander, died 'while establishing a tyranny among the *perioeci*'; perhaps a confused reference to Lycophron at Corcyra.

[140] Cypselus cannot be excluded; but he is less likely.

[141] The conjectures of van Groningen (*Theognis*, 341), that Periander was helping Eretria by attacking, from Potidaea, a Cerinthus that was part of the Chalcidian sphere, are based on a false date for the Lelantine War; but he refutes earlier views that the Cypselids are not Corinthian (ibid., 340-1). For conjectures concerning the affair, see Jeffery, *Archaic Greece*, 66.

Corcyraeans: it took place about 260 years before the same time.'[142]
The Corinthian thalassocracy is a product of fifth-century historio-
graphy; its date increases its credit, and the facts which Thucydides
derived from it are not to be doubted. It is a different matter with
Thucydides' absolute dates. They place Ameinocles and the sea
battle between Corinth and Corcyra a century before Periander's
time; but that is far too early. Thucydides argues that with economic
development tyrannies arose, and the Greeks took more interest in
the sea: the details of Corinthian naval affairs follow (i.13.1-5).
This sequence is stronger evidence than the absolute dates; the naval
developments were subsequent to the establishment of the Corinthian tyranny.[143]

Nicolaus' description of Periander's naval energy makes it probable
that he, rather than his father, was responsible for the Corinthian
'thalassocracy'. Thucydides places Ameinocles and his triremes[144]
forty years (i.e. a generation) before the battle with Corcyra,[145] and
Cypselus may therefore have built the first Greek triremes; but if so,
they probably had very little strictly military significance, for naval
affairs were dominated by penteconters in Greece for some time to
come.[146] Thucydides' source for naval affairs had a notion similar
to that of the compiler of the thalassocracy list in Eusebius: a
succession of powers enjoying primacy at sea.[147] The idea is too
schematic and too close to the Athenian experience: Periander
hardly exercised anything approaching the naval domination of
fifth-century Athens. But there does seem to have been a tradition
that Corinth under Periander employed her naval power on an
unprecedented scale, and this both supports and clarifies the more
general judgement of Aristotle: Periander's military energy was
concentrated on the sea, and he turned naval affairs in a new

[142] *CQ* xix (1969), 95-101. It is these details in Thucydides which make the Corinthians
a better emendation than Burn's Megarians (*JHS* xlvii (1927), 167-8); on palaeographical
grounds alone, the latter are just as probable (or improbable).

[143] Cf. Lloyd, *JEA* lviii (1972), 276-9. Lloyd's arguments from archaeological evidence
in *JHS* xcv (1975), 53, however, are of doubtful force: Basch, *JHS* xcvii (1977), 10.

[144] Formally speaking, Thucydides does not identify the vessels built by Ameinocles as
triremes; but it is excessive to insist (Rougé, *La Marine dans l'antiquité*, 93-4) that they
were not.

[145] This battle might in principle provide a fixed point; but it cannot be given a context
with confidence. Forrest (*CQ* xix (1969), 99, cf. 104, 106) suggests that it was a Corinthian
defeat which, for Eusebius' source, closed the Corinthian thalassocracy; Jeffery's suggestion
(*Archaic Greece*, 159 n. 3) that the battle marked the establishment of Periander's control
over Corcyra is no less plausible, and other contexts might be suggested (e.g. a defeat of
Corcyra by Periander after Lycophron's death). A date after the death of Periander is not
excluded.

[146] See esp. Basch, *JHS*, xcvii (1977), 6-8.

[147] Thuc. i.13.2-14.3; cf. Myres, *JHS* xxvi (1906), 86-7.

direction. There is little evidence either for Periander's aims or for
his methods. Thucydides mentions in particular the suppression of
piracy (i.13.5): that is particularly suitable for a naval power without
a predecessor, but it is doubtful whether Periander developed his
strength at sea only for such a purpose. Other factors were presumably involved, and the most likely is sheer ambition. Periander
inherited a string of colonies along the Adriatic coast. The opportunity
they presented and his own energy may well have suggested to him
a plan for domination of the waters of the western mainland. The
subjugation of Corcyra and the foundation of Apollonia and
Epidamnus may represent, at least in part, an extension to the north
of his ambitions, while Potidaea indicates that he was eager to look
even further afield.

   A few further scraps of information tend to support the view that
Periander cut a greater figure in the world than his father. He
arbitrated between Mytilene and Athens over the question of Sigeum;
he awarded the place to Athens by recognizing the status quo when
it was in Athenian hands.[148] Periander's arbitration shows both his
reputation among his contemporaries and that he was on bad terms
with neither party; more importantly, it indicates that he was thought
to have no concern in the Hellespont himself: interested parties make
bad arbitrators. His decision does not mean that he viewed Athens as
a potential ally in mainland Greece: it may have been a serious
attempt at a solution.[149] According to Herodotus Periander was a
particularly close friend of Thrasybulus of Miletus.[150] Periander
informed him about a Delphic oracle given to Alyattes, who was
then besieging Miletus; the news enabled Thrasybulus to reach a

[148] Hdt. v.95.2; Apollodorus *FGH* 244 F 27; possibly mentioned by Alcaeus: cf. Page,
Sappho and Alcaeus, 159 with n. 1. Tenedos 'used Periander as a witness' against the Sigeans
in the fourth century (Ar. *Rhet.* 1375 b 30-1); they probably used his statement of arbitration between Athens and Mytilene (Will, *Korinthiaka*, 560 n. 1) rather than anything
separate (as, apparently, Jacoby ad *FGH* 566 F 129, n. 538). Timaeus, according to Demetrius
of Scepsis (ap. Strabo 600), stated that Periander built Achilleum for the Mytilenaeans as a
protection against the Athenians (*FGH* 566 F 129). Timaeus' statement may rest on the fact
that Periander's arbitration left Achilleum in Mytilenaean hands (cf. Page, *Sappho and
Alcaeus*, 158 n. 2). If Timaeus is quoted correctly (which is doubtful), it is better to take
the statement that Periander supported Mytilene against Athens as a mistake than to suppose
(with Jacoby ad loc.) that he changed his allegiance during the long struggle between Athens
and Mytilene; Demetrius' argument, that one does not choose allies of disputants as
arbitrators, seems conclusive.
[149] It is unlikely that Athens would have accepted Periander as an arbitrator after the
Sacred War (below, 227-9); the arbitration therefore took place before that war began
c.595 (Forrest, *BCH* lxxx (1956), 33 with 34 n. 1). That accords with our other sources for
the chronology of the Sigean War (Page, *Sappho and Alcaeus*, 152-8), and indeed provides
useful confirmation that they are approximately correct.
[150] Thus the alignment of the Lelantine War was reversed (Andrewes, *Tyrants*, 50;
Forrest, *Emergence*, 119). That will not have concerned Periander.

settlement (Hdt. i.17-22). It is perhaps curious that at about the same time the shipwright Ameinocles was lent to the Samians (Thuc. i.13.3); but the friendship of Periander for Samos is rather confirmed than contradicted by the Samian rescue of 300 Corcyraeans from the fate prepared for them in Lydia by Periander, for the Corinthians clearly expected a welcome at Samos despite their gruesome business.[151] Ameinocles may have been sent to Samos by Cypselus; we might argue that he took Samos' part but his son preferred friendship with Miletus. But there is no obvious reason for such a change, and the story of the Corcyraean boys implies that Periander too enjoyed good relations with Samos. There were good reasons for a *rapprochement* between Samos and Miletus in the late seventh century, and there is even some evidence in favour of one (below, 226); Periander may have been able to be on good terms with both states at the same time.

Thrasybulus may have enabled Periander to open communications with Lydia. There is no evidence, despite what has often been claimed, that Corinth and Lydia were in contact before Periander's time;[152] but Periander sent the 300 Corcyraean youths to be castrated by Alyattes (Hdt. iii.48.2). It is excessive to deny any political significance to the episode on the ground that it was a particularly nasty form of slave-trading;[153] but the story does not prove close links. Periander's relations with Egypt and its rulers, on the other hand, may have been more important; there may have been a connection with Miletus here too. Our direct evidence is lamentably general, and consists merely of the name given (presumably by his father Gorgus) to Periander's nephew Psammetichus. The fact should mean something more than we have for Lydia; but its significance cannot be recovered.[154] Whether the last Corinthian tyrant was named after

[151] Cf. Will, *Korinthiaka*, 550. It remains possible that the Corinthian sailors, reluctant to carry out their orders, colluded with the Samians in order to avoid punishment. Plut. *Mor.* 860 B-C affirms on the authority of Antenor and of Dionysius of Chalcis that it was Cnidians who took the youths back to Corcyra, and that Cnidus enjoyed 'honours, exemptions, and decrees' at Corcyra as a result. Plutarch has been taken to deny Samian participation in the affair, and even as right to do so (Wickert, *Peloponnesische Bund*, 16); but Cnidus is not a suitable place to stop at on the way from Corinth or Corcyra to Sardis. Plutarch means not that the affair took place at Cnidus but that it was Cnidians who rescued the youths—at Samos. Whether or not that is true is unclear; Herodotus will have heard the story at Samos and may have falsely assumed that the heroes were Samian.

[152] The fact that Lydian offerings, including some of Gyges, were to be found in the Corinthian treasury in Herodotus' day (i.14.1-2; 50.3; 51.3) is nothing to the point; they were probably all placed there, like Croesus' lion (i.50.3), after the mid-sixth-century fire. Even then, the reason may only have been that it was one of the few buildings available (Will, *Korinthiaka*, 552-3).

[153] Ibid., 552.

[154] It was not a matter of Necho's use of Corinthian naval expertise, as argued by Lloyd, *JHS* xcv (1975), 45-61; see Basch, *JHS* xcvii (1977), 1-10. Nor is it likely that Corinth's

Necho's father Psamtik I or his son Psamtik II it is impossible to say
and hardly matters:[155] perhaps even Gorgus was not sure himself.
Whatever the nature of Periander's interest in Egypt, a connection
with Thrasybulus is extremely likely. Miletus probably enjoyed a
special position at Naucratis from the late seventh century,[156] and
Necho dedicated the garment which he had worn during the capture
of Cadytis in the sanctuary of Apollo at Branchidae (Hdt. ii.159.2-3).

The items which link Periander with Samos, Miletus, and Egypt
are tantalizingly suggestive. The presence of Samos causes the greatest
surprise, but it may be no accident that Samos and Miletus are
associated in an Egyptian context at Naucratis. Not only were they
two of the three states to possess separate sanctuaries under the
protection of the pharaoh: the sanctuaries were placed next to
each other.[157] We can only guess at the motives which lay behind
these connections; but the primary role may have belonged to
Thrasybulus. Of all the states involved, Miletus came under the
greatest threat: she experienced a long Lydian siege. Herodotus
informs us that the great advantage enjoyed by Miletus in the siege
was her control of the sea (i.17.3): Periander may have given more
help than his information from Delphi. To find Samos and Miletus
as allies is unusual; but the Lydian threat was not only directed
against Miletus, and the Samian possessions on the mainland were
close by. That fact was what normally made Samos and Miletus
enemies; but good sense dictated a common defence against Lydia.[158]
What Thrasybulus might have gained from Egypt is less clear; but the
friendship of another oriental power against Lydia will have done him
no harm, and Necho's dedication at Branchidae must be significant.

It is easier to reconstruct benefits Periander provided to these
allies than those he may have received. Thrasybulus offered him
advice as to how to secure his tyranny, and a pharaoh gave his name
to Psammetichus; the former is of doubtful truth and the latter of

triremes were modelled on those of Necho, unless they were of a pattern quite different
from the later Greek type: Necho's vessels were probably of the Phoenician form (Basch,
JHS xcvii (1977), esp. 3-6, 9-10). See now further Lloyd, *JHS* c (1980), 195-8; Basch,
JHS c (1980), 198-9.

[155] Contrast Lloyd, *JHS* xcv (1975), 55 with Berve, *Tyrannis*, 527.

[156] Milesian primacy (along with Samian and Aeginetan) is the obvious interpretation
of Herodotus' account of the separate sanctuaries of those states (ii.178.3) in contrast with
the general Hellenion (ii.178.2-3). Archaeology shows that Herodotus is wrong to date
Naucratis to the reign of Amasis (ii.178.1); the earliest material belongs to the last quarter
of the seventh century, and the Milesian sanctuary of Apollo has finds almost as old (Austin,
Greece and Egypt, 22-4).

[157] Ibid., 24 with n. 1 (p. 60). On Samians in Egypt, see further ibid., 27 with n. 1.

[158] Such collaboration might have been easier if Samos, like Miletus, was under the
control of a tyrant; at least an *aesymnetes* is to hand: the undated but probably early
Phoebias (Theodorus Metochites p. 668 Müller; cf. Barron, *CQ* xiv (1964), 211).

doubtful value. Lloyd suggests that Periander's external relations were an attempt to secure powerful friends against domestic difficulties;[159] but Corinthian enemies of the tyrant would not hold their hands for thought of such distant states, and his Egyptian name did not save Periander's nephew Psammetichus. Periander may have hoped to secure from Egypt the imports of corn that may have been necessary for the Corinthia by now; he was thought to have no interest in the Hellespont (above, 224), perhaps because he calculated that the Egyptian supply was sufficient. But the absence of Corinthians from Herodotus' list of those who shared in the sanctuaries of Naucratis is a serious impediment.

Only one advantage derived by Periander from these connections can be reconstructed; and it can be connected with an issue of Corinthian foreign policy which must have caused Periander grave concern. An isolated report in Frontinus records a successful attack by Thrasybulus of Miletus on the harbour of Sicyon (*Strat.* iii.9.7). It is difficult to avoid the conclusion that the episode was connected with the First Sacred War. In that war Cleisthenes of Sicyon, along with Athens and others, wrested control of Delphi from Corinth's ally Cirrha.[160] Corinth is not mentioned in connection with the war,[161] but Thrasybulus' attack on Sicyon will have been made at this time in the interest of Periander;[162] the Milesian fleet will, I take it, have reached the Corinthian Gulf by way of the diolkos.

The Sacred War led to changes in Apollo's allegiance; and this is reflected in the dedications of the Corinthian tyrants. Cypselus had extremely close links with Delphi; but for Periander we know only that early in his reign he reported to Thrasybulus the reply to Alyattes. The Cypselids seem to have diverted their attention to Olympia after Cleisthenes of Sicyon and his allies forced Apollo to change his stance.[163] Soon after the fall of the tyranny the Delphians

[159] *JHS* xcv (1975), 56.

[160] Forrest, *BCH* lxxx (1956), 33-52. I am not persuaded by Robertson (*CQ* xxviii (1978), 38-73) that the Sacred War was an invention of partisans of Philip of Macedon, although there is no doubt that almost all the details we have are imaginative reconstructions; see briefly Lehmann, *Historia*, xxix (1980), 242-6.

[161] Nic. Dam. *FGH* 90 F 61.5 reports that Cleisthenes accused Isodemus, his brother and predecessor in the tyranny, of plotting with the Cypselids of Corinth. The story is probably invented; in any case, the accusation was too early to have had anything to do with the Sacred War.

[162] Jeffery, *Archaic Greece*, 213, refers the attack to a mere border war between Corinth and Sicyon. This is less likely; Thrasybulus had derived benefit himself from Periander's contacts with Cirrhan Delphi.

[163] Herodotus' claim (vi.128.2), that Cleisthenes first chose Hippocleides as a husband for Agariste partly because of his relationship to the Cypselids, hardly argues against enmity between the Sicyonian and the Corinthian tyrants; and Herodotus' remarks might be a mere guess.

recognized the claim of the Corinthians to Cypselus' treasury; but Olympian Zeus rejected a similar request.[164] He may have had good reason. Two magnificent dedications offered ·at Olympia by the house of Cypselus—the colossus of gold and the 'chest of Cypselus' described by Pausanias—were probably given not by Cypselus but by his descendants, and precisely towards the end of Periander's reign.[165] The obvious conjecture is that Periander was no longer welcomed at Delphi after the Sacred War, and that he began to cultivate Olympian Zeus. It is likely that the large temple probably built by Periander in his last years (above, 202) was dedicated to the same god. It must have been in the region of the Gymnasium, where the few remaining fragments have been found. Pausanias records a burnt temple here, on the left of the road to Sicyon not far from the city, and gives two stories about it: that it was a temple of Apollo burned by Pyrrhus son of Achilles, and that the Corinthians built it for Olympian Zeus but it was destroyed 'by a sudden fire from somewhere' (ii.5.5). The latter is more plausible, for the former is mythical; and Pausanias presumably refers to the same temple at iii.9.2, where the Corinthians claim the burning of their Olympieium as an omen which prevented them from sending troops with Agesilaus to Asia Minor in 396 (below, 342). None of the links in this chain of evidence is complete; but the combination of the date and approximate location of the temple, the stories told to Pausanias, and the strong probability that Periander transferred his devotions from Apollo to Olympian Zeus after the Sacred War make a powerful case for identifying this large temple as his most costly attempt to secure Zeus' favour.[166] The god was impressed, and remained loyal to the Cypselids even after they were driven from power.[167]

[164] Plut. *Mor.* 400 D-F; cf. (for Delphi) Hdt. i.14.2.

[165] For the colossus, Servais, *AC* xxxiv (1965), 147-52; the date (after 600): ibid., 152. The chest (Paus. v.17.5-19) is unlikely on art-historical grounds to belong to the seventh century; but (not being preserved) it cannot be accurately dated. Schefold (*Myth and Legend in Greek Art*, 74) suggests that it was made *c*.570 for exiled Cypselids; *c*.590 and a dedication by an ageing Periander are just as possible on stylistic and more likely on historical grounds. Payne was clearly uncertain when to date the chest: contrast *Necrocorinthia*, 125 with 351 and n. 4. A third offering, the inscribed gold phiale dedicated by the Cypselids of (presumably) the Gulf of Ambracia, might belong to Cypselus' reign; but since a strong case can be made for a transfer of Periander's attention from Delphi to Olympia after the Sacred War, it is best to attribute the bowl to the same period or later.

[166] It is perhaps too fanciful to suggest that the mythical story in Pausanias, that the temple was dedicated to Apollo, is somehow connected with the change in the tyrant's allegiance; but Pausanias' attribution of the building of the temple of Olympian Zeus to 'the Corinthians' may reflect a change similar to that which the priests of Apollo allowed at Delphi.

[167] Servais, *AC* xxxiv (1965), 168 n. 66, declines to conclude that there was a change in 'la politique religieuse' of the tyrants. That is only proper if the Sacred War is not brought

So Periander derived some benefit during the Sacred War from his friendship with Thrasybulus; he may have hoped to derive more, and other help may have been given but not recorded. But it is unlikely that the connections with Thrasybulus, Samos, and Egypt were designed to secure a major Corinthian interest. It should not be ignored that Periander may have sold his naval expertise; it is perhaps therefore significant that the only areas to which he may have done so are far away from Corinth. To offer vessels (even at a high price) to close neighbours would have been dangerous; it may have been precisely because Periander believed that Corinth had no essential interests in the eastern Aegean that Samos and Miletus could enjoy the benefits of Corinthian experience. That would fit well with the implication of Periander's arbitration over Sigeum, that he had no interests in the Hellespont; paradoxically, the areas in which we have most evidence for Periander's friendships are those with which he was least concerned. Thrasybulus may have been a personal friend, and Periander or (perhaps more likely) Gorgus may have been proud of the connection with a distant pharáoh; but essential Corinthian interests were, in Periander's view, closer to home.

g. The Fall of the Tyranny

The end of the regime needs little discussion. When Periander died he had for some time faced growing opposition: his successor would face even more. Periander had no living sons and entrusted the tyranny to his nephew, Psammetichus son of Gorgus.[168] He ruled, according to Aristotle, for three years (*Pol.* 1315 b 26). 'He was tyrant over the Corinthians until some of them joined together and killed him after he had held the tyranny for a short while, and freed the city. The demos tore down the house of the tyrants and made public their property; they threw (Psammetichus') body out of the country without burial, dug up the graves of his ancestors, and cast out their bones' (Nic. Dam. *FGH* 90 F 60.1). Plutarch (*Mor.* 859 C-D) attributes responsibility for the overthrow of the tyranny to Sparta. It is no argument against this account that Nicolaus knows nothing of it, for his version inspires little confidence; but it is

into the account (as it is not by Servais); if it is, to resist the conclusion is excessively cautious.

[168] The name is given as Cypselus by Nic. Dam. when he refers to his rule at Corinth (*FGH* 90 F 60.1), and as Psammetichus at *FGH* 90 F 59.4; but the two references are clearly to the same man, who when he became tyrant preferred a famous Corinthian to a famous Egyptian name.

difficult to believe that Sparta was either capable of or interested in
the suppression of a tyranny so far away across a hostile Arcadia or
an equally hostile Argolid, and the signs are that the story was unknown to Herodotus.[169]

It is impossible to say how many Corinthians felt hostile to
Psammetichus. Nicolaus believed that those directly responsible
were few, but that the demos was happy to be freed and eager to
insult the body of Psammetichus and the bones of his ancestors;
but this is not serious evidence. We have no more; but the persistence
of the favourable tradition about Periander does at least demonstrate
that a significant section of Corinthian opinion remained favourable
to the end of his rule, and probably his nephew's. Whether that
meant that those who removed the tyrant faced serious opposition
from his supporters is doubtful, for the extent of the change represented by Psammetichus' fall is easily exaggerated. Far more than
Periander, he will have relied upon advisers, and they were probably
strongly represented among those who ejected him; if so, the end
of the tyranny may have meant little more than the murder of the
last tyrant: the formal institutions of government introduced by the
tyrants could have continued much as before. No doubt a few
personal friends and flatterers of Psammetichus suffered a similar
fate; but those who ran Corinth under the guidance of Periander
and his nephew probably continued to run the city after they had
removed the last guide. Some Corinthians may have regretted
Psammetichus' passing; but he was not to be brought back from the
dead. One thing, at least, is clear: the tyrants were not removed in
the interests of the Corinthian demos, or even of a more restricted
but still numerous group such as the hoplites; if such a group had
been so advanced in the early sixth century it could not have been
satisfied with the narrow opportunities it enjoyed under the Corinthian constitution for the next two and a half centuries.[170] Exceptional
but shadowy Corinthians helped Cypselus to power in order to secure
influence through him: equally exceptional, but unfortunately no
better known, Corinthians ejected Cypselus' grandson because he
now stood in their way.[171]

[169] Socles makes no reference to it when he argues that for Sparta to impose a tyrant on
Athens would be to populate the trees with fishes (below, 247; cf. Berve, *Tyrannis*, 530).
[170] Cf. ibid., 25.
[171] For all this, see above all Forrest, *Emergence*, 114–16. It is, regrettably, too fanciful
to make a direct connection between the fall of the tyranny and the establishment in the
second quarter of the sixth century of a hero shrine at the western end of the South Stoa
(Williams, *Hesperia*, xlvii (1978), 11–12).

XVI.   The Constitution

Formal Corinthian constitutional procedures are very imperfectly known. The only specific account is found in Nicolaus of Damascus. The text is corrupt, but has been satisfactorily cured by Will: the Corinthian demos, after the fall of the tyranny, 'set up a group of eight *probouloi* (men who undertake preliminary deliberation), and from the rest chose a council of nine men ⟨from each tribe⟩.' Each of the eight tribes (below, 413-9) probably provided one *proboulos*; and it is natural to suppose that the *probouloi*, whatever their precise function, served on the council ex officio. Thus the eight *probouloi* and the seventy-two ordinary members formed a council of eighty.[1] A Corinthian council of elders, which is presumably to be identified with the council of Nicolaus, is given a prominent part by Diodorus in his account of the dispatch of Timoleon to Sicily in 346/5.[2] A Corinthian assembly—though one of minor importance—is mentioned by Plutarch, who asserts, when explaining why Dion sent for help from Corinth when he was preparing a constitution for Syracuse in the mid-fourth century, that 'Corinth was more oligarchically governed, and dealt with little public business in the assembly' (*Dion* 53.2-4). This evidence might not give strong support for the existence of a Corinthian assembly if it stood on its own, since Plutarch may have applied to Corinth what he saw as a rule among oligarchies in general; but there was an assembly in early Hellenistic Corinth, as is shown by the decree from Delos now identified as Corinthian,[3] and Thucydides mentions in passing a Corinthian ξύλλογος in 421 which is almost certainly an assembly (v.30.5). Argive

---

[1] Nic. Dam. *FGH* 90 F 60.2: μίαν μὲν ὀκτάδα προβούλων ἐποίησεν, ἐκ δὲ τῶν λοιπῶν βουλὴν κατέλεξεν ἀνδρῶν θ ⟨ἐκ φυλῆς ἑκάστης⟩. Will, *Korinthiaka*, 609-15, following Busolt, *Griechische Geschichte*, i.658 n. 1 (accepted by Stroud, *CSCA* i (1968), 241 n. 26); for alternative suggestions, all of them far less satisfactory, see refs. in Stroud, ibid. Jones (*TAPA* cx (1980), 185-6 n. 28) has now offered a further conjecture which has a similar effect but introduces nine *oktades* of councillors, each consisting of one councillor from each tribe; it is difficult to see what function these *oktades* (as distinct from that of *probouloi*) might have performed.

[2] xvi.65.6,9 (γερούσια); it met, according to Diodorus, in a council-house (βουλευτήριον), and is also called a συνέδριον (xvi.65.8). This whole passage, however, is unreliable in detail (below, 384 n. 69). A council is attested in the late fourth-century Corinthian decree from Delos (below, n. 3).

[3] Robert, *Hellenica*, v (1948), 6, lines 9-10; see below, 413-4.

ambassadors went to Corinth during the diplomatic ferment that followed the Peace of Nicias and asked for an immediate alliance; but they were told to come to the next Corinthian ξύλλογος, which, to judge from Thucydides' usage elsewhere, should mean 'assembly'.[4]

We hear nothing of magistrates beyond those with military functions before the Hellenistic period. The *probouloi* are most unlikely, in view of the meaning of their title, to have been magistrates in the strict sense; there must therefore have been civil magistrates, but not even the title of the office (or priesthood) used for dating at Corinth is known before the late fourth century, when a decree is dated by the *grammatistas*.[5] The office may, but need not, have originated much earlier; the names and functions of other civil offices are quite unknown. Thucydides sometimes gives details of those who held military commands before and during the Peloponnesian War. In some cases he uses the probably untechnical verb ἄρχω (command);[6] but he uses the title *strategos* three times, and elsewhere employs the related verb στρατηγῶ (act as *strategos*): up to five *strategoi* for a single expedition are recorded.[7] Some support for the view that the title was *strategos* is afforded by an abacus with the inscription ΣΤΡΑΤΑ[in letters of the fifth century, found in a public building of Hellenistic date.[8] Herodotus is normally less concerned than Thucydides to use technically correct terms; but he gives the same title to Adeimantus, the Corinthian commander during the invasion of Xerxes.[9] Thucydides shows that five or more *strategoi* served at Corinth; that their term of office was annual is a natural assumption which receives some support from Xenophon's account of Agathinus and his successor in command of the Corinthian fleet in the early years of the Corinthian War.[10] It is easy to conjecture that

---

[4] Literally, the word means merely 'gathering', but where Thucydides uses it of a gathering of members of a single state (contrast ii.12.1, cf. 10.3) it always refers to an assembly, though there may in some passages be an implication that it is informal (esp. ii.22.1 with Gomme, *HCT* ii.76); Bétant, *Lexicon Thucydideum*, s.v. Plutarch implies that the assembly took part in the dispatch of Timoleon to Sicily; but this evidence has an even more doubtful value than *Dion* 52.4: see below, 385.

[5] Robert, *Hellenica*, v (1948), 6, line 2. For a *hypogrammateus* of uncertain date, see Stroud, *Hesperia*, xli (1972), 199 n. 4.

[6] ii.33.1 (three commanders); vii.7.1, 19.4, 34.2 (one each). Gongylus, on his arrival at Syracuse, is called εἶς τῶν Κορινθίων ἀρχόντων (vii.2.1), but the language is probably still untechnical. The ἄρχων of the garrison sent to Ambracia (iii.114.4) is, I take it, a different kind of officer, although the individual concerned had acted as *strategos* before (i.46.2).

[7] *Strategos*: i.46.2 (five); ii.83.4 (three); iv.43.1 (two; cf. Plut. *Nic.* 6.4). The verb: i.29.2 (five); i.60.1-2 (one: for the official status of this expedition, see below, 295 n. 35).

[8] Williams, *Hesperia*, xlvi (1977), 72-3 n. 29. Date and find-place: ibid., 53-7.

[9] viii.5.1, 59, 94.1 (where he is in ἡ στρατηγίς, the vessel of the *strategos*).

[10] See below, 353-4, 363 with n. 85. I take it that the word used by Xenophon—ναύαρχος— is descriptive rather than technical.

each of the eight Corinthian tribes had its own *strategos*; but Corinth may, like Athens, eventually have changed such a system so that *strategoi* could serve without restriction of tribe. What evidence we have indicates that Corinthian *strategoi* acted as a college, without an overall commander.[11]

I know of no other evidence which might be used to reconstruct the detailed provisions of the Corinthian constitution. What we have covers the long period from the fall of the tyranny until after the Macedonian occupation in 338, and there is nothing to prove that the constitution remained much the same for the whole of that time.[12] It would be surprising if the informal distribution of power between the various institutions did not alter between the early sixth century and the late fourth, for other states saw a great increase in the political consciousness of the demos during that period; but it is a reasonable hypothesis that such developments as took place at Corinth in this respect could be accommodated within the existing pattern. At least we have no contrary evidence; and some kind of positive argument is provided by the evident stability of the Corinthian regime. Doubtless there were minor changes in formal practice; but the broad legal framework probably remained constant.

Some sources, however, throw light on the general nature of the constitution. The most direct is Plutarch's characterization, quoted above, of mid-fourth-century Corinth as an oligarchy in which little public business was conducted in the assembly; and more than a century earlier Pindar wrote an ode for Xenophon of Corinth which provides stronger, even though less direct, evidence for a similar conclusion. He described Corinth as a city where

> Lawfulness dwells, and her sister,
> Safe foundation of cities,
> Justice, and Peace, who was bred with her;
> They dispense wealth to men,
> Golden daughters of wise-counselling Right.
> They wish to keep away
> Pride, the bold-spoken mother of Surfeit.[13]

[11] Cessation of tribal restriction at Athens: Fornara, *Athenian Board of Generals*, 19–27. At i.46.2 Thucydides refers to the Corinthian *strategos* Xenocleides as πέμπτος αὐτός. Similar expressions in Athenian contexts have been shown by Fornara (ibid., 28–39) to mean, not that the individual concerned had a formal superiority, but rather that the historian wished to emphasize the *strategos* thus singled out, even though his authority was constitutionally equal to that of each of his colleagues.

[12] The tyranny of Timophanes provided one brief interruption (below, 384–5). See also below, 355–7.

[13] *Ol.* xiii.6–10 (tr. Bowra). Xenophon won both the foot-race and the pentathlon in the Olympic Games of 464 (Pind. *Ol.* xiii.30; the date, Schol. Pind. *Ol.* xiii, inscr.).

Εὐνομία (Lawfulness, Good Order) was an oligarchic virtue, and Corinth must at the time have been oligarchically governed;[14] the same conclusion is indicated by two of the few constitutional details we have. *Probouloi* were regarded by Aristotle as peculiar to oligarchies;[15] and the small size of the council is a strong argument for its oligarchic nature.[16]

It may thus be confidently asserted that the Corinthian constitution was oligarchic; something of the character of the oligarchy may also be inferred. It was possible for an oligarchy to restrict political rights to fewer than all citizens,[17] though still perhaps to a majority (Ar. *Pol.* 1293 a 12-17); but in other respects to possess institutions of a democratic stamp, so that the limited number who enjoyed rights controlled affairs in much the same way as the demos controlled true democracies.[18] The *probouloi* and the small size of the council, however, demonstrate that Corinth was not an oligarchy of this type; neither institution is compatible even with democratic practice under a less than fully democratic franchise. Since the main decisions were therefore not taken in the assembly, those who controlled Corinthian affairs must have done so largely through the council; but this still allows enormous scope within the broad oligarchic limits. To indicate just a few of the more important questions to which we have no answers will both demonstrate the extent of our ignorance and indicate how wide the range of possibilities is.

Whether *probouloi*, councillors, *strategoi*, and other magistrates were elected and by whom is unknown, though the democratic practice of the lot is improbable. Nor can we tell whether any of these offices was subject to a property qualification. It is likely that councillors were able to serve for long periods, either because the term of office was itself long (perhaps for life) or because members were eligible for re-election or reappointment: annual or even shorter service, and prohibition or restriction of iteration, were characteristic of democratic councils.[19] Thus it was possible for individuals to maintain their hold on power through long membership

[14] Bowra, *Pindar*, 103.

[15] *Pol.* 1298 b 27-32; 1299 b 31-8; 1323 a 6-9; cf. 1322 b 15-17.

[16] A rule that democratic councils were relatively large is often referred to by modern commentators (e.g. Jones, *The Greek City*, 165); the converse, that oligarchic councils were relatively small, is equally likely. Cf. in general Ar. *Pol.* 1299 b 32-4.

[17] I use 'citizen' to denote something rather wider than Aristotle's definition (*Pol.* 1275 a 19-b 21); I include all those whose birth was such that they would, in a democracy, have been entitled to attend the assembly; briefly, all adult male Corinthians.

[18] Thus Aristotle calls the 'equals' who shared in rights under such a constitution 'a sort of demos' (*Pol.* 1308 a 13-19).

[19] Ar. *Pol.* 1317 b 23-5; cf. Busolt, *Griechische Staatskunde*, i. 467-8. The converse, that life office was uncharacteristic of democracy: *Pol.* 1317 b 41-1318 a 3.

of the council. We have no reliable evidence of the functions of the council. Diodorus represents it as taking a decision concerning foreign policy, when it sent Timoleon to Sicily; but that is not to say that it enjoyed the formal right to reach final decisions on such matters. Busolt concluded from the same passage that the council could act in a judicial capacity;[20] but the evidence derives, at least in this respect, from nothing more than the fertile imagination of Diodorus' source.[21]

The *probouloi* seem to have been of major importance, to judge from the emphasis given to them by Nicolaus of Damascus; but we have no evidence for their function beyond the meaning of their title. It has sometimes been supposed that the *probouleusis* which the title implies was undertaken before meetings of the council, so that they could guide the council itself;[22] but they may have carried out their *probouleusis* before meetings of the assembly, their informal role being to encourage the assembly to take decisions which conformed with the views of the oligarchic council. A combination of both functions is possible. Aristotle's general remarks on the nature of *probouloi* have sometimes been used to fill the gap in our knowledge of their functions at Corinth, but there is nothing to show that he had Corinth in mind.

The functions and composition of the assembly are no better known. It may or may not have taken part in elections of *probouloi*, councillors, and the rest. Thucydides (v.30.5) shows that it might be involved at some stage in the negotiations for a treaty, when he has the Corinthian authorities suggest to Argive ambassadors that they should 'come before the next (Corinthian) assembly'; but its exact role is unclear. It might have been necessary for treaties to be validated by the assembly, but there are signs that this suggestion was made in order to delay the progress of negotiations (below, 328); if so, the assembly need not have been required under the constitution to play any part at all. Even if it was, Aristotle shows that in an oligarchic state the assembly might act in a merely advisory capacity.[23] It is even unclear who could attend the assembly. There may have been a property qualification, perhaps restricting membership to hoplites; but there is nothing in the evidence to demand

---

[20] *Griechische Staatskunde*, i.363 n. 4 (on p. 364), cf. 368.

[21] Diod. xvi.65.2-8. The discussion in the council of what to do with Timoleon for murdering his brother certainly did not take place when Diodorus puts it, in 346/5 (below, 384 n. 69); a similar discussion might have been held twenty years earlier (cf. Plut. *Timol.* 5.1-2), but it would be rash to assert that it took place in the council.

[22] Kagan, *Politics and Policy*, 20.

[23] *Pol.* 1298 b 33-4; I take it that Aristotle is here describing the actual practice of some states.

this, and the possibility remains open that all citizens were entitled to attend.[24]

Our ignorance of details about the nature and role of the various organs of the Corinthian state could hardly be deeper; but at least one general inference seems solid enough. The Corinthian regime was remarkably stable: only the very brief tyranny of Timophanes, imposed by force in the mid-360s, interrupted the long domination of the oligarchy, and its stability demonstrates its broadly moderate character. I use the word moderate not in its technical sense, to indicate that the Corinthians who enjoyed rights were a relatively large proportion of the citizen-body; but rather descriptively, to mean that however decisions were taken they were reached with a careful eye to what the citizens in general could be persuaded, rather than forced, to accept. When conflict between oligarchs and democrats was all too common in Greek cities, those who controlled affairs at Corinth could not have taken decisions regularly in defiance of the general will without arousing significant opposition of a democratic character. That there was some democratic sentiment in Corinth cannot be proved, but is more than likely; Athenian ideas cannot have been excluded from a city which saw as many travellers as Corinth. But pressures in favour of democracy were, even in the fourth century, almost insignificant (below, 355–7, 385). The Corinthian regime certainly secured the acquiescence, and probably the active support, of the average Corinthian citizen. It may be appropriate to blame such a citizen for meekly following where the oligarchs led; but it is not possible to doubt that he did so.

The moderation of the Corinthian oligarchy is proved by its longevity alone; the skill of the oligarchs in manipulating the opinions of their fellow citizens is demonstrated by the major changes in foreign policy—the only sphere which can be tested— through which the average Corinthian was apparently happy to be guided. This is perhaps best seen in the events of the 360s. When Sparta became too weak to give any effective support to Corinth, and an arrangement with Athens which was distasteful to the

---

[24] Such a conclusion, since Corinth was an oligarchy, would conflict with Aristotle's formal definition of an oligarchy as a constitution in which the wealthy and well-born, being fewer than the whole citizen-body, control office (which includes membership of the assembly: *Pol.* 1275 a 19–b 21): *Pol.* 1290 b 17–20 (cf. 1279 b 17–1280 a 6, 1290 a 30– b 17, 1292 a 39–41; contrast, however, 1293 a 12–14). Aristotle himself, however, categorizes as an oligarchy a constitution which apparently does not fall within this definition (*Pol.* 1298 b 26–32); since he was well aware that the practical balance of power depends on more than mere rules (*Pol.* 1292 b 11–17), Aristotle no doubt called states oligarchies if power was in practice, if not in law, restricted to the wealthy and well-born (see also *Pol.* 1308 b 38–1309 a 2: a constitution democratic *de iure*, but *de facto* aristocratic).

oligarchs became possible, they were flexible enough to put their own loyalty to Sparta aside in order to prevent the possibility of mounting opposition. The Corinthians in general would not agree to continued alliance with Sparta; the oligarchs therefore established a position of neutrality (below, 379-81). If they could not lead the city where they wished to, at least they would lead her where she was prepared to follow. One general inference about the practical nature of decision-making at Corinth seems clear: that whoever took the decisions in a formal sense, public opinion was a major factor in the calculations they made.[25] For the practical effect of a constitution, as Aristotle points out (*Pol.* 1292 b 11-17), formal rules matter less than informal practice; and it is clear that the Corinthian oligarchs usually ensured that their decisions coincided with the popular will.

Such a conclusion allows tentative exploration of more detailed aspects of the constitution. If the oligarchy was moderate in the descriptive sense, it might have been narrow in the technical sense; but it is unlikely that a property qualification excluded more than a small minority of citizens from the assembly. To deny a majority of Corinthians membership of that body will have created tensions—especially in a city so open to foreign ideas—from which Corinth was apparently free.[26] There may have been a property qualification; but it is more likely that there was none at all. In the primitive assembly of the Greek city, all citizens were presumably entitled to attend. The restriction of the franchise found in many cities is a later development, devised specifically in order to exclude the poorest citizens; but such a device is improbable when the Corinthian assembly originated, presumably in the early sixth century at the latest. The exclusion will have resulted from either (or both) of two considerations: from a reaction against democratic practice; or from political theory, on the principle that citizen-rights were only to be enjoyed by those capable of serving the state.[27] Neither can have applied much before the mid-fifth century.[28] There was probably therefore no property qualification for the assembly. It may have been the very wealthy alone who were eligible to act as

---

[25] Thus the Corinthian oligarchs followed the sound advice of Aristotle that oligarchs should act on behalf of the general population (*Pol.* 1310 a 2-12).

[26] Cf. Ar. *Pol.* 1281 b 28-30: a city with numerous citizens who have no political rights is a city with many enemies.

[27] Both considerations affected the revolution at Athens in 411: for the second, cf. Thuc. viii.65.3; Ar. *Ath. Pol.* 29.5, 33.1, 2.

[28] Sparta seems to provide a counter-example, but the process there was different: it was a matter of ensuring that all citizens could be hoplites, not of excluding non-hoplites from citizen-rights.

probouloi, councillors, *strategoi*, or magistrates;[29] but we do
not know.

The few details we have suggest that the formal constitutional
rules may have helped the Corinthian oligarchs in their long and
successful manipulation of public opinion. The title of the *probouloi* implies that they undertook preliminary deliberation, though
whether before meetings of the council or of the assembly is unclear
(above, 235); but it would go some way to explaining the council's
long success in carrying public opinion with it if the *probouloi*
undertook preliminary deliberation for the assembly and guided
its decisions so that they followed those already made by the
council. Aristotle names no states in his discussions of *probouloi*;
but one of his passages illustrates admirably the way in which they
may have helped to secure the remarkable consensus between the
Corinthian council and the population at large.[30] He is discussing
what is appropriate for democracies and oligarchies in respect of the
deliberative element in a constitution, which is defined as 'sovereign
concerning war and peace, the making and ending of alliances, laws,
punishments of death, exile, or confiscation of property, and the
appointment of magistrates and the calling to account of those
appointed after their service' (*Pol.* 1298 a 2-7). He says that for
oligarchies it is right 'either to co-opt some men from the people
(to the deliberative body) or to institute an office like that which
some states call *nomophylaces* and others *probouloi*, and to allow
discussion (by the people in general) only on those matters which
these men have considered in advance. For in these ways the demos
will participate in deliberation, but will not be able to subvert any

---

[29] If this was the case, either Corinth was an exception to Aristotle's rule (as she was
an exception to many rules about oligarchies) that oligarchies are unstable if they have
a high property qualification for office but a low one (or none at all) for the electorate
(*Pol.* 1305 b 30-6; cf. 1264 b 7-10, 1316 b 21-3); or the councillors, *probouloi*, and others
were not elected by the assembly. The former is the more probable.

[30] Elsewhere (*Pol.* 1299 b 31-8), Aristotle draws a distinction between *probouloi*, which
he regards as oligarchic, and councils, which he sees as democratic. Will, *Korinthiaka*, 609-
10, argues that in these terms Corinth was 'a kind of compromise between democracy and
oligarchy, with the emphasis on the oligarchic element'; but this involves a supposition
which is neither true nor likely to have been thought true by Aristotle, namely that a
council as small as Corinth's could be democratic in character. In this passage Aristotle
was probably thinking of Athens after 413, when for a short while ten *probouloi* worked
alongside the democratic council of 500.

part of the constitution.'[31]

[31]*Pol.* 1298 b 27-32. That deliberation by the demos is in question is not stated, since χρηματίζειν lacks a subject; but it is implied by the nature of the argument. This interpretation demands no more alteration of the MSS text than the deletion of the superfluous καί before περὶ τούτων. Many scholars (particularly those who have tried to establish Corinthian practice on the basis of this passage) have changed the text further to eliminate the alternative between co-opting men from the demos and appointing *nomophylaces* or *probouloi*, on the ground that both must be part of the same process (Lutz, *CR* x (1896), 418-19; Will, *Korinthiaka*, 610-11); but the alternatives presented by the MSS are entirely plausible in themselves, and the further development of Aristotle's argument implies their existence. He goes on to discuss a second set of alternatives, introduced by ἔτι ἤ . . . ἤ; thus a first set, introduced by ἐν δὲ ταῖς ὀλιγαρχίαις ἤ . . . ἤ, is implied. The development of the argument is well clarified by Barker's translation (*The Politics of Aristotle*, 192-3).

XVII. Corinth and Sparta:
The Origins of the Peloponnesian League

For half a century after the fall of the tyranny our sources tell us nothing of Corinth; but in 525/4 the Corinthians joined Sparta in an unsuccessful expedition against Polycrates of Samos (Hdt. iii.46–56). This is the first trustworthy record we have of co-operation between Corinth and Sparta;[1] but there are grounds for supposing that they were already allies. We have no direct evidence for an alliance before 525/4; but the probability is that some arrangement had already been made when the Samian exiles arrived at Sparta to ask for help.[2] Herodotus says, literally, 'The Corinthians participated enthusiastically in the expedition against Samos that it should take place' (iii.48.1); thus he emphasizes the Corinthians' role in the decision to move against Samos almost at the expense of their participation in the force itself. Since there is no indication that the Samians approached Corinth first and that the two parties then made joint representations at Sparta, the implication is that Sparta consulted with Corinth before making her decision; that in turn implies that Sparta and Corinth were already in some sense allies.[3] A similar conclusion may be drawn from Herodotus' statement about Sparta's position in the Peloponnese c.550, when messengers from Croesus of Lydia went to discover the most powerful of the Greek states and to make an alliance with it (Hdt. i.53–56.1): at that time 'most of the Peloponnese was already subjected to (the Spartans)' (Hdt. i.68.6). These words imply that most of the Peloponnese had already made those arrangements with Sparta which formed the basis of the Peloponnesian League.[4] It is possible that Corinth was not one of the states concerned, so this argument is no more conclusive than the last; but it remains likely that Corinth and Sparta had reached some arrangement before 525/4, and probably already by c.550.[5]

---

[1] For earlier, more than doubtful, indications in our sources of Spartan help for Corinth and vice versa, see above, 68, 70 n. 61, 229–30.

[2] Hdt. iii.44–6. Schaefer, *Staatsform und Politik*, 201, argues unconvincingly that the alliance was made in order to undertake the Samian expedition.

[3] Cf. Wickert, *Peloponnesische Bund*, 16–17; (more general) Will, *Korinthiaka*, 626–7.

[4] Cf. de Ste Croix, 97; Forrest, *Sparta*, 74; below, 249.

[5] See Cartledge, *Sparta and Lakonia*, 139–40.

The nature of the arrangement is obscure. By the end of the century Corinth was a member of what is generally called the Peloponnesian League; the latter had its origin in a series of bilateral treaties between Sparta and other states of the Peloponnese (below, 249). There is only one clause from such a treaty preserved from the sixth century. In it the Tegeates promised not to make citizens of the Messenians but to drive them from Tegea;[6] but this can hardly be used to reconstruct the details of any alliance save that with Tegea. Sparta's fear of Messenian revolt was her main motive in making alliances with other Peloponnesian states; but this particular clause reflects rather the special circumstances of the case of Tegea than a general concern that Messenians should find no help in other states. The only remaining evidence is the way in which the Spartans and their allies behaved in the second half of the sixth century. It has been argued that from the earliest times Sparta secured alliances in which the other party promised 'to follow wherever the Spartans may lead, both by land and by sea, and to have the same friends and the same enemies as the Spartans';[7] but there are serious reasons to doubt whether the Spartans were able to impose so formal a hegemony at so early a date. It is not easy to see what might have persuaded Peloponnesian states—especially powerful Corinth—to subordinate their foreign policy to Sparta in such a way; and even if Sparta had persuaded (or forced) them to do so, it is difficult to imagine why Sparta did not make use of her allies, subordinate as they would have been, more frequently. We hear of numerous major Spartan campaigns in this period: the battles with Argos over the Thyreatis, the expedition against Polycrates, two against Hippias (of which the first was perhaps not very large), and one in order to install Isagoras in power at Athens; only for the last is there any sign that numerous allies marched with the Spartans. No doubt this evidence could be explained away; but it is simpler to conclude that there was as a rule no explicit obligation on Sparta's allies to follow wherever she led.

The treaties must have involved a promise by each ally to help Sparta if she were attacked, and presumably vice versa: that is the minimum requirement for an alliance not concluded for a specific

[6] Plut. *Mor.* 292 B; cf. 277 B-C. Explained by Jacoby, *CQ* xxxviii (1944), 15-16. *Staatsverträge*, ii, no. 112 (with refs). I see no reason to insist (with Cartledge, *Sparta and Lakonia*, 139) on separating this document from the alliance between Sparta and Tegea.

[7] De Ste Croix, 108-10; followed by Cartledge, *Sparta and Lakonia*, 148. The quotation is a translation of a treaty between Sparta and the Aetolian Erxadieis published by Peek (*Abh. Sächs. Akad. Wiss. Leipzig, phil.-hist. Kl.* lxv.3 (1974), 3-15). Peek dates the treaty c.500-470 on letter-forms, but this is an uncertain criterion (Cartledge, *LCM* i (1976), 90). For other examples of the same formula, see de Ste Croix, 108 (first for Athens in 404).

and limited purpose.[8] But what happened when Cleomenes tried to install Isagoras in power at Athens (Hdt. v.74-5) indicates that more than this may have been involved. Cleomenes was able to collect an army, Herodotus says,· 'from all the Peloponnese' (v.74.1) for a campaign which cannot have been presented as defensive. When Cleomenes' precise purpose was revealed the Corinthians declined to fight; their example was followed by the other allies when they saw that Demaratus also rejected the plans of his colleague (Hdt. v.75). Cleomenes may have been able to persuade or cajole the allies into sending forces against Athens even though the treaties were strictly defensive; but it is more likely, in view of the reluctance felt by the allies when the exact purpose of the campaign was made known, that he had been able to point to some clause in the treaties which might have been interpreted as obliging the allies to participate. Such a clause can be readily guessed at, for it figures in the preserved later formulations: a promise by each state to have the same friends and enemies as the Spartans—and, no doubt, a reciprocal promise by Sparta—fulfils the requirement exactly. Such a clause would have meant a formal equality between Sparta and each ally, and there would thus have been nothing to prevent a state as powerful as Corinth from swearing a treaty on these terms; yet it would have been imprecise enough to explain both why Sparta did not invoke the treaties before her attempt to secure power in Athens for Isagoras and why she tried to invoke it on that occasion. Other interpretations cannot be excluded; but it causes least difficulty if we suppose that Herodotus' statement that 'most of the Peloponnese was already subjected to' the Spartans *c*.550 reflects a series of bilateral treaties between Sparta and most other Peloponnesian states in which each party promised to have the same friends and enemies as the other. If so, Herodotus' word 'subjected' is perhaps too strong; but the treaties marked the beginning of Sparta's progress to hegemony which was complete by Herodotus' own time, and the exaggeration is understandable. Thus Corinth, probably already by *c*.550, had agreed to have the same friends and enemies as Sparta.

It remains to examine the motives of each party. As for the Spartans, they abandoned in the mid-sixth century the policy of conquest by absorption which they had attempted to extend from Laconia and Messenia to Tegea, and determined to achieve protection for themselves against their numerous suppressed peoples by making alliances with neighbouring states.[9] The new policy may

---

[8] Cf. Wickert, *Peloponnesische Bund*, 31.
[9] Cartledge, *Sparta and Lakonia*, 136-9.

have been devised first as a method of solving the problem of relations with Tegea; but if so, the Spartans quickly recognized that it had a far wider application, and used essentially the same method with many other states in order to prevent them from affording support to rebellious helots. This may have been one, perhaps the only, aspect of the alliance with Corinth which concerned Sparta at the time the agreement was reached. The first recorded action which resulted from the alliance, the expedition against Polycrates, was offensive; but this need not mean that the Spartans thought of anything more than defence when the alliance orginated. None the less, Corinth was a long way from Messenia; and part of the Spartan motive may have been a recognition among at least the more far-sighted Spartans that such alliances might be useful not only in defence but also in attack. The motives of the Corinthians are unclear. The initiative for the alliance probably came from Sparta; but if the Cypselid tyranny fell *c*.585 and the Spartans had no part in its destruction, the Corinthians did not accede to the Spartan request out of mere gratitude. Since the alliance was to all intents and purposes an equal one, and since it did not (as far as we know) commit Corinth to any immediate action, it may have been agreed to at least in part because there was no good reason to reject it;[10] but the usual interpretation, that it afforded Corinth some protection against Argos, was doubtless an important consideration: Sparta offered Corinth help against Argos in return for help against helots.[11]

None the less, the first joint action undertaken in virtue of the alliance was offensive: the expedition to depose Polycrates.[12] As has usually been recognized, the motives for the campaign given by Herodotus are unsatisfactory. The Samians, he writes, believed that Sparta attacked Polycrates out of gratitude for the help given by his Samian enemies against the Messenians, while Sparta and Corinth claimed to have made the expedition in order to avenge themselves: Sparta for the theft of presents sent to Croesus and to Amasis, and Corinth for the escape, arranged by the Samians, of 300 Corcyraean boys sent by Periander to Alyattes of Lydia to be made into eunuchs.[13] No doubt Herodotus reports what was said

[10] Compare, perhaps, the Spartan agreement to Croesus' proposal of alliance shortly afterwards: Hdt. i.69–70.1.

[11] Argive influence may already have reached Cleonae by this date, but this is uncertain; there is no evidence.

[12] Corinth may have provided vessels for Sparta's fleet intended to help Croesus against Cyrus (Hdt. i.83); but it is not to be ruled out that Sparta could provide sufficient transport herself.

[13] Hdt. iii.47–8; see further above, 225.

in Samos, Sparta, and Corinth in his time; but the last two stories were merely the excuses offered in public for what amounted to pure aggression.[14] Ancient commentators believed that Sparta made a practice of expelling tyrants,[15] and the attack on Polycrates may have been an attempt at adding another tyrant to the list. Modern scholars have suggested either that Sparta was concerned to prevent Persian expansion into the Aegean and tried to eliminate Polycrates because he had recently made his peace with Cambyses;[16] or that Polycrates was attacked because he was part of a loose 'Argive coalition' which included Peisistratid Athens and Lygdamis of Naxos.[17] But is is unnecessary to explain the attack by invoking such general principles.[18] The alliances concluded *c*.550 must have given Sparta a great deal of confidence; and it took no great imagination to see them as potentially powerful instruments for what might loosely be called imperialist expansion. Cleomenes, a few years after 525/4, certainly saw them as such; and already before his reign other Spartans were probably eager to grasp the opportunities they offered to extend Spartan influence. Croesus' offer of alliance perhaps gave the Spartans a greater idea of their importance than the facts justified. The attempt to spread Sparta's influence as far as Samos may seem improbably ambitious at this date; but it fits well with the alliance with Croesus, the decision to help him against Cyrus in virtue of the alliance,[19] and the command issued to Cyrus that he should keep his hands off the Greeks of Asia Minor (Hdt. i.152.3). As for Corinth, similar considerations may have affected her decision, and as a naval power she might well have gained more than Sparta from success; but the evidence for Corinthian attitudes to international affairs is less extensive than for Spartan, and only conjecture is possible. Since the Corinthians made their decision in advance of the Spartans, we cannot suppose that Corinth participated in order to secure her influence at Sparta: it was the suppression of Polycrates itself which appealed to Corinth. She may

[14] Despite Will, *Korinthiaka*, 634–5, the fact that Herodotus heard these versions is no argument in their favour: aggression has to be excused somehow, even two or three generations after the event.

[15] Perhaps already implied by Hdt. v.92 *a* 1; cf. Thuc. i.18.1; Plut. *Mor.* 859 C–D; Schol. Aeschin. ii.77.

[16] Hdt. iii.44.1; cf. esp. Andrewes, *Tyrants*, 122.

[17] Forrest, *Sparta*, 80–2.

[18] It is most unlikely that either principle was considered by Corinth to be a ground for attacking Polycrates: there is no sign that Corinth was concerned about Persia before 481, and she had small reason to wish to move against so loose an 'Argive coalition'. If Corinth was not so motivated, that perhaps makes it less likely that Sparta was.

[19] Hdt. i.83. There is no reason to doubt Herodotus here, with Will, *Korinthiaka*, 631 n. 2.

have hoped to step into the shoes of the main naval power in the Aegean; she may have seized the opportunity to act as policeman of the Aegean against the piratical activity of the tyrant of Samos. It has been argued that Corinth prevailed upon a reluctant Sparta to undertake the expedition, on the ground that such an adventure is incompatible with the 'natural' Spartan foreign policy of caution;[20] but caution hardly characterizes Sparta's policy in the last quarter of the sixth century. The Spartans, with their small fleet, may have needed the help of Corinth before they could commit themselves;[21] there can be little doubt that they were as enthusiastic as Corinth once they could be sure that they had the means.[22]

Despite the high hopes invested in the expedition, it failed (Hdt. iii.54-6). The Corinthians may have helped Sparta to remove Lygdamis of Naxos, for his deposition is probably to be dated to the time of the expedition against Polycrates; if so, it was presumably undertaken either as a preliminary to the main purpose of the campaign or as an attempt to gain some recompense for the fiasco at Samos;[23] but the success at Naxos was small consolation for the humiliating failure against Polycrates. Even Cleomenes made no similar attempt at extending Spartan influence by sea. The first action of his reign also involved Corinth, but in a very different way. In 519/18[24] 'Cleomenes and the Spartans happened to be in the vicinity'[25] to receive an appeal from Plataea for protection against Thebes. The Spartans pointed out that an alliance with so distant a state would give but cold comfort to Plataea and suggested an arrangement with Athens instead—hoping, according to Herodotus, to create difficulties

[20] Especially Will, *Korinthiaka*, 636-7; followed by Moretti, *Richerche sulle leghe greche*, 76.

[21] As noted by Will, *Korinthiaka*, 635. Will's observation is not invalidated by Wickert's argument (*Peloponnesische Bund*, 17) that the Samian exiles had forty ships themselves: these vessels were presumably too full of Samians to carry many Spartans. See in general Cartledge, *Sparta and Lakonia*, 142-3.

[22] Compare, with a different emphasis, Wickert, *Peloponnesische Bund*, 17.

[23] Plut. *Mor.* 859 D, cf. 236 C; Schol. Aeschin. ii.77.

[24] For the date, Thuc. iii.68.5. It has often been challenged (e.g. Wickert, *Peloponnesische Bund*, 20), but mainly because the suspicion of Athens presupposed by Herodotus' Spartan motive seems unlikely at this date. If the motive is false (below, 246), the date may be retained.

[25] Hdt. vi.108.2. Spartans can hardly have been in the vicinity without purpose, and two suggestions have been made: that they were there to arbitrate between Megara and Athens over Salamis (Will, *Korinthiaka*, 642-3; cf. Plut. *Sol.* 10); and that they went to the Megarid to conclude an alliance with Megara (Burn, *Persia and the Greeks*, 171; cf. already Dickins, *JHS* xxxii (1912), 28). The latter is the more likely; and in any case it is doubtful whether the Spartan arbitration over Salamis took place in the relevant period (Plutarch, at least, puts it in Solon's time). There is no evidence for the date of Megara's alliance with Sparta (Wickert, *Peloponnesische Bund*, 19); but there is no reason to deny that it was made as early as 519/18.

for Athens in Boeotia (vi.108.2–3). The Plataeans therefore appealed
to Athens, but the Thebans marched against them, and when the
Athenians came to give support to Plataea the Corinthians, who also
'happened to be in the vicinity', gave arbitration: they fixed the
boundaries between Thebes and Plataea and stipulated that the
Thebans should leave alone those Boeotians who did not wish to
belong to the Boeotian League. The Corinthians then retired, but
the Boeotians attacked the Athenians as they were withdrawing
and suffered a defeat; Athens followed up her victory and secured
more territory for Plataea than had been given by the Corinthian
arbitration (Hdt. vi.108.4–6).

It is by no means obvious what conclusions are to be derived from
this evidence for Corinthian policy. Corinthians are most unlikely
to have been present in such strength as to impose a settlement
of the Plataean question by force; the parties to the dispute must
originally have agreed to accept Corinth's arbitration, and that
demonstrates that she was thought to have no axe of her own to
grind. Corinth was probably following her own view of justice
instead of trying to benefit Athens under cover of neutrality: we
can hardly use this arbitration as evidence of Corinthian friendship
for Peisistratid Athens. On the other hand, the fact that the Corinthians were on hand to offer arbitration cannot have been the coincidence that it appears to be in Herodotus; the obvious conjecture
is that Corinth kept a watchful eye on the Plataean alliance with
Athens and took what action she could when difficulties arose.
Corinth had no interest in encouraging conflict between Athens and
Thebes; and she might gain friends by offering her services to secure
a peaceful settlement. If this is correct, Corinth acted in conflict
with the Spartan aim, asserted by Herodotus, of embroiling Athens
with Thebes. That would not be surprising if it were true. Corinth
hardly knew Sparta's dubious intentions, and will not have been
greatly concerned, in any case, if she knew she was acting against
Sparta's wishes; but the Spartan motive given by Herodotus should
be rejected. He cannot have had good evidence for secret Spartan
intentions; and fifth-century history offered powerful reasons for
inventing such a motive. The explanation provided in public for the
Plataeans, that Sparta was too far away to be a useful ally, was
entirely valid, as the sequel showed.[26] Whether Corinth acted by
previous agreement with Sparta is more difficult to determine.
Corinth herself would have gained friends if she had settled the
affair amicably; she may have made the attempt in her own interests

---

[26] Cf. the sensible note of Larsen, *CP* xxvii (1932), 147 n. 1.

alone. I argue below that her intention may have been precisely to diminish the influence of Sparta north of the Isthmus.[27]

The most fruitful evidence for Corinthian policy in the last quarter of the century is contained in Herodotus' account of the Spartan interventions in Athens. When Sparta followed the advice of the Delphic oracle to free Athens her first expedition, by sea under Anchimolius, was repulsed; but the second, led over land by Cleomenes, drove Hippias out (Hdt. v.62-5). A third force was led by Cleomenes to Attica to lend support to Isagoras in his dispute with Cleisthenes, but withdrew after being besieged for two days on the acropolis (Hdt. v.66-72). When Cleomenes led an army into Attica in Isagoras' interest once again, it was composed of forces 'from all the Peloponnese'; but just before battle was joined at Eleusis, 'first the Corinthians, after saying among themselves that they were not acting justly, changed their minds and withdrew, and then Demaratus did the same . . . and when the rest of the allies saw that the Spartan kings did not agree with each other, and that the Corinthians had deserted from the army, they too withdrew and went away' (Hdt. v.74-5). Finally, when the Spartans called a meeting of allied representatives to discuss the restoration of Hippias to the tyranny, the proposal was lost after Socles the Corinthian argued against it (Hdt. v.90-3).

There is no evidence for Corinth's attitude on any of these occasions except the last two, when Spartan intentions were thwarted as a result of Corinthian opposition. Cleomenes' purpose for his final expedition was 'to have revenge on the Athenian demos and to set up Isagoras as tyrant', though he did not reveal this to his allies (v.74.1); and when the Corinthians withdrew they did so after 'saying among themselves that they were not acting justly' (v.75.1). Their reasons are indicated by the later speech of Socles: he argues against destruction of ἰσοκρατία in Athens and the substitution of a tyranny (v.92 a 1), claims that to re-establish Hippias would be unjust (v.92 η 5), and supports his case by a long description of the misdeeds of the Cypselids (v.92 β-η 4). Since Herodotus was able to give the name of the Corinthian who made the speech—and his accuracy on this point need not be doubted—he may well have

---

[27] Below, 248-9. Will, *Korinthiaka*, 640-5, has a complicated discussion of the affair in which he suggests that Corinth and Sparta were pulling in different directions with respect to Athens during the decade before the expulsion of Hippias. The complications, however, are unnecessarily introduced by acceptance of Herodotus' anti-Athenian motive for Sparta over the Plataean question; and Will's account is further vitiated by the improbable assumption that arbitrator states used their arbitration to pursue their own foreign policy rather than judging the issues fairly as they saw them.

had valid information about the general tenor of what he said; and Corinth probably argued against the imposition not only of Hippias but also of Isagoras on the ground that to impose a tyranny on unwilling Athenians was unjust. Whether this was the real reason for Corinth's action is a different matter; Corinth could hardly present arguments of power politics in public.

By about 510, Sparta had held something approaching hegemony in the Peloponnese for more than a generation. Her leadership was informal, but none the less solid for that; and for Corinth there were dangers in allowing Sparta too great an influence outside the Peloponnese. We know of nothing specific which might have caused Corinth to suspect the Spartans, except perhaps the dangerous energy of Cleomenes and the alliances which may by now have been made with her enemies Megara and Aegina;[28] but a system of Spartan alliances with individual states from Elis to Attica must have given Corinth cause for general concern. It is true that Corinth marched with Cleomenes when his plan clearly was to intervene in Athens, even if he did not reveal his precise purpose; but she may have hoped to influence the settlement, and (perhaps more probable) her intention all along may have been to withdraw at the time when she calculated it would have the greatest effect. None of this can be demonstrated, but these were more powerful reasons than the hatred of tyranny which Corinth gave in public; some support can perhaps be found in the events of the first three Spartan interventions in Attica. On the first, Anchimolius went by sea. It has been suggested that the vessels may have been provided by Corinth;[29] but it is more probable that the less convenient sea route was chosen precisely because the Spartans were aware that they would not be welcomed in the Corinthia on their march to Athens. Cleomenes' next two expeditions went over the Isthmus; for it had been made clear that an approach by sea was risky. It is just possible that Corinth sent a contingent on the first occasion, even though Herodotus mentions nobody but Spartans and Athenian opponents of the tyrants; but Corinth was almost certainly not represented in Cleomenes' force when he was besieged on the acropolis.[30] Corinth probably refused help for each force because she did not wish Cleomenes to succeed. If so, new light is shed on the Plataea affair: Corinth may have acted then as she did precisely in order to *reduce* the possibility of Spartan involvement north of the

[28] Megara: above, 245 n. 25. The alliance with Aegina has no clear date; but it may have been concluded before the end of the sixth century: de Ste Croix, 123, 333–4 with references.

[29] Will, *Korinthiaka*, 646–7.

[30] Cf. Hdt. v.72.1: 'with no large force'.

Isthmus by settling the matter before any party could become obligated to Sparta. It was perhaps no coincidence that the Corinthian arbitration asserted, according to Herodotus, the right of a city to choose its own way in its relations with other states; the city for which the principle was enunciated was Plataea, but Corinth may have felt that it applied to her own relations with Sparta.

In the last decade, perhaps the last two decades, of the sixth century Corinth was much exercised over the danger of too great an extension of Spartan influence. When the two states made their original alliance it was an equal one; but Sparta's numerous allies now gave her a pre-eminence which caused concern at Corinth. The procedure adopted by the Spartans when they proposed the restoration of Hippias demonstrates that Corinth achieved considerable success in limiting Spartan power. The Spartans wanted allied help, but they submitted the matter to a vote and their plan was heavily defeated.[31] In addition to thwarting this particular attempt Corinth seems to have secured, whether deliberately or not, the acceptance of formal arrangements for consultation between Sparta and her allies which placed important restrictions on Sparta. Discussion of the Spartan proposal took place at a meeting which was very similar to those held by the Peloponnesian League in the fifth century; this marks the formal foundation of the League as such.[32] Before this time, Sparta enjoyed alliances with most Peloponnesian states on terms which were ill defined; but the fiasco of the invasion of Attica encouraged more careful definition of the rights and obligations of Sparta's allies. Precisely what was defined cannot be discussed here; but certain facts are clear.[33] The most important is that each ally was required, unless there were some religious impediment, to follow the decision of a majority in the League Congress.[34] In addition, the allies had bound themselves, probably in the original bilateral treaties, to Sparta without time-limit;[35] thus no ally could avoid the obligation to accept majority decisions of the Congress by abrogating its alliance.

These arrangements enabled Sparta to require compliance with any decision which she could persuade a majority of her allies to accept; they were the basis of Sparta's domination of the

---

[31] Sparta: Hdt. v.91; the reaction of the allies: v.92 ad init., esp. v.93.2.

[32] Cf. esp. Larsen, *CP* xxvii (1932), 138–45. It is doubtful whether all the rules about League Congresses which can be deduced from later practice were established so early (cf. de Ste Croix, 117–18); but the meeting to consider the restoration of Hippias was the beginning of an evolution which resulted in the formal practice of the League.

[33] The fundamental discussion is now that of de Ste Croix, 105–23 (with references).

[34] Thuc. v.30.1; cf. de Ste Croix, 115–20.

[35] De Ste Croix, 107–8.

Peloponnese for nearly a century and a half. None the less, the changes were probably viewed in the late sixth century (and for some time afterwards) in a very different light: as a serious impediment to Sparta.[36] The treaties under which Sparta called for contingents to install Isagoras may have been imprecise; but since the allies provided them, for a campaign with which they were out of sympathy, there must have been some feeling of obligation to march. The new arrangements, however, gave the allies—considered collectively—an absolute veto on the right to call for aid that Sparta had claimed. The first meeting of the Congress gave heavy emphasis to the allies' strength against Sparta: a Spartan proposal was roundly rejected. Corinth had led the allies in conflict with Sparta, and had won the victory. It was indeed possible to take another view: Spartans could now require unwilling allies to provide troops so long as a majority in the Congress approved a Spartan plan; but there can have been few Spartans so far-sighted as to recognize that the League which grew out of Sparta's recent defeats at the hands of her allies was a powerful weapon for the future. The allies will certainly have regarded the arrangements as a victory; and each state will have been encouraged in this view by a natural confidence, confirmed by Sparta's failures, that its own policy would be adopted by the majority.

Corinth, we may take it, shared this feeling. She might now be required to accept a decision with which she disagreed if she found herself in a minority; but she will have been so confident that the sympathy of the allies would remain with her that she took little account of this consideration. It was not until nearly a century later, with the Peace of Nicias, that it took effect against her. Corinth's central importance in preventing Spartan intervention in Athens cannot be doubted; but whether she worked deliberately for the more general restrictions on Spartan action is less certain. She may have been persuaded by the particular disagreement over Athens to seek general safeguards for the future; but the concessions may have originated in a purely Spartan desire to clear up the dangerous uncertainties of the past. If the ideas were not Corinth's, she still bore a good deal of responsibility for them: it was the opposition which she led that persuaded Sparta to make the new proposals.

Corinth probably took no part in Cleomenes' campaign against Argos *c*.494; the only allies mentioned in Herodotus' account are Aegina and Sicyon, and there is little doubt that only they were

---

[36] Cf. esp. Larsen, *CP* xxvii (1932), 146; Forrest, *Sparta*, 87-9; Cartledge, *Sparta and Lakonia*, 147.

involved.[37] It may be taken that Sparta, after the defeats of the late
sixth century, was uncertain of her ability to carry her allies with
her;[38] but it is probable both that Cleomenes' success had the effect
of damping anti-Spartan feeling in the League and that the campaign
was partly designed precisely to achieve that end.[39] We have no
evidence for Corinth's view of the attack on Argos; but if she
followed the same attitude as she had in the late sixth century she
will almost certainly have looked with disfavour on it. She had
originally concluded her alliance with Sparta partly to gain protection
against Argos; but now the subjection of Argos to Sparta presented
almost as many threats to Corinth as that of Athens would have
done. Will has suggested that Cleomenes' decision not to destroy
Argos was made partly out of deference to Corinth;[40] but if it does
not merely reflect a civilized horror of destruction for its own sake,
the most probable explanation is that Cleomenes preferred the
control of Argos to its destruction. If Corinth was considered at all
when the Spartan decisions about Argos were taken, it was as the
leader of the opposition within the League that the campaign was
partly designed to silence.

Corinthian action in the late sixth century was often beneficial
to the government in power in Athens at the time: the attempt to
settle the question of Plataea by arbitration, perhaps resistance to
Spartan efforts to overthrow the tyranny, and certainly the thwarting of Cleomenes' plans for imposing some form of puppet government after the reforms of Cleisthenes. In all these cases the essential
reason for Corinthian action concerned Sparta, and friendly acts
towards Athens were merely incidental; but the two states none the
less had common interests: they shared both strained relations with
Megara and enmity with Aegina. The chronology of the Athenian
wars with Aegina is disputed; but either just before or soon after
Marathon the Athenians fought a war against Aegina for which the
Corinthians hired or sold to Athens at a very low price—since it was
against the custom (or the law) to do so gratis[41]—twenty triremes,

[37] The campaign: Hdt. vi.76–81; Aeginetan and Sicyonian support: vi.92.1-2. Paus.
iii.4.1 mentions allies, but this will be either a false assumption or a reference to Aegina
and Sicyon.
[38] Wickert, *Peloponnesische Bund*, 31. Note the story of Hegesistratus of Elis (Hdt.
ix.37), which implies that at some time not long before Plataea Tegea was ill disposed
towards Sparta.
[39] That Sparta was the aggressor is shown by Hdt. vi.76.
[40] *Korinthiaka*, 639-40.
[41] This remark of Herodotus raises interesting possibilities; but we do not know (among
other things) whether the νόμος was a formal law or a custom, or whether it was purely
Corinthian or more widespread.

which the Athenians added to their own fleet of fifty and used to inflict a defeat on the Aeginetans.[42] This episode might be used to argue for positive friendship between Corinth and Athens at the time, and Herodotus emphasizes the good relations between the two states (vi.89). If so, Corinth's actions in defence of Athens might have been motivated not only by fear of excessive Spartan expansion but also by concern for Athens; but it is more likely that circumstances led Corinth to make common cause with Athens than that she helped the Athenians for friendship's sake. Aegina and Corinth, each with naval interests in the Saronic Gulf, were natural enemies, and Corinth's purpose was probably more to harm Aegina than to benefit Athens.[43] Herodotus is right to say that Corinth and Athens enjoyed excellent relations at this period; but it was more a matter of events throwing the two states into each other's arms than of close friendship. Herodotus probably remarked upon their good relations because of the contrast with the later fifth century. No Corinthians fought at Marathon.

[42] Hdt. vi.89, 92.1; Thuc. i.41.2. The wars between Athens and Aegina in general, Hdt. v.81-9; on the chronology, cf. (e.g.) Andrewes, *BSA* xxxvii (1936/7), 1-7; Hammond, *Historia*, iv (1955), 406-11; Jeffery, *AJP* lxxxiii (1962), 44-54. I find the compression of the events before Marathon in Herodotus intolerable; a powerful case can be made for placing the Nicodromus war of Hdt. vi.88-92 between Sepeia and Marathon, but note also Forrest, *GRBS* x (1969), 285.

[43] Will, *Korinthiaka*, 656-63 (cf. 643-5) explains almost all of Corinth's actions from 520 to the loan of twenty ships to Athens partly in the light of Corinth's hostility to Aegina; and he also puts the episode of the Aeginetan hostages (below, 253) into the same context. His argument is ingenious but unnecessary.

XVIII.   The Persian Wars

When the Persians landed at Marathon no members of the Peloponnesian League joined the Athenians in repelling them. As far as Sparta is concerned, that was no doubt because of the recent fall (if not the death) of Cleomenes, who had demanded hostages from Aegina in order to neutralize the island for the coming invasion;[1] but the absence even of the states of the north-east Peloponnese, including Corinth, demonstrates that if Cleomenes had been aware for some time of the Persian threat he had failed to persuade his allies of its importance. There is no sign that Corinth saw the danger from Persia as anything more than a private concern of Athens. None the less, Corinth was presumably one of the original states which conferred in 481 on the question of the defence of Greece.[2] It would be surprising if Corinthians were not among the ambassadors who failed to persuade Gelon of Syracuse to send help (Hdt. vii.153.1, 157-62); but it might have been tactless to allow a Corinthian to take part in the fruitless visit of the same embassy to Corcyra (Hdt. vii.168).

Corinth controlled some territory north of the Isthmus, the natural point for the defence of the Peloponnese; but the most important regions of the Corinthia were within the limits of the peninsula. Corinth therefore shares the credit that is due to all the Peloponnesian cities which sent forces north of the Isthmus in a vain attempt to defend the central Greek states; presumably she was motivated by a mixture of concern for her own territory outside the peninsula, calculation that the strategic situation demanded that Xerxes be halted as far north as possible, and fear of losing the enormous Athenian fleet.[3] Four hundred Corinthians fought at Thermopylae (Hdt. vii.202); no doubt most of them retired while

---

[1] It is perverse to deny (with Will, *Korinthiaka*, 659-63) that Cleomenes was concerned about Persia when he demanded the Aeginetan hostages; there is certainly no reason to believe that his purpose was closely bound up with Corinth's hostility to Aegina.

[2] Hdt. vii.145. It is unclear whether the Congress was held in Corinthian territory, at the Isthmus. Paus. iii.12.6 places it at Sparta, but subsequent meetings were held at the Isthmus (Hdt. vii.172, 175, etc.); cf. Wickert, *Peloponnesische Bund*, 36 n. 9. On the arrangements, see especially Brunt, *Historia*, ii (1953/4), 135-63.

[3] The best modern account of the invasion is in Burn, *Persia and the Greeks*; for the strategy, cf. esp. 352-7, 361-3.

Leonidas, his Spartans, and the Thespians died there (Hdt. vii.222).
Forty Corinthian vessels were present at Artemisium—less than a
third of the number provided by the Athenians, but still twice as
large as any other fleet (Hdt. viii.1). Herodotus has a story that
Themistocles, having been bribed by the Euboeans to ensure that
the Greeks fought at Artemisium, used three of the thirty talents
he had received to induce Adeimantus the Corinthian commander
not to withdraw (viii.4-5); but this is probably part of the 'Themistocles legend' and of the anti-Corinthian bias of the tradition
heard by Herodotus in Athens, both of which are to be observed
even more clearly in his account of Salamis. The Corinthians led the
fleet in the retreat from Artemisium after the news of Thermopylae
was learned: not because they had wanted to flee all the time, but
because they were the second largest contingent in the Greek force
(Hdt. viii.21.2).

Corinth either suffered little loss at Artemisium or was able to
repair her losses quickly, for she also provided forty ships for
Salamis (Hdt. viii.43); seven others came from Ambracia, and three
from Leucas.[4] The proportion of Corinthian vessels in the whole
fleet, however, was smaller than at Artemisium: Athens had increased her contribution to 180 and Aegina hers to thirty (Hdt.
viii.44.1, 46.1). Herodotus' account of Salamis and its preliminaries
reflects badly on Corinth: Adeimantus was gratuitously rude to
Themistocles when he attempted to persuade Eurybiades, the
Spartan commander-in-chief, to abandon the plan to withdraw to
the Isthmus (viii.57-63); and there was an Athenian tale—rejected
by the rest of the Greeks, who accepted the Corinthian claim to
have played a conspicuous part—that at the beginning of the battle
Adeimantus fled under sail in panic with his whole squadron, and
that after being turned back by a strange, possibly divine, vessel
they rejoined the main fleet after the victory had been won (viii.94).

Neither of these reports is likely to be well founded; they are
distortions which reflect the hostility felt at Athens for Corinth
after 460 and, to a lesser degree, the growth of anecdotes round the
character of Themistocles.[5] It is not even possible to be sure that
Adeimantus failed to grasp the naval strategy adopted by Themistocles of fighting in the narrow waters of Salamis and therefore
favoured withdrawal to the Isthmus, much less that he offered

---

[4] The number from Leucas is perhaps surprisingly low (cf., e.g., Thuc. i.27.2, 46.1: ten
for Leucimme and the same number for Sybota). This may not be significant, but Hippomachus of Leucas acted as seer for the Greek allies of Persia at Plataea (Hdt. ix.38.2). See
further below, 272.

[5] Cf. de Ste Croix, 211-12.

foolish insults to the commander of well over half the Greek fleet. The fact that Corinth helped in full force with the building of the Isthmus wall[6] —which is hardly surprising—does not mean that Corinth wished to withdraw to the Isthmus by sea; and Corinth, with much of her territory north of the Isthmus, had a direct interest in remaining at Salamis even if Adeimantus was not intelligent enough to appreciate the advantages of fighting in narrow waters.[7] The story of Corinthian panic and flight is even less credible. The Corinthians certainly hoisted sail and moved away from the main battle area, but they did so by design and not from fear; either to give the impression that the Greeks were in flight, or to deal with the Egyptian squadron at the western end of the Salamis sound.[8] The slanders heard by Herodotus in Athens can be corrected with the help of the inscriptions which commemorated the achievement of the Corinthians in the fleet—most importantly, that set up on Salamis and therefore with the permission of contemporary Athenians:

> Stranger, we once lived in the well-watered city of Corinth;
> But now we lie in Salamis, the island of Ajax.
> There we captured Phoenician ships, Persians
> And Medes; we defended holy Greece.[9]

When the Spartans were finally persuaded to lead their troops and those of their allies from the Peloponnese against those Persians who remained in central Greece under Mardonius,[10] 5,000 Corinthians marched with them, along with 300 from Potidaea, 500 from Ambracia, and 800 from Leucas and Anactorium (Hdt. ix.28.3, 5). There were more Corinthians present than any others save Spartans and Athenians (Hdt. ix.28.2-6). Whether they saw any fighting in the battle is not clear;[11] but if they did not, that was because they

---

[6] Hdt. viii.72. For a useful summary of the physical remains, with references, see Wiseman, 60-2: the wall used the ridge south of the Isthmus and was much longer than the shortest stretch between the two Gulfs.

[7] See the admirable discussion of Burn, *Persia and the Greeks*, 444-7, esp. 445.

[8] Ibid., 458-9.

[9] The Salamis inscription, Meiggs and Lewis, *GHI* no. 24. That Corinthians died in the battle and had this epitaph set up on their grave gives the lie to the hostile tale of the Athenians; and cf. Burn, *Persia and the Greeks*, 444. The inscription, along with others relating to the Corinthian performance, is quoted in an otherwise feeble discussion by Plutarch, *Mor.* 870 A-871 C.

[10] For balanced discussions of the Spartan delays, see Burn, ibid., 503-7; Forrest, *Sparta*, 97-8.

[11] At Hdt. ix.69.1 they leave their position at the Temple of Hera and rush forward without discipline over the foothills of Cithaeron to the Temple of Demeter, where much fighting took place (Hdt. ix.62-5); but they are mentioned no more. The indiscipline asserted by Herodotus may be true; but it may be part of the anti-Corinthian tradition he heard in Athens.

obeyed the orders of Pausanias, which had the effect of keeping them out of the conflict until it was over.[12] The importance of their contribution at Mycale, however, is in no doubt: with Troezen and Sicyon they shared second place only to the Athenians.[13] There is no indication that Corinth or her commanders were ever responsible for suggestions of strategic or tactical brilliance;[14] but her quantitative contribution, both at sea and on land, ranked behind only those of the far greater states of Sparta and Athens, and her forces carried out their orders with loyalty and determination. She deserved to be inscribed, along with Sparta and Athens, on the second coil of the Serpent Column at Delphi.[15]

[12] According to Hdt. ix.52 (cf. 60.1) the troops who moved to the Temple of Hera during the night before the battle did so in panic; in fact, they did so to set purpose and in good order (Burn, *Persia and the Greeks*, 531). Burn (ibid., 536-7) suggests plausibly that the Corinthians and others at the Temple of Hera performed the important service of ensuring that Artabazus did not engage his troops. Plutarch's account of Corinth's part in the award of battle honours after Plataea (*Arist.* 20. 1-3) is worthless.

[13] Hdt. ix.105, cf. 102.3. For the whole action, ix.90-105 (cf. also for Corinth ix.95).

[14] The importance of Adeimantus' contribution is not to be determined by the evidence of his epitaph (Plut. *Mor.* 870 F), which no doubt exaggerates.

[15] Meiggs and Lewis, *GHI*, no. 27.

XIX.   Corinth and Athens:
Through War to Peace

Almost immediately after Mycale there began to develop the clashes
of interest between Athens and Sparta and her Peloponnesian allies
which characterized the remainder of the century. The Peloponnesians suggested that the population of Ionia be transferred to the
territory of the Medizing states of the mainland; but this wildly
impractical scheme was successfully resisted by the Athenians, and
the island states were brought into the anti-Persian alliance (Hdt.
ix.106.2-4). The Greek fleet failed to capture the Persian bridge
over the Hellespont; and the Peloponnesians left for home while
the Athenians and the new members of the alliance laid siege to
Sestos.[1] More important differences were revealed in the winter of
479/8. The Athenians had started rebuilding their city, but Sparta—
urged on by allies who, according to Thucydides, 'were afraid of the
great size of the Athenian fleet, which had not existed before, and
of the confidence Athens had shown in the Persian War' (i.90.1)—
sent ambassadors to urge that the walls of Athens should not be
rebuilt, and indeed that all fortifications outside the Peloponnese
should be torn down. The Spartans defended their proposal by
saying that the Persians should not, if they returned, be given the
opportunity to use bases such as they had enjoyed for Xerxes'
invasion in Thebes; but Themistocles was well aware (as was
Thucydides) that the real motive was fear of Athens and her magnificent navy: he went to Sparta to delay matters until the walls were
defensible (Thuc. i.89.3-93). The Spartans accepted their defeat with
a good grace, at least in public (Thuc. i.92), and in the following
season twenty Peloponnesian vessels joined thirty Athenian and some
other ships for campaigns in Cyprus and Byzantium under the
command of Pausanias (Thuc. i.94); but he earned the displeasure
of the Ionians in particular and was recalled (Thuc. i.95.1-5). The
Spartans sent Dorcis in Pausanias' place, but he was not accepted by
the men he was to command; now, if not before, the Peloponnesian
forces returned home and left the Athenians to organize the Delian
League and to continue the war against the Persians.[2]

---

[1] Hdt. ix.114; Thuc. i.89.2.
[2] Thuc. i.95.6-96. The precise time of the departure of the Peloponnesians is not given.
See also Hdt. viii.3.2: less friendly to Athens, and probably more accurate.

The attitude of the Corinthians to these developments is noted in none of our sources; Corinthian enmity for Athens should not be too readily assumed. It must be taken that the Corinthians joined their fellow Peloponnesians when they returned home both in 479, while the Athenians and others remained in action at Sestos, and in the following year when the Ionians showed discontent with Spartan leadership; but these withdrawals are as likely to reflect war-weariness as hostility to Athens. Corinthians may have been among those Peloponnesians who advocated the transfer of the Ionian population to the mainland—no doubt in order to avoid further fighting in defence of Ionian freedom. It has sometimes been assumed that Corinth was one of the allies of Sparta who feared Athens and tried to prevent the rebuilding of her walls;[3] but this is improbable.[4] At some time shortly after the Persian Wars Themistocles acted as arbitrator between Corinth and Corcyra over rights at Leucas.[5] If Corinth had shared Sparta's views on the walls of Athens she would hardly have accepted Themistocles as arbitrator after his success in thwarting the plan to prevent the fortification of Athens. This argument of detail can be supported by consideration of Corinthian policy on a larger scale. In the years before 490 Corinth had been greatly concerned to limit the growth of Spartan power, and her actions to that end had often taken the form of co-operation with or support for Athens. This must have created a feeling of common interests, and it would have been logical, at least, if Corinth had positively welcomed the growth of Athenian influence as an effective counterweight to Sparta. Far more significant evidence, however, is provided by Corinth's rejection of Sparta's proposal to attack Athens during the Samian revolt in 440 (below, 281-2). Even after the bitterness of the First Peloponnesian War, Corinth was willing to tolerate Athenian control of the Aegean. In 479, after many years of co-operation with Athens in their efforts to limit Sparta, the Corinthians will certainly not have

----

[3] e.g. Burn, *Persia and the Greeks*, 556.

[4] Aegina is the only state specifically mentioned as having complained to Sparta (Plut. *Them*. 19.2). On Corinth see (briefly) de Ste Croix, 334–5; but his view that Megara—which had disputed with Athens over Salamis for more than a century—was not 'as yet seriously at odds with Athens' is improbable. Megara is a good candidate for the other state which justified Thucydides' use of the plural 'allies', even though any fortifications Megara had would have been destroyed by the same token. Thucydides' use of the plural may be inaccurate.

[5] Plut. *Them*. 24.1; *P. Oxy*. 1012, Fr. 9, 23–34 (from Theophrastus). The date should be after the Persian Wars, which gave Themistocles sufficient reputation to be chosen (cf. Oberhummer, 81). Piccirilli, *Arbitrati interstatali greci*, no. 13, in arguing for a date before the invasion of Xerxes, puts excessive weight on the stories in Herodotus of hostility between Themistocles and Adeimantus at Salamis (above, 254-5). See in general de Ste Croix, 212.

been alarmed by Athens' mere potential for growth, and they may positively have looked forward to the establishment of an Athenian influence in the Aegean which would create a more even balance of power in the Greek world.

Our sources also tell us nothing of Corinth's relations with Sparta after 479. Presumably Corinth looked with no greater favour on Spartan activity beyond the Isthmus shortly after 479 than on Cleomenes' interference in Athenian affairs before 500;[6] but Corinth probably took neither part nor pleasure in the difficulties that nearly engulfed Sparta in the late 470s and the 460s. Sparta had to face both Argive and Arcadian armies in the field; Elis may have been disaffected too.[7] When Sparta was just beginning to recover, an earthquake in Laconia provided the opportunity for a serious helot revolt.[8] It is unfortunate that we know very little of these events, for they must have been as important a factor behind the decisions that led to conflict between Athens and the Spartan alliance after 460 as the growth of Athenian power in the Aegean; but Corinth's position is hardly in doubt. Her sympathy must have been with Sparta. Argos was no less a threat to Corinth than to Sparta. A collapse of Spartan power in the Peloponnese might seem dangerous to Corinth after the rapid growth of Athenian influence in the Aegean; the principles of balance worked both ways. Whether Corinth afforded material help to Sparta during this period, as the terms of her alliance obliged her to do, is not recorded;[9] but an Argive defeat of Corinth, known only from the dedication of spoils at Olympia, fits epigraphically more easily in this period than during the First Peloponnesian War and was probably connected.[10] A Corinthian attack on Cleonae soon before 462 (Plut. *Cim.* 17.2) may also have been related, for Cleonae joined Argos in her attack on the Spartan ally Mycenae;[11] but although the Corinthians might have tried to detach Cleonae from her Argive alliance in order to help Sparta, they no doubt had reasons of their own for attempting to gain the allegiance of the place. Corinth probably enjoyed greater

---

[6] Leotychidas in Thessaly: Hdt. vi.72; Paus. iii.7.9; Plut. *Mor.* 859 D; Plut. *Them.* 20.1-2. Attempted reorganization of the Amphictyonic Council: Plut. *Them.* 20.3-4. Removal of tyrants in Thasos and Phocis (?): Plut. *Mor.* 859 D.

[7] On the details, see Andrewes, *Phoenix*, vi (1952), 1-5; Forrest, *CQ* x (1960), 221-32. For a brief and useful summary, Forrest, *Sparta*, 100-2.

[8] Sources in Hill, *Sources*, Index iv.2.8-9.

[9] Other allies are mentioned by most sources which describe the Spartan appeal for Athenian help against the helots at Ithome (Thuc. i.102.1; Diod. xi.64.2,4; Paus. i.29.8, iv.24.6; Plut. *Cim.* 17.3), but Corinth is not named specifically among them.

[10] Jeffery, *Local Scripts*, 169, no. 18; cf., however, de Ste Croix, 186.

[11] Strabo 377; cf. Forrest, *CQ* x (1960), 230-2.

success at Cleonae than in the engagement with the Argives,[12] but
it did not last: Cleonaeans fought with the Argives at Tanagra a few
years later (Paus. i.29.7).

Corinth did not share the jealousy of Athens' recent achievement
which Sparta shouted out when she insulted Cimon's troops at
Ithome in 462.[13] Plutarch records a minor altercation between
Cimon and a Corinthian Lachartus over Cimon's bad manners in failing
to gain permission to lead his insulted army back through Corinthian
territory. If it took place, the exchange was insignificant: Cimon had
more on his mind than protocol.[14] In 462 there were no reasons for
Corinth to review her earlier attitude of toleration towards Athens;[15]
but the insult at Ithome caused Athens to alter her view of Sparta,
and as a result Corinth was forced to go to war with Athens to
defend her own interests.

Thucydides calls attention to an 'intense hatred' conceived by
Corinth for Athens just before what we now call the First Peloponnesian War; it had its origin in an Athenian alliance with Megara in
the winter of 461/0.[16] Thucydides says, 'It was particularly from
this affair that the intense hatred of Corinth for Athens began to
exist.'[17] This emphasis of Thucydides provides strong evidence in
favour of a tolerant Corinthian attitude towards Athens before
462; but relations between the two states had probably already
changed significantly as a result of a quite separate episode. We
know of two developments in Athenian policy just before the
Megarian affair: the alliances with Argos and Thessaly,[18] and the

[12] For a different view, cf. Andrewes in Gomme, *HCT* iv.107; Forrest, *CQ* x (1960), 231.
Plut. *Cim.* 17.2 implies that Corinth was at least temporarily successful both at Megara and
at Cleonae. Schol. Pind. *Nem.* Hypoth. c, d asserts that Corinth at one time controlled the
Nemean Games; this is the only known historical context into which such a brief Corinthian
control will fit (cf. Jeffery, *Local Scripts*, 148-9). Paus. vii.25.6 reports that some of the
Mycenaeans who were driven out of their city after a long Argive siege took refuge in
Cleonae. This can be explained without assuming a change in the allegiance of Cleonae
(Andrewes and Forrest, locc. citt.); but in view of the other evidence Cleonae was probably
under Corinthian rather than Argive influence at the time.

[13] Thuc. i.102. The apology for Sparta offered by Holladay, *JHS* xcvii (1977), 54-5, is
unconvincing: that an insult is not deliberately intended as such does not make it any the
less insulting.

[14] Plut. *Cim.* 17.1-2; cf. de Ste Croix, 212. Gomme (*HCT* i.300) takes the anecdote to
show (if it is true) that Corinth was 'not anxious to help Sparta' at Ithome—presumably
because Lachartus was rude to Cimon when he was leading an army that had been intended
to help Sparta; I see no force in this argument.

[15] See however, below, on the date of the capture of Naupactus.

[16] I follow, in the main, the chronology of *ATL* iii.158-80, although I cannot accept that
Thucydides never deviates from strict chronological order when he moves from one theatre
to another; there is almost certainly one such case between the end of i.108 and the beginning of i.109 (Meiggs, *Athenian Empire*, 111 n. 1).

[17] i.103.4, cf. de Ste Croix, 181-2; the exact translation is significant.

[18] Thuc. i.102.4; see de Ste Croix, 182-3.

settlement of the helots at Naupactus.[19] The implications for Corinth of the alliance with Argos are uncertain, but at best worrying;[20] the action at Naupactus gave greater cause for concern. From Corinth's point of view, the settlement of the helots as such mattered little; what was disturbing was the fact that the Athenians had already captured Naupactus before the question of what to do with the helots arose. According to Thucydides (i.103.3) Athens had 'recently' taken Naupactus when the helots appealed to her; the city was not captured in order to settle the helots, but had already been taken.

We are left to guess at both the date and the purpose of the capture. Thucydides' word 'recently' will allow the seizure to have taken place either before or after the insult at Ithome.[21] To identify the purpose, however, will perhaps clarify the date. Athens' action must imply some threat to Corinth's domination of her Gulf. The presence, for the first time as far as we know, of Athenian ships in the Gulf must have alarmed Corinth; the capture by those ships of a city which could command its entrance was far worse. No such action is likely to have been undertaken before the rift with Sparta at Ithome; there was then no reason for Athens to threaten Corinth. Thucydides' view that it was the alliance with Megara that started Corinthian hatred of Athens cannot be taken to prove that Corinth was unconcerned about the capture of Naupactus. Doubtless that was not Corinth's main grievance against Athens; but even before the Megarian alliance, the capture of Naupactus showed that the new Athenian hostility against Sparta might be expressed in the form of interference with Corinth. There was little that Athens could do to harm Sparta directly, as the rest of the century shows; Corinth may well have feared (perhaps justly)[22] that Athens had determined

[19] Thuc. i.103.1-3. The date of this event is one of the most frequently discussed chronological problems in the fifth century; the literature is enormous (cf. McNeal, *Historia*, xix (1970), 306-25). Despite McNeal, ibid., 311, I can give no meaning to Thucydides' complaint about the chronology of Hellanicus' account of the Pentecontaetia (i.97.2) without supposing that he himself gave events in proper order (with the proviso mentioned above, n. 16); cf. *ATL* iii.160-4. Thus the settlement of the helots preceded the alliance with Megara.

[20] See Jeffery, *BSA* lx (1965), 52-3. Corinth will, at the very least, not have been unconcerned, especially if the defeat commemorated by the Argive dedication at Olympia was recent.

[21] The principle that Thucydides gives events in chronological order cannot be invoked to show that the capture was subsequent to the insult: the only event whose place in the chronological scheme is vouched for by Thucydides is the settlement of the helots.

[22] The best discussion of the Athenian attitude after Ithome (de Ste Croix, 182-3) is made incomplete by its author's failure to take account of the capture of Naupactus because of his uncertainty about the date (181). This act means that some Athenian agresssion (however understandable) must come into question besides the alarm and annoyance created by the insult at Ithome.

to harm Sparta through her allies, even before the Megarians made their appeal. The Megarian alliance must have seemed all too clear a confirmation of Corinth's fears.

Thucydides states that the occasion of the alliance between Megara and Athens was a border war with Corinth. Corinth initially had the advantage (Thuc. i.103.4), and she may therefore have been the aggressor; the anecdote in Plut. *Cim*. 17.2 shows, if it is true, that Corinth could be accused in 462 of aggression against Megara, probably recent. The Corinthian motive cannot be recovered; but the Megarian reaction must have been totally unexpected: she deserted the Peloponnesian League and appealed to the Athenians. They accepted their good fortune, built long walls from Megara to Nisaea, and installed a garrison. There is no record of whether the alliance with Athens enabled Megara to reverse her losses on the Corinthian border; but within a short while Athens and the Peloponnesian League were at war.

On the surface it seems that the First Peloponnesian War had its origin in the mere accident of Megara's decision to appeal to Athens against Corinthian aggression; and Gomme suggests that Corinth bears a heavy responsibility for being 'ready to risk the stability of the Peloponnesian League, not to mention the peace of the Greek world in general, rather than give up a claim to some strip of land'.[23] That Corinth was careless of the stability of the League is true; but she cannot be fairly accused of taking no thought for the peace of the Greek world in general. It could not have been predicted that Megara would take the steps she did to defend herself; Megarian hostility to Athens must have seemed almost as immutable as the enmity between Sparta and Argos. More importantly, Athens had already given Corinth good grounds for apprehension by capturing Naupactus; and the whole series of events had begun with the Spartan insult at Ithome. Sparta needed no encouragement from Corinth to be hostile to Athens.[24]

Technically, the Athenians were the aggressors in the war; their landing at Halieis was the first action.[25] But the question of which side started hostilities is scarcely important: neither party was loath to fight. When Athenians landed at Halieis war had probably already been declared by the Peloponnesian League;[26] even if it had not,

[23] *HCT* i.304.
[24] Cf. Kagan, *Outbreak*, 80–1. See further below, 420–1.
[25] Thuc. i.105.1: on the probable purpose of the landing at Halieis—to open lines of communication between Athens and Argos—see Jeffery, *BSA* lx (1965), 54; Meiggs, *Athenian Empire*, 97.
[26] Cf. de Ste Croix, 187–8. See further below, 420–1.

Athens had good ground to expect such a declaration, and her attack on Halieis will have been an attempt to gain an advantage by surprise in a war which had already all but started. However self-confident and keen to fight the Athenians were, it is unlikely that they would have struck the first blow, when they already had major forces committed in Egypt (Thuc. i.104), without good reason to believe that war would have broken out soon anyway.[27] The Peloponnesians were not caught unawares at Halieis; Corinthian and Epidaurian troops—almost certainly aided by 300 hoplite ἐπίκουροι 'of the Peloponnesians'—successfully disputed the landing.[28]

Whether Athenians or Peloponnesians were the aggressors in the subsequent naval battle of Cecryphaleia is obscure (Thuc. i.105.1). Corinthian ships were doubtless present, but the victory went to Athens, who now concentrated her energies on taking Aegina. In the previous war between these two states Corinth had helped Athens by providing twenty vessels (above, 251–2); her sympathies were now different, and despite the silence of Thucydides (i.105.2) on the identity of the allies of Aegina in the sea battle which was the first action in the Aeginetan War, Corinth must have been foremost among them. Altogether seventy Peloponnesian ships were taken in the battle, no doubt very many of them Corinthian.[29] Shortly afterwards the Peloponnesians attempted an invasion of the Megarid. The primary intention was to regain its allegiance, in the hope that Athenian forces could not be spared to defend her new ally; if that failed, it could, at least, be expected that Athens would have to withdraw from Aegina.[30] Myronides' army of the youngest and oldest falsified both hopes. The first invading force of Corinthians and unidentified allies could claim not to have been defeated by (among others) aged Athenians; but equally aged Corinthians stung their younger fellow citizens into returning on their own, and the insults merely succeeded in sending many to their deaths. Thucydides has a description of the final disaster which he must have had from an eyewitness: the Corinthians 'were returning after their defeat, and a not inconsiderable part of their forces came under pressure and missed the way. They entered a private estate which had a large ditch surrounding it; there was no way out. The Athenians saw

[27] One possible date for the battle of Oenoe would make that the first action of the war, and would mean that the Spartans were the technical aggressors, for Oenoe was in Argive territory; see below, 265.
[28] Thuc. i.105.1: for the ἐπίκουροι, i.105.3; the obvious occasion for them to have served with the Corinthians and Epidaurians is at Halieis. Sicyonians may also have been present (Holladay, *JHS* xcvii (1977), 57 n. 24).
[29] Thuc. i.105.2; Lys. ii.48.
[30] Thuc. i.105.3; Lys. ii.49.

what had happened and kept them in by facing them with their hoplites; they then placed their light-armed troops all round and stoned to death all those who were inside. This was a great disaster for the Corinthians; but the majority of their army got back home.' Megara remained Athenian, and Aegina continued under siege.[31]

The Spartans are not mentioned by Thucydides in any of these actions, and that must mean that they took no part in them; the Corinthians probably undertook temporary and informal responsibility for the co-ordination of Peloponnesian action. By this stage, if not before Halieis, war had almost certainly been declared by the Peloponnesian League; yet the Spartans took no positive action. Perhaps they had no time to take part in the naval battles in the Saronic Gulf, though that says little for Spartan efficiency; but the reason for the Spartan failure to participate in the invasion of the Megarid, which must have been planned in advance, can only have been that they believed it to have so small a chance of success that they refused to sanction it—or that they had for the time being abandoned the war effort altogether because Athenian tenure of the Megarid precluded the use of their only weapon, invasion of Attica.[32] Thucydides' description of the invading force as 'Corinthians with their allies' (i.105.3) implies that it was under Corinthian command; it seems that Corinth rejected Spartan faint-heartedness and organized an invasion with as many willing allies as she could find. Corinthian distress at the defeat[33] can only have been increased by the thought that success might have been achieved if only the head of the League had done her duty.

There must have been some discontent with Spartan leadership. This was perhaps one reason for the invasion of Doris which led to the costly Peloponnesian victory at Tanagra in 458 (Thuc. i.107.2-108.2); the Spartans wished to give the impression that they were doing something, even if it was not a direct attack upon Athens.[34] The army that crossed the Corinthian Gulf[35] was 11,500 strong—far larger than was needed for its ostensible object of helping Doris against Phocis;[36] but there seems to have been no definite plan for action against Athens. Diodorus' confused account[37] may suggest

[31] Thuc. i.105.3-106.2 (the quotation, 106.1-2); Lys. ii.49-53.
[32] De Ste Croix, 187-95.
[33] Cf. Thuc. i.106.2: 'this was a great disaster (πάθος μέγα) for the Corinthians.'
[34] Cf. Gomme, *HCT* i.314.
[35] See de Ste Croix, 190-5.
[36] Reece, *JHS* lxx (1950), 75-6, disputes Thucydides' figures, on insufficient grounds; cf. Jeffery, *BSA* lx (1965), 55 n. 58.
[37] For a useful summary, pointing out the difficulties, cf. Buck, *CP* lxv (1970), 219-20; Kagan (*Outbreak*, 90 with n. 38), in accepting Diodorus, does not seem to recognize them.

that part of the motive for the expedition was to help Thebes gain control of Boeotia, though Diodorus does not say that himself; but Thucydides indicates rather that once the Spartans had done their business in Doris they cast about for some means of returning home (i.107.3-4). An appeal made by Athenian oligarchs may have persuaded the Spartans to invade Attica while they had the opportunity —though the fears which led the Athenians to fight at Tanagra need not have been justified; the Peloponnesian losses in the battle were so heavy that there was no question of further operations.[38]

Sparta continued to fail Corinth. We hear of no offensives against Athens before the Five Years Truce—though an unsuccessful offence against Argos may have been involved in the battle of Oenoe.[39] Athens, however, maintained her momentum, not only by gaining Boeotia and much of central Greece after Oenophyta (Thuc. i.108.2-3), but also by pursuing the naval campaign with vigour, much to the detriment of Corinth. Aegina was finally defeated in 457, and her fleet removed from the already meagre naval resources of the Peloponnesian League (Thuc. i.108.4). The capture of Troezen perhaps took place now, and Athens concluded an alliance with Hermione probably in the latter part of the decade.[40] Tolmides, on his famous *periplous* in 457, took the Corinthian possession of Chalcis, on the northern shore of the entrance to the Corinthian Gulf, and won a victory near Sicyon (Thuc. i.108.5). Even after the disaster in Egypt Pericles led an expedition from Pagae, won a second battle against the Sicyonians, and then received Achaea into

[38] For Spartan caution in this whole episode, see Holladay, *JHS* xcvii (1977), 59-60; I cannot, however, share his conclusion that Sparta was not hostile to Athens (below, 420-1). For a dedication of spoils from Tanagra in Corinthian script, see Meiggs and Lewis, *GHI*, no. 36. It is unfortunately impossible to make any political sense of an inscription, dated about the mid-fifth century or rather later by letter-forms, in which the Corinthian Sotaerus is honoured by Thetonium near Pharsalus in Thessaly for saving 'gold and silver' (Jeffery, *Local Scripts*, 99, no. 10); his action may in any case have had no political implications.

[39] There are two plausible contexts for Oenoe: either almost immediately after the alliance between Athens and Argos (Meiggs, *Athenian Empire*, 469-72), or soon after Oenophyta (Jeffery, *BSA* lx (1965), 52-7). If we take the former it is difficult to explain why Thucydides omitted what was in effect the first action in the First Peloponnesian War (this difficulty is underestimated by Meiggs, *Athenian Empire*, 472); on the other hand, why after Tanagra and Oenophyta should the Athenians have been so proud of their victory at Oenoe that it was commemorated in the Stoa Poikile? The Athenians are more likely to have over-reacted to their first victory *over Sparta* in the field than Thucydides to have so distorted the war as to omit its first action. Corinth may have fought Argos independently at this time, if the dedication at Olympia belongs here, but an earlier date is more likely (above, 259). Andrewes (in Levick, *Ancient Historian and his Materials*, 9-16) has doubted the evidence for Oenoe, mainly on topographical grounds; but see Pritchett, *Studies in Ancient Greek Topography*, iii. 1-53, esp. 49-50.

[40] Troezen was Athenian in 446/5, when it was given up under the Thirty Years Peace (i.115.1); for Hermione, see Meiggs quoted by Jeffery, *BSA* lx (1965), 54 n. 54.

alliance; but he failed to take Oeniadae in Acarnania.[41] Molycreium, a Corinthian colony just west of Naupactus, may have been taken by Athens during these years (below, 277).

Athens might have applied naval pressure indefinitely had not matters in the Aegean claimed her attention; whatever effect the defeat of the Egyptian Expedition had on the members of the Delian League, the Athenians clearly had a great deal to do.[42] But the Peloponnesians could not even now devise any means of offence, and in winter 451/0 the Five Years Truce was signed.[43] The initiative may have come from Athens, for she probably wished to have her hands free of Peloponnesian trouble in order to wage a campaign against Persia and regularize her relations with the King. The Peloponnesians must in any case have welcomed a guarantee that Athens would undertake no offensive action, and it was not difficult for them to promise to continue the inactivity which the strategic situation imposed on them.[44] Whether Corinth voted for the Truce is not known. At about the same time Argos concluded a Thirty Years Peace with Sparta; but that took little pressure off Corinth, for she was not included.[45]

By early 447 the Peloponnesians may have regretted giving Athens a free hand in the Aegean; she had established a *modus vivendi* with Persia[46] and asserted her control over the Delian League.[47] Her recent successes on the mainland, however, were not so well secured as to be irreversible; and Peloponnesian intrigue went a long way towards reversing all gains made by Athens since 462. An arrangement was made with the anti-Athenian party in Megara that they

---

[41] Thuc. i.111.2-3. Diod. xi.85.1-2 (cf. Plut. *Per.* 19.3) states that Pericles won over the other cities of Acarnania, but this is not to be accepted; cf. Beloch, ii.1.174. Jacoby, *FGH* III B (Suppl.), ii.123, is right to point out that Pericles might have undertaken action in Acarnania proper; but the report of Diodorus is disproved by Thuc. ii.68.7-8, which shows that Phormio made the first alliance with Acarnania (for the date, see below, 422-3).

[42] The condition of the Aegean after the defeat of the Egyptian Expedition remains disputed; for a fully documented discussion, see Meiggs, *Athenian Empire*, 109-24.

[43] Thuc. i.112.1. There is no merit in the suggestion of Bengtson (212 with n. 2; *Staatsverträge*, ii. no. 143; cf. Gomme, *HCT* i.325) that a few words should be transposed in this passage to leave us with a date of *c.*453 for the Truce.

[44] For a different view, which fails to take account of Spartan inactivity in the war since Tanagra, cf. Kagan, *Outbreak*, 104-5.

[45] *Staatsverträge*, ii. no. 144.

[46] This will only have been apparent by 447 if the Peace of Callias was a public fact, as I believe; I have nothing to add to the unending debate. For a judicious discussion, cf. Meiggs, *Athenian Empire*, 129-51 (with a summary of the debate, 487-95).

[47] I do not discuss here the Congress Decree (Plut. *Per.* 17). Strong arguments have been urged in favour of rejecting it as a forgery of the 340s (Seager, *Historia*, xviii (1969), 129-41; Bosworth, *Historia*, xx (1971), 600-16); but the case remains unproved (Meiggs, *Athenian Empire*, 512-15). Even if demonstrably genuine, the Decree would tell us nothing about Corinth—and little about Sparta that we did not know already.

should revolt as soon as the Truce was over; Sparta could then at last invade Attica. Revolts in both Boeotia and Euboea were probably intended to take place at the same time; but the prompt action of Tolmides disrupted Peloponnesian plans. In winter 447/6 Boeotian exiles hostile to Athens gained control of some Boeotian cities (Thuc. i.113.1), and the Athenian assembly discussed the situation; Pericles argued for delay, but Tolmides persuaded the assembly to send him to meet the threat at once.[48] He lost his life and the whole of central Greece at Coronea (Thuc. i.113.1-4); but he had provoked the Boeotians into a mistimed rebellion. Euboea rebelled 'not long afterwards', and while Pericles was attempting to reduce the island he had to return to defend Attica against the Spartan invasion which Megara's revolt had made possible (Thuc. i.114.1). It cannot be proved that all these actions were originally intended to coincide; but circumstantial evidence is strong. Euboean exiles were among the allies of the Boeotian victors at Coronea (Thuc. i.113.2), and the Megarians were helped in their revolt by Corinthians, Sicyonians, and Epidaurians (Thuc. i.114.1). The Megarian revolt must have been timed to allow an invasion through the Megarid as soon as the Truce ran out; that the intention was for Boeotia and Euboea to rebel at the same time is only slightly less certain.[49] The involvement of Corinth with Megara is certain, and may be strongly suspected with at least Boeotia.

Athens was hard pressed by the invasion; but Pleistoanax led his force back home after advancing little further than Eleusis, Pericles subdued Euboea, and within a short while the Thirty Years Peace had been signed (Thuc. i.114.2-115.1). Sparta may have blamed Pleistoanax for his withdrawal, which allowed Athens to negotiate without immediate pressure (below, 297); but Corinth's attitude to the Samian revolt in 440 demonstrates that she, at least, viewed the Thirty Years Peace as a reasonable settlement of her differences with Athens.[50] Such a view was entirely logical. The reason for the 'intense hatred', the alliance with Megara, was now removed, and Athens promised to make no alliance with Megara or any other Spartan ally; Athens had managed to retain Pagae at the time of the Megarian revolt but she gave it up under the Peace,[51] as she gave up Nisaea, Troezen, and her alliance with Achaea. At the

[48] Plut. *Per.* 18.2-3; cf. Kagan, *Outbreak*, 122-3.

[49] Cf. de Ste Croix, 197 n. 94, mentioning only Euboea and Megara; there is no reason to exclude Boeotia from the conjecture (cf. *ATL* iii.303: less specific).

[50] On the terms of the Peace, see de Ste Croix, 293-4. The Corinthian attitude, ibid., 213-14; Alexander, *Potidaea*, 48-9. Contrast Holladay, *JHS* xcvii (1977), 60-1.

[51] For Athenian action in the Megarid at this time, see Meiggs and Lewis, *GHI*, no. 51; Diod. xii.5.2 is probably inaccurate in detail.

entrance to the Corinthian Gulf, Athens retained Naupactus, and probably Chalcis and Molycreium too.[52] The capture of Naupactus in the first place caused Corinth concern, but its retention after 446 will have been less worrying. Athens promised that she would not act with hostility towards Corinth; and any difficult that arose could, under the terms of the Peace, be submitted to arbitration. Naupactus was a potential threat, should Athens fail to observe her oaths; but for the moment there was no reason to fear that she might do so. The material concessions in the Peace were all made by Athens; and the recognition of Athenian domination in the Aegean, which was Sparta's main concession to Athens, had been given informally by the Corinthians long before. New Athenian interests in the far west— the alliance with Egesta and perhaps already with Rhegium and Leontini[53] —will not have disturbed Corinth a great deal. The friend-ship which Corinth felt for Athens before and perhaps after the invasion of Xerxes could not, of course, be restored; but the words which Thucydides gives to the Corinthians in the Corcyra debate in 433 summarize admirably the Corinthian attitude: 'we are neither your enemies, so that we should wish to harm you, nor your friends so that we should have frequent contact with you.'[54]

Paradoxically, Corinth's relationship with Sparta was probably harmed more by the war than her relationship with Athens was. It is easy to understand the Spartan failure to act decisively before 446; she could not do so while Athens garrisoned the Megarid. Corinth may have grasped that fact well enough after her own failure in the Megarid; but that will not have precluded her from feeling frustrated with a leader who was powerless to protect her, and there may have remained a suspicion that it was only Spartan unwillingness to participate that had prevented the success of the

[52] Gomme (*HCT* ii.217) suggests that Chalcis might have been returned under the Peace; it was certainly small enough for its return to have been omitted by Thucydides. It will have been worth Athens' while to gain the goodwill of Corinth by returning a possession which meant little to Athens while she held Naupactus; but at its next mention in Thucydides (ii.83.3) Chalcis is in Athenian hands. For Molycreium, see below, 277.

[53] Meiggs and Lewis, *GHI* nos. 37, 63-4, with discussion; the latter alliances might well have been made after 446.

[54] i.41.1. A second passage in this speech leads to a similar conclusion. The Corinthians mention (i.42.2) 'the suspicion we held of you before, over the issue of Megara', and urge the removal of that suspicion (by rejection of the alliance with Corcyra). There is no ques-tion here of *active* Corinthian suspicion of Athens, for it is specifically described as having existed before (ὑπαρχούσης πρότερον). They go on to say, 'for the most recent favour, done at the present time—even if it is a minor one—can eradicate a greater complaint'; there is some confusion in Thucydides' expression here, but he means that by rejecting the Corcyraean alliance Athens can remove the effect of the memory of the σφόδρον μῖσος, which is all that remains of it (cf. de Ste Croix, 230; Meiggs, *Athenian Empire*, 430; Tuplin, *CQ* xix (1979), 301-7).

invasion. Some of the responsibility for the war itself may have been placed on Sparta. Athenian actions against Corinth before the war were undertaken in fear of Sparta after the insult at Ithome, and after settling their differences with Athens some Corinthians may have been more inclined to blame Sparta for provocation than Athens for her response. Such criticism may have been forgotten because of the satisfactory nature of the Thirty Years Peace; but Thucydides makes a Corinthian speaker refer to one of these points at Sparta just before the Peloponnesian War itself: 'against the Athenians we survived in many respects not because of the help you gave us but because of the mistakes they made themselves; for there have already been cases in which those who took no precautions themselves because they trusted in you were destroyed because the hopes they had of help from you were not realized' (i.69.5).[55]

---

[55] The historian makes a similar point in his own person at i.118.2, though with no reference to Corinth: 'the Athenians established their empire on a firmer footing and made their own power very great; the Spartans recognized these developments but did little to prevent them, and for most of the time remained idle.' We can be confident that we know enough about relations between Corinth and Sparta during the reign of King Archidamus II to reject the identification of that king with the Archidamus who, at Polyaen. *Strat.* i.41.2, lays siege to Corinth and receives its surrender from wealthy Corinthians who were afraid that their poor fellow citizens might betray it to him first.

XX.   Corinth and Corcyra
in the North-West

'(The Corcyraeans), though they are our colonists, have in everything rebelled against us and are now at war. They say that they were not sent out in order to be maltreated; but we ourselves say that we did not found their city in order to be insulted by them, but rather to be leaders and to be treated with proper respect. At any rate our other colonies have a special affection for us.'

In these words, taken from the Corycra debate in 433, Thucydides (i.38.1-3) has the Corinthians describe, no doubt in part tendentiously, their relations with their colonies and the galling exception to the normal rule that Corcyra provided. The events which led to the outbreak of the Peloponnesian War began with a dispute between Corinth and Corcyra over rights at Epidamnus, but they cannot be understood without an examination of the character of Corinth's relationships with her Adriatic colonies before this time; what took place at Epidamnus was merely one of a series of conflicts between Corinth and Corcyra in the north-west.[1] Relations can first be traced in the time of the tyrants.

When the Bacchiads fled to Corcyra after Cypselus' revolution the traditional links of cult which Corinth enjoyed with all her colonies (below, 387) may have been broken; but by the tyranny of Periander at the latest they could be restored. Corcyra, Anactorium, Leucas, and Ambracia were ruled by relatives of the tyrant. No blood relations are recorded as having controlled the more northern colonies at Apollonia and Epidamnus, but they may have been governed by close associates (above, 212-3). The fall of Cypselus/Psammetichus in the metropolis no doubt deprived the tyrants in the colonies of much of their strength; but they did not necessarily fall along with him. Much as the Bacchiads, on their welcome in Corcyra after fleeing from Cypselus, naturally ruptured whatever links there had been with Bacchiad Corinth in the past, so the Cypselids of the Adriatic will have been no more tender towards those who had murdered Psammetichus; relationships with Corinth will have been temporarily

---

[1] After the work of Graham, *Colony and Mother City*, 118-39, it is no longer necessary to discuss the view of Kahrstedt, *Griechisches Staatsrecht*, i.357-63, that the inhabitants of the colonies retained Corinthian citizenship, and that the colonies were merely parts of the Corinthian state.

disrupted, perhaps until the tyrants fell in the colonies. At least in
the case of Ambracia, that seems to have been little less than half a
century after the death of Psammetichus in Corinth.[2]

Our next evidence for political relations is not before the fifth
century. The coin-types of Leucas show close dependence on
Corinth when her mint began operation perhaps a little before
500;[3] but this need have no political significance. From the beginning, as throughout the history of the mint, Leucas' types are distinguished from those of Corinth only by the addition of the ethnic
Λ on the obverse. The types of Greek cities are usually distinctive,
and no exactly similar relationship between the coins of one city
and those of another is known outside the Corinthian sphere; but
this should not lead us to conclude that the dependence of Leucas
on Corinth was politically as well as numismatically close. Apart
from Corcyra, Leucas was the first state of the north-west to issue
coins. Corinth was a natural source for technical assistance, and while
the choice of exactly the same type no doubt proves Leucas' filial
piety it does not demand the hypothesis of a closer control. The
Leucadians may have decided upon an issue of coins in order to
simplify the collection of dues at the canal which pierced their
isthmus;[4] probably no coins had earlier been given in payment
more frequently than Corinthian, and this may have influenced the
choice of type. The coins of Ambracia, although they begin rather
later than those of Leucas, show at first an even greater dependence
on Corinth; but this is of no more significance than the issues of
Leucas. The first Ambraciot coins do not only use Corinthian types,
but for the ethnic A on the obverse, but were also struck with
exactly the same reverse dies as contemporary Corinthian issues.
They must therefore have been struck in the Corinthian mint, but
this finds an easy explanation in the circumstances of the issue. It
was made *c.*480: presumably Ambracia found it necessary or

---

[2] Aristotle records two Cypselid tyrants of Ambracia. One, Archinus (specifically defined
as a Cypselid), must have ruled in the first half of the sixth century, for his widow married
Peisistratus of Athens (*Ath. Pol.* 17.4). The second, Periander, whose name shows him to be
Cypselid, was removed from power (*Pol.* 1304 a 31-3; 1311 a 39-b 1) by a combination of
the demos and those who resented his sexual appetites; Periander was presumably therefore
the last of the dynasty. Plut. *Mor.* 859 C-D claims that the Spartans were responsible for the
overthrow of the Cypselids in Ambracia as well as in Corinth. The latter is impossible (above,
229-30). Archinus' Argive wife is hardly enough to explain why, much less how, the Spartans
intervened as far away as Ambracia (contrast Huxley, *Early Sparta*, 75). Even if she were,
the Spartans failed in their object, for Archinus was not the last tyrant. There is no mention
of Spartans in Aristotle's account of the fall of Periander. The appearance of the Cypselids
of both Corinth and Ambracia in Plutarch's list is the result of overenthusiastic attempts to
improve Sparta's anti-tyrant credentials.
[3] For the numismatic details, Kraay, *Archaic and Classical Greek Coins*, 123.
[4] See above, 170-1, on the origins of Corinthian coins.

desirable to strike coins for use in connection with her participation in the campaign against Xerxes, and in the emergency asked her metropolis to undertake the production.[5]

The help offered to Corinth by her Adriatic colonies during the campaign against Xerxes is of more political interest than the coins of Ambracia which reflect it; but its implications are not clear. Ambracia, Leucas, and Anactorium all participated, and were inscribed on the Serpent Column at Delphi;[6] but their commitment was perhaps less than total. Herodotus says nothing of them before Salamis, to which Ambracia sent seven and Leucas three vessels; at Plataea there were 500 Ambraciots, while 800 men from Leucas and Anactorium fought in a single contingent.[7] It is doubtful whether these contributions adequately reflected the capacity of the colonies. They may have failed to provide contingents before Salamis because they were not asked in time, and even though they sent fewer vessels than are recorded later in the fifth century, the later figures may have been the result of construction after 480; but 500 is not a large force for a city the size of Ambracia which was under no immediate Persian threat,[8] and Hippomachus, who acted as seer for the Greek allies of Persia at Plataea, was a Leucadian (Hdt. ix.38.2). It is possible that the colonists felt it politic to retain part of their forces at home to meet a more local threat. Not only might Epirots or Acarnanians take advantage of the temporary absence of forces from their neighbouring cities; but Corcyra took an ambivalent attitude, and had fitted out a fleet of sixty vessels which remained in western waters (Hdt. vii.168).

It is unfortunate that the extent of the commitment of the colonies of the Ambracian Gulf region remains uncertain; for there is scattered evidence, which covers the whole period from the defeat of Xerxes to the Archidamian War,[9] for disputes between Corinth and Corcyra in most of the colonies along this coast. The most famous was at Epidamnus, because of what followed it; but Thucydides' account of it, along with scraps from other authors, indicates both that it was not the first clash of interest between Corinth and Corcyra and that Corinth had enjoyed success in all that had gone before. Themistocles had acted as arbitrator between Corinth and Corcyra over rights at Leucas shortly after the invasion of Xerxes, and his decision went

---

[5] For all this, see Kraay, *Archaic and Classical Greek Coins*, 82, 124.

[6] Meiggs and Lewis, *GHI*, no. 27, Coils 10–11. That the Corinthian colonies (including Potidaea on Coil 9) were inscribed close to each other may be significant; but Anactorium and Ambracia were originally separated by the Cythnians (Meiggs and Lewis, *GHI*, p. 59).

[7] viii.45; ix.28.5. It is not clear whether any colony sent forces to Mycale.

[8] Contrast the case of Potidaea, which sent 300: Hdt. ix.28.3.

[9] On all this, see especially Graham, *Colony and Mother City*, 118–53.

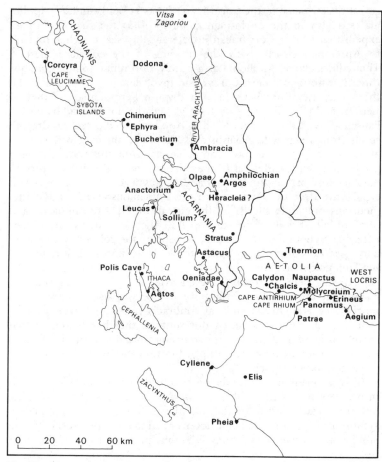

Fig. 17   The Corinthian Gulf and North-West Greece

against Corinth: she had to pay twenty talents and admit Corcyra to equal recognition as metropolis.[10] By 435, however, Corinth had wholly ousted any Corcyraean influence at Leucas, for the colony

[10] For references and discussion of the date, see above, 258. Gomme suggested that the story was invented to account for Thucydides' statement that Themistocles was a benefactor of Corcyra (*HCT* i.438); but that is excessively sceptical (Graham, *Colony and Mother City*, 129 with n. 1). What might have been invented in the absence of genuine tradition is indicated by the wretched scholiast on Thuc. i.136.1 (Themistocles prevents the punishment of Corcyra for neutrality against Xerxes).

gave full assistance to the Corinthian efforts at Epidamnus.[11] Apollonia was also in the Corinthian camp by 435: the first Corinthian expedition, fearing Corcyraean interference by sea, marched by land to Apollonia, clearly with the blessing of the colonists there.[12] Thucydides claims Apollonia as a purely Corinthian foundation, but three late sources record Corcyraean involvement too (above, 211); there may therefore have been a dispute here similar to that at Leucas, and Corinth seems to have gained the upper hand by c.450. Pausanias (v.22.2–4) records that Apollonia dedicated at Corinth spoils from a war with Abantis and Thronium; the inscription set up at Olympia, which records other spoils from the war, has been preserved in part, and dates to the third quarter of the fifth century.[13] At Anactorium, on the other hand, Corcyraean influence was still significant after the beginning of the Epidamnus affair. Thucydides mentions only one ship from the city in the Sybota campaign, and none at all at Leucimme; and in 433 the Corinthians, after their defeat at Sybota, felt it necessary to capture the colony by treachery and to settle Corinthian colonists there (Thuc. i.55.1). It is described by Thucydides as 'common to Corcyra and to (Corinth)', and the Corcyraean element remained even after 433: it was presumably responsible for the loss of the city to Corinth, again by treachery, nearly a decade later.[14] Only at Ambracia is there no evidence of a similar clash. In the state of our sources, that hardly means that there was none; if there was, it had been resolved in Corinth's favour, for Ambraciot help for Corinth in the Epidamnus affair was a true reflection of her capacity.[15]

It is impossible to recover with confidence the details of these disputes. Much of the evidence concerns the origins of the colonies; but there can be little doubt that the differing reports are merely symptoms of a more real conflict over influence between the Persian and Peloponnesian Wars. Thucydides may preserve a sign of Corinth's

---

[11] Thuc. i.26.1; 27.2; 46.1 (ten ships both for Leucimme and for Sybota).

[12] Thuc. i.26.2. Presumably they proceeded by sea from Apollonia to Epidamnus; if so, the vessels will have been Apolloniate. Cf. Gomme, *HCT* i.160.

[13] Jeffery, *Local Scripts*, 229. Beaumont has shown (*JHS* lxxii (1952), 65–6) that this war preceded 435; but it is too speculative to conclude, with him (ibid., 65, 68; cf. *JHS* lvi (1936), 170), that Corinth helped Apollonia in the war and that she did so precisely in order to keep open the land route used in 435; see Graham, *Colony and Mother City*, 130–1. Note also that the Apolloniate seer Deiphonus acted for the Greeks at Mycale, and that he was brought by the Corinthians (Hdt. ix.92.2–95). Graham's numismatic arguments in favour of an earlier Apolloniate connection with Corcyra (ibid.) can no longer be used: the earliest Apolloniate coins (closely similar to those of Corcyra) belong in the fourth century (Kraay, *Archaic and Classical Greek Coins*, 129).

[14] Thuc. iv.49; cf. Graham, *Colony and Mother City*, 132–3.

[15] Thuc. i.26.1; 27.2; 46.1 (eight ships for Leucimme, twenty-seven for Sybota).

attitude to her interests in this region in the speech he gives to the Corinthians in the Corcyra debate. They argue (i.40-3) that in 440 they established the principle that signatories to the Thirty Years Peace should be allowed to discipline their allies; and that just as Corinth enabled Athens to punish Samos then, so Athens should now allow Corinth to punish Corcyra. The argument is plainly false, for Corcyra was not listed as a Corinthian ally in the Peace;[16] but this gives it added importance as evidence for the Corinthian attitude. The argument is so central a part of the Corinthians' speech that Thucydides cannot have been true to his general principles of speech-writing if they did not use it;[17] but the Corinthians cannot have used it in the hope that it would persuade the Athenians even though they were not persuaded by it themselves, for it is so clearly invalid. They used it because they had deluded themselves into believing it; it thus illuminates Corinthian policy in the north-west: Corinth regarded the Thirty Years Peace as a full settlement of her differences with Athens, and her recognition of an Athenian sphere of influence in the Aegean encouraged her to view herself as enjoying a similar sphere in the north-west.

Such a conclusion is inevitably uncertain, and the dispute with Corcyra over Leucas, and perhaps Corinth's successful resolution of the clash at Apollonia, are to be dated before the Thirty Years Peace. Whether Corinth believed that that Peace entitled her to secure informal control of the north-west, where neither Spartan nor Athenian interests were heavily involved, is less important than the fact of the control itself; that, on the eve of the Epidamnus dispute, is clear at Leucas, Ambracia, and Apollonia, while at Anactorium it was established shortly after Sybota. It would make good sense for Corinth to devote a special effort to securing her influence in these waters after the defeat of Xerxes. In previous decades Corinth had enjoyed some success in limiting the growth of Spartan influence; she could not expect the threat of excessive Spartan control to diminish after her leadership of the Greek defence, and Corinthian naval weight could only be increased by an establishment of firm control in north-western waters. More specifically, perhaps, the addition of the votes of her colonies to the congress of the

---

[16] As the Corinthians in effect admit, Corcyra was an 'unlisted city'—ἄγραφος πόλις (Thuc. i.40.2).

[17] i.22.1; cf. below, 299 n. 54. De Ste Croix, 71, wonders 'whether the Corinthians did actually advance such a ludicrous argument, or whether Thucydides put these words into their mouth by way of demonstrating how weak their case was.' I doubt whether Thucydides placed such reliance on his readers' sense of absurdity; but he will hardly have invented this as one of those 'fitting' arguments which he was willing to supply himself, for it is so clearly *un*fitting.

Peloponnesian League would be a useful insurance against finding herself in a minority.[18] The Aegean, in view of Athenian developments, was hardly a suitable area for Corinthian naval enterprise; but Corcyraean ambiguity during the invasion made the north-west a fruitful area for exploitation. The Corcyraean navy could be presented as a potential threat if it was not an actual one; and the real links between a metropolis and her colonies already gave Corinth a firm foundation to build on.[19] Another was no doubt the assistance she could offer against Acarnanian hostility to Leucas and Anactorium.[20] If Thuc. i.47.3 is accurate, a similar argument could not be used with respect to Ambracia and the Epirots; but the good relations he reports Corinth as having enjoyed for a long time in 433 with the natives of these parts may have been based on the protection Corinth afforded them against Corcyra.

Circumstances made the north-west a particularly suitable area for Corinthian activity after 480; but disputes between Corinth and Corcyra probably did not begin so late. It should not be too readily assumed that Corcyra threw aside her filial piety as soon as it was no longer required by the force of a Cypselid tyrant. It is true that Periander had tried to wreak horrible revenge on 300 sons of Corcyraean families; but they had been saved, and in any case it was now possible to distinguish between Corinth and her tyrants. Equally, the only evidence we have for relations between the two cities from the early sixth century to Xerxes' invasion indicates, if anything, their co-operation: together they offered diplomatic assistance to Syracuse in the early fifth century.[21] But it would be rash to assert that the hostility which Herodotus noted as having existed 'ever since the original foundation' (iii.49.1) only began after 480; and it was probably the need to counter Corinthian influence in this area which caused Corcyra to build the second largest fleet of any Greek city outside Sicily by 480.[22] Corcyra then had a navy of at least sixty vessels. They were not built for

---

[18] It is unfortunately not clear what status, if any, the colonies had in the League Congress: cf. de Ste Croix, 124. The arguments of Wickert, *Peloponnesische Bund*, 79, do not establish that they were not members.

[19] It is noteworthy that more tenuous links were exploited by Athens in the Aegean; cf. Barron, *JHS* lxxxiv (1964), 46–8.

[20] Note the epitaph of Procleidas, written in Corinthian script of *c*.475–450 and found in North Acarnania, perhaps near Anactorium; he died 'fighting for his country' (Jeffery, *Local Scripts*, 229, no. 8). If Phormio's expedition to Acarnania is correctly dated to before 446 (below, 422–3), it will have been an attempt by Athens to support Acarnania against the Corinthian alliance.

[21] Below, 388–9. The sea battle reported by Thuc. i.13.4 cannot be used for this (or any other) context since its chronology is so uncertain: above, 218, 223 n. 145.

[22] The position of the Corcyraean navy was noted by Herodotus: vii.168.3.

nothing, and no local enemy could force the construction of such a
large armament.[23] Part of the reason for Corcyra's ambiguity in 480
may have been precisely that Corinth was committed to resistance.
Whether the contingents provided then by the other colonies were
relatively small because their commitment to Corinth was not as
complete as it was to become, or because they wished to fight in
greater strength but feared Corcyraean interference, it is impossible
to say. The great size of the fleet of Corcyra in 480 may well indicate that Corcyra had determined upon an effort to eradicate all
Corinthian naval influence in the region, at a time when Corinthian
energies were concentrated upon the difficult problems of relations
with her closer neighbours; Corinthian activity here after 480 may
have begun as a matter of self-defence.

The methods adopted by Corinth can only be guessed at; but an
attempt to defend and extend her influence in these waters provides
the best context for the Corinthian possessions of uncertain chronology which are recorded by Thucydides along the coast between
the Corinthian Gulf and Leucas. Molycreium is defined as a Corinthian colony, but is first mentioned in 429 as in Athenian hands, and
was probably seized during the 450s.[24] Sollium is described as a
πόλισμα and Chalcis a πόλις 'of the Corinthians'; the former was
captured by the Athenians in 431, and the latter had already been
taken by Tolmides on his famous *periplous* during the First Peloponnesian War and was probably not returned under the terms of the
Thirty Years Peace.[25] Of these three places only Chalcis can be
precisely located; but the general position of Molycreium near or
on Cape Antirhium is clear enough, and it is significant.[26] Among
all Corinthian colonies, it shares the character of the land it controlled only with Anactorium: both were sited for purely strategic
purposes, and had access to almost no good agricultural land. Just
as Anactorium was intended to secure the entrance to the Ambracian Gulf, so Molycreium was designed to provide Corinth with a
strong point at the mouth of the Corinthian. It is not clear exactly
what Thucydides means by the expressions πόλις and πόλισμα of the
Corinthians; but probably Sollium and Chalcis were captured and
subjected to Corinthian control without the establishment of enough

---

[23] Arniadas (above, 214) might have died in one of the early clashes between Corinth and
Corcyra in the Ambracian Gulf, and his death cannot be placed much later than c.550.
[24] ii.84.4; iii.102.2. Since the place was Athenian in 429 and Thucydides does not record
its capture during the previous two years, the best context for the seizure from Corinth is
the First Peloponnesian War, though that cannot be taken as certain.
[25] Thuc. ii.30.1; i.108.5; above, 268, n. 52.
[26] See above all Lerat, *Locriens de l'Ouest*, i.189–91.

permanent settlers to enable them to rank as colonies.[27] They did not therefore have the agricultural purpose of the majority of Corinthian colonies. It cannot be excluded that Molycreium was founded and Chalcis seized in the time of the tyrants; but the wider strategic considerations which they imply fit better in the fifth century, when Corinthian command of the entrance to her Gulf was under threat, than in the period of the tyranny, when Anactorium was founded for a more limited purpose of maintaining control over the entrance to the Ambracian Gulf. Since Sollium cannot be located, we cannot be sure of its exact purpose; but since it was not agricultural it was presumably strategic, and the signs are that it was intended to control the approaches to the Leucas channel.

Even if Chalcis and Sollium had originally been taken by the tyrants, the fact that Thucydides describes them as belonging to the Corinthians proves that control was maintained, or possibly re-established, in the fifth century; it is therefore certain that Corinth secured her influence in this area partly through strong points probably under garrison. Molycreium, even though a colony, will have been in a similar position. The maintenance of control through such strong points was already part of the Corinthian scheme before the First Peloponnesian War, for Chalcis and probably Molycreium were seized during that conflict by the Athenians; Sollium, a little to the north, may have been captured by the Corinthians later to take their place. A similar principle is probably to be observed in the Ambracian Gulf at Amphilochian Argos. When Phormio captured that place at some time before the Peloponnesian War he sold into slavery the Ambraciots who then held it; they had previously driven out the Amphilochians by whom they had originally been invited there (Thuc. ii.68.4-9). The chronology both of Phormio's expedition and of the previous activity of the Ambraciots at Argos is uncertain; but Phormio's action here cannot have been later than 432,[28] and when he arrived the Ambraciots must have held Argos for some time. They probably ejected the Amphilochians in order to secure their own, and through them Corinthian, control of the south-east corner of their Gulf. A different method may have achieved a similar effect for the Corinthians at Astacus. In the first year of the Peloponnesian War the Athenians drove Euarchus out of his tyranny there, and he was immediately reinstated by a large

---

[27] Graham (*Colony and Mother City*, 118-19; *Historia*, xi (1962), 251) seems to assume that both were colonies; that is to ignore the careful distinctions of terminology in Thucydides. For the location of Sollium, see Philippson, *Landschaften*, ii.2.382 with n. 4.

[28] I argue below, 422-3, for an earlier date, before 446.

Corinthian force (Thuc. ii.30.1; 33.1-2); that probably implies that he already had an understanding with the Corinthians before 431.[29]

Conjecture is necessary to make sense of the development of Corinthian interests in the north-west between 480 and 435 because Thucydides, perhaps reprehensibly, did not see fit to explain it;[30] but the inevitably uncertain character of the conjecture should not obscure the more general conclusions which are reasonably safe. During this period especially, and perhaps to a lesser degree before, Corinth secured a real control in north-western waters which was far greater than the influence that she derived from the normal relations between a metropolis and her colonies; and that control depended, not on inherited relations from the time of the foundation of the colonies, but on continued political and military activity. Control was maintained partly through strong points, sometimes captured from others (Chalcis, Sollium, and through the Ambraciots Amphilochian Argos) and sometimes small colonies founded for a strategic purpose (Molycreium and—a foundation of the tyrants—Anactorium); and partly through good relations with local inhabitants (the Epirots, Euarchus of Astacus). But these were less important than the maintenance of close ties with her colonies, especially Leucas and Ambracia but also Apollonia in the far north.[31] Exactly how these links were fostered remains unclear. They presumably depended to a considerable extent on personal relationships, which could be easily maintained in the context of inherited religious obligations and perhaps some secondary colonization;[32] the protection Corinth could afford against Corcyra and Acarnania provided powerful support, and could be used to draw not only her colonies close to Corinth but also the unrelated inhabitants of Epirus. But however Corinth secured the loyalty of her colonies, there can be no doubt that Corinthian skill in encouraging a real affection for her was a more potent factor than military strength. During the Peloponnesian War, and to an even greater extent in the fourth century, Corinth could not dispose of enough strength to require obedience;

[29] Larsen conjectures unnecessarily that the place may have been a Corinthian colony (*Greek Federal States*, 91).

[30] Compare his failure to discuss the Megarian Decrees (below, 425-6). Corinthian policy from 435 was heavily influenced by her earlier activity in the region; but Thucydides did not discuss these matters for fear of diverting attention from what he saw as the more important Spartan fear of Athens.

[31] It is doubtful whether the fact that the Corinthians brought Deiphonus to Mycale (Hdt. ix.95) can place strong Corinthian influence here before 480.

[32] On the possibility of more formal links suggested by the Potidaean *epidemiourgoi* see below, 393-4.

but the loyalty of the colonies remained (below, 394–5). The success of the Corinthian efforts in these waters, and no less the resentment which it caused at Corcyra, is an essential backdrop for the events which unfolded at Epidamnus.

XXI. Corinth and Athens:
From Peace to War

We have information about only one incident in Corinthian history
between the Thirty Years Peace and the beginning of events at
Epidamnus which led to the outbreak of the Peloponnesian War;
but that incident is of crucial importance. In 440 Samos revolted
against Athens, and Sparta called a Congress of the Peloponnesian
League to consider the question of helping the rebellion. But the
Corinthians openly opposed the proposal, and secured a majority
vote in favour of allowing Athens to coerce her ally without hin-
drance.[1] It is true that the evidence for these events comes in a
speech in which Corinthians tried to make the most of the benefit
they had conferred on Athens; but while they may have exaggerated
the extent of their influence, there can be no doubt that Sparta was
in favour of acting against Athens, that Corinth spoke and voted
against interfering, and that the proposal was rejected, at least partly
as a result of Corinth's opposition to it.[2]

This evidence illuminates Corinthian policy throughout the
Pentecontaetia; it proves that Corinth was willing, other things
being equal, to tolerate Athenian domination of the Aegean. Nothing
else can explain her failure to take advantage of an opportunity that
was most unlikely to recur. It is not enough to suggest that Corinth
was in principle in favour of war with Athens but judged that the
occasion was unsuitable and preferred to wait;[3] the occasion was
even more unsuitable in 433, when Corinth devoted all her energies
to provoking war. The Corinthian decision in favour of war was
taken immediately after Sybota (below, 292-3); at that time Athens
faced nothing so dangerous as the Samian revolt. Nor can Corinth
have felt more capable in 433 of persuading the other members of

---

[1] Thuc. i.40.5; cf. 41.2; 43.1. See Jones, *PCPhS* clxxxii (1952/3), 43-4; de Ste Croix,
200-3. De Ste Croix's account covers all possible objections; but Sealey has doubted the
conclusion (*CP* lxx (1975), 106-7). His argument is contrived, and he fails to take account
of the fact that a vote was taken (Thuc. i.40.5: ψῆφον; 43.1: ψῆφῳ); it is inconceivable that
Sparta would have allowed a vote without deciding for herself that she wished to help
Samos. The form of action which was proposed is not known, only that its purpose was to
give aid to Samos (Thuc. i.40.5; 41.2); it was presumably an invasion of Attica the Spartans
had in mind. To argue that the Corinthian claim was completely false (Raubitschek, in Kinzl
(ed.), *Greece and the Eastern Mediterranean*, 266-9) is excessive.

[2] Cf. Kagan, *Outbreak*, 174; but his interpretation of Sparta's attitude is unsatisfactory.

[3] Cf. de Ste Croix, 213-14.

the Peloponnesian League to fight: nothing had happened to persuade any state but Corinth to change its mind. After Sybota, Corinth was able to provoke Athens into providing her with arguments in favour of war at Potidaea; but such provocation was equally possible in 440. The only relevant difference was that in 433 Corinth's hatred for Athens, aroused by the Corcyra affair, gave her a will to war; in 440 she felt no need to fight.[4] The Corinthian decision in 440 is especially significant because it came only just after Athens' most ambitious intervention in the far west before the Peloponnesian War: the foundation of Thurii. Fortunately it is unnecessary to discuss the Athenian motives for this venture here;[5] the Corinthians themselves demonstrated in 440 that they were not unduly disturbed by what Athens had done. Corinth was willing for Athens not only to control the Aegean, but also to take a secondary interest in western affairs.

Corinthian confidence in Athens was shattered by the alliance between Athens and Corcyra in 433; thereafter events moved quickly towards war. The importance of Corinth's role has never been doubted, since the treatment of Thucydides himself;[6] but varying interpretations have been given of it, ranging from the view that Corinth forced the war on Sparta and Athens, neither of whom were willing to fight, to the suggestion that the war broke out because Athens acted with unnecessary aggression against innocent allies of Sparta, foremost among them Corinth.

The Corcyra affair began with an internal dispute at Epidamnus. Exiled oligarchs, in alliance with the Illyrians, were pressing the democrats, who in 435[7] appealed to Corcyra for help; but the request was rejected, for reasons which cannot be recovered (Thuc. i.24). Epidamnus, although a Corcyraean colony, had a Corinthian *oecistes*, and therefore sent to Delphi to ask if she might hand herself over to Corinth in return for Corinthian help; the oracle gave its blessing, and an embassy was sent to Corinth (Thuc. i.25.1-2). Thucydides continues, 'The Corinthians granted their request for help, both because they thought it legitimate to do so, since

---

[4] It could hardly be argued that the possibility of bringing Perdiccas of Macedon into the war (below, 292) was the decisive factor in persuading Corinth to fight in 433.

[5] Cf. Ehrenberg, *AJP* lxix (1948), 149-70; (succinctly) Meiggs, *Athenian Empire*, 185-6; Andrewes, *JHS* xcviii (1978), 5-8.

[6] There is no need for further discussion of Thucydides' account; cf. Andrewes, *CQ* liii (1959), 223-39; de Ste Croix, 50-63. De Ste Croix's account has not suffered from the criticism of Sealey, *CP* lxx (1975), 89-109, esp. 90-3, whom I cannot follow except in so far as he demonstrates that when X fears what Y is doing, it is the actions of Y which are necessarily prior (a fact of which Thucydides was well aware); cf. Andrewes, *CQ* liii (1959), 225.

[7] For the chronology of the Corcyra affair, see Gomme, *HCT* i.196-8.

they believed that the colony was their own no less than that of the Corcyraeans, and also because of their hatred of Corcyra; for the Corcyraeans took little account of Corinth even though she was their mother city: they did not give the usual offerings at the common festivals, nor did they reserve the first portions at sacrifices for a Corinthian as did the other colonies, but they despised them and relied on their own great wealth, their ability to compare with the richest states in Greece at that time, and their greater military resources' (i.25.3-4). The legitimacy of interfering was hardly a reason for doing so; it merely provided justification. Corinth's motive was jealousy of Corcyra; but her action fitted well not only with the known tension between metropolis and colony[8] but also with the pattern of disputes between the two states which had occupied much of the fifth century. The Epidamnus dispute must be judged against the background of similar conflicts at other places, all of which had been resolved in favour of Corinth.

In view of this background, a strong Corcyraean reaction when Corinth sent new colonists and a garrison to Epidamnus was only to be expected;[9] Corinth herself judged as much when she sent the expedition part of the way over land, to avoid the Corcyraean navy. Whatever the origins of the other Adriatic colonies, Epidamnus was admitted to be Corcyraean. In defence of her rights as metropolis, Corcyra sent a fleet to Epidamnus and demanded that the oligarchic exiles (who had meanwhile appealed to Corcyra) should be restored and the Corinthians expelled; her terms rejected, she laid siege to the city (Thuc. i.26.3-5). This firm response changed the situation radically. Until now, Corinth may have hoped that Corcyra would acquiesce in her action, if perhaps under protest; but when Corcyra demonstrated her determination to resist (perhaps to redeem her failures at Leucas and Apollonia), it would have been wise for Corinth to desist. She had some ground for anger at the fact that Corcyra had rejected the first Epidamnian appeal and only intervened out of spite, when Corinth herself had become involved (cf. Thuc. i.38.5); but any sober consideration of the issues would have shown that the risk was not worth taking—though it can be said in Corinth's favour that her failure to step down is understandable: from the Corinthian point of view, Corcyra had forfeited all

---

[8] I see no reason to doubt (with Beaumont, *JHS* lvi (1936), 183) the credibility of this explanation given by Thucydides; cf. Kagan, *Outbreak*, 219.

[9] At some time during the Epidamnus affair, the city appears to have minted an exceptional issue of coins, like the Corinthian issues of the time except for an epsilon (later altered, perhaps at Corinth's insistence, to koppa) with Pegasus on the obverse; see Kraay, *Archaic and Classical Greek Coins*, 84.

right to be considered as Epidamnus' metropolis by rejecting her colony's first appeal.

Corinth therefore prepared a second expedition, with new colonists and a large supporting force; the help she received from many states—Boeotia, Elis, and even Megara among them (Thuc. i.27)—shows that her credit in general stood high, whatever the merits of her case on this issue. In alarm Corcyra sent to Corinth to negotiate, and the ambassadors were given help by others from Sicyon and Sparta.[10] Thucydides gives no clue to Sparta's reasons. She might merely have been smarting over Corinth's rejection of the proposal to help Samos in 440 (Spartans were not notably forgiving), or she might already have feared Athenian involvement (cf. Thuc. i.28.3); but these do not exhaust the possibilities. The Corcyraeans first stated their maximum demands, for the withdrawal of both colonists and garrison sent by Corinth; but they also offered arbitration, either by Peloponnesian states acceptable to both sides or by Delphi. Finally, they warned that Corcyra would not shrink from war, and that if war came she might have to look for allies among states she would prefer to keep at arm's length—a clear reference to Athens (Thuc. i.28.1-3). It was not unreasonable of Corinth to refuse arbitration while the siege of Epidamnus was still being pursued; even the withdrawal of forces by both sides, which Corcyra suggested next, might have put Corinth at a disadvantage had she wished to dispute the arbitration award. But there were no reasonable grounds for rejecting the final suggestion: that both sides should remain as they were under truce until the arbitration had been completed (Thuc. i.28.4-5). On these terms it would have been easy for Corinth to accept arbitration without losing face, and without even putting herself into a position in which she would have to accept the decision of the arbitrators whatever it was; and the arbitrators offered by the Corcyraeans could hardly arouse Corinthian suspicions. By this stage, if not before, Corinth had ceased to base her policy on rational considerations; the possible gains were out of all proportion to the risks. The Corcyraean fleet was strong enough to make it impossible to predict the outcome with confidence; and the danger of bringing Athens in was a conclusive argument in favour of withdrawal.[11]

The Corinthians had no joy of their large expedition; it was defeated off Leucimme with the loss of fifteen ships. On the same day Epidamnus capitulated (Thuc. i.29). The Corinthians captured

---

[10] Thuc. i.28.1. Cf. Gomme, *HCT* i.162; but I see no difficulty in supposing that Sparta took the side of Corcyra.

[11] Cf. de Ste Croix, 68-9; Kagan, *Outbreak*, 226.

in the battle and after the siege were imprisoned in the hope that a settlement might eventually be reached; Corcyra followed up her successes by ravaging the territory of Leucas and burning Cyllene, the port of Elis, in revenge for the help Elis had given to the expedition. For the rest of the campaigning season of 435 the Corcyraean fleet was in action against Corinth's allies in the region; but in early summer 434 Corinth sent a fleet to their defence. For the rest of the summer the two forces remained in position without engaging; with the approach of winter, both fleets retired (Thuc. i.30). For two years after Leucimme the Corinthians prepared another force, far larger than before; as Thucydides says, 'they were furious at the way the war with Corcyra had gone' (i.31.1). By this time their intentions were clearly to bring Corcyra herself under their control, and no longer merely to gain Epidamnus.[12] Corcyra carried out her threat and asked Athens for an alliance; both Corcyraean and Corinthian ambassadors addressed an Athenian assembly on the subject.

It is unnecessary to analyse in detail the speeches of the Corcyraeans and the Corinthians as they appear in Thucydides (i.32–43); the central issues were simple. Scarcely an argument in the whole Corinthian speech carries conviction. Corinth was excessively belligerent over Epidamnus; her self-defence is specious, and consists of little more than repeated assertions that Corcyra should show more respect and let Corinth have her own way. On the more general issues, too, Corcyra has much the better of the argument. She asserts that since war between Athens and the Peloponnese is now inevitable (i.33.3; 36.1) it is in Athens' interest to ensure that the Corcyraean fleet is made available to her and not to the Peloponnesians (esp. i.36.3). War was hardly yet inevitable, but the attitude shown by Sparta in 440 obliged Athens to take the possibility seriously; she could not afford to allow Corinth to swallow up Corcyra and dominate the Adriatic (cf. Thuc. i.44.2). That would have been so dangerous for Athens if a war did break out that it was imperative for her to prevent it—even though an alliance with Corcyra might make war more probable. Corinth could only reply feebly that war was not a certainty (i.42.2); that was true, but it did not meet the case. As long as war was a closer than remote possibility Athens could not reject Corcyra's request—and Sparta's willingness to go to war in 440 made the possibility far more real than that. I have already discussed Corinth's attempt, which flies

---

[12] Compare the fears of Corcyra, Thuc. i.32.5. The Corinthians admitted as much when they claimed the right to do to Corcyra what they had enabled Athens to do to Samos: i.43.1.

in the face of the facts, to persuade Athens to allow her to discipline
Corcyra as Corinth had enabled Athens to suppress the Samian revolt
in 440 (above, 275). There is but one valid argument presented by
Corinth—apart from her references to past services done for Athens,
which she cannot have expected to cut much ice: her discussion of
the terms of the Thirty Years Peace.

The Peace allowed Athens to make any form of alliance she chose
with any state not included in the lists of allies appended to the
treaty; the Corinthians themselves admit, in practice, that the letter
of the treaty was no impediment to the alliance (i.40.2). They go on
to argue, however, that the Peace did not envisage a situation in
which an unlisted city asked for an alliance 'with the intention of
harming somebody', and that unlisted cities might legitimately be
accepted into alliance 'as long as it does not involve depriving another
party of its allegiance, and as long as the acceptance of the alliance
does not involve the substitution of war for peace' (i.40.2). To
clarify the argument here it must be expanded: 'it is all very well
for Corcyra, an unlisted city, to ask you for an alliance; but by
doing so she is asking you to commit yourselves to an alliance which,
while technically within the terms of the Peace, will lead you to
harm us, to deprive us of Corcyra's allegiance, and even to go to war
with us, since we are at war with Corcyra.'[13] There is much sound
argument here; for if the Athenians had made a full offensive and
defensive alliance with Corcyra they would have committed themselves to taking part in any aggressive action which Corcyra undertook against Corinth. It is precisely this point that the Athenians
took into account when they rejected the Corcyraean request for a
full *symmachia*, and gave them instead merely an *epimachia*: a
defensive alliance. Thus they avoided giving Corcyra the right to
commit Athens to war against Corinth (cf. Thuc. i.44.1), and gave
it instead to Corinth herself: if Corinth persisted in her attack on
Corcyra, in the full knowledge that Athens was bound to come to
Corcyra's assistance, then Corinth would have only herself to blame.
Athens therefore did more than preserve the letter of the Thirty
Years Peace; she went as far as her own interests allowed her to go
towards preserving its spirit, for she refused to make an alliance
that the terms of the Peace allowed her to make.

Thucydides reports that the Athenians held two assemblies to
discuss the Corcyraean alliance, and that at the first opinion tended
to favour the Corinthians; but at the second it was decided to conclude an *epimachia* with Corcyra (i.44.1). This should not be taken

---

[13] Cf. de Ste Croix, 71; Kagan, *Outbreak*, 231-2.

to imply that the Corinthian arguments were stronger than I have suggested, but to demonstrate that the Athenians gave due weight to the one valid point that had been made; and that they were, as their subsequent actions prove, anxious to avoid provoking Corinth. Athens could not afford to allow Corinth to overrun Corcyra; but many Athenians were so concerned to avoid giving offence to Corinth that they were willing to ignore their own interests and reject the alliance. De Ste Croix has made the very probable suggestion that at the first assembly the question was whether to accept a full *symmachia* with Corcyra, and that therefore many Athenians, realizing that it would force them, if Corcyra attacked Corinth, to break either the *symmachia* or the Peace, were unwilling to vote for it however much they feared the possibility of Corinth gaining Corcyra; but that on the second day the compromise of an *epimachia* was suggested which enabled the doubters in the assembly both to prevent a Corinthian defeat of Corcyra and to lay the responsibility for any breach of the Peace on Corinth.[14]

Even if the Athenians had been faced with a decision for or against a *symmachia* the objective arguments (though perhaps not a majority in the assembly) would have been in favour of it; if Corcyra had (improbably) declared a pre-emptive war on Corinth the Athenians could have chosen to abrogate their alliance with Corcyra rather than their Peace. Once an *epimachia* was proposed the issue could not be doubtful. Thucydides summarizes admirably (i.44.2): 'the war with the Peloponnesians looked as if it would take place anyway, and they did not wish to give up Corcyra to Corinth, seeing that the Corcyraean fleet was so large; they were happy for the two sides to weaken each other in the conflict, so that if war did come they would fight it with the Corinthians and the others in a weaker position in respect of naval power. They also thought it useful that Corcyra had such a good position on the coastal route between Italy and Sicily.'[15] The Callias decrees of 434/3 show clearly that Athens was preparing for war before the Corcyra debate —though not, perhaps, before it could be foreseen that Corcyra would ask for an alliance.[16] The alliance certainly brought war

[14] De Ste Croix, 72. Eckstein, quoted by Sealey, *CP* lxx (1975), 98, points out that the Athenians were trying to have their cake and eat it over Corcyra; that is true but not illuminating, since they had been placed in a dilemma in a situation not of their own making.

[15] This final factor is not to be taken as evidence that the Athenians had commercial considerations in mind; it was only for war vessels that Corcyra was useful, and this factor (in so far as it had any effect at all) was therefore only of strategic importance (Gomme, *HCT* i.171; de Ste Croix, 75).

[16] This has often been pointed out; cf. de Ste Croix, 74; Meiggs, *Athenian Empire*, 200-1. The decrees, Meiggs and Lewis, *GHI*, no. 58, with full discussion; the date of 434/3 has

closer; but if they had taken any other decision the Athenians would
have been placing far more trust in Sparta than she deserved after
what had happened in 440—an event to which the Corinthians
themselves had called untimely attention.

It is difficult to imagine how the Corinthians could have persuaded themselves that any other outcome was possible. However
confident they were of an Athenian desire to avoid conflict with
them—and such confidence was shown by the Athenians to be fully
justified—no rational consideration can have caused them to hope
that Athens would reject the Corcyraean appeal. There is a striking
parallel in the alliance between Megara and Athens which led to the
First Peloponnesian War. In each case, the request for an alliance
was made when war between Athens and the Peloponnese was a
distinct possibility; and in each case the advantages to be gained by
Athens in case of war were so great that she could not reject the
offer. Both situations were precipitated by Corinthian aggression;
but while Corinth cannot be accused of irresponsibility in the case
of Megara, Corcyra had given her fair warning and she had persisted
none the less. Corinthian policy in the Corcyra affair was not based
on a miscalculation,[17] but on no calculation at all; doubtless it was
hoped that the Athenians would not intervene, but the hope was
quite irrational. The hatred and jealousy Corinth felt for Corcyra
did not only cause her to adduce arguments that took no account
of reality; they caused her to hope that Athens would share her
view that black was white: that aggression was the defence of
legitimate interests.

Even the moderation of the Athenian decision failed to persuade
the Corinthians to desist. The Athenians, on the other hand, did all
they could to avoid needless provocation. They sent a mere ten
ships to Corcyra;[18] the event showed that this was too small a
number. Strict instructions were given to the commanders of the
contingent: 'They were not to engage with the Corinthians unless
they sailed to attack Corcyra with the intention of landing either
on the island or at any other place in Corcyraean territory; if that
happened, the squadron was to do its best to prevent it.' Thucydides
adds the self-evident comment, 'They gave these instructions in
order to avoid breaking the Peace' (i.45.3). The identity of one of
the *strategoi* chosen to command the ten ships—Lacedaemonius,

been challenged without being disturbed (cf. Meiggs, *Athenian Empire*, 519-23, 601; *contra*,
Sealey, *CP* lxx (1975), 89).

[17] Kagan, *Outbreak*, 234-7.

[18] Thuc. i.45.1; payments for the squadron are recorded in Meiggs and Lewis, *GHI*, no.
61, lines 7-12.

son of Cimon—is significant: 'he if anyone could be trusted to ensure that no armed conflict took place with Corinth or the other Peloponnesians unless it became absolutely necessary'.[19]

Despite her reckless persistence, Corinth was able to take with her not only contingents from her own colonies but also ships from Elis and Megara—the former no doubt in revenge for the burning of Cyllene and the latter perhaps because Megarians had suffered heavily at Leucimme.[20] The whole fleet amounted to 150 vessels, including ninety from Corinth herself;[21] it took up a position at Chimerium in Thesprotia, while a camp was made for the 110 Corcyraean ships and the ten triremes from Athens on one of the Sybota islands. Land forces supported either side (Thuc. i.46-7). The battle was not long delayed; but Athenian participation in it was. Neither Corinth nor Corcyra had learned much from Athenian developments in naval warfare, and Thucydides sneers, 'in the main it was like a battle on land' (i.49.2); but for a long time the ten Athenian ships avoided direct fighting: 'The Athenian vessels came to the support of Corcyraean ships that were in difficulties and put fear into their enemies; but the *strategoi* did not begin to fight for fear of exceeding their instructions' (i.49.4). In the end, however, they were forced to engage. The Corinthians had the advantage of numbers, and this was increased when twenty Corcyraean ships left the main battle in too eager a pursuit of a few defeated Corinthian allies; the Corinthians themselves began to gain the upper hand (Thuc. i.49.6), and even the circumspect *strategoi* could delay no longer. 'The Athenians, when they saw the Corcyraeans under pressure, came more readily to their aid; at first they avoided actually ramming enemy ships, but when the Corcyraeans were clearly in flight and the Corinthians were still pressing on, then they all joined in and made no further distinctions. The Corinthians and Athenians had thus been forced to come to blows with each other' (Thuc. i. 49.7).

[19] De Ste Croix, 76; cf. also Kagan, *Outbreak*, 243-4 (though the reasons of internal politics he adduces are less convincing).

[20] Probably not because of the Megarian decree, since that was still in the future; below, 424-6).

[21] The fleet as a whole was twice the size of that which fought at Leucimme (despite the losses sustained in that battle), and the Corinthian contingent had three times as many vessels; Corinth's effort was remarkable, but it has been seriously overestimated by Legon (*CP* lxviii (1973), 161-2), who says 'it is no exaggeration to rank the rebuilding of the Corinthian fleet in these two years among the most significant military developments of the fifth century.' Corinth's building programme was not enough to present 'a threat to Athens' naval supremacy' (cf. de Ste Croix, 66-7); and it is not to be explained by a tissue of speculation, some of it based on a serious misunderstanding of the nature of ancient commerce, such as is offered by Legon, *CP* lxviii (1973), 162-6.

The Corinthians had obliged the Athenians to engage, but the victory had gone to Corinth. The Corinthians cleared up some of the wreckage and prepared for a further engagement. If the first conflict had been a defeat for Corcyra, the second promised to be a disaster. Thucydides' figures indicate that there were some 120 Corinthian vessels remaining, many of them damaged, against a mere forty Corcyraean, also in part damaged, and perhaps the twenty that had pursued too far on the left wing; ten triremes, even if they were Athenian, could not have redressed such a balance.[22] In the event, however, the Athenian skills were not tested. The fleets were about to engage again when twenty ships appeared on the horizon; the Corinthians, fearing the truth, that they were Athenian reinforcements, gave up the battle (Thuc. i.50–51.1). The extra twenty vessels had arrived only just in time; if they had not done so Athenian attempts at keeping the conflict as restricted as possible would have suffered a severe set-back.

The twenty ships were just in time to prevent the Corinthians landing and all the dangers that might have ensued; and their arrival was enough to reverse the situation. The fleets put out once more the following day; but Corcyra had never wanted to go on the offensive, and the Corinthians were now prevented from doing so. They were, moreover, afraid that the Athenians might believe that the Thirty Years Peace had already been broken and try to prevent the Corinthian fleet from returning home (Thuc. i.52). They therefore sent messengers to discover the intentions of the Athenians. They began by accusing Athens of breaking the Peace by attacking them, and continued, 'If your intention is to prevent us from sailing against Corcyra or anywhere else we wish, thus breaking the Peace, take us as your first prisoners and treat us as your enemies' (i.53.2). Despite loud encouragement to put the Corinthians to death from those Corcyraeans who heard what was said, the Athenians replied: 'Peloponnesians, we are not beginning war, nor are we breaking the Peace; we came here to help these Corcyraean allies of ours. If you wish to sail anywhere else, we shall not prevent you; but if you sail against Corcyra or any other place in Corcyraean territory, we shall do our best to stop you' (i.53.4). Their final attempt to browbeat the Athenians having failed, the Corinthians left for home. On their way they took Anactorium by treachery, no doubt as a small consolation for their abject failure at Epidamnus and at Corcyra herself. After fulfilling, if only narrowly, their treaty

[22] There are, however, grounds for suspecting the figure for Corcyraean losses in the battle (Gomme, *HCT* i.191, 194); that would reduce the disparity, but a heavy Corinthian advantage cannot be doubted.

obligations to Corcyra, the Athenians also left for home (Thuc. i.55.1-2).

In the whole Corcyra affair the Corinthians had acted with thoughtless aggression, while Athens had been as conciliatory as she could. None the less, there was real truth in the accusation that the Athenians broke the Peace. During the battle of Sybota the Corinthians had not—as far as can be discovered from the narrative of Thucydides, which is very careful on this question—attacked any Athenian ships; they confined themselves to fighting the Corcyrae-ans. The first hostilities between Athenians and Corinthians were undertaken by Athenians, when they saw that Corcyra would be defeated unless they intervened. It is true that Corinthian aggression against Corcyra was indefensible, and that the Corinthians knew very well that they were attacking ships to whose defence the Athenians were bound to come; but the fact remains that Athenians struck the first blow. Technically the Corinthians were right when they accused Athens of breaking the Peace: its precise terms were on their side. Arbitration, which the Athenians later offered (Thuc. i.78.4; cf. 85.2, 145), might well have decided that Corinth was in the wrong; but from the Corinthian point of view there can have been no doubt about Athenian guilt. Hatred for Corcyra had so warped the judgement of Corinth that she believed herself to be in the right in chastising her rebellious colony—just as Athens had chastised Samos with Corinth's help a few years before. Thus in Corinthian eyes Athens was doubly in the wrong; not only had she broken the Peace by attacking Corinthian vessels going about their legitimate business, but she had done so despite the great benefit Corinth had conferred on her in 440. Corinth's help to Athens during the Samian revolt, far from making it difficult to explain Corinth's hostile attitude in 433, makes it the more understand-able. Athens had not only broken the Peace; she was ungrateful too.[23] A further cause for complaint may have been the fact that she now had in Corcyra a major ally in western Greece,[24] and could pose a threat to Corinthian interests there. Such a complaint can only have been half rational, for the Athenians made it clear to all those who had eyes to see that their alliance with Corcyra was not

---

[23] Cf. the remark made by the Corinthians in their speech at Athens, Thuc. i.43.1: 'We are now in the situation we referred to at Sparta when we advocated the principle that each side might punish its own allies; we now ask that you follow the same principle, and that you do not cast your vote to harm us in return for the benefit you received from our vote then.'

[24] Athens probably already had an alliance of sorts with Acarnania, made after the expedition of Phormio to Amphilochian Argos; but the chronology of the expedition is uncertain (below, 422-3).

an attempt at active expansion of her influence. But such a consideration can only have been in a few Corinthian minds;[25] Corinth was driven not by reason but by emotion.

Further causes for complaint between Athens and Corinth were not slow in developing. The Corinthian colony of Potidaea had been listed in the Thirty Years Peace as an ally of Athens; it was clearly against the Peace for any state to intervene there against Athenian interests. Shortly after the battle at Sybota (Thuc. i.56.1, 57.1) Athens sent demands to Potidaea:[26] 'to destroy that section of its wall which faces Pallene, to give hostages, and to expel and no longer to receive the *epidemiourgoi* whom the Corinthians sent to them each year' (i.56.2). In order to assess the importance of the affair at Potidaea for the Corinthian attitude, it is essential to determine what grounds Athens had for taking this action. The demands were plainly a cause for complaint to Corinth. If she had been uncertain after Corcyra of her attitude to Athens, these demands alone might have been enough to make her decide in favour of war; she must have been feeling especially tender on the subject of her rights as metropolis after the clash with Corcyra. The issue is whether Corinth was as yet uncertain and determined upon war because of what Athens did at Potidaea; or whether she was already committed to war after Sybota.

The events themselves do not help, and Thucydides does not tell us the answer directly; but he can be shown to have believed that Corinth was already eager for war before any demands were sent to Potidaea. At i.56.2 he gives as Athens' reason for the demands, 'since they were afraid that Potidaea might be persuaded to revolt by Perdiccas and the Corinthians, and that she might also bring into revolt their other allies towards Thrace.' On its own, this would allow either Corinthian attitude, for Athens had good reason to fear Corinthian hostility even if Corinth had not yet decided upon

---

[25] The renewal soon after Sybota of the old Athenian alliances with Rhegium and Leontini (Meiggs and Lewis, *GHI*, nos. 63-4) will have been even less significant, especially as the request for renewal came from the western cities (see the prescripts). The expedition of Diotimus to Naples cannot be securely dated (Davies, *Athenian Propertied Families*, 161); its importance must in any case have been small.

[26] These orders of 433 followed an increased tribute assessment on Potidaea. The first preserved record of 15 tal. tribute is in 433/2, after a constant 6 tal. since at least 445/4; but the increase probably belongs to 434/3 or even earlier (*ATL* iii.64-5; *contra*, Kagan, *Outbreak*, 275 with n. 8). Some have concluded that Athens was acting aggressively to Potidaea before 433 (*ATL*, loc. cit.; cf. Knight, *Studies in Athenian Politics*, 10-11 (extreme); Meiggs, *Athenian Empire*, 528-9), but it is unnecessary to take the increased assessment as Athenian pressure; there are signs that similar increases were imposed on other places nearby (Alexander, *Potidaea*, 43-6; on Athenian policy in this region in the 430s, *ATL* iii.318-19). On earlier relations with Athens, see below, 393 n. 31.

it; but in two other places Thucydides puts his own view beyond doubt. At i.57.1-2 he says, 'The Athenians made these preparations at Potidaea (i.e. the demands) straight after the naval engagement at Corcyra; for the Corinthians were already openly at odds with them'; and he introduces his account of events at Potidaea by saying, 'The Corinthians were taking action to revenge themselves, and so the Athenians, suspecting their hostility,'[27] issued their demands. He does not tell us what form the Corinthian 'action to revenge themselves' took; we are therefore unable to compare his conclusion with the evidence he had for it. But his authority stands high enough for us to accept that Corinth had already taken positive action against Athens when the orders were sent, as she had threatened during the Corcyra debate.[28] We must conclude that Corinth's decision in favour of war had already been taken as a result of the Athenian action at Sybota. The form taken by her overt hostile acts towards Athens must be guessed at; but conjecture is easy. Almost the only means open to Corinth of taking direct action against Athens was through her *epidemiourgoi* in Potidaea; that Athens' reaction to unspecified hostile acts by Corinth was a series of demands made to Potidaea makes it next to certain that Corinth was agitating there for rebellion.[29]

The Corinthian intrigue at Potidaea which made it necessary for Athens to take measures to prevent rebellion was already a breach of the Peace; what followed was far worse, and involved not only Corinth but Sparta. Athens made her demands probably in late summer 433;[30] probably during the winter of 433/2 Potidaea sent an embassy to Athens but had no joy of it, for an expedition that

[27] i.56.2. The Greek is quite explicit about the Corinthians: they were actually taking action (πρασσόντων) to revenge themselves, and not merely planning revenge. If we translate πρασσόντων as 'negotiating' rather than 'taking action', the effect will be the same, for Corinth had no action open to her beyond negotiating (perhaps rather 'intriguing'). Whether the Athenians already knew of the actions Corinth had taken is less clear, since at i.56.2 Thucydides asserts merely that they suspected (ὑποτοπήσαντες) Corinthian hostility; but cf. i.57.1, where the Corinthians are 'already openly at odds' (φανερῶς ἤδη διάφοροι).

[28] Thuc. i.40.6. Cf. de Ste Croix, 80-1; contrast Meiggs, *Athenian Empire*, 202. For what it is worth, Diodorus reports Corinthian incitement to rebellion before any Athenian action at Potidaea (xii.34.2); but the Athenian demands are not so much as mentioned in his account, so no conclusion can be drawn from the fact that the Corinthians (and Perdiccas) take the first action.

[29] See further below, 429 Endnote B.

[30] Thuc. i.57.1; cf. 56.1. These expressions allow a gap of a few months—sufficient to allow for Corinthian agitation—between Sybota and the demands; cf. Gomme, *HCT* i.199. The whole chronology of the Potidaea affair, and with it that of the Spartan assembly and the League Congress which declared war, remains in dispute; for a judicious discussion, cf. de Ste Croix, 318-22.

was sailing against Perdiccas of Macedon in spring 432 was ordered to see that the demands were put into effect (Thuc. i.57.6, 58.1). Potidaean ambassadors to the Peloponnese, however, had much greater success. Perdiccas himself had earlier sent both to Sparta to try to provoke war between Athens and the Peloponnesians and to Corinth to ask for help for a revolt at Potidaea (Thuc. i.57.4). The Potidaeans were accompanied by Corinthians, and they obtained a promise from 'the authorities at Sparta'[31] that Attica would be invaded if Athens attacked Potidaea.

The precise terms of the promise are not often noticed; but they are significant. Sparta did not undertake to help Potidaea if she rebelled, but if Athens attacked her; in such a case the Spartans could invade Attica under the fair pretext of protecting an innocent Athenian ally from aggression, and they could at the same time be sure that Potidaea would resist the Athenian force sent to coerce her. From the Spartan point of view, this would have been far more satisfactory than what actually occurred; for the Potidaeans, encouraged by the sympathy they received at Sparta but misinterpreting it, rebelled at once. They were joined by the Chalcidians and the Bottiaeans and secured help from Perdiccas (Thuc. i.58). The Spartans could hardly claim that Athens was unjustified in attacking a rebellious ally; they therefore did not invade Attica at once. Their plans had been put out of joint by the premature revolt, which made the promise impossible to fulfil in the precise terms in which it had been given.[32]

Corinth, however, did send aid: a force commanded by Aristeus son of Adeimantus, who had always been a close friend of Potidaea (Thuc. i.60.2), consisting of 1,600 hoplites and 400 light-armed troops, volunteers from Corinth and mercenaries from the Peloponnese.[33] We do not know whether the force took the land or the sea route. Corinth must also, at about this time, have made a formal alliance with the rebel states. Corinthians later refer to oaths which they had sworn to the cities that rebelled with Potidaea (Thuc. v.30.2); oaths were not part of the normal diplomatic machinery,

---

[31] Thuc. i.58.1. The promise may have been made by the assembly (Andrewes in Gomme, *HCT* iv.135); but I think it more likely that the ephors, or the ephors and the gerousia, were responsible (de Ste Croix, 204).

[32] In their speech at Sparta the Corinthians urge the fulfilment of the promise made to Potidaea (Thuc. i.71.4), but this cannot be taken to imply that Sparta had undertaken to help a Potidaean revolt; that would controvert Thucydides' words at i.58.1, and the Corinthians were not above special pleading.

[33] Thuc. i.60. An extraordinary issue of coins, in which Pegasus is ridden by Bellerophon and the letter Π appears on both obverse and reverse, presumably has some connection with this force; see Kraay, *Archaic and Classical Greek Coins*, 84–5.

and the reference must be to some formal alliance, although its nature cannot be recovered.[34] Both this alliance and the sending of a Corinthian force were clear breaches of the Thirty Years Peace.[35] The events of the Potidaea campaign can be briefly summarized.[36] The rebel states chose Aristeus to command all their land forces, and Athens eventually laid siege to Potidaea. Aristeus advised that only a small force should be left behind with him to man the walls while the rest of the defenders attempted to slip out; but his sound advice was not accepted. He therefore evaded the blockade himself and remained for some time in the area, encouraging the rebels outside Potidaea and maintaining contact with the Peloponnese. In the second year of the Peloponnesian War itself he was still doing so; he was captured while on an embassy to Thrace, where he was attempting to secure the help of the Thracian king Sitalces. He was executed without trial by the Athenians 'because before this time he seemed to have been responsible for everything that had happened at Potidaea and the Thraceward region'.[37]

Athenian action at Potidaea was undertaken, from the beginning, under heavy provocation. The original demands, not in themselves severe, were made as a result of Corinthian agitation through her *epidemiourgoi*; but the orders, which were intended to prevent rebellion, were rather an encouragement to it. Corinth was doubtless delighted to be given further ammunition to persuade her colonists to revolt.[38] Sparta's promise to invade Attica in case of an Athenian attack on Potidaea gave Corinth more ammunition, even if the precise terms of the undertaking were (perhaps deliberately) misunderstood. Since Corinth had already decided upon war with Athens before the Potidaean affair began, it must not be seen as a reason for Corinthian participation in the Peloponnesian War. Corinthian action at Potidaea was the first action in a private war Corinth was waging against Athens.[39] It is true that the war was

---

[34] De Ste Croix, 84; cf. Thuc. i.58.1: the rebels swear oaths, but Corinth is not mentioned.

[35] It has often been supposed that the force commanded by Aristeus was an unofficial expedition, made up of volunteers and without the sanction of the state of Corinth; see, e.g., Gomme, *HCT* i.224-5; Kagan, *Outbreak*, 282-3. If that were true, it would mean only that Corinth broke the spirit rather than the letter of the Peace; and in any case de Ste Croix (82-5) has shown that ἰδίᾳ at Thuc. i.66 means rather that Corinth was acting separately from the other members of the Peloponnesian League.

[36] Thuc. i.59-65; cf. Alexander, *Potidaea*, 67-71.

[37] Thuc. ii.67; cf. Hdt. vii.137.3. If the Athenians were right, this would give us the name of the leader of the Corinthian faction which agitated for war; but it is hardly reliable evidence. On Aristeus, see Westlake, *Essays*, 74-83.

[38] Some ammunition probably already existed in the increased tribute assessment on Potidaea (above, 292 n. 26).

[39] Cf. Wickert, *Peloponnesische Bund*, 72; Andrewes in Gomme, *HCT* iv.26.

not declared, and that Corinth did not admit that she had broken the Thirty Years Peace; but if she had done so it would have been more difficult to secure a vote in the League Congress that Athens was in the wrong, and her failure to make a formal declaration of war does not show that she did not believe herself to be at war in practice.[40] Corinth was in clear breach of the Peace in all she did at Potidaea. As de Ste Croix has pointed out, Athens was acting entirely within the Peace *'even if Athens' action against (Potidaea) was not justified'*;[41] for even though Potidaea was a colony of Corinth, she had been listed in the terms of the Peace as an Athenian ally. The terms of the Peace enabled Corinth to ask for arbitration if she thought Athens to be in the wrong;[42] but in the circumstances no arbitrator would have given judgement against Athens, for her demands were sent as proper (indeed, moderate) self-defence after Corinthian attempts at fomenting rebellion. After the rebellion took place Corinth would, if she had taken the same attitude as she had over Samos, have admitted Athens' right to suppress it.

Events at Potidaea did not cause Corinth to decide in favour of war with Athens; but they must have confirmed her in the decision she had already taken, and the increasingly active Athenian commitment at Potidaea, where both Corinthians and other Peloponnesians were now under siege, had given Corinth extra grounds—if specious ones—for agitating against Athens in the Peloponnese. Corinth therefore urged her fellow members of the League to send to Sparta and try to persuade her to go to war. The Spartans held an assembly, and allowed embassies from other states to address it. Thucydides mentions in particular the Megarians, who came to complain—among other things—about the Megarian Decree (Thuc. i.67.1-4).[43] The only speech of an ally which Thucydides gives in detail is that of the Corinthians. When foreigners had been excluded from the assembly, Archidamus the experienced Eurypontid king opposed war, and the ephor Sthenelaidas spoke in favour of it; the Spartans then voted heavily for war (Thuc. i.67.5-88).[44]

---

[40] Because war had not been declared, Gomme (*HCT* i.224-5) argues that Corinthian action at Potidaea was throughout unofficial (above, 295 n. 35); but states which are at war do not always openly confess as much.

[41] De Ste Croix, 82: his italics.

[42] Sealey (*CP* lxx (1975), 99) argues against de Ste Croix, but only because he misunderstands his case, which is not that Corinth 'could put forward no further claim on the city', but that any complaint Corinth had over Potidaea should have been submitted to arbitration, and that her military intervention was therefore unjustified.

[43] See below, 424-6.

[44] Kagan (*Outbreak*, 305, 310) supposes that the vote was not for war but merely 'that the Athenians had broken the Peace'. Some passages of Thucydides (e.g. i.87.6; 118.3) refer only to the latter, but i.88 ('that the Peace had been broken and that they should go to war', cf. 86.5) demonstrates that the vote was for the former as well.

The Corinthian speech (Thuc. i.68–71) has frequently been mis-interpreted. It contains much vituperation of Athens; but Sparta herself equally comes under attack for her lethargy. This has encouraged the conclusion that Sparta was reluctant to fight, and that she was aroused by the efforts of the Corinthians;[45] but this is false method. The fact that the Corinthians use strong language does not show that strong language was necessary. The Corinthians would hardly have moderated their arguments merely because they knew they were preaching to the converted; modern party leaders do not speak in notably moderate words to their party conferences or conventions. The Corinthians wished the majority in favour of war to be overwhelming; their reasons were no doubt the same as those of Sthenelaidas, who used a novel method of voting specifi-cally in order to demonstrate the size of the majority (Thuc. i.87.2-3). The essential question about the role of the Corinthians is the extent to which they altered Spartan attitudes; that can be deter-mined better by looking at the Spartan stance before the assembly than by analysing the Corinthian speech.

If there was any consistency in Sparta's attitude, there was a 'natural' majority in favour of making war on Athens—so long as the opportunity was favourable.[46] It is true that in 446/5 Sparta agreed to the Thirty Years Peace; but there was then no favourable opportunity, for the revolt in Euboea had been suppressed.[47] What is more, Pleistoanax, whose rapid withdrawal from Attica had enabled Athens to subdue Euboea, had been tried and forced into exile on a charge of bribery.[48] His condemnation may merely indicate his guilt; but in view of subsequent Spartan policy, it is more likely that part of the reason was that the king had, from his own motives (whether of policy or of greed), prevented the use of the excellent opportunity that had been arranged for kicking Athens while she was down. Most significantly, the Spartans wished to help the revolt of Samos in 440; but the proposal was rejected by the League Congress. The next occasion when we have evidence for Sparta's attitude to an Athens under pressure is similar: the promise to invade Attica given to Potidaea.[49] If those who made

---

[45] Cf. esp. Kagan, *Outbreak*, 307–10.

[46] For all that follows, cf. de Ste Croix, 196–210; below, 420–1.

[47] This important fact (noted by de Ste Croix, 187–200) is ignored by Holladay in his account (*JHS* xcvii (1977), 60).

[48] For the sources, see Hill, *Sources*, index s.vv. Cleandridas, Pleistoanax; cf. de Ste Croix, 197–9.

[49] At some time before 431 Mytilene asked for Spartan help to revolt from Athens, but was refused (Thuc. iii.2.1; 13.1); that merely proves that the lesson of 440 had been learned (if the appeal was made after 440; but such a date should not be taken for granted, as

the promise were called upon to fulfil it, an exactly similar situation would have obtained to that which Sparta had tried to use in 440 and perhaps exiled Pleistoanax for failing to use in 446.[50]

All this is very strong evidence that, at the least, Sparta was likely to seize the first favourable opportunity for attacking Athens.[51] The events of 440, however, showed that a mere favourable opportunity was not enough; Corinth herself demonstrated that willing support from the allies was also necessary. In 432 there was every prospect of fulfilling both requirements. Athens was under pressure in the Thraceward region. The temper of the allies could not be tested in the Congress of the League without a previous decision by Sparta that she was willing to go to war; but many allies had preceded the Corinthians in making complaint against Athens, and Corinth herself was now urging war. If the Spartans ran true to form they would be eager to fight; and the support of Thucydides can be claimed for this view. He says that the Spartans made their decision 'not so much because they were persuaded by the speeches of their allies as because they were afraid that Athens would become more powerful, observing as they did that the majority of Greece was already subject to her' (i.88). Westlake has shown that in a number of passages in which Thucydides says 'not so much because of X as because of Y', X is a 'widely accepted, conventional, or seemingly obvious reason', while Y is 'a latent reason . . . now advanced by Thucydides himself . . . by virtue of a deeper study and more penetrating understanding of the situation.'[52] This exactly fits the circumstances of the Spartan assembly. A superficial interpretation (and one which has appealed to many scholars) is that the Spartans were persuaded to fight by the complaints of their allies; but Thucydides knew of a more important reason which he emphasizes because it is less obvious: that Sparta was afraid that Athens would grow greater. He admits both reasons, but asserts that the Spartans fought primarily out of fear, and only secondarily because of the speeches of their allies. The point is almost exactly the same as that made by Thucydides when he introduces his account of the origins of the war (i.23.6): that the 'most genuine cause' was the

Meiggs, *Athenian Empire*, 194), not that she was in principle unwilling to help (cf. de Ste Croix, 204-5). Even if the appeal was made before 440, it proves no more than that Sparta was careful about choosing her opportunity.

[50] See also de Ste Croix, 320-2, on the evidence provided by Spartan elections to the ephorate.

[51] It has often been argued that the Spartans demonstrated that they were unwilling to fight by delaying the fulfilment of their promise to Potidaea (cf., e.g., Kagan, *Outbreak*, 280, 307); but this is to fail to take into account the precise terms of the promise.

[52] *Essays*, 161-7; quotation from 165.

increasing power of Athens and the fear that this induced in the
Spartans; he does not deny importance to the grievances he is about
to discuss, but asserts that the fear was the most significant factor.[53]

The carefully considered judgement of Thucydides, stated both
as an introduction and as a conclusion to his account of the events,
was that Sparta had her own reasons for going to war before the
allies spoke at the assembly; and the previous actions of Sparta
amply confirm his view. The Corinthian speech is therefore to be
assessed as an attempt not at persuading unwilling Spartans to fight,
but at confirming the majority in their opinion and at converting
as many of the minority as possible. The first task was not difficult;
the speech is directed towards the second object. Its main burden
is an elaborate contrast between the confident, grasping energy of
the Athenians and the selfish, careful sloth of Sparta; this much,
at least, can be taken to reflect what was actually said by the
Corinthians,[54] and they probably also made a threat to join a different alliance if Sparta made the wrong decision (i.71.4-6). The
complaints about past Spartan lethargy are hardly justified. They
presumably refer both to the Spartan failure to take the side of
Corinth over Corcyra[55] and to Spartan inactivity in the First
Peloponnesian War (i.69.5); but in the case of Corcyra the Spartans
had every justification for believing that Corinth had 'made partisan
accusations on the basis of private grievances' (Thuc. i.68.2; cf. also
68.1), while in the First Peloponnesian War the Spartans had not
been inactive through choice but because there was no action open
to them. That the Corinthian attack on Sparta was deficient in
logic, however, need not have diminished its emotional effect, and
some Spartans may have been shamed into voting for war; others,
who were rightly unimpressed by Corinth's claims to have been
the object of Athenian aggression at Corcyra and Potidaea, may
have been more concerned by the description of Athens as a state
which proceeds in its offensive by almost imperceptible degrees,

---

[53] The only difference between the two formulations is negligible: at i.23.6 the fear is
induced by an observed increase in Athenian power which is already taking place (μεγάλους
γιγνομένους), while at i.88 the Spartans fear a possible future increase (μὴ ἐπὶ μεῖζον
δυνηθῶσιν); one fear led to the other, and they were both part of the same attitude.

[54] Whatever Thucydides meant by his declaration of principle about the speeches in his
work (i.22.1), his claim to have kept something of the original cannot be valid unless at least
this much of what was actually said was preserved in his version. De Ste Croix, 7-11, has
made a strong case for supposing that only this much (what he calls the 'main thesis', the
ξύμπασα γνώμη of i.22.1) may reflect the original speech; to believe less is to convict
Thucydides of deliberate misrepresentation.

[55] Thuc. i.68.2. The reference is not clear; but it fits the Corcyra affair better than the
First Peloponnesian War, which is the only other possible reference (cf. de Ste Croix, 111
n. 59).

and must be opposed before it is too late.[56] The threat that Corinth might be forced to join a different alliance was perhaps the most persuasive point of all.[57] Thucydides does not define the 'different alliance'; but Athens is a more likely candidate than Argos. Corinth's earlier friendship for Athens would make the threat plausible, especially for Spartans who remembered 440; and it would be logical to prevent Athenian help for Corcyra—if Sparta was not willing to assist—by coming to an arrangement with Athens.[58] It is fortunate, however, that no major question turns on the extent to which the speech was able to achieve its object; no accurate assessment can be made. Thucydides admits that the speeches of the allies in general had some effect, but his words do not allow us to quantify it.

After the proposal to go to war was carried at Sparta, the same issue was put to the Congress of the Peloponnesian League. Corinth sent embassies to every member state to canvass votes. The majority of states which spoke at the Congress urged war, according to Thucydides (i.119); but he only gives a version of the speech of the Corinthians. The mood of the allies in general is more difficult to judge than that of the Spartans before their assembly. In 440, a majority had voted with Corinth against intervention; now, when Corinth urged war, the Congress voted for it. That argues for considerable Corinthian influence which was quite independent of Sparta; but Corinth's influence cannot be compared with that of Sparta, although the fact that Thucydides gives a Corinthian speech shows that he believed her influence to have been greater than that of any other Spartan ally.[59] We may take it that Corinth's influence was extensive, but it is impossible to say whether it was decisive or overwhelming. But although Corinth's direct influence on the votes

[56] Thuc. i.69.3. Kagan, *Outbreak*, 287-93, has a useful discussion of the aims of the speech, but I cannot accept his view of the mood of the Spartans before it was made (see 287).

[57] Contrast Brunt, *Phoenix*, xix (1965), 255-6. We cannot avoid convicting Thucydides of irresponsibility if the threat was not actually made.

[58] Cf. de Ste Croix, 60. I am not persuaded by Westlake (*LCM* v (1980), 121-5) that a *rapprochement* between Corinth and Athens was inconceivable; but his suggestion of a coalition against Athens including Boeotia is plausible. To attempt to make the Corinthian threat precise when Thucydides leaves it vague is perhaps to miss the point: the plethora of modern conjectures (see Westlake, ibid.) demonstrates admirably that those Spartans who were still reluctant to fight were given a good deal to think about.

[59] The fact that Thucydides gives a Corinthian rather than a Spartan speech might indicate that he believed Corinth's influence to have been greater than that of Sparta. But it is possible that no Spartan speech was made; if so, Thucydides could hardly have given one. Sparta provided the chairman for the Congress, but she may have had no vote (de Ste Croix, 111-12); she may have left the speaking to others, since her view was known by the fact that a proposal was before the Congress (ibid., 110-11).

remains unclear, it should be noted that Corinthian provocation led to almost all the events which might have persuaded members of the League who had opposed war in 440 to change their minds in 432. Elis suffered during the Corcyra affair; if she voted for peace in 440 and war in 432, she changed her vote because of Corinth's quarrel with Corcyra. Megara also helped Corinth at Sybota; but she had a grievance of her own in the Megarian Decree.[60] The other states involved over Corcyra had only helped when Athens was not involved, in 435—Epidaurus, Hermione, and Troezen with ships,[61] and Boeotia[62] and Phleious with money (Thuc. i.27.2); but some of them, and perhaps others who were never directly involved, may still have changed their votes as a result of the Corcyra dispute. Some states may have altered their stance because of events at Potidaea; but that affair too grew out of Corinthian provocation. The only matters which might have led members of the League to change their minds in which Corinth, as far as we know, played no part were the Megarian Decrees and the complaint of Aegina.[63]

The version Thucydides gives of the Corinthian speech at the Congress (i.120-4) is much more clearly intended for an audience which was already inclined to vote in the way the Corinthians wished than the speech he gives to Corinth at the Spartan assembly. This may reflect what the Corinthians actually said; in any case, Thucydides would not have composed this speech if he had not believed that most of the allies were already in favour of war.[64] The Corinthians attempt to ensure unanimous support for the war, first by claiming that those inland states (especially, presumably, the cities of Arcadia) who had not suffered directly at Athens' hands should not stand back on those grounds, for they would soon come under attack;[65] there follows an optimistic forecast of the way in which

---

[60] Megara probably voted for war in 440 in any case: at least, her colony Byzantium was in rebellion at the same time (cf. Gomme, *HCT* i.175).

[61] I omit Same in Cephallenia; she sent four ships, but we do not know whether she was a member of the League. If any of the Corinthian colonies which fought at Leucimme and Sybota (Leucas, Ambracia, and Anactorium) were members (see above, 276 n. 18), they presumably voted with Corinth both in 440 and 432.

[62] There is some dispute about whether Boeotia was a League member; de Ste Croix, 335-7, makes it more than likely that she was.

[63] Thucydides records that Aegina agitated for war on the grounds that Athens had not given her the autonomy she had promised (i.67.2); but this need not have referred to any specific event between 440 and 432 (cf. de Ste Croix, 66 with n. 9). For the Megarian Decrees, see below, 424-6.

[64] Cf. also Thuc. i.119: the majority of speakers in favour of war. The fact that Thucydides give no speech against war is a strong indication that those who opposed fighting were a minority so small that they could be almost ignored.

[65] Thuc. i.120.2-4; 120.5 loses the thread of the argument, cf. Gomme, *HCT* i.415.

a Peloponnesian victory can be expected (Thuc. i.121–122.1). Finally, they make an explicit plea for unanimity, 'If we do not act all together—all our races and every single city—and defend ourselves against them with complete unity of purpose, they will have no difficulty in subduing us in our divided state' (Thuc. i.122.2); and they support their plea with rhetorical appeals to freedom and justice (Thuc. i.122.3–124). The speech failed to achieve its object, however; 'the majority voted for war' (Thuc. i.125.1), and there must have been some dissenters, though they cannot be identified and they were probably few.

Thucydides does not mention the Corinthians again before the outbreak of war; they were presumably happy to leave the organ- ization of the war to the Spartans. There is but one issue arising out of events between the League Congress and the Theban attack on Plataea which requires discussion here; the purpose of the embassies sent by Sparta to Athens in the winter of 432/1. The first, in which the Spartans formally demanded the expulsion of those involved in the Cylonian curse, was mere ritual; the Athenians replied in kind (Thuc. i.126.1–128.2). The last, when the Spartans simply demanded that Athens should 'allow the Greeks their autonomy' (Thuc. i.139.3), was so general that it cannot have been a serious attempt at nego- tiation.[66] But in between, more than one embassy made specific demands and may have been a real effort to avoid the war the Spartans had already declared. The Spartans 'sent embassies to Athens to demand the end of the siege of Potidaea and the granting of autonomy to Aegina. But the most important and the clearest point they made was that war would not take place if the Megarian Decree were to be repealed' (Thuc. i.139.1); had it been rescinded, it would have been difficult for Sparta to go to war without some further pretext. In the event, the demands were rejected; but the fact that they were made has often encouraged false conclusions. It is too simple to conclude that Sparta was reluctant to go to war, and that she did so particularly because of the Decree. Quite apart from the fact that such a conclusion stultifies the whole of Thucy- dides' account,[67] the Spartans cannot have fought in order to redress the grievances of their allies; they could have done that by accepting the Athenian offer of arbitration, as Archidamus urged (Thuc. i.85.2). By rejecting arbitration and issuing an ultimatum, the Spartans declared that they were no longer willing to observe the terms

[66] Cf. Thuc. i.126.1: the Spartans sent embassies, 'so that they might have the best possible pretext (πρόφασις) for war, in case the Athenians failed to comply.'

[67] It is worth noting that Thucydides included this second set of embassies in his assess- ment (above, n. 66) that the Spartans were merely looking for pretexts for war.

of the Thirty Years Peace. If the mere threat of war had been enough to force Athens' submission on one issue, however minor, the balance established by the Peace would have been disturbed and Sparta would have forged a powerful weapon for future use.[68] It is self-evident that Sparta did not wish to go to war if she could gain her ends by other means; and Athenian submission would have shown that Sparta could coerce Athens without fighting. The demands were not an attempt at negotiation but an ultimatum; as Thucydides has Pericles say, 'If you give way to their demand they will at once make a greater one, because they will believe that you gave way in this case out of fear.'[69] The Athenians sent the appropriate answer: 'that they would do nothing under compulsion, but were ready to go to arbitration, on terms of absolute equality, as the Peace laid down.'[70]

Assessment of Corinth's role in the outbreak of the Peloponnesian War depends on the part played by the other states involved. It has often been concluded that the representations of Corinth forced a reluctant Sparta to fight; but this is at variance both with the considered judgement of Thucydides that Sparta was not persuaded to go to war so much by the speeches of her allies as by her fear of increasing Athenian power (i.88), and with the strong evidence that Sparta was eager to make war so long as she could be sure of the support of her allies. None the less, Corinthian responsibility for the Peloponnesian decision to undertake the war was heavy. The Corcyra affair assumed major proportions as a result of Corinthian aggression, while the trouble at Potidaea was caused by Corinthian agitation. It is true that Sparta was in principle eager to fight; but that is not to deny a major, even a decisive, role to Corinth. In the first place, it was Corinthian action over Corcyra and Potidaea which created the conditions necessary for a Spartan declaration of war: fear or hatred of Athens among Sparta's allies (including Corinth) and a revolt in the Aegean to be exploited. More importantly, Corinthian support gave Sparta confidence that she could pursue her own inclinations without risking defeat in the Congress of the League. It was perhaps mainly Corinthian efforts which prevented war at the time of the Samian revolt; but now Corinth was urging war,

---

[68] Cf. Kagan, *Outbreak*, 328-9; de Ste Croix, 256-7.

[69] i.140.5. There can be little doubt that this reflects accurately what Pericles said, for this must have been the 'main thesis' of his speech; cf. above, 299 n. 54. The fact that the speech is, in Thucydides, made after the final Spartan embassy rather than after those which demanded the repeal of the decree makes no difference; the assembly at which the speech was made discussed the whole range of issues (Thuc. i.139.3: ἅπαξ περὶ ἀπάντων).

[70] Thuc. i.145; see further below, 425 with n. 5.

and her influence, along with the effect of the Corcyra and Potidaea affairs for which she was responsible, may have been decisive both in persuading Sparta that the effort to induce her allies to fight was worth while and in delivering the support of the more hesitant members of the League. This is to go beyond the view of Thucydides, for although he emphasizes the Corinthian role he makes no explicit statement about it;[71] but it complements rather than contradicts his assessment, and it is strongly supported by the fact that on the two occasions when Sparta proposed war to the Congress, it voted against in 440 and for in 432. In each case the majority followed Corinth's lead.

It remains to assess the influence exerted by Corinth on Athenian policy. It has been argued that Athens (at least, Pericles) did not intend to observe the Thirty Years Peace faithfully, for it had been imposed in a time of stress: 'Athens had recoiled to jump better.'[72] If this is right, Corinth was merely responsible for providing, in the Corcyra affair, the first effective opportunity for Athenian expansion, and her role was but superficially important. More frequently it has been supposed that Athens was initially willing to observe the Peace, but altered her policy as a result of the Corcyra affair and undertook aggressive action—especially against Potidaea and Megara —with small concern for the probability that she would provoke war.[73] Corinth's responsibility will then have been more significant. The Corcyra affair—which was the occasion of the change in Athens' attitude—resulted from Corinthian aggression; and while Athens will have had reasons of her own for the change, a significant factor may have been that she believed war to be unavoidable if Corinth was in favour of it. These interpretations cannot be disproved by pointing out that throughout the preliminaries to the war Athens was extremely careful to avoid breaking the terms of the Peace; her care might have reflected not a genuine desire to maintain the Peace but

[71] The emphasis he gives to Corinth is greater than was imposed upon him by the events, for he might have given versions of speeches made by other states both at the Spartan assembly and the League Congress; and he draws careful attention to Corinthian canvassing for war when it was not strictly necessary to do so (i.67.1; 119).

[72] Wade-Gery, *Essays*, 253-5; quotation from 253. The suggestion, though powerfully presented, has received little support; cf. Sealey, *CP* lxx (1975), 90; Kagan, *Outbreak*, 158-60; esp. *ATL* iii.305 n. 20. Knight, *Studies in Athenian Politics*, 1-12, also takes Pericles' policy after 446 to be aggressive; he will persuade far fewer readers than Wade-Gery.

[73] Cf., e.g., Meiggs, *Athenian Empire*, 201-4. Kagan (*Outbreak*, 251-85, esp. 272, 279; 310; 352-3) varies this view by arguing that Athenian policy in 432 was designed to prepare for the war Athens believed to be possible, and increasingly likely; but that while she was prepared for war with Corinth, she expected to be able to avoid fighting Sparta. Such a policy is curiously inept; the calculation that Athens could fight Corinth without embroiling Sparta can hardly have been made with any confidence after what had happened in 440.

only a wish not to be seen to break it. Two other factors, however, make any view which imputes aggressive intent to Athens unlikely. First, at Potidaea, at least, Athens did not act with unprovoked aggression but was reacting to Corinthian hostility; much the same is probably true of the Megarian Decree: it was the Athenian answer to Megarian provocation.[74] Far more important is the fact that Pericles could not have hoped for anything more than survival in the war he is alleged to have been careless about provoking. It is conceivable that the average Athenian voter was more optimistic; but that Pericles positively welcomed a war in which he had no hope of victory but only of avoiding defeat defies belief.[75] Athens' offers of arbitration may therefore be taken at their face value: Athens was trying to avoid the war, while at the same time refusing to give way to Spartan pressure. This makes Corinthian responsibility far greater. The Athenians were reluctant to fight; but at Corcyra and Potidaea Corinthian aggression presented Athens with a choice between allowing her interests to be undermined and undertaking actions which brought an unwanted war closer. Not only did Corinth exert her influence to persuade Sparta and her League to go to war, but she also compelled Athens against her will to give the Peloponnesians reasons to fight; and all this because Athens had prevented Corinth from having her revenge on Corcyra.

[74] See further below, 424–6.

[75] De Ste Croix, 208–10; cf. Brunt, *Phoenix*, xix (1965), 259. The fact that Pericles is said by Thucydides to have 'urged the Athenians on to the war' (i.127.2) does not imply that he was eager for war; it merely shows that he preferred war to the alternative of caving in before Spartan threats—especially as he is represented as urging the Athenians on to *the* war (i.e. the one already declared by Sparta); cf. de Ste Croix, 65.

XXII. Impotence

There is little profit in discussing here the general course of the Archidamian War; but some theatres were of particular concern to Corinth and deserve special consideration. The Corinthian part in Peloponnesian campaigns on land rarely rates a mention in Thucydides, though doubtless two-thirds of the Corinthian force, as of other forces, helped in the regular invasions of Attica in the first years of the war (ii.10.1–2 etc.). Corinth's main contribution was at sea: she led the Peloponnesian naval effort. Thucydides does not give figures which enable us to calculate the proportion of Corinthian to other ships in Peloponnesian fleets; but Corinth is named first in the list of Spartan naval allies at ii.9.3, and she probably provided something like half the total. Her colonies of Leucas and Ambracia doubtless took the contribution of Corinth and her colonies together to well over a half.[1]

Before the outbreak of the war the Corinthians made, according to Thucydides, a wildly optimistic assessment of the naval capacity of the Peloponnesians when they were trying to persuade the League Congress to vote in favour of war. They may not have made exactly the forecast Thucydides gives (i.121.3–5); if they did, they may not have fully believed it, for their case demanded an optimistic forecast. If they did make anything like the speech in Thucydides, they were deceiving either themselves or their audience. All their points concerning naval possibilities were proved false in the event. There is no sign that borrowing from Olympia and Delphi was ever attempted.[2] An inscription shows—if it belongs to the Archidamian War—that exiguous funds could be provided by voluntary contributions;[3] but the Peloponnesian states could not contribute enough to attract skilled rowers from the Aegean, and even if funds could be found it is doubtful whether many men would risk exile for the sake of a few extra drachmae.[4] The Corinthians try to minimize the disparity in skill between Peloponnesian and Athenian oarsmen, but this was

---

[1] See below, 430 Endnote C.
[2] i.121.3,5; cf. Brunt, *Phoenix*, xix (1965), 260–1.
[3] Meiggs and Lewis, *GHI*, no. 67; its date is, however, uncertain, and it may not belong to the Peloponnesian War at all (Lewis in Meiggs and Lewis, *GHI*, p. 184).
[4] Thuc. i.121.3. The Corinthian point is met by Pericles at i.143.2.

the most important factor making for Peloponnesian naval failure; Athenian fleets frequently overturned odds that were numerically overwhelming.[5]

Whatever we make of the speech in Thucydides, the naval actions undertaken by the Corinthians during the war demonstrate that they were over-optimistic: they had to learn their almost total incapacity by bitter experience. Their first action was an attempt to repair the damage done by an Athenian *periplous* in 431. Even if the precise character of Corinthian interests in the north-west cannot be defined (above, 272-80), there is no doubt of their existence, and the first Athenian naval action of the war was designed to put pressure on Corinth in this area. Immediately after the outbreak of war the Athenians sent embassies in particular to Corcyra, Cephallenia, Acarnania, and Zacynthus 'because they realized that if these places were confirmed in their friendship, they would be able to make war all round the Peloponnese' (ii.7.3); shortly afterwards an expedition was sent here: a large fleet of a hundred Athenian vessels and fifty from Corcyra (ii.25.1). Brief landings were made in Messenia and Elis (ii.25), but the later activity of the expedition was harmful to Corinth in particular: Sollium was captured, Euarchus was driven out of Astacus, and Cephallenia—which had not been among the allies of Athens when the war began (ii.9.4)—was brought into alliance (ii.30). All three places where the Athenians acted had links with Corinth.[6] The Corcyraeans who joined in the expedition were no doubt delighted to help to weaken Corinth in this region; and by giving the captured Sollium to the Acarnanians Athens confirmed their alliance with the second major anti-Corinthian power of the north-west.

Corinth reacted vigorously in winter 431/0; without waiting either for Spartan help or for the next campaigning season, she attempted to undo all that Athens had done. Euarchus 'persuaded the Corinthians to sail to restore him with forty ships and 1,500 hoplites, and he himself paid for extra mercenaries' (ii.33.1); in this respect Corinth was successful, but all her other efforts miscarried. The 'other places on the Acarnanian coast' which the Corinthians vainly tried to take (ii.33.2) must have included Sollium: a landing on Cephallenia was equally without success, for the force met with stiff local resistance, re-embarked with difficulty, and sailed for

[5] On all this, see especially Brunt, *Phoenix*, xix (1965), 259-61. The attempts to counteract Athenian naval supremacy in ways not mentioned by the Corinthians proved equally fruitless in the Archidamian War: ibid., 261-3.

[6] Above, 277-9 (Sollium, Euarchus); i.27.2 (Cephallenia provides four ships for Leucimme).

home (ii.33.3). Even the restoration of Euarchus gave Corinth little joy, for either he was soon removed again or he changed sides: when Astacus is mentioned for the next (and only other) time in Thucydides an Athenian force landed there in winter 429/8 and marched inland without effective opposition (ii.102.1). The fact that this Corinthian expedition was independent need occasion no surprise. Since Corinth still retained some naval confidence she may have felt it unnecessary to involve Sparta—especially as a naval expedition on such a scale was hardly to be expected in winter.

When the Spartans did become involved in naval activity in the west, it was in order to advance general Peloponnesian, and not specifically Corinthian, interests there. Two invasions of Attica, and even the plague, had failed to force Athens to submit; and Sparta perhaps began to realize that the war might last far longer than she had expected. She therefore undertook, perhaps with Corinthian encouragement, naval action which she had probably thought unnecessary in 431.[7] Well into the summer of 430 a fleet of 100 vessels under Spartan command attacked Zacynthus; but although almost the whole island was ravaged the islanders refused to come to terms and the expedition returned home (ii.66). Thucydides does not indicate the purpose of the attack in strategic terms; but it must have been to make Athenian naval raids on the Peloponnese more difficult by removing one of her bases.[8] The Athenian reply was to send Phormio with twenty ships to Naupactus, where he 'guarded against ships sailing either out of or into Corinth and the Crisaean Gulf' (ii.69.1). Thucydides' formulation demonstrates that Corinth was a main target of the blockade, but its effect is difficult to estimate; it can only have been partial, since the entrance to the Gulf was not blocked with a boom. Polyaenus v.13.1 may record a successful Corinthian attempt to protect a convoy of corn ships from Athenian attack (above, 130 with n. 11). If the Athenians believed that the blockade served a useful purpose, it will have been maintained in subsequent years, although Thucydides mentions it no more; there were usually triremes stationed at Naupactus.

Failure at Zacynthus did not discourage the Spartans; for their next efforts in this area, if Thucydides is to be trusted, were part of a grandiose plan for the total elimination of Athenian influence near the entrance to the Gulf. In 429 Cnemus was sent to Acarnania with 1,000 hoplites as a result of representations made by Ambracia

---

[7] See, on the Spartan attitude, esp. vii.28.3; cf. iv.85.2.
[8] Cf. ii.7.3; esp. ii.80.1; for the necessity of bases for *periploi*, see Gomme, *JHS* liii (1933), 16-24. Cf. in general Kagan, *Archidamian War*, 93-4.

and the Chaonians of Epirus, with strong support from Corinth (ii.80.1,3). Thucydides asserts that the Spartans were persuaded by arguments that 'if (the Spartans) came to help both by land and by sea, the Acarnanians of the coast would be unable to join in the defence, and Acarnania would be easily captured; Zacynthus and Cephallenia would then be taken, and the Athenians would no longer be able to make *periploi* round the Peloponnese as they had in the past. There was also some hope of taking Naupactus' (ii.80.1). We cannot judge whether Thucydides had access to good information about the arguments used by the Ambraciots, Corinthians, and Chaonians, or about the Spartan motives for agreeing to the proposals; but the plan seems most unreal. It was possible to hope (no more than that) for the conquest of Acarnania, and the attempt was revived in 426; but that would have made it no easier to take Zacynthus or Cephallenia, although Spartan tenure of Acarnania might have made it more difficult for the Athenians to defend Naupactus. Thucydides may have exaggerated the hopes the Spartans had of the expedition; but it is doubtful whether they would have invested such resources in Acarnania if they had not expected far-reaching benefits. Both Corinth and Ambracia had private reasons for encouraging Spartan intervention, for Corinth was clearly unable to restore her position here without assistance and Ambracia had made a fruitless attack on Amphilochian Argos in the previous year (ii.68); but we cannot say whether Corinth or her colony led Sparta into false hopes for her own purposes, or shared those hopes themselves.[9]

The plans failed in every respect. Cnemus acted without waiting for naval support (ii.80.4,8), and his local allies were so heavily defeated at Stratus that he quickly withdrew to Leucas (cf. ii.84.5) through the territory of the Oeniadae, his only friends among the Acarnanians (ii.80.8-82; cf. ii.102.2). Worse followed. The main naval force, coming from Corinth and consisting of forty-seven ships, was forced to battle by the twenty Athenian triremes that were guarding Naupactus under Phormio. The result was disastrous. Phormio made skilful use of his knowledge both of local weather conditions and of the inexperience of the enemy, who allowed themselves to be bunched into a confused group in rough water; they lost twelve vessels with most of their crews (ii.83-4). The remnant limped to Cyllene, where they were joined by Cnemus,

---

[9] Kagan (*Archidamian War*, 107) assesses the affair differently: 'the appeal was persuasive, and the prospects seemed good'. That is perhaps true of the possibilities in Acarnania, but it hardly holds good for the broader aspects of the plan; cf. Beaumont, *JHS* lxxii (1952), 63.

now returned from Leucas (ii.84.5); preparations were begun for a second naval battle against Phormio.

Seventy-seven ships were gathered at Cyllene (ii.86.4), but Thucydides does not make specific the Peloponnesian intentions; he merely says that the Peloponnesians were ordered to 'make better preparations for a second naval battle, and not to be driven off the sea by a few ships' (ii.85.1). They left Cyllene for Panormus in Achaea, inside the Gulf (ii.86.1), and when Phormio placed his twenty ships at Molycreian Rhium (Antirhium), doubtless just outside the narrows (cf. ii.86.5), the Peloponnesian fleet sailed along its own coast to Rhium (ii.86.2-4); for a week or so the two fleets stayed opposite each other, neither wishing to move from its own position and thus give the advantage to the enemy (ii.86.5). Phormio placed himself so as to prevent the Peloponnesians from proceeding north-westwards; he therefore believed, as was natural, that their intention was still to make a landing in Acarnania (he had received, and been unable to comply with, requests for help from the Acarnanians when Cnemus had threatened them: ii.81.1). This was probably the original intention of the Spartans: if they had planned all along to attack Naupactus there would have been no reason to delay for a week as they did—especially as reinforcements from Athens might have arrived at any moment. Their aim was probably to make Phormio believe that Naupactus was their target by coasting to Panormus, and then to slip out of the Gulf to Acarnania while Phormio was concentrating upon the defence of Naupactus. He guessed their intentions, but in thwarting them he left Naupactus vulnerable, and the Peloponnesians sensibly changed their plan and attacked it. Phormio was forced, much against his will (ii.90.3), to come to its defence, for it had been (inexcusably) left without a garrison. The Peloponnesians were at first victorious, having drawn Phormio out of position; but they gave chase in disorder. A single Athenian vessel doubled back round a merchant ship at anchor and sank a pursuing vessel from Leucas; the remaining Athenian triremes saw their opportunity and won a spectacular victory. The defeated Peloponnesians made for Corinth (ii.90-93.1).[10] Phormio spent the following winter securing Athenian interests in Acarnania (ii.102.1-2).

These defeats in the Gulf were disastrous in terms of both material and morale. Eighteen ships were taken—nearly a quarter of the total number; some of the crews were killed and the rest captured (ii.84.4; 92.2), though the free prisoners were exchanged the following winter (ii.103.1). Far more important was the loss of all rational

---

[10] On these battles, see esp. Gomme, *HCT* ii.216-34.

hope of effective naval action. Before the war Corinth had, according
to Thucydides, made light of the disparity in naval skill between
Athenians and Peloponnesians; she claimed that the first naval
victory won by the Peloponnesians was likely to mean the end of
the war (i.121.4). There were many flaws in that argument; and in
any case the battles against Phormio demonstrated that there was
almost no chance of ever winning such a victory. The first defeat
was perhaps excusable, though it was over-optimistic for the Corinthians to fail to prepare for battle merely because they took superiority
in numbers to be sufficient protection (ii.83.3). In the second the
Peloponnesians enjoyed all the advantages: there were odds of
almost 4 to 1 to their favour. Phormio had not been given the rapid
reinforcements he needed and, having left Naupactus without a
garrison, had been manœuvred into an inferior position; but the
technical incompetence and indiscipline of the Peloponnesian crews
nullified a skilfully conceived plan of battle. The effect on Peloponnesian naval confidence was disastrous: almost at once a daring and
equally skilfully conceived scheme to attack the Peiraeus miscarried
because Peloponnesians could not trust themselves to put it into
effect (ii.93-4).

Naval incompetence proved a serious impediment to the Spartan
war effort in the following year, when the revolt of Lesbos offered
the opportunity to attack Athens where she had most to lose, in
the Aegean; Corinth was unable to help Sparta to exploit it. Geographical factors made it difficult for the Peloponnesians to operate
in the Aegean. Of Sparta's naval allies only Corinth and Megara had
ports facing east. Even the Corinthian vessels which went to help
Lesbos in 427 sailed from Lechaeum round the Peloponnese, not
from Cenchreae (iii.29.1), and the forty ships from the Megarian
docks at Nisaea which were used in the abortive attempt on the
Peiraeus had been out of use for so long that they were no longer
serviceable.[11] The panic caused at Athens on this one occasion
when Peloponnesian ships did appear in the Saronic Gulf merely
reinforces the impression: the Athenians were so confident of their
control of their Gulf that they had taken no steps to guard the
Peiraeus (ii.93-4). It was technically possible for the geographical
problem to be solved by use of the diolkos. The Mytilenaeans asked
for a second invasion of Attica to help their rebellion in 428, and

[11] Gomme (*HCT* ii.238) suggests that Cenchreae would have been a better base for the
attack, but that it could not be used because there were no vessels there. Cenchreae,
however, was more than twice as far from the Peiraeus as Nisaea, and the distance might
have prevented the use of such triremes as were there; there are unlikely to have been many,
but there were some in winter 419/18 (below, 330).

initially enthusiastic preparations were made by the Spartans for a
fleet to help in the invasion after crossing the Isthmus on the diolkos
(iii.15; cf. 13.4); but in the end it was decided, partly because the
fleets of Sparta's allies were slow in preparing themselves (iii.15.2),
to send instead forty ships under Alcidas round Cape Malea to help
at Lesbos itself (iii.16.3). Even this fleet did not sail that summer;
and in the following year it progressed so slowly that Mytilene had
surrendered before it arrived (iii.29.1). Alcidas scuttled for home,
despite much advice (Corinthian?) that he should attempt some
daring action while he was there (iii.29.2-33.1). Part of the reason
for the failure of the expedition may have been the incompetence
of Alcidas;[12] but his keen desire not to face an Athenian fleet was
sound judgement, born of Peloponnesian experience at sea in the
west.[13] He was fortunate not to have been forced into battle before
discovering that the revolt of Lesbos had failed. With no rebellion
in progress there was no point in taking any positive action. It could
only have ended in the defeat and capture not only of the ships but
also of their crews; there was no friendly shore to which the men
might escape.[14]

Meanwhile, events in the north-west brought some small comfort
to the Corinthians. The Acarnanians asked for an Athenian force
under the command of a son or a relative of Phormio; his son
Asopius was sent. After ravaging the coasts of Laconia he led an
Acarnanian army against Oeniadae, the one Acarnanian city which
did not adhere to Athens; but Oeniadae survived. Asopius sailed to
Leucas and landed on the island at Nericus; but on his return he
himself and many of his men were killed by the Leucadians and
'some troops of the garrison'—probably Corinthians posted in
permanent defence of their colony.[15]

It was perhaps at about the same time as the defeat of Asopius,

---

[12] Gomme, *HCT* ii.294.

[13] For a very different assessment, see Kagan, *Archidamian War*, 148-51. His comparison
of the situation in 427 with that faced by Athens after the defeat of the Sicilian expedition
seems to me highly inaccurate.

[14] Kagan, ibid., 150, points out justly that the ships would not have been a great loss,
for in 425 Peloponnesian naval activity ceased altogether; then, however, it was only the
ships that were lost. Kagan's suggestion that the men might have escaped inland to Asia
Minor would have involved an extremely risky journey home.

[15] iii.7. In 425, 500 Corinthians were on garrison duty in Leucas and Ambracia (iv.42.3),
and 300 had been sent to Ambracia in winter 426/5 (iii.114.4); thus, there were probably
200 at Leucas in 425 (Beaumont, *JHS* lxxii (1952), 63 n. 21) That does not prove that
there was a garrison of Corinthians at all in 428, much less that it consisted of 200 men; but
it is difficult to see which other state is likely to have sent garrison troops to Leucas, and
the garrison are plainly distinguished in Thucydides from 'those who came from there to
help'.

or shortly afterwards, that Corinth set in motion an ambitious but fruitless plan to make up for her recent losses in the north-west by achieving control of Corcyra.[16] Ever since the battle of Sybota Corinth had held 250 Corcyraean captives, 'and treated them with great consideration in the hope that they might return to Corcyra and bring the city over to them; most of the captives were men of power and importance in the city' (i.55.1). These prisoners were now sent back to Corcyra, ostensibly after payment of a large ransom,[17] but in fact with the intention of handing the city over to Corinth (iii.70.1). They began by arguing, in private conversation with other Corcyraeans, that Corcyra should sever her links with Athens. The issue was debated in the assembly, which was addressed not only by Athenian but also by Corinthian ambassadors; but the decision was made 'to remain an ally of Athens under the existing terms, but to be friendly to the Peloponnesians as before' (iii.70.1–2). This was hardly logical; but it proved that Corcyra felt that she still needed Athenian protection against Corinth. Corcyra felt no special friendship for Athens: her only recorded action during the war so far was to send fifty ships to help the first Athenian *periplous* in 431. The Corcyraeans voted positively in favour of friendship with the Peloponnese, and may have wished, in principle, to return to the position of neutrality they had enjoyed before 435 (i.32.4–5); but they felt unable to do so in the face of Corinthian threats. The Corinthian ambassadors, far from setting their case forward, had done the opposite; their presence demonstrated that Corinth's designs on her colony were as active as ever.

The Corinthian ship which had brought the ambassadors now left;[18] open Corinthian support was harming the chances of those Corcyraeans who were doing Corinth's work. Persuasion having failed, different methods were attempted. Peithias, *prostates tou demou* and a leading pro-Athenian in Corcyra, was prosecuted on a charge of 'enslaving Corcyra to Athens': but he turned the tables

---

[16] Thucydides gives no date for the first step in the scheme, the return of the captives taken at Sybota. It has usually been conjectured (refs. in Gomme, *HCT* ii.359; cf. Kagan, *Archidamian War*, 175) that the attempt was intended to coincide with the trouble the Corinthians hoped Athens would face in the Aegean from the rebellion of Lesbos and the fleet sent to the Aegean under Alcidas: this would give a date of winter 428/7 at the earliest. An equally plausible conjecture would be that the Corinthians hoped to take advantage of Athens' reduced capacity to act in the west which followed the loss of Asopius; that would give a rather earlier date.

[17] Not, probably, 800 talents, as the MSS of Thuc. iii.70.1 have it; Gomme, *HCT* ii. 359–60.

[18] This is not stated by Thucydides, but must be assumed. It would surely have rated a mention in the narrative of the later violence had it taken part in it; presumably it would have done so had it still been at Corcyra.

and had heavy fines imposed on five of his richest opponents for sacrilege (iii.70.3-4). Learning, according to Thucydides, that Peithias intended to press for a full *symmachia* with Athens, the five organized an armed attack on the council, of which Peithias was a member: sixty councillors and others, among them Peithias himself, were killed; a few of Peithias' sympathizers escaped to the Athenian trireme which had brought ambassadors from Athens and was still in the harbour (iii.70.6), and they were taken to Athens for safety.[19] A resolution was forced through the Corcyraean assembly, that 'neither (Sparta nor Athens) should be received except on peaceful terms and in one ship only; any more would be considered as enemies.' Ambassadors were sent to Athens, but they were arrested and taken to Aegina (iii.71-72.1). In the meantime, a Corinthian trireme carrying Spartan ambassadors reached Corcyra. It was probably timed to arrive when, according to the plan, Peithias had been condemned in the courts and his opponents could propose the motion they in fact had forced through the assembly; but events turned out differently, and when the trireme came 'those who held power in Corcyra' attacked the demos. After a few days' fighting the demos gained the upper hand. The Corinthian ship slipped away (iii.72.2-74), and on the following day Nicostratus brought twelve Athenian vessels from Naupactus and tried to arrange a settlement between oligarchs and democrats which involved a full *symmachia* with Athens; a few days later fifty-three Peloponnesian ships under Alcidas arrived—having failed to take the opportunity of attacking Naupactus in Nicostratus' absence.[20]

The nature of the Corinthian scheme is clear enough. Two main weapons were to be used by the Corcyraean ex-prisoners: fear of enslavement to Athens, and oligarchic revolution, which was to be supported by a Peloponnesian fleet. It is naïve to suppose that oligarchic revolution was not part of the initial plan merely because the first actions were directed towards abrogation of the alliance with Athens;[21] there would have been no hope of success if revolutionary intentions had been open from the start. The whole scheme was devised by Corinth, and there was no hope of achieving her ultimate aim of controlling Corcyra without securing a change of government. Equally, while 'patriotic Corcyraeans could reasonably have reached the conclusion that it was in the best interests of their

[19] This is not mentioned by Thucydides, but must be assumed from iii.71.2-72.1; cf. Gomme, *HCT* ii.361-2.
[20] Gomme, *HCT* ii.363-4.
[21] As Bruce, *Phoenix*, xxv (1971), 108-12.

city to avoid active participation in the war',[22] the ex-prisoners must have expected a return for handing Corcyra over to Corinth: political control for themselves. Thucydides shows at i.55.1 that the prisoners were men of exactly the kind we should expect to be oligarchs: 'men of power and importance in the city'; there can be no doubt that they hoped first to sever Corcyra's links with Athens and then, with the help of a Peloponnesian force, to change the government to suit themselves. With that achieved, Corinth would be able to exert through them the control she had failed to gain at Sybota. But force had to be employed sooner than was intended, and Peloponnesian help came too late to be of any use.

The direct Spartan interest in Corcyra is evident, if perhaps small: it was of some advantage to detach the Corcyraeans from Athens, even though they had taken little part in the war. But the main impetus behind the intervention was Corinthian. The plan originated in Corinth; indeed, the first steps may have been taken without Spartan approval. Sparta was not involved even diplomatically at the first stage; when the Athenian alliance was discussed in the assembly only Corinthian ambassadors were present. If the scheme had been evolved with Spartan agreement from the start, we should have expected the Spartans themselves to send representatives. Spartans did come at a later stage; but by then the time for merely diplomatic assistance was past, and when more powerful help came, the oligarchs were already on the run. Sparta seems, then, to have been drawn into a plan she had no part in preparing; perhaps Corinth was uncertain of Spartan willingness to help, so she set events in train on her own initiative and then demanded support. If this is right, the lack of consultation was probably part of the reason for failure. The scheme in itself was not unreal; but for success it demanded careful timing, little or no public involvement of Corinth herself, prompt and well-co-ordinated action by Peloponnesian forces, and no small amount of luck. In the event it enjoyed none of these advantages, not least because Corinth did not trust the Spartans to do as she wished without being forced to.

After the arrival of the Peloponnesian fleet the Corcyraean democrats panicked and lost a number of ships; but Brasidas, who had been sent to advise Alcidas, could not persuade him to make any serious effort to take the city in the face of the twelve Athenian vessels under Nicostratus. They gave a good account of themselves in defensive action against even more overwhelming odds than

---

[22] Bruce, ibid., 110; this is, in practice, what the Corcyraean assembly freely decided at its first meeting: iii.70.2.

Phormio had faced in the Gulf; and when sixty Athenian vessels
under Eurymedon were sighted the Peloponnesians very properly
fled, dragging their ships over the isthmus of Leucas to avoid being
caught (iii.75-81.1). An appalling massacre of the Corcyraean
oligarchs followed (iii.81.2-83), but some of them escaped to the
mainland, from where they mounted damaging raids on the island
and caused a famine. They failed to get help from Sparta and
Corinth, and in the end hired mercenaries and established themselves
at Mount Istome on the island itself (iii.85). In 425 a fleet of sixty
ships was sent to their assistance (iv.2.3); but it had to leave to
defend Pylos, where it was captured in its entirety by the Athenians
(iv.8.2; 8.4-23.1). Shortly after the affair at Pylos, an Athenian
fleet came to help the Corcyraean democrats; Istome was taken
and the oligarchs slaughtered almost to a man (iv.46-48.5).

Athens continued to harry Corinth in the north-west. In 426
Demosthenes commanded thirty ships on a *periplous*, and after
destroying some troops of the garrison of Ellomenus on the Peraea
of Leucas,[23] he landed on the island itself with the help of Acarnanians, Zacynthians, Cephallenians, and fifteen ships from Corcyra.
He was urged by his Acarnanian (and, I should guess, his Corcyraean) allies to institute a regular siege (iii.94.1-2); but instead he
followed the advice of the Messenians of Naupactus to attack the
Aetolians who, it was alleged, were threatening Naupactus. That
decision deprived him of the majority of his forces, for the Acarnanians and Corcyraeans left for home now that their own interests were
no longer involved; he was thoroughly defeated (iii.94.3-98).

Probably even before the attack of Demosthenes, the Aetolians
tried to secure help for an attack on Naupactus by sending ambassadors not only to Sparta but also to Corinth (iii.100.1). After
the experience of the early years of the war, Sparta judged that it
would be far too risky to try to reach Aetolia by sea through
Oeniadae; 3,000 allied hoplites, with the Spartan Eurylochus and two
Spartan subordinates in command, assembled at Delphi in autumn
426 (iii.100.2-101.1). In view of the interest of Corinth in the
expedition, she may have provided a significant proportion of the
force; but there is no mention of Corinthians in Thucydides.
Eurylochus marched through Ozolian Locris and ravaged the land
round Naupactus in concert with the Aetolians. He captured the

---

[23] There is some uncertainty about the correct reading of Thucydides here, but Λευκαδίας
(E), meaning the part of the mainland controlled by Leucas as distinct from the island
itself, is probably correct against Ἀρκαδίας (*cett.*), which is impossible; cf. Dover, *CQ* iv
(1954), 79 n. 2, modified by Gomme, *HCT* ii.399-400. As for the garrison, it is possible
that it was manned by Corinthian troops; but it was probably Leucadian.

portion of the city outside the walls and gained possession of Molycreium, the Corinthian colony west of Naupactus which had previously been captured by Athens.[24] In the meantime Demosthenes raised a force of 1,000 Acarnanians, despite his failure to take their advice about Leucas, and brought them into Naupactus; Eurylochus therefore gave up his attempt (iii.102.3–5).

He did not, however, return to the Peloponnese; the Ambraciots asked him to revive the plan for a Spartan offensive in the northwest that had been unsuccessfully attempted by Cnemus in 429. This time Thucydides does not mention Corinthian representations in support of their colonists' plan; but it would be surprising if they were not made (iii.102.5–7). Eurylochus marched through Acarnania and joined 3,000 Ambraciots who had come to attack Ampilochian Argos at Olpae (iii.105–6); but Demosthenes inflicted a serious defeat on the combined Ambraciot and Peloponnesian armies. Both Eurylochus and his second in command Macarius were killed; the remaining Spartan, Menedaeus, was left without any means of retreat for his Peloponnesian troops.[25] Demosthenes, wishing to thin out the forces opposed to him, but more particularly hoping to gain for the Spartans a reputation for saving their own skins without concern for their local allies, made a secret agreement to allow the Peloponnesian forces to withdraw under truce (iii.109.2); but confusion in its implementation led to further casualties before the Peloponnesians got away (iii.110.1; 114.2). Finally, Demosthenes overwhelmed a force from Ambracia which had heard nothing of the first battle (iii.112). The number of Ambraciot casualties in all these actions together that was given to Thucydides was so great that he did not report it for fear of exaggeration; he does, however, allow himself to comment: 'this was the greatest disaster to fall upon a single Greek city in an equal number of days throughout this war' (iii.113.6).

Fortunately for Corinth, the conflicting interests of her enemies prevented the total loss of Ambracia. Demosthenes wished to capture the city and invited his Acarnanian and Amphilochian allies to join him in doing so; but they rejected his proposal 'because they were afraid that the Athenians, if they held Ambracia, would be worse neighbours than they had already' (iii.113.6). This is good (if superfluous) evidence for the nature of Athenian relations with Acarnania and Amphilochia: it was merely an alliance of convenience,

---

[24] iii.101–102.2; on Molycreium, above, 277.
[25] iii.107–109.1; evidently Menedaeus put no trust in the ability of the Ambraciot fleet to help him to retreat in the face of the twenty Athenian vessels Demosthenes had with him (cf. Gomme, *HCT* ii.421).

encouraged by common resistance to Corinthian efforts to secure
control in the north-west. In the case of minor sites, it was useful
for Athens to give them to the Acarnanians, for her interest was
essentially to deny them to Corinth.[26] But Ambracia was in neither
Acarnanian nor Amphilochian territory, and Athens might wish to
hold such an important site for herself; to help Athens to take it
would be to encourage too positive an Athenian interest. The
Amphilochians and Acarnanians therefore made a peace for 100
years with Ambracia which required each party to defend the other's
territory except, in practice, in case of a Peloponnesian attack on
Acarnania and/or Amphilochia or an Athenian attack on Ambracia.[27]
Despite the treaty or perhaps because of its exclusions, Corinth felt
it necessary to send a garrison of 300 to Ambracia; and they had a
difficult journey by land, for they could not trust to their ability
to reinforce their colony by sea. The commander of the garrison
was Xenocleides son of Euthycles (iii.114.4) who had been singled
out by Thucydides among the five *strategoi* in command of the
Corinthian fleet at Sybota (above, 233 n. 11); he was presumably
an expert on north-western affairs. Because of her special weakness,
Ambracia was forced to agree to a clause under which she promised
not to give aid to Anactorium (iii.114.3); this clause bore fruit in the
following year. The place was captured by Acarnanian and Athenian
forces and settled by Acarnanians (iv.49), who no doubt increased
the difficulties of communication with Ambracia, for the site of
Anactorium had originally been chosen precisely in order to secure
the entrance to the Ambracian Gulf (above, 217). Thus the last
Corinthian possession on these coasts save Ambracia herself and
Leucas was lost; Oeniadae was forced to join Athens the following
year (iv.77.2). The whole coast from Naupactus to Ambracia was
now hostile to Corinth, with the possible but unimportant exception
of Molycreium.[28]

Until 425 Corinthian participation in the war had, at any rate,
been active. But in that year the greater part of her fleet was captured
or destroyed at Pylos (above, 316); her offensive capacity was
reduced almost to nothing. Her geographical position did, at least,
enable her to provide 2,700 of the 6,000 or so hoplites raised by

---

[26] Sollium, ii.30.1; Anactorium, below.

[27] iii.114.3; cf. Gomme, *HCT* ii.429. Kagan, *Archidamian War*, 217, misrepresents the
terms of the treaty as attempting to 'keep the region free of further involvement in the great
war'; Beaumont, *JHS* lxxii (1952), 63, also summarizes the effects of the treaty inaccurately.

[28] At its last mention in Thucydides this place was in Peloponnesian hands (above, 317);
either it was recaptured by Athens but the fact was too unimportant for Thucydides to
record, or the Athenians did not think it worth while to recapture it.

Brasidas to defend Megara in 424,[29] and to help the Boeotians in the recapture of the fort at Delium after the battle (iv.100); but for the rest of the war she appears mainly as the target of Athenian attacks, especially when Nicias invaded the Corinthia in 425. She had advance warning from Argos (iv.42.3); but not in sufficient time to secure help. Since it was not known which part of the Corinthia would be attacked, the Corinthian forces had to be divided: the troops who lived 'outside the Isthmus' stayed to defend their home area,[30] while the rest gathered at the Isthmus.[31] Nicias approached the coast at night, and landed at dawn with 2,000 hoplites and 200 cavalry on the long beach 'between Chersonese and Rheitus' (above, 31-2). Signals had informed the Corinthians at the Isthmus that an attack was in progress; but darkness and then Mt. Oneion had prevented observation of the landing—evidently there was not yet even an observation post at Stanotopi, where a fort was built in the fourth century.[32] The forces at the Isthmus were therefore themselves divided: half went to Cenchreae in case Crommyon should be attacked, and Battus and Lycophron led the other half southwards (iv.42.1-2,4). They arrived too late to dispute the landing, but engaged with the Athenians close to the beach. There was hard hand-to-hand fighting: the Corinthian left was at first forced back to higher ground, but then used the slope—and stones from a wall built on it—to return to the attack and drive the Athenians right back towards their ships. But they were again pushed back, and finally the Corinthians, having no cavalry to oppose that of the Athenians, retreated to defend the unfortified settlement at Solygeia. The Athenians put up a trophy, but the force that had been left at Cenchreae and the older Corinthians still capable of bearing arms came towards Solygeia when they saw the dust of the battle rising above Oneion. Nicias, thinking that these were general Peloponnesian reinforcements, withdrew to islands just off the coast. He left 212 Corinthian dead, including the *strategos* Lycophron—and two Athenians of the just under fifty who had died in the battle; these remaining two were recovered under a truce when Nicias realized that he had left them behind.[33] He landed near Crommyon, laid waste land

---

[29] iv.66-74; the Corinthians, 70.1.

[30] Thuc. iv.42.3 seems to imply that these troops were not called out at all; but his meaning is probably merely that they did not take part in the action at Solygeia that he is about to describe, because their duty was to defend the northern Corinthia.

[31] iv.42.3; cf. Stroud, *CSCA* iv (1971), 239-41. Polyaen. *Strat.* i.39.1 is scarcely compatible with Thucydides, and should be rejected (Stroud, ibid., 227 n. 2).

[32] Cf. Stroud, *Hesperia*, xl (1971), 139.

[33] iv.43-4. Two lead sling-bullets, inscribed with the name Lycophron and said to have been found 'at Corinth', are now in the Ashmolean Museum (Foss, *AR* 1974/5, 41, nos.

there, and spent a night on shore; he then withdrew and fortified Methana in the Argolid before returning to Athens.[34]

Corinth's part in the Archidamian War was thus merely to suffer; as between Corinth and Athens the war was an almost unbroken series of Athenian successes, especially in the north-west. It was her special claim to influence in this region which had driven Corinth to fight, but the war had all but eradicated her strength here, and meanwhile her naval credentials had been exposed for the anachronism they were. In the face of all this, and of the fall of Potidaea (ii.70) and Nicias' attack on the Corinthia itself, Athenian activities in the far west, pursued with varying success from 427 to 424 and briefly in 422, must have seemed but a minor irritation. The Athenian intention, according to Thucydides, was 'to prevent the import of corn (from Sicily) to the Peloponnese, and to make a preliminary survey to see whether it might be possible to bring affairs in Sicily under their control' (iii.86.4). Corinth, one of the major Peloponnesian importers of Sicilian corn (above, 129–30), was one of the main targets, as she was of the blockade at Naupactus (above, 308); but Athenian hopes were not fulfilled, and the Peloponnesian corn supply was probably little, if at all, affected.

Thucydides gives little information on the relationship between Corinth and Sparta during the war. In 421 Corinth rejected the Peace of Nicias; but relations were seriously strained well before that. Corinth had been enthusiastic in urging Sparta to war; when expectations of an easy victory proved unfounded it would be surprising if Sparta had not directed some of the anger her frustration caused her against Corinth—especially as Corinthian naval incompetence was the most important reason for some of the more spectacular Peloponnesian failures and was partly responsible for the capture of the Spartans on Sphacteria (cf. ii.85.2). As for Corinth's attitude to Sparta, we do not know whether Corinth concurred in the general Peloponnesian criticisms of Archidamus' lethargy on the first invasion (ii.18.3–5); but there are possible early signs of tension. The Spartan expedition to Acarnania in 429 was intended by the

3–4). Despite the fact that slingers are not mentioned by Thucydides, they might have been used; but Corinth is not Solygeia, and these bullets may have been prepared for some earlier action in which Corinthian slingers were led by Lycophron. It would be interesting to find slingers from Corinth attested in the Archidamian War, whether they fought at Solygeia or not; but the identification with the Lycophron who fought this battle is uncertain, and with it the date of the bullets.

[34] iv.45. It has been suggested that Nicias' intention in landing in the Corinthia was to capture and fortify Solygeia, as he later fortified Methana; and that Corinth, despite losing the battle, was thus able to thwart him. Solygeia, however, was too far inland to be suitable for such a purpose; Nicias' intention was probably merely to harass (Stroud, *CSCA* iv (1971), 245–7).

Corinthians to restore their lost influence in the area, but they may have misrepresented their hopes for the expedition because they could not trust Sparta to take their part if they were to present the case honestly. The case for supposing that Corinth initiated her scheme for the subversion of Corcyra without reference to Sparta is stronger; the reason will have been the same. These instances are not certain; but there can be no doubt that Sparta was almost powerless to counter the pressure exerted by Athens on Corinth. It was but small recompense that after 424 Sparta was able, through Brasidas in the north, to inflict serious damage on Athens; this area was of little concern to Corinth after the fall of Potidaea.

If Corinthian mistrust of Sparta over the conduct of the war is merely probable, Spartan negotiations for peace made it profound—and resoundingly justified. Already in 427 the Spartans may have believed that it might be necessary to conclude a peace which would re-establish, in broad terms, the pre-war situation. Thucydides reports that at the time of the fall of Plataea Sparta wanted the city to surrender instead of being taken by storm, 'so that if peace was ever to be concluded with the Athenians on the terms that each side should give up those places they had won during the war, Plataea need not be given up on·the ground that it had gone over (to the Spartans) voluntarily' (iii.52.2). If Thucydides is not here merely drawing unjustified conclusions from what was actually agreed about Plataea in the Peace of Nicias,[35] that does not mean that Sparta was already in favour of such a peace; but it does show that she was considering the possiblity that she might have to reach such an agreement.[36]

The first firm proposals for peace made by Sparta were far worse.[37] When the Spartans were trapped on Sphacteria, an embassy offered Athens terms which not only ignored the pre-war grievances of Corinth and others, but also made no mention of returning places Athens had taken since 431.[38] These terms meant for Corinth, at this date, the loss of Sollium; worse followed, for when Athens rejected the offer and demanded Nisaea, Pagae, Troezen, and Achaea

[35] v.17.2. There is ground for suspicion here: Thucydides might not have had access to such inner Spartan counsels. But the difficulty that is explained by these orders—that Sparta preferred to negotiate a surrender rather than to risk troops in storming the city— is not so great that Thucydides might have invented the orders to explain it.

[36] Cf. Kagan, *Archidamian War*, 171-2.

[37] It has been suggested that Aristophanes (*Ach.* 652-4) refers to peace proposals made in 426 but not mentioned in Thucydides; but this is improbable (Gomme, *HCT* ii.391; Kagan, *Archidamian War*, 82-3).

[38] iv.16.3-20; see esp. 17.4: 'you may keep what you now hold and gain honour and a good reputation besides'.

as well Sparta was prepared to continue discussions (iv.21–22.1).
Sparta was no doubt unwilling to concede all these Athenian demands;
but Corinth must have been alarmed that negotiation about Athenian tenure of Pagae in particular was not rejected outright. Sparta
showed herself willing to make concessions against the interests of
her allies, even beyond what Athens had already won during the war,
in order to secure peace for herself and the release of her citizens on
Sphacteria; she was merely unwilling to risk causing disaffection
among her allies by making concessions that would be unacceptable
to them without a guarantee that Sparta herself could have what she
wanted in return.[39] When the Spartans on Sphacteria were finally
captured there were further attempts to conclude peace; the terms
Sparta offered are not known, but they were presumably more
favourable to Athens than those that had been recently rejected
(iv.41.3–4).

The terms eventually agreed between Athens and Sparta in the
Peace of Nicias were even worse for Corinth; in the meantime she
had lost Anactorium. When a year's truce was signed in 423 to allow
negotiations for a more permanent peace (iv.117–19), Corinth was
not opposed to peace in principle, for she signed the truce (iv.119.2).
That may mean that by 423 she accepted that Athens could not be
chastised for her actions at Corcyra and Potidaea and was willing
to return to the pre-war situation; in 423 it was impossible to hope
for better terms. In the event, Sparta made no effort to achieve even
so much. Thucydides believed that disaffection among her allies was
one of the reasons which persuaded Sparta to make the Peace of
Nicias. The Thirty Years Peace between Sparta and Argos was to
expire in 420;[40] the Argives refused to renew it unless they received
Cynouria in return. Thucydides claims not only that the Spartans
thought themselves incapable of fighting Athens and Argos together,
but also that they suspected that some cities in the Peloponnese
might desert Sparta and go over to Argos (v.14.4). Corinth was
probably not among the cities whose loyalty to Sparta was suspect;
they will rather have been cities which had no quarrel of their own
with Athens, especially those of Arcadia and Elis.[41] Sparta had
been willing to ignore the wishes of Corinth, Boeotia, and Megara
to make peace from at least 425; when she began to fear that other

[39] iv.22.2–3. See Gomme, *HCT* iii.462. We cannot say what concessions Sparta might
have made; she may have intended to make none but wished to drag the negotiations out
in the hope that something might turn up to save the men on Sphacteria (cf. Kagan,
Archidamian War, 236).

[40] For the date, see most concisely Brunt, *Phoenix*, xix (1965), 277 n. 77.

[41] Ibid., 277.

members of her alliance might desert her if she did not make peace, she had no hesitation in doing so.

Sparta's selfish attitude was emphasized by one clause in particular of the Peace of Nicias: Sparta and Athens together, acting alone, might alter the text of the treaty.[42] In detail, it was agreed that Athens and Sparta should hand back what they had captured from each other during the war; but many of the places Athens had taken from Sparta's allies were not mentioned in the treaty, and indeed Sparta went so far as to promise the return to Athens of Panactum, for the capture of which Boeotians alone were responsible (v.3.5). Corinth, since she had never been able to take anything from Athens, could not be subjected by Sparta to such an insult; but she was expected to accept the loss of Sollium and Anactorium. On these grounds in particular, according to Thucydides, she rejected the settlement.[43] Boeotia, Elis, and Megara did the same. It is difficult to see what arguments Sparta can have used when she tried for a second time to persuade the four allies to accept the terms. When this pressure proved without effect Sparta determined to protect herself against the anger of her erstwhile allies by concluding a defensive alliance with Athens; that doubtless only increased the allies' concern (v.22-4).

[42] v.18.11. Gomme (*HCT* iii.677) aptly compares the final words of the Spartan speech asking for peace during the Pylos affair: 'for it is evident that when your city and ours are in agreement, the rest of Greece, which is weaker than us, will honour us for our strength' (iv.20.4). See in general Gomme, *HCT* iii.677-8, 695.

[43] v.30.2. Thucydides implies that there were other points on which Corinth thought she had short measure from Sparta; but he does not specify what they were, and we cannot guess.

XXIII.   Corinth and Sparta:
From Conflict to Victory

When the Peace of Nicias was signed Corinth set about exploiting the opportunity presented by the imminent expiry of the Thirty Years Peace between Sparta and Argos. The Corinthian ambassadors who had been to Sparta to discuss the Peace of Nicias and the alliance between Sparta and Athens did not return home at once; they went instead to Argos, where they made informal contact with 'some of those in authority'. They complained about the Peace and the Spartan alliance with Athens, and urged Argos to 'consider how the Peloponnese might be saved' and invite cities to join a defensive alliance to that end (v.27.2). When the Corinthians returned home, their Argive contacts made a formal proposal before the Argive assembly, and the alliance was put into effect;[1] the first states to join were the Mantineans and their allies (v.29.1).

Thucydides reports that many Peloponnesian states began to move in a similar direction (v.29.2-4). Sparta recognized Corinth's responsibility and sent ambassadors to Corinth to prevent her from joining. To do so, they argued, would be to break the oaths Corinth had sworn as a member of the Peloponnesian League; Corinth was already in the wrong for having refused to be bound by the League decision in favour of the Peace of Nicias (v.30.1). In reply, the Corinthians did not mention their real reason for rejecting the Peace—the failure of Sparta to secure the return of Sollium and Anactorium—but argued that to accept it would be to break the oaths they had sworn to their allies in Thrace when Potidaea rebelled; as to the alliance with Argos, they had not yet taken a decision (v.30.2-4). Shortly afterwards an embassy from Elis arrived at Corinth to make an alliance and went on to join the Argive coalition (v.31.1-5); at once Corinth did the same, along with the Chalcidians of Thrace (v.31.6).

Boeotia and Megara had also voted against the Peace of Nicias; but they did not join the Argives (loc. cit.). Approaches were made by Argos and Corinth to Tegea; but she rejected them, on the ground that she did not wish to act against Sparta (v.32.3-4). Corinth, in fear that momentum might be lost, approached Boeotia; but the

---

[1] v.28.1; the Argive motives, v.28.2.

negotiations failed (v.32.5-7). As the summer of 421 wore on, suspicion between Athens and Sparta grew, as neither side was able or willing to make the restorations stipulated in the Peace (v.35.2-8). At the beginning of winter a new board of ephors took office at Sparta; at least two of them were opposed to the Peace (v.36.1). They made private contact with Boeotian and Corinthian ambassadors who were in Sparta, and urged them to arrange for Boeotia to join Argos; the whole coalition could then approach Sparta (v.36.1-2). The Argives were naturally eager for at least the first step in this scheme; but full information was not given to the Councils of Boeotia, and nothing came of the attempt, although a separate alliance was subsequently arranged between Sparta and Boeotia.[2] At about this time the Corinthians refused to join Argos, Elis, and Mantinea in making 'their alliance offensive as well as defensive.[3] A defensive treaty (the Quadruple Alliance) was made in the following summer between Athens, Argos, Elis, and Mantinea (v.43-7); but Corinth did not take part. According to Thucydides, she 'turned towards the Spartans again';[4] when Argos and her allies tried again to gain the adherence of Corinth, their overtures were rejected (v.50.5).

Thucydides gives few indications of Corinthian motives in these complicated diplomatic transactions. It has been argued that Corinth followed a 'totally negative policy designed solely to diminish Sparta';[5] but it is unlikely that Corinth had no positive aims, even though her methods may have been sadly misdirected. Corinthian hatred for Athens remained undiminished: now that the Spartans had made peace, Corinth tried in two ways to resuscitate the war. First, the expiry of the Thirty Years Peace between Argos and Sparta led her to hope for a new anti-Athenian alliance led by Argos; thus Corinth asked Argos to 'consider how the Peloponnese might be saved'. It is superficially plausible that Corinth wanted Argos to save the Peloponnese from the threat of an active alliance between Sparta and Athens; Thucydides has the Corinthians argue at Argos that Sparta had signed the Peace of Nicias and the alliance with Athens 'not for the good of the Peloponnese, but to enslave it' (v.27.2), and he reports fears in the Peloponnesian cities that Sparta might enslave them with Athenian help (v.29.3). But it is

---

[2] v.37-8. We should not accept the view of Plutarch (*Alc*. 14.5) and perhaps Diodorus (xii.77.3), against Thucydides, that Sparta made a separate alliance not only with Boeotia (Thuc. v.39) but also with Corinth (cf. Andrewes in Gomme, *HCT* iv.52).

[3] v.48.2: the date is not given accurately.

[4] v.48.2-3; cf. Diod. xii.77.3.

[5] Seager, *CQ* xxvi (1976), 254.

most unlikely that Corinth genuinely entertained such a fear: her concern was that Athens might enslave her with Spartan conniv-ance.[6] Other states, especially Mantinea (v.29.1; cf. 33) and Elis (v.31.1–5; cf. 34.1, 49–50), had strong grounds to fear Spartan aggression; but Corinth merely objected to Sparta's decision to make peace with Athens, and the Corinthian oligarchs—unlike the demo-crats of Mantinea and Elis[7] —had no reason to fear Spartan interven-tion in their internal affairs. None the less, the unpopularity of Sparta gave Corinth a powerful argument: when the plan was first suggested to the Argives great play was made with the anti-Spartan element in it, and the Corinthians claimed that 'many cities would join out of hatred for Sparta' (v.27.2). But for the Corinthians this was a matter of mere propaganda; they had no difference with Sparta except over policy towards Athens.

For many members of the coalition, however, hostility to Sparta was far more than the mere facade it was for Corinth; this seriously reduced the chances of Corinthian success. Argos, Elis, and Mantinea all hated or feared the Spartans; but none had much reason to quarrel with Athens. They might be persuaded to join together by means of anti-Spartan propaganda; but it would be a far greater task to direct the energies of the alliance towards war with Athens.[8] Moreover, the anti-Spartan tone of the Corinthian propaganda was a serious impediment to other important states which shared Corinth's hostility to Athens: they hesitated to break with Sparta. Boeotia and Megara calculated that it was wiser to try to change Sparta's policy from within her alliance. Boeotia rejected the initial Corinthian request to join the Argive coalition (v.32.6); the later plans of the Spartan ephors were disturbed by the refusal of the Councils of Boeotia to conclude a defensive alliance with Corinth, precisely because the Councils were unwilling to join a city that was in rebellion against Sparta (v.38.1–3). Tegea rejected the over-tures of Corinth and Argos for similar reasons (v.32.4).

The democratic nature of the Argive constitution created further problems for the Corinthian scheme. The natural sympathy between democratic states would make it difficult to persuade Argos, Mantinea, and Elis to fight Athens (cf. esp. v.44.1). The same coin had another side: Thucydides writes, 'The Boeotians and the

---

[6] Cf. Westlake, *AJP* lxi (1940), 414–16; Kagan, *AJP* lxxxi (1960), 296–7; Seager, *CQ* xxvi (1976), 254. Contrast Griffith, *Historia*, i (1950), 236–7.

[7] Mantinea: v.29.1. Elis: Andrewes in Gomme, *HCT* iv.60–1.

[8] For Argos, cf. esp. v.40.2. As for Elis, she had voted against the Peace of Nicias (v.17.2), but her reason was probably fear of Sparta rather than hostility towards Athens; cf. Brunt, *Phoenix*, xix (1965), 277; Seager, *CQ* xxvi (1976), 250.

Megarians . . . thought that the Argive democracy was less congenial
to them, oligarchically governed as they were, than the Spartan
constitution.'[9] At Corinth the oligarchs were in such firm control
that they had no need to concern themselves with the internal
implications of their foreign-policy decisions;[10] but in Boeotia and
Megara they had to take seriously the possibility that Argos might
give support to their democrats.[11] The Corinthians may have had
a plan for meeting this difficulty. The arrangements for the coalition,
suggested by Corinth, had a strongly oligarchic character: negotiations
for membership were to be conducted in secret, and twelve Argives
were chosen with full powers to admit or reject any state save
Athens or Sparta (v.27.2–28.1). It has been argued that these were
concessions made by Argive democrats to the sensitivities of oligarchic Corinthians;[12] but the purpose was probably rather to aid
Argive oligarchs. They might expect significant benefits from the
prestige they would gain from the creation of a coalition with Argos
at its head. There must be a strong suspicion that the unidentified
'Argives in a position of authority' approached informally by the
Corinthians were precisely the oligarchs, and that the Corinthians
caused them to hope that the success of the coalition might create
conditions for an oligarchic revolution.[13] Certain Argives, probably
these very oligarchs, were already in touch with Corinth in 425
(above, 319).

None the less, the obstacles in the way of the Corinthian scheme
were large. It was perhaps unrealistic to hope even for an oligarchic
revolution in Argos; the whole scheme was even less plausible. The
Corinthians were probably misled into an over-optimistic plan by
the coincidence that the expiry of the Thirty Years Peace between
Sparta and Argos brought a new potential ally on to the international
scene just as they felt a need for one. It would have been more

[9] v.31.6. A similar motive may have been involved at Tegea, though Thucydides does not
mention it; cf. Griffith, *Historia*, i (1950), 238. There was a party in Tegea in favour of
joining Argos (v.62.2; 64.1); it was presumably a democratic one under an oligarchic regime.
[10] Cf. Griffith, *Historia*, i (1950), 239. I am not persuaded by Kagan's attempt, based on
no evidence, to distinguish between 'oligarchic' and 'aristocratic' parties at Corinth in this
period; see further below, 405.
[11] Athens had tried to use the help of democrats in both Megara (iv.66–74) and Boeotia
(iv.76.2–5) in the recent past; in Megara the oligarchic regime was of very recent origin
(iv.74.2–4).
[12] Griffith, *Historia*, i (1950), 237–8. Kagan, *AJP* lxxxi (1960), 294–6, argues that
secrecy was important for the Corinthian ambassadors because they were of an 'oligarchic'
party in Corinth which was uncertain of its ability to persuade 'aristocratic' Corinthians
to join them in an alliance with Argos; but see above, n. 10.
[13] Compare the Corinthian plans for Corcyra: above, 312–5. If Corinth hoped to secure
an oligarchic revolution at Argos that will answer the objections raised by Seager, *CQ* xxvi
(1976), 254, esp. n. 43.

328 Corinth and Sparta: From Conflict to Victory

realistic to work for an arrangement with Boeotia and Megara; a defensive alliance between Corinth, Boeotia, Megara, and the Chalcidians of Thrace would have been concluded had it not been for the reluctance of the Councils of Boeotia to make an alliance with Corinth after she had rebelled against Sparta.[14]

A second possible Corinthian aim—not incompatible with that of persuading Argos to lead an anti-Athenian coalition—was to frighten Sparta into changing her policy towards Athens.[15] Even though Corinth had taken the first steps towards the Argive coalition herself, her own signature (v.31.6) came some time after the foundation of the alliance (v.28–29.1), perhaps because Corinth wished to give the Spartans the chance to alter their stance before she committed herself. When Sparta sent to Corinth to complain of her responsibility for the Argive alliance and to try to prevent her from joining it, the Corinthians arranged for the discussions to take place in the presence of representatives from those allies who had joined Corinth in rejecting the Peace of Nicias (v.30.1). The intention was presumably to put pressure on the Spartans; but they took the wind from the Corinthian sail by protesting that to join Argos would be to break the oaths which Corinth had sworn when she joined the Pelopon-nesian League. Thucydides' use of the word προεῖπον (they suggested *in public*) when Corinthians advised Argive ambassadors to come to the next meeting of the Corinthian assembly (v.30.5) may imply that he thought they were playing for time. If Corinth was not committed to the Argive alliance from the start, she can be partially absolved of the charge that her policy was unrealistic; but she must be condemned at the same time for short-sightedness. Tension arose between Sparta and Athens over the implementation of the terms of the Peace of Nicias; but by that time the energy of the Corinthians in vituperating Sparta had borne such fruit that Sparta faced too many enemies to give attention to the Athenians.

The grandiose plans of the Corinthians did far more than merely fail: they positively hindered the creation of an effective anti-Athenian alliance. Corinth did not, of course, generate alone the turmoil in the Peloponnese which followed the Peace of Nicias: Sparta's own treatment of Mantinea and Elis played an important role, Athens—especially Alcibiades—stirred the pot vigorously, and the Argives might have acted much as they did without Corinthian encouragement. But Corinthian responsibility for the opportunities

---

[14] v.38.1–3. The Boeotian attitude to Corinth cannot be tested, since no approach was made until Corinth had already deserted Sparta; but Boeotia was, at least, willing to offer Corinth diplomatic support at Athens (v.32.5–7).

[15] Cf. Kagan, *AJP* lxxxi (1960), 297–8.

exploited by Alcibiades was heavy, and Corinthian policy was so double-edged that it might be thought to have been nicely calculated to achieve precisely the opposite of what was intended.[16] Too late, Corinth recognized something of her mistake: when she was urged by Argos, Elis, and Mantinea to strengthen the original defensive alliance and make it offensive she declined. Corinth's attempt to conclude the limited alliance with Boeotia, Megara, and the Chalcidians of Thrace was probably a further sign of her repentance; but even this relatively simple matter foundered, precisely because of Corinth's earlier machinations.[17] In the longer run, her wild plots helped to encourage such hostility to the Spartans that they had no opportunity, however willing they may have been, to concern themselves with Corinth's grievances against Athens.

After her brief and foolish flirtation with Argos, Corinth settled down to play, in the land warfare generated by the Quadruple Alliance, the same insignificant role that she had played in the last years of the Archidamian War; Thucydides rarely thinks her part worth mention. A special Corinthian interest was involved when Alcibiades persuaded Patrae to build long walls to defend their approach to the sea, and attempted to build a fort near Achaean Rhium, at the entrance to the Corinthian Gulf; Corinth, along with Sicyon and other interested states, prevented his success at Rhium, though they could do nothing at Patrae (v.52.2). An Argive attack on Epidaurus was devised by Alcibiades and the Argives, according to Thucydides, 'partly in order to keep Corinth quiet' (v.53); and the Corinthian concern for Epidaurus is demonstrated by Thucydides' report of a demand made by the Corinthian Euphamidas, at a general conference at Mantinea, that the forces before Epidaurus should be withdrawn before genuine discussion was possible (v.55.1). Corinth had been equally concerned about this region at the time of the outbreak of the First Peloponnesian War, again just after an alliance between Athens and

[16] Cf. Seager, *CQ* xxvi (1976), 254.

[17] This aspect of the plan of the two ephors was perfectly plausible, even if the whole plot was little more realistic than Corinth's earlier schemes (cf. Andrewes in Gomme, *HCT* iv.41). Kagan (*AJP* lxxxi (1960), 302-5) argues that Corinth did not wish the ephors' plan to succeed, on the grounds that the Spartans would be unlikely to make war on Athens if they enjoyed peace with Argos; he suggests that the alliance between the Isthmian states, Boeotia, and the Chalcidians was proposed by the Corinthians because they knew that it would meet opposition in Boeotia and prevent further progress. But Sparta was *more* likely to fight Athens if she could achieve an accommodation with Argos: Thucydides believed that the fear of Argos induced by the impending expiry of the Thirty Years Peace was a major factor in the Spartan acceptance of the Peace of Nicias. It is perverse to suggest that Corinth was insincere in proposing the alliance—if the initiative came from her, as Kagan assumes without justification; in itself it had much to recommend it (cf. Seager, *CQ* xxvi (1976), 257-8).

Argos,[18] but the precise reason for her interest is obscure. The Corinthian interest in this area was probably not merely a sentimental tie with Epidaurus; but Thucydides gives no explanation on either occasion, and conjecture is difficult.[19] After many false alarms (v.54.1-2; 55.3) the Spartans garrisoned Epidaurus, surprisingly enough by sea, presumably from Cenchreae and therefore in Corinthian vessels (v.56.1). In 418 Sparta invaded the Argolid along with her allies, among whom the Corinthians gave an adequate account of themselves in preliminary skirmishing before Agis, the Spartan commander, and two Argives negotiated a truce, much to the annoyance of their troops (v.57-60). It is difficult to say whether the Corinthians, fresh from their Argive alliance, were among those allies of Sparta who bitterly condemned Agis for giving up a splendid opportunity to crush the Argives (v.60.2-4). Corinth took no part in the subsequent Mantinea campaign, in which Sparta with a few Arcadian allies defeated the forces of all the states of the Quadruple Alliance but Elis (v.62); but the failure of Corinth to participate was not due to any lack of enthusiasm, for she had been given short notice of the campaign and had great difficulty in crossing hostile territory to the rendezvous at Mantinea.[20]

After Mantinea, affairs in the Peloponnese began to settle again (cf. esp. v.75.3): Sparta and Argos made a Fifty Years Peace (v.76-9), the Argives required the Athenians to evacuate the position from which they threatened Epidaurus (v.80.3), and Mantinea reached an agreement with Sparta.[21] But conflict was prolonged by internal struggles in Argos and by Spartan support for the Argive oligarchs. In both winter 417/16 and winter 416/15 Sparta mounted invasions of the Argolid with all her allies except, Thucydides remarks on each occasion, the Corinthians (v.83.1-2; vi.7.1). The reason for Corinth's refusal can only be the subject of conjecture. Probably Corinth believed that the Mantinea campaign and the subsequent treaty with democratic Argos had settled Peloponnesian affairs sufficiently to enable Sparta to resume vigorously the offensive war against Athens; she therefore resented diversions in support of Argive oligarchs.[22]

[18] Above, 263. The attack on Epidaurus made by Pericles in 430 may also have been intended to put pressure on Corinth; but Thucydides says nothing of Corinth here (ii. 56.1-4).
[19] Andrewes in Gomme, *HCT* iv.72-3. Seager (*CQ* xxvi (1976), 263, cf. 265) perhaps exaggerates Corinth's importance.
[20] v.64.4; 75.2. Cf. Seager, *CQ* xxvi (1976), 267-8.
[21] v.81.1. Cf. also Xen. *Hell.* v.2.2, and Andrewes in Gomme, *HCT* iv.148.
[22] It may be significant that the absence of Corinthians in later Spartan invasions of the Argolid is not recorded (vi.95.1; 105.1); by this stage the Spartans had decided to take stronger action against Athens. Kagan, *AJP* lxxxi (1960), 309, argues that the Corinthians positively wished the expeditions of 417/16 and 416/15 to fail, since Sparta would be less

The Peace of Nicias and the alliance between Sparta and Athens had been in practice void since the Quadruple Alliance; but Sparta herself took no offensive action. Even when the Athenian garrison at Pylos took extensive plunder from their territory in 416, the Spartan reaction was merely to 'announce that any of their allies who wished might plunder the Athenians' (v.115.2). This was doubtless too feeble for the belligerent Corinthians, but they responded as best they could on their own: 'The Corinthians made war on Athens because of certain private grievances; but the other Peloponnesians remained quiet' (v.115.3). Corinth had remained technically in a state of war with Athens since 421.[23] Thucydides' words, if taken literally, imply that Corinth now, for the first time since 421, attacked Athens in some way. He says that they went to war (ἐπολέμησαν),[24] while the Spartan announcement merely allowed plunder (λῄζεσθαι). The distinction may be oversubtle; if more than mere raids on Athenian shipping was involved there is no way of telling the nature of the action. Nor can the 'private grievances' be identified;[25] but Corinth's desire for war with Athens was as intense as ever. Her allies—Sparta included—were both less enthusiastic and more cautious.

Athens herself gave Corinth the opportunity to stir her allies: in 415 she launched the Sicilian Expedition.[26] There is little sign in Thucydides that the expedition was intended to give extra weight to Athens for use in mainland Greece; the conquest of Sicily was seen as an end in itself.[27] However that may be, success in Sicily

---

likely to fight Athens if there was a pro-Spartan faction in control of Argos. In general, Kagan makes too much of Corinthian fears of an arrangement between Sparta and Argos (see above, n. 17); it could have been predicted that an accommodation between the two states would have been one result of success for the Spartan invasion of the Argolid in 418, for which Corinth sent 2,000 troops.

[23] Cf. v.32.7: 'Corinth had an informal (literally 'without the swearing of oaths') truce with Athens.' The Athenians claimed that Corinth was included in the Peace of Nicias as a Spartan ally (v.32.6), but this argument was of doubtful validity. The Peace included provision for the exchange of oaths not only between Athens and Sparta, but also between Athens and Sparta's allies (v.18.9–10); no such exchange had taken place between Athens and Corinth.

[24] Cf. vi.10.3, with Dover in Gomme, *HCT* iv.232.

[25] On all this, see Andrewes in Gomme, *HCT* iv.188.

[26] The Athenian motives, vi.1.1; 24.2–3; compare iii.86.4, iv.65.3 (similar motives for the expedition of 427). See Dover in Gomme, *HCT* iv.229–30.

[27] Contrast the expedition of 427, where part of the motive was to prevent the shipment of corn from Sicily to the Peloponnese (iii.86.4). The advantages over Sparta that might be gained in Sicily are conspicuously absent from Thucydides' account of the debate; Alcibiades does refer to them briefly (vi.18.4), but they are given no prominence. In his speech at Sparta, Alcibiades is made to emphasize Athens' intention of exploiting the anticipated conquest of Sicily in her struggle against Sparta (vi.90.2–4); that was natural, since he was trying to persuade Sparta to intervene.

would certainly have enhanced Athens' prospects in the mainland; and the alarm this gave rise to in Corinth can only have been increased by the ties she enjoyed with Syracuse. Some sources (though not Thucydides) report that the Corinthians had a hand in the mutilation of the Hermae which caused such consternation at Athens before the expedition sailed;[28] but it is very doubtful whether the allegations were true.[29] Even if Corinthians were implicated, their role can only have been minor.

Corinth readily complied when the Syracusans asked for support at Sparta in their request for renewal of the war in mainland Greece.[30] When Alcibiades, now in flight after accusations of impiety, added his (possibly not very great) weight to that of Corinth and Syracuse, the Spartans acceded to all the requests. They decided to invade Attica and fortify Decelea (although the decision was not actually carried out for a year) and sent Gylippus to co-ordinate the defence of Syracuse.[31] He asked the Corinthians to arrange for two ships to go at once to Asine,[32] and for others to make ready at Corinth (vi.93.3).

The two Corinthian ships were joined by two Spartan; Gylippus next turns up in Thucydides at Leucas with two Spartan and ten Corinthian ships, eight of the latter presumably having arrived direct from Corinth.[33] The total is small compared with fleets provided by Corinth at other times, doubtless because a long campaign was in prospect. When Gylippus was at Leucas he heard false reports that Syracuse had been successfully invested and gave up hope of saving Sicily; but he crossed quickly to Taras with two Spartan and two Corinthian vessels and the Corinthian Pythen, to try to save Italy.

---

[28] Plut. *Alc.* 18.7; Cratippus *FGH* 64 F 3; Philochorus *FGH* 328 F 133; cf. the confused entry of Photius, s.v. Ἑρμοκοπίδαι.

[29] Andoc. i.61 proves a significant interval between the decision to mutilate the Herms and its implementation; that demonstrates that the affair was not mere drunken vandalism (cf. Dover in Gomme, *HCT* iv.284-6) but had some (presumably political) purpose (Macdowell, *Andokides on the Mysteries*, 192). This makes room for a Corinthian role; but convincing explanations based on internal Athenian considerations can be offered (e.g. Macdowell, ibid. 192-3; Hatzfeld, *Alcibiade*, 186-9), and modern commentators have rightly doubted whether Corinthians were involved, especially on the ground that Thucydides says nothing of the allegations: (e.g. Macdowell, ibid., 192-3; Jacoby, *FGH* III b i, 506 with n. 15 = III b ii. 408-9). An accusation of Corinthian complicity was almost inevitable.

[30] vi.73.2, cf. 34.3; vi.88.7-8.

[31] vi.88.9-93.2; vii.18-19.2. It is doubtful whether Thucydides' emphasis on the importance of Alcibiades is justified (cf. Brunt, *REG* lxv (1952), 59-96, esp. 71).

[32] Despite Dover in Gomme, *HCT* iv.367, there is no means of telling whether this was Asine in Messenia or the place of the same name mentioned by Strabo 363 as being near Gytheium.

[33] The ten Corinthian ships of vi.104.1 *include* the two which went with Pythen under Gylippus ahead of the rest; cf. Dover in Gomme, *HCT* iv.376. There seems to have been no Athenian fleet at Naupactus (Dover in Gomme, *HCT* iv.393).

Three Ambraciot and two Leucadian ships were to be manned and to follow him with the eight Corinthian ships he left behind (vi.104). On discovering that all was not yet lost at Syracuse he beached his ships at Himera and set out for the city by land (vii.1); but the first Peloponnesian to arrive in Syracuse was the Corinthian Gongylus, who had been the last to set out but had overtaken the others (vii.2.1). He arrived just in time. The Syracusans were about to discuss how to end the war, but he encouraged them with the news that more ships were on their way and that Gylippus had been sent to help them (vii.2.1). The Syracusans sent a force to meet Gylippus (vii.2.2-3), and shortly afterwards the twelve remaining vessels from Leucas arrived under Erasinides;[34] but by that time Gylippus had already succeeded in pushing the Syracusan counter-wall beyond the line of the Athenian fortification (vii.6), though the crews of the vessels did help to complete it (vii.7.1).

After the arrival of Gongylus and Gylippus almost everything fell to the advantage of Syracuse. Corinth and Sparta were asked for reinforcements, and Thucydides remarks on the confidence of the Corinthians as they and the Spartans prepared to send extra hoplites in merchant vessels (vii.17.3). Sparta made active preparations for an invasion of Attica (vii.18). Corinthian confidence had often been misplaced before; but this time her action was more effective. Twenty-five vessels were made ready to offer battle to the Athenian fleet of twenty at Naupactus and to protect the merchant vessels which carried the reinforcements for Sicily;[35] in spring 413 the reinforcements—including the Corinthian contribution of 500 hoplites, partly Corinthian and partly Arcadian mercenaries—evaded the Athenians at Naupactus (vii.19) and eventually reached Syracuse.[36]

The Corinthian plan was well laid. The transports for Sicily, in order not to be sighted by the Athenians at Naupactus, sailed from Pheia in Elis;[37] the war fleet stationed itself, with Corinthian and other land forces in support, well inside the Gulf at Erineus,[38] in a position to threaten Naupactus from the east if the Athenians tried to intercept the transports in the west.[39] More significantly, the same Corinthian squadron, with a few reinforcements (vii.34.1), gave

[34] vii.7.1 (v. l. Thrasonides).
[35] vii.17.4; the Athenian fleet, vii.17.2.
[36] vii.50.1-2; cf. Polyaen. *Strat.* vi.23.
[37] Cf. vii.31.1: a Corinthian transport destroyed by Demosthenes at Pheia. Presumably the Corinthian and Sicyonian forces went by land to Pheia, picking up Arcadian mercenaries *en route*, and there met the force that had set out from Taenarum (vii.19.3-4).
[38] vii.34.1-2. This was the position of the forces for the sea battle that took place shortly afterwards; we may assume that they had been there for some time.
[39] Cf. Dover in Gomme, *HCT* iv.414.

a good account of itself under Polyanthes (vii.34.2) shortly afterwards against a slightly larger Athenian fleet of thirty-three based
on Naupactus. Conon did not think his eighteen vessels sufficient
to meet the Corinthians, and he secured ten more from Demosthenes
and Eurymedon as they passed on their way to Sicily (vii.31.4-5); his
judgement was vindicated when his successor Diphilus, who had
brought reinforcements from Athens, offered battle, for the result
was inconclusive (vii.34). The contrast with Phormio's achievement
in 429 is plain. Part of the reason was probably that many of the
Athenian ships and their crews were inferior; the best had doubtless
been sent to Sicily,[40] although the ten left by Demosthenes and
Eurymedon were of high quality (vii.31.5). More significantly, the
Corinthians had devised a technical improvement which was to be
used to great effect at Syracuse: seven Athenian vessels were disabled by being rammed head-on by the Corinthians, who had
strengthened their prows for precisely this purpose (vii.34.5). The
immediate results of the battle were unimportant: three Corinthian
vessels were lost, and although the Corinthians disabled seven of their
opponents' the Athenians regained possession of them because the
wind took them out to sea; no prisoners were taken on either side
(vii.34.6). But the battle demonstrated the success of the Corinthian
technical advance and the ability of the crews to make use of it—
despite Thucydides' sneer that 'the Corinthians thought it a victory
not to be thoroughly defeated, and the Athenians thought it a
defeat not to be thoroughly victorious' (vii.34.7).

Meanwhile Nicias fortified Plemmyrium in order to facilitate the
delivery of supplies to the Athenian forces before Syracuse (vii.4.4-
6); but in the following year the fortifications were lost, and Thucydides attributes the beginning of Athenian decay to this (vii.21-4).
A Corinthian, whom the Syracusans sent among others for help
from other parts of Sicily (vii.25.9), brought 1,500 troops to
Syracuse after considerable losses in a Sicel ambush (vii.32). The
Syracusans won a victory at sea in the Great Harbour. First—presumably on Corinthian advice—the technique employed by the Corinthians in the Gulf was used to establish an approximate equality
between the two fleets (vii.36-39.2); then victory was accomplished
by a trick devised by Ariston, 'a Corinthian, and the best steersman
serving in the Syracusan fleet'.[41] After a second day's inconclusive

[40] Cf. ibid., 411.
[41] vii.39.2; cf. Polyaen. *Strat.* v.13.2. At *Strat.* v.32.1, however, a similar trick is credited
to the Corinthian Telesinicus (deviser of victory). Ariston is also credited, almost inevitably,
by Plutarch (*Nic.* 25.4) and Diodorus (xiii.10.2) with the improvements to Corinthian prows
already used near Naupactus.

battle he enabled the Syracusans to take their meal quickly and to drive the unfed and unprepared enemy to the shore. Seven Athenian ships were sunk and many others disabled; only two Syracusan vessels which had pursued too eagerly were lost (vii.39.2-41). Demosthenes' arrival with large reinforcements brought momentary hope to the Athenians, but he failed to capture Epipolae and advised withdrawal; Nicias demurred despite the support of Eurymedon for Demosthenes (vii.42-9). After two further naval battles, in the second of which the Corinthian vessels under Pythen were disposed in the centre (vii.70.1), the Athenians tried to retreat by land, but suffered almost total destruction (vii.50-87). Nicias himself surrendered to Gylippus, in the hope that his life might be spared; but his hopes were unfulfilled, partly because 'others, especially the Corinthians, were afraid that he might bribe somebody, for he was wealthy, and escape to do them some further harm; so after persuading their allies to agree they put him to death' (vii.86.4).

Corinth was prominently involved in Peloponnesian efforts on behalf of Syracuse; but her role was scarcely decisive. The bulk of the forces used in the defence were either Syracusan or at least Sicilian. A few ships came from Corinth, and there were some Peloponnesian troops, but these are not likely to have altered the balance of forces significantly; in a quantitative sense the victory was almost exclusively Syracusan. The main Corinthian contribution was less tangible: encouragement and technical expertise; the effects of these factors were of varying strength. It was after representations from Corinth that Sparta sent help to Syracuse, and Gylippus' leadership was a major factor in the final victory; but Corinth had been joined by Syracuse and Alcibiades in begging Sparta to act, and in any case Sparta probably needed little persuasion beyond that provided by the events themselves. The first help to reach Syracuse was brought by the Corinthian Gongylus, who was just in time to prevent a Syracusan capitulation; but Gylippus was already very close. More important was Corinthian technical advice. Thucydides emphasizes the strengthening of their prows as a factor in the Syracusan success. This practice had been developed at Corinth and was first used by Corinthian vessels in the battle in the Gulf;[42] and the first Syracusan sea victory was gained through the advice of the Corinthian Ariston. The effect of these Corinthian contributions was to prevent a successful Athenian withdrawal at a time when the capture of Syracuse was already out of the question. Corinth's

---

[42] Cf. Morrison and Williams, *Greek Oared Ships, 900-322 B.C.*, 229; Dover in Gomme, *HCT* iv.415.

achievement was therefore most significant in precisely that sphere
which had the greatest long-term effect: by enabling the Syracusans
to annihilate the Athenian force, Corinth contributed to an alteration
of the balance of power in mainland Greece which made the final
Athenian defeat possible.

Corinth's part in the last phase of the Peloponnesian War is difficult
to assess; our sources rarely specify contributions made by individual
allies of Sparta. The decisive factor was the naval conflict in the
Aegean; but Corinthian action is recorded in one other sphere and
may be guessed at in another. In 410, Corinthian forces (with some
help from Boeotia) were besieging the Athenian fort at Oenoe in
retaliation for the destruction of a group of Corinthians on their
return from Decelea by the garrison of the fort; when the regime
of the 400 fell at Athens Aristarchus fled to Oenoe and secured the
surrender of the Athenians to the Boeotians before what had
happened in the city became known (viii.98.2-4). Diodorus reports
stasis at Corcyra in 410/9 in which an oligarchic plan to hand over
the city to Sparta was thwarted, with much bloodshed, by the
democrats with the help of an Athenian force under Conon (Diod.
xiii.48). The Corcyraean oligarchs might have been urged on by
Corinth, as they were in 427; but Diodorus does not tell us so.
Both these episodes, if Corinth was involved in the second, were
Corinthian offensives. Athenian attacks on Corinth in particular
are hardly to be expected at this stage; but Athens held Naupactus
until the end,[43] and may have maintained a small fleet there to
harass Peloponnesian shipping at the entrance to the Gulf.[44]

Corinth's part in the remainder of the war was mainly to provide
vessels to serve in the Aegean under Spartan command; the first
action demonstrated that Sparta's main naval ally was unable to
meet what was required. After the Athenian defeat in Sicily, various
plans for the prosecution of the war were proposed to the Spartans;
but it was finally decided to send the fleet from the Isthmus in two
halves, one after the other, to the Aegean to help rebellions of
Athenian allies. Twenty-one vessels crossed the Isthmus by way of
the diolkos.[45] Most of them were probably Corinthian, for the naval
construction which resulted from Spartan requisitions in the previous

---

[43] The Messenians were finally expelled in 399: Diod. xiv.34.2.

[44] Conon took 600 Messenians from Naupactus to Corcyra in 410/9, and presumably
came from Naupactus himself, where his fleet will have been based: Diod. xiii.48.6.

[45] This may have been the occasion for improvements at its western end which are
archaeologically dated *c.*400 (Verdelis, *Praktika*, 1960, 136-43). Repairs at one other
point on its course were made at a similar date (Verdelis, *Praktika*, 1962, 48-50), perhaps
after Spartan sabotage during the Corinthian War (below, 363); the improvements at the
Corinthian-Gulf end may, but need not, have been undertaken for similar reasons.

winter (below, 338) had presumably not yet borne fruit. At Corinthian insistence, they did not sail from Cenchreae until the Isthmian Games were over. That enabled the Athenians, who had been invited to the Games, to make counter-plans (Thuc. viii. 7–10.1). Initially, the Peloponnesians 'held the powerlessness of the Athenians in contempt, for there was no evidence that they had anything much for a navy' (viii.8.4); but when they sailed from Cenchreae they would not be drawn on to the open sea to face an equal number of Athenian and Chiot vessels. The Athenians withdrew, but returned with thirty-seven ships and followed the Peloponnesians as they sailed along the coast of the Corinthia; after destroying one of the enemy vessels, the Athenians drove the rest into Speiraeum, now the Bay of Korphos (Pl. 9). The Peloponnesians came to anchor in the Bay; but they were attacked and driven ashore: most of the vessels were disabled and the Spartan commander Alcamenes lost his life.[46] The Athenians suffered little loss themselves, and even landed on the coast; after leaving enough ships to maintain an effective blockade, they withdrew and camped on a nearby island (viii.10.2–11.1).

Corinthian land forces arrived to help on the day after the battle, but they found no comfort in the situation. 'They did not know what to do. They saw the difficulty of garrisoning such a remote place, and first considered burning the ships; but they then decided to drag them on to the shore and leave their land force there to guard them until some useful means of escape should present itself' (viii. 11.2). The Spartans were horrified when they heard the news: 'they no longer thought of sending ships out, but rather of recalling some of those which had already been sent' (viii.11.3). Alcibiades, however, persuaded them to send him with Chalcideus and a small force, and he procured the revolt of Chios. The Athenians reduced the blockading force at Speiraeum to twenty, in order to send a fleet into the Aegean (viii.12–5); and eventually the twenty Peloponnesian vessels broke out, captured four enemy ships, and returned to Cenchreae (viii.20.1).

These events made it clear that Corinth was quite incapable of posing a significant threat to Athens on her own. In his account of the action at Speiraeum Thucydides does not mention the technical improvements which had helped the Corinthians in the previous year in the Corinthian Gulf and at Syracuse; the Athenians may by now have found an answer to them. The Peloponnesian failure at Speiraeum may have been partly a matter of over-confidence, and in

---

[46] Korphos is the only bay in the south-eastern Corinthia with room for an action of this kind; see further above, 5–6.

the end they inflicted more losses than they suffered; but although
the immediate Spartan reaction to the initial defeat was too pessimistic, the whole episode demonstrated that it was necessary to
work for naval domination—and that Corinthian resources were
quite unequal to the task. Corinth rapidly lost her primacy in the
naval affairs of the Spartan alliance: during the Ionian War the
proportion of Corinthian vessels was far smaller than it had been
before.

The size of Corinth's quota is not to be gauged by the fact that
she was only asked to provide fifteen out of the hundred vessels
requisitioned by Sparta in winter 413/12 (viii.3.2); what is in question
here is the building of new ships, and the fifteen from Corinth were
additional to what she already possessed.[47] Just under thirty vessels
had survived the battle in the Gulf in 413, and of the fifteen which
returned to Corinth from Sicily in 412 (viii.13) at least eight were
Corinthian.[48] If Corinth built the fifteen ships she was asked for in
413/12, she will have had about fifty at her disposal; but it is unlikely that Corinth and her Adriatic colonies provided even a third
of the Peloponnesian fleets, much less the half that they had contributed in the Archidamian War. Of the fleet of ninety-four which
stayed at Rhodes for eighty days in 411 (viii.44.2, 4), sixty had some
origin other than Corinthian, and it is improbable that more than
two-thirds of the remaining thirty-four came from Corinth or her
Adriatic colonies. Perhaps less than a quarter of the whole fleet came
from Corinth; probably Sparta herself contributed more vessels than
her greatest naval ally of the Archidamian War.[49] If anything, the
proportion of Corinthian contingents will have diminished towards
the end of the Ionian War. Details cannot be traced from the meagre
information given by Xenophon and Diodorus; but as the Peloponnesian fleet increased in size, so the proportion of Corinthian vessels
in it must have decreased. Corinth will hardly have been able to
provide crews for anything like a quarter of the large fleets of the
last years of the war—even if the pay was provided by the Persians.[50]

[47] Contrast de Ste Croix, 344; Kagan, *PP* xvi (1961), 336; Lewis, *Sparta and Persia*, 88;
Morrison and Williams, *Greek Oared Ships, 900–322 B.C.*, 230.

[48] Seventeen had gone to Sicily: ten Corinthian, two Spartan, and five from Leucas and
Ambracia manned by Corinthians (above, 332–3). One was lost at Syracuse, for only sixteen
set out on the return journey (viii.13); a second was lost on the way back (ibid.). Even if
both losses were Corinthian there were still eight left.

[49] Of the vessels at Rhodes, twenty-two were from Sicily: viii.26.1; one from Megara, one
from Hermione, and three (?) from Sparta: viii.33.1, cf. 31.1; six from Sicily, Italy, or
Sparta: viii.35.1–3; twenty-seven from Sparta: viii.39.1.

[50] Callicratidas had 140 vessels in 406 (Xen. *Hell.* i.6.3; Diod. xiii.76.3), and 170 later in
the year (Xen. *Hell.* i.6.16). No source gives a figure for the fleet at Aegospotami, but
Lysander had over 200 shortly afterwards (Diod. xiii.107.2).

Corinthian losses are recorded at Cynossema (Thuc. viii.106.3) and
Aegospotami (Xen. *Hell.* ii.1.31). Two Corinthians were among the
many commanders whose portraits stood in the group which commemorated Aegospotami at Delphi; Leucas and Ambracia were also
represented.[51]

We have a brief record of apparently independent action by the
Corinthian Timolaus in 411. He 'plundered many islands under
Athenian control with a fleet of five ships', and 'sailed with two
triremes to Amphipolis, manned four ships locally, and defeated
the Athenian strategos Simichus in a sea battle . . . ; he captured five
enemy triremes and the thirty vessels they were escorting. After
this, with . . . ships, he sailed to Thasos and made it revolt from
Athens.'[52] A Corinthian may have been chosen for this action
because of the close relationship Corinth had enjoyed with the
Chalcidians of Thrace since the revolt of Potidaea (cf. esp. v.30.2;
31.6; 38.1).

The reduction in the proportion of Corinthian vessels no doubt
caused a decline in Corinth's importance among Sparta's allies, but
it can scarcely be used to demonstrate a slackening of Corinthian
enthusiasm for the war; it resulted rather from increased contributions
by Sparta and her other allies than from a reduction in the number
of Corinthian ships. It can nevertheless be argued that Corinth and
Sparta had serious differences towards the end of the war. Corinthian hostility to Sparta can be documented as early as 403, when she
refused to supply a contingent for Pausanias' campaign in Attica.
The reason for Corinthian suspicion of Sparta was that she did not
wish the Spartans to use Athens for their own purposes (below,
344-5); similar considerations were relevant as early as 412. During
the Ionian War Corinth twice acted in ways which might indicate
some reluctance to serve. In 412 a Peloponnesian fleet was being
prepared to help the rebellion of Chios; Corinth delayed its departure
by refusing to sail until the Isthmian Games were over (viii.7-9.2).
In the following winter an attempt at revolt by Lesbos failed miserably
(viii.22-23.5); the Spartan commander Astyochus wished to support
a second attempt, but 'the Corinthians and the other allies were
unenthusiastic because of the previous failure', and no help was
given (viii.32.1).

There were strong grounds for Corinth to revise her policy towards
Athens in 412. Her hatred had its origin in the Corcyra affair, and

---

[51] Paus. x.9.7-10; Meiggs and Lewis, *GHI*, no. 95.
[52] *Hell. Oxy.* 7.4; cf. Thuc. viii.64.2-4. See Meiggs, *Athenian Empire*, 574-7. *IG* xii.
8.402 is presumably a funerary inscription for two of the Corinthians who fought under
Timolaus.

during the Archidamian War her influence in north-west Greece was further diminished. But after the defeat of the Sicilian Expedition, Athens would have been more than happy to withdraw from the west in return for a free hand in the Aegean. Corinth could in principle return to the policy of coexistence with Athens she had pursued after the Thirty Years Peace. It would have been sound to do so. To continue the war until Athens was broken meant to take her empire; but that was to entrust it to Sparta, and events since 431 had given Corinth ample grounds for fearing what the Spartans might do with it. If Corinth did think in this way, that would explain the delays she made in the naval campaign in 412. No contrary argument is afforded by the Corinthian demand for the destruction of Athens in 404. If Corinth wanted an arrangement with Athens in 412, her reason was that she feared Sparta; in 404 that same fear made the total destruction of Athens preferable to her surrender to Sparta to use for her own purposes.

Sparta showed after 404 that such a policy would have been wise; but Corinth was probably not so clear-sighted so soon. The only signs that she may have been less than whole-hearted in her support of Sparta are the two delays of 412; and they can both be explained by the immediate circumstances. There may have been a genuine religious concern behind the first: the Isthmian Games were doubtless especially important for Corinth. Equally, rational calculation may have persuaded not only Corinth but also the other allies that Astyochus' plan to help Lesbos was inadvisable. We have no further evidence of procrastination. Corinth maintained a squadron in the Peloponnesian fleet until the end of the war; if she had serious reservations we might have expected her not to serve. Immediately after the defeat in Sicily, at least, Sparta had no doubt about Corinth's loyalty: hostages taken from various central Greek states were placed by Agis for safe keeping at Corinth (viii.3.1); but any difference Corinth may have had with Sparta may not have been apparent so early. It is impossible to prove that Corinth had no serious differ-ence with Sparta before 404; but we should perhaps have expected more evidence of divergence had it existed. More importantly (since this is an argument from silence), Corinth was probably unable, in the very moment when revenge upon Athens at last became possible, coolly to calculate her response to the new situation. For twenty years her policy towards Athens had been determined not by reason but by passion. It would have been logical to revise her attitude; but for twenty years she had acted in defiance of logic. When she could hope for the destruction of Athens she would hardly have paused to consider the consequences. Even a less impulsive state might now have been forgiven for pursuing her hatred of Athens to the end; Corinth would not stand back and think out her policy afresh.

Nevertheless, serious differences arose in 404. When Athens was defeated, 'Corinth and Thebes in particular, but also many others of the Greeks, spoke against coming to an agreement with Athens and advocated her destruction';[53] but Sparta argued that Athens had performed great services for Greece in the past, and she was allowed to survive (Xen. *Hell*. ii.2.20). It is difficult to believe that Sparta's professed reason for saving Athens was the real one: Lysander intended to exploit an Athens which he could now control.[54] It is less easy to determine the motives of Boeotia and Corinth. In 403 Sparta called out her League forces ·to support the oligarchic faction at Athens; Corinth and Thebes refused to serve because they wanted to deny Sparta her own way in Athens (below, 344–5). The same motive has been suggested for 404: they wished to wipe Athens out and prevent Sparta from exploiting her as a puppet state.[55] There is no evidence to disprove such a view; but Corinth, at least, was probably motivated by nothing but hatred of Athens. If Corinth did not look beyond the end of her vengeful nose in 412, she will have been no more far-sighted after suffering eight more years of difficult warfare—especially as Sparta had given no serious sign in the meantime that she would use her victory against the interests of Corinth. The activity of Lysander in the Aegean was a dangerous pointer to the future; but Corinthians were probably unable to read the signs. They will rather have rejoiced at the removal of the democratic regimes which had been such a major factor in Athenian control. The Corinthians would have been well advised to try to prevent Sparta from exploiting too selfishly the fruits of her victory; but their recent record of short-sightedness makes it most unlikely that they did so.

[53] Xen. *Hell*. ii.2.19. Isocrates (xiv.31) suggests that Thebes was alone in demanding that Athens be destroyed; this tendentious remark cannot stand against the clear statement of Xenophon.

[54] Cf. de Ste Croix, 343; I see no reason to accept the complicated account of Lysander's attitude in Hamilton, *Sparta's Bitter Victories*, 49–54.

[55] De Ste Croix, 343.

XXIV.   Corinth and Sparta:
From Victory to Conflict

a.   The Origins of the Corinthian War

Ten years after Sparta's victory in 404, she found herself fighting
against Corinth, Argos, Athens, and Boeotia in the Corinthian War;
tension between Sparta and Corinth had been evident as soon as
the defeat of Athens was achieved. Corinth, along with other Spartan
allies, wished Athens to be destroyed, but Sparta ensured her survival
(above, 341). Corinth was among the states which ignored the
Spartan demand that all refugees from the Athenian regime of the
Thirty be given up: Aeschines (ii.148; cf. 78) claims that his parents
spent their exile at this time in Corinth.[1] In 403 Pausanias led a
Spartan army into Attica, at the request of the Athenian oligarchs;
Corinth and Boeotia both refused to march with him (Xen. *Hell.*
ii.4.29-30). Shortly afterwards the Spartans mounted an expedition
against Elis; again Boeotia and Corinth failed to join them.[2] When
Thibron went in 399 to defend the freedom of the Greek cities of
Asia Minor against the Persians, it is uncertain whether Corinth was
represented in his forces. Xenophon (*Hell.* iii.2.25) merely identifies
his allies as Peloponnesians, but Diodorus (xiv.36.2), although he is
silent about the origins of Thibron's troops, states that he summoned
them to meet him at Corinth and that he set sail from there. That
does not necessarily imply that Corinth sent forces with him or that
her vessels were used for transport; her refusal to help at Athens, at
Elis, and later under Agesilaus in Asia makes Corinthian aid to
Thibron improbable. But there is no reason to deny that Thibron
collected his forces at Corinth; that was convenient for his purpose,
and Sparta may have chosen Corinth with the specific intention of
putting pressure on the city to join the expedition. If so, the attempt
was probably unsuccessful. In 396 Agesilaus sailed for Asia to
continue the campaign; Corinth declined to send forces with him
(Paus. iii.9.1-2). Pausanias claims that the Corinthians were eager to
go, but did not do so because they considered the recent burning of
their temple of Olympian Zeus to be an omen; this need not be taken

---

[1] For the Spartan order and the reaction of other states, see Diod. xiv.6.1-3; Xen. *Hell.*
ii.4.1; Lys. xii.17.

[2] Xen. *Hell.* iii.2.25; Diod. xiv.17.7.

Fig. 18   Central Greece and the North-East Peloponnese

seriously as an indication of Corinth's true motive, but it shows that she was not yet prepared to resist Sparta's demands without a plausible reason. No doubt similar excuses were found for Corinth's rejection of Sparta's other recent requests.

Agesilaus was unable to pursue his campaign in Asia for long. Timocrates the Rhodian offered Persian gold to leading men in the major Greek cities to make war on Sparta; two Corinthians were among the recipients,[3] and before long Agesilaus had to be recalled because war had broken out in Greece. It was provoked by a faction in Boeotia: they persuaded some Phocians to invade territory in dispute between Phocis and Locris; Locris asked Boeotia for help,

---

[3] *Hell. Oxy.* 7.2–5 (I cite Bartoletti's numeration throughout); Xen. *Hell.* iii.5.1; Paus. iii.9.8. The chronology is uncertain: between 397 and spring 395; see Bruce, *Commentary*, 58–9, 66–72.

and the Boeotians invaded Phocis after rejecting a Spartan demand that they desist.[4] The Spartans sent Lysander to march with their allies from central Greece to Haliartus in Boeotia, where he was to meet with a Peloponnesian force under Pausanias; meanwhile the Boeotians gained an alliance with Athens. Before the two Spartan armies could join hands Lysander was killed before the walls of Haliartus; and Pausanias was forced to conclude a truce under which he withdrew from Boeotia.[5] Corinth had not yet taken positive steps to oppose Sparta, although she had refused to join Pausanias (Xen. *Hell.* iii.5.17,23); but soon after Haliartus she committed herself: Boeotia, Athens, Corinth, and Argos made an alliance.[6] It was not a declaration of war on Sparta, for it was defensive in form (below, 348–9); hostilities followed in the next year.

Corinth's attitude to Sparta progressed from disagreement over the settlement with Athens, through discontent demonstrated by the failure to supply contingents for Spartan campaigns, to a conditional declaration of war. Apparently Corinth did not fight in order to right a particular wrong of her own; at least our sources preserve no record of Spartan action taken directly against Corinth, although she may perhaps have resented the activity at Naupactus as an interference in her own sphere.[7]

The Boeotian conflict with Phocis had nothing to interest Corinth; her willingness to go to war must have depended on other consider-ations. Four specific suggestions are made by our sources. Xenophon states, with respect to the Corinthian refusal to march with Pausanias in 403, that Corinth and Thebes 'said that they believed that they would be breaking their oaths if they marched against the Athenians, who had done nothing contrary to the treaty; but in fact they took their action because they recognized that the Spartans wished to make Athens their own loyal possession' (*Hell.* ii.4.30). Justin records that after the Peloponnesian War Thebes and Corinth sent ambassadors to Sparta to demand a share of the booty, but that their claims were rejected (v.10.12–13).[8] Xenophon attributes the

---

[4] *Hell. Oxy.* 18; for other versions and discussion, cf. Bruce, *Commentary*, 118–22 (but see below, 347 n. 19).

[5] Xen. *Hell.* iii.5.4–24; Diod. xiv.81.1–3; Plut. *Lys.* 28–9; Paus. iii.5.3–5, 9.10–11.

[6] Diod. xiv. 82.1; Andoc. iii.22.

[7] Diod. xiv.34.2. It might be possible to derive a Corinthian grievance from the anecdote in Plut. *Lys.* 22.5. But the details—Corinth revolts from Sparta and is besieged by a Spartan force under Lysander—are so much at variance with what we know of Corinthian relation-ships with Sparta during Lysander's lifetime that Corinth may appear in the text only as a result of corruption. In any event, there must be serious confusion in the report.

[8] There is a trace of a similar complaint in the speech given to the Thebans at Athens in 395 by Xenophon: *Hell.* iii.5.12.

war to the bribery of Timocrates;⁹ and finally, the Oxyrhynchus
Historian (P) argues against this facile interpretation and points out
that the men who received the money had long been seeking war:
those in Argos and Boeotia 'hated the Spartans because they supported their political opponents', those at Athens wanted the
opportunities for enrichment that the war would provide (*Hell. Oxy.*
7.2), while at Corinth 'those who wished to change the present state
of affairs were all hostile to the Spartans in the same way as the
Boeotians and the Argives, but for Timolaus, who was an enemy of
theirs for private reasons'.¹⁰ To these more specific assertions may
be added the general cause of the war adduced by Diodorus (xiv.
82.2) who ultimately relies on P: 'for because the Spartans were
hated by their allies as a result of the heavy nature of their control,
(the allies) thought that it would be easy to overthrow their supremacy if the greatest cities were to agree together.'

None of these reasons convinces except the last; and it would be
helpful to have more flesh for Diodorus' bones.¹¹ The first is plausible
as a reason for the refusal to join Pausanias—to which Xenophon
restricts it—but it can have no importance after 403. When the
request was made, Sparta was ostensibly responding to a plea for
help from Athenian oligarchs against democrats under Thrasybulus:
Corinth and Boeotia might well turn it down on exactly the grounds
offered by Xenophon. But Pausanias' settlement gave the democrats
control of the city, against Lysander's wishes; there was no reason
for Corinth or Boeotia to object to such a moderate arrangement¹²
—except perhaps because it gained in Athens a willing ally for Sparta.
Justin's story need not be doubted, and resentment of Sparta's greed
may have been powerful; but it can have had little direct influence
on the Corinthian decision to go to war. P's explanation has the
merit of recognizing that a mere fifty talents in the palms of venal
politicians were insufficient to generate war unless there were strong
independent reasons to fight; but he does not attempt, in the preserved portion of his work, to give the arguments by which these
men persuaded their fellow citizens to fight Sparta. It was these

⁹ *Hell.* iii.5.1–2; iv.2.1; cf. Paus. iii.9.8.
¹⁰ *Hell. Oxy.* 7.3. The papyrus text is corrupt: I translate the conjecture of Grenfell and
Hunt. P compares the Corinthians who were hostile to Sparta with the Boeotians and the
Argives. The conjecture of Grenfell and Hunt, ⟨παραπλησίως⟩, makes the comparison refer
to the reasons for the enmity to Sparta; that of Castiglioni, ⟨πάλαι παραπλησίως⟩, makes it
concern the long-standing nature of the enmity as well.
¹¹ For recent discussions, with references, see Perlman, *CQ* xiv (1964), 64–81 (but see
below, 347 n. 17); Hamilton, *Sparta's Bitter Victories*, 99–208.
¹² Cf. de Ste Croix, 343; Hamilton, *Sparta's Bitter Victories*, 85–6. The latter's reconstruction of Spartan factions, however, goes far beyond the evidence.

arguments—rather than the possibly personal motives of those who took the money—which really counted.[13]

The two Corinthians who received the bribes of Timocrates both gave valuable service to Sparta in the Peloponnesian War. In the case of Timolaus, P notes the change in his attitude: 'he was an enemy of (the Spartans) for private reasons, although before he had been very well disposed towards them and an enthusiastic Laconizer' (*Hell. Oxy.* 7.3). The nature of the private grievance cannot be recovered and is unimportant: if it was private, it concerned none but Timolaus. Polyanthes, too, had served well: he commanded the Corinthian fleet in the Gulf which enabled Syracuse to be reinforced in 413 (above, 334). The Spartan refusal to share the proceeds of victory will have seemed especially irksome to those Corinthians who had given loyal service during the war. Not only was Corinth denied these more tangible rewards of victory. Sparta's refusal to destroy Athens prevented satisfaction of the powerful emotional need which had driven Corinth for thirty years; and even a rational calculation of the balance sheet of the war showed that Corinth lost far more by it than she won: her only gain was the doubtful comfort of being on the winning side. It is hardly surprising, even if it was not entirely logical, that Corinth's frustration at the result of the Peloponnesian War turned to hatred and resentment of Sparta. Once Sparta had saved Athens there was little that she could have done to retain Corinth's goodwill; but her astoundingly selfish attitude to the spoils of war might have been nicely calculated to increase the ill feeling that would have developed even without it.

Passion, as often before, played a significant role in Corinth's policy; but hatred and resentment are far from being a sufficient cause for war. They will adequately account for Corinth's refusal to fulfill her obligations as a member of the Peloponnesian League; but they cannot on their own have been responsible for the decision to fight. Such decisions are not always—perhaps not often—based on a careful consideration of possible gains; but we should seek a more compelling reason than mere hatred. The most obvious is that adduced by Diodorus: the Spartan behaviour after 404, which made Corinth fear for her own safety. This is adduced by Xenophon to explain the Corinthian refusal to accompany Pausanias in 403; Pausanias' settlement may have calmed such fears, but subsequent Spartan activity was more then enough to arouse them again. Elis had much of her territory removed.[14] Corinth will not have feared such action against

[13] Cf. Andrewes, *Phoenix*, xxv (1971), 223-4, for a concise statement of this argument with respect to Boeotia.
[14] Xen. *Hell.* iii.2.21-31; Diod. xiv.17.4-7; Paus. iii.8.3-5.

herself, for she had no similar perioecis; but the attack was a clear indication of what Sparta was capable of. She had also attempted to extend her control in northern and central Greece, although the details here are far from certain.[15] Moreover, Spartan activity in the east gave cause for alarm. During the final phase of the Peloponnesian War Sparta undertook to allow Persia control of the Greek cities of Asia Minor in return for help against Athens; but when she was called upon to honour the agreement she sent Thibron, Dercyllidas, and finally Agesilaus to defend the freedom of the cities against the King. It is perhaps unfair to suppose that the Spartan motives were entirely selfish;[16] but it is easy to imagine the effect on an already resentful Corinth of the prospect of success for Sparta when she had already demonstrated her determination to dominate the Peloponnese and to extend her influence north of the Isthmus. No doubt Corinth declined to join these expeditions partly because of a general unwillingness to serve Sparta; but her decision will have been reinfórced by fear of the consequences of Spartan success: namely, a stranglehold on the Aegean and Asia Minor equal to that enjoyed by Athens at her most powerful.[17] Corinth was not, as far as we can tell, directly threatened by Sparta; in this she was perhaps alone among the four allies. But the potential threat was felt so strongly that Corinth went to war without direct provocation.[18]

Corinth's attitude to Sparta can be traced through various stages. Until Agesilaus left for Asia, she merely rejected Spartan demands, both for troops and for the surrender of refugees from Athens. But when Timocrates reached Greece he must have judged that there was sufficient feeling at Corinth against Sparta to make it worth spending the King's gold there. When Ismenias and his party provoked the quarrel which led to war,[19] P (18.1) asserts that he relied on help from Athens, Corinth, and Argos as well as on Persian money; if that is not hindsight Ismenias, with far more at stake than Timocrates, made the same judgement that Corinth was ready to fight. He was mistaken. When Sparta invaded Boeotia the Corinthians did not join Pausanias; but they did not help Boeotia either:

---

[15] Cf. Andrewes, *Phoenix*, xxv (1971), 217–26; Hamilton, *Sparta's Bitter Victories*, 120–1.

[16] Cf. Lewis, *Sparta and Persia*, 108–43.

[17] Perlman, *CQ* xiv (1964), 64–81, properly emphasizes the importance for all Sparta's opponents of the offensive against Persia; but he undervalues other factors.

[18] Bruce, *Commentary*, 117–18.

[19] Bruce (*Emerita*, xxviii (1960), 80–6) argues that Ismenias and his friends did not deliberately provoke war. I am not persuaded, but even if he is right it makes little difference to my argument: Ismenias relied on support from Corinth whether he provoked war or accepted it when it was threatened.

she made an alliance with Athens, but otherwise had to face the Spartans alone. There must have been enough hostility to Sparta at Corinth to give Ismenias cause for hope; but the Corinthians were not sufficiently confident actually to fight until there was a reasonable prospect of success. It is not possible to be sure of the event which tipped the scale. It might have been the Boeotian alliance with Athens, which ensured a powerful coalition if Corinth were to join; if so, there will not have been time to negotiate an agreement between Boeotia and Corinth before Haliartus. Alternatively, Haliartus itself, in association with the Athenian alliance, may have been needed before Corinth could be finally persuaded.[20]

The Corinthian decision to fight can thus be explained without adducing internal political struggles; it remains to assess the validity of P's version, in which such considerations seem to have played a decisive role.[21] Other factors must have been mainly responsible for the war in the sense that they were the basis for the decision of the majority of those who voted for it; but the motives of those who led the agitation are by no means insignificant. It would be natural, especially in a context of debate over the attitude to be taken to Sparta, for the Spartans to support their friends;[22] their opponents will have seen this as a threat to their own position, and in some cases this motive may have become dominant. With respect to Corinth, P's account has almost always been taken to refer to democrats who hated Sparta for her intervention on behalf of their oligarchic opponents;[23] this would make his assertion more specific (though perhaps curiously vague in expression) and increase the importance of this factor. But I argue below (355–7) that there was no democratic faction of any significance at Corinth.

The establishment of the anti-Spartan alliance can be reconstructed from Diodorus: 'the Boeotians and the Athenians, and in addition the Corinthians and the Argives, made an alliance . . . And they first set up a common council at Corinth' (xiv.82.2–3). The alliance between Boeotia and Athens is preserved,[24] and was

---

[20] I take it that Boeotia attempted to gain an alliance with Corinth at the same time as she approached Athens, and that the reason for the initial failure was not mere lack of time. There was room for successful negotiation between Boeotia and Athens; other signs that Boeotia had ample warning are noted by Bruce, *Commentary*, 120.

[21] Above, 345. It is to be noted that P's preserved account is incomplete: *Hell. Oxy.* 7.5 (προαιρημέναις) proves that Corinth and Argos (the cities referred to) were at least mentioned before, and they may have been more fully discussed there.

[22] Bruce, *Emerita*, xxviii (1960), 79–80.

[23] Cf. esp. Griffith, *Historia*, i (1950), 238–41; Kagan, *Historia*, xi (1962), 447–53; Hamilton, *Sparta's Bitter Victories*, 262–8. Contrast Perlman, *CQ* xiv (1964), 69–70.

[24] Tod, ii, no. 101; Staatsverträge, ii, no. 223.

concluded first, before Haliartus (above, 344). It has been argued that the rest of Diodorus' sentence also reflects the chronological order of alliances: that Corinth joined first and then Argos;[25] I should hesitate to trust Diodorus on such matters, but the order is scarcely important. A subsequent alliance between Athens and East or West Locris is preserved;[26] in its preamble it is stated that the terms are the same as those of an already existing alliance between Athens and Corinth.[27] The alliances with Boeotia and Locris are closely comparable with each other: they take the regular form of defensive alliance. That with Corinth must have been of the same kind, and thus each of the four states seems to have concluded a bilateral treaty with each of the others.[28] Diodorus further shows that they went on to make arrangements for a council, but their nature is unknown.

The council sent ambassadors throughout Greece to gain adherents.[29] Diodorus lists the whole of Euboea, Leucas, Acarnania, Ambracia, and the Chalcidians of Thrace (loc. cit.). Both the Locrides and Malis may be added from Xenophon's list of states which sent troops in the following year to the Nemea (*Hell.* iv.2.17), and Megara probably joined too.[30] Corinth presumably secured the adherence of Leucas and Ambracia, and perhaps also that of the Chalcidians of Thrace: Timolaus will have made good use of the connections he established in Thrace during the Peloponnesian War (above, 339). All efforts to persuade the Peloponnesian allies of Sparta to join, however, were fruitless (Diod. xiv.82.4). The allies gained some successes in central Greece before the campaigning season of 395 ended,[31] in the particular interest of Boeotia; but only the Argives and the Boeotians, of the four major powers in the coalition, were militarily involved (Diod. xiv. 82.5-9).

---

[25] Accame, *Ricerche*, 54-5; apparently followed by Perlman, *CQ* xiv (1964), 68-9 n. 13.

[26] Tod, ii, no. 102; Staatsverträge, ii, no. 224.

[27] And, perhaps, either the Boeotians or the Argives: the space on the stone fits either exactly. The Boeotians may have been mentioned earlier in the preamble, and the Argives at the same point as the Corinthians; cf. critical note in Tod, ii, ad loc.

[28] Accame, *Ricerche*, 55.

[29] It is not known whether these adherents were represented at the council; Accame, *Ricerche*, 55-6, argues on insufficient grounds that they were not.

[30] Ibid., 61-2. Megara ignored the demand of Sparta that all Athenian fugitives from the Thirty be given up (Xen. *Hell.* ii.4.1; Lys. xii.17), and Plato suggests that Megara would be a suitable place for Theaetetus to rest after having been wounded at the Nemea (*Theaet.* 142 C); Agesilaus' later campaign in the Peiraeum is better understood if Megara was not a Spartan ally (below, 365 with n. 97).

[31] On the chronology, cf. Accame, *Ricerche*, 57.

350   *Corinth and Sparta: From Victory to Conflict*

The form of the alliances on which the coalition was based was defensive, and in theory the purpose of its members was to protect themselves against Spartan aggression; but they could hardly achieve that by remaining quiet: Sparta would have to be intimidated into a less aggressive stance.[32] In spring 394 they gathered at Corinth,[33] and the battle of the Nemea was eventually fought close by; but the strategy of the campaign is unclear. The nature of the war might have led either side to take the offensive; but the late date—early July—of the battle of the Nemea makes it likely that neither actually did so.[34] Some time after Haliartus, Sparta recalled Agesilaus from Asia Minor (Xen. *Hell.* iv.2.2), but according to Xenophon the Spartans also mobilized for an immediate campaign in Greece (*Hell.* iv.2.1-2). This is not impossible; but to reject Xenophon's assertion makes better sense of the campaign. If Sparta intended to take the offensive in Greece, her army should have marched well before early July; but there were good reasons to postpone an encounter. It was doubtful whether Spartan forces were adequate without Agesilaus; and the young Agesipolis now occupied the throne after the exile of his father Pausanias.[35] There was every encouragement to wait for Agesilaus: when he returned, the allies' position at the Isthmus could be threatened by a joint attack from north and south; and an immediate offensive was a serious risk when there was no experienced commander to hand. It is to be noted that Sparta failed to take advantage of the victory at the Nemea (below, 353): had the purpose of the campaign been offensive, some attempt would probably have been made to exploit the success more effectively.

The actions of the allies are also better explained if the Spartans hoped to delay matters. Xenophon records that the ephors mobilized the Spartan forces and placed them under the command of Aristodemus, Agesipolis' guardian; afterwards the Corinthian Timolaus—who had wide experience of Spartan military affairs, as his advice indicates—persuaded the allies that since Spartan forces were like a river, which grows in strength as tributaries of allies are added to it, the best course was to 'burn out the wasps in their nest', and fight in Spartan territory, or at least as close to it as possible.[36] But

[32] Cf. Hamilton, *Sparta's Bitter Victories*, 212-13.
[33] Diod. xiv.82.10; Xen. *Hell.* iv.2.10 does not specify where they convened.
[34] For the date of the battle, cf. Accame, *Ricerche*, 65. His calculation should not be disturbed by Tod, ii, no. 105, the stele of Dexileos, an Athenian cavalryman who died 'at Corinth' in the archon year 394/3; he died either some time after being wounded at the Nemea or in a different, subsequent action.
[35] Xen. *Hell.* iii.5.25; Paus. iii.5.6-7; Diod. xiv.89.1; Plut. *Lys.* 30.1.
[36] Xen. *Hell.* iv.2.10-13; Accame, *Ricerche*, 80-2, rejects this, on quite inadequate grounds: (i) that invasion of Laconia is inconceivable before Epaminondas' invasions after

disagreements in the allied camp wasted time, and in the end the battle was fought close to Corinth (Xen. *Hell*. iv.2.14-15). We should certainly have expected Timolaus' admirable suggestion to be put into effect earlier than July; but if Sparta tried to postpone serious conflict everything falls in place. The allies expected Sparta to march in the spring: they therefore secured the Isthmus. But as the weeks wore on it became clear that Sparta was waiting for Agesilaus; the danger for the allies of staying where they were was patent. They therefore decided to attack Laconia at once. There was some delay in putting the decision into effect—enough to give rise to Xenophon's account at *Hell*. iv.2.13. It was probably only now that the Spartan army was called out; but the allies had allowed time for their invasion to be forestalled, and they got no further than Nemea (Xen. *Hell*. iv.2.14). There can be no doubt about how the allied intention was divulged: there was a significant pro-Spartan party in Corinth (below, 354-62).

Aristodemus marched rapidly, picking up troops at Tegea and Mantinea (Xen. *Hell*. iv.2.13). According to a probable emendation of the text of Xenophon he took the route from Mantinea to Sicyon through Alea.[37] Since the obvious way for the allies was through Nemea,[38] his intention seems to have been not to dispute their passage but to draw them back to defend the Isthmus (see Fig. 18). He marched from Sicyonian into Corinthian territory; but the allies returned from Nemea along the river of that name, and their light-armed troops forced the Spartans to continue their work of devastation further towards the sea, out of range of missiles from the heights above the plain. The main force of allies retired towards Corinth and encamped on the east bank of the steep-sided Longopotamos; the Spartans made their camp some ten stadia to the west.[39]

There was some delay before the battle took place. It was in the Spartan interest to wait: they had prevented the invasion of Laconia, they could both live off the rich land of the enemy and destroy what they had no need of, and all the while Agesilaus was approaching. For much the same reasons the allies had to fight soon; there was also a pro-Spartan faction in Corinth which could only gain strength if the allies failed to engage. They had already taken up a strong

Leuctra (as if successes are only conceivable after their achievement); (ii) that an attack on Laconia is ruled out by the late date of the battle of the Nemea (see below). The decision of the allies to march on Sparta can only be rejected if we also reject Xenophon's statement that they reached Nemea (*Hell*. iv.2.14): if their intention was to hold the Isthmus there was no point in advancing so far south.

[37] Loc. cit.; cf. Pritchett, *Studies in Ancient Greek Topography*, ii.79-80.
[38] Ibid., 76-7.
[39] Xen. *Hell*. iv.2.14-15; Pritchett, ibid., 77-83 with esp. pl. 51.

defensive position in order to protect Corinth itself; that achieved—at least in the short run—they were forced to abandon their advantage.[40] They crossed the river-bed and attacked. The Spartans were not aware of the advance until they heard the enemy Paean, because their vision was obstructed by what grew in the area—no doubt much higher than corn; none the less, they had ample time to prepare for battle (Xen. *Hell.* iv.2.18-19).

The precise number of troops engaged cannot be determined, for our sources are defective;[41] but it was the largest yet seen in a battle of Greeks against Greeks. There were more than 20,000 hoplites on each side; the opposing forces must have been of approximately equal strength, though the Spartans were perhaps slightly outnumbered.[42] Corinth provided 3,000 for the allied force. The Boeotians, on the right wing, attacked at speed with their phalanx (as earlier at Delium and later at Leuctra) massed deeper than usual. Initially almost the whole allied front was victorious and set off in pursuit; but the Spartans extended their right wing, consisting of the Spartans themselves, well beyond the Athenians on the allied left, wheeled round their extended troops, and formed a second phalanx at right angles to the main line of battle which swept across the field and inflicted heavy casualities on the enemy as they returned in disorder from the pursuit. Diodorus reports 1,100 dead on the Spartan side and 2,800 on the allied, which seem reasonable figures (xiv.83.2); it is even possible that the eight strictly Spartan dead recorded by Xenophon is accurate.[43]

The defeated allies fled to Corinth; but Xenophon reports that they were 'shut out by the Corinthians, and camped again in their old camp' (*Hell.* iv.2.23). Demosthenes (xx.52-3) has more details of this remarkable episode: those in the city would not receive the fugitives and even entered into negotiations with the victorious Spartans. Demosthenes' claim that the Spartans 'controlled the corridor'—presumably that between the city and Lechaeum, defended by the Long Walls—is an exaggeration for his own rhetorical purposes, since the Corinthians in the city will have commanded the Long Walls along with the rest of the city's fortifications. But the claim serves to emphasize how disastrous would have been the strategic

---

[40] Thus it is unnecessary to invoke (with Pritchett, ibid., 83-4) topographical considerations to explain the Spartan failure to attack and the allied initiative.

[41] Xen. *Hell.* iv.2.16-17; Diod. xiv.82.10-83.1.

[42] Pritchett, *Studies in Ancient Greek Topography*, ii.73-4; Anderson, *Military Theory and Practice*, 143-4; Roy, *PP* xxvi (1971), 439-41; Hamilton, *Sparta's Bitter Victories*, 221.

[43] Xen. *Hell.* iv.3.1. For the details of the battle, ibid. iv.2.18-22, with especially Anderson, *Military Theory and Practice*, 144-50; also Pritchett, *Studies in Ancient Greek Topography*, ii. 83-4.

consequences for the allies if the Spartans had reached an agreement with the men who now controlled the city: neither the Athenian nor the Boeotian troops could have reached home without serious difficulty, for the Spartans would have commanded the Isthmus. But it did not come to that. The Corinthians who had fought at the Nemea had the gates opened, either in defiance of the original decision or after it had been rescinded; the defeated army entered the city—and no doubt secured the Long Walls for the allies. Certainly the pro-Spartan faction in Corinth was unable to control policy for long; a Corinthian contingent fought at Coronea little more than a month after the Nemea.[44]

Nemea brought negligible results, doubtless precisely because the victors had fought it for defensive purposes. The Spartan forces were dismissed, though a single Spartan *mora* crossed the Corinthian Gulf to fight with Agesilaus at Coronea;[45] the allies left the Isthmus to defend Boeotia against Agesilaus. At Coronea the Spartans remained masters of the field; but according to Diodorus (xiv.84.2) they lost some 350 men while accounting only for rather over 600 of the enemy. Agesilaus withdrew through Delphi across the Corinthian Gulf and so back to Sparta.[46]

Sparta had won two technical victories; but 394 ended with little advantage to either side. Agesilaus had returned to Sparta, but she launched no serious offensive in 393.[47] Desultory warfare continued near Corinth; but elsewhere the affairs of the allies improved. Not long before Coronea, Pharnabazus and Conon had inflicted a decisive defeat on the Spartan fleet at Cnidus;[48] in the following year they raided Laconia, garrisoned Cythera, and then conferred with the allies at Corinth.[49] After encouraging them to continue the war against Sparta and handing over all the money they had left, Pharnabazus returned to Asia while Conon went to help with the rebuilding of the walls at Athens.[50] The Corinthians put the money to good use. In 394 Agesilaus had returned from Coronea across the

[44] Xen. *Hell.* iv.3.15; Griffith, *Historia*, i (1950), 240 n. 16.

[45] Xen. *Hell.* iv.3.15; Plut. *Ages.* 17.2 gives two (without mentioning the half-*mora* Agesilaus took from the garrison at Orchomenus: Xen. loc. cit.), but Xenophon is more likely to be right on such a point, since he took part in the battle himself. Compare the vaguer report of Diodorus, xiv.84.1.

[46] Xen. *Hell.* iv.3.10–4.1; *Ages.* ii.6–16; Diod. xiv.84.1–2. Cf. Pritchett, *Studies in Ancient Greek Topography*, ii.85–95; Anderson, *Military Theory and Practice*, 150–3.

[47] Xen. *Hell.* iv.4.1. The chronology of the Corinthian War has been much disputed; cf. Ryder, 165–9. I follow his System II and add comments when necessary.

[48] Xen. *Hell.* iv.3.11–12; Diod. xiv.83.4–7.

[49] For all these developments, see Hamilton, *Sparta's Bitter Victories*, 227–32.

[50] Xen. *Hell.* iv.8.1–10; Diod. xiv.84.3–5; 85.2–3. That the reconstruction began before Conon's arrival seems to be proved by Tod, ii, no. 107 A; but cf. Pritchett, *The Greek State at War*, ii.120–1 n. 21.

Corinthian Gulf;[51] but now the Corinthians manned a fleet with their Persian money and appointed Agathinus to command it. A unique issue of gold coins was probably produced by the Corinthian mint from metal supplied by the King, and used to finance the operations of Agathinus.[52] He engaged the Spartans with some success, and established mastery of the Gulf, for Xenophon records the death of the Spartan commander Podanemus and the wounding of his second in command Pollis (*Hell*. iv.8.10-11). But the allies, like the Spartans, were unable to break the deadlock on land.

b.   Revolution at Corinth

Warfare in the Corinthia, even if inconclusive on the large scale, had serious effects at Corinth. The shutting of the gates of the city to the allies after the Nemea and the betrayal of the plan to invade Laconia demonstrate internal dissension at Corinth already in 394. Xenophon asserts that the 'majority and the best' of the Corinthians came to desire peace when they saw that they were suffering while their allies were able to cultivate their lands unhindered (*Hell*. iv.4.1). The trouble came to a head in spring 392 when a revolution was carried out by those Corinthians who favoured continuing the war, with help from their allies. They chose the last day of the festival of Artemis Eucleia,[53] because then—according to Xenophon—'they expected to find more people in the agora to kill'. They killed 'one man while he was standing with others, another while he was sitting, another in the theatre, another while he was sitting as a judge'—no doubt of a performance associated with the festival. Those who were able fled to the holy places of the agora, where they were none the less slaughtered, to the horror, Xenophon asserts, of right-minded Corinthians. 'Many of the older men were killed here', but a younger group, led by Pasimelus who 'suspected what would happen', was in the gymnasium at Craneion near the Cenchrean Gate.[54] They heard, both with their own ears and from fugitives, what was happening, withdrew up the slopes of Acrocorinth, and there beat off an attack by Argives who were helping the revolutionaries; but when they sacrificed after 'the capital had fallen off a (votive?) column even

---

[51] Xen. *Hell*. iv.4.1: ἀπέπλευσε. Cf. Accame, *Ricerche*, 96.

[52] Ravel, *NC*[5] xv (1935), 1-6; for the chronology, Kraay, *Archaic and Classical Greek Coins*, 86 n. 2.

[53] For the date, cf. Beloch, iii.2.219.

[54] Only the place Craneion is vouched for by Xen. *Hell*. iv.4.4; but a famous gymnasium was to be found there later in the fourth century, and it was probably here that these young βέλτιστοι were gathered: refs. and discussion in Wiseman, 86. It is impossible, with the evidence at our disposal, to locate Craneion exactly.

though there was neither earthquake nor wind', the omens favoured descent from their position. They left the city; but some returned under promise of amnesty from those now in control (Xen. *Hell.* iv.4.2–5). Diodorus, in a shorter, less vivid, and less indignant account (xiv.86.1–2), gives the number of dead as 120 and exiles as 500. It is legitimate to suspect Xenophon, whose sympathies were with the victims, of having exaggerated the horrors; but Diodorus confirms that the attack was made during a festival. The only other control we have is the fact of the amnesty, admitted by Xenophon and later put to good use by Pasimelus against those who had offered it; this gives further reason for somewhat toning down Xenophon's pious revulsion.

These events have often been discussed in recent years. The purpose was to remove the pro-Spartan faction from Corinth; but most have agreed that the massacre was followed at once by the introduction of democracy.[55] The direct evidence for this view consists of nothing more than an emendation of a corrupt passage in Diodorus. At xiv.86.1 the manuscripts all give Ἐν δὲ τῇ Κορίνθῳ τινὲς τῶν ἐπιθυμίᾳ κρατούντων συστραφέντες ἀγώνων ὄντων ἐν τῷ θεάτρῳ φόνον ἐποίησαν καὶ στάσεως ἐπλήρωσαν τὴν πόλιν. Wurm read δημοκρατίας ἐπιθυμούντων for ἐπιθυμίᾳ κρατούντων: 'In Corinth some (of those who were eager for democracy) gathered together while contests were taking place in the theatre, conducted a massacre, and filled the city with revolution.' This is a possible emendation; but it is hardly 'very probable'.[56] There is no sign in the rest of Diodorus' account that he regarded the revolution as democratic; and Wurm's conjecture is too far from the manuscript reading to be imposed by purely palaeo-graphical considerations. The indirect evidence which might support the introduction of democrats by emendation is weak. P describes the leaders of the anti-Spartan faction at Corinth as 'those who wished to change the state of affairs' (οἱ μεταστῆσαι τὰ πράγματα ζητοῦντες: *Hell. Oxy.* 7.3). This might mean that they were demo-crats;[57] but it need mean nothing more than that they wished to change the dependence of Corinth on Sparta. Xenophon, in describ-ing the programme of his Corinthian friends after the revolution, says that they wished to secure the return of *eunomia* (*Hell.* iv.4.6). The word has a strong oligarchic flavour; but it shows only that those who used it were oligarchs, not that they wished to overthrow a democracy. Other sources characterize the recipients of Timocrates'

---

[55] Cf., with references to earlier discussions, Kagan, *Historia*, xi (1962), 447–53; Griffith, *Historia*, i (1950), 239–41; Hamilton, *Sparta's Bitter Victories*, 261–8.

[56] Hamilton, *Sparta's Bitter Victories*, 267.

[57] Cf. Griffith, *Historia*, i (1950), 239.

gold in general as 'demagogues';[58] but this may merely reflect the
Athenian orientation of the sources: at least the Boeotians concerned
were probably not democrats.[59]

The revolution can easily be explained without invoking constitutional considerations.[60] The party of Timolaus and Polyanthes had
already suffered from opposition; the devastation of the Corinthia
in 393 must have strengthened that opposition, and there was little
prospect of decisive military action. Xenophon's description of the
pro-Spartans as a majority is presumably an exaggeration; but they
were by no means weak in 394, and they must have been stronger
by spring 392. There was every likelihood that more Corinthians
would come to favour peace; those who favoured war took the all
too obvious course. None of this provides an argument against a
democratic element; but the amnesty is not likely to have been
offered by democrats who were inevitably, given Corinth's history,
only precariously in power.[61] Moreover, if there had been a significant democratic movement at this time it cannot have been eradicated when the pro-Spartan exiles returned to Corinth after the
King's Peace; if they existed at all, Corinthian democrats were very
weak at a later date (below, 385). It cannot be quite excluded that
there was a democratic aspect to the revolution; but if it was present
at all, other factors were probably more significant. Certainly the
passage of Diodorus into which emendation has introduced democrats is better elucidated otherwise. The change of one letter, θύσι for
θυμι, will direct the sense quite differently. This conjecture is very
strongly encouraged by Xenophon's emphasis on the sacrilegious
nature of the revolution, which involved violence at a sacrifice
(θυσία), and Diodorus clearly refers to these events in the words
immediately after the corruption: 'they conducted a massacre while
contests were taking place in the theatre'. I lack the skill to suggest
a full emendation with confidence; but I am grateful to Dr Keith
Sidwell for suggesting to me a change in word order which demands
the alteration of no more letters in the manuscripts: τινὲς τῶν
κρατούντων ἐπὶ θυσίᾳ συστραφέντες: 'In Corinth some of those in power
gathered together at a sacrifice while contests were taking place in
the theatre, conducted a massacre, and filled the city with revolution.'
Once θυσίᾳ had been corrupted to θυμιᾷ, it was easy to understand it

[58] Plut. *Ages.* 15.8; Polyaen. *Strat.* i.48.3.
[59] Bruce, *Emerita*, xxviii (1960), 78.
[60] Cf. Grote, vii.494–8: still a valuable discussion.
[61] Kagan's description of the revolution, 'long-suppressed class hatred bursting forth with
a fierce and sudden passion' (*Historia*, xi (1962), 453), is hardly supported by the fact of
the amnesty.

as ἐπιθυμᾷ and take that with τῶν κρατούντων, 'of those in power because of their desire'; a scribe altered the word order accordingly.

Xenophon's description of the reaction of the exiles who returned under the amnesty gives us more information about the consequences of the revolution, although it is highly tendentious. 'They saw that the city was being governed by tyrants, and realized that it was being wiped out by the removal of boundary-stones and that their fatherland was being called Argos instead of Corinth. They were being forced to share in the rights of citizenship at Argos—for which they had no desire—and they were less powerful in their own city than metics' (*Hell.* iv.4.6). Similar phrases occur in Xenophon's account of subsequent years;[62] clearly arrangements were made between Corinth and Argos which allowed Sparta and her Corinthian and 'historian' friends to claim that the Corinthian identity was swamped by Argos. That the arrangements were formal is proved by the fact that the Isthmian Games of 390 were conducted by the Argives jointly with the Corinthians (below, 358): the Argives must have had some standing in the Corinthian state. At *Hell.* iv.4.6 Xenophon implies that these changes were made shortly after the revolution in spring 392, for he makes them a motive for treachery by pro-Spartan Corinthians soon after their return under the amnesty; and at iv.8.15 he shows that they were at least projected, and probably already effected, when the conference met at Sardis later in 392 (below, 364 n. 90). It has been suggested that this chronology is inaccurate: that Xenophon antedated the 'union' with Argos precisely in order to provide an acceptable motive for the Corinthian traitors, with whom he sympathized. But the arguments for a later date for the 'union' are not compelling;[63] and the obvious time for the 'union', since it was intended to strengthen the anti-Spartan element at Corinth (below, 362), is immediately after the revolution. Argive troops had played a direct role at the time of the Eucleia;[64] probably an arrangement with Argos had been envisaged from the very beginning.

The nature of the 'union' is far more important than its date;

[62] *Hell.* iv.5.1: 'as if Corinth were Argos'; iv.8.15: 'to possess Corinth as Argos'; iv.8.34: 'made Corinth into Argos'; v.1.34 (when the arrangements were finally dissolved): 'Corinth came under her own control once more'; and v.1.36: 'The Argives made Corinth their own'.
[63] Griffith, *Historia*, i (1950), 242-52, argues that Xenophon's chronology for the 'union' is contradictory; that he dates it to 392 but also gives information which proves that Corinth cannot have 'become Argos' until well after that date (see below). He concludes that there were two stages to the 'union': the first in 392, which did not involve Corinth 'becoming Argos', and the second later, which did. The chronological problem dissolves if, as I argue below, Corinth never 'became Argos'.
[64] Xen. *Hell.* iv.4.4; Diod. xiv.86.1.

but on this question the evidence is woefully inadequate. We are restricted to the propaganda faithfully recorded by Xenophon and reflected by other writers[65] to the effect that Corinth was swallowed up by Argos; the joint celebration of the Isthmia by Argives and Corinthians in 390;[66] and the complaints of the Corinthians at Xen. *Hell.* iv.4.6. That Corinth really 'became Argos' in 392, in the sense that Corinth was merged into the Argive state, is impossible: she sent separate representatives to Tiribazus later in 392 and to Athens later still (below, 363–4). Joint celebration of the Isthmia proves only that some arrangement was made, and that it was relatively far-reaching since it involved religious matters; for other aspects of the scheme we are left only with the tendentious complaints of the Corinthians who opposed the 'union' in Xenophon.

Griffith has demonstrated that the arrangements attacked in the final part of Xenophon's most detailed passage (*Hell.* iv.4.6) were an isopolity agreement between Corinth and Argos; the complaint takes on a precise, indeed telling, meaning if it refers to an agreement under which Argives might exercise citizen-rights at Corinth and vice versa. Xenophon says that his Corinthian friends 'were being forced to share in the rights of citizenship at Argos—for which they had no desire—and they were less powerful in their own city than metics': the Corinthians were indeed being forced to share in Argive citizenship, and had at best no greater, if not strictly a smaller, influence in their own state than Argives, whom they considered as mere metics. Whether more than an isopolity agreement was involved is doubtful. Such agreements in the Hellenistic period had a very limited political effect,[67] and were largely a matter of convenience (and economic advantage) for individuals. But it would be a mistake to interpret such an agreement between Corinth and Argos in the early fourth century in the same light, and to suppose that it was a 'mere courtesy exchange of local voting rights'.[68] The military situation demanded the presence of many Argives in service at Corinth; they would now be able to exercise direct influence as of

---

[65] Diod. xiv.92.1 (below, 367; for the chronological implications, n. 112); Plut. *Ages.* 21.3.

[66] Whatever the arrangements between Corinth and Argos were, it is impossible to accept the natural implications of the words of Xenophon (*Hell.* iv.5.1–2) and Plutarch (*Ages.* 21.3–6) that the Argives celebrated the Games alone; joint celebration with the Corinthians would in any case have to be assumed, and is in fact attested by Paus. iii.10.1.

[67] Griffith, *Historia*, i (1950), 252–3, and refs. at p. 248 n. 40. Gawantka, *Isopolitie*, esp. 113–64.

[68] Tomlinson, *Argos and the Argolid*, 133; he argues, on the basis of this false definition, that there must have been more to the 'union' than such a 'mere' isopolity agreement (below, 360).

right over Corinthian decisions, and it could be taken that they would act with hostility to Sparta. This alone will account both for the passionate opposition which the scheme aroused among the Spartans and their friends and for the attractions it held for their Corinthian opponents.[69] It is perhaps more difficult to explain why the average Corinthian accepted it.[70] That he did so is demonstrated by the fact that after the King's Peace Agesilaus had to use the threat of force against Corinth to secure the dissolution of the 'union'.[71] The agreement must have passed through the normal constitutional process at Corinth; whether the revolution during the Eucleia had involved a change to democracy or no, the 'union' must have been placed before the Corinthian assembly, which ratified treaties in the fifth century (above, 235). If Corinth was now a democracy, the support that democratic Argos would bring to the new constitution might have been a powerful factor; but the need to ensure that a majority of votes in the Corinthian assembly remained in favour of the war may well have been sufficient on its own. If, as I believe, it was the latter motive alone which operated, that is a clear indication of the strength of feeling against Sparta at Corinth.

The details of the agreement cannot be recovered. Presumably Argive citizens might register themselves with the authorities at Corinth and then act as if they were Corinthian citizens, and vice versa. Special arrangements may have been made to allow for Argive participation in Corinthian religious affairs; but it is more likely that the Argives participated in the celebration of the Isthmia in 390 purely in virtue of their tenure of Corinthian citizenship. It would have been difficult to secure acceptance of the scheme at Corinth if all its religious and other implications were precisely defined from the beginning. The oligarchic nature of the constitution at Corinth may have created some difficulty: Argos was democratic. But the Corinthian rules of (among other things) property qualification could be applied to 'Argive' citizens of Corinth just as they were to

[69] Paus. iii.9.8, in describing the visit of Timocrates, calls Timolaus and Polyanthes 'those Corinthians who were favourable to Argos'. This has been taken as an indication that the 'union' was already planned before the war broke out (Bruce, *Commentary*, 58). It is more likely that Pausanias defines these men by reference to their future actions, and that the scheme was conceived far later.

[70] The average Argive will probably have been less alarmed, since the military situation did not demand the regular presence of numerous Corinthians at Argos.

[71] Below, 369. At this time there may have been even more to the 'union' than an isopolity agreement (below, 367-8, n. 112); if so, we might have expected even greater reluctance among the Corinthians.

'Corinthian' citizens, and the Argive rules to 'Corinthian' Argives.[72]

An isopolity agreement will explain all the known consequences of the 'union'; but it has been suggested that something more was involved:[73] that a parallel is to be found in the mid-fifth-century arrangement between Argos and two Cretan cities, Cnossus and Tylissus, under which (among other things) neither Cnossus nor Tylissus might make a treaty without the approval of a πλῆθος in which the Argives cast a third share of the votes.[74] Thus the Argives may have cast (e.g.) a third share of the votes in the Corinthian assembly. Other aspects of the Argive/Cretan arrangements might have suited the Argive/Corinthian situation of 392, especially the emphasis on religious affairs; that would explain the Argive celebration of the Isthmia. But there cannot have been a precise parallel, for the Argive/Cretan πλῆθος is a separate institution; in our case there is no question of a third assembly, distinct from those of Corinth and Argos.[75] Since the parallel is not precise we cannot look to the Argive/Cretan documents for guidance.

It remains to discuss the first items in Xenophon's account: 'that the city was being governed by tyrants, and . . . was being wiped out by the removal of boundary-stones and that (it) was being called Argos instead of Corinth' (*Hell.* iv.4.6). Almost all writers have taken these words seriously, and have concluded that Corinth did indeed 'genuinely "become Argos"', that the boundaries between the two territories were removed, and the name of Corinth ceased to be employed'; and that Corinth 'ceased to have a separate existence'.[76] Kagan dates this destruction of the Corinthian state to 392; but

[72] It might have been more difficult to determine whether property in Argos would count for the purposes of establishing the rights of an Argive at Corinth. One would guess not—which would mean that Argives would have little influence at Corinth beyond their votes in the assembly. If the Corinthian franchise was restricted to hoplites (above, 235-7), 'Argive' Corinthians would have to prove hoplite status before they could vote at Corinth; but the wearing of hoplite gear could have been taken as sufficient evidence. We do not know how 'Corinthian' Corinthians demonstrated their status as hoplites for this purpose, if such a restriction existed.

[73] Tomlinson, *Argos and the Argolid*, 133-6.

[74] Meiggs and Lewis, *GHI*, no. 42; the πλῆθος, ll. 6-11.

[75] That the 'union' was a federal state, with a third, federal, assembly, is formally possible; but it is suggested by nothing in the evidence, it would not by itself explain the participation by Argives in the celebration of the Isthmia, and if it were the case, we should have expected the propaganda of the Corinthians at Xen. *Hell.* iv.4.6 to concentrate more on the obviously obnoxious elements of a federal state (e.g. the usurping by federal institutions of Corinth's foreign policy) than on the isopolity agreement which might have accompanied such a federal scheme.

[76] The expressions are those of Griffith, *Historia*, i (1950), 252, 253. Compare, among recent writers, Kagan, *Historia*, xi (1962), 453: 'voluntarily give up its identity and autonomy'; Hamilton, *Sparta's Bitter Victories*, 275, 276: 'the Argive incorporation of Corinth as part of the Argive state', 'complete subjugation of Corinth to Argos', 'total Argive domination'.

Griffith, and after him Hamilton, have shown that this is impossible, for the separate existence of Corinth in that year is demonstrated by Corinthian diplomatic activity (above, 358). They conclude that the 'union' had two stages: the first, in 392, an isopolity agreement alone, followed by the total absorption of Corinth by Argos at a later stage.[77] All these conclusions are highly improbable. Corinthians in general favoured the 'union': Agesilaus had to theaten force to secure its dissolution (below, 369). I cannot conceive of any circumstances in which the average Corinthian would accept the wholesale abolition of his state. We should therefore ask if the words of Xenophon which have encouraged this conclusion can be interpreted differently; the answer is evident. Xenophon here records the propaganda of the enemies of the 'union'; his remark about tyrants is clearly tendentious. For the rest he does little more than expand, in a graphic way, his general condemnation of the scheme expressed elsewhere more succinctly by phrases like 'as if Corinth were Argos'.[78] It is easy to imagine how this propaganda arose if only an isopolity agreement was in question: 'The Argives now have the same rights at Corinth as we true Corinthians, and the boundary-stones between Argos and Corinth have been removed;[79] we might just as well call Corinth Argos.' The propaganda is skilful; but it did not deceive contemporary Corinthians.[80] It is evidence for nothing more than the natural abhorrence of those Corinthians against whose position in the city the 'union' was directed.[81]

The Argives had to take action to protect the 'union' later; but they need not have done anything more than confirm the isopolity agreement (below, 367 with n. 112). Since it is surprising enough that even so much was accepted by Corinth it is unlikely that more

[77] Kagan, *Historia*, xi (1962), 453; Griffith, art. cit., 242-52; Hamilton, *Sparta's Bitter Victories*, 267-78.

[78] Xen. *Hell*. iv.5.1; cf. for other examples above, 357 n. 62.

[79] It is not clear to me whether the boundary-stones were in fact removed. Xenophon states that they were, and that would have been a suitably symbolic act after an isopolity agreement. Xenophon may, however, have been misled by the propaganda of his Corinthian friends—'we might as well remove the boundary-stones'—into believing that they were removed when they were not.

[80] Similar phrases to those of Xenophon in Diodorus and Plutarch (above, 358 n. 65) are to be interpreted in the same way. Andoc. iii.26,27 has remarks which might be adduced in this connection, but prove nothing. Andocides is speaking at Athens in favour of peace in winter 392/1 (below, 364), and argues that (26) if war is continued victory will only have the effect of 'securing the land of the Corinthians for the Argives' and that (27) Argos hopes by continuing the war to 'take Corinth'; taken by themselves, these passages suggest nothing more than that Argos wished to gain control of Corinth—which it suited Andocides' case to claim.

[81] All scholars who have accepted Xenophon's evidence remark on the extraordinary nature of the conclusion it leads to; it would have been better to question its validity.

was involved; that cannot be excluded, given the state of our evidence, but it would be difficult to guess what was added. The scheme has often been greeted as a refreshing attempt to break free of the constraints of the particularism of the city.[82] The experiment was certainly bold; but to turn it into a serious attempt to cast off the shackles of local loyalties is to exaggerate. The intention was quite specific and limited: to strengthen the anti-Spartan element in Corinth. A few far-sighted souls may have foreseen the possibilities for future development; but clearly the immediate party advantages were paramount. The potential of such a politically effective isopolity union was probably greater than that of a federal state: Argives could now participate in Corinthian affairs across the whole range of city life—and vice versa—while in a federal state common participation was possible only in the limited, if important, range of affairs subjected to federal control. But such potential can have been seen by only a few, if any, participants; the 'union' may have been accepted in spite of, rather than because of, its more far-reaching possibilities.[83] The scheme may have been devised precisely because it seemed *less* far-reaching than a federal state, in which Argos and Corinth as such would lose control over their foreign policy. None the less, the importance of the development is not to be minimized: if it was only the immediate advantages which recommended it, the potential remained; and even though it was accepted for party reasons, its adoption was a sign of flexibility which might have been exploited had not Sparta killed the 'union' like a deformed child exposed on Taygetus.

c.   The Corinthian War and the King's Peace

Incensed by the isopolity agreement, and exploiting the amnesty, two pro-Spartan Corinthians whose names—Pasimelus and Alcimenes —Xenophon was able to report, communicated with Praxitas, the Spartan commander at Sicyon, by 'wading through a torrent'—thus, presumably, still in spring (*Hell*. iv.4.7). They admitted him with a force of Spartans, Sicyonians, and 150 Corinthian exiles into the Long Walls between Corinth and Lechaeum, where a stockade was built for protection. After a day the Corinthians were joined by Argive hoplites (the Argive force permanently stationed at Corinth cannot have been very great) and Athenian mercenaries under Iphicrates; in the ensuing battle the Spartans employed a similar

---

[82] Griffith, *Historia*, i (1950), 252-6; Hamilton, *Historia*, xxi (1972), 37; Bengtson, 267.
[83] Cf. Griffith, art. cit., 253.

tactic to that which had gained them victory at the Nemea, the allies were routed, and the Spartans took Lechaeum despite the Boeotian garrison in the port.[84] Praxitas destroyed a section of the Long Walls, marched through the gap, and captured Sidous and Crommyon beyond the Isthmus; he left garrisons there, built a fort at Epieiceia on the frontier between Corinth and Sicyon, and then withdrew to Sparta (Xen. *Hell.* iv.4.13, cf. iv.2.14). His activity in the Isthmus region may have included sabotage of the diolkos: repairs were made to the installations *c*.400, and they may have been necessitated by such enemy action (above, 336 n. 45). The loss of Lechaeum made allied control of the Isthmus less secure; but it also deprived Corinth of the mastery of the Gulf established by Agathinus (above, 354). His successor Proaenus abandoned Rhium, which Agathinus had presumably controlled; the place was taken over by the Spartans under Herippidas.[85] At about the time of their success at Lechaeum—the precise chronology is unclear—the Spartans attempted to end the war by negotiation. It was impossible to fight both against Persia and against the Greek allies; Sparta naturally chose to abandon her efforts in the east. That choice presented an opportunity for ending the war in Greece too; the King might be induced to cease his help for the allies and at best Sparta might gain his assistance in imposing a solution.[86] Thus Antalcidas was sent to Tiribazus in Sardis; he recognized the Persian claim to the cities of Asia Minor, and suggested that peace be imposed in Greece on the basis of autonomy for all states.[87] Sparta's main enemies were also represented before Tiribazus, and each city protested against the proposals: the Athenians because they would lead to the loss of Lemnos, Imbros, and Scyros, the Boeotians because they would mean the dissolution of their League, and the Argives (and presumably the Corinthians as well, though Xenophon does not specify their complaint) because they knew Sparta would use the autonomy clause to suppress the 'union' (Xen. *Hell.* iv.8.12–15). The conference broke up.

Shortly after this, if not before, the Spartans took Lechaeum; but that did not disturb their judgement that a negotiated peace was preferable to an attempt at military victory. Further proposals were

[84] Xen. *Hell.* iv.4.7–12; Diod. xiv.86.2–3. Diodorus has the Spartans take Lechaeum itself before the battle, but Xenophon's account is preferable.

[85] Xen. *Hell.* iv.8.11. The chronology of these events is not clear in Xenophon, but Corinth cannot have controlled the Gulf for long after the loss of Lechaeum. Agathinus' command probably belongs in 393; Proaenus will have succeeded him in 392.

[86] Cf. ibid. iv.8.12: 'they could either bring Tiribazus to change sides, or at least prevent him from continuing to support Conon's fleet.'

[87] Ryder, 27–31; Lewis, *Sparta and Persia*, 145.

soon made by Sparta, probably in winter 392/1.[88] The Athenians were to be allowed to retain their three islands and the Boeotian League was to continue—though Orchomenus, already detached by Lysander before Haliartus, was to remain separate (Andoc. iii.12–14, 20). It is most improbable that concessions were made to Argos and Corinth. Sparta could not abandon her control of the Peloponnese, and in particular its gates at Corinth. She will have continued to insist on the dissolution of the Argos/Corinth 'union', if on nothing else.[89] This Spartan priority was natural and obvious; indeed, the first Spartan effort to secure peace, through Antalcidas, was probably made precisely because of the alarm caused by the Argos/Corinth 'union'.[90] It is no wonder that embassies from both cities spoke forcibly at Athens against acceptance of the proposals (Andoc. iii.24,27).

For the moment, however, the Spartan proposals were rejected and the war continued.[91] The Corinthia suffered in 391 from raids by the Spartans and Corinthian exiles now based in Lechaeum, as it had suffered before from raids based on Sicyon; but the Athenians marched in full force with craftsmen to the Corinthia and rebuilt the Long Walls (Xen. *Hell.* iv.4.18). The allies laid siege to the Spartans at Lechaeum and probably held the place briefly;[92] but Agesilaus, after invading the Argolid and devastating it, soon recaptured the port with the help of his half-brother Teleutias, who commanded about twelve vessels in the Gulf.[93]

In 390 Agesilaus led the first major Spartan offensive of the war.

[88] Ryder, 31–3. It is often suggested (e.g. Smith, *Historia*, ii (1953/4), 277–8) that these milder proposals were the work of a different Spartan faction; this is hardly necessary, since the attempt at Sardis had failed. Cf. Hamilton, *Sparta's Bitter Victories*, 255 (but contrast 274).

[89] Cf. Beloch, iii.1.81–2 (despite his failure to distinguish the two sets of terms properly); Hamilton, *Sparta's Bitter Victories*, 255, 274.

[90] Only the ambiguity of Xen. *Hell.* iv.8.15 raises doubts. The Argives object to the Sardis terms 'because they would then not be able to possess Corinth as Argos, which they wanted to do'; they might be expressing a wish either to retain a 'union' that already existed or to achieve one that was merely projected. The former is the natural meaning (despite Accame, *Ricerche*, 114; Griffith, *Historia*, i (1950), 243 n. 28, gives the phrase the latter meaning, but for reasons connected with his unnecessary hypothesis that there were two stages to the 'union'); but the latter cannot quite be excluded.

[91] For Boeotia, see Andoc. iii.13, 20, 24, 28. His claim that the Boeotians agreed to the proposals is sometimes accepted (e.g. Smith, *Historia*, ii (1953/4), 277 with n. 8). But Andocides' case was helped by the claim, which may have been based only on the fact that they had not yet declined. Boeotia helped Corinth in 391, at least according to Diodorus (xiv.86.4); none the less, a certain decrease in Boeotian activity is to be detected.

[92] Xen. *Hell.* iv.4.18 has the allies rebuild the Long Walls; Diod. xiv.86.4 has the Spartans under siege at the port. At *Hell.* iv.4.19 Xenophon records that Teleutias later captured the 'ships and dockyards', which implies that Lechaeum had temporarily been lost to the Spartans (Beloch, iii.1.80). To repair the Long Walls will have been dangerous if the Spartans still held Lechaeum.

[93] Xen. *Hell.* iv.4.19; *Ages.* ii.17; Plut. *Ages.* 21.2 (lacunose text); cf. Diod. xiv.86.4.

It was, significantly, directed against allied tenure of the Isthmus. His army reached the Corinthia when the Argives were sharing the celebration of the Isthmia with the Corinthians; they fled in mid-sacrifice at his approach,[94] and he gave protection to the Corinthian exiles as they celebrated the Games.[95] He then marched towards the Peiraeum. He had discovered from the exiles that the livestock of the Corinthians had been evacuated to that place, and that supplies were being provided from there for those in the city;[96] but the most important reason for his attack on the peninsula is revealed by Xenophon (*Ages.* ii.18) as strategic: Boeotian (we might add, Athenian) support for Corinth came from this direction. Sparta already held Sidous and Crommyon (above, 363); capture of the Peiraeum would close the land route,[97] and although the Boeotians had access to the sea at Creusis (Xen. *Ages.* ii.18) Spartan control of Lechaeum would make the sea route almost impossible. The Spartan intention may also have been offensive: to facilitate an invasion of Boeotia. The allies were well aware of the importance of the Peiraeum; Iphicrates was there with his peltasts.[98] Agesilaus therefore turned about and made camp by the city itself. Remembering 392, the Corinthians feared that Sparta had come to some arrangement with traitors inside the city and hurriedly recalled Iphicrates. He arrived during the night[99] and was unable to defend the Peiraeum when Agesilaus led his troops back there on the following day. The Spartan march towards Corinth was evidently intended to draw Iphicrates away from the Peiraeum.[100] Agesilaus captured the now almost

[94] Since they fled 'along the road to Cenchreae' (Xen. *Hell.* iv.5.1) he must have marched towards the sanctuary from the west.

[95] Ibid. iv.5.1-2; Plut. *Ages.* 21.3-4; Paus. iii.10.1; Diod. xiv.86.5.

[96] Xen. *Hell.* iv.5.1; *Ages.* ii.18.

[97] Had Sparta been able to count on the allegiance of Megara, an attack on the Peiraeum would have been unnecessary; but Megara was probably hostile (above, 349). For the road through the northern Megarid here referred to, cf. Hammond, *BSA* xlix (1954), 103-20 (though he does not note this passage). His towers A, B, D, E, and G (ibid., 108-11) may have been built during the Corinthian War (cf. 110).

[98] This is not recorded but can be deduced. At Xen. *Hell.* iv.5.3 Agesilaus withdraws from the Peiraeum to threaten Corinth and the Corinthians summon aid from Iphicrates and his peltasts; in fact they came from the Peiraeum (Xen. *Ages.* ii.19). Cf. Underhill, *Commentary*, 144.

[99] This is probably the occasion of Iphicrates' successful defence of the city against an attempt by Corinthian exiles, who were admitted by traitors, to capture the city-walls (Diod. xiv.91.2); 300 exiles were killed. Diodorus places the episode 'some days' before Iphicrates' destruction of the Spartan *mora* (below, 366). Cf. also Polyaen. *Strat.* iii.9.45.

[100] Xen. *Hell.* iv.5.3; *Ages.* ii.18-19. At *Ages.* vii.6, Corinthian exiles expect an attack on the city but Agesilaus disappoints them. The reason reported by Xenophon—that Greek cities should not be enslaved but rather taught to behave themselves—is tendentious, but the reference is probably to this time. The real reason will have been that the threat to the city had been a feint in the first place.

undefended peninsula with ease. Iphicrates had brought 'most of' his peltasts to Corinth with him (Xen. *Hell*. iv.5.3); those that were left behind do not figure in Xenophon's accounts of Agesilaus' success, but he thought it necessary to secure the heights of Mt. Loutraki on the first night of his attack while he camped at Therma (Loutraki). He earned Xenophon's praise by sending up fire to his men on the heights to warm themselves on a cold night; he might rather have been blamed for not ensuring that they took both fire and warm clothing in the first place (Xen. *Hell*. iv.5.4). On the following day, the men from the heights descended to capture the fort at Oenoe, near the border with Megara. Agesilaus himself marched by the coast road to the Heraeum, where the inhabitants of the peninsula had fled at his approach; they soon surrendered. He 'decided to hand over to the exiles those who had taken part in the massacre, and to have all the rest sold'.[101] Meanwhile Iphicrates' peltasts made up for their failure to defend the Peiraeum by cutting to pieces a Spartan *mora*;[102] Agesilaus hurried to do what he could and then returned to the peninsula to complete his grisly business there. After devastating the coastal plain[103] he returned home.[104] Iphicrates had nullified a potentially major Spartan success. While Agesilaus was in the Peiraeum, Boeotian ambassadors had come to treat for peace. Agesilaus would not listen to them then; but after the destruction of the *mora* they took heart and asked only for permission to withdraw to Corinth. Their proposals for peace were never made.[105] The Spartans might still have been able to secure the Peiraeum and to take advantage of it had they not been severely discouraged by their defeat. They garrisoned Oenoe before Agesilaus left; but Iphicrates recaptured not only that fort but also Crommyon and Sidous, which had been taken in 392 by Praxitas (Xen. *Hell*. iv.5.19). The Spartans were only able to maintain their hold on Lechaeum. Meanwhile, the Argives and Corinthians celebrated under their own auspices the Isthmian Games that had already been conducted once by the Corinthian exiles.[106]

The Spartans and Corinthian exiles remained in Lechaeum; they

---

[101] Xen. *Hell*. iv.5.3–8; cf. Wiseman, 32–3. The quotation, iv.5.5. Xenophon is more likely to have played down Agesilaus' brutality than to have exaggerated it; so much for Agesilaus' desire not to enslave a Greek city (above, n. 100). Cf. Xen. *Ages*. ii.19; Plut. *Ages*. 22.1.

[102] Xen. *Hell*. iv.5.11–17; Diod. xiv.91.2; Plut. *Ages*. 22.3–4; Paus. iii.10.1. The site of the action is plausibly identified by Wiseman, 99, as the hill of Agios Gerasimos.

[103] Xen. *Hell*. iv.5.7–10; Plut. *Ages*. 22.7.

[104] Xen. *Hell*. iv.5.18; Plut. *Ages*. 22.8.

[105] Xen. *Hell*. iv.5.6–10; Plut. *Ages*. 22.1–7.

[106] Xen. *Hell* iv.5.2; Plut. *Ages*. 21.5–6; Paus. iii.10.1.

made occasional raids but had been much subdued by the destruction of the *mora* (Xen. *Hell*. iv.5.19). There was also political trouble at Corinth. Xenophon, when he explains why Iphicrates and his peltasts were available for service in the Hellespont in 388, writes, 'since the Argives had made Corinth into Argos, they said that they no longer had need of them (sc. the peltasts at Corinth); for (Iphicrates) had also killed some of the partisans of Argos, and for that reason he returned to Athens and was at home.'[107] Iphicrates cannot have left Corinth before 389; Xenophon's explanation would be stultified if the interval between his service at Corinth and in the Hellespont had been greater, and he will hardly have been left idle in Athens for long.[108] Diodorus (xiv.92.1-2: under 393/2) adds more: 'The Argives marched in full force under arms to Corinth, seized the acropolis, secured the city for themselves, and made Corinthian territory Argive. Iphicrates the Athenian also considered seizing the city, since it was convenient for control of Greece; but when the Athenians prevented him, he gave up his command, and the Athenians sent Chabrias to Corinth as a general to replace him'.[109] No doubt Iphicrates gained much popularity in Corinth from his exploits— not only the cutting to pieces of the *mora* and the recapture of Oenoe, Sidous, and Crommyon but at least one other success at Corinth (above, 365 n. 99) and yet more at Phleious, in Arcadia, and at Sicyon;[110] presumably he hoped to derive some advantage from his activities for himself or for Athens. He killed, or at least was accused of killing, some prominent Corinthian supporters of the 'union' with Argos; but the Argives marched to Corinth in full force, secured his dismissal before he could do any further harm,[111] and the 'union' was preserved.[112]

[107] *Hell*. iv.8.34. The introductory ἐπεί here is normally translated in a temporal sense; that would imply that the 'union' came only a little before Iphicrates' dismissal (Griffith, *Historia*, i (1950), 243-4). But since Xenophon plainly dates the 'union' far earlier than this (above, 357) it is preferable to translate it in a causal sense. If the meaning had been temporal and Xenophon had intended to imply a short interval between the 'union' (in its final stage) and Iphicrates' dismissal, we might have expected the aorist and not the pluperfect ἐπεποίηντο.

[108] Griffith, ibid., 244.

[109] Aristeid. *Panath*. 270 (praise of Athens for taking no advantage of her control of Acrocorinth) may refer to Athens' refusal to entertain this proposal of Iphicrates; but it may merely call attention to the long presence of Iphicrates' peltasts in the city, without knowing of (or deliberately omitting) the dubious end to his service there.

[110] Phleious and Arcadia: Xen. *Hell*. iv.4.15-16; Phleious and Sicyon: Diod. xiv.91.3 (misdated). Cf. Aristeid. *Panath*. 291. On Iphicrates' force at Corinth, see in general Pritchett, *The Greek State at War*, ii.117-25.

[111] The Argive purpose may not only have been to exert military pressure against Athens but also to cast numerous 'Argive' votes in the Corinthian assembly.

[112] In Diodorus' sequence, what lies behind the propaganda that 'Corinth became Argos' took place after the destruction of the *mora*; Griffith, *Historia*, i (1950), 245, uses this as

Spartan efforts after the destruction of the *mora* were concentrated in the east. After some military action and much diplomacy the King agreed to the bargain Antalcidas had first proposed in 392. In 387 ambassadors were called from the various states to Sardis. Tiribazus read out what had been agreed between Sparta and the King, as follows, 'Artaxerxes the King thinks it right that the cities in Asia shall belong to him, and of the islands Clazomenae and Cyprus; and that the other Greek cities, both small and great, shall be left free but for Lemnos, Imbros, and Scyros: they shall belong to Athens as in the past. Whichever side rejects the peace,[113] I shall make war on them, in alliance with those who accept it, by land and by sea, with ships and with money'.[114]

The decisions in Greece which followed the 'sending down' of these terms by the King are made obscure by the failure of Xenophon to discuss them carefully. The precise implications of the autonomy clause may have been made clear at Sardis;[115] but that is not likely; and the Spartans, now allies of the King, were probably allowed to interpret the clause as they wished. Further negotiations were therefore necessary, for at one stage in the recent past Sparta had been prepared to tolerate the continued existence of the Boeotian League (above, 364), and it might have been hoped that they would offer similar concessions elsewhere to obtain a secure settlement. If they were to insist on the most rigid application of the clause possible—dissolution of both the Boeotian League and the Argos/Corinth 'union'—there was no way of predicting the decisions of the allies. The Athenians were the most likely to accept the settlement, since their possession of the three islands was already agreed; but they might have been encouraged to continue resistance if the alliance could remain firm, and Boeotia, Corinth, and Argos had stronger reason to do so. They would certainly lose the support of the King; but that had in any case been of little use. It is true that the allies had enjoyed no great success during the war; but there were signs that disaffection existed in the Peloponnese to be

evidence that there were two stages in the 'union', and supposes that Diodorus here refers to the second stage, the true incorporation of Corinth in Argos. Diodorus must be wrong in placing his first reference to the 'union' after the joint celebration of the Isthmia (xiv. 86.5). His report may reflect some strengthening of the 'union' as a result of Iphicrates' plot; but it is just as likely that it refers merely to successful resistance against Iphicrates' threats to the previous arrangements, which Diodorus had failed to record in their proper place.

[113] For this translation, see Lewis, *Sparta and Persia*, 147.

[114] Xen. *Hell*. v.1.31; cf. Diod. xiv.110.2–4.

[115] It might be argued that they were—on the ground that one such implication, the status of the three Athenian islands, was specified. But this was the one issue which might concern the King; it does not follow that the other details were also given so early.

exploited,[116] and it cannot be ruled out that the allies, even without the Athenians, might have tested the sincerity of the King's promise to give active help to Sparta in enforcing the terms she chose.

In these circumstances, it is unfortunate that Xenophon is not more precise. Agesilaus took charge of the Spartan side of the negotiations. The Boeotians were willing to make peace if their League were to remain;[117] but Agesilaus insisted that each city take the oath separately. The Boeotian ambassadors protested that they had no mandate to agree to such terms; he sent them home to get ratification and meanwhile persuaded the ephors to prepare an army. Boeotia caved in before it left Tegea, so it was disbanded along with the Boeotian League.[118] The Corinthians, Xenophon goes on, 'did not send away the Argive garrison'; evidently they wished to maintain their 'union'. But Agesilaus threatened both cities with war, and the Argives withdrew from Corinth, which 'came under her own control once more'; the 'murderers and those who shared their guilt decided themselves to go into exile', and those who had been in exile returned.[119]

Thus Boeotia, Corinth, and Argos accepted Sparta's rigid interpretation of the Peace under threat of force. It may have been their failure to achieve any offensive success since 395 which persuaded them to do so; but it is possible that Agesilaus' unscrupulous skill in manipulating the negotiations prevented them from rejecting the terms in concert and then continuing resistance. From a strict interpretation of Xenophon's account, it seems that the only point initially at issue was that of Boeotia. He claims that 'all the other cities swore to accept the terms'; since Corinth and Argos objected at a later stage to the dissolution of their 'union', the implication is that they were led to believe that the 'union' was not under threat. In that case it is hardly surprising that they were prepared to agree: the 'union' would provide a powerful defence against the threat of the very Spartan interference which they had entered the war to prevent. With acceptance of the Peace achieved at Athens, Corinth, and Argos, Agesilaus could threaten a lonely Boeotia; and once she had submitted he could unveil his intentions with regard to Corinth and Argos. It was naïve for Corinth and Argos not to

---

[116] Achaea: Xen. *Hell.* iv.6.1-3 (cf. Anderson, *BSA* xlix (1954), 86). Arcadia: Xen. *Hell.* iv.5.18; v.2.1-2; perhaps iv.4.16-17; Plut. *Ages.* 22.8.

[117] Xen. *Hell.* v.1.32; I take it that this is the truth behind Xenophon's tendentious expression.

[118] Ibid., v.1.32-3; cf. Plut. *Ages.* 23.5.

[119] Xen. *Hell.* v.1.34. That the Corinthians received back the pro-Spartan exiles willingly, as is asserted by Xenophon, is in the words of Griffith (*Historia*, i (1950), 253-4 n. 55) 'mere humbug' (cf. Grote, vii.550); but that is no reason to change the text.

gain assurances from Sparta about her precise intentions or (more
likely) to accept assurances dishonestly given; but it is possible
that they agreed to the terms in the knowledge that they involved
the dissolution of the 'union' and still tried to prevent their implementation.

Once it became clear that Sparta would insist on the dissolution
of the 'union', even the sympathy of their fellow citizens for the
Corinthians who had controlled policy for a decade or more was
feeble protection against the anger of the Laconizing exiles—despite
the autonomy clause. They fled.

XXV.   Exhaustion

a.   Corinth, Sparta, Thebes, and Philip

Our sources provide no more than occasional illumination of Corinthian policy in the tumultuous half-century after the King's Peace. That makes a coherent account impossible to write; but it also reflects a significant change. The history of the city from the Corcyra affair to 387 is that of impotent, often hysterical protest against domination of the Greek world by more resourceful states. After the King's Peace such protest ceased: Corinth behaved in accordance with the implication of her history, that she was no longer fitted to occupy even a small part of the centre of the Greek stage. With a few exceptions—one a fruitful and more than honourable enterprise—Corinth was merely passive.

It was natural after the King's Peace for Corinth to act as an obedient ally of Sparta. The city had suffered more than any other during the Corinthian War;[1] and despite the hostility towards Sparta that Corinthians had demonstrated when they tried to retain the 'union' with Argos, the arguments in favour of loyalty were overwhelming. It is doubtful, however, if those who controlled Corinthian policy made a conscious decision to avoid independent action: their stance will have been determined by the history of their faction. They returned from exile only under threat of Spartan force, and they were bound to ensure that their city played the insignificant role that Sparta demanded, even if only to secure their own internal position. Their decision to support Sparta during the Corinthian War may have been made on the honourable, if faint-hearted, ground that resistance to Sparta was futile; that argument was now even stronger, but it is more likely that they had opposed action against Sparta for purely factional reasons.

In the years immediately after the King's Peace they no doubt faced serious difficulty in the attitudes of their fellow citizens. The leading opponents of Sparta were in exile;[2] but they had enjoyed majority support, and Corinthian sentiment cannot have been

---

[1] Cf. Diod. xv.23.4: Corinth (and Argos) had been 'laid low' by the previous wars; Diodorus refers to the period when Sparta held the Cadmea at Thebes.
[2] Cf. Diod. xv.40.3 (Argos); Dem. xx.51–7 (Athens).

favourable either to Sparta or to her recently restored friends. None the less, the argument for loyalty was unanswerable, and Xenophon remarks on the faith of Corinth c.380 (*Hell.* v.3.27: πιστοτάτους).

Our sources rarely mention any specific allies of Sparta during the campaigns undertaken to enforce her oppressive interpretation of the autonomy clause of the King's Peace—the separation of Mantinea into its constituent villages, the coercion of Phleious, and the dissolution of the Chalcidian League[3] —and Corinth is not mentioned at all; but she presumably provided help whenever it was asked for —even against the Chalcidians of Thrace, with whom she had enjoyed a special relationship ever since the revolt of Potidaea. When Phoebidas occupied the Cadmea at Thebes with the treacherous help of Leontiades,[4] Corinth was probably represented among the 1,500 Spartans and allies who made up the garrison (Diod. xv.25.3); it is not recorded whether the Corinthian who sat in judgement on Ismenias voted with the majority to condemn him to death for fighting against Sparta in alliance with Corinth a decade before (Xen. *Hell.* v.2.35-6).

Xenophon (*Hell.* v.3.27) and Diodorus (xv.23.3-5) both remark on the favourable position of Sparta after the settlement with the Chalcidians. At some time in the 380s the alliance was organized into ten sections; each was to provide an equal contingent for campaigns undertaken by the alliance or to pay cash in lieu at a specified rate. Corinth's importance in the alliance, despite the losses of half a century's warfare, remained considerable—in so far as any ally was important: she made up, with Megara, a whole section, and may well have provided a greater proportion of the allied forces than any other single city save Sparta herself and Elis.[5] Spartan success, however, was as short-lived as it was (temporarily) complete: the garrison in the Cadmea was forced to withdraw.[6] At Athens the response was more definite than Xenophon's account indicates; she took action when Sphodrias unsuccessfully attempted

---

[3] Mantinea: Xen. *Hell.* v.2.1-7; Diod. xv.5. Phleious: Xen. *Hell.* v.2.8-10; 3.10-17, 21-5; Diod. xv.19.3. Chalcidian League: Xen. *Hell.* v.2.11-24, 37-3.9; 3.18-19,26; Diod. xv. 19.2-3, 20.3-23.4. On Spartan policy in this period, see Ryder, 39-48; Cawkwell, *CQ* xxvi (1976), 71-80.

[4] Xen. *Hell.* v.2.25-35; Diod. xv.20; Plut. *Ages.* 23.6-11.

[5] Sparta and Elis were the only cities to make up single sections on their own. Corinth will have provided a greater proportion of her section than Megara; probably no single Arcadian city provided a greater proportion of either of the two Arcadian sections. The details are given by Diod. xv.31.2, under 377/6, when Boeotia had been replaced by the Chalcidians of Thrace; but the basic pattern is presupposed by Xen. *Hell.* v.2.20-1, 37 (cf. Diod. xv.19.3); it must therefore belong to the mid-380s.

[6] Xen. *Hell.* v.4.1-12; Diod. xv.25-7.

a raid on the Peiraeus.[7] Thebes countered all Spartan attempts to regain control of the city, and before long the Athenians had secured numerous members for what is now known as the Second Athenian Confederacy, which had the specific intention of ensuring that the Spartans 'should allow the Greeks to live at peace in freedom and autonomy and to possess all their own territory in security', and that 'the Common Peace which the Greeks and the King swore according to the agreements should be valid and last for ever.'[8] These developments may have increased the difficulties faced by those in power at Corinth, for they made possible a renewal of the alliance which had fought Sparta in the Corinthian War; but Corinth remained firmly in the Spartan camp, whether by conviction or under duress. Corinthians may have been among those Spartan allies who insisted, against the wishes of the Spartans themselves, on surrendering the Cadmea before help could arrive from the Peloponnese, and who thus unnecessarily added to Sparta's difficulties (Diod. xv.27.2); if so, they probably acted from fear rather than disaffection. The adherence of Corinth gave Sparta the opportunity she did not have in the Corinthian War of an easy route to Boeotia (cf. Xen. *Hell.* v.4.19), but she made little effective use of it.[9] In both 375 and 371, when the Spartans invaded Boeotia or helped their Phocian allies, they went by sea across the Corinthian Gulf, probably with Corinthian help.[10]

Corinth is rarely mentioned among Sparta's allies in actions between the foundation of the Second Athenian Confederacy and the battle of Leuctra; but the one reference we have is significant. Most of Sparta's allies contributed money instead of men for the expedition of Mnasippus to Corcyra;[11] but Corinthians served in person, and Corinth and her colonies of Leucas and Ambracia are named first in Xenophon's list of the allies who contributed to the fleet of sixty vessels (*Hell.* vi.2.3). It will have been easy to persuade Corinthians to act against Corcyra—out of jealousy rather than because they retained their fifth-century ambitions. More importantly, this probably reflects an attempt to restore Corinth's position as

[7] Xen. *Hell.* v.4.20-1; Diod. xv.29.5-6; Plut. *Ages.* 24.4-8; *Pelop.* 14.2-6.

[8] Tod, ii, no. 123 (*Staatsverträge*, ii, no. 257), lines 9-15. For Athenian policy at this time, and the stages in the foundation of the Confederacy (a process which began before the raid of Sphodrias), see Cawkwell, *CQ* xxiii (1973), 47-60.

[9] Xen. *Hell.* v.4.13-18, 35-41, 47-55, 59; Diod. xv.27.3, 32-33.4, 34.1-2; Plut. *Ages.* 24.3, 26.2-4; *Pelop.* 13.2, 14.1.

[10] Xen. *Hell.* vi.1.1; cf. 2.1 (375); below. Xenophon does not state specifically that the army of Cleombrotus in Phocis in 371 had got there by sea (vi.4.2), but it is next to certain that it had.

[11] Ibid. vi.2.16; cf. Diod. xv.47.1-7.

Sparta's main naval ally. Immediately after Leuctra Sparta and Corinth together manned a fleet and prepared to transport an army under Archidamus across the Corinthian Gulf (Xen. *Hell*. vi.4.17-18); Corinth will therefore presumably have taken part in the transport of Spartan armies across the Gulf earlier in the 370s. No doubt Corinth was represented in the fleet commanded by Nicolochus against Timotheus at Corcyra, as were the Ambraciots even though their six ships arrived so late that they joined a fleet already worsted.[12] Corinthians may have been foremost among the allies who complained at Sparta in 376 that the war was being fought without vigour and suggested that a fleet be manned either to blockade Athens or to transport troops by sea to Boeotia (Xen. *Hell*. v.4.60). At any rate, the proposal implied Corinthian support, for it probably involved the use of the diolkos to transport at least part of the fleet from the Corinthian to the Saronic Gulf or vice versa. The proportion of Corinthian vessels in the fleet of sixty or more that was raised as a result of this proposal and commanded by Pollis is unknown; but although the fleet had some success at first, it was defeated by Chabrias off Naxos.[13]

Corinth therefore went some way towards re-establishing her position as the most important naval ally of Sparta; but her success was hardly greater than in the Archidamian War. All the naval honours in the 370s went to Athens, and in the Common Peaces that were agreed in 375 and early in 371 Sparta made concessions.[14] Diodorus records that the Peace of 375 quickly gave rise to an attempt at revolution in Corinth by exiles living at Argos (xv.40.3). It was, he says, part of a general movement in the Peloponnese against those who controlled their cities in the Spartan interest (xv.40), but probably these events are misdated and took place after Leuctra.[15] Even if Diodorus is right, the attempt at Corinth failed.[16] The Peace of 371 specified that all armies within foreign territory must be withdrawn (Xen. *Hell*. vi.3.18), but the Spartans

[12] Xen. *Hell*. v.4.65-6; cf. Diod. xv.36.5.

[13] Xen. *Hell*. v.4.61 (sixty ships); Diod. xv.34.3-6 (sixty-five).

[14] On all this, see Ryder, 58-70. Whether Corinth was subjected before 371 to a Spartan harmost, and thus gained directly from the clause in the Peace of that date under which all harmosts were withdrawn (Xen. *Hell*. vi.3.18; cf. Ryder, 67), is unknown.

[15] Cf. esp. xv.40.1, 'during the hegemony of the Spartans', implying that at the time Diodorus is speaking of, that hegemony is no more. Diod. xv.40 probably goes with the previous section and stands with it outside the annalistic order, despite the apparent return to that order at the end of xv.39.3. Cf. Stern, *Geschichte der spartanischen und thebanischen Hegemonie*, 93-9, 155; Cawkwell, *CQ* xxvi (1976), 77 n. 53. *Contra*, Lauffer, *Historia*, viii (1959), 318 n. 5; Roy, *Klio*, lv (1973), 135-9. Certainty on such a question is unattainable.

[16] On the events of the revolution, see below, 383-4.

sent Cleombrotus, who was at the time leading an army in Phocis, to his defeat and death at Leuctra.[17] Our sources do not tell us whether the Corinthians provided money for the campaign, as they were allowed to do, or fought in person; but the latter seems more likely in view of their enthusiastic service in Archidamus' army immediately after the battle.[18]

In the few years after Leuctra Corinth offered Sparta material help. The allies who had served in the battle were not prepared to renew the fight (Xen. *Hell.* vi.4.14–15); but Xenophon names Corinth, along with Tegea, Mantinea, Sicyon, Phleious, and Achaea, as having willingly provided forces for the army Archidamus led to the rescue. Corinth also manned triremes for transport across the Gulf (*Hell.* vi.4.18). But help was not needed. Jason of Pherae enabled the Spartan army to withdraw (Xen. *Hell.* vi.4.20–6), and when it met with Archidamus' force at Megara he led all his troops to Corinth and disbanded them (Xen. *Hell.* vi.4.26). The Corinthian reaction to Leuctra is most unlikely to have been carefully calculated, for the effects of the battle could not have been predicted at once; help was probably sent to Sparta more out of habit than anything else. Corinth will hardly be numbered among those allies of Sparta who were not disturbed by Leuctra or (as Jason of Pherae claimed) contemplated desertion (Xen. *Hell.* vi.4.15,24). As events unfolded it became clear that the choice for Corinth was no longer between an attempt to revive the coalition of the Corinthian War and continued loyalty to a decreasingly threatening Sparta; it was now between a Sparta no longer capable of serious interference and a Boeotia whose ultimate intentions may have been unknown but were strongly suspect. Corinth's decision could not be doubted: she helped Sparta. It was not long before even Athens took the same decision.

For some five years after Leuctra, Corinth gave Sparta devoted service while the Boeotians invaded the Peloponnese and tried to gain allies by securing independence for those cities which wished to be free of Spartan control.[19] When Sparta asked for Athenian aid and alliance against Boeotia, Corinthian support was given before the Athenian assembly and is represented by Xenophon as having been significant.[20] He also notes Corinthian actions on other occasions

[17] Xen. *Hell.* vi.4.1–15; Diod. xv.51.3–56; Paus. ix.13.3–12; Plut. *Ages.* 28.5–8; *Pelop.* 20–3.

[18] Below. On Leuctra itself, in which the Spartan allies played but a small part, see Anderson, *Military Theory and Practice*, 192–220; Pritchett, *Studies in Ancient Greek Topography*, i.49–58.

[19] For the Peloponnesian policy of Boeotia in this period, see Roy, *Historia*, xx (1971), 569–99.

[20] *Hell.* vi.5.33–7; cf. vii.1.1 (Corinth not named).

during the early 360s;[21] but it was Corinth's geographical position rather than her military assistance that was most important to Sparta, even if it was never exploited very effectively. Corinthian territory formed the exit from the Peloponnese for Spartan campaigns in Boeotia before 371; after that date it saw traffic in the opposite direction. In 370 the first Spartan priority was to guard the Isthmus. Xenophon (*Hell.* vi.5.11) records that a force of mercenaries gathered at Corinth; it was perhaps 1,000 strong.[22] That was only sensible before Boeotian intentions were known. Trouble in Arcadia soon became pressing (Xen. *Hell.* vi.5.3-11), and the troops left Corinth to give help at Orchomenus.[23] Thus the Isthmus lay open when Epaminondas invaded. Iphicrates the Athenian attempted to bar the exit of the Boeotians on their return, and his failure earned Xenophon's criticism;[24] when they invaded the Peloponnese a second time the attempt to prevent their passage was equally unsuccessful.[25] On the third invasion, Epaminondas did not risk trying to force the pass at Oneium; he persuaded the Argives to secure his route in advance, and their success demonstrates remarkable negligence on the part of the defending forces.[26] Although the efforts to defend the Oneium passes had no success, it is likely that a force was kept in Corinth for the purpose during at least part of the intervals between invasions. The troops sent by Dionysius of Syracuse to help Sparta in 368 are said by Xenophon to have arrived at some unspecified place from where, after deliberation among the allies already there, they left for Laconia; Corinth seems the obvious place—and fits Xenophon's language well.[27]

---

[21] *Hell.* vi.5.29; vii.2.2 (the first Boeotian invasion; cf. Diod. xv.65.6); vii.1.25 (help for Epidaurus against Argos); vii.2.17-23 (help for Phleious; cf. Aeschin. ii.168). Cf. Plut. *Timol.* 4.1-3: Corinthians fight against Argos and Cleonae. Corinth and Sparta's other allies in the region had to face not only Boeotian but also independent Argive aggression during this period: Roy, *Historia*, xx (1971), 572.

[22] The force is clearly Spartan, not Corinthian. Xenophon gives no number but names Polytropus as having taken an army of mercenaries from Corinth to Orchomenus in Arcadia. Diod. xv.62.1 has Polytropus take 1,000 Spartan citizen troops along with 500 Argive and Boeotian exiles to Orchomenus. Diodorus cannot be right in claiming that the 1,000 were Spartans; the obvious conclusion is that they were the mercenaries mentioned by Xenophon, and were joined by the Argive and Boeotian exiles for operations in Arcadia.

[23] Xen. *Hell.* vi.5.11-14; Diod. xv.62.1-2.

[24] Xen. *Hell.* vi.5.51-2, cf. vii.5.16; Plut. *Pelop.* 24.10. Cf. Stroud, *Hesperia*, xl (1971), 139. Cf. perhaps Polyaen. *Strat.* iii.9.28.

[25] Xen. *Hell.* vii.1.15-17; Diod. xv.68, cf. 72.1. Cf. Stroud, ibid., 139-40.

[26] Xen. *Hell.* vii.1.41-2; cf. Stroud, ibid., 140-1.

[27] Xen. *Hell.* vii.1.28, following the suggestion of Cawkwell, *CQ* xxvi (1976), 77 with n. 55: 'they sailed round . . . to Sparta' is exact for a journey from Lechaeum through the Corinthian Gulf and on to Laconia (or, indeed, for one over the diolkos and through the Saronic Gulf). Dionysius' first force certainly arrived at Corinth (Xen. *Hell.* vii.1.20; Diod. xv.70.1).

Corinth's importance for the defence of the Peloponnese made it as desirable to Boeotia to secure a change in her allegiance as it was vital for Sparta to retain it; Epaminondas, unable to persuade Corinth, tried to force her. He ravaged the Corinthia on his first invasion,[28] but made a more serious attempt during the second. After passing through Oneium he successfully attacked Sicyon and Pellene,[29] and laid waste the territory of Epidaurus and Troezen;[30] but he reserved his most serious effort for Corinth—or at least it is upon Corinth that Xenophon and Diodorus concentrate. Epaminondas probably won a minor action near Lechaeum,[31] and then tried to rush the Phleiasian Gate in the west city-wall; but his forces were repulsed by light troops who made skilful use of the advantage of height they gained by climbing both the slopes in this rough terrain and funerary monuments by the road.[32] Over the next few days the Boeotians ravaged the plain but suffered considerably from Chabrias' Athenians on the higher ground above it. A force sent by Dionysius of Syracuse which included cavalry inflicted further damage, and before long the invaders left.[33]

Despite the damage Boeotia could inflict on her almost with impunity, Corinth gave Sparta good service in the diplomatic sphere as well as in the military. In 367[34] Pelopidas persuaded the King to send down new terms for a Common Peace which accorded with

---

[28] Xen. *Hell.* vi.5.37. The claim is made by the Corinthian Cleiteles in a speech at Athens in which he attempts to persuade the Athenians to join the resistance to Boeotia; but there is no good reason to doubt its truth.

[29] Ibid., vii.1.18 merely records the attacks and not their outcome, but at vii.1.22 Sicyon is in alliance with Boeotia. At vii.2.11 Pellene is too (and cf. vii.2.2-3); but she did not go over to Epaminondas before sharing in a defeat at his hands near Lechaeum (below, n. 31). Diodorus records Boeotian success at Sicyon, Phleious, and other cities (xv.69.1); but in view of Xen. *Hell.* vii.2.2 and esp. 5-9, he is unlikely to be right about Phleious.

[30] Xen. *Hell.* vii.1.18 (Epidaurus); Diod. xv.69.1 (both).

[31] Paus. ix.15.4. This victory over Spartans, Pellenaeans, and Athenians under Chabrias will not fit into the first or fourth invasions; while on the third Pellene was in alliance with Boeotia (Xen. *Hell.* vii.2.11; she only returned to her old allegiance later, vii.2.18). Pausanias may refer to Pellenaean exiles, but no other source mentions action near Corinth during the third invasion, and while Chabrias is known to have commanded the Athenians at Corinth during the second (below), he is not recorded as having done so during any of the others (cf. Pritchett, *The Greek State at War*, ii.72-7). Diodorus (xv.69.1) has a Boeotian victory over the Corinthians as the first engagement in the Corinthia, and this may be Pausanias' action; Xenophon's silence about this Boeotian success is no argument against it.

[32] Xen. *Hell.* vii.1.18-19. Diod. xv.69.1 relates that some Boeotians entered the city and the Corinthians fled to their houses; but Chabrias killed or drove out the enemy. If this is the action at the Phleiasian Gate, Xenophon's account is to be preferred, in view of his access to Corinthian sources; but Diodorus may be reporting a different incident.

[33] Xen. *Hell.* vii.1.20-2; Diod. xv.69.2-70.1. Diodorus seems to believe that he is reporting a pitched battle, but the details imply rather that Chabrias used his force to harass the Boeotians in their work of destruction.

[34] On the chronology of the ²60s, see Roy, *Historia*, xx (1971), 590-4.

Boeotian interests;[35] but the Thebans failed to gain agreement to the terms at a general conference (Xen. *Hell.* vii.1.33-9). They tried to secure acceptance by approaching cities individually; but Corinth, the first city to receive Theban ambassadors, resisted and set the pattern for the reaction of others (Xen. *Hell.* vii.1.40). It may be significant that the ambassadors went to Corinth first. In view of what happened shortly afterwards (below, 379-81), they may have done so because the feeling for peace was particularly strong in that city; but geography is as plausible an explanation. Athens stood to lose more than most from the proposed terms and it would not have been wise to approach her first; Megara's agreement (if not already secured) was not a major priority.[36]

Boeotia was not alone in trying to win Corinth. Athenian policy after 369 was directed by Callistratus, who favoured resistance to Boeotia in concert with Sparta and what remained of her alliance; but in 366 Athens lost Oropus[37] and felt herself under direct threat for the first time since Leuctra. She appealed to her allies for help, but received none (Xen. *Hell.* vii.4.1); Callistratus was discredited,[38] and the Athenians reviewed their policy. In 369 it had seemed reasonable to resist Boeotian expansion by a Spartan alliance; but small success had been achieved. An alternative was now offered by the Arcadian Lycomedes, and an agreement was negotiated.[39] It remained as vital as ever to hold the Isthmus against Boeotian invasions; but Corinth, as a loyal ally of Sparta, might react unfavourably to the new arrangement. The Athenians therefore decided (perhaps by agreement with Lycomedes?) to try to gain control of the entrance to the Peloponnese for themselves; they planned to use the forces they had kept in Corinth for some time as a result of their alliance with Sparta. Unfortunately the proposal was mentioned in the Athenian assembly. The Corinthians reacted quickly: all Athenians on garrison duty in various parts of the Corinthia were replaced. They gathered in the city itself, and when Chares approached Cenchreae with a fleet he was politely refused entrance;

[35] Detailed references in Ryder, 136.

[36] Megara's stance in the years after Leuctra is not clear. She may not have decided positively in favour of the Boeotians, but she was hardly in a position to resist them; cf. Isoc. v.53. Megarian help for Sparta in 369 is recorded by Diod. xv.68.2, but this is almost certainly false: cf. Roy, *Historia*, xx (1971), 574 n. 33. Note Isoc. viii.117-18 (Megarian neutrality, but not precisely dated; see below, 381).

[37] Xen. *Hell.* vii.4.1; Diod. xv.76.1.

[38] References in Beloch, iii.1.190; see also Cawkwell, *CQ* xi (1961), 84 (but cf. below, 427-8).

[39] Xen. *Hell.* vii.4.2-3; the Athenian concern for Sparta reported by Xenophon is perhaps imaginary.

the Athenians who had served in the garrisons were sent home (Xen. *Hell.* vii.4.4-6).

Athens had not attempted to win Corinth by force once her plans were known; but it could hardly be assumed that no such attempt would be made in future, and mercenaries, both cavalry and foot, were raised.[40] Aristotle (*Pol.* 1306 a 21-4) states that the force was recruited because the Corinthian oligarchs could not trust the demos. They may have feared democratic revolution; but another possibility is that the general Corinthian population could not be trusted to remain loyal to Sparta. Aristotle's assertion may be mere assumption; but if he is right, what the oligarchs feared may have been precisely a further Athenian attempt on Corinth with support from within the city. There were Corinthian exiles in Athens (above, 371 n. 2); they will have retained some sympathy in their home city after their popularity before the King's Peace, and for those outside the Corinthian ruling circle there was a certain logic in joining Athens. Loyalty to Sparta was no longer dictated by Spartan strength, and Athens was a more attractive ally than an aggressive Boeotia; it may therefore have been in order to prevent the growth of feeling in favour of Athens that the Corinthian oligarchs devised a plan to extricate the city from her difficulties by diplomatic means.

Unfortunately our two sources conflict over the details. According to Xenophon, the Corinthians sent to Boeotia to ask for peace; the response was encouraging. They therefore sent to Sparta to ask if she too would cease fighting and, if not, to ask permission to do so alone. The Spartans would not make peace themselves, but did not obstruct Corinth,[41] so ambassadors went again to Boeotia and concluded, not an alliance as the Boeotians asked, but an agreement to be at peace. Corinth seems to have reached the same arrangement with Argos, and possibly with other Boeotian allies;[42] Phleious, Epidaurus, and perhaps some other cities made similar agreements.[43] Diodorus, however, reports (in far less detail) that Artaxerxes sent ambassadors and persuaded the Greeks in general to make a Common Peace (xv.76.3). It has usually been taken that we have here two versions of the same events, and there has been controversy over which to follow. For an interpretation of Corinth's role, the difference is considerable: either she took the initiative in proposing to

---

[40] Ibid., vii.4.6; cf. Plut. *Timol.* 4.4.

[41] Xenophon represents Sparta as giving her agreement willingly, but this is more than doubtful; cf. Isoc. vi.11-14, 90-1.

[42] Argos: Xen. *Hell.* vii.4.11; cf. Roy, *Historia*, xx (1971), 582. Others: Schaefer, *Demosthenes und seine Zeit*, i.114; Roy, ibid., 597.

[43] Xen. *Hell.* vii.4.6-10; Epidaurus: Isoc. vi.91.

Boeotia and getting accepted at Sparta a position of neutrality for herself and for some of her neighbours (Xenophon), or she merely accepted a Common Peace sponsored by the King in the Boeotian interest (Diodorus). Many have followed Diodorus; but his very vague report cannot stand against the detail given by Xenophon; it is best to reject Diodorus altogether as a misplaced and misconceived account of the intended Boeotian Peace of 367, which does not appear in the correct place in Diodorus' narrative.[44]

It has been suggested[45] that during these negotiations Boeotia secured acceptance, among the cities concerned, of the terms worked out by Pelopidas and the King two years before. This is true in the sense that Corinth and the cities which followed her lead now recognized, in effect, Messene's independence of Sparta; but it gives a seriously misleading impression of the responsibility for the arrangements. Xenophon's account has the Corinthians, and not the Boeotians, take the initiative; there is no reason to doubt him.[46] Corinth was in a position of extreme difficulty after dismissing the Athenians. She had not defended herself at all effectively during the second Boeotian invasion when she had enjoyed Athenian help; she was even less likely to be able to do so now, especially as there may have been a threat that the city would be betrayed to Athens from within. Those in power in Corinth defended themselves by withdrawing from the international scene altogether.[47]

The initiative of the Corinthian oligarchs was made because of their own exposed position; but it deserves more credit than it has usually been given.[48] For Corinth herself and for some of her neighbours it secured peace; it might have been even more fruitful. The implication of the arrangements was that small states might remain neutral in quarrels between the great powers. This was a principle which, if it could not eradicate the larger power struggles, at least might have helped to restrict their effects to those states

[44] Cf. Beloch, iii.2.241; according to his chronology, however, Diodorus is not wrong as to the date but merely as to the matter. See further below, 426-7.

[45] Ryder, 83, summarizing his earlier treatment in *CQ* vii (1957), 203-4.

[46] Ryder seems to characterize the agreement as he does partly in order to explain the mistaken reference in Diodorus to a Common Peace (*CQ* vii (1957), 204); the same problem is solved in a different, though no less unsatisfactory, way by Roy, *Historia*, xx (1971), 597-8. It is simpler to conclude that Diodorus was in error. If Isocrates can be trusted to show that the status of the cities of Asia Minor was an issue (which I doubt: below, 427), then Corinth offered acceptance of the terms of 367 in return for a recognition of Corinthian neutrality; but Xenophon still shows that the initiative came from Corinth.

[47] Another factor may have been Epaminondas' capture of Naupactus during his third invasion (Diod. xv.75.2); but this was hardly a major consideration.

[48] See, for example, Grote, viii.276-8; Beloch, iii.1.191; Bengtson, 282-3; Ryder, 83. For the affair from the Spartan point of view, see Cartledge, *Sparta and Lakonia*, 301.

which insisted on taking part in them. The principle is summarized well by Xenophon (*Hell.* vii.4.7): 'so that they might make the peace with those who wanted it, and let those who wished to make war do so.' The least that can be said is that Phleious and Epidaurus (and perhaps others too) were able to take advantage of the Corinthian initiative; at best, the Corinthians attempted (even if not with full consciousness) to secure general acceptance of a principle that would have allowed the lesser states of Greece to withdraw into peace after generations of disputes in which their own essential interests were not involved.[49] No doubt this interpretation is too simple to reflect the whole truth, for it ignores the effect of factional disputes;[50] but the principle would at least have achieved the resolution of such disputes within cities in a way which reflected local conditions. The advantages of neutrality are directly attested for Megara by Isocrates: in the *De Pace*, of 355, he drew attention to her peace and prosperity in the midst of war and poverty.[51]

At least until the death of Epaminondas[52] it appears that Corinth maintained her neutrality and that it was respected by other states. Corinth is not mentioned in Xenophon's *Hellenica* after 365, nor does she appear in Diodorus' account; to conclude that she was not involved is dangerous, but the silence is probably significant. Corinth does not figure among the recorded combatants at Mantinea.[53] Of the states which negotiated neutrality in 365, Phleious and Epidaurus might have been omitted even if they had been present; but Corinth is less likely to have been ignored. Corinth seems to have allowed troops from each side to pass through her territory without molestation;[54] she was presumably taking advantage of her neutrality rather than merely accepting the inevitable—though the two perhaps amount to much the same thing.[55]

[49] It is possible that not only the former enemies of Boeotia but also at least one of her allies benefited. Phocis did not take part in the final invasion of the Peloponnese by Epaminondas, on the ground that her alliance with Boeotia only required her to help in defending Boeotia, not in attacking her enemies (Xen. *Hell.* vii.5.4; cf. Diod. xv.85.2). Phocis may have used whatever excuse she could find, and her argument was not the same as Corinth's had been; but she may have been encouraged by Corinth's success in negotiating neutrality some years before.

[50] For a judicious assessment of this effect, cf. Roy, *Historia*, xx (1971), 588–90.

[51] viii.117–18. Megara may have been one of the unnamed cities which took advantage of the opportunity Corinth's initiative provided.

[52] Xen. *Hell.* vii.5; Diod. xv.82–8.

[53] Xen. *Hell.* vii.5.18; Diod. xv.84.4, 85.2. Diodorus mentions minor states opposed to Boeotia without naming them; this permits belief in Corinthian participation, but it hardly encourages it.

[54] Attested specifically for Athens: Xen. *Hell.* vii.5.15; for Boeotia, cf. vii.5.6.

[55] Unlike Corinth, Phleious did not remain neutral for long: she joined with Athens, Arcadia, Achaea, and Elis in a treaty probably made immediately after the second battle

After Epaminondas' death there was less pressing reason for Corinth to maintain neutrality to preserve her safety; the cockpit of Greek international politics transferred to central Greece during the Sacred War, when Phocis took control of the temple at Delphi and was challenged by Boeotia and finally crushed by Philip of Macedon. We have very little information about Corinth's stance in these years. When Philip settled the affairs of Delphi in 346 he deprived Corinth of her traditional role there on the ground that she had shared in Phocian impiety.[56] His accusation is apparently justified by Corinth's frequent appearance in the *naopoioi* lists at Delphi during the years of Phocian control,[57] but the implications of this evidence are difficult to assess. Philip chose to claim that Corinth had been guilty of complicity in the Phocian sacrilege; but he may have been right only in the technical sense that Corinth had participated in the affairs of the temple while it was under Phocian control. This might have been the result of a strict neutrality which was interpreted by Philip, perhaps because of pressure from his allies, as hostility when he imposed his settlement in 346.[58] On the other hand, Corinth may have maintained her relations with Phocian Delphi because she positively supported Phocis: it would have been natural for Corinth, if she made a decision at all, to take the side of Phocis along with Sparta and Athens. It is impossible to reach a definite conclusion;[59] but even if Corinth did ally herself with the Phocians, it is unlikely that she took more than a minor part in the hostilities.[60]

of Mantinea (Tod, ii, no. 144; *Staatsverträge*, ii. no. 290). If the commonly printed restoration of line 30 of the text is correct, the reason was probably that Phleious regained a democratic constitution after 365; it is unnecessary to doubt (with Roy, *Historia*, xx (1971), 587 n. 95) that τὸν] δῆμον . . . [τὸν Φλειασίων . . . , especially in such a context, implies that the city was a democracy.

[56] Diod. xvi.60.2. The Corinthians are mentioned here, but not Phocis' more important allies; a lacuna has often been suspected (cf. Schaefer, *Demosthenes und seine Zeit*, ii. 286 n. 2). There are no grounds, however, for emending Corinth out of the text.

[57] Most conveniently in *SIG*³ 241, lines 1-70 *passim*.

[58] This may have been connected with the presence of Phalaecus and some of his mercenaries in Corinth at about this time (Schaefer, *Demosthenes und seine Zeit*, ii.286 n. 2); some of the mercenaries took service with Timoleon in Sicily: Plut. *Timol.* 30.7-8; cf. Diod. xvi.61.4. In view of Plut. *Timol.* 30.8 (cf. *Mor.* 552 F), I see no reason to doubt (with Talbert, *Timoleon*, 57 with n. 1) that Timoleon recruited some of the mercenaries who had served with Phalaecus. Since he and his men cannot have been in Corinth for long when the decision to punish the city was taken, the chronology is a little tight; but not impossibly so.

[59] It has sometimes been supposed that Corinth did take Phocis' part: Ellis, *Philip II and Macedonian Imperialism*, 74, 93. But this ignores the establishment of Corinthian neutrality in 365; the evidence is not sufficient to prove that she abandoned it—except in the eyes of the committed enemies of Phocis.

[60] Note Plut. *Timol.* 3.1: Corinth enjoyed peace and leisure when Timoleon was sent to Sicily; but this is as likely as not to be a construction of Plutarch's.

Corinth figures among the allies who joined Athens in 340 and fought Philip at Chaeronea.[61] Thus, even though she may have stood aside from the quarrels of the recent past, she joined Demosthenes in the crisis of Greek independence. She may have recognized that the Macedonian threat was of a quite different order from that posed by any city; but she had private reasons too. Part of her motive will have been that she was excluded from the organization of the Pythia in 346; she will also have remembered Philip's interference with her Adriatic colonies in 343/2.[62] After Philip's victory Corinth prepared initially to resist (Lucian, *De Hist. Conscr.* 3), but surrendered instead.[63] Philip convened a congress at Corinth which confirmed Macedonian domination of Greece, but the arrangements have no place in the history of an independent Corinth: Acrocorinth was garrisoned by Macedonian troops,[64] and with a few intervals remained in Macedonian hands until Flamininus' settlement of Greece in 196 BC.

b. Internal Affairs

In the early years after the King's Peace, those who held power in Corinth relied heavily on Spartan support; it is therefore to be expected that Spartan weakness after Leuctra would have encouraged change. No such change is recorded immediately after 371, but a report of Diodorus concerning internal conflict at Corinth in 375/4 probably refers to this time (above, 374). Diodorus gives his account as one example of a general trend of attacks on those who had control of their cities under Spartan leadership,[65] but he says nothing more about the issues involved. Numerous Corinthian exiles living in Argos were admitted to the city, but killed each other when they were discovered; others were accused of complicity and either

[61] Athens, Corinth, and Boeotia are the only states named by Strabo 414. Cf. Dem. xviii.237; Plut. Dem. 17.5 (both also giving Leucas and Corcyra); (Plut.) *Mor.* 851 B.
[62] Cf. Dem. ix.34. It is doubtful, however, whether a formal alliance was made between Corinth and Athens as early as the time of the Athenian expedition to Acarnania in 343/2 (as Beloch, iii.1.545-6), and as far as I am aware there is no evidence for the often repeated view that Corinth, after an appeal for help from her colonies, herself approached Athens (cf., e.g., Beloch, ibid.; Pickard-Cambridge in *CAH* vi.249; Ellis, *Philip II and Macedonian Imperialism*, 158). See rather Griffith in Hammond and Griffith, *History of Macedonia*, ii.508 n. 1.
[63] Aelian, *Var. Hist.* vi.1; cf. Roebuck, *CP* xliii (1948), 83.
[64] Polyb. xxxviii.3.3; Plut. *Arat.* 23.4. Cf. Griffith in Hammond and Griffith, *History of Macedonia*, ii.612 n. 3. It is unclear whether the garrison was imposed as soon as Corinth surrendered (as Schaefer, *Demosthenes und seine Zeit*, iii.40), or not until the congress had completed its business; the question is important, but speculation is without point.
[65] xv.40; Corinth, xv.40.3.

put to death or exiled. Argos was a natural place of refuge for those Corinthians who had been responsible for the recent 'union' with Argos, and it is possible that the ultimate aim of the revolutionaries was to revive the scheme in the hopeful circumstances created by Leuctra, perhaps with Boeotian support;[66] but this is mere speculation. There are no signs that Epaminondas could call on help from within the city during his attempt on Corinth; it is unlikely that a significant pro-Boeotian faction developed, but in the absence of evidence we cannot be sure.[67] It would be even more hazardous to attempt to identify the exiles from Argos as democrats. An incidental remark of Xenophon's helps to show that the Laconizing faction which gained power in Corinth after the King's Peace remained in control until 366: Pasimelus, named by Xenophon as having betrayed Corinth's Long Walls in 392 (above, 362), was still giving service to Sparta more than twenty-five years later, when he was summoned from Corinth by Euphron of Sicyon to take over that city's port in the Spartan interest.[68]

The mercenaries raised in the crisis of 366, however, gave their commander an opportunity to take Corinth over by force. Timophanes the brother of Timoleon was appointed to lead them[69] and, perhaps following the example of Euphron in Sicyon,[70] he gained control of the city for himself[71] and put many leading citizens to death without trial.[72] Whether more was involved in Timophanes' tyranny than

[66] These events, if they are correctly placed after Leuctra, were probably approximately contemporary with the horrific massacre of the scytalism at Argos (Diod. xv.57.3–58); there may have been some connection between the two revolutions—if only in the desire of the Corinthian exiles, who were probably oligarchically inclined, to escape implication in the murderous events at Argos; but if there was it cannot be recovered. If Diodorus' date is right, that will make little difference: the Corinthian exiles had reason to hope for success already in 375/4, though Athens (where there were other Corinthian exiles: above, 371 n. 2) may have been a more probable source of help than Boeotia.

[67] It might be argued that the attempt of the exiles from Argos was timed to coincide with Epaminondas' attack; but there are no points of contact between our accounts of the two events.

[68] *Hell.* vii.3.2; cf. Cawkwell, *CQ* xxvi (1976), 77.

[69] Plut. *Timol.* 4.4. Diodorus' account (xvi.65.3–8) places the events in 346/5; but Plutarch's version, in which Timoleon lived a private life for about twenty years after murdering his tyrant brother (*Timol.* 7.1), accords with Xenophon's context for the raising of the mercenaries (*Hell.* vii.4.6; that the two sources refer to the same force is clear from Plut. *Timol.* 4.4), and must be correct (cf. Beloch, iii.1.192 n. 2). Diodorus' account results from a double process of distortion: first, a source was misunderstood to give a false date for Timophanes; then, details were invented to dramatize the choice of Timoleon for the expedition to Sicily by placing it in the very middle of discussion of what to do with him for murdering his brother.

[70] Beloch, iii.1.192.

[71] Ar. *Pol.* 1306 a 21–4; Plut. *Timol.* 4.4–5; cf. Diod. xvi. 65.3.

[72] Plut. *Timol.* 4.5. It seems likely that these events took place *after* the negotiations for neutrality in 365 (above, 379–81); but there is no evidence.

mere personal ambition is doubtful. Diodorus' version implies that
he was a tyrant of the demagogic type; but this receives no support
elsewhere.[73] Since Diodorus' account contains details invented in
order to dramatize the choice of Timoleon to go to Sicily (above,
n. 69), it may be strongly suspected that it also contains details
invented in order to force Timophanes into one accepted pattern
of tyranny. It cannot be excluded that Timophanes tried to build
his tyranny on the foundation of popular support;[74] though if he
did, that does not show that there was a strong democratic movement in Corinth for him to exploit. The foundation he chose was
too shallow, and the Corinthian demos was unable to prevent
Timoleon from assassinating his brother[75]—either with his own
hand (Diod. xvi.65.4) or through the agency of others (Plut. *Timol.*
4.5-8). The oligarchs regained control almost at once.[76] Plutarch's
account of the choice of Timoleon to go to Sicily implies that the
city had a democratic constitution;[77] but this has been correctly
regarded as an attempt to 'create the impression that Timoleon was
a popular choice for the mission of liberating Syracuse'.[78] Unless
Corinth had only recently become democratic, Plutarch's narrative
here conflicts with his own statement that Dion sent for help from
Corinth when he wished to devise an oligarchic constitution for
Syracuse 'because he saw that Corinth was more oligarchically
governed, and dealt with little public business in the assembly'.[79]

[73] Aristotle (*Pol.* 1306 a 21-4) mentions the demos, but only in so far as it was mistrust
of the demos that persuaded the oligarchs to hire mercenaries; since the context was a crisis
of foreign policy, the mistrust is as likely to have been caused by fear that the demos would
not accept the oligarchs' foreign policy (above, 379) as by a fear of democratic revolution.
Xenophon's account of the activity of the mercenaries implies that they were not used to
keep the demos under control, but for operations against foreign enemies (*Hell.* vii.4.6).

[74] The implications of Diodorus' account have often been accepted; cf. Beloch, iii.1.192;
Berve, *Tyrannis*, i.304; Roy, *Historia*, xx (1971), 582 n. 71.

[75] The account of Sordi, *Timoleonte*, 6-8, in which Timoleon kills his brother in the
interests of Boeotia and democracy, is pure fantasy.

[76] We can conclude nothing for the history of classical Corinth from an anecdote
preserved by Aelian (*Var. Hist.* xiv.24) about two wealthy Corinthians, Theocles and
Thrasonides (and also about Praxis of Mytilene), who cancelled debts owing to them and
were thus spared when other creditors were killed. The moralizing tendency of the story
makes it suspect, and it is in any case without a date. There are no points of contact with
known events in fourth-century Corinth. That the name of a Corinthian commander at
Syracuse in the late fifth century is given by one MS as Thrasonides (above, 333 n. 34) is
mere coincidence.

[77] *Timol.* 3.2: nomination of Timoleon by 'one who stood up from the crowd', presumably in the assembly; cf. 5.2 and 7.2.

[78] Talbert, *Timoleon*, 131.

[79] *Dion*, 53.2-4. Diod. xvi.65.6-9 (discussion of the case of Timoleon by the Corinthian
gerousia) implies that Corinth was an oligarchy when Timoleon was sent to Sicily. I hesitate
to use this evidence, for it contains invented material (above, n. 69); but this aspect may
well be genuine.

The evidence is insufficient for certainty; but it is unlikely that the Corinth upon which a Macedonian garrison was imposed was anything other than oligarchically governed.[80]

[80] Macedonian partisans, among them perhaps Demaratus and Deinarchus (below, 391), may have been installed in power when Corinth surrendered to Philip or even before; but there is no evidence (cf. Griffith in Hammond and Griffith, *History of Macedonia*, ii.613–14 n. 3).

XXVI.   Corinth and her Colonies

Corinth no doubt enjoyed those relations with her colonies—with the exception of Corcyra—that were normal for Greek metropoleis. These were most frequently to be observed in the religious sphere. Thucydides states, as part of the explanation of Corinth's action at Epidamnus in 435, that the Corcyraeans 'did not give the usual offerings at the common festivals, nor did they reserve the first portions at sacrifices for a Corinthian as did the other colonies'.[1] The precise character of the religious obligations of Corinthian colonies may have been special; but close co-operation in matters of cult with the metropolis is widely attested in Greek colonies, and it is clear that Corcyra was an exception to the rule not just in the Corinthian sphere.[2] The ties that these regular joint celebrations represented were powerful, as is shown by the emphasis Thucydides placed on the failure of the Corcyraeans to maintain them; but although they provided admirable opportunities for more specifically political links, they could not by themselves guarantee more than a strong common sentiment. Even that might be overridden, as the Corcyraean case shows, by other considerations. It would be interesting to know if the temporary rupture between Corinth and her Adriatic colonies which followed the expulsion of the Cypselids from Corinth (above, 270-1) had the effect of stopping, for a while, such common celebrations; but we have no evidence.

A common right of the metropolis to send extra drafts of colonists after the original foundation may have been of more practical importance. There is no evidence of such a general right in the Corinthian sphere; the cases of Epidamnus (itself a Corcyraean and not a Corinthian colony), Anactorium (above, 274), and Syracuse in Timoleon's day (below, 391-2) were special. But reinforcements of this kind are known in sufficient numbers to make it likely that a general right of reinforcement was normal.[3] Its significance, however,

---

[1] i.25.4. The precise translation of the first item is not clear. It could refer to festivals held either in the metropolis and attended by representatives of all colonies, or in the colonies and attended by Corinthians; cf. Graham, *Colony and Mother City*, 161. The difference matters little for the present purpose.

[2] Cf. Graham, *Colony and Mother City*, esp. ch. viii.

[3] Graham, *Colony and Mother City*, Index s.v. reinforcement.

cannot be assessed in the absence of evidence for the frequency with
which it was exercised. Since the land of the colonies was never
unlimited—even though in the case of Syracuse it eventually became
very extensive—it can hardly be true that any Corinthian could
approach the authorities in one of the Corinthian colonies with a
demand for a plot of land and be confident of receiving one. The
character of the restrictions on free access will have differed from
case to case, and cannot be recovered; but they will normally have
depended, in the nature of the case, on the availability of resources
in the colony rather than on the requirements of the metropolis.
The serious losses sustained by Ambracia during the Archidamian
War created a situation in which the colony might have welcomed
such a reinforcement; but none is recorded. Thucydides informs us
rather that Corinth sent a garrison of 300 to defend her colony
(above, 318); such a temporary reinforcement may have been all
Corinth felt able to offer when she was under extreme military
pressure herself. If Corinthians did settle from time to time in the
colonies, that would have served to strengthen the ties of sentiment
already made powerful by shared cult celebrations; but it is unlikely
that the reinforcements were so frequent and so numerous that the
colonies provided, not only temporary relief of the pressure on
Corinthian land at the time of their foundation, but also a permanent
solution. Once a colony was established within a defined territory
it will normally have faced much the same population problems as
the mother city.

In the case of Syracuse the relationship between metropolis and
colony is not likely to have gone beyond the feelings of filial regard
fostered by traditional religious practice; but the strength of the
feeling is shown by the number of occasions on which even our
meagre evidence records minor benefits conferred, usually by the
parent on the child. That nothing is preserved for the archaic period
depends on the character of our sources;[4] as soon as they become
more informative we begin to hear of expressions of the relationship.
Syracuse was saved by the intervention of Corinth and Corcyra
from any more distressing consequence of her defeat at the hands
of Hippocrates of Gela than the cession of her own colony of

[4] Dunbabin, *Western Greeks*, 244, suggested that the late arrival of Attic pottery at
Syracuse (in comparison with other western sites) which he detected is to be attributed
to an especially close commercial connection between Syracuse and Corinth. The amount
of published material from Syracuse is not yet large enough to base conclusions on; if
Corinthian was sold for longer at Syracuse, the explanation is probably that the traditional
mechanisms of distribution were especially strong there (above, 115), rather than that
Syracusans were more inclined to buy Corinthian. Sentiment is not likely to have affected
commercial judgement.

Camarina.[5] A decade later, however, when the Greeks made an appeal to Syracuse for help against Xerxes, none was given, for the city was now under the control of Gelon (Hdt. vii.153-63). In the mid-fifth century the Syracusans sent into exile at Corinth the Sicel king Ducetius; there can be little doubt that Corinth was chosen because of her close relationship to Syracuse. Soon after, he returned to Sicily and founded a colony at Cale Acte on the north coast. Diodorus reports that he broke his agreement with Syracuse by doing so; Corinth seems therefore to have shown scant regard for her colony by allowing him to escape.[6]

It was natural for Syracuse to approach Corinth with a request for aid against the Sicilian Expedition 'because of their relationship' (Thuc. vi.88.7); but Corinth's enthusiastic response depended more on her own passionate hatred for Athens than on concern for her colony (above, 332). When a request had passed in the opposite direction in 431 the Syracusans had been notably silent.[7] When the Sicilian Expedition had drawn them into the conflict they participated in the Ionian War: 'Hermocrates of Syracuse had been especially prominent in urging that they should join in what was left of the task of destroying Athens, and twenty ships arrived from Syracuse' (Thuc. viii.26.1). Corinth may have afforded official help to Dionysius a little later; but the individual Corinthians of whom we hear may rather have acted in a private capacity.[8] Dion is reported by Diodorus (xvi.6.5) to have left from Corinth on his mission to liberate Syracuse from the tyranny of Dionysius II, and to have asked for Corinthian help; but it is not recorded that he received any, and Plutarch says nothing of Corinth but gives Zacynthus as the rendezvous (*Dion* 22.8; 23.4). The truth about Timoleon (below) may have distorted Diodorus' account of Dion.[9] Once in power at Syracuse, Dion sent for legislators from Corinth (Plut. *Dion*, 53.2-4); this may, but need not, imply official Corinthian assistance.[10]

These scraps prove no more than that the traditional ties between

[5] Hdt. vii.154.3; cf. Graham, *Colony and Mother City*, 143-4.

[6] xii.8. The reconstruction of Rizzo, *La Repubblica di Siracusa nel momento di Ducezio*, 153-69, in which Ducetius' foundation is to the advantage of Syracuse, is too conjectural.

[7] Thuc. ii.7.2 represents the Spartans as asking for 500 ships from Italy and Sicily—a difficult number to credit; presumably the Corinthians supported whatever request the Spartans actually made at Syracuse.

[8] See Talbert, *Timoleon*, 53-4, for references and discussion. Since the thirty ships, some of them Peloponnesian, which reached Syracuse in answer to Dionysius' request were led by a Spartan (Diod. xiv.63.4), it is perhaps unlikely that Corinthian vessels were among them at a time (396) when relations with Sparta were seriously strained; but Corinthian regard for Syracuse may have been stronger than her reluctance to serve with Sparta.

[9] Compare the story of Archias: above, 65-6.

[10] Cf. Talbert, *Timoleon*, 54.

colony and metropolis often encouraged Syracuse to turn to Corinth when she was in difficulty; Corinth was happy to offer diplomatic assistance, or a home in exile to a Ducetius; but she would only respond with positive commitment if she could hope to advance her own interests by doing so. Similar conclusions may be drawn from her role in the activity of her most spectacular gift to Syracuse: Timoleon.[11] Corinth played little part in mainland affairs between 365 and 340; but it would be difficult to argue that Timoleon's mission represented from the first an attempt by Corinth to exploit her colony in order to make up in the west for what she had lost in the mainland. On the contrary, she took only a minor interest in Timoleon until he gained such success that he was worth cultivating. When an appeal for help came from Syracusan exiles,[12] Corinth sent Timoleon with her blessing, at least if he had any success;[13] but since he had taken no part in public life for twenty years after murdering his brother (above, 384 with n. 69) the choice of Timoleon hardly indicates heavy involvement. He was also provided with vessels—seven only, which were joined by two from Corcyra and one from Leucas;[14] but Corinth probably gave neither crews for the vessels nor enough money to enable the mercenaries who sailed in them to be properly paid.[15] It was but a small contribution to provide ships alone, especially as the hulls are likely to have been idle for years in any case, but even this minor involvement needs explanation, and no obvious one presents itself.[16] Corinth can hardly have hoped to gain anything positive, since the help she gave was minimal; so we should perhaps ask rather what Corinth feared to lose than what she hoped to gain. The answer is then clear enough: Timoleon and the vessels were in any case idle; if they never returned nothing much would have been lost. Sentimental ties will have inclined Corinth to a favourable answer if one were possible; and she probably responded to the Syracusan appeals because there was no reason not to: both her ships and Timoleon were already rotting in retirement.

A stronger commitment was made when it began to appear that Timoleon might achieve some success. After being welcomed to

[11] The political involvement of Corinth in Syracusan affairs under Dion and Timoleon is consistently overestimated by Seibert, 'Metropolis und Apoikie', 114-21.

[12] Despite the impression given by Plut. *Timol.* 2, the help was asked for against Dionysius II and not the Carthaginians: cf. Westlake, *Essays*, 265-75; Talbert, *Timoleon*, 122.

[13] Plut. *Timol.* 7.2; Diod. xvi.66.2.

[14] Plut. *Timol.* 8.4; Diod. xvi.66.2. Ps.-Ar. *Rhet. ad Alex.* 1429 b 18-22 gives nine vessels all told, but it is not clear whether the reference is to the original force or to the reinforcements (below).

[15] On all the details, cf. Talbert, *Timoleon*, 55-7.

[16] Talbert, ibid., 54 (cf. also 201-2), leaves the question open.

Tauromenium,[17] he won the battle of Adranum;[18] and when he was well on the way to taking all Syracuse[19] Corinth sent large reinforcements: 2,000 hoplites, 200 cavalry (Plut. *Timol.* 16.3), and ten ships (Diod. xvi.69.4). This was a very large force, given the resources of the city and the distance from home at which it was to operate: only 3,000 hoplites had been provided by Corinth for the Battle of the Nemea in her own territory in 394. Corinth now evidently hoped for considerable rewards from Timoleon, but exactly what her expectations were it is impossible to say. I take it that the romantic notions of defending freedom and attacking tyrants, which Plutarch (*Timol.* 2.2) adduces when Timoleon was originally sent, are irrelevant; there is no other evidence, and Corinth's hopes were probably no more precise than to derive what material and political advantage she could from the venture.[20] It is perhaps more than a coincidence that the leaders of the Corinthian reinforcements, Deinarchus and Demaratus,[21] are named by Demosthenes as agents of Philip of Macedon in Corinth.[22] It is an obvious conjecture that Philip's men in Corinth ensured that she was unable to resist him very effectively by denuding her of forces just at the critical time.[23]

There were rapid and possibly extensive material benefits for Corinth from her investment. Timoleon sent booty to Corinth, and on the inscription set up with it, which has been partially preserved, drew attention to the relationship between the city of his origin and that which he had saved; but the exact restoration remains uncertain.[24] He also offered the opportunity of settling in Sicily to

[17] Plut. *Timol.* 10.6-8; Diod. xvi.68.7-8.
[18] Plut. *Timol.* 12; Diod. xvi.68.9-10.
[19] For discussion (inconclusive) of the differing accounts of Plutarch and Diodorus, see Talbert, *Timoleon*, 97-110.
[20] It can hardly be argued that the purpose was to enable Timoleon to recruit settlers from Corinth and thus ease population problems (below).
[21] Plut. *Timol.* 21.3; 24.4; 27.6.
[22] xviii.295. The appearance of the two names together, even though the contexts are quite different, makes the identification almost certain; it has already been made by Schaefer, *Demosthenes und seine Zeit*, ii.350 n. 2; iii.39. For their subsequent careers, see Berve, *Das Alexanderreich*, ii, nos. 248, 253.
[23] On the chronology (343), see Talbert, *Timoleon*, 49. Sordi, *Timoleonte*, 10-12, suggests that Timoleon, Demaratus, and Deinarchus were all Macedonian partisans, sent to Sicily by the anti-Macedonian government of Corinth in order to get them out of the way. It might have been useful to remove Macedonian sympathizers; but hardly to deprive the city of 2,000 hoplites, 200 cavalry, and ten ships at the same time.
[24] Κτιστῆρα Κόρινθον, 'the founder Corinth', is preserved, but it is not clear whether the reference is to the city itself or to an eponymous hero. If the most probable restoration of the dedication is correct it includes, significantly, only Corinthian colonies (Leucas, Ambracia, Corcyra, and Apollonia), apart from Corinth herself, even though many other cities had by this stage contributed (above, 174). For references, see Talbert, *Timoleon*, 76-7; for a general account of the booty, Plut. *Timol.* 29.

(among others) any Corinthians who wanted it;[25] it is not recorded
how many Corinthians took up the offer.[26] Timoleon personally
showed a natural regard for Corinth when he sent deposed tyrants
there—presumably for safe keeping, as the Syracusans had done with
Ducetius over a century before[27]—and when he was assisted in
constitutional matters by the Corinthians Cephalus and Dionysius.[28]
Corinth no doubt derived more benefit than most mainland cities
from the revival of Sicilian prosperity and increased trade across
the Adriatic.[29] But if the Corinthians hoped to make any significant
political gains they were disappointed: Philip deprived them of any
chance to exploit Timoleon's success almost as soon as it had been
achieved.

Potidaea was special among Corinthian colonies, both because she
was not a western foundation and because she was a member of the
Delian League; she is also the only colony for which we have clear
evidence of a formal institutional link between metropolis and
colony in the *epidemiourgoi* 'whom the Corinthians sent each year'
(Thuc. i.56.2) to the city. We know nothing of Potidaea after her
foundation until the invasion of Xerxes. The city contributed,
perforce, to the armaments of Xerxes (Hdt. vii.123.1); but she
revolted as soon as she was able, successfully defended herself
against a long siege by Artabazus (Hdt. viii.126.2-129), and sent
a small force to Plataea, where it stood alongside the Corinthians
(Hdt. ix.28.3). For these services the Potidaeans were inscribed on
the Serpent Column at Delphi (above, 272 n. 6). Since she had
already fought against the Persians, Potidaea was probably a founder
member of the Delian League.[30] Her enthusiastic resistance against
Artabazus and her participation at Plataea may or may not have
been influenced by the knowledge that her metropolis was fighting
on the same side; but her association with Athens will have caused
no difficulties in her relationship with Corinth until the First
Peloponnesian War. It is not recorded in the extant lists that she
paid tribute to Athens until after the Thirty Years Peace; but we
cannot know whether that is because of the incomplete preservation
of the stones, because she was still contributing ships, or because

---

[25] Plut. *Timol.* 22.4-23.6; Diod. xvi.82.3,5. For discussion, Westlake, *CHJ* vii (1941-3),
81-4.
[26] Diod. xvi.82.3 does not mean (despite Wiseman, 12) that 5,000 colonists were Corinthian: Westlake, ibid., 81 n. 40.
[27] Dionysius II: Plut. *Timol.* 13.3-15; Diod. xvi.70.1-3. Leptines: Plut. *Timol.* 24.2; cf.
Diod. xvi.72.5.
[28] Plut. *Timol.* 24.3; Diod. xiii.35.3; xvi.82.6. See Talbert, *Timoleon*, 130-43, esp. 133.
[29] For the implications of all this for the Corinthian mint, see above, 174.
[30] *ATL* iii.223.

she was for at least part of the time in rebellion.[31] Even in the latter case, Potidaea's decisions may have been taken with little regard to Corinth. Potidaea must have been listed as an Athenian ally in the Thirty Years Peace even though we have no specific evidence; thus when Corinth agitated for rebellion through her *epidemiourgoi* after Sybota she was in clear breach of her treaty obligations (above, 292-6). When Corinth subsequently supported the rebellion she had fomented, she was pursuing her own interests perhaps in flagrant disregard of those of her colony: her purpose was to provide further arguments in favour of war with Athens to present to her Peloponnesian allies. Corinth enjoyed success; Potidaea suffered destruction.

None of this information enables us to reconstruct the character of Corinth's relationship with her single Aegean colony. Presumably Potidaea was among the colonies from which Thucydides has the Corinthians claim that they received a proper respect (i.38.3). The colony was persuaded to rebel in 432; but the local assistance of Perdiccas[32] may have been a more powerful argument than those of the Corinthians. Certainly Corinth could exert no pressure in the Aegean. The extent of her influence will have depended on nothing but her arguments and the degree of affection in which she was held; the latter cannot be quantified. The information about the *epidemiourgoi* provides the most tantalizing evidence; but it is impossible to make much of it. The office was annual, and held by Corinthians;[33] it is not quite clear from the words of Thucydides whether there was more than one *epidemiourgos* each year. The functions of the office are unknown,[34] and may have been little more than ceremonial: to be, for example, the Corinthian for whom the first portions at sacrifices were normally preserved (Thuc. i.25.4). But the potential use of the office is powerfully demonstrated by the Potidaean Revolt. If other Corinthian colonies received similar officers, the mechanisms by which Corinth secured and maintained her influence in north-western waters (above, 274-80) would be easy to guess at; but it is possible that *epidemiourgoi* were sent to Potidaea—perhaps

---

[31] Even a resolution of the general controversy over the interpretation of the early lists (for one view, with references, see Meiggs, *Athenian Empire*, 109-24) would not help to reconstruct the case of one particular state. There are no grounds for supposing, with *ATL* iii.321 with n. 88 (cf. Alexander, *Potidaea*, 48), that certain passages in the *Eumenides* of Aeschylus refer to trouble at Potidaea at this time; cf. Kagan, *Outbreak*, 274 n. 5.

[32] Thuc. i.56.2; 57.4; 58.2.

[33] Note ἔπεμπον, 'they sent', at Thuc. i.56.2.

[34] It is dangerous in principle to search for guidance in the functions of magistrates with similar titles elsewhere (as, e.g., Alexander, *Potidaea*, 22-3); the fact that the Potidaean *epidemiourgoi* were sent to the city by Corinth makes them unique in our evidence.

first at a stage well after the foundation—precisely because there was so little regular contact between the metropolis and this isolated colony that maintenance of ties of cult could not be guaranteed unless a special arrangement was made. The office is suggestive; but none of the suggestions can be confirmed.

Corinth's relationships with her Adriatic colonies in the mid-fifth century are fully treated above, 274-80, where they find their proper place in the narrative. In this region, to which Corinth had easy maritime access, she was able to exploit her traditional links with the colonies of the tyrants for political gain, and she established an informal control, with the full co-operation of her colonies—although that control was so resented by Corcyra that she broke even the ties of cult. It might seem that the more independent position of Syracuse is to be explained by her longer history: since she was founded so early, the relationship between Syracuse and her metropolis was less well defined. But the distinction was rather one of geography than of chronology. Corcyra was also founded in the eighth century; but it was closer to home, and in fact was subjected to Corinth under Periander, if not before (above, 218-9, 224). During the rule of Periander, Corcyra was in the same position as Leucas, Ambracia, and Anactorium: all were governed by rulers related to the tyrant of Corinth (above, 212). The later independence of Corcyra was the result of subsequent developments, not of her different status as an early foundation. The lack of importance for later relationships of the conditions which obtained at the time of foundation is demonstrated also by the specially close links Corinth enjoyed in the fifth century with her faithful Adriatic colonies. Since these were in origin ruled by relatives of the Corinthian tyrants, there was of necessity a shift when the last tyrant of Corinth was deposed; the ties between metropolis and colonies which existed in the fifth century were established when personal motives for hostility were no longer relevant after the overthrow of the colonial tyrants. The precise character at any time of the relationship between metropolis and colony did not depend on links preserved from the distant past, but on contemporary political conditions.

Those conditions were disastrous for Corinth after the outbreak of the Archidamian War, which the Corinthians urged Sparta to undertake precisely because in their view Athens had prevented them from subjugating Corcyra: the war deprived Corinth of almost all her strength in the north-west. But even though Corinth's capacity to exploit the credit she had won here was seriously diminished, the credit remained and bore fruit well into the fourth century. Corinth was assisted in her efforts against the Sicilian Expedition and during the Ionian War by both Ambracia (despite her heavy losses) and Leucas.[35] It is hardly surprising that her colonies should have joined Corinth in these actions, for they had themselves suffered from Athenian attacks; but Corinth was also able to secure their allegiance in all the changes of direction in her foreign policy during the fourth century. Both Leucas and Ambracia adhered to the anti-Spartan alliance in the Corinthian War (above, 349), although their military assistance is not recorded; and when Corinth returned to her Spartan loyalties her colonies followed and gave practical help in the Adriatic naval actions of the 370s.[36] Leucas even fought along-side her metropolis at Chaeronea (above, 383 n. 61). Both Corcyra and Leucas took part in the first stage of Timoleon's expedition (above, 390); help at this early stage, when there can have seemed little hope of success, is far more important than their representation, along with Ambracia, among the later reinforcements, for by that time very many states in north-west Greece were making con-tributions.[37]

Corcyra's willingness to participate in an expedition under Corinthian leadership is significant. Even in the 370s, when the Corinthian threat was sadly diminished, Corcyra had taken the part of Athens against Sparta—though not necessarily any longer because she feared Corinth, for there were ample reasons for suspicion of the Spartans themselves. The continued help provided, most consistently by Leucas but for most of the time by Ambracia too, through all the changes of Corinthian policy after the Pelopon-nesian War is remarkable, and testifies to the exceptional strength of the connection; but the Corcyraean vessels which sailed with Timoleon demonstrate that it was a connection of sentiment alone. If Corinth had retained the slightest pretensions to political control in north-western waters, it is difficult to believe that Corcyra would have joined Timoleon, even though he was a spent force in Corinth-ian politics and his mission was to assist her sister Syracuse. Even Corcyra judged that Corinth no longer entertained Adriatic ambitions by the mid-fourth century. The assistance afforded by Leucas

[35] Sicily: Thuc. vi.104 (cf. vii.7.1). It is not quite clear at vi.104.1 whether these vessels (three Ambraciot and two Leucadian) were manned by Corinthians, by colonists, or by a mixture of both; but Ambraciots and Leucadians are enumerated among the forces at vii.58.3, and Ambraciot diplomatic assistance is recorded at vii.25.9. Ionian War: Thuc. viii.106.3 (Cynossema).

[36] Above, 374. The temporary absence of six Ambraciot vessels during Nicolochus' expedition (Xen. *Hell.* v.4.65–6) is hardly a serious sign of reluctance to serve.

[37] Ambracia does not figure in the literary sources, but is a very probable restoration in Timoleon's victory monument (above, 391 n. 24). For numismatic evidence for the re-inforcements, see above, 174 n. 16.

and Ambracia was given without compulsion, out of a sense of filial piety; it is even possible that by now the Corcyraeans had resumed their obligations of cult and sentiment.

XXVII. Corinth in the Greek World

In 464 Xenophon of Corinth won both the stadion and the pentathlon at Olympia.[1] Pindar was commissioned to compose two works in celebration of the unique achievement; he wrote lines which reveal a remarkable sensitivity to Corinthian realities. Pindar's values were those of the old world, already under serious threat in the mid-fifth century; but he recognized them at Corinth:

> I shall come to know fortunate Corinth,
> Poseidon's porch on the Isthmus,
> Glorious in its young men.
> There Lawfulness (Eunomia) dwells, and her sisters,
> Safe foundation of cities,
> Justice, and Peace, who was bred with her;
> They dispense wealth to men,
> Golden daughters of wise-counselling Right.
>
> They wish to keep away
> Pride, the bold-spoken mother of Surfeit.
> (*Ol.* xiii.3–10, tr. Bowra.)

More than two centuries before 464, Corinth had begun a period of development perhaps more rapid and intense than that taking place anywhere else in the comtemporary Greek world; but the city of Xenophon had not lost sight of Pindar's values. They had been presided over by the aristocratic Bacchiads and then by the tyrants, who for all their hostility to exclusive Bacchiad control shared a similar outlook; it was no different with the succeeding oligarchs. The flavour of Corinth was created in the early archaic period, when aristocratic ideals were strong enough to assimilate substantial change while society retained its well-ordered nature. Eunomia was an aristocratic virtue.

Pindar was perhaps not entirely comfortable with Corinth. He may have seen a danger of Pride and Surfeit, and later he writes,

> Be not grudging to our prayers
> For the whole of time, Father Zeus.
> Guide this people out of harm
> And give a straight wind to Xenophon's fortune.
> (*Ol.* xiii.25–8, tr. Bowra.)

[1] I generally omit cross-references in this chapter; see the Index.

His pointed silence on the fate of Bellerophon, who fell to his death while attempting to ride Pegasus to the heavens, is no doubt a warning (*Ol.* xiii.91). He may already have sensed the threat to the structure of the Greek world presented by Athens; or he may have feared that what he approved at Corinth could not indefinitely survive the tensions of a society far more diverse that that which was familiar to him. In fact Corinth retained her political and social stability; but eventually she proved unable to face the challenge of change in the wider Greek world.

Corinth stood out among Greek cities in some obvious ways. The second of Pindar's poems, unfortunately preserved only in part, was directly connected with a unique feature of Corinthian life. Xenophon had vowed a hundred sacred prostitutes to Aphrodite if he was successful; and Pindar composed an ode for their dedication.

> Young women, hostesses to many, handmaidens
> Of Attraction in wealthy Corinth,
> Who burn the golden tears of fresh frankincense,
> Often you soar in your thoughts
> To Aphrodite in the sky,
> The mother of loves.
>
> She gave to you, girls, without blame
> To pick the fruit of soft youth
> In beds of desire.
> With compulsion all is fair . . .
>
> But I wonder what the masters of the Isthmus
> Will say of me, who have found
> Such a start to a honey-hearted catch
> To consort with consorting women (tr. Bowra).
>
> We have shown how to test gold by a pure touchstone . . .
> Queen of Cyprus, here to your sanctuary
> Xenophon has brought a herd of a hundred grazing girls,
> And takes delight
> In the fulfilment of his vows.
>
> (Fr. 107 Bowra; 122 Snell.)

Pindar, with delicacy and no little humour,[2] celebrates the increase of a company without parallel in the Greek world—one which contributed much to the Corinthian reputation for licentiousness. The origins of sacred prostitution cannot be recovered. The practice is known in the east, and Aphrodite herself has strong eastern connections. It is likely enough that this aspect of the cult reached

---

[2] See esp. Bowra, *Pindar*, 388-9.

Corinth from the east, perhaps immediately from Cyprus; but the date of its arrival remains uncertain.[3] It was well established by Pindar's day, and Periander's attack on secular prostitution more than a century before may have been undertaken in order to protect Aphrodite's girls from competition. It is perhaps dangerous to argue that since the practice suited a city which, from the seventh century onwards, saw as many travellers as Corinth did, it can only have been introduced at some time during that period; it may have originated earlier in quite different conditions.[4]

Strabo explains the wealth of Corinth partly by these temple prostitutes: 'the temple of Aphrodite was so rich that it owned more than a thousand temple slaves, courtesans, whom both men and women had dedicated to the goddess. It was because of these women that the city became crowded and wealthy; for ship captains easily spent all their money on them, and there arose a proverb, "Not every man can make the voyage to Corinth"' (378). The proverb was already known to Aristophanes.[5] The number reported by Strabo may be somewhat exaggerated, but his mention of ship captains serves well to emphasize how appropriate it was that the only known Greek cult of this kind was to be found in the city which saw perhaps more travellers than any other. The formally religious function of Aphrodite's 'hostesses to many' hardly prevented them from contributing heavily to a Corinthian reputation for licence. Two glosses of the verb κορινθιάζομαι (I act the Corinthian) in a fragment (354) of Aristophanes are preserved: ἐταιρεῖν (to be a prostitute) and μαστροπεύειν (to pimp, procure).[6]

Aphrodite, however, did not enjoy a monopoly of sexual service for payment in Corinth. If Periander was trying to eliminate private competition for Aphrodite when he 'threw the madams into the sea'[7] he had no lasting success, if any: secular prostitutes flourished in Corinth and may have contributed more to the Corinthian

---

[3] Burkert, *Griechische Religion*, 238–43, esp. 239; Will, *Korinthiaka*, 223–33. Conzelmann, *Nachr. Akad. Wiss. Göttingen, phil.-hist. Kl.* 1967, 247–61, doubts the sacred character of the prostitution; but Pindar's verses, along with his evident embarrassment, make it clear enough.

[4] Neither the Geometric vases, probably dedications, nor the late seventh-century temple from the summit of Acrocorinth (Blegen, *Corinth*, iii.1, 3–4) can help with the chronology of sacred prostitution, for it is not clear whether it was practised at this sanctuary or some other one less exhausting to reach. See now Williams, 'Corinth and the Cult of Aphrodite' (forthcoming, in *Essays for D. A. Amyx*).

[5] Fr. 902 a. Translated into Latin by Horace: *Ep.* i.17.36. A version appears on a fifth-century Attic RF skyphos: οὐ παντός ἐστι Κόρινθος (Panofka, *Arch. Zeit.* v (1847), 21*-2*).

[6] Steph. Byz. s.v. Κόρινθος; Hesych. s.v. κορινθιάζειν; Macar. v.18. The title of at least two comic plays, Κορινθιαστής (Poliochus fr. 1, Philetaerus fr. 5 Edmonds), presumably had a similar connotation.

[7] Ar. fr. 611.20 Rose; cf. Hermippus *FHG* iii.40, fr. 16.

reputation than their counterparts in Aphrodite's service. It was no coincidence that Neaera began her career as a slave in Corinth,[8] or that many of the wealthy men who enjoyed her in her early youth were not Corinthian (Ps.-Dem. lix.18-32). Lais was the name of three courtesans who spent most of their lives at Corinth, and the name came to be used as a type;[9] that of Ocimon appears to have been almost equally well known:

> I came to Corinth. There I somehow enjoyed
> Tasting the fresh, green Ocimon, and was destroyed.[10]

The anonymous women who served Aphrodite probably usually performed the hectic task of satisfying the desires of numerous ordinary Corinthians and others; but the famous—or infamous—individual slaves and courtesans of whom we hear will have delighted in the main a higher class of lover, even though the younger Lais is said not to have distinguished between rich and poor.[11] Neaera was sold for half a talent, and was later able to raise twenty minae from her men as the price of her freedom when her Corinthian owners offered it to her at a reduced rate.[12] These women were partly responsible for a more general Corinthian reputation for luxurious living:

> Such things, Syrus, neither Corinth nor Lais provided,
> Nor the good food given on groaning tables by Thessalian hosts.
> (Eriphus fr. 6, 1-2 Edmonds.)

The fame of the Corinthian Cydon's hospitality was great enough to reach the status of a proverb.[13] Apollodorus, when he imagines a life far better than the present, has the Athenian *hippeis* 'march for ten days' revelling in Corinth, crowned and perfumed before the dawn' (fr. 5 b, 6-8 Edmonds). It is not impossible that Pindar's slight discomfort in Corinth is to be partly attributed to his distaste for what he may have seen as an excess of gracious living.

Besides her athletic prowess, Pindar, in his ode for Xenophon, praises Corinthian inventiveness:

[8] Contrast Finley, *Ancient Economy*, 134.
[9] For references and discussion, see Geyer, *RE* s.v. 1-2.
[10] Eubulus fr. 54, 1-2; cf. Anaxandrides, fr. 9 (also Lais), Nicostratus fr. 21 Edmonds.
[11] Athen. 588 E; that the elder Lais is described as equally undiscriminating in her old age is hardly significant (Epicrates fr. 2-3, 18-19 Edmonds).
[12] Ps.-Dem. lix.29-32. Finley, *Ancient Economy*, 134, properly emphasizes the importance of income from prostitution in Athens; but in Corinth Aphrodite had probably deprived the secular whore-masters of much of their business at the cheap end of the market.
[13] Macar. i.32; Apostol. xvi.59.

Many times, sons of Alatas,
Has the brightness of victory been given to you
From men who surpass on the heights of success
In the holy Games,
And many wise devices of old
Were set in the hearts of men

By the flower-laden Hours.
Each thing belongs to its finder.
Whence came the delights of Dionysus
With the ox-driving Dithyramb?
Who added the bridle to horses' harnesses?
Or the king of birds
Fore and aft on the God's temples?
There the Muse breathes sweetly; there Ares flowers
Among young men's deadly spears.

(*Ol.* xiii.14–23, tr. Bowra.)

The poet chooses items which interest him;[14] but he was right to emphasize Corinthian originality, for, in the main, the special features of Corinthian society were created by the skills and enterprise of her citizens. It is too simple to rely on brute geographical determinism for explanation of the unique nature of the Corinthian economy. The position of the city at the Isthmus was of minor importance— despite the emphasis given to it by Thucydides (i.13.5). Corinth's advantages were in this respect unrivalled, for Pagae was a considerable distance from Megara; but it is doubtful whether Corinthian primacy is to be attributed to this factor. Before the construction of the diolkos, no significant exchanges over the Isthmus from sea to sea can be traced; and the signs are that whatever Periander may have hoped for from his installation, it did not achieve a great deal. Corinthians may have derived greater profit from the fact that all land traffic between the Peloponnese and central Greece had to pass through their territory. In view of the prohibitive expense of transport by land in antiquity, exchange of goods by this route was probably of small significance; but the services, both sexual and material, that were required by travellers themselves provided considerable opportunities for profit. The Corinthian reputation for good living may have been won in part by the enthusiasm with which these opportunities were seized.

[14] The 'king of birds' refers either to the gables (originally, hips) of the roof or perhaps to the sculptured decoration which stood in them; cf. Cook, *BSA* lxv (1970), 17–19. For the dithyramb, see however Schol. Pind. *Ol.* xiii.25 a, where it is asserted that Pindar also ascribed its invention to Naxos and to Thebes.

The real achievements of the Corinthians were positive rather than parasitic. The skills of the potter, the dyer, and the weaver, of metal and woodworking, and of architecture (noted by Pindar himself) owed little to the special advantages of Corinth's position: the ready availability of a fine, distinctive clay was offset by the absence of metals. It is true that few, if any, of these skills would have been developed as fully as they were without the extra stimulus provided by the possibility of export, and that the commercial skills which were acquired so early at Corinth depended on her location near the coast; but the heavy concentration of Corinthian trade in the west shows that access to the western routes was a more significant factor than her position on the Isthmus itself, and in general most of the exchanges which supported Corinthians were generated in the Corinthia. Equally, the availability of both seas to Corinth was less significant than what was probably the city's greatest debt to nature: the fertility of her soil, which both provided a sufficient surplus to support the creative and commercial skills of her citizens and fuelled a substantial proportion of the exports.

Corinthians exploited these advantages so effectively that the economy of the city was more diverse than that of any other city in the Greek world with the exception of Athens in the fifth century and later. We are unable to trace in detail the social effects of the changes as they occurred, and most of the evidence is negative; but in the classical period Corinthian society seems to have been remarkably stable. There are no signs of serious political instability even in the fourth century: the only disputes recorded originated in the ambitions of Timophanes (who failed precisely because his coup was not an attempt to solve pressing problems) or in the real political question of relations with Sparta. It is unlikely that Corinth suffered serious unrest at other times without leaving a trace in our evidence; and there are some positive indications of stability in the extensive changes of foreign policy through which the citizens were happy to be led in the early fourth century. Pindar's lines for Xenophon in the mid-fifth hardly describe an unstable city, and in a quite different way Herodotus' observation of relaxed Corinthian social attitudes (ii.167.2) offers evidence which is all the stronger for its explicit comparison with other states: Herodotus' experience was remarkably wide.

The explanation for this extraordinary combination of an exceptionally diverse economy with enviable social and political stability is mainly to be found in the early date at which the changes were accomplished. Already by the mid-seventh century many of the skills which were to be practised for centuries in the Corinthia or from its ports were well established. What is more significant, they were exercised in the main by citizens. This had two immensely stabilizing effects. It ensured that the status of such activities was relatively high; and, since the citizens would not willingly give up their land, it encouraged the development of a pattern of part-time involvement in the new skills by men who retained the ownership of at least small plots. It is perhaps unlikely, however, that the precise equivalence between citizens and plots achieved by Pheidon in the eighth century persisted into the fourth.

The early establishment of the basic pattern of Corinthian society and the Corinthian economy was also responsible for the maintenance of the values which enabled Pindar to praise the city so highly. The domination of the well-born was threatened neither by the establishment nor by the overthrow of the house of Cypselus, and the new skills were assimilated without encouraging a challenge to traditional social deference—perhaps especially because few of those who learned them entirely lost those links with the land which are a powerful restraint on new modes of thought. Aristocratic values enjoyed a vigorous life at Corinth which is amply attested. The athletic ideal was prominent not only in the Isthmian Games, the only Panhellenic festival directly administered by a major state, but also in the activities indicated by archaeological remains from the centre of the city. From the late sixth or early fifth century a race-track covered much of the area of the later Roman agora, while a ring for boxing, wrestling, and the pancration stood close by.[15] The symposion, another major feature of aristocratic life, was no doubt the context of much of the luxury which gave Corinth her reputation; and it is much in evidence in the material remains. From Early Corinthian, banqueting scenes are an extremely popular subject on Corinthian vases.[16] The numerous dining-rooms of the sanctuary of Demeter and Kore on the north slope of Acrocorinth, which begin in the sixth century,[17] are an eloquent testimony to the wide popularity of the symposion, at least in a religious context; the identification of a dining-room at Perachora makes our first evidence at least seventh-century and perhaps even earlier (above, 59 with n. 15).

The early establishment of the pattern of the Corinthian economy was a considerable encouragement to stability. New practices which made for stress in the fifth century elsewhere, especially when they were associated with radical political developments as at Athens,

[15] Williams, *Hesperia*, 1 (1981), 2-21.
[16] Payne, *Necrocorinthia*, 118.
[17] Bookidis, *Hesperia*, xliii (1974), 267-302, with refs. to earlier reports, 267 n. 1.

were already traditional at Corinth. But much of the responsibility for the continued stability of Corinthian society remains none the less with the sound sense and moderation of leading Corinthians. Some of their success was no doubt accidental. A great deal of tension was caused in Athens and elsewhere by the continued importance in political life of hereditary ties which had outgrown contemporary opinion. In Corinth the kinship tribes were replaced for political purposes by a territorial organization after the fall of the Bacchiads. It is improbable that Cypselus' intention was precisely to do away with hereditary privilege; but the change, made for quite different reasons, had the effect of freeing Corinth from the problems suffered later elsewhere. It seems, moreover, to have served, even in detail, as a model for Cleisthenes at Athens. Similarly, the *probouloi*, whether they were introduced by Cypselus or after the fall of his grandson, were probably not intended to perform the tasks of moulding and representing public opinion; but the institution was admirably suited to fulfil such roles when the expression of popular will became more insistent in the fifth century.

Those who ruled in Corinth used the advantages they had been given with considerable skill. We cannot trace the development of the constitution in detail, and indeed it may have undergone little formal change after its establishment by the Cypselids; but Corinth did not suffer from the debilitating disputes between oligarchs and democrats which tortured many cities, often her close neighbours, in the fifth and fourth centuries. The reason can hardly have been that the general citizen-body was so docile that the popular will was insignificant; rather, those who governed Corinth were intelligent enough to ensure that their decisions accorded with the views of the majority. The exceptionally relaxed social attitudes noted by Herodotus in the city may have made the oligarchs both less contemptuous of public opinion and more capable of sensing what it was. No doubt individuals or groups among the leading men of Corinth were often disappointed at their failure to gain office or at the adoption of a particular item of policy. But either such minorities resisted the temptation to appeal, like Cleisthenes at Athens, for popular support; or, if they did not, the majority had been skilful enough to ensure that public opinion was behind it. Corinthian history after the fall of the tyrants is generally anonymous. That no doubt reflects in part the state of our evidence; but it may also be explained by a broad unanimity among the ruling class which discouraged attention to individuals. When the oligarchs were bitterly divided over the attitude to adopt towards Sparta during the Corinthian War and force was used for the first recorded time in internal Corinthian affairs since the overthrow of the tyrants, we cannot be sure whether the faction of Timolaus and Polyanthes had majority support among the oligarchs for their anti-Spartan policy. If they did not, they perhaps provide the only case in Corinthian history since Cypselus of a successful appeal to popular opinion (along with force) by a minority, for there is no doubt that the majority of the population sympathized with them; but it is more likely that the revolution was directed against a Laconizing minority among the ruling group which might all too easily have been tempted to appeal to (Spartan) arms itself. The skills of the pro-Spartan faction were amply demonstrated after their return from exile by their ability to lead a reluctant population into loyalty to Sparta and, when Spartan weakness made change imperative, into neutrality.

The only division of opinion among the oligarchs which can be traced is that of the early fourth century. No doubt there were others; but the attempt of Kagan to trace two lasting factions—of controlling 'oligarchs', who derived their wealth from 'commerce and manufacture', and less numerous 'aristocrats', who lived off landed estates—is both unnecessary and wholly unpersuasive.[18] Not only is it based on no evidence, either for the factions themselves or for the issues and interests that divided them; it is also impossible to square with what evidence we have. Pindar would hardly have praised the city of Xenophon if its destiny had been controlled by men who gained their wealth, however great, by means which were contemptible to the class for which he wrote. Corinth was indeed less hostile to craftsmen than any other Greek city; but that hardly entitles us to guess that her leading citizens supported themselves, even indirectly, from commerce and manufacture when such activities were so alien to their counterparts elsewhere. The hypothesis also depends on the false view that agriculture was a relatively insignificant feature in the Corinthian economy; if the majority of Corinthians supported themselves from their land, the proportion of the leading citizens who did so must have been even greater.

Those Corinthians who determined the city's policy will thus certainly not have taken commercial considerations into account for the sake of their own private interests; but it has been persistently suggested that such factors played a significant role, from the foundation of the colonies in the eighth and seventh centuries, through the expedition against Polycrates, to the Peloponnesian War itself.[19] I have consistently explained Corinthian policy without

---

[18] *AJP* lxxxi (1960), esp. 294–5.

[19] I select only two recent examples: Hamilton, *Sparta's Bitter Victories*, 28; Murray, *Early Greece*, 141–7, 211.

adducing the commercial motive, and in my view the only plausible case to be made for it is in the siting of some, probably not all, of the colonies of the tyrants. Even then, there is nothing to show that this factor was considered, and if it was it played little if any part in the decision to found new colonies; its only effect was to help, along with the far more important requirement of the availability of good agricultural land, to determine the location of some of them. Periander devoted enormous resources to improving conditions for commerce by excavating the harbour at Lechaeum and constructing the diolkos; but that is quite different from determining foreign policy on commercial grounds. Part of his intention will have been to serve the convenience of merchants working from the port; but his main motive was probably to raise income. The diolkos assisted commerce originating outside rather than inside the Corinthia; while trade from Lechaeum was already substantial before the harbour was built. If Corinthian policy was ever affected by any commercial consideration other than the need to secure vital imports, the city was unique in the Greek world. The traditional patterns of trade established by the seventh century and never disturbed, along with the unrivalled access Corinth enjoyed to Sicilian and North African corn, were probably sufficient to ensure that in peace time no special measures were necessary; certainly no such action is recorded. Since citizens were more heavily involved in commerce at Corinth than at Athens, it is possible that private interests in trade might have carried greater weight in public opinion; but if this had any significant effect on Corinthian policy when the city determined to fight Athens, Thucydides would be as guilty of serious misrepresentation in the Corinthian case as in the Athenian if similar considerations affected Athenian decisions. It is true that many Corinthians lived at least in part by commerce; but trading interests were negligible in the determination of Corinthian policy.

Political and social attitudes at Corinth were characterized by a remarkable intelligence, moderation, tolerance, and sensitivity on the part of the oligarchs towards the citizens in general; similar qualities can be observed in the role played by the city in international affairs, under the guidance of the oligarchs, until the Peloponnesian War. Corinthian power reached its height in the reign of the ambitious Periander, before Sparta achieved a preponderant position in the Peloponnese after the mid-sixth century; but for more than a century after the Corinthians concluded an alliance with Sparta, their influence was exercised with consistent success in favour of balance, first between the interests of Sparta and her less powerful allies, and later also between the two great powers of

Athens and Sparta. Corinth joined in the expedition of Sparta against Polycrates of Samos, perhaps in the hope that as a naval power she would gain more from success than Sparta; but in the late sixth century she recognized the threat of too great an extension of Spartan influence and led the opposition within the alliance to interference in Athenian affairs. This forced Spartan acceptance of that formal consultation of her allies which marks the foundation of the Peloponnesian League. It is unfortunately impossible to determine whether the Corinthian contribution extended to the arrangements themselves, which would make them the inventors of the first and only mechanism which had any lasting success in restricting the power of the leader of a Greek alliance; but Corinthian minds are at least as likely to have been responsible as Spartan.

After her honourable part in the Persian Wars, for nearly half a century Corinth played a major, sometimes a decisive role in preventing total war between the two great powers. She had secured an effective balance of power within the Peloponnesian League; she now sought equilibrium on a wider scale.[20] She was not unduly disturbed by her replacement by Athens as the leading naval power of the Greek mainland, and was content to maintain her position as the leading naval ally of Sparta. Indeed, she probably welcomed the establishment of an Athenian balance for Spartan power: her interests were overwhelmingly concentrated in the west, where Athenian intervention could not be expected. By 462 she had probably already begun the informal consolidation of her naval control in north-western waters by careful exploitation of her colonial links and the Corcyraean threat; that process might also have had advantages for her position within the Spartan alliance if her colonies joined it as full members. The balance was seriously disrupted, but not ultimately shaken, by the First Peloponnesian War; but although at first sight Corinth bore a heavy responsibility for that conflict, more careful analysis shows that she fought it in order to maintain her position within the delicate equilibrium of the Greek world established after 478. The Megarian alliance with Athens, which was the major immediate antecedent of the war, had its origin in a border dispute between Corinth and Megara; but the ultimate origin of the war is to be sought earlier, in the Spartan insult to Cimon at Ithome and the consequent Athenian exertion of pressure on Sparta's allies. Corinth's naval control in the west was already threatened by Athenian tenure of Naupactus when Megara's allegiance changed.

---

[20] For balance as an aim of Corinthian policy, see in general Griffith, *Historia*, i (1950), 236-7.

It was Corinthian action against Megara which led to the war in the immediate sense; but responsibility for the more general changes in the international scene lay elsewhere.

Corinth suffered heavily during the First Peloponnesian War. Loss of men and ships cannot be quantified but must have been great; in addition, Chalcis and probably Molycreium were captured by the Athenians. None the less, her commitment to the principle of balance was not affected; she accepted the Thirty Years Peace as a formal establishment of it, and it is possible that an important consideration in the decision of the Spartans to agree to the Peace—to which they were not necessarily committed by Pleistoanax—was the knowledge that Corinth was satisfied with it and would oppose further hostilities. Nor was Corinthian acceptance merely grudging, for it was conclusively demonstrated in 440 when the city voted against intervention during the Samian Revolt. Corinth was prepared to view Athenian promises as honestly given and to exert her possibly decisive influence to ensure that the balance established by the Peace was not broken by Sparta at the first opportunity.

But it was a change in Corinth's position which precipitated the final conflict. In 435 she attempted to exploit the opportunity afforded at Epidamnus to extend her own influence within the general equilibrium created by the Thirty Years Peace; but she was shortly to be found exerting her considerable influence in favour of war between the Peloponnesian League and Athens. She did not cease her agitation for the destruction of Athenian power until the goal was achieved. It is not difficult to understand Corinthian intransigence as the affair developed, even though once Corcyra intervened Corinthian policy was determined by nothing but aggression and hatred of Corcyra: her hostile colony had been given an opportunity to act and failed to take it, while even when Athens became involved the Corinthians could be forgiven for imagining that their moderation over Samos entitled them to special consideration.

From an early stage in the Epidamnus affair, Corinth could only have served her general policy of pursuing balance in the international scene by complete withdrawal; the events serve admirably to demonstrate the ultimate futility of her persistent attempt to achieve equilibrium over the previous decades. Had the only issue been that of the relationship between Corinth and Athens, there would have been no reason for Athenian intervention; but Athens could not allow Corinth to subjugate Corcyra, precisely because of Spartan hostility. The Corinthians had attempted for forty years to maintain a balance between two powers at least one of which—Sparta—was essentially hostile to the other; in addition, the only serious means of offence Athens had against Sparta was through her allies, foremost among them Corinth. Corinth showed that in these circumstances it was possible to limit or postpone conflict; but since Sparta was eager for war and thus forced Athens to consider it a serious threat, it was almost impossible to avert it altogether. What is remarkable is not that in 433 Corinth, unable to tolerate the strain, turned to bitter hostility towards Athens; it is rather that she had been able to maintain the attempt at balance for so long. She was helped by powerful factors: Megarian adherence to Athens during the First Peloponnesian War, which denied to the Spartans those invasions of Attica which were their main weapon against Athens; and the similarly tolerant views of two kings of Sparta, Pleistoanax and Archidamus. But Spartan belligerence and the fear it provoked in Athens were too strong to be denied their effect; it was perhaps only the Megarian alliance with Athens—for which Corinth was also, if unwittingly, responsible—that prevented the First Peloponnesian War from being the last.

According to Thucydides (i.71.4-6), in the speech in which they urged war at Sparta the Corinthians threatened that if they did not achieve their object they would join a different alliance. If the reference is to an arrangement with Athens, to carry out the threat would no doubt have allowed them to have their way over Corcyra; but it would have been no solution to the general problem. There were now long-standing, if sometimes strained, links between Corinth and Sparta, and Thucydides makes the Corinthians refer to a preference for Spartan leadership which was probably based on a shared oligarchic outlook. But even if these factors had been ignored, the balance which Corinth had worked for would have been shattered by such an alteration of allegiance. It would have been far more significant than the earlier Megarian volte-face; and in any case Corinth could not hope for a similar position in alliance with Athens to that which she enjoyed in the Peloponnesian League. Her influence at Sparta as the most powerful naval member of the alliance was strong; but her vessels would be negligible in an Athenian fleet, and while initially Athens could be expected to treat her with deference, time would inevitably diminish her weight. Few Corinthians can really have favoured adherence to Athens unless their hatred for Corcyra had driven all long-term considerations out of their minds.

Once Corinth had determined upon war, her success in achieving it was impressive; but her talents were extremely ill suited to it when it came. Her military and diplomatic efforts during the Archidamian War were feeble or worse; and her wild schemes to resuscitate war after the Peace of Nicias merely succeeded in postponing an effective renewal of the conflict. It is difficult to understand in detail how Corinth could have hoped to achieve her aim; but a significant general factor may have been her view of history since the late sixth century, which encouraged her to overrate her influence. For the whole of this period, until the Peace of Nicias was signed against her wishes, Corinth had secured the adoption by the Peloponnesian League of her own policy, whether it was to restrain Sparta or to make war or peace with Athens. That was a powerful encouragement to Corinthians to view their influence as decisive. I have indeed argued that it was; but it was so only in the limited sense that the balance of votes in the Congress of the League was such that small changes could have a disproportionate effect. Corinth can perhaps be forgiven for supposing that she had secured decisions in the past through her own weight; but other states saw more clearly, especially after Corinthian impotence in the Archidamian War.

If a balance between the two great powers had been difficult to achieve in the mid-fifth century, the possibilities were greater in 421 or after the failure of the Sicilian Expedition. The Archidamian War proved to Sparta that her main weapon of invasions of Attica was blunt; while Athenian belligerence, increased by her successes in the Archidamian War, had little to feed it after 413. But on each occasion Corinth was too bitter against Athens to resume her efforts for equilibrium. That need occasion no surprise; but it will certainly have occasioned regret in those Corinthians who reflected after 404 on the opportunities they had missed. Sparta had with Corinthian help been raised to exactly that position of domination which Corinth's policy had for a century been designed to prevent; and that at a time when the use to which Sparta might put her preponderant power had been made all too evident, especially during the Archidamian War. The earliest Corinthian actions against Sparta after 404 are perhaps to be explained partly by mere pique at Sparta's refusal to have Athens destroyed; but within a decade those Corinthians who had been prominent in the prosecution of the war were attempting to create a new balance in which Sparta's weight could be countered by both her allies and her enemy of the Peloponnesian War. It is doubtful whether Timolaus and his faction felt themselves consciously to be the inheritors of the fifth-century Corinthian policy of equilibrium: the principle was the same, but the circumstances were now quite different. But for nearly a decade they showed a similar moderation, flexibility, and intelligence.

It is true that they used force in the revolution of 392. But their opponents had already barred the city to their defeated army after the Battle of the Nemea and might well have appealed to Spartan arms; and the amnesty offered (and treacherously used by Pasimelus and Alcimenes) was in these conditions generous. It is perhaps not surprising that Corinth made common cause not only with Argos but even with Athens; but the 'union' with Argos was an experiment with considerable potential, and it was almost certainly devised by Corinthians. Even after the coalition of the Corinthian War had been disbanded, the 'union' would have been a powerful weapon, especially given the geographical position of its members; Sparta recognized as much, and insisted on its dissolution. But perhaps the most significant Corinthian contribution was the least obvious: advice which was not accepted. The greatest chance of long-term success for the coalition was to exploit Peloponnesian discontent with Spartan leadership. None were better placed than Corinthians to do so, and the speech of Timolaus in 394 recorded by Xenophon (*Hell*. iv.2.10–13) is a strong indication that he was well aware of the crucial significance of this factor; but he was unable to persuade his Boeotian, Athenian, and Argive colleagues. They were less well versed in Sparta's Peloponnesian difficulties, and may have relied too heavily on Persian help— which, as the events proved, was most unlikely to be maintained once the Spartans recognized that they could not defend their own position in the mainland and the freedom of Asia Minor at the same time. It may be significant that it was while Iphicrates was based at Corinth that he undertook action in Arcadia, at Phleious and at Sicyon: the intention must have been precisely to encourage hostility to Sparta in those parts.

Corinth's efforts during the war which bears her name were her last attempt to introduce stability into the world of the cities as it fell into chaos. She suffered more extensively now than at any other period—perhaps even more significantly in the loss of her last leaders of independent stamp than in the destruction of her territory and resources. But even the Laconizing faction which returned to power after the King's Peace was able to show something of the qualities which had characterized the Corinthian contribution to Greek affairs—with the disastrous exception of the Peloponnesian War— since the sixth century when they persuaded Thebes and Sparta to allow not only Corinth but also many of her neighbours to withdraw into neutrality from the debilitating conflicts of the great powers. It is fitting that the last major Corinthian action before the victory of Philip at Chaeronea was the expedition of Timoleon, for it illustrates the longest-lasting effect of Corinthian moderation. When Timoleon—who himself possessed the Corinthian virtues to no small degree—first sailed on what must have seemed an almost hopeless task he was able to take with him contingents both from

Corcyra and from Leucas. Ever since 480, skilful Corinthian exploitation of the traditional links between colony and mother city had ensured that the city enjoyed the consistent support of a majority of her Adriatic colonies in whatever policy she herself adopted; by the time of Timoleon, when Corinthian Adriatic ambitions were long past, even Corcyra offered assistance. But the expedition also illustrates the weakness of Corinthian moderation in the face of the interests of the great powers: Macedon prevented the gathering of any of the political fruits of success.

Appendix I.
The Corinthian Local Tribes

The only explicit notice of the tribal structure of classical Corinth is given by the *Suda* s.v. πάντα ὀκτώ, 'eight of everything': one explanation of the catchphrase was that 'when Aletes synoecized Corinth in obedience to an oracle he divided the citizens into eight tribes and the city into eight parts.' The only other clear example of the number in Corinthian institutions is given by Nicolaus of Damascus (*FGH* 90 F 60.2), who records that there were eight *probouloi*. The parallel division of both the citizen-body and the city itself into eight parts demonstrates that the tribes were local in character;[1] how the eight tribes were arranged had long been the subject of conjecture before the discovery of four inscriptions from Corinth. These have been interpreted by von Gaertringen, Dow, and Stroud to yield evidence for tribal structure; the problems have been considerably complicated by Jones's recent identification of a Hellenistic decree from Delos as Corinthian and his thorough re-examination of the evidence.

The earliest document to be studied was probably inscribed in the second half of the third century, and was identified by Dow as a casualty list. It contains unequal groups of names, and each group is headed by an abbreviated rubric as follows: ΣΙ-Π, ΛΕ-Ε, ΛΕ-Π, ΚΥ-F.[2] Von Gaertringen was the first to associate this document with the Corinthian tribal system: he pointed out that the abbreviation ΚΥ might stand for the Κυνόφαλοι, the only Corinthian tribe given a name by a literary source.[3] Similar or the same rubrics occur over numerals (ἕν, δύο: one, two) at the head of stones, dating apparently to the fifth century, which have turned up near the east course of the city-wall: ΛΕΠ, ΣΙΠ, ΣΥF.[4] There is a similar abbreviation in a decree in the Doric dialect found at Delos. It honours two Athenians, and the relevant lines read as follows:[5]

20   τὰν δὲ
        βουλὰν διακλαρῶσαι εἰς
        ἡμιόγδοον καὶ τριακάδα

---

[1] Jones, *TAPA* cx (1980), 177-8 (cited below by page numbers only), makes unnecessary objections to this obvious interpretation; but he continues to view the tribes as locally based. I am extremely grateful to Dr Jones for allowing me to see his article in advance of publication.

[2] Dow, *HSCP* liii (1942), 90-106 (with earlier references); corrections by Stroud, *CSCA* i (1968), 237-8.

[3] *Phil. Woch.* lii (1932), 362. For the meaning of the name (Hesych., s.v.), cf. Dow, *HSCP* liii (1942), 98-9; that it was insulting now seems most unlikely.

[4] Stroud, *CSCA* i (1968), 233-7.

[5] Robert, *Hellenica*, v (1948), 5-15; xi-xii (1960), 562-9; Jones, 165-6, with corrections by Stroud.

καὶ φυλὰν καὶ φάτραν. Διεκλα-
ρώθην· ἡμιογδόου vv ΑΣ vv F
25 [ἀ]ρχαίας vv φυλᾶς vv Ἀορέων·
[φ]άτρας vv Ομακχιάδας.

'And the council shall allocate (them) to *hemiogdoon* and *triakas* and tribe and *phatry*. They were allocated: to the *hemiogdoon* ΑΣ F; the ancient tribe of Aoreis; the *phatry* (H)Omacchiadae.' The identity of the issuing state is not given in the decree; but Jones has made a powerful case for identifying it as Corinth.[6] The correspondence between what we know of Corinthian practice, including the abbreviations, and the decree is so close that until contrary evidence is found the text must be assumed to be Corinthian. The abbreviations must therefore all refer to the same system.

Even before the identification of this decree as Corinthian, the fact that the abbreviation KY could represent the only known Corinthian tribe, the Κυνόφαλοι, gave strong grounds for supposing that the two-letter abbreviations stood for tribes, while the single letters represented tribal subdivisions. Recent excavations in the Gymnasium at Corinth have uncovered an inscription which would firmly establish this conclusion if it were not for difficulties about its chronology. The stone has letters on all four sides, but only one has a text of any substance: it reads ΦΥΛΗΣΑF.[7] The digamma of this document, preceded either by the genitive φυλῆς (tribe) and a single-letter abbreviation or (more probably)[8] by the nominative φυλή and a double-letter abbreviation, makes it so close to the casualty list, one of the fifth-century markers, and the Delos decree that there is a strong prima-facie case for relating this inscription to the same system. This conclusion is further strengthened by the presence of the word δύο on face B of the stone, which is paralleled on the same fifth-century marker; and like the markers, the document was found close to the course of the city-wall. The letter-forms, however, give some reason for doubt. Such an argument cannot be conclusive on a stone which is neither tidily cut nor—since it was designed to be read at a distance—of normal character; but such indications as there are point to a date in the Roman period, when the tribal pattern of Corinth had long been disused.[9] None the less, it demands a lively faith in the malevolence of chance to attribute to mere coincidence, not only the agreement between the first two letters of the tribe Cynophali and one of the two-letter abbreviations, but also the remarkable similarities between the Gymnasium inscription and our other evidence. Only the chronological difficulties presented by the lettering of the stone from the Gymnasium prevent us from conclusively

[6] Jones, 165–72.
[7] Wiseman, *Hesperia*, xli (1972), 33–8. Both facsimile and photographs (ibid., fig. 11, pls. 10c, 11) make it plain that the last letter is digamma—which should hardly be dotted—despite numerous efforts to resist this obvious reading (Wiseman, ibid., 37–8; id., in Temporini (ed.), *Aufstieg und Niedergang*, ii.7.1, 498 n. 221; Jones (also quoting Dow), 175). All attempts to remove the digamma are mere special pleading.
[8] Despite the differing depth of the final two letters, for which cf. Dow *apud* Jones, 175.
[9] Wiseman, *Hesperia*, xli (1972), 36–7.

identifying the two-letter abbreviations as tribes and the single-letter as tribal subdivisions; as it is, the case for doing so remains powerful.

At first sight, however, the Delos decree points in a different direction: the abbreviations ΑΣ F follow immediately after ἡμιόγδοον, and must clearly refer at least to it, and perhaps to the τριακάς too, since it is mentioned with the ἡμιόγδοον in l. 22. Jones assumes that since the abbreviations refer to these units, they must be abbreviations of their names; he therefore rejects as coincidence the considerable evidence that the two-letter abbreviations stand for tribes.[10] But this assumption—which is the basis of Jones's whole interpretation —is invalid. The word ἡμιόγδοον (half-eighth) demonstrates that the unit to which it refers was part of the tribal system, in which the importance of the number eight was great enough to give rise to the phrase 'eight of everything'. In that case, it is possible that both a *hemiogdoon* and a *triakas* could be identified by an abbreviation which defined first the tribe (ΑΣ) and then its subdivision (F). We might have expected three abbreviations in such a case: the first for the tribe, and one each for *hemiogdoon* and *triakas*. That there are only two, however, could be easily explained if there was only one *triakas* in each *hemiogdoon*. Membership of a particular *hemiogdoon* would thus carry with it membership of a particular *triakas*—so long as the individual concerned belonged to a *triakas*, for not all those in a *hemiogdoon* need necessarily have been members of its *triakas*.

This interpretation is encouraged by the fact that although the council is ordered to allocate the Athenians to *hemiogdoon* and *triakas*, the latter is not named in the allocation itself. Jones argues that it is to be found in the single-letter abbreviation F. This is a possible view, so long as ΑΣ does not stand for a tribe; but it is better to suppose that since every other type of group in the order to the council—*hemiogdoon*, tribe, and phatry—is specified in the allocation clause, the *triakas* would also have been specified unless allocation to it was redundant because it would follow automatically from allocation to a *hemiogdoon*. The reason for the reference to the *triakas* in the clause instructing the council was probably that it was a restricted (privileged?) group within the *hemiogdoon*; a guarantee was made to the honorands that they, unlike some other members of the *hemiogdoon* to which they were allocated, would be enrolled in its *triakas*. Since, therefore, the abbreviation ΑΣ F refers to the *hemiogdoon* alone, and to the *triakas* only indirectly, we should interpret the first two letters as defining the tribe to which it belonged, and only the last, single letter as indicating the *hemiogdoon*.

This conclusion, however, that ΑΣ refers to the local tribe, is impossible if Jones's interpretation of the following words in the allocation clause, ἀρχαίας φυλᾶς Ἀορέων, is correct. He identifies this as one of the eight local tribes, and ΑΣ can hardly be an abbreviation for it; but the definition of the Aoreis as an ancient (ἀρχαίας) tribe makes this interpretation extremely improbable.[11] It is

---

[10] Jones, 172-5.

[11] Cf. Jones, 173, for arguments in favour of associating ἀρχαίας with φυλᾶς rather than the (understood) τριακάδος represented, in his view, by F. They are persuasive even if F stands for the *triakas*; if it does not, they are incontrovertible, for the adjective cannot agree with a noun that is not even to be understood. Cf. also Calligas, *BSA* lxvi (1971), 88-9.

perverse to identify a tribe explicitly described as ancient as one of the eight local tribes; for these were undoubtedly of a more *recent* origin than the only other Corinthian tribes, the kinship tribes of the early aristocratic state. If, on the other hand, the kinship tribes maintained themselves, no doubt for religious reasons, even after they had been replaced for other purposes by the eight local units, a grant of citizenship might require allocation both to a local and to a kinship tribe. We have exactly such a case here: allocation to a *hemiogdoon* carried with it *ipso facto* membership of the local tribe represented by the abbreviation AΣ; allocation to a kinship tribe, and associated phatry, follows— and it is most improbable that the phatry was anything other than a kinship group. The order of both the instruction to the council and the allocation clause itself supports such an interpretation: in each case, the local units precede those based on kinship. The name Aoreis has connections which are particularly appropriate for a Corinthian kinship tribe. Recently published evidence from Corcyra gives Ἀϝορῶν (genitive) as a large population division in that Corinthian colony, perhaps a tribe; this is easier to accept as a kinship tribe which reached Corcyra, along with the Dorian Hylleis, Pamphyli, and Dymanes (above, 57 with n. 11), at the time of the foundation of the colony than as a local unit, introduced at a later date.[12] The name is suitable for a non-Dorian tribe of the north-east Peloponnese, for Pausanias (ii.12.5) refers to an early king of Phleious named Aoris.[13] This gives us the name of one (perhaps the only) non-Dorian tribe of Corinth. It would be appropriate for the Ionian citizens of Athens honoured in the Delos decree to be allocated to such a tribe.

The Delos decree, on internal evidence alone, is thus best interpreted as making allocations to units of two quite distinct kinds: the local *hemiogdoon* Ϝ of the tribe AΣ, and the ancient kinship groups Aoreis and (H)Omacchiadae. Internal evidence alone does not exclude other possibilities—especially that the abbreviations represent *hemiogdoon* and *triakas*, as Jones has argued; but the fact that the decree, if interpreted as I have suggested, accords with all our other evidence, is an almost conclusive argument in favour of this interpretation. It remains only to make use of the unsatisfactory evidence at our disposal for determining the nature of the subdivisions of the eight local tribes. The Ϝ unit is found in each of the tribes ΚΥ(νόφαλοι), ΣΥ, AΣ, and perhaps—from the Gymnasium inscription—ΣΑ; while Π appears in both ΛΕ and ΣΙ. The tribe ΛΕ, on the other hand, is known to have contained both Ε and Π subdivisions. Stroud concluded reasonably that each tribe contained at least three subdivisions, Ε, Π, and Ϝ.[14] He conjectured further that these subdivisions were part of a *trittys* arrangement similar to that of Cleisthenes in Attica; and that, as in Attica, each Corinthian tribe was made up of three *trittyes*, each from a different part of the Corinthia. The *Suda*, he suggested, in referring to the division of the city into eight parts, preserves an echo of the fact that one regional division

[12] Calligas, ibid., 79–93, esp. 86–90; contrast, for the date of introduction at Corcyra, Jones, 167–8, 192.
[13] Cf., attributing the Delian decree (with caution) to Phleious, Robert, *Hellenica*, v (1948), 13–15.
[14] *CSCA* i (1968), 238.

of the Corinthia was, again as in Attica, the city. He guessed that the other two regions were divided at the Isthmus. Stroud's guess can be strongly supported by a passage in Thucydides. When Nicias invaded the Corinthia in 425, the historian remarks, all the Corinthians 'except those outside the Isthmus' and those on garrison duty elsewhere took part in the defence of the southern Corinthia (iv.42.3). Those who lived outside the Isthmus, it may be inferred, stayed in their own area; for it could not be known where Nicias would attack (above, 319-20). It is possible that the forces were divided on this occasion in an exceptional way, in order to ensure that each man would be defending his home area; but the obvious conclusion is that the normal division of Corinthian forces facilitated the separation of men who lived north of the Isthmus. The abbreviated rubrics can easily be made to fit with such a reconstruction: Ἐ(ντὸς τοῦ Ἰσθμοῦ), Π(έρα(ν) τοῦ Ἰσθμοῦ), and F(άστυ).[15] It is possible that there were more than three regions of the Corinthia, and thus more than three subdivisions for each tribe; but there will not have been many more than three, or we should have expected our eight (or, with the Gymnasium document, nine) items of evidence to offer more single-letter abbreviations than they do.[16]

Since our evidence is hardly explicit, much of this remains a matter for conjecture; but it is certain that, at least once, the Corinthian forces were divided at short notice[17] into groups living inside and outside the Isthmus. The probability is very strong indeed that the army fought in locally based contingents, and that one boundary between regions of the Corinthia defined for this purpose was the Isthmus. Stroud's is not the only reconstruction which fulfils this criterion; but it is the most likely. It is possible that two or three tribes lived wholly outside the Isthmus and five or six wholly inside. The E, Π, and F rubrics might then stand for deme names, and the demes might have been subdivisions of the tribes;[18] but it is unlikely that the six or seven demes for which we should then have evidence[19] all shared only three initial letters. No other explanation of the single-letter abbreviations presents itself if they represent demes. The casualty list and the boundary markers would allow each tribe to have a single block of territory if the single-letter abbreviations stood for age groups within the tribal contingents; but the Delos decree could not be accommodated to such a pattern. It might be suggested that each of the eight Corinthian tribes had a single region to itself and was divided into groups each made up of men who belonged to one of the old kinship tribes.[20] At

[15] For the latter suggestion I am indebted to Robert Jordan.
[16] Cf. Jones, 180-1.
[17] Despite the Argive warning (Thuc. iv.42.3), Corinth can have had little time to prepare.
[18] There is little evidence for local units such as demes in the Corinthia. Hdt. v.92 β 1 gives the origin of Cypselus' father Aetion as 'the deme Petra', and Thucydides (iv.42.2) and Theopompus (*FGH* 115 F 173-4) refer to Corinthian κῶμαι; but we cannot tell whether either word had a technical meaning. That an inhabitant of Cromna (above, 24) in the late fourth or early third century appears to have been called a Cromniate on his tomb (Wiseman, *Hesperia*, xxxii (1963), 249, 257 with 258 Fig. 4) hardly proves that Cromna had a formal identity as a unit of local administration. See further Wiseman, 10 with n. 8.
[19] One each from the tribes ΣΙ, ΣΥ, ΑΣ, ΚΥ(νόφαλοι), and perhaps ΣΑ; and two from ΛΕ.
[20] Compare the pattern suggested for Sparta by Forrest, *Sparta*, 43-5.

least the Π rubric could stand for the Dorian tribe of Pamphyli; but there is no correspondence between the other rubrics and the Dorian Hylleis and Dymanes or the Aoreis. A further alternative was suggested originally by Wallace:[21] that the abbreviations indicate military function, perhaps Ε(πίλεκτοι), Π(ελτασταί), and Ϝ(ίλαι: i.e. cavalry). At least the last of these is made less likely by the information given by Thucydides (iv.44.1), that Corinth had no cavalry in 425; and it is doubtful whether it was appropriate to place the Athenians whom Corinth honoured in the Delos decree in a military unit. Some, probably most, of our documents which carry abbreviations relate to military affairs (below); but that is probably only because the units to which they refer provided contingents for the Corinthian army, not because they were defined by their military function.

The reconstruction of a system of *trittyes* (or perhaps *tetartyes*) on the lines indicated by Stroud is the best available guess at present, although it can hardly yet rank as established. It is not contradicted by the term *hemiogdoon*, apparently analogous to the Attic *trittys*, revealed by the Delos decree. We might perhaps have expected τριτόγδοον, a *third* part of one of eight local tribes, if the Corinthia had been divided into three regions, each of which contributed an eighth of itself to make up a tribe; but the *hemiogdoon* is not incompatible with a threefold division of the Corinthia. The boundaries of the Ϝ(άστυ) region might, for example, have been fixed in such a way as to ensure that its population was roughly equal to that of the other two regions put together; each tribe might then contain two *hemiogdoa*: one from its block in the city, and the other from its blocks within and beyond the Isthmus.[22] Alternatively, there might have been four regions (Ε, Π, Ϝ, and ?) in the territory, but for certain purposes each of the four subdivisions within a tribe was combined with one other to make up a *half*-eighth; in such a case, the same pair of subdivisions would have made up a *hemiogdoon* in each tribe, or the formula of the Delos decree would not have defined the *hemiogdoon* to which the Athenians were allocated. Other possibilities might be imagined; but the *hemiogdoon* can be accommodated to a system in which each tribe had more than two subdivisions, and in the absence of further evidence speculation is pointless.

Little can be said of the functions of either *hemiogdoon* or *triakas*. Since the former occurs nowhere else, and the latter in many places and many different forms,[23] the practices of other states give no help in reconstructing that of Corinth. The casualty list shows that the subdivisions indicated by the abbreviations provided contingents for the Corinthian forces—presumably by land;[24]

[21] *Hesperia*, xvi (1947), 119 n. 14; see also Jones, 180.

[22] It is perhaps significant that both the Ϝ marker from the fifth century and the Gymnasium inscription, which also has Ϝ, carry the numeral 'two'; while the two fifth-century markers with Π carry rather 'one'. This might mean that the Ϝ groups had to perform twice the function of the Π groups; but the argument is hardly conclusive. The casualty list is not sufficiently representative to allow it to be used to test the hypothesis that the Ϝ subdivisions were large.

[23] Robert, *Hellenica*, v (1948), 10–12.

[24] The standard number of vessels in a Corinthian fleet seems to have been forty: Hdt. viii.1, 43 (Artemisium and Salamis); Thuc. ii.33.1 (restoration of Euarchus of Astacus).

and there is much attraction in Stroud's conjecture that the fifth-century markers (to which the Gymnasium document may perhaps be added), since they were all found near the course of the city-wall, were connected with the duties of the units to which they refer in the defence or the maintenance of the wall.²⁵ But it is hardly likely that the functions of the units were solely military: there will have been some other purpose to this aspect of the allocation in the Delos decree. The subdivisions probably had some functions in local administration; but what they were cannot be known in the absence of evidence. The *triakas*, in view of the meaning of the word, must in origin have been a group of thirty—though not necessarily of thirty men, for thirty families is a possibility.²⁶ It was probably not a military unit: its place in the Delos decree suits rather some other restricted—and probably privileged—group within the *hemiogdoon*. If Stroud's general reconstruction is correct, our evidence strictly only implies that each tribal subdivision within the F(άστυ) region possessed a *triakas*; but clearly the others are likely to have done so too. If so, the *triakades* may have been in some way connected with whatever responsibilities the subdivisions possessed in local administration; but such a possibility cannot be confirmed without further evidence.

Probably each tribe manned five ships in these fleets; but how, if at all, the tribal subdivisions were involved is impossible to determine. Of the two Corinthian fleets which saw action at the time of the Sicilian Expedition—ten ships in Sicily and about thirty in the Corinthian Gulf (above, 332-4)—the first cannot have had equal tribal representation in it; the second may have had if it contained thirty-two vessels.

²⁵ *CSCA* i (1968), 239-40. See also Jones, 183-4.
²⁶ Cf. Robert, *Hellenica*, v (1948), 11-12. Jones, 182-3, argues plausibly enough that subsequent developments might have led to changes in the size of the group without being reflected in the nomenclature; but change on such a scale as he supposes is perhaps unlikely.

Appendix II.

Spartan Policy Towards Athens, 479–431, and the First Peloponnesian War

Throughout my treatment of 479–431 I have suggested that the Spartans were consistently jealous of, and hostile to, Athens, and that when conditions were suitable they were eager to fight her. This view has been challenged, with special reference to the First Peloponnesian War, by Holladay, *JHS* xcvii (1977), 54–63. Spartan participation in hostilities against Athens *c*.460–446 was certainly minimal; but to concentrate on this period alone gives a false impression. We have sufficient knowledge of Spartan[1] attitudes at various points in the Pentecontaetia (the walls of Athens in 479, the promise to Thasos, the insult at Ithome, the invasion of 446, the wish to help Samos in 440, the promise to Potidaea, and the declaration of war in 432) to make an overwhelming case for consistent hostility—which would, of course, only result in action if circumstances were favourable. Holladay treats such cases as special: the Spartans 'would only occasionally swing into a "hawkish" mood under the influence of . . . some startling event (Thasos, Samos, Potidaea).' But they are only special in the sense that they induced the Spartans to move from latent to active hostility (or, sometimes, the promise of active hostility). It is special pleading to argue that these episodes are exceptions to a rule of toleration—even if grudging—of Athenian domination in the Aegean; on the contrary, they prove a quite different rule. On almost every occasion when the Spartans had an opportunity to demonstrate or actively pursue their hostility to Athens, they either took it or promised to do so but were prevented by some other consideration;[2] it is perverse to view these occasions as lapses from an otherwise unbroken—and, except in the special circumstances which led to the signing of the Thirty Years Peace (above, 297), unattested—policy of acceptance of Athenian power.

It is in this broad context that Spartan inactivity in the First Peloponnesian War must be viewed. It is possible that Sparta was reluctant to fight over the issue of the Megarian alliance with Athens; but if she ran true to form her reluctance was caused not by general unwillingness to fight, but by the particular military difficulty of acting when the Megarid was under Athenian control.[3] It is more likely that Sparta herself declared war, and secured a similar declaration from her allies, immediately after the Athenian alliance with Megara;[4] but that the construction of the long walls from Megara to Nisaea caused the

---

[1] Some of these cases may reflect the view of some body other than the assembly; we cannot often be sure.

[2] For one possible (but not certain) exception, see above, 297–8 n. 49.

[3] De Ste Croix, 187–95.

[4] This would have the advantage of helping to explain Athens' attack on Halieis at a time when her forces were heavily committed elsewhere; above, 262–3.

Spartans to calculate that their expected means of putting pressure on Athens, an invasion of Attica, was not worth attempting.[5] The alternative is to suppose that Sparta did not declare war until after Tanagra, or perhaps even after Tolmides' attack on Gytheium;[6] this is less probable, since it would imply that the Spartans declared a war which they knew they had no immediate means of prosecuting. No change in the general strategic situation comparable to the building of the long walls took place now (as far as we know) to dissuade Sparta from any action she might have had in mind.

It remains curious that Sparta did not act at least against Argos, even if she thought herself incapable of attacking Athens.[7] This is to be explained partly by the fact that the Argives did not undertake any offensive action against Sparta in virtue of their alliance with Athens;[8] in addition, Sparta did not want concessions from Argos at this time, and thus had no reason—as far as her relationship with Argos alone went—for án offensive.[9] None the less, an invasion of the Argolid would have been a useful means of, at the least, embarrassing Athens—though it might not have been easy to persuade allies, perhaps especially Corinth, to attack Argos when they were mainly concerned with the war against Athens.[10] The Spartans' conduct of the war was less than efficient, perhaps because of a general feeling of helplessness induced by their inability to use their major weapon of an invasion of Attica; but as soon as they were given the opportunity by Megara, they acted with vigour.[11]

[5] Holladay, writing of the Corinthian invasion of the Megarid, finds it 'inconceivable that the Spartans should have refused to lead an expedition which the Corinthians were not frightened to undertake' (*JHS* xcvii (1977), 58); but it was not a matter of bravery but rather of calculation. Had the Spartans participated, Athens would no doubt have avoided open battle; and it was reasonable for the Spartans to judge that no benefit would come from an invasion of the Megarid when Athens could hold the long walls. The Corinthians were able to seize the passes over Geraneia for their invasion (Thuc. i.105.3), and the same could have been achieved as a preliminary to a general Peloponnesian invasion; but the long walls would have blocked its progress further east. Before the Corinthian invasion, the Geraneia passes were defended by Athens (and Megara) either ineffectively or not at all; but the lesson was learned well before the time of Tanagra (Thuc. i.107.3).

[6] Holladay, ibid., 61 with n. 41.

[7] Ibid., 61. The action which led to Oenoe is not sufficient to remove this difficulty; ibid.

[8] The treaty may have been merely defensive; cf. Tomlinson, *Argos and the Argolid*, 112–13. The use by Aeschylus in the *Eumenides* of συμμαχία and its cognates (de Ste Croix, 184) does not prove that it was more than defensive; but we do not have evidence to answer the question.

[9] After 421 things were different, for Argos sought the return of Cynouria (Thuc. v.14.4; 41; 44.1); Sparta therefore invaded the Argolid to induce acceptance of her terms (Thuc. v.57). Forty years earlier Sparta and Argos were strictly in a state of war (Thuc. i.102.4); but that Sparta was satisfied, in principle, with the current position is demonstrated by her acceptance of a Thirty Years Peace in 451 on terms which (since neither side had any significant success in the mean time) presumably reflected the informal situation in 461, and by her desire to renew the treaty on similar terms when it expired (Thuc. v.14.4; 41.2).

[10] Cf. above, 330, on the events of 417/16 and 416/15.

[11] Pleistoanax was hardly vigorous; but his attitude was probably exceptional: above, 267, 297.

Appendix III.

Phormio at Amphilochian Argos

The chronology of the Athenian expedition of thirty ships under Phormio to Amphilochian Argos (Thuc. ii.68.7-8) has been much disputed. Thucydides reports that at some time before the Peloponnesian War the Amphilochians and the Acarnanians appealed to Athens, and that Phormio was sent to help them against some Ambraciots who had taken control of Argos; these men were enslaved, and the first alliance between Athens and Acarnania followed. All this must have taken place after Pericles' expedition to Acarnania in 454 (above, 266 n. 41); various dates between then and 432 have been proposed.

Whatever the date of the expedition, we can at least be confident that it did not cause a significant shift in Corinthian policy towards Athens. If it took place either before 446[1] or after Sybota,[2] Corinth was already hostile. If Phormio's activity was between 446 and 440, she was not unduly disturbed by it, for in the latter year she rejected the proposal to help the Samian Revolt (above, 281-2). Had the expedition been sent in the early 430s,[3] Thucydides would surely have made the Corinthians mention it in their speech in the Corcyra debate if he thought they had been greatly concerned by it; we can hardly do other than accept his judgement.

The date of the expedition can best be determined by looking at it from the Athenian point of view. Between 446 and 432, there was little purpose to such an intervention in this area: it could hardly have been connected with the Athenian tenure of Naupactus. It is difficult to avoid the conclusion that the Athenian intention was to exert pressure on Corinth;[4] thus Phormio was sent either during the First Peloponnesian War or after Sybota, for in the interval there was no reason to exert such pressure. Of these two dates the earlier is preferable, on two grounds, neither of them quite conclusive: if the expedition took place in 432 it is more difficult to explain why Thucydides failed to mention it in its proper chronological place; and no payments are preserved for Phormio in *IG* i.² 295, 296+309a.[5] Phormio might have sailed at any time between 454 and 446, for the Five Years Truce presumably did not cover activity of this kind. The general Athenian purpose was no doubt to deprive

---

[1] Gomme, *HCT*, esp. ii.416.
[2] Wade-Gery, *Essays*, 253-4; cf. *ATL* iii.320; Beaumont, *JHS* lxxii (1952), 62-3; Kagan, *Outbreak*, 252, 385.
[3] Jacoby, *FGH* IIIb (Suppl.), i.128-9; ii.122-3.
[4] De Ste Croix, 85-8, exaggerates the extent to which Corinth could view the expedition with equanimity. More significantly, Athenian intervention in this 'rather isolated area' (ibid., 87) would have been without point if it was not intended to diminish Corinthian influence; Athens had no positive interests here (cf. above, 307).
[5] On this argument, see ibid., 87, 330.

Corinth of another of the strong points through which she exercised her influence in north-west Greece: Chalcis and probably Molycreium, near the entrance to the Corinthian Gulf, were seized at about the same time (above, 278).

Appendix IV.
The Megarian Decrees

The Megarian Decrees remain the subject of intense debate. They have no relevance to the question of what Corinthian policy was, or to that of how it was determined: Corinth's decision to fight Athens was taken on quite different grounds, probably before the passing of the main Megarian Decree.[1] But they have crucial significance for general assessment of the Corinthian role in the outbreak of the Peloponnesian War. I have argued (above, 304–5) that Athens attempted to avoid war, but that Corinth forced her to give the Peloponnesians reasons to fight. The Megarian Decrees, however, have often been taken to demonstrate Athenian aggression; if they do, then the Corinthian (and Spartan) responsibility for the war will be correspondingly reduced.

Discussion of the Decrees must now begin from the fundamentally new treatment by de Ste Croix, 225–89, 381–401. This is not the place for a full analysis, but I hope here to defend the view I have taken above, that they do not establish Athenian belligerence.[2] The main Decree can hardly have been contrary to the letter, at least, of the Thirty Years Peace, in view of the quite specific claim put into Pericles' mouth by Thucydides at i.144.2.[3] De Ste Croix has shown conclusively that it was not designed to inflict serious economic harm, whatever the impression created by Aristophanes. He has also argued that the words of our sources are to be interpreted very precisely, and that the Megarians were excluded only from the civic agora of Athens and the harbours of the empire: not from other parts of the empire, nor from the Peiraeus or even the commercial agora of Athens. This is the minimum which our sources allow. Since they make no attempt to reproduce the actual wording of the Decree, it is dangerous to insist that the Megarians were excluded only from those places which are explicitly mentioned. Thucydides might well have written what he did if Megarians were denied access to both the Peiraeus and the commercial agora of Athens; but in view of the emphasis on the *harbours* of the empire, the Decree may not have attempted to ban Megarians from other parts of it. The Decree may therefore have been more rigorous than the minimum which de Ste Croix has established; but there can be little doubt that the Athenians could have passed a much stronger measure by extending the exclusion to all those trading to or from Megara.

---

[1] See on the date most concisely Meiggs, *Athenian Empire*, 430–1.

[2] For reactions to de Ste Croix's discussion, see (e.g.) Sealey, *CP* lxx (1975), 89–109, esp. 103–5; Fornara, *YCS* xxiv (1975), 213–28; Gauthier, *Historia*, xxiv (1975), 498–503; French, *Historia*, xxv (1976), 245–9. Wick, *AC* xlvi (1977), 74–99, seems to me thoroughly misconceived.

[3] *ATL* iii.304 n. 15; Kagan, *Outbreak*, 266–7; de Ste Croix, 256.

It is unfortunate that the intended damage cannot be defined more accurately, for the crucial question in determining the Athenian attitude to the war is whether the Decree was a reasonable, or an exaggerated, response to the alleged Megarian provocation. The occasion for the Decree was an allegation that Megarians had cultivated sacred and other land on the border between the Megarid and Attica, and that they were harbouring fugitive slaves from Attica (Thuc. i.139.2). We can hardly doubt that there was some substance to the accusation, even if the second item was little more than routine. Since neither the degree of pressure exerted upon Megara by the Decree nor the amount of land in question can be determined, we are unable to balance the provocation against the Athenian reaction; but there are strong signs of moderation in the Athenian behaviour. De Ste Croix has argued convincingly that the main Decree, of which the Megarians complained, was preceded by a Decree in the name of Pericles which provided for a herald to be sent to Megara and to Sparta, and which made what Plutarch (*Per*. 30.2-3) calls a 'reasonable and courteous' case.[4] Thus the main Decree was only passed when Athens' initial protests failed to achieve their object. Even if the main Decree was more damaging than de Ste Croix has argued, it was certainly less severe than it might have been; and of course the Athenians offered to repeal it—so long as the Spartans made a concession in their turn, for there could be no question of yielding to an ultimatum.[5] The last, and most hostile, stage in Athens' dispute with Megara was reached in the Charinus Decree, recorded by Plutarch (*Per*. 30.3), which promised death to all Megarians who set foot in Attica and added a clause which required the *strategoi* to swear an oath to invade the Megarid twice each year. This no doubt followed the Theban attack on Plataea; it may well have been passed after the Spartan invasion of Attica in 431.[6]

The Megarian Decrees can certainly therefore be reasonably interpreted in a way which does not imply Athenian aggression. There are two reasons of a more general kind for accepting this interpretation. First, Athenian belligerence cannot be detected in any of the other immediate antecedents to the war; on the contrary, what evidence we have points in a quite different direction (above, 304-5). The Athenians might have calculated that after the affairs of Corcyra and Potidaea it was no longer possible to avoid war, and passed the main Decree now for that reason; but if so, we should have expected its terms to be more severe than they were. Secondly, and more importantly, to take the Decree as aggressive is to convict Thucydides of a serious misjudgement. This is not merely a matter of balance and emphasis. On the surface, the final Spartan ultimatum made the Megarian Decree the crucial issue in the negotiations before the war (above, 302-3); but Thucydides gives it very little space. That is why it has generated so much discussion; but his failure to explain it properly must have been the result of deliberate choice, because he believed that it had no great

[4] De Ste Croix, 248-51; see also Fornara, art. cit.
[5] Thuc. i.144.2. There is no reason to doubt that the offer was serious, for Pericles' whole argument was that the Decree itself was a small matter, and that the real issue was that Athens should not give way to an ultimatum, whereas arbitration or negotiation was acceptable; see de Ste Croix, 289, and above, 302-3.
[6] See ibid., 248.

importance—perhaps as a protest against contemporary public opinion.[7] He would have served the truth better by explicitly countering the prevailing view, as he did on the question of the fall of the Peisistratids (i.20.2; vi.54–9). He does not give the evidence on which he based his decision; but I am prepared to rely on his judgement.

Since the affair began with Megarian action, the implications of the Megarian cultivation of the land in question must be considered. After the Battle of Sybota, the Corinthians agitated for war and themselves took action to that end at Potidaea, in the hope that the Athenian reaction would provide arguments in favour of war which could be presented to possibly reluctant allies. The action of the Megarians is surely to be seen in a similar light. We have no means of judging whether the Megarians favoured war before the passing of the Megarian Decrees; but if they did, they chose an admirable stratagem; it would either win them extra land (if the Athenians did nothing) or force the Athenians to provide further arguments in favour of war.[8] As at Potidaea, Athens was placed in an impossible position: either she ignored the provocation and her own interests, or she made more likely the conflict she did not wish to fight. At least her initial reaction, the sending of a herald to present a 'reasonable and courteous' case, was outstandingly moderate; no doubt she felt her interests at Potidaea were more vital. Megara had provided ships to help Corinth both at Leucimme and at Sybota (Thuc. i.27.2; 46.1). It is perhaps not entirely fanciful to conjecture that the Corinthians may have suggested the Megarian action: they knew what dire consequences border disputes with Megara might have!

---

[7] Cf. Meiggs, *Athenian Empire*, 203, 431.
[8] Cf. Völkl, *Rh. Mus.* xciv (1951), 335–6; de Ste Croix, 255.

Appendix V.
Corinthian Neutrality in 365

For a full discussion of the contrary accounts of the negotiations which led to Corinthian neutrality in 365,[1] see Ryder, *CQ* vii (1957), 199–205; Cawkwell, *CQ* xi (1961), 80–6, with a reply by Ryder, *Koine Eirene*, 138–9. Cawkwell tries to discredit Xenophon's account by comparing it with Isocrates' *Archidamus* (vi), which professes to be the speech made by Archidamus at the Spartan assembly which discussed the request of Corinth and others to be allowed to withdraw from the fighting. At vi.26–7 Archidamus attacks the Boeotians for recognizing Persian control over Asia and yet also demanding Messenian independence; for, he argues, Sparta controlled Messenia long before Persia won Asia. This, in Cawkwell's view, shows that the King's right to the cities of Asia Minor was an issue in the negotiations; and Xenophon omits it. Even if the reference is to the cities, and not to Persian rule over Asia in general—which is not at all clear—the real context of this invented speech was probably a less important factor in Isocrates' insertion of this argument than his own interests. This passing reference is best interpreted as an attack on the terms negotiated by Pelopidas with the King two years before.[2] Even if Cawkwell is right, Xenophon is merely convicted of a minor omission. If, however, Xenophon is recording the negotiations for a Common Peace that Diodorus reports, he positively misleads by representing the Corinthians as taking the initiative; that is less probable.

If a Common Peace was signed as in Diodorus, then Athens must have accepted it, at least temporarily. It is clear from Xenophon that Sparta rejected it; but if both Sparta and Athens, not to mention Arcadia,[3] stood aside there can be no question of believing Diodorus' account. Cawkwell shows that Isoc. vi does not prove that Athens rejected the Peace; but his argument that she accepted it is weak. At vi.58, Archidamus represents his opponents as asking where Sparta could hope to gain support. Such a question, Cawkwell argues, was superfluous so long as Athens resisted the Boeotian Common Peace; he therefore suggests that she had agreed to it. Athens, however, had recently concluded an alliance with Arcadia; she could hardly be relied upon to defend Sparta, and the question was pertinent (above, 378). Cawkwell's view implies an improbable change in Athenian policy. In 366 she made an alliance with Arcadia in order to detach Arcadia from Boeotia (Xen. *Hell*. vii.4.2); is it likely that she would agree to a Boeotian Common Peace so soon, before making any serious effort to explore the new possibilities? Cawkwell argues that the

---

[1] Xen. *Hell*. vii.4.6–10; Diod. xv.76.3. See above, 379.
[2] Above, 377–8; cf. Ryder, *Koine Eirene*, 138.
[3] Ryder, *CQ* vii (1957), 202; cf. Roy, *Historia*, xx (1971), 582.

discrediting of Callistratus' policy of alliance with Sparta (above, 378) brought his policy of rejecting a Boeotian Common Peace into equal disfavour. That was a possible option; but in fact Athens chose a different anti-Boeotian alliance—with Arcadia.[4] Nothing had happened between the alliance and the supposed Common Peace proposals to make her change her mind.[5]

[4] Arcadia, however (perhaps because of the death of Lycomedes), did not positively turn against Boeotia yet; cf. Roy, *Historia*, xx (1971), 596.

[5] Cf. Ryder, *Koine Eirene*, 83 n. 1.

Endnotes

A (171 n. 5)

Kraay, *Archaic and Classical Greek Coins*, 313-16, suggests that the various items of ancient evidence which relate to Aeginetan coins, Pheidon, and the use of spits as currency in the period before coinage are to be explained by supposing that Pheidon fixed the relationship between spits and silver bullion for his territory (perhaps at a time when silver was coming into common use as a means of exchange?), and that the weights he specified became the basis for the subsequent Aeginetan standard; some such explanation is necessary to account for the anomalous use of obol (spit) and drachma (handful—hardly of coins) as coinage denominations. It is doubtful, however, whether we may posit an equivalence in value between silver obol and iron spit for every area which used such terms for their coins (ibid., 315): that would imply a highly improbable fluctuation between the values of spits and/or silver from place to place, for the Corinthian silver obol weighed less than half the Aeginetan. Probably the names for coin denominations were derived from Aegina (where the standard was indeed based on Pheidon's spit/silver relationship); but the weights at Corinth were determined by current local weight-standards and thus bore a different relationship to the spit currency. There is in any case no sign that Corinth ever used spits as a currency; the dedication of a drachma of them at Perachora was merely one of spits for use (Jeffery, *Local Scripts*, 123-4; esp. Tomlinson, *BSA* lxxii (1977), 200).

B (293 n. 29)

Thuc. i.55.2 provides, at first sight, an argument against a Corinthian decision in favour of war before the events at Potidaea: 'This was the first grievance for the Corinthians against the Athenians which led to the war: that Athens had fought a naval battle against Corinth on behalf of Corcyra when the Peace was in force.' This could be taken to imply that other grievances were needed to account for the Corinthian decision; but Thucydides does not deny that Corcyra was a sufficient grievance, and his narrative shows that he believed it was. In his whole work he explains not just why Corinth went to war but why the whole Peloponnesian League did so; and for the League the Corcyra affair was not a sufficient grievance. He fails to distinguish here between Corinthian grievances and those held by other Peloponnesians; and in fact he goes on at once to introduce his discussion of the Potidaea affair, which he characterizes as 'a further cause for complaint' (i.56.1), not this time for the Corinthians but for the Peloponnesians. He is thinking in terms of a series of grievances affecting members of the League, and Corcyra was the first of the series, which affected (in the main) Corinth alone; hence his wording at i.55.2.

C (306 n. 1)

During the Archidamian War the size of a Corinthian fleet is given only once, for an independent Corinthian expedition: forty ships went to restore Euarchus tyrant of Astacus (ii.33.1). That figure compares badly with the ninety Corinth sent to Sybota, even though some of the ninety will have been destroyed in that battle. Gomme suggests (*HCT* i.193) that Corinth scrapped the Sybota fleet after learning how useless old-style triremes were, and that this is one reason for the smaller numbers found in the Archidamian War. But there is no sign that Corinth had learned the necessary lesson; compare her confidence against Phormio in 429 (above, 309–11). A better explanation is that mercenary rowers could not be hired from the Aegean after 431, as they certainly were for Sybota (cf. Brunt, *Phoenix*, xix (1965), 259); it was not only hulls that were needed, but men to man them. Corinth may have been able to man more than forty vessels for the largest Peloponnesian fleet, that of a hundred which attacked Zacynthus in 430 (ii.66); but forty will be too many for most of the other fleets, which range from forty for the help of Lesbos in 428 and 427 (iii.16.3 etc.) to seventy-seven for the second battle with Phormio in 429 (ii.86.4). The forty at iii.16.3 etc. did not include vessels from the Corinthian colonies (cf. iii.69.1). In 429 the forty-seven ships for the first battle with Phormio came only from the states on the Corinthian Gulf (ii.83.1, cf. 80.3), that is, Corinth and Sicyon (ii.80.3), and probably Megara and/or Pellene (cf. ii.9.3); Corinthian predominance in this fleet is demonstrated by the fact that it is called 'the Corinthians and their allies' (ii.83.3), and Thucydides gives the names of the Corinthian commanders only (ii.83.4).

Bibliography

Bibliographical details of works cited by author's name and short title, and by author's name alone are given below. Works cited by author's name alone are asterisked.

ACCAME, S., *Ricerche intorno alla guerra corinzia* (Turin, 1951).
AGOSTINO, B. D., 'Osservazioni a proposito della guerra lelantina', *DdA* i (1967), 20-37.
— 'Tombe della prima età del ferro a S. Marzano sul Sarno', *MEFR* lxxxii (1970), 570-619.
ALEXANDER, J. A., *Potidaea: its History and Remains* (Athens, Ga., 1963).
ALEXANDRESCU, P., *Histria*, iv: *La Céramique d'époque archaïque et classique (VIIe-IVe s.)* (Bucharest, 1978).
AMANDRY, P., 'Vases, bronzes et terres cuites de Delphes', *BCH* lxii (1938), 305-31.
— 'Petits objets de Delphes', *BCH* lxviii/lxix (1944/5), 36-74.
AMYX, D. A. and LAWRENCE, P., *Corinth*, vii.2: *Archaic Corinthian Pottery and the Anaploga Well* (Princeton, 1975).
ANDERSON, J. K., 'A Topographical and Historical Study of Achaea', *BSA* xlix (1954), 72-92.
— 'Old Smyrna: the Corinthian Pottery', *BSA* liii/liv (1958/9), 138-51.
— *Military Theory and Practice in the Age of Xenophon* (Berkeley and Los Angeles, 1970).
ANDREWES, A., 'Athens and Aegina, 510-480 B.C.', *BSA* xxxvii (1936/7), 1-7.
— 'The Corinthian Actaeon and Pheidon of Argos', *CQ* xliii (1949), 70-8.
— 'Sparta and Arcadia in the Early Fifth Century', *Phoenix*, vi (1952), 1-5.
— *Probouleusis: Sparta's Contribution to the Technique of Government* (Oxford, 1954).
— *The Greek Tyrants* (London, 1956).
— 'Thucydides on the Causes of the War', *CQ* liii (1959), 223-39.
— 'Two notes on Lysander', *Phoenix*, xxv (1971), 206-26.
— 'Could there have been a Battle of Oinoe?', in LEVICK (ed.), *Ancient Historian and his Materials*, 9-16.
— 'The Opposition to Perikles', *JHS* xcviii (1978), 1-8.
ASKEW, H. E., see STILLWELL, R.
AUSTIN, M. M., *Greece and Egypt in the Archaic Age* (Cambridge, 1970).
BAKHUIZEN, S. C., *Chalcidian Studies*, iii: *Chalcis-in-Euboea, Iron and Chalcidians Abroad* (Leiden, 1976).
BARKER, E., *The Politics of Aristotle: Translated, with an Introduction, Notes, and Appendices* (Oxford, 1946).

432   *Bibliography*

BARRON, J. P., 'The Sixth Century Tyranny at Samos', *CQ* xiv (1964), 210-29.
— 'Religious Propaganda of the Delian League', *JHS* lxxxiv (1964), 35-48.
BASCH, L., 'Trières grecques, phéniciennes et égyptiennes', *JHS* xcvii (1977), 1-10.
— 'M. le Professeur Lloyd et les trières: quelques remarques', *JHS* c (1980), 198-9.
BEAUMONT, R. L., 'Greek Influence in the Adriatic Sea before the Fourth Century B.C.', *JHS* lvi (1936), 159-204.
— 'Corinth, Ambracia, Apollonia', *JHS* lxxii (1952), 62-73.
BELOCH, K. J., *Die Bevölkerung der griechisch-römischen Welt* (Leipzig, 1886).
*BELOCH, K. J., *Griechische Geschichte* (2nd edn., Strassburg, 1912-27).
*BENGTSON, H., *Griechische Geschichte von den Anfängen bis in die römische Kaiserzeit* (4th edn., Munich, 1969).
BENSON, J. L., *Die Geschichte der korinthischen Vasen* (Basel, 1953).
— 'Some Notes on Corinthian Vase Painters', *AJA* lx (1956), 219-30.
BENTON, S., 'Excavations in Ithaca, III', *BSA* xxxv (1934/5), 45-73.
— 'Excavations at Ithaca, III: The Cave at Polis, II', *BSA* xxxix (1938/9), 1-51.
— 'Note on Spectacle Fibulae and Horses', *JHS* lxxii (1952), 119.
— 'Further Excavations at Aetos', *BSA* xlviii (1953), 255-361.
BÉRARD, C., 'Architecture éretrienne et mythologie delphique: le Daphnéphoréion', *AK* xiv (1971), 59-73.
BERNABO-BREA, L. and CAVALIER, M., *Mylai* (Novara, 1959).
BERVE, H., *Das Alexanderreich auf prosopographischer Grundlage* (2 vols., Munich, 1926).
— *Die Tyrannis bei den Griechen* (2 vols., Munich, 1967).
BÉTANT, E. A., *Lexicon Thucydideum* (2 vols., Geneva, 1843-7).
BINTLIFF, J. L., *Natural Environment and Human Settlement in Prehistoric Greece* (Oxford, 1977).
BLAKEWAY, A., 'Prolegomena to the Study of Greek Commerce with Italy, Sicily and France in the Eighth and Seventh Centuries B.C.', *BSA* xxxiii (1932/3), 170-208.
— '"Demaratus": a Study in Some Aspects of the Early Hellenisation of Latium and Etruria', *JRS* xxv (1935), 129-49.
BLEGEN, C. W., 'Corinth in Prehistoric Times', *AJA* xxiv (1920), 1-13.
— *Korakou: a Prehistoric Settlement near Corinth* (Boston and New York, 1921).
— 'Corinth in Prehistoric Times: Dr. Blegen's Reply', *AJA* xxvii (1923), 156-63.
— *Zygouries: a Prehistoric Settlement in the Valley of Cleonae* (Cambridge, Mass., 1928).
— 'Gonia', *MMS* iii.1 (1930), 55-80.
— 'Prosymna: Remains of Post-Mycenaean Date', *AJA* xliii (1939), 410-44.
BLEGEN, C. W., BELLINGER, A. R., BRONEER, O., and STILLWELL, R., *Corinth*, iii.1: *Acrocorinth: Excavations in 1926* (Cambridge, Mass., 1930).
BLEGEN, C. W., BOULTER, C. G., CASKEY, J. L., and RAWSON, M., *Troy: Settlements VIIa, VIIb and VIII*, iv (Princeton, 1958).
BLEGEN, C. W., PALMER, H., and YOUNG, R. S., *Corinth*, xiii: *The North Cemetery* (Cambridge, Mass., 1964).

BLINKENBERG, C., *Lindos: Fouilles de l'acropole 1902-1914*, i: *Les Petits Objets* (Berlin, 1931).

BOARDMAN, J., 'Pottery from Eretria', *BSA* xlvii (1952), 1-48.

—— 'Early Euboean Pottery and History', *BSA* lii (1957), 1-29.

—— 'Old Smyrna: the Attic Pottery', *BSA* liii/liv (1958/9), 152-81.

—— 'Evidence for the Dating of Greek Settlements in Cyrenaica', *BSA* lxi (1966), 149-56.

—— *Excavations in Chios 1952-1955: Greek Emborio* (London, 1967).

—— 'Reflections on the Greek Pottery Trade with Tocra', in GADALLAH (ed.), *Libya in History*, 89-91.

—— *The Greeks Overseas: their Early Colonies and Trade* (3rd edn., London, 1980).

BOARDMAN, J. and HAYES, J., *Excavations at Tocra, 1963-1965* (2 vols., London, 1966-74).

BOER, W. DEN, 'The Delphic Oracle Concerning Cypselus (Hdt. v, 92 β 2)', *Mnemosyne*[4], x (1957), 339.

BOGAERT, R., *Banques et banquiers dans les cités grecques* (Leiden, 1968).

BON, A., CARPENTER, R., and PARSONS, A. W., *Corinth*, iii.2: *The Defenses of Acrocorinth and the Lower Town* (Cambridge, Mass., 1936).

BOOKIDIS, N., 'The Sanctuary of Demeter and Kore on Acrocorinth: Preliminary Report V: 1971-1973', *Hesperia*, xliii (1974), 267-307.

BOSWORTH, A. B., 'The Congress Decree: Another Hypothesis', *Historia*, xx (1971), 600-16.

BOUCHER, E., 'Céramique archaïque d'importation au Musée Lavigerie de Carthage', *Cahiers de Byrsa*, iii (1953), 11-85.

BOURGUET, E., *Fouilles de Delphes*, iii: *Épigraphie*, fasc. 5: *Les Comptes du IVe siècle* (Paris, 1932).

BOWRA, C. M., 'Two lines of Eumelus', *CQ* xiii (1963), 145-53.

—— *Pindar* (Oxford, 1964).

BRANIGAN, K., *Aegean Metalwork of the Early and Middle Bronze Age* (Oxford, 1974).

BRANN, E. T. H., *The Athenian Agora*, viii: *Late Geometric and Protoattic Pottery* (Princeton, 1962).

BRAVO, B., 'Une lettre sur plomb de Berezan. Colonisation et modes de contact dans le Pont', *DHA* i (1974), 110-87.

—— 'Remarques sur les assises sociales, les formes d'organisation et la terminologie du commerce maritime grec à l'époque archaïque', *DHA* iii (1977), 1-59.

BROADBENT, M., *Studies in Greek Genealogy* (Leiden, 1968).

BROCK, J. K. and YOUNG, G. M., 'Excavations in Siphnos', *BSA* xliv (1949), 1-92.

BRONEER, O., *Corinth*, x: *The Odeum* (Cambridge, Mass., 1932).

—— 'Excavations in the Agora at Corinth, 1933', *AJA* xxxvii (1933), 554-72.

—— 'A Sandstone Head from Corinth', *AJA* xl (1936), 204-9.

—— 'Hero Cults in the Corinthian Agora', *Hesperia*, xi (1942), 128-61.

—— 'Investigations at Corinth, 1950', *Hesperia*, xx (1951), 291-300.

—— *Corinth*, i.4: *The South Stoa and its Roman Successors* (Princeton, 1954).

—— 'Excavations at Isthmia: Third Campaign, 1955-1956', *Hesperia*, xxvii (1958), 1-37.

— 'Excavations at Isthmia: Fourth Campaign, 1957-1958', *Hesperia*, xxviii (1959), 298-343.

— *Isthmia*, i: *The Temple of Poseidon* (Princeton, 1971).

— *Isthmia*, ii: *Topography and Architecture* (Princeton, 1973).

BROWN, W. L., *The Etruscan Lion* (Oxford, 1960).

BRUCE, I. A. F., 'Internal Politics and the Outbreak of the Corinthian War', *Emerita*, xxviii (1960), 75-86.

— *An Historical Commentary on the 'Hellenica Oxyrhynchia'* (Cambridge, 1967).

— 'The Corcyraean Civil War', *Phoenix*, xxv (1971), 108-17.

BRUNT, P. A., 'Thucydides and Alcibiades', *REG* lxv (1952), 59-96.

— 'The Hellenic League against Persia', *Historia*, ii (1953/4), 135-63.

— 'Spartan Policy and Strategy in the Archidamian War', *Phoenix*, xix (1965), 255-80.

BUCHNER, G., 'Pithekoussai, Oldest Greek Colony in the West', *Expedition*, viii.4 (1966), 4-12.

— 'Mostra degli scavi di Pithecusa', *DdA* iii (1969), 85-101.

— 'Recent Work at Pithekoussai (Ischia) 1965-1971', *AR* 1970/1, 63-7.

BUCHNER, G. and BOARDMAN, J., 'Seals from Ischia and the Lyre-Player Group', *JdaI* lxxxi (1966), 1-62.

BUCK, R. J., 'The Athenian Domination of Boeotia', *CP* lxv (1970), 217-27.

BURFORD, A., *The Greek Temple Builders at Epidaurus: a Social and Economic Study of Building in the Asclepian Sanctuary during the Fourth and Early Third Centuries B.C.* (Liverpool, 1969).

BURKERT, W., *Griechische Religion der archaischen und klassischen Epoche* (Stuttgart, 1977).

BURN, A. R., 'Greek Sea-Power, 776-540 B.C., and the "Carian" Entry in the Eusebian Thalassocracy List', *JHS* xlvii (1927), 165-77.

— 'The so-called "Trade Leagues" in Early Greek History and the Lelantine War', *JHS* xlix (1929), 14-37.

— *The Lyric Age of Greece* (London, 1960).

— *Persia and the Greeks: the Defence of the West, c.546-478 B.C.* (London, 1962).

BUSOLT, G., *Griechische Geschichte bis zur Schlacht bei Chaeroneia* (3 vols., Gotha, 1893-1904).

— *Griechische Staatskunde*, i (Munich, 1920).

CALLIGAS, P., 'An Inscribed Lead Plaque from Korkyra', *BSA* lxvi (1971), 79-94.

CARPENTER, R., *Discontinuity in Greek Civilization* (Cambridge, 1966).

CARPENTER, R., *see* BON, A.

CARTLEDGE, P., 'A new Fifth-century Spartan Treaty', *LCM* i (1976), 87-92.

— *Sparta and Lakonia: a Regional History 1300-362 B.C.* (London, 1979).

CASKEY, J. L., 'The Early Helladic Period in the Argolid', *Hesperia*, xxix (1960), 285-303.

CASKEY, J. L. and AMANDRY, P., 'Investigations at the Heraion of Argos, 1949', *Hesperia*, xxi (1952), 165-221.

CASSON, L., *Ships and Seamanship in the Ancient World* (Princeton, 1971).

CASSON, S., 'Early Greek Inscriptions on Metal: some Notes', *AJA* xxxix (1935), 510-17.

CATLING, H., 'Excavations at the Menelaion, Sparta, 1973-76', *AR* 1976/7, 24-42.

CAWKWELL, G. L., 'The Common Peace of 366/5 B.C.', *CQ* xi (1961), 80-6.

—— 'The Foundation of the Second Athenian Confederacy', *CQ* xxiii (1973), 47-60.

—— 'Agesilaus and Sparta', *CQ* xxvi (1976), 62-84.

CHADWICK, J., 'Who were the Dorians?', *PP* xxxi (1976), 103-17.

CHADWICK, J., KILLEN, J. T., and OLIVIER, J.-P., *The Knossos Tablets* (4th edn.), Cambridge, 1971).

CHARITONIDES, S. I., 'A Geometric Grave at Clenia in the Corinthia', *AJA* lix (1955), 125-8.

—— 'More Geometric from the Corinthia', *AJA* lxi (1957), 169-70.

CLEMENT, P. A. and THORNE, M. M., 'From the West Cemetery at Isthmia', *Hesperia*, xliii (1974), 401-11.

COLDSTREAM, J. N., (*GGP*) *Greek Geometric Pottery: a Survey of Ten Local Styles and their Chronology* (London, 1968).

—— (*GG*) *Geometric Greece* (London, 1977).

COLDSTREAM, J. N. and COLLEDGE, M. A. R. (eds.), *Greece and Italy in the Classical World: Acta of the XI International Congress of Classical Archaeology, 1978* (London, 1979).

COMPERNOLLE, R. VAN, 'La Date de la fondation d'Apollonie d'Illyrie', *AC* xxii (1953), 50-64.

CONZELMANN, H., 'Korinth und die Mädchen der Aphrodite', *Nachr. der Akad. der Wiss. in Göttingen*, phil.-hist. Kl. 1967, 247-61.

COOK, J. M., 'Mycenae 1939-1952 III: the Agamemnoneion', *BSA* xlviii (1953), 30-68.

COOK, R. M., 'Die Bedeutung der bemalten Keramik für den griechischen Handel', *JdaI* lxxiv (1959), 114-23.

—— 'Reasons for the Foundation of Ischia and Cumae', *Historia*, xi (1962), 113-14.

—— 'The Archetypal Doric Temple', *BSA* lxv (1970), 17-19.

—— *Greek Painted Pottery* (2nd edn., London, 1972).

—— 'Archaic Trade: Three Conjectures', *JHS* xcix (1979), 152-5.

COULTON, J. J., *The Architectural Development of the Greek Stoa* (Oxford, 1976).

—— *Greek Architects at Work* (London, 1977).

COURBIN, P., *Tombes géométriques d'Argos*, i (Paris, 1974).

DAKARIS, S., *Cassopaia and the Elean Colonies* (Athens, 1971).

DAVIES, J. K., *Athenian Propertied Families 600-300 B.C.* (Oxford, 1971).

—— *Democracy and Classical Greece* (London, 1978).

DAWKINS, R. M. (ed.), *The Sanctuary of Artemis Orthia at Sparta* (London, 1929).

DEONNA, W., 'L'Ex voto de Cypsélos à Delphes: le symbolisme du palmier et des grenouilles', *RHR* cxxxix (1951), 162-207; cxl (1951), 5-58.

DESBOROUGH, V. R. D'A., (*PGP*) *Protogeometric Pottery* (Oxford, 1952).

—— Mycenae 1939-1954 VI: Three Geometric Tombs', *BSA* l (1955), 239-47.

—— *The Last Mycenaeans and their Successors: an Archaeological Survey c.1200-c.1000 B.C.* (Oxford, 1964).

—— 'The Greek Mainland, c.1150-c.1000 B.C.', *PPS* xxv (1965), 213-28.

—— *The Greek Dark Ages* (London, 1972).

DICKINS, G., 'The Growth of Spartan Policy', *JHS* xxxii (1912), 1-42.

DICKINSON, O. P. T. K., *The Origins of Mycenaean Civilization* (Göteborg, 1977).

DIELS, H. (ed. KRANTZ, W.), *Die Fragmente der Vorsokratiker* (Zurich and Berlin, 1964).

DILTS, M. R., *Heracleides Lembus: Excerpta Politiarum* (Durham, NC, 1971).

DIMITRIU, S. and COSA, M., 'La Céramique archaïque et les débuts de la cité pontique d'Histria', *Dacia*, ii (1958), 69-92.

DÖHL, H. and others, *Tiryns: Forschungen und Berichte*, vi (Mainz, 1973).

DÖRIG, J., 'Frühe Löwen', *AM* lxxvi (1961), 67-80.

DOVER, K. J., 'The Palatine Manuscript of Thucydides', *CQ* iv (1954), 76-83.

DOW, S., 'Corinthiaca I: the Month Phoinikaios', *AJA* xlvi (1942), 69-72.

—— 'Corinthiaca', *HSCP* liii (1942), 89-119.

DRAGENDORFF, H., *Thera*, ii: *Theräische Gräber* (Berlin, 1903).

DRERUP, H., *Griechische Baukunst in geometrischer Zeit* (Göttingen, 1969).

DREWS, R., 'The Earliest Greek Settlements on the Black Sea', *JHS* xcvi (1976), 18-31.

DUCAT, J., *see* LE ROY, C.

DUGAS, C., *Exploration archéologique de Délos*, x: *Les Vases de l'Héraion* (Paris, 1928).

—— *Exploration archéologique de Délos*, xvii: *Les Vases orientalisants de style non mélien* (Paris, 1935).

DUNBABIN, T. J., ''Εχθρη Παλαίη', *BSA* xxxvii (1936/7), 83-91.

—— *The Western Greeks: the History of Sicily and South Italy from the Foundation of the Greek Colonies to 480 B.C.* (Oxford, 1948).

—— 'The Early History of Corinth', *JHS* lxviii (1948), 59-69.

—— *The Greeks and their Eastern Neighbours: Studies in the Relations between Greece and the Countries of the Near East in the Eighth and Seventh Centuries B.C.* (London, 1957).

—— (ed.), *Perachora: the Sanctuaries of Hera Akraia and Limenia*, ii: *Pottery, Ivories, Scarabs and other Objects from the Votive Deposit of Hera Limenia* (Oxford, 1962).

DUNBABIN, T. J. and ROBERTSON, C. M., 'Some Protocorinthian Vase-Painters', *BSA* xlviii (1953), 172-81.

DYGGVE, E. and POULSEN, F., *Das Laphrion: der Tempelbezirk von Kalydon* (Copenhagen, 1948).

EHRENBERG, V., 'The Foundation of Thurii', *AJP* lxix (1948), 149-70.

ELIOT, C. W. J. and M., 'The Lechaion Cemetery near Corinth', *Hesperia*, xxxvii (1968), 345-67.

ELLIS, J. R., *Philip II and Macedonian Imperialism* (London, 1976).

FINKELSTEIN, M. I., ''Έμπορος, ναύκληρος and κάπηλος: a Prolegomena to the Study of Athenian Trade', *CP* xxx (1935), 320-36.

FINLEY, M. I. (ed.), *Slavery in Classical Antiquity: Views and Controversies* (Cambridge, 1960).
—— *A History of Sicily*, i: *Ancient Sicily* (London, 1968).
—— *The Ancient Economy* (London, 1973).
FORNARA, C. W., *The Athenian Board of Generals from 501 to 404* (Wiesbaden, 1971).
—— 'Plutarch and the Megarian Decree', *YCS* xxiv (1975), 213–28.
FORREST, W. G., 'The First Sacred War', *BCH* lxxx (1956), 33–52.
—— 'Colonisation and the Rise of Delphi', *Historia*, vi (1957), 160–75.
—— 'Themistocles and Argos', *CQ* x (1960), 221–41.
—— *The Emergence of Greek Democracy: the Character of Greek Politics, 800–400 B.C.* (London, 1966).
—— 'Two Chronographic Notes', *CQ* xix (1969), 95–110.
—— 'The Tradition of Hippias' Expulsion from Athens', *GRBS* x (1969), 277–86.
—— *A History of Sparta, 950–192 B.C.* (2nd edn., London, 1980).
FOSS, C., 'Greek Sling Bullets in Oxford', *AR* 1974/5, 40–4.
FOSSEY, J. M., 'The Prehistoric Settlement by Lake Vouliagmeni, Perachora', *BSA* lxiv (1969), 53–69.
FOWLER, H. N. and STILLWELL, R., *Corinth*, i: *Introduction: Topography, Architecture* (Cambridge, Mass., 1932).
FRANKE, P. R., *Die antiken Münzen von Epirus* (Wiesbaden, 1961).
FREDERIKSEN, M. W., 'Archaeology in South Italy and Sicily, 1973–76', *AR* 1976/7, 43–76.
FRENCH, A., 'The Megarian Decree', *Historia*, xxv (1976), 245–9.
FREYBERG, B. VAN, *Die Geologie des Isthmus von Korinth* (Erlangen, 1973).
FRICKENHAUS, A., MÜLLER, W., and OELMANN, F., *Tiryns: die Ergebnisse der Ausgrabungen des Instituts*, i (Athens, 1912).
FRÖDIN, O. and PERSSON, A. W., *Asine: Results of the Swedish Excavations 1922–1930* (Stockholm, 1938).
FURTWÄNGLER, A., *Aegina: das Heiligtum der Aphaia* (Munich, 1906).
GADALLAH, F. F. (ed.), *Libya in History* (Benghazi, 1968).
GAERTRINGEN, H. VON, Review of Merritt, *Corinth*, viii.1 (1931), *Phil. Woch.* lii (1932), 361–4.
GAJDUCEVIC, V. F., *Das bosporanische Reich* (Berlin, 1971).
GAUER, W., *Olympische Forschungen*, viii: *Die Tongefässe aus den Brunnen unterm Stadion-Nordwall und im Südost-Gebiet* (Berlin, 1975).
GAUTHIER, P., 'Les Ports de l'empire et l'*agora* athénienne: à propos du décret mégarien', *Historia*, xxiv (1975), 498–503.
GAWANTKA, W., *Isopolitie: ein Beitrag zur Geschichte der zwischenstaatlichen Beziehungen in der griechischen Antike* (Munich, 1975).
GEBHARD, E. R., *The Theater at Isthmia* (Chicago, 1973).
GHALI-KAHIL, L., *Études thasiennes*, vii: *La Céramique grecque (fouilles de 1911–1956)* (Paris, 1960).
GJERSTAD, E., *Swedish Cyprus Expedition*, iv.2: *The Cypro-Geometric, Cypro-Archaic and Cypro-Classical Periods* (Stockholm, 1948).
—— (ed.), *Greek Geometric and Archaic Pottery found in Cyprus* (Stockholm, 1977).

438   Bibliography

GOLDMAN, H. (ed.), *Excavations at Gözlü Kule, Tarsus*, iii: *The Iron Age* (Princeton, 1963).

GOMME, A. W., 'A Forgotten Factor of Greek Naval Strategy', *JHS* liii (1933), 16-24.

—— (*HCT* i-iii) *A Historical Commentary on Thucydides*, i-iii (Oxford, 1945-56).

—— 'The Slave Population of Athens', *JHS* lxvi (1946), 127-9.

GOMME, A. W. (*HCT* iv), ANDREWES, A., and DOVER, K. J., *A Historical Commentary on Thucydides*, iv (Oxford, 1970).

GOW, A. S. F., *Machon: the Fragments* (Cambridge, 1965).

GRAEVE, V. VON, 'Milet: Bericht über die Arbeiten im Südschnitt an der hellenistischen Stadtmauer', *IM* xxiii/xxiv (1973/4), 63-115.

GRAHAM, A. J., 'Corinthian Colonies and Thucydides' Terminology', *Historia*, xi (1962), 246-52.

—— *Colony and Mother City in Ancient Greece* (Manchester, 1964).

—— 'Patterns in Early Greek Colonisation', *JHS* xci (1971), 35-47.

GREGORY, T. E., 'The Late Roman Wall at Corinth', *Hesperia*, xlviii (1979), 264-80.

GREIG, J. R. A. and TURNER, J., 'Some Pollen Diagrams from Greece and their Archaeological Significance', *JAS* i (1974), 177-94.

GRENFELL, B. P. and HUNT, A. S., *The Oxyrhynchus Papyri*, x (London, 1914).

GRIERSON, P., 'Commerce in the Dark Ages: a Critique of the Evidence', *Trans. Royal Hist. Soc.*⁵ ix (1959), 123-40.

GRIFFITH, G. T., 'The Union of Corinth and Argos (392-386 B.C.)', *Historia*, i (1950), 236-56.

GRONINGEN, B. A. VAN, *Aristote: le second livre de l'Économique* (Leiden, 1933).

—— *Theognis: le premier livre édité avec un commentaire* (Amsterdam, 1966).

GROTE, G., *History of Greece* (new edn., 10 vols., London, 1888).

GSCHNITZER, F., 'Prytanis', *RE* Suppl. xiii (1973), 730-816.

HÄGG, R., *Die Gräber der Argolis in submykenischer, protogeometrischer und geometrischer Zeit*, i: *Lage und Form der Gräber* (Uppsala, 1974).

HAMILTON, C. D., 'The Politics of Revolution in Corinth, 395-386 B.C.' *Historia*, xxi (1972), 21-37.

—— *Sparta's Bitter Victories: Politics and Diplomacy in the Corinthian War* (Ithaca, N.Y, 1979).

HAMMOND, N. G. L., 'The Heraeum at Perachora and Corinthian Encroachment', *BSA* xlix (1954), 93-102.

—— 'The Main Road from Boeotia to the Peloponnese through the Northern Megarid', *BSA* xlix (1954), 103-22.

—— 'Studies in Greek Chronology of the Sixth and Fifth Centuries B.C.', *Historia*, iv (1955), 371-411.

—— *Epirus: the Geography, the Ancient Remains, the History and the Topography of Epirus and Adjacent Areas* (Oxford, 1967).

HAMMOND, N. G. L. and GRIFFITH, G. T., *A History of Macedonia*, ii: *550-336 B.C.* (Oxford, 1979).

HARVEY, F. D., 'The Maritime Loan in Eupolis' "Marikas" (P. Oxy. 2741)', *ZPE* xxiii (1976), 231-3.

HATZFELD, J., *Alcibiade: étude sur l'histoire d'Athènes à la fin du Vᵉ siècle* (2nd edn., Paris, 1951).

HERRMANN, H.-V., 'Werkstätten geometrischer Bronzeplastik', *JdaI* lxxix (1964), 17-71.

—— *Olympische Forschungen*, vi: *Die Kessel der orientalisierenden Zeit*, i (Berlin, 1966).

HILL, B. H., 'Excavations at Corinth, 1926', *AJA* xxxi (1927), 70-9.

—— *Corinth*, i.6: *The Springs: Peirene, the Sacred Spring, Glauke* (Princeton, 1964).

HILL, G. F., *Sources for Greek History between the Persian and Peloponnesian Wars* (new edition by R. MEIGGS and A. ANDREWES, Oxford, 1951).

HOLLADAY, A. J., 'The Followers of Peisistratus', *Greece and Rome*, xxiv (1977), 40-56.

—— 'Sparta's Role in the First Peloponnesian War', *JHS* xcvii (1977), 54-63.

HOOKER, J. T., *Mycenaean Greece* (London, 1976).

HOPE-SIMPSON, R., *A Gazetteer and Atlas of Mycenaean Sites* (London, 1965).

HOPE-SIMPSON, R. and DICKINSON, O. P. T. K., *Gazetteer of Aegean Civilization in the Bronze Age*, i: *The Mainland and the Islands* (Göteborg, 1979).

HOPE-SIMPSON, R. and LAZENBY, J. F., *The Catalogue of Ships in Homer's Iliad* (Oxford, 1970).

HUMPHREYS, S. C., *Anthropology and the Greeks* (London, 1978).

HUXLEY, G. L., *Early Sparta* (London, 1962).

—— *Greek Epic Poetry from Eumelos to Panyassis* (London, 1969).

—— 'The Malian Boat (Aristotle F 544)', *Philologus*, cxix (1975), 140-2.

JACOBY, F., 'ΧΡΗΣΤΟΥΣ ΠΟΙΕΙΝ (Aristotle fr. 592 R.)', *CQ* xxxviii (1944), 15-16.

JEFFERY, L. H., *The Local Scripts of Archaic Greece: a Study of the Origin of the Greek Alphabet and its Development from the Eighth to the Fifth Centuries B.C.* (Oxford, 1961).

—— 'The Campaign between Athens and Aegina in the Years before Salamis (Herodotus, vi, 87-93)', *AJP* lxxxiii (1962), 44-54.

—— 'The Battle of Oinoe in the Stoa Poikile: a Problem in Greek Art and History', *BSA* lx (1965), 41-57.

—— *Archaic Greece: the City-States c.700-500 B.C.* (London, 1976).

JOHANNOWSKY, W., 'Problemi relativi alla "precolonizzazione" in Campania', *DdA* i (1967), 159-85.

JOHANSEN, K. F., 'Exochi: ein frührhodisches Gräberfeld', *Acta Archaeologica*, xxviii (1957), 1-192.

JOHNSTON, A. W., 'The Rehabilitation of Sostratos', *PP* xxvii (1972), 416-23.

—— 'Two-and-a-Half Corinthian Dipinti', *BSA* lxviii (1973), 181-9.

—— 'Trademarks on Greek Vases', *Greece and Rome*, xxi (1974), 138-52.

—— 'Rhodian Readings', *BSA* lxx (1975), 145-67.

—— *Trade Marks on Greek Vases* (Warminster, 1979).

JONES, A. H. M., *The Greek City from Alexander to Justinian* (Oxford, 1940).
—— 'Two Synods of the Delian and Peloponnesian Leagues', *PCPhS* clxxxii (1952/3), 43-6.
—— *Athenian Democracy* (Oxford, 1957).
JONES, N. F., 'The Civic Organisation of Corinth', *TAPA* cx (1980), 161-93.
KAGAN, D. 'Politics and Policy in Corinth, 421-336 B.C.' (diss., Ohio State University, 1958).
—— 'Corinthian Diplomacy after the Peace of Nicias', *AJP* lxxxi (1960), 291-310.
—— 'The Economic Origins of the Corinthian War (395-387 B.C.)', *PP* xvi (1961), 321-41.
—— 'Corinthian Politics and the Revolution of 392 B.C.', *Historia*, xi (1962), 447-57.
—— *The Outbreak of the Peloponnesian War* (Ithaca, NY, 1969).
—— *The Archidamian War* (Ithaca, NY, 1974).
KAHRSTEDT, U., *Griechisches Staatsrecht* (Göttingen, 1922).
KARAGEORGHIS, V., *Salamis*, iii-v, vii. *Excavations in the Necropolis of Salamis*, i-iv (Nicosia, 1967-78).
KARDARA, C., 'Dyeing and Weaving Works at Isthmia', *AJA* lxv (1961), 261-6.
KELLY, T., *A History of Argos to 500 B.C.* (Minneapolis, 1976).
KINCH, K. F., *Vroulia* (Berlin, 1914).
KINZL, K. H. (ed.), *Greece and the Eastern Mediterranean in Ancient History and Prehistory: Studies Presented to Fritz Schachermeyr on the Occasion of his Eightieth Birthday* (Berlin, 1977).
KLEIN, J. J., 'A Greek Metalworking Quarter: Eighth Century Excavations on Ischia', *Expedition*, xiv.2 (1971/2), 34-9.
KNIGGE, U., *Kerameikos, Ergebnisse der Ausgrabungen*, ix: *Der Südhügel* (Berlin, 1976).
KNIGHT, D. W., *Some Studies in Athenian Politics in the Fifth Century B.C.* (Wiesbaden, 1970).
KOEHLER, C., 'Evidence around the Mediterranean for Corinthian Export of Wine and Oil', *Proceedings of the 9th Conference on Underwater Archaeology, San Antonio, 1978* (Texas Antiquities Committee Publications, viii, Austin, 1978), 231-9.
KOSMOPOULOS, L. W., *The Prehistoric Inhabitation of Corinth* (Munich, 1948).
KRAAY, C. M., *The Composition of Greek Silver Coins: Analysis by Neutron Activation* (Oxford, 1962).
—— 'Hoards, Small Change and the Origin of Coinage', *JHS* lxxxiv (1964), 76-91.
—— *Greek Coins and History: Some Current Problems* (London, 1969).
—— 'A Note on the Carosino and Ionian Shore Hoards', *MN* xvi (1970), 23-30.
—— *Archaic and Classical Greek Coins* (London, 1976).
—— 'Timoleon and Corinthian Coinage in Sicily', *Actes du 8éme Congrès Internationale de Numismatique, New York and Washington, 1973* (Paris and Basle, 1976), 99-105.
—— 'The Asyut Hoard: Some Comments on Chronology', *NC* cxxxvii (1977), 189-98.

KRAIKER, W., *Aigina: die Vasen des 10. bis. 7. Jahrhunderts v. Chr.* (Berlin, 1951).

KRAIKER, W. and KÜBLER, K., *Kerameikos, Ergebnisse der Ausgrabungen*, i: *Die Nekropolen des 12. bis 10. Jahrhunderts* (Berlin, 1939).

KRITSAS, Ch. B., 'Κατάλογος πεσόντων ἀπὸ τὸ "Ἀργος', ΣΤΗΛΗ, 497-510.

KÜBLER, K., *Kerameikos, Ergebnisse der Ausgrabungen*, vi.1: *Die Nekropole des späten 8. bis frühen 6. Jahrhunderts* (Berlin, 1959).

KURTZ, D. C., *Athenian White Lekythoi: Patterns and Painters* (Oxford, 1975).

KURTZ, D. C. and BOARDMAN, J., *Greek Burial Customs* (London, 1971).

LAGRAND, C. H., 'Un habitat côtier de l'age du fer à l'Arquet, à La Couronne (Bouches du Rhône)', *Gallia*, xvii (1959), 179-201.

LARSEN, J. A. O., 'Sparta and the Ionian Revolt: a Study of Spartan Foreign Policy and the Genesis of the Peloponnesian League', *CP* xxvii (1932), 136-50.

— *Greek Federal States: their Institutions and History* (Oxford, 1968).

LAUFFER, S., 'Die Diodordublette XV 38 = 50 über die Friedensschlüsse zu Sparta 374 and 371 v. Chr.', *Historia*, viii (1959), 315-48.

LAVEZZI, J. C., 'Prehistoric Investigations at Corinth', *Hesperia*, xlvii (1978), 402-51.

LAWRENCE, A. W., *Greek Aims in Fortification* (Oxford, 1979).

LAWRENCE, P., 'Five Grave Groups from the Corinthia', *Hesperia*, xxxiii (1964), 89-107.

LEGON, R. P., 'The Megarian Decree and the Balance of Greek Naval Power', *CP* lxviii (1973), 161-71.

LEHMANN, G. A., 'Der "erste heilige Krieg"—eine Fiktion?', *Historia*, xxix (1980), 242-6.

LEHMANN-HARTLEBEN, K., *Die antiken Hafenanlagen des Mittelmeeres* (Leipzig, 1923).

LERAT, L., 'Fouilles de Delphes (1934-1935): rapport préliminaire', *RA*⁶ xii.2 (1938), 183-227.

— *Les Locriens de l'Ouest* (2 vols., Paris, 1952).

— 'Fouilles à Delphes, à l'Est du grand sanctuaire (1950-1957)', *BCH* lxxxv (1961), 316-66.

LE ROY, C. and DUCAT, J., *Fouilles de Delphes*, ii: *Topographie et architecture: les terres cuites architecturales; la sculpture décorative en terre cuite* (Paris, 1967).

LEVICK, B. (ed.), *The Ancient Historian and his Materials: Essays in Honour of C. E. Stevens* (Farnborough, 1975).

LEWIS, D. M., 'Cleisthenes and Attica', *Historia*, xii (1963), 22-40.

— *Sparta and Persia* (Leiden, 1977).

LLOYD, A. B., 'Triremes and the Saïte Navy', *JEA* lviii (1972), 268-79.

— 'Were Necho's Triremes Phoenician?', *JHS* xcv (1975), 45-61.

— 'M. Basch on triremes: some Observations', *JHS* c (1980), 195-8.

LO PORTO, F. G., 'Ceramica arcaica dalla necropoli di Taranto', *Annuario*, xxxvii/xxxviii (1959/60), 7-230.

— 'Satyrion (Taranto)', *NS* 1964, 177-279.

—— 'Gli scavi sull'acropoli di Satyrion', *BA* xlix (1964), 67-80.

LUTZ, H., 'The Corinthian Constitution after the Fall of the Cypselids', *CR* x (1896), 418-19.

MACDOWELL, D., *Andokides on the Mysteries* (Oxford, 1962).

MACINTOSH, J., *see* WILLIAMS, C. K.

MCNEAL, R. A., 'Historical Methods and Thucydides I.103.1', *Historia*, xix (1970), 306-25.

—— 'The Greeks in History and Prehistory', *Antiquity*, xlvi (1972), 19-28.

MCPHEE, I. D., 'Attic Red Figure of the Late Fifth and Fourth Centuries from Corinth', *Hesperia*, xlv (1976), 380-96.

MALLWITZ, A. and SCHIERING, W., *Olympische Forschungen*, v: *Die Werkstatt des Pheidias in Olympia* (Berlin, 1964).

MARINATOS, S., ''Ανασκαφαὶ ἐν Πύλῳ', *Praktika*, 1953, 238-50.

—— ''Έρευναι ἐν Σάμῃ τῆς Κεφαλληνίας', *AE* 1964, 15-27.

MATTUSCH, C. C., 'Corinthian Metalworking: the Forum Area', *Hesperia*, xlvi (1977), 380-9.

MEIGGS, R., *The Athenian Empire* (Oxford, 1972).

MEIGGS, R. and LEWIS, D. M., (*GHI*) *A Selection of Greek Historical Inscriptions to the End of the Fifth Century B.C.* (Oxford, 1969).

MELE, A., *Il Commercio greco-arcaico: prexis ed emporie* (Naples, 1979).

METZGER, H., *Fouilles de Xanthos*, iv: *Les Céramiques archaïques et classiques de l'acropole lycienne* (Paris, 1972).

MILCHHÖFER, 'Der "Apollo" von Tenea', *Arch. Zeit.* xxxix (1881), 54-5.

MOREL, J.-P., 'Les Phocéens en Occident, certitudes et hypothèses', *PP* xxi (1966), 378-420.

—— 'Les Phocéens en Occident: dix années de recherches (1966-75)', *BCH* xcix (1975), 853-96.

MORETTI, L., *Richerche sulle leghe greche (peloponnesiaca-beotica-licia)* (Rome, 1962).

MORGAN, C. H., 'Excavations at Corinth, 1935-1936', *AJA* xl (1936), 466-84.

—— 'Excavations at Corinth, 1936-1937', *AJA* xli (1937), 539-52.

—— 'Investigations at Corinth, 1953—a Tavern of Aphrodite', *Hesperia*, xxii (1953), 131-40.

MORRISON, J. S. and WILLIAMS, R. T., *Greek Oared Ships, 900-322 B.C.* (Cambridge, 1968).

MOSSÉ, C., *La Tyrannie dans la Grèce antique* (Paris, 1969).

MURRAY, O., *Early Greece* (London, 1980).

MYRES, J. L., 'On the "List of Thalassocracies" in Eusebius', *JHS* xxvi (1906), 84-130.

NACHOD, H., 'Therikles', *RE* v A (1934), 2367-8.

NAUMANN, R. and TUCHELT, K., 'Die Ausgrabungen im Südwesten des Tempels von Didyma 1962', *IM* xiii/xiv (1963/4), 15-62.

NICHOLLS, R., 'Architectural Terracotta Sculpture from the Athenian Agora', *Hesperia*, xxxix (1970), 115-38.

NICHOLS, M. L., 'Geometric Vases from Corinth', *AJA* ix (1905), 411-21.

*OBERHUMMER, E., *Akarnanien, Ambrakia, Amphilochien, Leukas im Altertum* (Munich, 1887).

OOST, S. I., 'Cypselus the Bacchiad', *CP* lxvii (1972), 10–30.

ORLANDINI, P., 'Scavi archeologici in località Incoronata presso Metaponto', *Acme*, xxix (1976), 29–39.

ORLANDOS, A. K., *Les Matériaux de construction et la technique architecturale des anciens Grecs* (2 vols., Paris, 1966–8).

PAGE, D. L., *Sappho and Alcaeus: an Introduction to the Study of Ancient Lesbian Poetry* (Oxford, 1955).

— *History and the Homeric Iliad* (Berkeley and Los Angeles, 1959).

PALMER, H., *see* BLEGEN, C. W.

PANOFKA, T., 'Archäologisches aus Italien', *Arch. Zeit.* v (1847), 17*–28*.

PARKE, H. W., *The Oracles of Zeus: Dodona, Olympia, Ammon* (Oxford, 1967).

PARKE, H. W. and WORMELL, D. E. W., *The Delphic Oracle* (2 vols., Oxford, 1956).

PARSONS, A. W., *see* BON, A.

PAYNE, H. G. G., *Necrocorinthia: a Study of Corinthian Art in the Archaic Period* (Oxford, 1931).

— *Perachora: the Sanctuaries of Hera Akraia and Limenia*, i (Oxford, 1940).

PEASE, M. Z., 'A Well of the Late Fifth Century at Corinth', *Hesperia*, vi (1937), 257–316.

PEEK, W., 'Ein neuer spartanischer Staatsvertrag', *Abh. der Sächs. Akad. der Wiss. Leipzig, phil.-hist. Kl.* lxv.3 (1974), 3–15.

PELEKIDIS, S., 'Ἀνασκαφὴ Φαλήρου', *AD* ii (1916), 13–64.

PEMBERTON, E. G., 'The Vrysoula Classical Deposit from Ancient Corinth', *Hesperia*, xxxix (1970), 265–307.

PERDRIZET, P., *Fouilles de Delphes*, v: *Monuments figurés: petits bronzes, terres cuites, antiquités diverses* (Paris, 1908).

PERLMAN, S., 'The Causes and the Outbreak of the Corinthian War', *CQ* xiv (1964), 64–81.

PFUHL, E., 'Der archaischer Friedhof am Stadtberge von Thera', *AM* xxviii (1903), 1–290.

PHILIPPSON, A., 'Der Isthmos von Korinth', *ZGEB* xxv (1890), 1–98.

— *Das Klima Griechenlands* (Bonn, 1948).

— *Die griechischen Landschaften, eine Landeskunde* (4 vols., Frankfurt am Main, 1950–8).

PICCIRILLI, L., *Gli Arbitrati interstatali greci* (Pisa, 1973).

PLEKET, H. W., 'The Archaic Tyrannis', *Talanta*, i (1969), 19–61.

POMTOW, H. R., 'Gesteinsproben von den delphischen Bauten und Weihgeschenken', *Philologus*, lxvi (1907), 260–86.

POWELL, J. E., *A Lexicon to Herodotus* (2nd edn., Cambridge, 1938).

POWELL, J. U., *Collectanea Alexandrina* (Oxford, 1925).

PRICE, M. and WAGGONER, N., *Archaic Greek Coinage: the Asyut Hoard* (London, 1975).

PRITCHETT, W. K., *Studies in Ancient Greek Topography* (3 vols., Berkeley and Los Angeles, 1965–80).

— *The Greek State at War*, ii (Berkeley and Los Angeles, 1974).

PROTONOTARIOU-DEILAKI, E., 'Ἡ Σφίγξ τῆς Κορίνθου', *AAA* vi (1973), 181–8.

RAUBITSCHEK, A. E., 'Corinth and Athens before the Peloponnesian War', in KINZL (ed.), *Greece and the Eastern Mediterranean*, 266-9.

RAVEL, O., 'Rare and Unpublished Coins of Corinthian Types', *NC*⁵ xv (1935), 1-15.

REECE, D. W., 'The Battle of Tanagra', *JHS* lxx (1950), 75-6.

RENFREW, C., *The Emergence of Civilisation: the Cyclades and the Aegean in the Third Millennium B.C.* (London, 1972).

RIDDER, A. DE, 'Fouilles d'Orchomène', *BCH* xix (1895), 137-224.

RIDGWAY, D., 'Scavi della necropoli di Quattro Fontanili a Veio ii: coppe cicladiche da Veio', *St. Etr.* xxxv (1967), 311-21.

RIDGWAY, D. and DICKINSON, O. P. T. K., 'Pendent Semicircles at Veii: a Glimpse', *BSA* lxviii (1973), 191-2.

RIZZO, F., *La Repubblica di Siracusa nel momento di Ducezio* (Palermo, 1970).

ROBERT, L., 'Un décret dorien trouvé à Délos', *Hellenica*, v (1948), 5-15.

—— 'Addenda aux tomes I-X: tome V: décret dorien trouvé à Délos', *Hellenica*, xi/xii (1960), 562-9.

ROBERTSON, C. M., 'Excavations in Ithaca, V: the Geometric and Later Finds from Aetos', *BSA* xliii (1948), 1-124.

—— *A History of Greek Art* (Cambridge, 1975).

ROBERTSON, N., 'The Myth of the First Sacred War', *CQ* xxviii (1978), 38-73.

ROBINSON, H. S., 'Excavations at Corinth, 1960', *Hesperia*, xxxi (1962), 95-133.

—— 'A Sanctuary and Cemetery in Western Corinth', *Hesperia*, xxxviii (1969), 1-35.

—— 'Excavations at Corinth: Temple Hill, 1968-1972', *Hesperia*, xlv (1976), 203-39.

ROEBUCK, C. A., 'The Settlements of Philip II with the Greek States in 338 B.C.', *CP* xliii (1948), 73-92.

—— *Ionian Trade and Colonization* (New York, 1959).

—— 'Some Aspects of Urbanization in Corinth', *Hesperia*, xli (1972), 96-127.

ROEBUCK, M. C., 'Excavation at Corinth: 1954', *Hesperia*, xxiv (1955), 147-57.

ROLLEY, C., *Fouilles de Delphes*, v: *Monuments figurés*, fasc. 2: *Les Statuettes de bronze* (Paris, 1969).

—— *Fouilles de Delphes*, v: *Monuments figurés*, fasc. 3: *Les Trépieds à cuve clouée* (Paris, 1977).

ROSE, H. J., 'Stesichorus and the Rhadine-Fragment', *CQ* xxvi (1932), 88-92.

ROUGÉ, J., *La Marine dans l'antiquité* (Paris, 1975).

ROUSSEL, D., *Tribu et cité: études sur les groupes sociaux dans les cités grecques aux époques archaïques et classiques* (Paris, 1976).

ROUX, G., 'Κυψέλη. Où avait-on caché le petit Kypsélos?', *REA* lxv (1963), 278-89.

ROY, J., 'Arcadia and Boeotia in Peloponnesian Affairs, 370-362 B.C.', *Historia*, xx (1971) 569-99.

—— 'Diodorus Siculus xv.40—the Peloponnesian Revolutions of 374 B.C.', *Klio*, lv (1973), 135-9.

RUBENSOHN, O., *Das Delion von Paros* (Wiesbaden, 1962).

RUSCHENBUSCH, E., ΣΟΛΩΝΟΣ ΝΟΜΟΙ: *Die Fragmente des Solonischen Gesetzeswerkes mit einer Text- und Überlieferungsgeschichte* (Wiesbaden, 1966).

RUTTER, J. B., 'The Late Helladic IIIB and IIIC periods at Korakou and Gonia in the Corinthia' (diss., University of Pennsylvania, 1974).

—— 'Ceramic Evidence for Northern Intruders in Southern Greece at the Beginning of the Late Helladic IIIC Period', *AJA* lxxix (1975), 17-32.

—— '"Non-Mycenaean" Pottery: a Reply to Gisela Walberg', *AJA* lxxx (1976), 187-8.

—— 'The Last Mycenaeans at Corinth', *Hesperia*, xlviii (1979), 348-92.

RYDER, T. T. B., 'The Supposed Common Peace of 366/5 B.C.', *CQ* vii (1957), 199-205.

*RYDER, T. T. B., *Koine Eirene: General Peace and Local Independence in Ancient Greece* (London, 1965).

*STE CROIX, G. E. M. DE, *The Origins of the Peloponnesian War* (London, 1972).

—— 'Ancient Greek and Roman Maritime Loans', in EDEY, H. and YAMEY, B. S. (eds.), *Debts, Credits, Finance and Profits: a Collection of Essays Presented to W. S. Baxter* (London, 1974).

*SAKELLARIOU, M. and FARAKLAS, N., *Corinthia-Cleonaea* (Athens, 1971).

SALMON, J. B., 'The Heraeum at Perachora and the Early History of Corinth and Megara', *BSA* lxvii (1972), 159-204.

—— 'Political Hoplites?', *JHS* xcvii (1977), 84-101.

—— 'Periander and the Commercial Installations of Corinth', in COLDSTREAM and COLLEDGE (eds.), *Greece and Italy in the Classical World*, 197.

SCHACHERMEYR, F., 'Periandros', *RE* xix (1937), 704-17.

—— *Die ägäische Frühzeit. Forschungsbericht über die Ausgrabungen im letzten Jahrzehnt und über ihre Ergebnisse für unser Geschichtsbild* i: *Die vormykenischen Perioden des griechischen Festlandes und der Kykladen* (Vienna, 1976).

SCHAEFER, A., *Demosthenes und seine Zeit* (3 vols., Leipzig, 1885-7).

SCHAEFER, H., *Staatsform und Politik: Untersuchungen zur griechischen Geschichte der 6. und 5. Jahrhunderts* (Leipzig, 1932).

—— 'Polemarchos', *RE* Suppl. viii (1956), 1097-134.

—— 'πρόβουλος', *RE* xxiii (1957), 1221-31.

SCHAMP, J., 'Sous le signe d'Arion', *AC* xlv (1976), 95-120.

SCHEFOLD, K., *Myth and Legend in Early Greek Art* (London, 1966).

SCRANTON, R. L., *Corinth*, i.3: *Monuments in the Lower Agora and North of the Archaic Temple* (Princeton, 1951).

SCRANTON, R. L., SHAW, J. W., and IBRAHIM, L., *Kenchreai, Eastern Port of Corinth*, i: *Topography and Architecture* (Leiden, 1978).

SEAGER, R. J., 'The Congress Decree: Some Doubts and a Hypothesis', *Historia*, xviii (1969), 129-41.

SEAGER, R. J., 'After the Peace of Nicias: Diplomacy and Policy, 421-416 B.C.', *CQ* xxvi (1976), 249-69.

SEALEY, B. R., 'The Causes of the Peloponnesian War', *CP* lxx (1975), 89-109.

446   *Bibliography*

SEIBERT, J., 'Metropolis und Apoikie: historische Beiträge zur Geschichte ihrer gegenseitigen Beziehungen' (diss., Würzburg, 1963).

SERVAIS, J., 'Le "colosse" des Cypsélides', *AC* xxxiv (1965), 144-74.

—— 'Hérodote et la chronologie des Cypsélides', *AC* xxxviii (1969), 28-81.

SHEAR, T. L., 'Excavations in the North Cemetery at Corinth in 1930', *AJA* xxxiv (1930), 403-31.

—— 'The Excavation of Roman Chamber Tombs at Corinth in 1931', *AJA* xxxv (1931), 424-41.

SMITH, E. A., 'Prehistoric Pottery from the Isthmia', *Hesperia*, xxiv (1955), 142-6.

SMITH, R. E., 'The Opposition to Agesilaus' Foreign Policy 394-371 B.C.', *Historia*, ii (1953/4), 274-88.

SMITHSON, E. L., 'The Protogeometric Cemetery at Nea Ionia, 1949', *Hesperia*, xxx (1961), 147-78.

SNODGRASS, A. M., *Early Greek Armour and Weapons from the End of the Bronze Age to 600 B.C.* (Edinburgh, 1964).

—— *The Dark Age of Greece: an Archaeological Survey of the Eleventh to the Eighth Centuries B.C.* (Edinburgh, 1971).

—— *Archaic Greece: the Age of Experiment* (London, 1980).

SORDI, M., *Timoleonte* (Palermo, 1961).

SPARKES, B. A. and TALCOTT, L., *The Athenian Agora*, xii: *Black and Plain Pottery of the Sixth, Fifth and Fourth Centuries B.C.* (Princeton, 1970).

STARR, C. G., *The Economic and Social Growth of Early Greece* (New York, 1977).

STERN, E. VON, *Geschichte des spartanischen und thebanischen Hegemonie vom Königsfrieden bis zur Schlacht bei Mantineia* (Dorpat, 1884).

STILLWELL, A. N., 'Eighth Century B.C. Inscriptions from Corinth', *AJA* xxxviii (1933), 605-10.

—— *Corinth*, xv.1: *The Potters' Quarter* (Princeton, 1948).

STILLWELL, R., 'Excavations at Corinth, 1934-1935', *AJA* xl (1936), 21-45.

—— *Corinth*, ii: *The Theater* (Princeton, 1952).

STILLWELL, R., see FOWLER, H. N.

STILLWELL, R., MACDONALD, W. L., and MCALLISTER, M. H., *The Princeton Encyclopaedia of Classical Sites* (Princeton, 1976).

STILLWELL, R., SCRANTON, R. L., and FREEMAN, S. E., with contributions by ASKEW, H. E., *Corinth*, i.2: *Architecture* (Cambridge, Mass., 1941).

STRONG, D., *The British Museum: Catalogue of the Carved Amber in the Department of Greek and Roman Antiquities* (London, 1966).

STROUD, R. S., *Drakon's Law on Homicide* (Berkeley and Los Angeles, 1968).

—— 'Tribal Boundary Markers from Corinth', *CSCA* i (1968), 233-42.

—— 'Thucydides and the Battle of Solygeia', *CSCA* iv (1971), 227-47.

—— 'An Ancient Fort on Mt. Oneion', *Hesperia*, xl (1971), 127-45.

—— 'Greek Inscriptions at Corinth', *Hesperia*, xli (1972), 198-217.

STUCCHI, S., *L'Agora di Cirene*, i (Rome, 1965).

—— *Cirene 1957-1966: un decennio di attività della missione archeologica italiana a Cirene* (Tripoli, 1967).

TALBERT, R. J. A., *Timoleon and the Revival of Greek Sicily 344-317 B.C.* (Cambridge, 1974).

TEMPORINI, H. (ed.), *Aufstieg und Niedergang der römischen Welt* ii.7.1 (Berlin, 1979).

THEOCHARIS, D. R. (ed.), *Neolithic Greece* (Athens, 1973).

*TOD, M. N., *A Selection of Greek Historical Inscriptions*, ii: *from 403 to 323 B.C.* (Oxford, 1948).

TOMLINSON, R. A., 'Perachora: the Remains Outside the two Sanctuaries', *BSA* lxiv (1969), 155-258.

—— *Argos and the Argolid from the End of the Bronze Age to the Roman Occupation* (London, 1972).

—— 'The Upper Terraces at Perachora', *BSA* lxxii (1977), 197-202.

TOMLINSON, R. A. and FOSSEY, J. M., 'Ancient Remains on Mount Mavrovouni, South Boeotia', *BSA* lxv (1970), 243-63.

TRIAS DE ARRIBAS, G., *Ceramicas griegas de la Péninsula Ibérica* (2 vols., Madrid, 1967-8).

TUPLIN, C., 'Thucydides 1.42.2 and the Megarian Decree', *CQ* xix (1979), 301-7.

UNDERHILL, G. E., *A Commentary with Introduction and Appendix on the Hellenica of Xenophon* (Oxford, 1900).

URE, P. N., *Aryballoi and Figurines from Rhitsona in Boeotia* (Cambridge, 1934).

VALLET, G., *Rhégion et Zancle: histoire, commerce et civilisation des cités chalcidiennes du détroit de Messine* (Paris, 1958).

VALLET, G. and VILLARD, F., 'Céramique et histoire grecque', *Rev. Hist.* ccxxv (1961), 295-318.

—— *Mégara Hyblaea*, ii: *La Céramique archaïque* (Paris, 1964).

—— 'Les Phocéens en Méditerranée occidental à l'époque archaïque et la fondation de Hyélè', *PP* xxi (1966), 166-90.

VATIN, C., *Médéon de Phocide, rapport provisoire* (Paris, 1969).

VENEDIKOV, I. (ed.), *Apoloniya. razkopite v nekropola na Apoloniya prez 1947-1949* (Sophia, 1963).

VERDELIS, N. M., 'Der Diolkos am Isthmos von Korinth', *AM* lxxi (1956), 51-9.

—— 'Ἀνασκαφὴ εἰς τὴν ἀρχαίαν Σολύγειαν', *Praktika*, 1958, 135-45.

—— 'Ἀνασκαφὴ τοῦ Διόλκου', *Praktika*, 1960, 136-43.

—— 'Ἀνασκαφὴ τοῦ Διόλκου', *Praktika*, 1962, 48-50.

—— 'A Sanctuary at Solygeia', *Archaeology*, xv (1962), 184-92.

VILLARD, F., *La Céramique grecque de Marseille (VIe-IVe siècle)* (Paris, 1960).

VILLARD, F. and VALLET, G., 'Géométrique grecque, géométrique sicéliote, géométrique sicule: étude sur les premiers contacts entre Grecs et indigènes sur la côte orientale de la Sicile', *MEFR* lxviii (1956), 7-27.

VOCOTOPOULOU, I., 'Πολεοδομικὰ τῆς ἀρχαίας Ἀμβρακίας', *AAA* iv (1971), 332-6.

—— 'Ἀρχαιολογικαὶ εἰδήσεις ἐξ Ἠπείρου', *AAA* vi (1973), 215-29.

—— 'Le Trésor de vases de bronze de Votonosi', *BCH* xcix (1975), 729-88.

VÖLKL, K., 'Das megarische Psephisma', *Rh. Mus.* xciv (1951), 330-6.

WAAGE, F. O., 'An Early Helladic Well near Old Corinth', *Hesperia*, Suppl. viii (1949), 415–22.

WADE-GERY, H. T., *Essays in Greek History* (Oxford, 1958).

WALBERG, G., 'Northern Intruders in Myc. IIIC?', *AJA* lxxx (1976), 186–7.

WALDSTEIN, C., *The Argive Heraeum* (2 vols., Boston and New York, 1902–5).

WALLACE, W., 'The Demes of Eretria', *Hesperia*, xvi (1947), 115–46.

WALLENSTEIN, K., *Korinthische Plastik des 7. und 6. Jahrhunderts vor Christus* (Bonn, 1971).

WALTER, H., 'Korinthische Keramik', *AM* lxxiv (1959), 57–68.

WEINBERG, G. D., *Corinth*, xii: *The Minor Objects* (Princeton, 1952).

WEINBERG, S. S., 'Remains from Prehistoric Corinth', *Hesperia*, vi (1937), 487–524.

—— 'Excavations at Corinth, 1938–1939', *AJA* xlii (1939), 592–600.

—— 'What is Protocorinthian Geometric Ware?', *AJA* xlv (1941), 30–44.

*WEINBERG, S. S., *Corinth*, vii.1: *The Geometric and Orientalizing Pottery* (Cambridge, Mass., 1943).

—— 'A Cross-Section of Corinthian Antiquities (Excavations of 1940)', *Hesperia*, xvii (1948), 197–241.

—— 'Investigations at Corinth, 1947–1948', *Hesperia*, xviii (1949), 148–57.

—— 'Terracotta Sculpture at Corinth', *Hesperia*, xxvi (1957), 289–319.

—— *Corinth*, i.5: *The Southeast Building, the Twin Basilicas, the Mosaic House* (Princeton, 1960).

—— 'Excavations at Corinth, 1959, Part II', *Hesperia*, xxix (1960), 240–53.

—— 'KTΛ from Corinth', *Hesperia*, xliii (1974), 522–34.

WELWEI, K.-L., *Unfreien im antiken Kriegsdienst*, ii: *Die kleineren und mittleren griechischen staaten und die hellenistischen reiche* (Wiesbaden, 1977).

WESTERMANN, W. L., 'Athenaeus and the Slaves of Athens', *HSCP* Suppl. i (1940), 451–70.

WESTLAKE, H. D., 'Corinth and the Argive Coalition', *AJP* lxi (1940), 413–21.

—— 'Timoleon and the Reconstruction of Syracuse', *CHJ* vii (1941–3), 73–100.

—— *Essays on the Greek Historians and Greek History* (Manchester, 1969).

—— 'A Corinthian Threat of Secession', *LCM* v (1980), 121–5.

WICK, T. E., 'Thucydides and the Megarian Decree', *AC* xlvi (1977), 74–99.

WICKERT, K., *Der peloponnesische Bund, von seiner Entstehung bis zum Ende des archidamischen Krieges* (Erlangen, 1961).

WILL, E., *Korinthiaka: recherches sur l'histoire et la civilisation de Corinthe des origines aux guerres médiques* (Paris, 1955).

—— 'Limites, possibilités et tâches de l'histoire économique et sociale du monde grec antique', *Ét. arch.* i (1963), 153–66.

WILLEMSEN, F., *Olympische Forschungen*, iii: *Dreifusskessel von Olympia, alte und neue Funde* (Berlin, 1957).

WILLIAMS, C. K., 'Excavations at Corinth', *AD* xxiii.B (1968), 134–6.

—— 'Excavations at Corinth, 1968', *Hesperia*, xxxviii (1969), 36–63.

—— 'Corinth, 1969: Forum Area', *Hesperia*, xxxix (1970), 1–39.

—— 'Corinth 1976: Forum Southwest', *Hesperia*, xlvi (1977), 40–81.

—— 'Pre-Roman Cults in the Area of the Forum of Ancient Corinth' (Diss., University of Pennsylvania, 1978).

—— 'Corinth 1977: Forum Southwest', *Hesperia*, xlvii (1978), 1–39.
—— 'Corinth 1978, Forum Southwest', *Hesperia*, xlviii (1979), 105–44.
—— 'Corinth Excavations, 1979', *Hesperia*, xlix (1980), 107–34.
—— 'Demaratus and Early Corinthian Roofs', ΣΤΗΛΗ, 345–50.
—— 'Corinth: Excavations of 1980', *Hesperia*, 1 (1981), 1–33.
WILLIAMS, C. K. and FISHER, J. E., 'Corinth, 1970: Forum Area', *Hesperia*, xl (1971), 1–51.
—— 'Corinth 1971: Forum Area', *Hesperia*, xli (1972), 143–84.
—— 'Corinth 1972: the Forum Area', *Hesperia*, xlii (1973), 1–44.
—— 'Corinth 1974: Forum Southwest', *Hesperia*, xliv (1975), 1–50.
—— 'Corinth 1975: Forum Southwest', *Hesperia*, xlv (1976), 99–162.
WILLIAMS, C. K., MACINTOSH, J., and FISHER, J. E., 'Excavation at Corinth, 1973', *Hesperia*, xliii (1974), 1–76.
WINTER, F. E., *Greek Fortifications* (London, 1971).
WISEMAN, J. R., 'A Trans-Isthmian Fortification Wall: Notes on Hellenistic Military Operations in the Corinthia', *Hesperia*, xxxii (1963), 248–75.
—— 'Excavations at Corinth, the Gymnasium Area, 1965', *Hesperia*, xxxvi (1967), 13–41.
—— 'Excavations at Corinth, the Gymnasium Area, 1966', *Hesperia*, xxxvi (1967), 402–28.
—— 'Ancient Corinth: the Gymnasium Area', *Archaeology*, xxii (1969), 216–25.
—— 'The Gymnasium Area at Corinth, 1969–1970', *Hesperia*, xli (1972), 1–42.
*WISEMAN, J., *The Land of the Ancient Corinthians* (Göteborg, 1978).
—— 'Corinth and Rome I: 228 B.C.–A.D. 267', in TEMPORINI (ed.), *Aufstieg und Niedergang*, ii.7.1, 438–548.
WÖRRLE, M., *Untersuchungen zur Verfassungsgeschichte von Argos im 5. Jahrhundert vor Christus* (Erlangen, 1964).
WORMELL, D. E. W., 'Studies in Greek Tyranny, i', *Hermathena*, lxvi (1945), 1–24.
YOUNG, R. S., *see* BLEGEN, C. W.
ZAPHEIROPOULOS, N., 'Ἀνασκαφικαὶ ἔρευναι εἰς περιφέρειαν Φαρῶν Ἀχαίας', *Praktika*, 1952, 396–412.
*ZÖRNER, G., 'Kypselos und Pheidon von Argos: Untersuchungen zur frühen griechischen Tyrannis' (diss., Marburg, 1971).

Index

No distinction is made between text and footnotes

Sources Discussed

(i) *Authors*

Passages merely cited as evidence for events etc. are not normally included;
see the General Index

General

References in bold type are to Figures

Acarnania, Acarnanians, **17**, 91, 210-11,
 213-14, 266, 272, 276, 279, 291, 307-10,
 312, 316-18, 320, 349, 383, 422-3

Achaea, Achaeans, **1**, 89, 265-7, 321, 369,
 375, 381
Acrocorinth, **2**, **6**, 1, 4, 8, 14-15, 20, 23,

Argolid, 13, 45, 49-51, 82, 107, 110; *see*
  Argos
Argos, Argives, 1, 18, 3, 5, 38-9, 47-54,
  65-6, 71-2, 82, 107, 110, 123-4, 129,
  131, 146, 165-6, 218, 232, 235, 241,
  243-4, 250-1, 259-62, 265-6, 300, 319,
  322, 324-31, 342-5, 347-54, 357-71,
  374, 376, 379, 383-4, 411, 417, 421;
  see Pheidon
Argos, Amphilochian, 17, 278-9, 291, 309,
  317, 422-3
Arieus, 55
Arion, 141, 197
Aristarchus, 336
Aristeus, 294-5
Aristocracy, 149-54, 397, 403, 405; *see*
  Bacchiads
Aristodemus I, 52
Aristodemus II, 350-1
Aristomachus, 39
Ariston, 130, 334-5
Arniadas, 214, 277
Artabazus, 256, 392
Artaxerxes, 368, 379
Artemis, 107, 121, 354
Artemisium, 18, 167, 254, 418
Aryballos, 90, 107, 110, 113-14, 117-18
Asia Minor, 108, 144; cities of, 244, 342,
  347, 350, 363, 368, 380, 411, 427
Asine, 3, 18, 14, 82
Asopius, 312
Asopus, 62
Asprokambos, 5, 26, 31; temple, 26
Assembly, 57, 231, 234-5, 237-8, 328,
  359-60, 367, 385
Astacus, 17; *see* Euarchus
Astyochus, 339-40
Athena, 172, 219
Athens, Athenians, Attica, 1, 18, 31, 50,
  56-8, 129-31, 141, 175, 186, 208, 224,
  241-2, 245-69, 275-8, 281-345, 347-54,
  356, 358, 362-84, 389, 392-5, 398,
  406-11, 413, 415-16, 418, 420-9;
  economy, 107, 109-10, 115-16, 121-4,
  129, 131, 141, 143, 147-55, 159-63,
  172-3, 400, 403-4, 406
Athikia, 2, 27, 37, 48, 58, 156
Attic, *see* Pottery
Attica, *see* Athens
Autonomy, 363, 368-70, 372-3
Bacchiads, 46-7, 55-74, 93, 171, 186-95,
  198, 205-7, 209, 216, 218-19, 270, 397
Bacchis, 46-7, 55-6
Bacchius, 70
Banker, 149
Barley, *see* Cereals
Basileus, 57, 188, 190, 207
Basilica, Lechaeum, 6, 134

Battus, 319
Bellerophon, 294, 398
Bissia, 2, 26
Black Sea, 14, 62, 109, 127, 144
Blockade, 129-30, 177, 308, 320
Bluff, 8, 20-1, 23-5, 35, 126, 221
Bodyguard, 188, 195, 197-8
Boeotia, Boeotians, 18, 82, 94, 99, 106-7,
  110, 121, 147, 165-6, 245-9, 265, 267,
  284, 301-2, 319, 322-9, 336, 341-5,
  347-54, 356, 364-9, 371-84, 411, 427-8
Booty, *see* Spoils
Bottiaea, Bottiaeans, 294
Bottomry Loan, 148-52
Branchidae, 226
Brasidas, 165, 315, 318-19, 321
Brielthi, 4, 17
Bronze, 12, 75, 78, 84-7, 89, 91, 94, 99,
  118-19, 128-9, 173
Bucephalus, 6
Buchetium, 17, 214
Bucchero, *see* Pottery
Budorum, 177
Building, Public, 59-62, 78-9, 170-1, 180-4,
  201-2, 220-1; skills, 61, 82, 97-9, 120-5,
  142, 150, 155, 401
Burial, *see* Grave
Byzantium, 1, 257, 301
Callicratidas, 338
Callistratus, 378, 427-8
Cale Acte, 12, 389
Calydon, 17, 120-1, 142
Camarina, 12, 388-9
Canal, Isthmus, 134, 202; Leucas, 134,
  209-11, 217, 271
Capua, 12, 86
Carians, 222
Carpentry, 82, 99, 152, 402
Carthage, 14, 105-6, 140-1, 146, 390
Caunus, 1, 195
Cavalry, 68, 166, 319, 391, 418
Cecryphaleia, 18, 263
Cemetery, *see* Graves, North Cemetery
Cenchreae, 3-5, 6, 31, 35, 37, 143-7, 155,
  157, 177, 311, 319, 330, 337, 365, 378
Centaur Bath, 16, 181
Cephallenia, 17, 91, 204, 301, 307-9, 316
Cephalus, 392
Cereals, 20, 22-8, 34, 82, 130-1, 154, 165;
  imports, 34, 90, 129-32, 135, 141-2,
  144, 147, 155, 159, 177, 227, 320, 406
Cerinthus, 18, 222
Chabrias, 367, 374, 377
Chaeronea, 18, 383, 395, 411
Chalcideus, 337
Chalcidians (Thrace), 292-5, 324, 328-9,
  339, 349, 372
Chalcis (Aetolia), 17, 92, 213, 265, 268,
  277-9, 408, 423

Neutrality, Corinthian (365), 178, 237,
379-82, 384, 405, 411, 427-8
New Corinth, **2**, **4**, 21-24, 36, 47
Nichoria, **1**, 91
Nicias, 27, 32, 166, 175, 177, 319-20,
334-5, 417;*see* Peace of Nicias
Nicolochus, 374, 395
Nicostratus, 314-15
Nisaea, **18**, 262, 267, 311, 321, 420-1
Non-Dorians, 51, 57, 186, 189, 192-3, 208,
416
North Building, **16**, 181, 184
North Cemetery, **6**, 15, 22, 34, 42-5, 83,
100, 110, 176, 179
North Stoa, **16**, 180
Obsidian, 10-11, 13, 28
Ocimon, 400
Oecist, 63, 65, 67, 209-13, 215, 218, 282
Oeniadae, **17**, 266, 309, 312, 316, 318
Oenoe (Argolid), **18**, 263, 265, 421; (Attica),
18, 336; (Corinthia), **5**, 1, 26, 366-7
Oenophyta, **18**, 265
Oil, 88, 90, 95, 117-18, 127, 136, 178
Olbia, **14**, 109, 127
Oligaethidae, 208
Oligarchy, Oligarchs, 56, 180, 191-2, 206-7,
231-9, 327, 355-6, 359, 379-80, 383-6,
397, 404-6, 409
Olive, 13, 17, 20, 22, 24-8, 32, 95, 130,
156, 178;*see* Oil
Olpae, **17**, 317
Olympia, **1**, 72, 107, 119, 121, 140, 188-9,
196, 213, 220, 227-8, 259, 261, 265,
274, 306, 397-401
(H)Omacchiadae, 208, 414, 416
Oneion, Mount, **2**, 1, 20, 23, 26-7, 29-30,
37, 319, 376-7
Oracle, 22, 38, 58, 66, 72-3, 165, 186-7,
190-2, 219-20, 224, 227, 247
Orchomenus (Arcadia), **18**, 376; (Boeotia),
18, 107, 364
Orsippus, 71
Pagae, **18**, 1, 265, 267, 321-2, 401
Painted Building, **16**, 180-1
Pamphyloi, 51, 416, 418
Panormus, **17**, 310
Partheniae, 22, 73
Pasimelus, 354-5, 362, 384, 411
Patrae, **17**, 329
Patrocleides, 57, 188, 190, 207
Pausanias, 256-7
Pausanias (King), 339, 342, 344-7, 350
Peace, of Callias, 266; of Nicias, 176, 232,
250, 320-31, 409-10;*see* Common,
King's, Thirty Years
Pegasus, 172, 283, 294, 398
Peiraeum, **5**, 1, 26, 28, 30-1, 36-7, 48, 120,
135, 157, 178, 349, 365-6

Peiraeus, 311, 372-3, 424
Peirene,*see* Spring
Peisistratus, Peisistratids, 186, 196, 200-3,
206, 209, 244, 271, 426
Peithias, 313-14
Pellene, **18**, 377, 430
Pelopidas, 377-8, 380, 427
Peloponnese, 52, 107, 129-131, 141, 144,
307-9, 320, 364, 368, 374-81, 406, 411;
see League, Peloponnesian
Peloponnesian War, 31-2, 109, 128, 172-3,
179, 184, 232, 270, 279, 281-341, 346,
394, 405-6, 408-11, 424-6, 429;*see*
Archidamian War, Ionian War, Sicilian
Expedition
Peloponnesian War, First, 166-7, 178,
258-69, 277-8, 288, 299, 329-30, 392,
407-9, 420-2
Penteskouphi, **2**, 4, 25, 29, 34; village, **2**, 3,
25, 27;*see* Plaques
Perachora,*see* Heraeum; peninsula, *see*
Peiraeum; village, **2**, 26, 28, 36
Perantas, 55
Perdiccas, 282, 292-4, 393
Perdikaria, **4**, 17
Perfume, 90, 117-18, 153, 400
Periander, 37, 78-80, 133-9, 142, 148, 153,
180, 195-207, 211-30, 270, 276, 394,
399, 401, 406
Periander (Ambracia), 271
Pericles, 265-7, 304-6, 330, 422, 424-5
Periplous, 265, 277, 307, 309, 313, 316
Persia, 173, 177, 244, 253-7, 266, 271-2,
338, 342, 347, 353-4, 363, 368-9, 373,
377-80, 389, 392, 407, 411, 427-8
Petra, 186, 417
Phalaecus, 382
Phalerum, 107
Phalius, 211-13
Pharnabazus, 353
Phatry, 208, 414-16
Pheia, **17**, 333
Pheidon (Argos), 65, 71-3, 193-4, 221, 429;
(Corinth), 57, 63-5, 72, 96, 126, 154,
194, 403
Philip, 382-3, 386, 391-2, 411-12
Philolaus, 64
Phleious, **18**, 34, 131, 301, 367, 372, 375,
377, 379, 381-2, 411, 416
Phocaea, Phocaeans, **1**, 140
Phocis, **18**, 107, 110, 264, 343-4, 373, 375,
381-2;*see* Medeon
Phoebias, 226
Phoebidas, 372
Phoenicia, 146-7
Phormio, 129-30, 266, 276, 278-9, 291,
308-12, 316, 334, 422-3, 430
Phoukas, Mount, **4**, 27;*see* Apesas

PLATES

1. The Coastal Plain from Acrocorinth

2. The Perachora Peninsula from Acrocorinth

3. The Isthmus from Acrocorinth

4. From Acrocorinth East

5. The Leukon Valley from Acrocorinth

6. The Spathovouni Plain

7. Ravines West of Penteskouphi

8. The Coast South of Korphos

9. Korphos Harbour from the South

10. Acrocorinth and Bluff East of Corinth

11. Acrocorinth and Bluff North of Corinth

12. Leukon Valley East of Corinth

13. South-East Gate and East City-Wall

14. Barley and Olives beneath the North Face of Oneion

15. Vines and Olives North-West of Chiliomodion

16. The Longopotamos Valley from the South

17. Vines beneath Penteskouphi

18. The Potters' Quarter Plateau

19. Towards Acrocorinth from Duo Vouna East

20. Towards Oneion from above Athikia

21. Oneion from Alamannos

22. East from Solygeia

23. Skiona from Acrocorinth

24. Olives on the North Slope of Acrocorinth

25. Barley and Olives near Sophiko

26. Acrocorinth from the Isthmus

27. Acrocorinth from the North-East

28. Acrocorinth and the Temple of Apollo

29. Acrocorinth and Penteskouphi from Lechaeum

30. Cenchreae and the Isthmus from Stanotopi

31. Aleppo Pines South-East of Sophiko

32. Erosion West of Penteskouphi

33. Forest in the South-East Corinthia

34. Olives and Forest in the South-East Corinthia

35. The Isthmian Gate, from the North

36. Central Corinth, Graves 9–10 (left), 18–19

37. Central Corinth, Grave 1

38. Central Corinth, Submycenaean Grave

39. Early Corinthian Pyxis
(Manchester III C 58)

40. Middle and Late Corinthian Vases
(Oinochoe: Manchester III C 64. Kotylai: Manchester III C 96A (back), 1963. 125)

41. Aryballoi (Manchester III C 19, 16, 17 (left to right)) and
Miniature Kotyle (Manchester III C 66)

42. Painted Plaque from Pitsa

43. Spoil Mounds at Lechaeum

44. Potters' Quarter Plateau and Ravines, from Acrocorinth